The Politics of Genocide

Volume 2

THE POLITICS
OF GENOCIDE

The Holocaust in Hungary, Volume 2

RANDOLPH L. BRAHAM

COLUMBIA UNIVERSITY PRESS
New York
1981

Library of Congress Cataloging in Publication Data

Braham, Randolph I.
The politics of genocide.

Includes bibliographical references.
CONTENTS: v. 2. The holocaust in Hungary.
1. Jews in Hungary—Persecutions. 2. Holocaust,
Jewish (1939–1945)—Hungary. 3. Hungary—Ethnic
relations. I. Title.
DS135.119B74   323.1′1924′0439   80-11096
ISBN 0-231-04496-8 (the set)
0-231-05208-1 (vol. 1)
0-231-04388-0 (vol. 2)

COLUMBIA UNIVERSITY PRESS
NEW YORK   GUILDFORD, SURREY

Contents

List of Tables

List of Figures and Maps

The Politics of Genocide

Volume 2

CHAPTER NINETEEN

DEPORTATION

IN POLAND, the Jews were allowed to linger in ghettos for several years before they were deported to various extermination camps; in Hungary they were only held in ghettos for a relatively short time. A few days before the beginning of the deportations, the Jews of many smaller ghettos were relocated and concentrated in brickyards and deserted mills and factories that had railroad sidings. These were normally located at the outskirts of larger cities and served as convenient points for the inconspicuous and efficient entrainment of the Jews. However brief the ghettoization and concentration period was, it proved sufficient for the dejewification authorities to achieve their immediate objectives:

- The demoralization of the Jewish masses to prevent the possibility of resistance.
- The "unearthing" and confiscation of "hidden Jewish wealth."
- The finalization of the deportation plans.

Demoralization of the Jews

By the time of the German occupation, the masses of Hungarian Jewry had already been considerably impoverished and discriminated against under the various anti-Jewish measures, including the major anti-Jewish laws adopted between 1938 and 1942. The rapid succession of further anti-Jewish acts and decrees adopted immediately after the German occupation deprived the Jews not only of their livelihood, but also of their dignity. By the time they were ordered into the ghettos beginning with the Jews in Carpatho-Ruthenia on April 16, they were atomized, isolated, and marked. With many of the able-bodied men serving in the labor companies, and with their national and local leaders preoccupied with the fulfillment of official orders, the Jewish masses did not even contemplate resistance and very few Jews toyed with the idea of escaping. The possibilities of escape within Hungary were minimal. A limited number of provincial Jews were able to escape to the capital and to survive by hiding or by acquiring false Aryan identification papers. But in contrast to such countries as France, Poland, or

Yugoslavia, there were no partisan forces in Hungary to join, and very few Hungarians dared to take the risk of hiding Jews. There was a chance for the more daring to escape to Romania or Slovakia, which had a more tolerant policy at the time. But very few Jews dared to leave their families behind and most of them, understandably, decided to share a common fate.

Within the ghettos and the concentration camps the Jews were over-crowded and many of them were compelled to live outdoors. Exposed to the weather, deprived of sanitary facilities, robbed of all their posses-sions, undernourished and diseased, the Jews became demoralized. They no longer had the strength or the spirit to revolt after the ordeals they had suffered in the ghettos and camps, and when their turn ar-rived for deportation most of them entered the freight cars convinced that they were bound to be better off at their unknown destination than in the ghettos and entrainment centers they were forced to leave.

During their captivity in the ghettos and the camps, those Jews sus-pected of having any property were subjected to a cruel "interrogation program" under the experienced hands of the Hungarian police and gendarmerie. Although the extent of the interrogations and the degree of brutality varied from ghetto to ghetto depending on the attitude of the local authorities, the technique employed in many of the camps was basically similar to the one used in Nagyvárad.

Finalization of the Deportation Plans

While the details of the deportation program were not finalized until early May 1944, the basic decision had been agreed to a month earlier. It was reached *in camera* by some of the leaders of the Hungarian dejewification program, including Secretaries of State László Baky and László Endre, and by the representatives of the Eichmann-*Sonderkom-mando* in accordance with the directives of the RSHA.

The master plan for the implementation of the deportation decision called for a two-pronged approach:

(1) The exploitation of the agreement involving Horthy and the Hungarian and German governments relating to the delivery of several hundred thousand Hungarian Jews "for war pro-duction purposes" (chapter 11).

(2) The "removal of the danger" represented by the large con-centration of Jews in the northeastern parts of the country, which were declared to have become military operational zones (chapter 17).

As we have seen, Horthy consented at Schloss Klessheim (March 18, 1944) to the delivery of at least 100,000 "Jewish workers" for the German war effort. These were to be employed by the *Todt* Organization for the building of an underground aircraft factory in the Protectorate of Bohemia and Moravia within a few months. This quixotic plan was designed to overcome the losses suffered by the *Luftwaffe* and to compensate for the destruction of the German aircraft industry by the Allies. On the basis of the Klessheim agreement, Edmund Veesenmayer took up the question of the 100,000 "Jewish workers" immediately after arriving in Budapest as the Plenipotentiary of the Third Reich. During the early phase of the occupation, his primary diplomatic function in this respect was to assure the speedy delivery of the workers. Cognizant of the obligations undertaken by the Regent in the name of the Hungarian state, the new Sztójay government proved fully cooperative in fulfilling them. By April 9, Hitler was already in a position to inform Field Marshal Erhard Milch, the State Secretary in the Air Ministry and armaments chief of the *Luftwaffe*, that the needed 100,000 Hungarian Jews would be arriving. Five days later, Veesenmayer reported to Ribbentrop that he had received a "binding assurance" from Sztójay to this effect. The Hungarian Prime Minister assured him that Hungary would place at the disposal of the Reich 50,000 able-bodied Jews within two weeks, and an additional 50,000 able-bodied Jews by the end of the next month. Sztójay's assurances were reinforced by the concurrence of the Regent, the cooperation offered by the *Honvédség* (Hungarian Armed Forces) and the Ministry of the Interior, and the measures already taken by the *Sicherheitsdienst* and the Hungarian police.[1] The following day, on April 15, Veesenmayer reported to the Foreign Office that the *Honvédség* was ready to provide 5,000 Jews at once and additional groups of 5,000 every three or four days until the figure of 50,000 was reached. With the Jews at his disposal, Veesenmayer began to discuss the problem of their transportation with Otto Winkelmann, the Higher SS- and Police Leader in Hungary, and asked Berlin for instructions as to where in Germany the transports should be directed.[2] On April 19, Veesenmayer urged Berlin to provide the freight cars needed to transport the 10,000 Jews which the Hungarian Ministry of Defense had already made available.[3]

Veesenmayer's communications were relayed by Thadden to Eichmann the following day together with a summary of his discussion with Rolf Günther, Eichmann's deputy, on the same subject. According to Thadden, Günther maintained that all problems relating to the transportation of the Hungarian Jews would be solved by Eichmann's office as soon as the final directive regarding the disposition of the Jews was received from the Chief of the Reich Security Main Office, Ernst Kaltenbrunner. Thadden hastened to inform Veesenmayer as well as Ribbentrop and Ritter about this important development.[4]

However, on April 23, Veesenmayer suddenly recommended to the German Foreign Office that the deportation of the first installment of 50,000 able-bodied Jewish workers put together by the *Honvédség* be delayed in order not to jeopardize the large-scale *Aktion* that had begun in Carpatho–Ruthenia on April 16 and that was to continue in Northern Transylvania and the rest of Hungary. He coupled his recommendation with the information that transportation facilities had been secured for the shipment to Auschwitz of 3,000 Jews daily beginning on May 15, 1944.[5] Concurrently, the Foreign Office also received an answer to Veesenmayer's earlier inquiry about the destination of the transports in Germany. Writing in behalf of the RSHA, Günther informed Thadden on April 24 that the Hungarian Jews could be shipped to any of the concentration camps under the jurisdiction of the *Reichsführer-SS*, but could not be employed freely in German territory because that would render Germany's cleansing of Jews "illusory."[6]

While Veesenmayer, the German Foreign Office, and the RSHA were scheming with the Eichmann-*Sonderkommando* and the Endre-Baky group to fuse the "legally" agreed upon shipment of 100,000 Jewish workers with the deportation of *all* the Jews, the *Honvédség* was still proceeding with the plan for fulfilling the obligations that had been undertaken by Horthy.

The Council of Ministers met on April 26. In addition to approving the ghettoization program as reported by the Minister of the Interior Andor Jaross, it also approved the recommendations of the Deputy Minister of Defense, General Imre Ruszkiczay-Rüdiger, who appeared in behalf of Minister of Defense Lajos Csatay. Ruszkiczay-Rüdiger informed the Council that the Germans wanted 50,000 stablemen, 10,000 men for fortification work, 3,000 more Hungarian workers in Serbian mines to join the 3,000 already there, and 50,000 Jewish labor servicemen. The Council gave its immediate approval to the delivery of the 50,000 servicemen "and their families."[7]

The following day, Veesenmayer alerted the Foreign Office about the imminent deportation to Auschwitz of two groups of 2,000 Jews that had already been made available by the *Honvédség*. The first transport left Kistarcsa on April 29 with 1,800 Jews and the second transport, with 2,000 Jews, left Topolya the following day.[8] Both contained only able-bodied Jews ranging in age from 16 to 50. These transports constituted the first installment toward the Germans' *bona fide* demand for the 100,000 agreed-upon Jews.

By this time the concentration of all the Jews in Carpatho-Ruthenia and northeastern Hungary for "national security reasons" was already in full swing and the plans for the concentration of the Northern Transylvanian Jews were finalized. While ghettoization was taking place in these northeastern provinces of Hungary, the Hungarian dejewification experts devoted part of their attention to the technical and organizational details of the deportation. Their German counterparts were primarily concerned with the problem of transportation.

After April 23, Veesenmayer's diplomatic pursuit of the "legitimate objectives" inherent in the Hitler–Horthy agreement became gradually intertwined with the RSHA's ideological goals relating to the Final Solution. Veesenmayer was now fulfilling his functions both as SS-*Brigadeführer* and as *Gesandter und Bevollmächtigter des Grossdeutschen Reiches*—as representative of both the SS and the German Foreign Office. Having already arranged the immediate delivery of at least 100,000 Jewish workers and their families, he now lent his services to the scheme for the deportation of all the Jews. Toward the end of April, Veesenmayer approached Sztójay with the "request of the *Wehrmacht*" that the Jews concentrated in the military operational zones in the northeastern and southern parts of the country be removed to the interior. Sztójay relayed the request to Minister of the Interior Jaross, who in turn forwarded it to Endre, "the person entrusted with the handling of Jewish questions." In accordance with the scenario already agreed upon, Endre reported that the fulfillment of the *Wehrmacht*'s request was impossible because of the great number of Jews in Carpatho-Ruthenia. However, he reminded his superior that the Germans had offered to take over all Jews and that they had promised to put the able-bodied men and women in labor camps and those not fit for labor, including the children and the aged, into concentration camps. Endre recommended acceptance of the German offer, because in his view "Hungary could not support such a large number of Jews." Jaross forwarded the recommendation to Sztójay.[9]

According to another version, the deportation process was set in motion by a suggestion by the Gendarmerie Commander in Máramarossziget. He advised that in view of the inadequate space and sanitary facilities in the ghettos, either the ghettoization should stop or the "surplus Jews" should be sent to Western Hungary or to Germany. The suggestion was conveyed to Wisliceny, who was in Munkács supervising the ghettoization in Carpatho-Ruthenia. Wisliceny went immediately to Budapest in the company of Meggyesi, Ferenczy, and Lullay. Upon their arrival they met in Baky's office with Colonel Győző Tölgyesy, the Prefect of Máramarossziget, Eichmann, Hunsche, and Novak. Baky placed before Eichmann the matter of the situation in Máramarossziget and allegedly asked him whether the ghettoization should be stopped or whether he was ready to take over the Jews. Eichmann, who helped work out the scenario, naturally opted for the latter. After the meeting, which lasted only 15 minutes, Lullay and Novak were empowered to go to Vienna to make arrangements for transportation with the leaders of the German Railways.[10]

Operational Directives

Convinced that his anti-Jewish recommendations would be routinely approved by the government, Endre began to work on the technical and organizational details of the deportation. Early in May, he issued the following memo to his immediate subordinates:

To implement the Jewish action in the territory of Gendarmerie District Kassa, (i.e., Carpatho-Ruthenia) the Germans—8 officers and 40 men—will leave for Munkács in 10 cars on May 11.

Munkács will serve as the headquarters of the staff. On the German side, the staff will include *Haupsturmführers* Wisliceny and Novak, 5 subgroup leaders (of sub-officer rank), and 5 soldiers. On our part, Lieutenant-Colonel Ferenczy, Royal Prosecutor Meggyesi, and Chief Inspector László Koltay will be included.

Committees will operate in Kassa, Ungvár, Sátoraljaujhely, Munkács, Beregszász, Nyiregyháza, Máramarossziget, Nagyszőllős, Huszt, and Mátészalka.

In the above cities, we shall entrust the following persons with the direction of the action in conjunction with the German committees: In the cities, the competent commander of the police and the commander of the gendarmerie subdivisions; in localities where there are no gendarmerie subdivision commanders, the competent gendarmerie wing commanders; in localities where there are no police commands, the competent chief constable and wing commander.

Upon their arrival, the German committees will immediately establish contact with the committee members assigned by us. (Courtesy, thoughtfulness, tact, information and guidance are to be offered; assistance is to be given in feeding and quartering; and, when necessary, interpreters are to be provided.)

The German and Hungarian committee operating centrally in Munkács will be located at that city's police headquarters; all contacts and communications should be directed there.[11]

The details of this memo were also discussed at a conference in Munkács on May 8 attended by the top administration, police, and gendarmerie officers of the various counties and county seats. The conference, chaired by László Ferenczy, heard an elaboration on the procedures to be used in the entrainment of the Jews and the final schedule for the planned transports from the various ghetto centers. (Specific details relating to the entrainment and deportation were normally given by Ferenczy in the field.[12])

The plans for the deportation of the Hungarian Jews were finalized by the German and Hungarian dejewification authorities at Munkács on May 9. They called for the deportation of the Jews of Carpatho-Ruthenia and Northern Transylvania between May 15 and June 11.[13] It was also at Munkács that the final written instructions for the mayors of the ghetto centers were worked out. These confidential instructions read as follows:

On May [illegible] a meeting was held at the police headquarters of Munkács under the chairmanship of Gendarmerie Lieutenant-Colonel László Ferenczy, with the participation of Gendarmerie Captain Dr. László Uray and Gestapo Captain Dr. Márton Zöldi on the part of the Germans.

The meeting discussed the removal of the Jews that will begin on May 14.

An exception will be made for Jews of foreign citizenship, namely British, American, Polish, Russian, Romanian, Bulgarian, Slovak, Finnish, Swiss, Swedish, Spanish, Portuguese, and Turkish citizens, who are to be removed in advance and placed in police custody so that they will not witness the removal of the others.

The Jews will be transported in 110 trains to the station at Kassa where the transports will be taken over by German police. Marking [on the trains]: "D.A.-Umsiedler" [German Worker Resettlement].

Each train will transport 3,000 persons. It will consist of 45 cars, each with 70 persons plus baggage, and two C cars at the front and the back of the train for the guards.

The commander of the loading station will be a German or a Hungarian gendarmerie officer; this will require that the stationmaster make available cars and loading areas, at a place removed from the station, five hours in advance.

The Jews will be able to take along only limited luggage, and no beds or mattresses. Name lists are to be prepared in duplicate. One copy is to remain with the transport and the other copy is to be sent to the police headquarters at Munkács for the commander of the loading area.

If the train leaves at night, the Jews must be loaded during the day.

The gendarmerie will supervise the transfer from the camp to the station, and the police will guard street crossings. The area will have been closed off previously by the gendarmerie and the streets by the police; the same procedure is to be followed at the loading site.

The camp, ghetto, and road are to be under strict guard; the road is to be closed to traffic while the Jews are marched. They are to be marched in groups of 500, walking four in a row. The seriously ill and their relatives are to be taken to the site as part of the last group. There will be a hospital train with a doctor and nurse, which will also hold the members of the Jewish Council and persons of doubtful citizenship.

Shelter [workers] and labor servicemen, and physicians and pharmacists, will also be included.

With respect to the labor servicemen, the Ministry of Defense will take separate action.

The number of persons in a filled car will be marked in chalk on the outside of the car.

In each car, one person will be selected as Council member and will be in charge of acquisition of water, etc.

Mayoral responsibility

The persons to be transported are to be supplied with bread for two days. The two days' supply per person is 400 grams. Taking along of additional food is prohibited. During the day of loading, coffee for the trip will be distributed in the camp kitchens; if this is not possible, the transport must be supplied with water. The bread is to be provided and delivered by the Mayor.

The Mayor will also see to it that each car is provided with a covered bucket (for sanitary purposes) and with a can suitable for drinking water.

It is the responsibility of the Mayor to supply 90 locks with keys per transport, possibly with the help of the Council.

It should be remembered that the transports will also include German cars which cannot be locked unless a 30-centimeter chain is first used, which will then be locked.

The Mayor will also see to the provision of chalk for marking the wagons.

It is also his responsibility to provide keychains and tags on which the number of the car can be identified.

The transfer and takeover of the transports will take place at Kassa; rollcall is not to take place.

Mayor's task: After removal of the inmates, camp locations are to be disinfected by the administrative authorities (military physician).

During the transfer, individual additions and actions are to be avoided.

Captain Dr. Uray: If necessary, as many as 100 may be put in a car. They can be loaded like sardines, since the Germans require hardy people. Those who cannot take it will perish. There is no need in Germany for ladies of fashion.

Nagybánya schedule: May 30, 8 P.M. to 2 A.M.

June 11, 2 P.M. to 2 A.M.

Discussion: Pál Szehor, Mayor of Nyíregyháza: Not a single Jew should be left behind. Let them all go.

Lieutenant-Colonel Ferenczy: Only absolutely indispensable physicians and their families are to be left behind. These will be identified by the German advisers, who can do this expertly; they know how to do this and the selection will be their responsibility.

Christians who, on appeal, return within 48 hours anything accepted from Jews, will be exempted from the consequence of internment, etc.[14]

Transportation Arrangements

While the Hungarian experts were completing the technical organizational details, the Germans were concerned with settling the problem of transportation, including the acquisition of the freight cars and the determination of the deportation route. Because of the high priority attached to building the aircraft factory and the other military-related projects in which the able-bodied Jews were to be employed, the *Wehrmacht* was very cooperative in releasing the rolling stock demanded by the SS; the latter were, of course, primarily motivated by their ideological concern. The singlemindedness with which the Nazi leaders pursued their objective of the Final Solution overshadowed even the military requirements of the Reich. They continued to attach a greater priority to the deportation of the Jews than to the transportation needs of the *Wehrmacht* even when Soviet troops were rapidly approaching the Carpathians.[15]

The Nazi leaders' concern for the priority solution of the Jewish question was shared by Theodor Ganzenmüller, the executive director of the *Deutsche Reichsbahn* (German Railways). He cooperated fully with the Eichmann-*Sonderkommando* and especially with Franz Novak, its chief transportation expert, by providing the rolling stock needed for the scheduled deportation of the Hungarian Jews.[16]

The schedule of the deportations and the route plan were finalized at a conference in Vienna on May 4–6 attended by the representatives of the railroad, the Hungarian gendarmerie, and the *Sicherheitspolizei.* The chief representative of the gendarmerie was Dr. Leó Lullay, Ferenczy's aide, and that of the Eichmann-*Sonderkommando* was Franz Novak.

Prior to the conference three alternative deportation routes appear to have been considered. The first one, which was generally preferred, led through eastern Slovakia; the others were through Lemberg (Lvov) and via the Budapest–Vienna route.

On the eve of the conference, Thadden asked Hanns Elard Ludin, the German Minister in Bratislava, whether there would be any political objection to the shipment of the Hungarian transports through eastern Slovakia. Ludin's original reaction was that there would be such an objection.[17] Thadden, however, insisted on the proposed plan because the two other possible routes were no longer acceptable. The route through Lemberg, "while the shortest," had become "extraordinarily difficult for military reasons" and the transportation of the Jews via Budapest–Vienna, it was felt, would make the Jews of the Hungarian capital restless.[18]

Ludin's political objections were overruled. The Vienna Conference decided to begin the deportation of the Hungarian Jews on May 15 and to carry it out in four trains daily through eastern Slovakia following the Kassa, Prešov, Muszyna, Tarnow, and Cracow route to Auschwitz.[19]

With the transportation schedule and route settled, only one additional problem had to be solved before the launching of the deportation. This involved the avoidance of complications that might arise from the inclusion of Jewish citizens of enemy and neutral states in the general Hungarian anti-Jewish program, and from the handling of the property of the deported Jews. To help in the prevention and solution of these potential complications, the German Foreign Office had suggested on April 6 that Adolf Hezinger and Ambassador Saucken, both associated with the *Inland II* section, be sent to Budapest for four to eight weeks to act as "advisers on the solution of the Jewish question."[20] On April 12, Veesenmayer requested the assignment of Hezinger to act as liaison between the Legation and the German and Hungarian authorities in charge of the Final Solution.[21] With Ribbentrop's approval,[22] Hezinger arrived in Budapest toward the end of April.[23] He stayed in Hungary until the middle of June, when he was replaced by Theodor Horst Grell.[24] During his stay Hezinger visited the ghettos and concentration camps, from which he selected from 100 to 200 Jews of foreign citizenship.[25] As a well-trained *Inland II* officer, Hezinger was concerned not only with the identification and selection of these Jews but also with delicate liaison matters involving the German Legation and Eichmann's *Sonderkommando.* His effectiveness and "tactful" services were appreciated by both German agencies in Hungary. Indeed, they asked Horst Wagner, the chief of *Inland II,* to extend his tour of duty at least until the completion of the deportation of the Jews of Budapest. Representatives of both agencies expressed doubt about the abilities of Grell to assume Hezinger's responsibilities.[26]

Deportation: Zones I and II

The deportations from Gendarmerie Districts VIII, IX, and X (Carpatho-Ruthenia and Northern Transylvania), which were identified as

Dejewification Operational Zones I and II, began on schedule on May 15 with four trainloads daily. Each train carried about 3,000 persons crammed into freight cars, each car being supplied with two buckets: one with water and the other for excrements. One of the first ghettos to be cleared was that of Kassa, the rail hub through which all the deportation trains left the country. Then came the turn of Munkács, Nagyszőllős, Máramarossziget, and the other ghettos of Carpatho-Ruthenia followed by those of Northern Transylvania.

The deportations were carried out with sickening brutality. This is how Lévai described the entrainment and deportation of the Jews of Munkács on May 22:

On May 22, the ghetto of the city of Munkács was also emptied and most of Munkács' 12,000 Jews were driven on the route from the ghetto to the brick-yard by guards using whips, machine-guns, and rifle butts. There they were compelled to lay down their baggage and undress—men, women, and children alike. Stark naked, they were then ordered to move back a few steps, and the women, who were called in specially, together with Gestapo men, policemen, and gendarmes went through their baggage and clothing, even opening stitches to discover whether the Jews had hidden anything. Those who did not undress or step back fast enough were beaten. Most of the people were bleeding and stood silently, naked, and numbed. The searchers, however, were all the more loud. The clothes were then returned, the personal documents were torn, and everybody became a non-person. They were then driven by night sticks and rifle butts to get dressed. The crush of the desperate crowd and the frenzied confusion were terrible. Here, 90 persons were crowded into a freight car: *obviously there were too few cars and too many Jews!* The cars were then chained and padlocked. Each got a bucket full of water and an empty one for the excrements. The train, however, was left standing in the station during the hot May day and was allowed to leave only the following day. By that time many became mad and even more died, since the Jewish hospital patients were also included. The doors were not opened the day of departure. The corpses were removed three days later at Csap, where also the mad were clubbed or shot.[27]

The agony of the Jews assembled for deportation after weeks of dehumanizing treatment in the ghettos and entrainment centers was described by Samu Stern, the head of the central Jewish Council, as follows:

[Searching for the valuables of the Jews] no brutality, no method of torture was spared to make them confess. Wives were beaten under the eyes of their hus-bands, and when this was of no avail, children were tormented in front of their parents. The favorite methods of the Hungarian gendarmes to make these un-fortunates speak up one way or another were tying up the victims, beatings with rubber truncheons, the use of electrical devices, blows with sticks upon the soles of the feet and the palms of the hands, boxing the ears, puncturing under the nails, and kicking. When the detectives were through with their job, the SS men of Wisliceny and Zöldi's special unit put in an appearance. They surrounded the ghetto with loaded machine-guns in hand watching with the eyes of lynxes until the trains rolled in. Hereupon they drove the unfortunate people with whips and rifle-butts to the station. At the beginning this was done in the early hours, for they were anxious to avoid sensation; later on, when the pace had to be accelerated, they did not care any more, chasing their victims across the towns in broad daylight. At this sight kindhearted Christians could often not help bursting into tears, but they had to hide them lest some gendarme might notice their pity and assault them with rifle-butts and foul language. We heard about an instance when a good-natured peasant woman tried to hand over edibles to the poor creatures crammed into freight cars. A gendarme caught her in the act and pushed that kind woman into the car which then, carefully sealed, went on with an additional victim.

One car had to hold—depending upon the number of deportees and cars—60 to 80 persons. . . . In the burning heat of summer, sealed in cattle wagons with two buckets per car, they started their journey via Kassa to Auschwitz, the terminal.[28]

The horrors of the entrainment and deportation of the Jewish community of Kassa were detailed in a moving letter addressed to Mrs. Horthy by Mrs. Sámuel Gotterer, the head of the Jewish Women's Association of that city. Mrs. Gotterer had been exempted from the anti-Jewish regulations because her husband was a 75 percent war invalid. Her letter of May 17, written at the request of the Jewish Council, had requested that the First Lady intervene to halt the deportations or at least try to prevent the deportation of those under 18 and over 60 (50 in the case of women), who "would be unfit for useful labor beyond the country's borders anyway."[29]

The Higher SS and Police Leader's office, on the other hand, was informed daily about the progress of the operations by the men in charge. Its reports, which were also submitted to the German Legation, were forwarded to the German Foreign Office by Veesenmayer as soon as they were received. According to these reports, the number of persons deported reached 23,363 within two days. By May 18, it reached about 51,000. With each passing day the number of those deported continued to climb dramatically: May 19, 62,644; May 23, 110,556; May 25, 138,870; May 28, 204,312; May 31, 217,236; June 1, 236,414; June 2, 247,856; June 3, 253,389; and June 8, 289,357.[30] The transport of June 7, which was reported the following day, was the last one from Zones I and II. With it, the dejewification experts fulfilled their target. Within 24 days, they had deported 289,357 Jews in 92 trains (table 19.1)—a daily average of 12,056 and an average of 3,145 per train.

TABLE 19.1.

DATA RELATING TO THE GHETTOIZATION AND DEPORTATION OF HUNGARIAN JEWRY BY OPERATIONAL ZONES AND GENDARMERIE DISTRICTS

Operational Zone	Gendarmerie District	Area of Hungary	Number of Ghettos or Concentration Centers	Date of Ghettoization or Concentration	Date of Deportation	Number of Trains	Deportation Figures	
							Ferenczy's	Veesenmayer's[a]
I	VIII. (Kassa)	Carpatho-Ruthenia	16	Apr. 16–	May 15–June 7	92	288,333	289,357
II	IX. (Kolozsvár) X. (Marosvásárhely)	Northern Transylvania	11	May 3–			[275,415][b]	50,805
III	II. (Székesfehérvár) VII. (Miskolc)	Northern Hungary[c]	6 5	June 5–10	June 11–16	23	23,725 28,104	50,805
IV	V. (Szeged) VI. (Debrecen)	Southeastern Hungary[d]	4 3	June 16–20	June 25–28	14	21,489 19,016	41,499
V	III. (Szombathely)	Western and Southwestern Hungary	5	June 30–July 3	July 4–6	10	17,667 11,889	55,741
	IV. (Pécs)		3					
VI	I. (Budapest)	(Suburbs)	2	June 30–July 3	July 6–8	8	24,128	
	Total		55			147	434,351	437,402

SOURCE: Ferenczy Reports May 3–July 9, 1944.

[a] *RLB*, Docs. 174, 182, 193.

[b] In his report of June 8, 1944, Ferenczy lists the number of those deported from Gendarmerie Districts VIII, IX, and X as 275,415. His later reports, however, brought the figure closer to that of Veesenmayer.

[c] North of Budapest from Kassa to the frontier of the Third Reich.

[d] East of the Danube, not including Budapest.

[e] West of the Danube, not including Budapest.

Extraordinary Deportations

Concurrently with the deportations from Zones I and II, which, like the subsequent deportations from the other zones, were carried out by the gendarmerie, around 21,700 Jews in the areas adjacent to Croatia and Occupied Serbia were deported by the Hungarian and German military authorities[31] in an independent action presumably designed as a "precautionary measure" in the war against Tito's partisans. These Jews do not appear in Ferenczy's reports on the ghettoization and deportation progress; most of them had been placed into ghettos and concentration camps during the second half of April. Among the major camps from which these Jews were deported during the second half of May were those of Nagykanizsa, Baja, Horgos, and Barcs. These entrainment centers included the Jews from the neighboring communities as well. The Barcs camp, for example, included the Jews of Sziget-vár.[32] The ghettoization and deportation of the Jews in these areas were carried out under the immediate command of Lieutenant-Colonel Ferenc Zalasdi (Zalostyál) of the gendarmerie, under the usual cruel circumstances. On the way to Auschwitz, for example, the Jews in the two transports that left Baja on May 25–27 were locked in their freight cars for three and a half days. When the doors were first opened at Gänsendorf, 55 of them were dead and about 200 had gone mad.[33]

The Jews of the Bácska and Baranya regions not included in these early transports were deported in conjunction with the liquidation of the Jews in Zone IV (see chapter 21).

In addition to the extraordinary deportations from Zala County and other parts in Southern Hungary, the Hungarian Ministry of the Interior, according to a dispatch by Veesenmayer, also decided to deport the Jews of Gödöllő, the summer residence of Horthy, in a similar fashion. The suggestion for this special *Aktion* in Gödöllő, which because of its location northeast of Budapest should actually have taken place as part of the operations in Zone III, if not Zone IV, allegedly came from within the Governor's circle. The objective apparently was to enable Horthy to walk around the town without having to see any Jews and "to make it possible for him to personally experience the consequences of the anti-Jewish measures."[34]

The Mission of Eberhard von Thadden

One week after the beginning of the mass deportations, Eberhard von Thadden, the specialist on Jewish Affairs in *Inland II*, visited Budapest to assess the activities of the German agencies involved in the anti-Jewish operations. He summarized his findings in two reports dated May 25 and 26. After a brief progress report on the deportations in the northeastern parts of Hungary, Thadden noted that with the completion of that phase of the *Aktion* the anti-Jewish measures would be extended to the other parts of the country, including Budapest. According to the master plan, the campaign was to have been completed by the end of July with the deportation of around one million Jews. The deportation of the Budapest Jews was planned for the middle or the end of July in "a large-scale one-day *Aktion*" for which the German authorities expected the continued full cooperation not only of the Hungarian government, the gendarmerie, and police, but also of the mailmen and chimney sweepers. All traffic in Budapest was to be halted for that day.

With reference to the deportees from the northeastern parts of the country, Thadden reported that only one-third of them "were found suitable for work" upon their arrival in Auschwitz. He attributed the success of the deportation operations to the wholehearted cooperation of Endre and Baky. He revealed that the Jews in the other parts of Hungary continued to remain calm because the "Jewish Council of Budapest was forced to announce that these measures applied only to Jews of the eastern areas, who had been preserving their Jewish peculiarities." [35]

Thadden's assessment concerning the condition of the deportees from the northeastern parts of Hungary was confirmed by SS-*Obergruppenführer* Oswald Pohl, the chief of the SS Economic and Administrative Main Office (*Hauptamt Verwaltung und Wirtschaft—VWHA*), which was in charge of all concentration camps. In a telegram to Himmler dated May 24, Pohl complained that even of those able to work 50 percent were women. He requested authorization for the employment of these women in construction work under the auspices of the *Todt* Organization. The request was, of course, granted by Himmler, who also advised that the women be fed raw vegetables, including "plenty of garlic from Hungary." [36]

German Camouflage Attempts

Fearing negative world reaction to the deportations from Hungary, Paul Karl Schmidt, Chief of the Information and Press Division of the German Foreign Office, proposed on May 27 that the German and

Hungarian dejewification authorities provide "external causes and reasons" for the "current and planned operations" against the Jews of Hungary, especially in connection with the planned deportation from Budapest. He suggested "the discovery of explosives in Jewish clubs and synagogues, the unearthing of sabotage organizations, attempts at coups, attacks on police, and involvement in foreign currency dealings designed to undermine the Hungarian food supply system." Schmidt's suggestions for the camouflaging and justification of the anti-Jewish operations were forwarded by Thadden to Veesenmayer,[37] who rejected them as unnecessary. As events proved, he correctly pointed out that world public opinion would be no more shocked by the proposed measures against the Jews of Budapest than it had been by the deportations from Carpatho-Ruthenia and Northern Transylvania.[38] Moreover, he reminded Berlin, Schmidt's suggestions would sound "incredible" in view of the close surveillance under which the Jews were held.[39]

Schmidt's suggestions were probably motivated by the desire to overcome the possible impact of revelations about the brutalities committed against Jews in the course of their deportation. And indeed, there were several incidents involving Germans who were seen by civilians along the deportation route killing and robbing Hungarian Jews in the trains and railroad stations. Such an "incident" took place on May 24 at the Slovakian railroad station of Kysak.[40] The incident was "investigated" by the competent German authorities, who found little basis for the "allegations." Hezinger assured Thadden that reports about the robberies at Kysak were false because the Jews had already been stripped of all their possessions before entrainment.[41] Eichmann claimed that the incident might have occurred because of the inexperience of the *Volksdeutsche* who had been recruited into the SS from the Bácska and the Banat.[42] Veesenmayer assured the Foreign Office that the shooting incident reported by Ludin was an accident resulting from "the cleaning of a pistol by a member of the *Wehrmacht*."[43] The issue was settled by Ribbentrop, who requested that the Slovak authorities be informed about the "untruthfulness" of the whole incident.[44]

A German Film on the Deportations

The Germans managed to win one brief victory in the propaganda battle for the protection of their tarnished image. During the deportations from Nagyvárad, the Nazis produced a film showing the brutality of the Hungarian gendarmes in contrast to the "humanitarian" and "civilized" behavior of the Germans.

The "documentary" film, produced by the Nazi firm of Tobis-Klang, was in two parts. The first part showed the Hungarian gendarmes at work beating women with rifle butts, chasing lagging children with whips, and tearing wedding bands off the helpless victims. It also focused on the omnipresent cock-feathered gendarmes pressing the Jews into the freight cars like cattle and on the two buckets that were placed in each car, one with water and the other for excrements. No Germans were shown in these scenes. They appeared only in the second part, filmed partially in Kassa, where the Germans took over the transports. In contrast to the brutality associated with the Hungarians, this part of the film, produced by Eberhard Taubert, the film and propaganda expert in Goebbels's Ministry, showed how German Red Cross nurses threw open the sealed cars and, horrified and scandalized, removed the corpses, distributed fresh water and provisions to the emaciated victims, and bathed and disinfected the afflicted. Once they were refreshed and rested, the Jews were shown being led away supposedly to some easy job somewhere in Germany.

The film was shown in several neutral countries under the sponsorship of the German authorities. Early in July 1944, it was also shown at a reception given by Otto Koecher, the German Minister in Berne, for the diplomats representing the Axis-allied and neutral states in Switzerland. It was on this occasion that the film was seen by Imre Tahy and László Rakolczay, the Secretary and Military Attaché, respectively, of the Hungarian Legation in Berne. After the screening, the German Minister and his associates, including Fürst Urach, the Press Attaché, and Bibra and von Nostitz, Legation Counselors, took pains to explain the "real" position of the Third Reich on the Jewish question as against the "malicious rumors" spread by its enemies all over the world.[45]

However, the Germans soon found that the film was in fact counterproductive. By that time the world could no longer be fooled by propaganda gimmickry; it was already fully aware of the realities of the Nazis' Final Solution program. Moreover, the Hungarian representatives abroad who saw the film alerted the Foreign Ministry in Budapest, contributing to Horthy's decision shortly thereafter to suspend the deportations (see chapter 25). The showing of the film in Switzerland was suspended by the Germans after Baron Károly Bothmer, the Hungarian Chargé d'Affaires in Berne, lodged a protest at the request of Mihály Arnóthy-Jungerth, the Deputy Foreign Minister.[46]

While the film was obviously designed to put the Germans in a good light before world public opinion at the expense of the Hungarians, its message was not totally devoid of substance. The Hungarian gendarmerie was in fact very brutal throughout the entire ghettoization, concentration, and deportation process. Without the wholehearted support of the gendarmerie, the Germáns could not possibly have carried out their Final Solution program in Hungary. The Hungarian Nazis' zeal in the anti-Jewish drive was practically unmatched anywhere else in German-dominated Europe. There was much to what Wisliceny said to Freudiger in one of his confessional moments: "The Hungarians really seem to be the offspring of the Huns; we never would have succeeded like this without them." [47]

Ferenczy's Deportation Progress Reports

On the Hungarian side, the deportations were carried out by the gendarmerie in cooperation with the local police and civil service under the overall immediate command of Lieutenant-Colonel Ferenczy. In his first major report on the deportations from Carpatho-Ruthenia and Northern Transylvania, dated May 29, 1944, Ferenczy not only gave an accounting of how many Jews had been deported by that time, but also revealed that he might have been aware of the realities of Auschwitz. He asserted that it was the wish of the German Security Police that the Hungarian Jews be supplied with food for five days because "after the selection effectuated upon their arrival in Auschwitz they are immediately dispatched by train to various labor camps." [48]

Ferenczy issued his final report on the deportations from Gendarmerie Districts VIII, IX, and X on June 8. He informed the Minister of the Interior that by June 7, 275,415 Jews had been deported from Carpatho-Ruthenia and Northern Transylvania in 92 trains and that with the exception of Jews in mixed marriages and their descendants those areas had become *Judenrein*. He portrayed a glowing picture of the positive effects of the deportations on the political, economic, and security affairs of the affected areas. Ferenczy, using the typical anti-Jewish tone in vogue at this time, emphasized the decline in food prices, the virtual elimination of the black market, the disappearance of horror propaganda, and the dramatic decline of court cases. [49]

On the basis of the experience gathered by the German and Hungarian dejewification experts in the course of ghettoization and deportation of the Jews of Carpatho-Ruthenia and Northern Transylvania, Ferenczy suggested that:

- The rounding up and concentration of the Jews be effectuated by suitable gendarmerie and police forces covering smaller territorial units.

- The deportations begin immediately after the completion of the concentration.
- The internal command of the camps and the technical supervision of entrainment continue to be the responsibility of the German Security Police while the external security and guarding of the camps become the task of the Hungarians.[50]
- Meetings be held in the Ministry of the Interior with the concerned county prefects and gendarmerie commanders only a few days before the launching of an operation in a particular territory, and meetings with the local mayors and police officials only one day before the beginning of the operation.
- The ill, the aged, and their families be deported in the first transports rather than in the last as had been the case earlier.[51]

Hungarian Official Camouflage

Although the press was absolutely silent about the character and scope of the deportations, the population at large was well aware of the atrocities and horrors associated with the ghettos and concentration camps and the brutalities perpetrated in the course of the deportations. The number of those who dared to demonstrate their opposition was pitifully small. While most of the Christians adopted an attitude of passivity, some took advantage of the deportation of the Jews by breaking into their homes or by having their businesses expropriated. This attitude of the general population was fostered by the public pronouncements of government officials who reassured the people that no physical harm would befall the Jews.

The beginning of the deportation coincided with the inauguration of new county prefects, which was exploited by various members of the Sztójay government to elaborate on the anti-Jewish measures. Speaking in Székesfehérvár on May 12 at the inauguration of Dr. Árpád Toldi as the new Prefect of Fejér County, Baky emphasized in the presence of Béla Jurcsek, Bálint Hóman, and Kálmán Hubay that the thorough and final solution of the Jewish question would assure the unity of the home front and final victory.[52] Three days later, he was more specific about the objectives of the anti-Jewish measures. He stated:

First and foremost, we must rid the Hungarian people of Jewry. Segregation of the Jews has partly taken place. As a final result of all these operations, we shall remove every Jew from the country; not a single one is going to stay here. On the territory east of the Tisza, so far 320,000 Jews have already been taken into concentration camps.[53]

Having been notified of the intention to remove all the Jews from the country, the Hungarian population had to be assured that no physical harm would befall them. This task was assumed by Lajos Szász, Minister of Industry. Speaking in Nyíregyháza on May 22 at the inauguration of Pál Thuránszky as the Prefect of Szabolcs County, Szász declared:

The radical and final solution of the Jewish question will not and could not bring about any disturbance in the Hungarian economy because the government considers the maintenance and the continuity of production even more important than the solution of the Jewish question. In general, in connection with the solution of the Jewish question let us be clear about the following: Nobody aims at the extirpation, destruction, or tormenting of the Jews. The government has not taken any measures so far that would induce one to believe that it is pursuing goals unworthy of Hungarians. The guide in the solution of the Jewish question cannot be a hate-fed anti-Semitism, but only and exclusively a love-imbued defense of race. Nobody wants to extirpate the Jews from the world; we only want to save our race from their harmful influence. I believe that all of us who are the fighters and workers for, and the followers of, the idea of race defense will and would be very happy if the unlucky people of Ahasuerus were to find a home somewhere on this globe, where it would build its own state far away from our borders. But there is need for great seriousness, deliberation, and calm in the solution of the Jewish question because it cannot be anybody's aim to arouse our people's compassion and pity for Jewry.[54]

Szász spoke on the day the railroad station of Nyíregyháza was in use for the criminal entrainment of Jews who had lived in the midst of their Christian neighbors for many centuries. Thuránszky refused to heed the advice of Lajos Erdőhegyi, the outgoing prefect, that he protest against the obvious lies uttered by the Minister.[55]

In his inaugural speech in the lower house of the Hungarian Parliament on May 25, Prime Minister Sztójay was more laconic but also more emphatic. He stated: "We want to implement all the theoretical and practical objectives of the politics of . . . race defense, including the radical solution of the Jewish question."[56]

The cynical statements by Szász and his colleagues designed to deceive Hungarian public opinion achieved their objective. This was partially also due to the failure of the leaders of the Hungarian Jewish community to do anything effective to counteract them. Already in possession of the Auschwitz Protocols and fully aware of the extermination program, these leaders kept on bickering about the possible harmful consequences for themselves and the remaining community if they were caught in "illegal propaganda activities." They were well aware that their contacts and acquaintances still in the Sztójay government had allied themselves with the Nazi position and would not lend themselves to persuasion by Jews. Pető, for example, upon hearing the first news about the deportations in Carpatho-Ruthenia called on Lajos Reményi-Schneller, the Minister of Finance, who had served in the same capacity in the Kállay government, "to verify the deportation decision" and to try to influence him. Pető informed Reményi-Schneller about the realities of Auschwitz, the cruelties perpetrated by the gendarmerie, and the news on the deportations from Carpatho-Ruthenia and asked him to use his influence in the Council of Ministers to halt the deportations. The opportunistic minister responded in a deceitful fashion stating that although he had also heard some complaints from his own electoral district in Baja, the Council of Ministers did not discuss the question of deportations and "if such a thing were in preparation he also would have to know about it."⁵⁷

The members of the Council were eager to get in touch with Baky and Endre to "enlighten" them also about the realities of Auschwitz. They were never received by them. However, they did manage to see Albert Takács, Endre's secretary, soon after the completion of the deportations from Carpatho-Ruthenia and Northern Transylvania. Takács denied that the Jews had been taken out of the country, asserting that they had merely been removed from the operational zones in the northeast at the request of the Germans and relocated somewhere in the country's interior. He assured the Jewish leaders that there would be no further concentrations and that the Jews would be merely placed into ghettos. The deportations, of course, continued unabated; when the Jewish leaders reproached him a week later, he laughingly reminded them that his promise was dependent upon the "good behavior" of the Jews. He claimed cynically that the Jews had plotted to kill a certain stage director by the name of Vaszary and had also plotted to kill Endre.⁵⁸

While the Hungarian government leaders were busy swaying public opinion with declarations of their noble intentions and the Jewish leaders were paralyzed by their impotence and frustration, the German and Hungarian dejewification experts proceeded with the Final Solution in accordance with the preestablished schedule.

Notes

1. *RLB*, Doc. 134. The contents of this message were relayed to Eichmann by both Ritter and Thadden. See *NA*, Microcopy T-120, Roll 4355, Frames K213629-630.

2. *RLB*, Doc. 135. Veesenmayer's telegram was relayed to Eichmann the following day. *Ibid.*, Doc. 136.

3. *Ibid.*, Doc. 138.

4. *Ibid.*, Docs. 139, 141, 143.

5. *Ibid.*, Doc. 145.

6. *Ibid.*, Doc. 147. This information was conveyed to Veesenmayer by Ritter on April 27. *Ibid.*, Doc. 149.

7. *Vádirat*, 1:136.

8. *RLB*, Docs. 148, 150. See also the following personal narratives by those in this first group of deportees from Kistarcsa: Mrs. Joseph Weiser (YIVO, File no. 771/3276) and Mrs. A. Koltay (771/3523).

9. Lévai, *Zsidósors Magyarországon*, p. 107.

10. *Der Kastner-Bericht*, pp. 300–301.

11. Lévai, *Zsidósors Magyarországon*, p. 118.

12. During May 18–20, 1944, for example, Ferenczy held a conference with the top civilian, police, and gendarmerie officers of the counties and county seats of Northern Transylvania to finalize the plans for the entrainment and deportation of the Jews from Gendarmerie Districts IX and X. *Tribunalul Poporului, Cluj*, pp. 146–47.

13. Ferenczy Report of May 9, 1944. Israel Police, Bureau 06, Eichmann Trial Doc. 1316.

14. Ferenczy Report. Israel Police, Bureau 06, Eichmann Trial Doc. 1318. This particular copy of the instructions had been addressed to the Mayor of Nagybánya.

15. See also Martin Broszat, *German National Socialism, 1919–1945* (Santa Barbara, California: Clio Press, 1966), p. 52.

16. During his trial in 1961, Eichmann claimed that he could never have completed his deportation program without the complete and consistent support of Ganzenmüller. Ganzenmüller was indicted by the Düsseldorf Assize Court (*Schwurgericht*—File 8 Ks 1/71) on June 21, 1971, but was soon released on bail. Because of his "illness," the court consistently postponed his trial, including those scheduled for October 17, 1972, and May 3, 1973. As of August 1979, no new trial date had been set. Communication by *Zentrale der Landesjustizverwaltungen* (Central State Administrations of Justice) of Ludwigsburg, dated August 24, 1979. See also *HJS*, 3:284–85.

17. *RLB*, Docs. 151, 152.

18. *RLB*, Doc. 154. Thadden forwarded an identical communication to Veesenmayer. See Doc. 155.

19. *Ibid.*, Docs. 156–57. Most of the Jews of Carpatho-Ruthenia, northeastern Hungary, and Northern Transylvania were deported through this main route. The dejewification units also used the following four alternate routes leading to Auschwitz: Sátoraljaujhely–Leginamieh Wlany–Michalovce–Medzilaborce; Munkács–Lavoczne; Galánta–Sered–Leopoldstadt–Novemesto–Trencin; and Vrutky–Zilina. See telegram 4041, dated June 24, 1944, from Roswell McClelland, WRB representative in Berne, to U.S. Secretary of State.

Shortly after the conclusion of the Nazis' transportation agreement, Rabbi Michael Dov Weissmandel of the Bratislava *Vaada* alerted the Hungarian Jewish leaders about it and about the imminent deportation of the Hungarian Jews. For details, see chapters 23 and 29. See also *Der Kastner-Bericht*, p. 82.

20. *RLB*, Doc. 132.

21. See Veesenmayer's telegram No. 159 of April 12, 1944; Inl. II/662g. *NA*, Microcopy T-120, Roll 4355, Frame K213633.

22. Thadden requested Ribbentrop's concurrence on April 14, 1944. *Ibid.*, Frame K213634.

23. He was assigned to *Inland II* in February 1940; claims that he asked for his transfer from Hungary because he was disgusted with what he had seen in the camps he visited.

(NG-4457). Hezinger was not charged after the war and in the 1970s he was still active as a businessman in the Federal Republic of Germany. *HJS*, 3:286.

24. *RLB*, Doc. 170.

25. NG-4457. For details on the treatment of foreign Jews, see chapter 27.

26. *RLB*, Docs. 164, 166.

27. Lévai, *Fekete könyv*, pp. 142–43.

28. Samu Stern, "A Race With Time": A Statement. *HJS*, 3:19–20.

29. Munkácsi, *Hogyan történt?*, pp. 82–83.

30. *RLB* Docs. 267–79.

31. Lévai, *Zsidósors Magyarországon*, p. 467.

32. The Jews of Szigetvár were concentrated in a ghetto on April 26 on the basis of the lists prepared by Béla Löbl, Ernő Kelemen, and László Beck, the three leading officials of the community. Details about the expropriation of the Jews were revealed during the postwar trial of Berend. For further details, see chapter 14.

33. Lévai, *Zsidósors Magyarországon*, p. 150.

34. *RLB*, Doc. 276.

35. *Ibid.*, Docs. 164, 166.

36. *Ibid.*, Docs. 163, 167.

37. *Ibid.*, Docs. 168, 169.

38. The world press, including the American one, allotted only scanty space to the anti-Jewish measures in Hungary. *The New York Times*, for example, "informed" its readers about the ghettoization of 800,000 Jews in Hungary by referring in three short paragraphs to a dispatch by the Nazi *Transkontinent* news agency, under the headline, "Hungary Herds All Jews," buried in column 4 of page 5 in the May 17, 1944, issue.

39. *RLB*, Doc. 172.

40. Although Hanns Elard Ludin, the German Minister in Bratislava, did not inform the German Foreign Office about the May 24 incident until June 14 (*RLB*, Doc. 176), intelligence reports must have reached Berlin soon after its occurence.

41. *RLB*, Doc. 177.

42. This was revealed by Veesenmayer in his telegram of June 20, 1944. See *NA*, Microcopy T-120, Roll 4664, Serial K1509/K350960-.

43. *RLB*, Docs. 181, 185.

44. *NA*, Microcopy T-120, Roll 4664, Serial K1509/K350960-.

45. Jenő Lévai, *Abscheu und Grauen vor dem Genocid in aller Welt* (Abhorrence and Dread for Genocide All Over the World). (New York: Diplomatic Press, 1968), pp. 222–24.

46. Lévai, *Zsidósors Magyarországon*, p. 264. From the resignation of Minister Baron György Bakách-Bessenyey until Bothmer assumed his duties in the summer of 1944, the Hungarian Legation at Berne was led by Imre Tahy, the Legation Secretary. *Ibid.*, p. 213.

47. Philip Freudiger, *Five Months*, manuscript dated November 21, 1972, p. 15.

48. Ferenczy reported that by May 28, 184,049 Jews had been deported in 58 trains. Israel Police, Bureau 06, Eichmann Trial Doc. 1319.

49. Ferenczy Report of June 8, 1944. Israel Police, Bureau 06, Eichmann Trial Doc. 1321.

50. The reason for strengthening the external guarding of the camps was the discovery of "collusion" between some of the leaders of the Ungvár ghetto with local officials, including Dr. Szendrődi, the deputy public notary, and Dr. Török, a Police Counselor. See chapter 17.

51. Ferenczy Report of May 29, 1944. Israel Police, Bureau 06, Eichmann Trial Doc. 1319.

52. *Magyarság*, May 13, 1944.

53. *Ibid.*, May 16, 1944.

54. Lévai, *Zsidósors Magyarországon*, pp. 138–39.
55. *Ibid.*, p. 140.
56. *Ibid.*
57. Statement by Ernő Pető. *HJS*, 3:52.
58. "Néptörvényszék a Zsidó Tanács felett" (Popular Tribunal on the Jewish Council), in *Fehér könyv* (White Book), Eds, Sándor Bródy, *et al.* (Budapest: Globus, 1945), pp. 76–77.

CHAPTER TWENTY

ZONE III:
NORTHERN HUNGARY

The Concentration of the Jews

IN THE MASTER PLAN for the dejewification of Hungary, Zone III encompassed the area of northern Hungary extending from Kassa to the borders of the Third Reich north of Budapest. Zone III covered the territories of Gendarmerie Districts II (Székesfehérvár) and VII (Miskolc), including the counties of Bars, Borsod, Fejér, Győr, Heves, Komárom, and Nógrád (see map 13.1).

The operational details for the concentration of the Jews in order to entrain them were discussed at a conference in the Ministry of the Interior on May 25. Held under the chairmanship of László Baky, the conference was attended by the prefects and the gendarmerie and police chiefs of the particular counties, the SD commander, and the leaders of the *Sonderkommando,* including Eichmann. The participants decided to begin the concentration of the originally estimated 65,000 Jews gathered in the ghettos in Zone III on June 5 and to carry out the deportations between June 11 and 16.[1] The launching of the anti-Jewish operations in this Zone was envisioned to coincide with the completion of the deportations from Northern Transylvania.

In accordance with the resolutions adopted on May 25, Lieutenant Colonel László Ferenczy, who was in charge of the ghettoization-deportation process, called a meeting of the officials to be involved in the operations for June 3. Held at the headquarters of the gendarmerie's investigative unit in Budapest, the meeting was attended by the mayors of the communities as well as by two top police officials and three transportation experts in the affected area.

In contrast to the procedures followed in Carpatho–Ruthenia and Northern Transylvania, it was decided that in Zone III and all subsequent operational zones the Jews were to be concentrated in centers with adequate rail and entrainment facilities only a few days before their scheduled deportation.[2]

For the direction of the anti-Jewish operations in Zone III, the dejewification squads set up their headquarters in Hatvan, northeast of

Budapest. By the time the concentration began on June 5, the Jews had lived in ghettos for several weeks. The rural Jews were first taken to their local synagogues and then, usually after a few days, transferred to the ghetto of the neighboring larger community, often the county seat. Among the larger ghettos whose populations were transferred to the entrainment centers after June 5 were those of Sajószentpéter, Ózd, Gyöngyös, and Galánta.

The ghetto of Sajószentpéter included the Jews of the rural communities in the district bearing the same name. Its population was transferred to Miskolc for entrainment.[3] The same was true of the ghetto of Ózd, which included the Jews of Bélapátfalva.[4] The ghetto of Gyöngyös was located near the railroad and the military barracks and included approximately 1,600 local Jews.[5] It had a Jewish Council composed of Dr. Ármin Vajda (chairman), Dezső Hajdu, L. H. Feigl, Jungreisz, and Jakobovits. The ghetto of Galánta, which was located in and around the synagogue, included approximately 1,100 local Jews and 600 from the neighboring rural communities. They were transferred to Komárom for entrainment.

Among the smaller ghetto centers relocated after June 5 were those of Párkány, Nagysurány, and Losonc. The Jews in the ghetto of Párkány were transferred to Léva. The ghetto of Nagysurány, which also included the Jews of the rural communities in the districts of Érsekujvár and Tardoskedd, was transferred to Komárom.

The concentration of the Jews began on schedule at 5:00 A.M. on June 5; by June 10, 51,829 Jews had been transferred to 11 entrainment centers. Of these, six centers were in the area of Gendarmerie District II, 5 centers in that of Gendarmerie District VII as shown in Table 20.1.

The living conditions in these centers, as was the treatment of the Jews both prior and during their entrainment, were generally the same as elsewhere in the country.

Gendarmerie District II

Dunaszerdahely. The local ghetto was established in and around Bacsák and Csillag streets. It had a population of 2,840, including the Jews from 72 small rural communities in Komárom County. Approximately 350 Jews were brought in from Somorja and another 350 from Nagymagyar. The ghetto was administered internally by a Jewish Council headed by József Wetzler whose main aide was József Spitzer, a Council

TABLE 20.1.
NUMBER OF JEWS IN THE GHETTOS AND
ENTRAINMENT CENTERS
IN GENDARMERIE
DISTRICTS II AND VII

Gendarmerie District II (Székesfehérvár)		Gendarmerie District VII (Miskolc)	
Dunaszerdahely	2,840	Balassagyarmat	5,820
Érsekujvár	4,843	Eger	2,744
Győr	5,635	Hatvan	3,800
Komárom	5,040	Miskolc	13,500
Léva	2,624	Salgotarján	2,240
Székesfehérvár	2,743	Total	28,104
Total	23,725		

SOURCE: Ferenczy Reports of June 7 and 12, 1944.

member. While in the ghetto the Jews were subjected to the usual searches for valuables, which were conducted under the direction of Ernő Bárki and Jenő Benkő, two police officers. The ghetto was relocated on June 8, when the Jews were transferred to the local synagogue for entrainment. The deportation of the Jews concentrated in Dunaszerdahely took place on June 15.[6]

Érsekujvár. The local Jews were concentrated in a ghetto within the city while those in the various communities of the districts of Érsekujvár, Galánta, and Végsellye, including those of Csuz and Udvard, were detained within the Kurzweil Brick Works.[7] The number of Jews entrained in Érsekujvár was 4,843.

Győr. The ghetto in this ancient city in Győr-Moson County was located in the Sziget District (Győrsziget). Of the more than 5,600 Jews concentrated in Győr by May 23, all but approximately 1,000 were from the city itself. The remainder were from the neighboring communities in the county, including Ferencháza, Győmőre, Mosonmagyaróvár, and Tét. The ghetto consisted of buildings with about 430 rooms previously occupied by around 1,200 people. The overcrowding and the inclusion of the Christian Jews in the general anti-Jewish measures induced the Bishop of Győr, Baron Vilmos Apor, to write a protest letter to Jaross. In it, he stated:

The *Győri Nemzeti Hirlap* [The National Journal of Győr] made public your decision, which nullifies the humane and calming measures of the local city authorities relating to individuals identified as Jews, and which aims to concentrate into ghettos, irrespective of age and sex, all those who are considered Jews under a variety of Ministerial decrees. In practice, this means that in the 430 rooms currently inhabited by 1,200 people, 3,500 more people will have to be crowded, which means the crowding of 10 people in a room. As the Bishop of this ancient city of Győr I raise my voice to protest against this measure, which is in conflict with humanitarianism and the Christian spirit and which punishes innocents, including children incapable of crime, without a just and objective judgment and I make you, Mr. Minister, responsible before God and Hungarian and world history for all the illnesses and deaths and for all the contempt and condemnation that will come in the wake of this measure.[8]

Although Jaross threatened him with internment, Bishop Apor continued to raise his voice against the injustices committed against the Jews, and especially the converted ones. He urged Jusztinián Cardinal Serédi, the Prince Primate of Hungary, to speak up in behalf of the Jews and did everything in his power to alleviate the position of the Jews concentrated in Győr. His efforts, however, were mostly in vain, for the local authorities, headed by Mayor Jenő Koller and including the police, the Gestapo, and the ghetto commanders refused to heed his pleas or warnings.[9]

Fate played an especially cruel game with the communities of Győr and Komárom. The Jewish community of Győr was to have been one of the beneficiaries of the Eichmann-Kasztner deal under which about 30,000 Jews—15,000 from Budapest and 15,000 from the provinces—were to be placed "on ice" in Strasshof, Austria, pending the fulfillment of the obligations assumed by "World Jewry." Eichmann insisted that the Jews of Carpatho-Ruthenia and Northern Transylvania, who had already been deported by that time, could not be included among the provincial contingent because they "represented procreative and ethnically valuable elements." Under the agreement a trainload of about 3,000 Jews from Győr and Komárom was to have been directed toward Austria. However, the *Scharführer* in charge of the train mistakenly directed it toward Kassa—the usual destination for such trains. It was only there that he discovered his mistake and asked Eichmann for instructions. Motivated by a concern for efficiency rather than the fulfillment of "legal agreements," Eichmann suggested that as long as the train was at the Slovakian border it might as well go on to Auschwitz. Instead of the train from Győr, one from Debrecen was directed to Austria. Among the 3,000 victims of Győr and Komárom was Dr. Emil Roth, the noted rabbi of Győr.[10]

As everywhere else, the Jews of Győr were subjected to a search for valuables, which began on June 7 in a school building. Shortly thereafter they were transferred to some military barracks about three miles from the city which had served as a POW camp during World War I. It is from here that the entrainment began, on June 11.[11]

Komárom. The local ghetto was established in a fort and included not only the approximately 2,000 Jews of the community[12] but also those of a number of neighboring communities. Among these were the Jewish communities of Baracska, Biatorbágy, Bicske, Ercsi, Esztergom, Galánta, Guta, Kajászó, Kolta, Martonvásárhely, Oroszlány, Pusztazámor, Sóskut, Szár, Tárnok, Tata, Tatabánya, and Vereb. Before their transfer to Komárom, these communities were used as centers for the concentration of Jews from their neighboring villages. Their average stay in Komárom before entrainment for Auschwitz was 10 days.[13]

Léva. The over 2,600 Jews concentrated here included the about 1,200 local Jews. The others were brought in from the neighboring communities, including Csata, Leker, Mikula, Nagysalló, Oroszka, Párkány, Sáró, Verebély, and Zseliz, and crowded into the military barracks at 2 Vakbottyán Street.[14] The local Jewish Council was headed by Gyula Klein.[15]

Székesfehérvár. The local Jews were first placed in a temporary ghetto within the city. After a short while they were transferred to the Szabó Tile Factory and the cavalry barracks located at the edge of the city. The new ghetto areas were terribly overcrowded; they held 2,743 Jews, of which a little over 2,000 were from the city itself.[16] The others were brought in from the neighboring communities in Fejér County, including Dunapentele, Kápolnásnyék, Mór, and Polgárdi. The well-to-do members of the various Jewish communities were taken to the local police and Gestapo headquarters on Kegel György Street, where they were subjected to the usual interrogation in search for hidden valuables—a search that became especially cruel after June 5, when the police guarding the ghetto were replaced by gendarmes.[17] The local Jewish Council was headed by Dr. Imre Neuhauser. Like his counterpart in Győr, the Bishop of Székesfehérvár, Lajos Shvoy, raised his voice against the ghettoization and deportation of the Jews, and especially of the converted ones. His interventions with Colonel Árpád Toldy, the gendarmerie officer appointed as prefect by his friend László Baky, were as vain as those with László Endre. The Bishop continued his humanitarian activities even after the deportation of the local Jews, for which he was interned during the *Nyilas* era by Prefect József Pintér.[18] Of the once comparatively large, prosperous, and historically important Jewish community of Székesfehérvár only four families are known to have been exempted from the anti-Jewish measures. These were the families of Frigyes Somogyi, József Singer, Pál Takács, and László Bernstein, who had distinguished themselves as heroes in World War I or as counterrevolutionaries.[19]

As was the case with the community of Győr, fate played a cruel trick with the "prominent" Jews of Székesfehérvár. In line with the Kasztner-Eichmann deal, the leading figures of the community were to have been taken to Budapest and from there to Austria "to be laid on ice" (see chapter 21). However, the 30 Jews who were eventually brought to Budapest were not those on Kasztner's original list. Instead, they were persons whose names were among the 80 on a supplementary list brought to Budapest by László Bernstein, one of the four exempted Jews in the community. This supplementary list was also handed over to Wisliceny, who bungled his mission; instead of the 30 "prominent" Jews, 30 mostly elderly men and women were brought to Budapest. Among the "prominent" Jews taken to Auschwitz as a consequence was the well-known Rabbi of Székesfehérvár, Dr. Pál Hirschler.[20]

Gendarmerie District VII

Balassagyarmat. The 5,820 Jews who were concentrated in the city included the local community of about 2,000 Jews;[21] the others were brought in from the neighboring rural communities in Nógrád County, including Nógrádbercel and Szécsény.[22]

The Jewish Council was composed of Mihály Lázár, Chairman, Dezső Sándor, Pál Sándor, Ferenc Hajdu, Imre Léván, and János Weltner. Just before deportation, the Jews were relocated in the tobacco barns at Nyírjespuszta about 5 kilometers from the city. The local police leader, Oszkár Oriás, was among those who distinguished themselves by their cruel behavior.

Eger.[23] The ghetto was located in and around Ujvilág, Káptalan, Patak, Gólya, Uszoda, and Almagyar Streets and Szunyog and Piac (Market) Squares. It included 2,744 Jews of whom around 2,000 were from the city itself. About 1,500 Jews from the various communities of Heves County, including Füzesabony and Heves, were taken into the workers' quarters of a deserted mine called Bagólyuk, which belonged to the *Egercsehi Kőszénbánya és Portlancementbánya* (Coal and Portland Cement Mine of Egercsehi) located near Egercsehi and Szücs, northwest of Eger.[24] The approximately 1,500 Jews of Heves and of the rural communities in the district were transferred to Bagólyuk on

May 9. Technically, the transfer of these Jews was illegal, for under the ghettoization decree the city, which had a population of over 10,000, would have had to establish its own ghetto.[25] The ultimate result would, of course, have been the same.

Gyula Czapik, the local archbishop, tried to alleviate the persecutions by intervening in behalf of the Jews with the local authorities. He even had the pastoral letter of Jusztinián Cardinal Serédi read in all the churches in his parish despite the Cardinal's decision to recall it in the wake of his agreement with Prime Minister Sztójay.[26]

Before entrainment, the Jews were concentrated for a few days in the brickyards at Kerecsend. They were deported on June 8 from the Maklár railway station. Soon after the completion of the deportations, the local population invaded the camp site and removed the belongings of the Jews.[27]

Hatvan. The headquarters of the dejewification squad in operational Zone III, Hatvan, a city in Heves County, had about 3,800 Jews concentrated in the local sugar factory.[28] During their loading for deportation, which began on June 12, a train with about 600 Jewish labor servicemen from Budapest stopped at the station en route to its destination. Captain Márton Zöldi, one of the commanders of the dejewification program, ordered that the cars with the labor servicemen be attached to the deportation train, which was, of course, directed to Auschwitz.[29] Another morbidly interesting aspect of the tragedy of the Jews of Hatvan was the case of Baroness Alexandra Hatvany, the daughter of Baron Ferenc Hatvany, the Hungarian sugar magnate. According to a report by Ferenczy, the Baroness was hidden by Gendarmerie Captain Endre Nagy as his fiancée. He married her in Budapest on May 29. Ferenczy had the Baroness arrested and the Captain subjected to legal action.[30]

Miskolc. Of the 13,500 Jews in the ghetto a little over 10,000 were from the city itself.[31] The ghetto was located in and around these streets: Arany János, Csizmadia, Jósika, Kőműves, Rákosi Jenő, Vörösmarty, Asztalos, Esztergályos, Kalapos, Lakatos, Rostás, Vilma, Bádogos, Villányi, Kárpitos, Mészáros, Szatócs, Ács, Bors Vezér, Gubacs, Kovács, Molnár, Zöldfa, Bognár, Cukrász, Hadirokkant, Kölcsey, Petőfi, Zrinyi and Margit Streets. The local Jewish Council was headed by Mór Feldman and Elemér Banet. The concentration of the city Jews and of those in the neighboring communities in Borsod County was carried out cruelly and with the closest cooperation of Emil Borbély-Maczky, the Prefect.[32]

On the day of the concentration, the local authorities resorted to a vicious anti-Jewish propaganda technique. The police of Miskolc made public an announcement warning the local Christian population against "actions" directed against it:

We warn the Hungarian Christian public that certain individuals have placed poisoned lump-sugar by house gates with which they want to endanger the life and health of Hungarian Christian children.[33]

The Jews from the districts of Edelény, Mezőcsát, Mezőkeresztes, Mezőkövesd, Miskolc, Ózd, and Sajószentpéter in Borsod County as well as those of some of the neighboring communities in the District of Szerencs in Zemplén County, the District of Szikszó in Abauj-Torna County, and the District of Putnok in Gömör-Kishont County were concentrated in the local brickyards. Among the largest of the Jewish communities that were concentrated in Miskolc prior to their deportation were those of Abaujszántó, Bánréve, Diósgyőr, Edelény, Encs, Gőnc, Hejócsaba, Hidasnémeti, Mád, Mezőcsát, Mezőkeresztes, Mezőkővesd, Monok, Ózd, Putnok, Sajószentpéter, Szerencs, Szikszó, Tállya, Tisza-Eszlár, Tiszaluc, and Vilmány.[34] A number of physicians from Miskolc and Borsod County who were not deported in June were taken to Pusztavám in August, where they were executed by the SS.[35]

Salgótarján. The 2,240 Jews concentrated in the local ghetto were not only from the city but also from a number of rural communities in Nógrád County, including Cered, Etes, Somoskőujfalu, Zagyvapálfalva, and Zagyvarékás.[36] The ghetto population was housed in the stables of the local mining company. The rounding up and interrogation of the Jews were the responsibility of 50 gendarmes brought in from another area. They performed their task in a particularly brutal fashion, the details of which were described in a report of June 7 addressed to the Central Jewish Council.[37]

Reaction of the Jewish Council

The deportation of the Jews concentrated in Zone III began on schedule on June 11—one day after the completion of the concentration. By noon on June 12, six trains with 16,238 Jews had already left the area for Auschwitz. The operation was completed by June 16; 51,829 Jews were deported in 23 trains.[38]

The alarming reports that came in from the Jewish concentration areas in Zone III had a sobering effect on the leaders of the Central Jewish Council. Most of its members had rationalized the deportations from Kistarcsa and Topolya late in April because they involved "only" able-bodied Jews between 16 and 50 years of age and, like many other Jews, they tended to "understand" the necessity of removing the Jews from the "military operational zones" in Carpatho-Ruthenia and Northern Transylvania; however, the ghettoization and deportation of the Jews from Hungary proper awakened them to the reality of the ultimate intentions of the dejewification experts engaged in the Final Solution. Ironically, even at this late hour the leading members of the Central Jewish Council were fearful about taking any "illegal" measures to safeguard the remaining Jews, lest they jeopardize the chance to win the race with time. This fear and paralysis extended even to blocking a flyer calculated to inform the Hungarian-Christian society about the realities of the deportations and Auschwitz. They continued to rely on techniques they had successfully employed under relatively normal conditions—the filing of complaints and petitions with Horthy or leading government officials.

When the deportations were ended in northeastern Hungary and Northern Transylvania, the Jewish Council decided to follow the example of some factories and local and central governmental organs, including the Ministry of Defense. Motivated partly by humanitarian concerns and partly by their own interests and manpower needs, a number of governmental agencies and enterprises came to the assistance of the beleaguered Jews, demanding the exemption of some individuals or categories of Jews from the general anti-Jewish measures. These were usually Jews who were personally known to the local authorities or who possessed specialized skills of great interest to the particular factories or communities. This was especially the case for Jewish physicians, who were often the only ones serving a particular locality.[39]

Parallelling these non-Jewish initiatives, the Council submitted a lengthy memorandum to Sztójay on June 7, urging that the Jews be retained in the country and employed on projects of vital interest to the nation. The memorandum identified specific projects for which Jews could be employed, following procedures like those in Slovakia, where, after the first wave of deportations in the spring of 1942, the remaining Jews were placed in special work camps.[40]

Around June 10, just before the beginning of the deportations from Zone III, the Council addressed a memo to some members of the government:

We are aware that over 300,000 of our brethren have so far been taken to strange, faraway places, into deportation, where, beyond harsh physical suffering, the catastrophe of destruction is threatening them. According to the data at our disposal, which cover the period up to June 6, 303,000 persons have so far been deported. The deportations are still continuing and the number of deportees by this time may be established at 320,000 at least; there is also the threat that this number will continuously increase.

Also shocking are the circumstances in which the Jews were first concentrated into ghettos and in which they were subsequently evacuated, that is deported, from there. We do not wish to detail the various phases of this sad process, but we had to determine shockingly from all this that the Jews already concentrated in the provincial ghettos have been faced by the direst and most primitive conditions. (The Nyír area, Carpatho-Ruthenia, the Upper Province, Transylvania, the rear of the Tisza, and the Délvidék.)

In certain areas, they were placed in brickyards (where they were under a roof, but without walls, exposed to the vicissitudes of weather, rain, and wind), mills, warehouses, factories, or barracks located in the outskirts of cities, where there was neither water nor toilets. (Győr, Székesfehérvár, Komárom, Bicske, and Miskolc.) Under the open sky or with barely a roof, they have become the victims of rats, mice, vermin, and worms.

In some ghettos, the gendarmes interrogated the Jews who were well off and those who were suspected of hiding their valuables; these were seriously manhandled; neither the elderly nor the ill were spared so that many died as a result of the maltreatment.

It was after such antecedents that the totally despoiled Jews were crammed into locked freight cars, 70 to 80 per car, irrespective of age, sex, or health and without the most essential clothing, blankets, or food; each car was supplied with one full bucket and one empty one. The departure was effectuated under the most adverse conditions, usually at night. In many cases, many people died en route in the wake of the extreme overcrowding so that when the sealed doors were opened corpses fell out of the cars.

It must be emphasized that the deportation of the Jews removed from the ghettos was not restricted to the able-bodied. In the Kistarcsa camp only those over 16 and under 50 were taken away; the ill and those outside these age groups were not deported. It was this circumstance that filled their concerned relatives with the hope that they had been taken away for purposes of labor. However, there was no such selection during the deportations from other places. They entrained the very old, even those over 80; what is more, in some cities, including Beregszász, the Jews in the homes for the aged were the first ones to be taken to the stations. Even the infants were taken away. That the deportation of the Jews in these areas has taken place irrespective of age, sex, or health—that is, irrespective of their capacity for labor—leaves their relatives still in the country and Jewry as a whole in a state of extreme concern and almost drives them to despair.[41]

"Revolt" Against the Council

While the Council became clearly mired in its own inertia, though visibly frustrated by its failure to win the race with time in the provinces, many of the Jews of Budapest became increasingly restless and adopted a more militant position toward it. Unaware of the desperate attempts of the Council members to save what was still to be saved, these Jews saw only one thing: the Council had cooperated with the authorities. They saw the Council's active involvement in the concentration of the Jews in special quarters and apartments, the issuance of internment summonses, the distribution and enjoyment of immunity certificates, and the requisitions of goods. Tension between the two factions became unbearable when the Council revealed its total impotence in the course of the deportations from the provinces. Many of the Jews of Budapest had friends and relatives in the provinces who managed to keep them posted about the cruelties of the ghettoization and deportation program.

A confrontation took place around June 10, when a delegation composed of labor servicemen and leftist and resistance-oriented Jews appeared before the Council in Samu Stern's office. Their spokesman was Dr. Imre Varga, a young physician of Budapest, who in an impassioned speech implored the Council to change its course and adopt more suitable methods to prevent total catastrophe:

Don't you see, don't you want to understand that our fathers, mothers, and brothers are crammed into freight cars by gendarmes' bayonets, 70 in a car, where they are taken in human manure to unknown places, to extermination? Can one tolerate this further, is it permissible to be satisfied with petitions and servile requests, would it not be desirable to reveal all this before Christian society? We have to shout out to the whole world that they are murdering us, we have to resist, and stop further cowardly submission!

The audience was visibly shaken by the emotional impact of the speech, but apparently was soon disarmed by Stern's cool reply:

The Jewish Council is doing everything in its power. It has spoken about the deportations to each and every governmental and church official from whom it could expect assistance. Unfortunately, the Germans are in command and the Hungarian authorities either cannot or do not want to resist. Jewish resistance would be a useless sacrifice that would be crushed within minutes and would unimaginably aggravate the situation of the others. The Council has done and will continue to do its duty.[42]

Seeing the hopelessness of the situation, Dr. Varga committed suicide the following day.

The encounter, however, was not a total failure for those clamoring for greater militancy. It galvanized some of the middle-echelon officials of the Council into action. A group composed of Dr. Lajos Gottesmann and Dr. Sándor Braun, members of the "provincial department" (*vidéki osztály*), which was headed by József Goldschmied, Ernő Munkácsi, and György Polgár of MIPI, convened soon after the encounter to discuss the possibility of preparing and distributing an appeal to the Hungarian intelligentsia. Almost concurrently, but acting independently, Sándor Somló, the head of the Council's Food Section (*élelmiszerosztály*), also appealed to the Central Jewish Council to issue such an appeal. A draft appeal was prepared by Munkácsi, who read it before the Council the following day. Although Stern was initially inclined to go along, upon hearing the texts, he adopted a totally negative position against involvement in any "illegal" activity. He expressed willingness to go along only if the appeal had the approval of the censorship authorities, which was, of course, totally absurd. The other members of the Council followed Stern's leadership and opposed the "illegal" issuance of the appeal. They even refused to allow the mailing of the appeal in the form of a letter, which technically did not fall under the censorship regulation.

Gottesmann and Munkácsi, however, passed the text to Rabbi Fábián Herskovits, who edited it slightly in conjunction with Sándor Somló and then mimeographed it in cooperation with Professors Fülöp and Jenő Grünwald.[43] The mimeographing and distribution of the appeal was the first overt act of defiance of any importance. The appeal, addressed to Hungarian Christian society, read partially as follows:

In the 24th hour of its tragic fate, Hungarian Jewry turns to Hungarian Christian society and raises a beseeching plea. It is turning to those with whom we have lived for a thousand years through good times and bad times, in this country in whose dust lie our forefathers, grandfathers, and fathers.

We did not speak up when we were deprived of our wealth and lost our human dignity and civic honor. And we did not take this final step when we were taken away from our family hearths. Now, however, it is a matter of our very lives. What is more, even the writing of this sentence is painful because we are talking about only part of Hungarian Jewry.

We must reveal before Hungarian Christian society that hundreds of thousands of Hungarian Jews have been deported under such tragic and cruel circumstances as have no parallel in world history.

Hungarian Jewry, from the first moment it was deprived of its rights to the present day, has borne its terrible lot in silent resignation, but the death trains have nevertheless departed from all parts of the country. So far, almost 500,000 persons have been deported.

Although the pertinent governmental decree spoke only about the placement of the Jews into separate parts of the cities, in fact the separated areas (ghettos) mentioned in the Decree became terrible concentration camps from which the provincial Jews were taken under even worse conditions to brickyards and the ruins of deserted mills located in the outskirts.

It was from these concentration camps that they were taken to the deportation trains, where 70 to 80 were jammed into each freight car by rifle butts, bayonets, and whips. The only air inside was what came through the inefficient ventilating slots. These unfortunates traveled for days in such sealed cars, deprived of all goods and money, without blankets or even straw. For food they were given a few loaves of bread; in addition, there were two buckets, one full of water and the other for sanitary needs. This is how they left for foreign countries.

We would have been a little less concerned if our able-bodied brethren had been taken for labor. But the elderly and infants were crowded into these cars as well, without any selection. Moreover, seriously ill persons just after an operation, and pregnant women were taken into the cattle cars on stretchers. This was done under terribly cruel conditions. These people were not being taken for labor!

According to the May 23 issue of the *Uj Nemzedék* (New Generation), three women passengers of the "Jewish train" from Nagykanizsa died at the railway station of Szombathely. One was 104, another 102, and the third 92. The 102-year-old died of pneumonia. Obviously, these people were not taken for labor. The old, the sick, and infants would only consume food abroad, and consequently we have no doubt about the fate that awaits them—destruction.

Hungarian society could not have witnessed these terrible happenings with indifference had it known about them. However, experience shows that a considerable segment of Hungarian public opinion knows nothing about these horrors. This is even more the case because the press is silent on the matter.

Will it be possible to justify before history that 8 percent of Hungary's citizens, almost one million people, were condemned to deportation and destruction without a hearing and a legal judgment?

Today we have no time and especially no means to defend ourselves against one-sided accusations. But we hold our heads high and look the accusers in the eye. If we had faults, they stemmed not from our specific sins but from that system of production which has guided the world, including Hungary, for a century, and of which every production force was a part, Christian and Jewish alike.

Those who know history know that the nation is permanent and the political direction is variable. Today this is seen as political justice, tomorrow it will be something else. But beyond political trends there is a lasting human justice, and he who sins against it cannot hold his place before the lord of history, the Almighty God of us all.

It is possible that the Hungarian nation approves of eradicating Jewry from its body. But how could the merciless extermination of helpless old people, infants, limbless and sightless veterans, and unarmed defenseless people be reconciled with the always chivalrous Hungarian nation?

Let a means be found, in conjunction with the neutral states, so that the few hundred thousand remaining Hungarian Jews can emigrate.

In the name of our children, the aged, and defenseless women, in the name of all of us who face final destruction, we raise our beseeching voice to the Hungarian Christian society.

We believe in the sense of justice of the Hungarian nation, which is awaiting and demanding justice from the people of the world, and which could not possibly desire or permit this terrible destruction of innocents.

But if our beseeching voice, appealing for our bare lives, is in vain, then we only request the Hungarian nation to put an end to our suffering here at home before the deportation with its accompanying horrors and cruelties, so that we can at least be buried in the land of our birth.[44]

The emotional tone of the appeal was geared to the presumed psychological makeup and receptiveness of the Hungarian intelligentsia. It is almost impossible to determine its impact. The four Jewish intellectuals involved in the mimeographing and distribution were arrested shortly after the first copies were mailed out[45] and were not freed until the Lakatos era, after considerable effort by the leaders of the Hungarian Jewish community, especially Ottó Komoly (see chapter 29).

The belated act of resistance took place almost simultaneously with the translation and selective distribution of the so-called Auschwitz Protocols, which accurately described the processes and dimensions of the mass murder committed in the concentration camp. Why these elements of Hungarian Jewry did not enlighten Hungarian public opinion until the deportation of provincial Jewry was virtually completed, and why the Protocols, which were dictated on April 25, were not distributed earlier remains one of the most baffling enigmas requiring elucidation if one is to understand the extent of the catastrophe in Hungary.[46]

While this heroic group of Hungarian Jews was engaged in this act of resistance, an act which required considerable courage but was basically useless, the dejewification experts were completing their operation against the Jews in Zone III and were finalizing their plans for the implementation of the same program in Zone IV.

Notes

1. Veesenmayer telegram to the German Foreign Office dated May 25, 1944. *RLB,* Doc. 165. The actual number of Jews entrained for deportation from Zone III was only close to 52,000 (see below).

2. Ferenczy Report of May 29, 1944. Israel Police, Bureau 06, Eichmann Trial Doc. 1319.

3. Some of the details on this and several other ghettos and entrainment centers discussed in this chapter were taken from a Jewish Council document reproduced in Lévai, *Zsidósors Magyarországon,* pp. 407–21. For further details on Sajószentpéter, see Rav Slomo Paszternák, *Miskolc és környéke mártirkönyve* (The Memorial Book of Miskolc and Its Environs) (Tel Aviv: The Author, 1970), pp. 76–77.

4. According to the census of 1941, Ózd, in Borsod County northwest of Miskolc, had a Jewish population of 721 representing 3.4 percent of the city's total. In 1949, the community had 113 members and was led by Béla Sárosi and Péter Groszmann. By 1957, the community was reduced to 69. Zsidó Világkongresszus, no. 4 (April 15, 1947), pp. 4–5; no. 13–14 (May 1949), p. 17. Uj Élet, August 1957. See also statement by Mrs. Lewis Vidor at the YIVO, Archives no. 3192, File 775; and Paszternák, Miskolc és környéke mártirkönyve, pp. 71–73.

5. In 1941, Gyöngyös, a community in Heves County, had a Jewish population of 2,071, representing 8.6 percent of the city's total. In 1946, the community numbered 461 Jews, including survivors who moved in from the neighboring communities. By 1949, the community was reduced, to an Orthodox congregation with 102 and a Status Quo congregation with 312 members. Zsidó Világkongresszus, no. 4 (April 15, 1947), pp. 2–3; no. 13–14 (May 1949), pp. 11, 25.

6. A dunaszerdahelyi hitközség emlékkönyve (The Memorial Book of the Jewish Community of Dunaszerdahely), ed. Alfred Engel. (Tel Aviv: A Dunaszerdahelyi Emlékkönyv-Bizottság, 1975), pp. 124–35. The book also contains a general history of the community, a list of its martyrs (pp. 319–429) as well as briefer accounts of Somorja (pp. 150–54) and Nagymagyar (pp. 155–57). See also the personal narratives of Charlotte and Rose Fleischmann at the YIVO, Archives File no. 774/2715.

7. Lévai, Zsidósors Magyarországon, p. 412. See the accounts by Esther Kalisch (YIVO, 769/1084) and Charlotte Adler (YIVO, 773/1695) for additional information on the camp in Érsekujvár. According to most sources, the Jews of the town of Galánta were transferred for entrainment to Komárom.

8. Lévai, Zsidósors Magyarországon, pp. 145–46.

9. Lévai, Szürke könyv magyar zsidók megmentéséről (Gray Book on the Rescuing of Hungarian Jews) (Budapest: Officina, n.d.), pp. 44–45, 72, 79.

10. Der Kastner-Bericht, pp. 113–14, 121–22. According to the census of 1941, Győr had 4,688 Jews, representing 8.2 percent of the population. By 1946, there were 950 or 1.5 percent. In 1949, it had a Congressional community with 459 members and an Orthodox congregation with 72 members. They were led by Elek Fleischmann and Jakab Grünzweig respectively. As a result of the campaign against Zionism and cosmopolitanism and the Hungarian Revolution of 1956, the community gradually declined. According to Dr. Tibor Klein, the Rabbi of Győr, who came to America after the events of 1956, the estimated number of the Jews residing in the city was just over 150 in 1957. Zsidó Világkongresszus, no. 4 (April 15, 1947), pp. 2–3; no. 13–14 (May 1949), pp. 12 and 24. For a personal account of the ghetto see Lévai, Zsidósors Magyarországon, p. 414. See also the personal narratives of Mrs. Dezső Krausz (YIVO, 768/3635) and Martha Haász (YIVO, 775/3148). The latter also deals with the community of Mezőkövesd.

11. Pinkas ha'kehilot, pp. 240–43. See also István Domán, A győri izraelita hitközség története, 1930–47 (The History of the Jewish Community of Győr, 1930–47) (Budapest: A Magyar Izraeliták Országos Képviselete, 1979), 69 pp.

12. Lévai, Zsidósors Magyarországon, p. 413. In 1941, Komárom had a Jewish population of approximately 1,800 out of a total population of 17,000. After the war the community's membership dwindled to under 100 and it was led by Imre Kálmán. Zsidó Világkongresszus, no. 4 (April 15, 1947), pp. 2–3; no. 13–14 (May 1949), p. 14. For additional details, see the personal narratives of G. Berger (YIVO, 768/3634), Stephen Pál (YIVO, 773/1735), and M. Weiss (YIVO, 776/27). See also Pinkas ha'kehilot, pp. 484–86.

13. Personal communication by Margit Pressburger Halmenschlager, a former deportee from Bicske, dated June 4, 1978.

14. The Jews of Párkány were taken to Léva on June 6 together with the Jews of Esztergom who had previously been transferred to Párkány. Munkácsi, Hogyan történt?, p. 114. The 80 to 85 Jewish families of Verebély, together with the Jews from the neighbor-

ing villages, were first concentrated in the local steam-mill on May 9. Five or six privileged families were concentrated in the synagogue, but these too were transferred to the mill on June 8. Two days later the entire ghetto population was transferred to Léva, where their entrainment began on June 13. Personal communication by Rachel Herzog of Tel Aviv, a survivor of the Verebély ghetto.

15. Lévai, *Zsidósors Magyarországon*, p. 412.

16. In 1941, Székesfehérvár had 2,075 Jews representing 4.3 percent of the city's population. By 1946, the community dwindled to 289, or 0.6 percent. With the immigration of survivors from the neighboring rural areas, the community increased and by 1949 the Congregational group had 346 members and the Orthodox one 30 members. They were headed by Ármin Gerőfi and M. Győző Adler respectively. A decade later, the membership of the community was estimated at 300. The lay leadership was provided by Gerőfi; the spiritual needs of the community were taken care of by Rabbi Mór Schwartz of Budapest who paid regular visits to the city. Lévai, *Zsidósors Magyarországon*, pp. 413–14; *Zsidó Világkongresszus*, no. 4 (April 15, 1947), pp. 2–3; no. 13–14 (May 1949), pp. 20 and 25; *Uj Élet* (New Life), Budapest, April 15, 1959.

17. Munkácsi, *Hogyan történt?*, p. 114.

18. Lévai, *Szürke könyv*, p. 77.

19. Lévai, *Zsidósors Magyarországon*, p. 413.

20. *Der Kastner-Bericht*, pp. 120–21. See also *Pinkas ha'kehilot*, pp. 408–11.

21. In 1941, Balassagyarmat had 1,712 Jews representing 13.9 percent of the city's total. Their number declined to 221 or 1.8 percent by 1946. In 1949, the community was headed by Jenő Büchler. By the late 1950s, the city had only around 70 Jews under the leadership of Ignác Elfer. *Zsidó Világkongresszus*, no. 4 (April 15, 1947), pp. 2–3; no. 13–14 (May 1949), pp. 8 and 24; *Uj Élet*, April 1, 1958.

22. See personal account by George Zilczer, one of the leaders of the Balassagyarmat community (YIVO, 768/3550). See also the accounts of Dr. Elisabeth Schenck (YIVO, 768/3551), Mrs. Oscar and Anikó Weisz (YIVO, 768/3552), and Mrs. Mór Bleyer, et al. (YIVO, 771/3549). See also *Pinkas ha'kehilot*, pp. 173–75.

23. In 1941, Eger had a Jewish population of 1,787 Jews representing 5.5 percent of the total. By 1946 there were but 215 or 0.6 percent. In 1949, the community had 294 members under the leadership of Dr. Lajos Kraj. With a relatively stable membership, the community's leadership was reorganized in November 1959 as follows: Dr. Miklós Fischer, Chairman; Endre Székely, Executive Officer; László Kardos, Secretary; and Simon Deutsch, Treasurer. *Zsidó Világkongresszus*, no. 4, April 15, 1947, pp. 2–3; no. 13–14, May 1949, pp. 10, 24, and 25. *Uj Élet*, December 15, 1958 and August 15, 1959.

24. Lévai, *Zsidósors Magyarországon*, p. 411. See also *Pinkas ha'kehilot*, pp. 128–31.

25. The Jewish Council brought this fact to the attention of the authorities, including Zsigmond Székely Molnár of the Jewish Department in the Ministry of the Interior, and the Gestapo on May 12. Munkácsi, *Hogyan történt?*, pp. 68–69. See also *Pinkas ha'kehilot*, pp. 262–63.

26. Lévai, *Szürke könyv*, p. 76. For details on the agreement between Cardinal Serédi and Sztójay, see chapter 30.

27. For a history of the Jews of Eger see *Egri zsidók* (The Jews of Eger). Edited by Arthur Ehrenfeld, et al. (Jerusalem: Az Egri Zsidók Emlékbizottsága, 1975), 100+ 92 pp. The list of the community's martyrs is on pp. 88–100. See also Veesenmayer telegram no. 280 of June 27, 1944. *RLB*, Doc. 285.

28. In 1941, Hatvan had a Jewish population of 541, representing 3.4 percent of the city's total population of 16,020. *Pinkas ha'kehilot*, pp. 263–64.

29. Statement by Imre Reiner. Israel Police, Bureau 06, Eichmann Trial Doc. 347. Many of these labor servicemen were on route to their stations at Jászberény. See the personal narratives by the following servicemen deported from Hatvan: Endre Guttmann,

Dr. Alexander Puder, Tibor Nathan, Jósef Sprunz, Alexander Ecker, and Ernő Klein in YIVO 768/3587, 770/225, 772/2128, 772/2435, 773/2114, and 774/2874, respectively.

30. Ferenczy Report of June 7, 1944. Israel Police, Bureau 06, Eichmann Trial Doc. 1320. For an account on the postwar case relating to the Hatvany art collection, see *HJS*, 3:281–83.

31. In 1941, the city had 10,428 Jews representing 13.5 percent of the total. By 1946, the number of survivors, including those who came in from the neighboring rural communities, amounted to 2,353 or 3.0 percent of the city's population. On July 30–31, 1946, the city was the scene of a Communist-condoned pogrom that claimed a number of Jewish victims. By 1959, the community was reduced to about 500 families led by Dr. György Havas (Chairman), Márton Weisz (Rabbi), and Mrs. Imre Révész (Chairman of the Ladies' Chapter). *Zsidó Világkongresszus*, no. 4 (April 15, 1947), pp. 2–3; no. 13–14 (May 1949), pp. 16, 24, 27–29; Eugene Duschinsky, "Hungary," in *The Jews in the Soviet Satellites*, ed. P. Meyer (Syracuse: Syracuse University Press, 1953), pp. 427–29.

32. Three Jews (Mark Tyrnauer, Sándor Klein, and Hofbauer) are known to have died as a result of the maltreatment suffered during the concentration. Munkácsi, *Hogyan történt?* p. 113. Shortly after the war, Borbély-Maczky was beaten to death by a mob in the Népkert (People's Garden) in Miskolc. Elek Karsai, *Itél a nép* (The People Judge). (Budapest: Kossuth, 1977), p. 14.

33. *A tizhónapos tragédia* (The Ten Months Tragedy), vol. 2, eds. Ervin Szerelemhegyi, István Gyenes, Károly Kiss, and Jenő Lévai (Budapest: Müller Károly, 1945), p. 42.

34. For a historical account of the Jewish community of Miskolc and some of the larger communities in Borsod County see Rav Slomo Paszternák, *Miskolc és környéke mártirkönyve* (The Memorial Book of Miskolc and Its Environs). (Tel Aviv: The Author, 1970), 277 + 38 + 14 pp. Pages 103–276 contain the lists of the martyrs of Miskolc and of 220 neighboring towns, villages, or hamlets. See also Lévai, *Zsidósors Magyarországon*, pp. 105 and 410, and the following personal narratives available at the YIVO: Violet Keil (Archives no. 770/151) and Mrs. László Adler (771/3501).

35. *Pinkas ha'kehilot*, pp. 359–64.

36. The Jewish population of Salgotarján represented about 6.2 percent of the city's total in 1941. By 1946, the number was reduced to 852 or 1.2 percent of the total. In the late 1950s the community consisted of 138 Jews led by Izidor Berkovics. *Zsidó Világkongresszus*, no. 4 (April 15, 1947), pp. 2–3; no. 13–14, (May 1949), pp. 19 and 24; *Uj Élet*, August 1957, March 15, 1958; *Pinkas ha'kehilot*, pp. 518–20.

37. Munkácsi, *Hogyan történt?*, pp. 84–85 and 114.

38. Ferenczy Report of June 7, 1944. Israel Police, Bureau 06, Eichmann Trial Doc. 1320; Ferenczy Report of June 12, 1944. In his telegram of June 30, 1944, Veesenmayer reported that 50,805 Jews had been deported from Zone III and that the total number of Jews deported from Zones I–III was 340,162. *RLB*, Doc. 182.

39. For examples of such petitions submitted by local governmental organs and factories, see *FAA*, 2:499–502, 507–10, 513–14, 516–17, 519–32, 556–65, and 644–47.

40. For the text of the memorandum, see *ibid.*, pp. 540–48.

41. Munkácsi, *Hogyan történt?*, pp. 114–16.

42. *Ibid.*, pp. 118–19.

43. *Ibid.*, pp. 119–21. Fábián Herskovits gives a somewhat different version of the origin of the appeal. He claims that the draft appeal was drawn up by him and Somló, who was his neighbor, and that the Jewish Council approved it and handed it over to Munkácsi for rewording. Herskovits claims that he then used the text prepared by Béla Pásztor, who was also concerned about the issuance of such an appeal. Herskovits' corrected version was retyped by Mrs. Tibor Faragó in the "rabbinical offices" and then 2,000 copies were mimeographed. Statement by Fábián Herskovits, YIVO, 768/3581.

44. Munkácsi, *Hogyan történt?*, pp. 121–23.

45. Herskovits claims that the arrest of the conspirators was the consequence of a denunciation by a school teacher who had received a copy of the appeal from Dr. Dénes Láczer, a Professor of Religion, who had obtained a few copies for distribution from Professor Jenő Grünwald. Statement by Fábián Herskovits. For further details see section on "Resistance" in chapter 29.

46. For an evaluation of the controversial question of what the Jewish leaders knew about the realities of the concentration camps and when they learned about them, see chapter 23.

CHAPTER TWENTY-ONE

ZONE IV:
SOUTHERN HUNGARY EAST
OF THE DANUBE

The Ghettoization Process

THE ANTI-JEWISH operations in Zone IV affected the Jews living in Gendarmerie Districts V (Szeged) and VI (Debrecen). The zone included the southeastern parts of Trianon Hungary extending from the Danube and the formerly Yugoslav-held area of the Délvidék (see map 13.1).

As was the case in the other anti-Jewish operational zones, the Jews of these gendarmerie districts were systematically rounded up shortly after the adoption of the ghettoization decree of April 26. The Jews of the rural communities were assembled in the local synagogues and after a first round of expropriation were taken to a nearby large ghetto center, usually the district seat. The population of these ghetto centers was transferred after a few weeks to the nearest entrainment centers from where they were deported, together with the other Jews assembled there, within a few days.

The ghettoization, concentration, and deportation operations in Zone IV were directed from Kiskunfélegyháza, where the dejewification squads had their headquarters.[1] The speed, efficiency, and inhumanity with which these operations were carried out were identical with those displayed in the other zones. Although the assembled Jews lived in the entrainment centers for only a few days, they were emaciated and dispirited by the conditions under which they lived in the ghettos and the brickyards and above all by the cruel treatment at the hands of the gendarmes and detectives searching for hidden valuables.

The deportation of the Jews from this zone began on schedule on June 25, shortly after the transfer of the Jews from the various ghettos into the entrainment centers. It was completed on June 28 with the removal of 40,505 Jews in 14 trains.[2]

Gendarmerie District V

The larger ghettos in Gendarmerie District V whose populations were eventually transferred to the entrainment centers were those of Hódmezővásárhely, Kalocsa, Kecel, Kiskőrös, Makó, Nagykáta, Szarvas, and Szentes.[3]

Hódmezővásárhely. Hódmezővásárhely, a city in Csongrád County, in 1941 had a Jewish population of 1,501, representing 2.4 percent of its total population.[4] With the inauguration of anti-Jewish measures after the German occupation, the local Jews were at first quite lucky, for the city administration refused to force them into a separate ghetto. They were allowed to remain in their apartments until June 16, when on orders of the area dejewification unit they were ordered into the local synagogue, where they were deprived of their valuables. On June 19, they were transferred to Szeged for entrainment.[5]

Kalocsa. In 1941, the town had 360 Jews, representing 2.9 percent of the local population. There were two small ghettos in the locality: one consisting of a number of buildings on Tomori and Hid Streets; the other located in a paprika mill on Buzapiac Square. The former had 617 Jews, including those of the town and a few localities in Dunavecse District; the latter housed the Jews from the neighboring rural communities, including those of Bátya, Dragszél, Dunaszentbenedek, Dusnok, Érsekcsanád, Foktő, Géderlak, Hajós, Miske, Nemesnádudvar, Sükösd, and Szakmár. The local Jewish Council was headed by Dr. Mátyás Wolf and included Dr. Gyula Szekeres and Dr. Elemer Link representing the Jews of Kalocsa, Sándor Tápai those of Kalocsa District, and Ferenc Faragó the Jews of the communities from Dunavecse District. József Grösz, the Archbishop of Kalocsa, tried to intervene in behalf of the Jews, but, like his colleagues elsewhere in the country, was unsuccessful. The Jews of Kalocsa were deported on June 18.[6]

Kecel. A town in Pest-Pilis-Solt-Kiskun County, located between Kecskemét and Baja, Kecel had a Jewish population of 110 (0.4 percent) in 1941. Following their round-up in late April 1944, the Jews were concentrated in three buildings in Rákóczi Ferenc II Street. The 92 local Jews were joined by 26 Jews brought in from neighboring Császártöltés. Until June 17, when they were transferred to Szeged, they were led by a Jewish Council composed of György Vető (chairman), József Weisz, Ferenc Weisz, and Dávid Klein.[7]

Kiskőrös. Located just north of Kecel, Kiskőrös had a Jewish population of 509 (3.9 percent) in 1941. Shortly after the German occupation, 22 local Jews were taken to the Topolya internment camp. The ghetto which was established toward the end of April in and around the synagogue contained 582 Jews, including those brought in from the neighboring villages. Until the transfer of its population to Kecskemét on June 21, the ghetto was led by a Jewish Council composed of Mór Ruder, Vilmos Lebovits, Sándor Gottlieb, Izsák Spiegel, Mór Kupfer, and Mózes Blumenthal.[8]

Makó. A city in Csanád County renowned for onion-growing, Makó had a Jewish population of 1,881 (5.3 percent) in 1941. The ghetto, which was reportedly set up as early as April 15, included approximately 3,000 Jews. Among these were also the Jews of the neighboring communities of Apátfalva, Csanádpalota, Földeák, Kiszombor, Magyarcsanád, Nagylak, Pitvaros, and Szőreg. Early in June the Jews were transferred to Szeged, from where many were deported to Strasshof.[9]

Nagykáta. Located east of Budapest, Nagykáta was a military labor service recruitment center; 10 to 12 companies were sent from there to serve along the frontlines in the Ukraine. One of the commanders, Lieutenant-Colonel Lipót (Metzl) Muray, a notorious sadist, was aptly named "the hangman of Nagykáta" for he was responsible for the death of a large number of labor servicemen (see chapter 10). The ghetto was located in and around Count István Tisza and Damjanich Streets and included 628 Jews. Among these were the approximately 200 local Jews. The others were brought in from the surrounding communities, including Gyömrő, Kóka, Maglód, Tápióbicske, Tápiógyörgye, Tápiósáp, Tápiósüly, and Tápiószele. The Jewish Council was composed of Rabbi Soma Breuer, István Székely, Vilmos Schwarz, Imre Relle, and Imre Sebestyén. Early in June, the ghetto population was transferred for entrainment to Kecskemét.[10]

Szarvas. The Jews of Szarvas, who numbered 636 (2.7 percent) in 1941, were reportedly ordered into the ghetto as late as May 15. Their deportation took place from Szolnok, to which they were transferred early in June.[11]

Szentes. The ghetto of Szentes, a city located north of Szeged, was situated at the northern side of the Vásártér (Market Square) and the adjacent Vecseri Street. It had 530 inhabitants, of which close to 500 were local and the others from Szeghalom. The Jewish Council was composed of Dr. József Berend, the Chief Rabbi (Chairman), Dr. Imre Balázs, and Jenő Bárdos. Some of the prominent members of the community, including Sándor Gunst, the president, were interned in April at Topolya, from where they were among the first to be deported to

Auschwitz that same month. The ghetto population was transferred to the entrainment center at Szeged on June 16.[12]

Gendarmerie District VI

In Gendarmerie District VI there were also a number of ghettos from which the Jews were transferred during the middle of June into the entrainment centers, of which by far the most important one was that of Debrecen. Several of these ghettos were in the so-called Hajdu towns in the vicinity of Debrecen, namely in Hajduböszörmény, Hajdudorog, Hajduhadház, Hajdunánás, and Hajduszoboszló.

Hajduböszörmény. On May 27, 1944, the town's Jews were ordered into the ghetto, which was established in and around the synagogue. On June 15 they were first taken to the local pig market, where they were deprived of their valuables, and then transferred for entrainment to Debrecen. According to one account, 653 of the Jews perished in the wake of the deportation.[13]

Hajdudorog. The ghetto was located at the northwestern end of the main square on Jackovits Mihály Street and in and around the synagogue. It included approximately 350 Jews, of which around 300 were local. The others were brought in from Hajduszováta and Józsa. The Jewish Council was for a while headed by Dr. László Hercz. The Jews were transferred to Debrecen on June 17, on the train that also carried the Jews of Hajduböszörmény and Hajdunánás.[14]

Hajduhadház. As was the case with the other Hajdu cities, the Jews of Hajduhadház, numbering 471 (3.78 percent) in 1941, were placed in a ghetto which consisted of the synagogue and the adjacent buildings. They were transferred to Debrecen during the middle of June.[15]

Hajdunánás. Here too the ghetto, which was established on May 14, was located in and around the synagogue. The Jews were transferred to Debrecen on June 17.[16] The wife of the Mayor of Hajdunánás, Mrs. Mihály Pénzes, committed suicide upon being suspected by H. Szabó, a gendarmerie investigator, of being of Jewish origin.[17]

Hajduszoboszló. The close to 500 Jews in the community were ordered into a ghetto around the middle of May. They were transferred to Debrecen on June 15.[18]

In addition to the ghettos in the Hajdu towns, the area of Gendarmerie District VI also included the ghettos of Karcag and Téglás.

Karcag. The ghetto of Karcag, a town situated between Szolnok and Debrecen, was established on April 24 between the cemetery (Temető) and Vágóhid Street. It included close to 1,300 Jews. Among these were the approximately 800 local Jews; the others were brought in from the neighboring communities, including Kúnmadaras and Tiszaszentimre. On June 18, the ghetto population was transferred to the sugar plant at Szolnok, and entrained shortly thereafter.[19]

Téglás. In this town located just north of Debrecen, the ghetto was established at the Bácsi-Puszta. Because of the conditions in the ghetto, the well-to-do Jews arranged to be transferred to the Debrecen ghetto. In addition to the local Jews, the ghetto of Téglás also included the Jews of Hajdusámson and Vámospércs. Before the deportation, Téglás had 172 Jews, Hajdusámson 188, and Vámospércs 298. Around June 17, the entire ghetto population was transferred to the brickyards of Debrecen.[20]

The Délvidék

Although the Jews of the Délvidék shared the ultimate fate of the Jews in Gendarmerie District V, they were rounded up and placed into ghettos much earlier than those in the Trianon section of the District. The anti-Jewish measures adopted in this region must have been a lesser surprise to the local Jews than to their brethren in the other parts of Hungary, for they had already had a foretaste of them a few years earlier.[21]

Because the region was inhabited by a large number of pro-Nazi and highly anti-Semitic *Volksdeutsche* elements and was strategically close to Tito's partisan forces, the Jews of the Délvidék were subjected to extraordinary "precautionary" measures. Even before the German occupation, a large number of the "politically suspect" Jews were interned at Bácska Topolya, where they shared the fate of other Jews from Hungary proper.[22] After the occupation, the internment camp was taken over by the SS and transformed into a deportation center.

As elsewhere in occupied Hungary, the Germans began their anti-Jewish drive in the Délvidék with a series of individual killings and mass arrests.[23] They were wholeheartedly assisted in these drives by their Hungarian hirelings and the *Volksdeutsche.*

In accordance with an April 19 resolution of the Baky group in the Ministry of the Interior, the ghettoization of the Délvidék Jews began on April 26.[24] The usual procedure was followed. The details relating to the ghettoization were spelled out in ordinances that were posted the day before. The Jews were warned not to leave their residence as of

5:00 A.M. of the day of the roundup and the Christians were urged to surrender within 48 hours all the valuables they might have received from Jews for safekeeping.[25]

Almost everywhere, the local synagogue and the community buildings around it were designated as the ghetto. With the exception of the ghetto of Szabadka and the internment camp at Bácska Topolya, the Délvidék ghettos were in existence only a few days—long enough to enable the gendarmerie and police officers to interrogate the Jews and confiscate their property.

The concentration of the Jews from the various ghettos was carried out on a territorial basis. Those in the communities along the western bank of the Tisza River in the eastern section of the Bácska were taken to Szeged. Among the Délvidék Jewish communities transferred to Szeged were those of Ada, Mohol, Szenttamás, Török Kanizsa, and Zenta.[26] The Jews of Szentamás were first taken to Óbecse, from where, together with the local Jews, they were taken either to Szeged or to Bácska Topolya.

Those living in the central zone of the Bácska were concentrated in Szabadka. Among these were the Jews of Ujvidék, who had suffered especially discriminatory treatment practically since the beginning of the Bácska's reacquisition by the Hungarians. Shortly after the city's occupation by Hungarian troops in April 1941, the commander of the city, General Ferenc Bajor, imposed a ransom of 50 million *Dinars*[27] on the Jews "because they had not contributed to Hungarian causes during the Yugoslav occupation." At first the leaders of the Jewish community were required to deliver the money within 48 hours. However, when the officers involved in the collection became convinced that the Jews could not possibly collect all that cash within the short time assigned to them, they were willing to accept the 3.4 million *Pengős* the Jewish leaders had offered. The Hungarian officers blackmailed the Jews into delivering the money immediately by the threat that otherwise they would be handed over to the dreaded Ustashi, the Croat Nazis. The bulk of the ransom money was divided by Bajor among his fellow officers; 100,000 *Pengős* were allegedly given to Miklós Bonczos, then the Undersecretary of State in the Ministry of the Interior.[28]

The Jewish community of Ujvidék had also suffered the brunt of the massacres perpetrated by the Hungarian military in January 1942 (see chapter 6). Greatly depleted in the wake of the massacres, the Jewish community at the time of the ghettoization was composed of around 1,900 Jews. The roundup of the Ujvidék Jews was carried out under the immediate supervision of Mayor Miklós Nagy and Chief of Police Gyula Zombory. Transferred to Szabadka, the Jews were housed in a flour mill from where most of them were transferred to Baja on May 13. Most of the Jews of Ujvidék were deported on May 25–26 together with the other Jews in Baja.[29]

The Jews living in the communities situated along the Danube in the western parts of the Bácska and in the Baranya region along the Drava River were taken to Baja for entrainment.[30] Among these were the Jews of Zombor, who were first collected in the local Silk Factory (*Selyemgyár*), which served as a ghetto, and then taken to Bajmok, from where they were eventually transferred to Baja.[31] A part of the Zombor Jews were taken to Bácska Topolya, from where they were deported to Auschwitz. Just before the deportations began in Baja on May 25, many of the Délvidék Jews concentrated in Szeged and Szabadka, including most of the Ujvidék Jews, were also relocated to Baja for entrainment.

The major ghetto and concentration centers from which the Délvidék community of around 21,000 was deported were those of Bácska Topolya, Baja, Szabadka, Szeged, and Bácsalmas.

Bácska Topolya. The camp was originally established by the Hungarians for political prisoners. Following the German occupation, its scope was expanded by the SS and it was used primarily for the concentration of Jewish hostages. Most of these came from the Délvidék, but a considerable number were also brought in from other parts of Hungary. All in all about 3,000 Jews were detained in and deported from the camp. It was from this camp that one of the first two transports of around 2,000 "able-bodied Jews" was directed to Auschwitz on April 30, 1944.[32]

While in camp the internees were subjected to all kinds of humiliation designed to drain their mental and physical energy. They were used instead of draft animals in the plowing of land around the camp and after work they were compelled to do calisthenics, mostly for the amusement of the guards.[33]

Baja.[34] During the second half of May, around 8,000 Délvidék Jews were "housed" in three camps in Baja. Two of these camps contained the Jews from Ujvidék; the third, the other Jews from the Délvidék not concentrated in Bácska Topolya, Szabadka, and Szeged. During the ten days in Baja, 65 of the Jews died or committed suicide. The deportations from Baja started on May 25, a month before the general deportations in Zone IV, with the usual cruelty. According to an eyewitness, when the doors of the freight cars were first opened at Gänsendorf a few days later, 45 corpses were found along with a number of Jews who went mad as a result of the ordeal.[35]

The local Jews were concentrated in the streets around the synagogue and the other institutional buildings. The mayor, Dr. Sándor Bernhardt, was quite a decent man; he refused to establish a formal ghetto or to prohibit the relatively free circulation of the Jews for shopping and other purposes. The Germans, who had occupied the institutional buildings, set up a number of workshops in the Jewish school and in the adjacent areas in which they employed Jewish skilled workers. These were housed in five buildings on Madách and Szent László Streets and together with their families, numbering from 140 to 150 persons, managed to escape the deportations. Baja, according to an account by a postwar Jewish leader of the community, was the only provincial town where nonexempted Jews were permitted to remain. Their survival apparently was to a large extent due to the benevolent attitude of a local SS officer, First Lieutenant Rumpf.

The deportation of the local Jews took place in three phases. The first phase involved the arrest on April 14 of around 150 Jews, including many of the communal leaders and professionals. These were taken to Bácska Topolya from where they were deported at the end of the month. The second phase involved the mass deportations of May 25–27 which included 640 local Jews. Following this *Aktion,* the number of Jews still remaining in the city was reduced to approximately 400; among these were labor servicemen from Northern Transylvania and Eastern Hungary. They were all transferred to Bácsalmás on June 17 and deported together with the other Jews in the camp on June 25.[36]

Szabadka. The 3,000 to 3,500 Jews of Szabadka were placed into a special ghetto early in May, almost a week after the ghettoization of the other Jews in the Délvidék. The ghetto was located near the railroad station and was fenced off from the rest of the city. The Jews that were brought in from the central Bácska, including Ujvidék, were placed into an abandoned four-story flour mill. For a while they were fed by the Jewish community of Szabadka, which was then under the leadership of a Jewish Council headed by Dr. Zoltán Loránt. Endre visited the city on May 2 and in the company of Mayor Dr. Jenő Székely inspected the flour mill and the area designated as the ghetto.[37]

For purposes of deportation, the central Bácska Jews were transferred to Baja on May 15. The Jews of Szabadka remained in their ghetto until June 16, when most of them were transferred to Bácsalmás.[38]

The Concentration of the Jews

The concentration process in Zone IV began at 5:00 A.M. on June 16, the very day the deportations from Zone III were completed. It terminated within five days with the establishment of seven concentration centers: four in Gendarmerie District V and three in Gendarmerie District VI. The original plan called for these centers to be located in Békéscsaba, Berettyóujfalú, Debrecen, Kecskemét, Szabadka, Szeged, and Szolnok and for the deportations to begin on June 21, the day after the completion of the concentration.[39] The revised plan called, among other things, for the replacement of Szabadka by Bácsalmas as one of the major entrainment centers and for delaying the deportation date by four days.

As a result of the drive, 40,505 Jews were concentrated in the seven entrainment centers of the zone. Of these, 21,489 were concentrated in the four centers in Gendarmerie District V and 19,016 in the three centers in Gendarmerie District VI, as shown in table 21.1. The deportation of these Jews took place between June 25 and 28, 1944. The Jews transferred from the neighboring ghettos remained in the entrainment centers for only a few days. During this time, they were subjected to another round of searches for valuables. The condition and treatment of the Jews in these centers were uniformly deplorable.

TABLE 21.1.
NUMBER OF JEWS IN THE GHETTOS AND
ENTRAINMENT CENTERS
IN GENDARMERIE
DISTRICTS V AND VI

Gendarmerie District V (Szeged)		Gendarmerie District VI (Debrecen)	
Bácsalmás	2,793	Békéscsaba	3,113
Kecskemét	5,413	Debrecen	13,084
Szeged	8,617	Nagyvárad	
Szolnok	4,666	(Bihar County)[a]	2,819
Total	21,489	Total	19,016

SOURCE: Ferenczy Report of June 29, 1944

[a] Includes only Jews from the rural communities in the county after the Jews of Nagyvárad had been deported.

Bácsalmás. Located in the southern part of Hungary between Szeged and Baja, the concentration and entrainment camp of Bácsalmás contained 2,793 Jews.[40] Among these were many from Baja, Madaras, Jánoshalma, Szabadka and the neighboring communities in northern Bácska. The camp was supervised by a group of *Volksdeutsche* SS-men from the Bácska; they were especially cruel. However, many of the Jews who left Bácsalmás in the transport of June 25 were quite lucky: when the train reached Szeged, a few freight cars with around 700 Jews, who, it turned out, came mostly from Szabadka, were detached and coupled to another train, which was directed to Strasshof.[41]

Békéscsaba. The ghetto was established in the local tobacco factory and its environs and included 3,113 Jews, of which about 2,500 were from the city proper.[42] The others were brought in from the neighboring villages and towns, including Bánhegyes, Battonya, Békés, Endrőd, Gyula, Mezőkovácsháza, Orosháza,[43] Szarvas, and Tótkomlós. Apparently the pre-occupation relationship between the local authorities and the Jewish community was quite good, for the mayor, Dr. Gyula Jánossy, and some of the police officers, including Ladányi, Sitkai, and Szokolai, had been denounced by Ferenczy for harboring the interests of Jewry.[44] The entrainment of the Jews concentrated in Békéscsaba took place on June 25. The Jews of Békéscsaba were placed on a train directed to Auschwitz; the others were taken to Strasshof, where most of them survived the war.[45]

Debrecen. The capital of Hajdu County, Debrecen had a large Jewish community before World War II.[46] The ghetto was established in the western part of the city by Mayor Sándor Kölcsey (Order No. 21838). The mayor himself was opposed to the ghettoization and was soon relieved by the anti-Semitic Prefect, Lajos Bessenyei. However, many individuals were enthusiastic about their role in the implementation of the anti-Jewish measures in the city. Among these were Chief Police Counselor Gyula Szabó, the commander of the ghetto, and Colonel Gyula Szilády, the nemesis of the Jews of Debrecen and Hajdu County.[47] The ghetto consisted of two parts, the "large" and the "small" ghettos, divided by Hatvan Street. It encompassed Csapó, Szécsenyi, Zsák, Zugó, Csók, Simonffy, and József Kir. Herceg Streets. The Jewish Council was headed by Dr. Pál Weiss and included Miksa Weinberger, Bernfeld, and Waldmann as members. Health services were provided under the leadership of Dr. Dezső Fejes Friedmann; the ghetto police was headed by Béla Lusztbaum, a former Captain. On June 21, the Jews were relocated to the Serly Brickyard, where their coreligionists from the neighboring communities, including those of Balmazujváros, Hajduböszörmény, Hajdudorog, Hajduhadház, Hajdunánás, Hajdusámson, Hajduszoboszló, Téglás, and Vámospércs were also concentrated.

The Jews of Debrecen, like those of several other communities in Gendarmerie Districts V and VI, were lucky. The two transports that left Debrecen on June 26 and 27 from the entrainment center at Szentgyörgypuszta with 6,841 Jews ended up in Austria where many of the families survived intact.[48]

Kecskemét. The city had a relatively small Jewish community before the German occupation.[49] Following the entry of the Germans, the Jews were subjected to a particularly humiliating treatment: some 60 Jews were selected by the Nazis to destroy the local synagogue and transform it into a stable to be used by the German troops. Thirty other Jews were picked up and taken to Kistarcsa, from where they were among the first to be deported to Auschwitz. The entrainment center included 5,413 Jews, of which close to 1,500 were from the city. The others were brought in from the neighbo;ing ghettos of Abony, Cegléd, Jászkarajenő, Kiskőrös, Kiskúnfélegyháza, Nagykőrös, Soltvadkert, and Törtel.[50] The Jewish Council was under the leadership of Dr. Dezső Schönberger. The Jews were concentrated in an unused plant at the outskirts of the city, which also served as the entrainment point.[51]

Szeged. The capital of Csongrád County, Szeged had one of the most active Jewish communities before the occupation.[52] When a concentration center, Szeged had 8,617 Jews, of which more than half were from the city itself. The others were from the neighboring communities, including Apátfalva, Csanádpalota, Csongrád,[53] Dunapataj, Éjkécske, Földeák, Halas, Hódmezővásárhely, Horgos, Kalocsa, Kecel, Kiskundorozsma, Kiskunhalas, Kistelek, Kiszombor, Magyarcsanád, Makó, Mindszent, Pitvaros, Szentes, Szőreg, and Ujkécske.[54] The Jewish Council was headed by Dr. Róbert Pap and included M. Reizer, M. Gross, L. Fenyő, and Dr. L. Wilhelm as members. The ghetto police of 40 Jews was headed by Sándor Gerle. The ghetto for the local Jews was located around the synagogue and the Jewish schools, and in Margit, Korona, and Bús Péter Streets. (It was in the building of the Jewish community at 20 Margit Street that the gendarmerie and police made their search for valuables.) Like most ghettos, it was surrounded by a wall of wooden boards, in this instance put up under the supervision of Szilárd Markovitcs, a member of the Municipal Board of Szeged. At the request of the local Catholic and Protestant clergy, the converted Jews were housed in private buildings located at 11 Kelemen Street, 24 Polgár Street, and in the Bors Hotel.[55] In a way the lot of the converted Jews was even worse than that of the Jews in the ghetto, for they were virtually locked in and isolated within the buildings, which were guarded by the police day and night. About 2,000 Jews from the rural communities were for a while "housed" in the pigsties of the sausage plant at Dorozsma.

On June 16–17, the ghetto of Szeged was liquidated; the Jews were transferred to the Rókus sports field and to the brickyards that already "housed" the Jews from the neighboring communities. The three transports from Szeged left between June 25 and 28 from the Rókus Railway Station. Of these, two were directed to Strasshof, where many of the deportees survived.

The despicable operation was carried out with the wholehearted cooperation of Police Chief Sándor Takács, Police Counselor Keresztes, Police Officer Gombosi, Prefect Magyary-Kossa, and Szeged's mayor, Béla Tóth, [56] who had just replaced the rather moderate József Pálffy. The gendarmes in the ghetto were under the command of Captain Imre Finta.[57] Expert advice on the handling of the Jews was provided by SS-Captain Argermayer.

Appalled by the horrors of the ghettoization and concentration processes in the city and elsewhere, Endre Hamvas, the Bishop of Csanád, protested repeatedly against the injustices committed against the Jews. On May 12, he first intervened in behalf of the Christian Jews; then on June 16 he protested in a telegram to Sztójay and Jaross against the impending deportation. On June 25, he even approached Horthy via Gyula Ambrózy, the head of the Cabinet Office. As a result of his interventions he managed to save about 200 converted Jews from deportation.

Also saved were many of the 5,739 Jews in the two transports from Szeged who arrived in Strasshof on June 30.[58] One of these transports had actually been directed to Auschwitz, but since a trainload of Jews from Kecskemét that was originally designed to go to Austria had inadvertently and routinely been ordered to Auschwitz the Germans allowed the Szeged train to proceed to Austria instead.[59]

As a result of pressure exerted by Hungarian academicians and church leaders and above all the initiatives of Miklós Mester, who sponsored many of the exemption applications filed by Jews (see chapter 25), Drs. Béla Purjesz and István Rusznyák, two well-known professors of medicine at the University of Szeged, were brought back after their deportation to Strasshof.[60]

Szolnok. The ghetto of Szolnok, the capital of Jász-Nagykún County, was located in and around the synagogue, the Jewish school, and the adjacent community building. On June 16, the ghetto population was transferred to the facilities of the local sugar factory, which was used as the concentration and entrainment center for the Jews of the neighboring communities as well. Before the deportations began, the sugar plant held 4,666 Jews, of which approximately half were from Szolnok.[61] The others were from the neighboring communities including Dévaványa, Endrőd, Gyoma, Karcag, Kisujszállás, Kőrösladány, Kunhegyes, Kunmadaras, Mezőtúr, Szarvas, Szeghalom, Szentimre, Túrkeve, and Vésztő. While in Szolnok, 29 Jews died in the ghetto and the sugar plant. The deportations took place on June 29, with one transport of 2,567 Jews directed to Strasshof and the other to Auschwitz. From among those directed to Strasshof, a relatively large percentage survived the war.[62]

Nagyvárad. About three weeks after the liquidation of the original ghetto, with the 35,000 Jews of Nagyvárad and environs, the city's entrainment facilities were used once again, this time to deport the Jews in the section of Bihar County in Trianon Hungary that was in Zone IV. On June 16–17, 2,819 Jews from the small communities south and southeast of Debrecen, including Derecske and Konyár, were concentrated in Nagyvárad.[63]

"Laying on Ice" in Strasshof

The Jews that lived in Gendarmerie Districts V and VI fared relatively better than their counterparts in the other provincial gendarmerie districts. This was due to a combination of good luck and a new element introduced in the so-called "blood for trucks" negotiations between Kasztner and Eichmann (see chapter 29). Although contact between the *Vaada* and the Eichmann-*Sonderkommando* was established shortly after the German occupation of March 19, Eichmann's "blood for trucks" offer was not made until shortly before the beginning of the mass deportations on May 15. The negotiations over this grandiose plan went hand-in-hand with an even more intensive bargaining for the rescue of close to 1,700 "prominent" Jews.

On June 14, during the deportations from Zone III, Eichmann unexpectedly informed Kasztner that he was willing to allow 30,000 Hungarian Jews to be "laid on ice" in Austria as a demonstration of his good will and sincerity. He set one stipulation: the immediate payment of five million Swiss Francs. Since the Jews of Carpatho-Ruthenia and Northern Transylvania had already been deported, he insisted that only Jews from Trianon Hungary could be considered for the transfer. He referred to the former as "ethnically and biologically valuable elements" whom, according to Kasztner, he would not allow to remain alive. Half of the 30,000 Jews were to come from Budapest, half from the provinces. Since large sums of money were involved, Kasztner revealed the details of the Eichmann offer to the Jewish Council on June 14, 1944.[64]

While the transfer of the Jews to Austria was technically effectuated within the framework of the Kasztner–Eichmann negotiations, it appears that Eichmann was guided in the offer and in the conduct of these negotiations by the instructions he had received from Kaltenbrunner. The chief of the RSHA was besieged by Austrian entrepreneurs operating war industries and by government officials, including SS-*Brigadeführer* Blaschke, the Mayor of Vienna, with requests to provide them with desperately needed slave labor. Since Hungarian Jewry was at the time still the one relatively untapped reservoir of Jewish labor, Kaltenbrunner instructed Eichmann to have a few transports of deportees diverted to Austria.[65]

From the Germans' point of view the deal with Kasztner offered a number of distinct advantages:

- It provided an opportunity for a demonstration of good will in the "blood for trucks" negotiations.
- It supplied the Austrian industrial and agricultural entrepreneurs and local government officials with needed slave labor.
- It enriched the coffers of the *Sonderkommando*.[66]
- It contributed to the "solution" of the Jewish problem by eliminating those "unable to work."[67]

The selection of the Jews for the Strasshof transports appears to have been the responsibility of the Zionist or other well-known Jewish leaders in the concentration and entrainment centers in Zone IV. These leaders, in turn, seem to have been designated for the task by the Kasztner-dominated *Vaada* group in Budapest. In the case of Szeged, it worked as follows. On June 20, the last day of the ghettoization in the city, SS-*Hauptsturmführer* Argermayer appeared at the gate of the ghetto and summoned Dr. Leopold Löw, Dr. Jenő Frenkel, Ernő Kertész, Dr. Adolf Silberstein, and Dr. József Radó and handed them a letter from Ernő Szilágyi, a leading member of the *Vaada*. Writing in German, Szilágyi asked them to select 3,000 Jews from among the ghetto inhabitants, giving priority to:

- Families with many children.
- Families of labor servicemen.
- The relatives of prominent Jews.

Appended to the letter was a list of 160 prominent Jews in the Szeged ghetto, which had been compiled in Budapest. The five-man commission was given two days to complete its task. To facilitate its work, Argermayer placed at its disposal the membership list of the Jewish community, which had been prepared earlier, as well as the necessary typewriters, stationery, and carbon paper. On June 21, Argermayer reduced the number of Jews eligible for inclusion in the special transport to 2,400, half from Szeged itself and half from among the other Jews in the Szeged ghetto. He further stipulated that, in addition to the eminent, the list should include primarily children up to 12 and adults above 50 years of age. The selection of the 1,200 Jews outside Szeged was made the responsibility of the Jewish leaders from Hódmezővásárhely. In the end, the number of Jews taken to Strasshof from the Szeged entrainment center exceeded 5,000. It is not clear whether this was due to a subsequent directive from Budapest or the bribing of local officials. Sixty-six of the prominent Jews were included in the special Kasztner group which eventually ended up in Switzerland via Bergen Belsen.[68]

Kasztner had expected that the first trainload of Jews would be leaving from Győr and Komárom, the areas from which Jews were being deported at the time. Although this plan apparently had the approval of Eichmann, all the transports from Gendarmerie Districts II and III, including of course those from Győr and Komárom, were routinely directed to Auschwitz, presumably due to the inertia of some of the SS-*Scharführer* in charge of the transports. When the *Scharführer* responsible for the transport from Győr failed to notice that the train's number was not on his ledger until after the transport had reached the Slovakian border, he called Eichmann for instructions. Motivated by a concern for efficiency rather than moral obligation, Eichmann apparently instructed the *Scharführer* that as long as the transport was already at the Slovakian border it might as well continue on to Auschwitz.[69] He decided to "compensate" Kasztner by a transport from another part of Hungary. Since the deportation from Zone III had been completed by

June 16, it was the good luck of many Jews from Zone IV to be destined for work in Austria.

The concentration of the Jews in the communities in Zone IV began the very day the deportations ended in Zone III. With the concentration process completed by June 20, the deportations were scheduled for June 25–28. It was during these deportations that six or seven trainloads of Jewish deportees were directed to Strasshof, a camp near Vienna. According to one source, 20,787 Jews were directed to Strasshof.[70] These came from the following concentration centers:

Baja	5,640
Debrecen	6,841
Szeged	5,739
Szolnok	2,567

After their arrival in Strasshof during the first days of July, the Jews were sent to labor in industrial and agricultural enterprises in a number of communities in eastern Austria, including Gmünd, Weitra, Wiener-Neustadt, and Neunkirchen. Many of them worked under the auspices of the *Todt* Organization. Their treatment varied with the disposition of the individual employers and foremen. On the whole they were often treated quite humanely and around 75 percent of them, including children and the elderly, survived the war.[71] Approximately 1,000 of the Jews died of natural causes or illnesses incurred while in the camps. Close to 170 were transferred to Bergen-Belsen and an indeterminate number were ordered deported by Krumey to Auschwitz as punishment for infractions, including the possession of money, the use of barbers, or going to the movies.[72]

The Hungarian Jews in Austria were under the control of a central administrative office in Vienna headed by SS-*Obersturmbannführer* Hermann A. Krumey, one of Eichmann's closest collaborators. Located at 35 Kasteletzgasse, the office was officially known as *Der Höhere Befehlshaber der SS und Polizei in Ungarn—Sondereinsatzkommando—Aussenkommando Wien* (The Higher SS and Police Commander in Hungary—Special Commando—Foreign Commando Vienna). Krumey was assisted by SS-*Hauptsturmführer* Siegfried Seidl and SS-*Hauptsturmführer* Schmitzhofen; the clerical personnel included eight Hungarian Jewish women.[73]

While the Hungarian Jews in and around Strasshof were deprived of much, including their liberty, they were definitely among the lucky ones. They were in relative safety, while the remainder of the provincial Jews were being concentrated and deported.

With the deportation of the 40,505 Jews from Zone IV, the dejewification squads completed the removal of 380,660 Jews from Hungary in 129 trainloads.[74]

Reaction of the Jewish Council

The concentration and deportation of the Jews from Zone IV took place simultaneously with the concentration of the Jews of Budapest into special "starred houses" (csillagos házak) (chapter 24). The relocation of these 250,000 Jews took place between June 17 and 25. The authorities at this time chose not to establish a territorially contiguous ghetto for fear that the Allies would then have a freer hand to bomb the rest of the capital. Nevertheless, the central Jewish leadership had every reason to believe that the establishment of the starred houses was the prelude to the deportation and liquidation of the Jews of Budapest.

It was around this time, during the deportations from Zone IV, that postcards were first brought back from Auschwitz for delivery to the relatives and friends of many of those deported earlier. Postmarked "Waldsee," a fictitious geographic name, the cryptic messages ("Arrived safely. I am well.") were often written by the victims just before they were gassed. The objective of the Germans was, of course, to lull the Jews still awaiting deportation in Hungary into a false sense of security.[75]

One such batch of cards was handed over for distribution to Fülöp Freudiger, a leading member of the Jewish Council. He noticed that on one of them the word "Waldsee" was written on an erased spot on the postcard. He doublechecked the erased word with his thread-counter magnifying glass, a tool he frequently used in his textile manufacturing plant, and noticed that the original word had ended with "witz." He revealed his findings to Krumey who allegedly told him: "Freudiger, I know you for a clever man; you shouldn't see everything!" Around June 25, Freudiger himself got such a "Waldsee" card from Joseph and Samuel Stern, the brothers of his plant manager Edmund Stern. They signed their name as Joseph R'evim (Hebrew for "hungry") and Samuel Blimalbish (Hebrew for "without clothing").[76]

The Jewish Council became frantic. In a desperate effort to save the remaining provincial Jews, (they were to be found only in the western and southwestern parts of the country) and to forestall the deportation that now threatened the Jews of Budapest, it once again resorted to its traditional weapon. On June 22, the Council filed an imploring petition with Prime Minister Sztójay, the copies of which were also submitted to some other members of the government. The text read as follows:

The Provisional Committee of the Association of the Jews of Hungary, which in accordance with Government Decree No. 1,520/1944. M.E. is the legal representative organ of the Jews, is taking the liberty of respectfully revealing before Your Excellency and the Royal Hungarian Government the terrible situation which threatens Hungarian Jewry and which is causing despair for all of us in the wake of the deportation of hundreds of thousands of Jews of the Israelite and Christian faith which began in May and which has seemed to continue ever since. In the last hour of our tragic fate and in the name of the principles of humanity we beseech you in perturbed spirit and implore Your Excellency and the Royal Hungarian Government to immediately end the removal of hundreds of thousands of innocent people from the country.

The Jews of Hungary have borne with resignation the strokes of fate that have recently befallen them in quick succession. We bowed without a murmur before the many governmental decisions which deprived us of our wealth, family hearths, and civic honor and which excluded us not only from the national, but so-to-speak also from the human community. We cried out in pain only when they began to concentrate the Jews along the country's borders who were in the ghettos and deprived of everything into deserted factories and fields and subsequently to deport them from the country without regard to age or sex. At the beginning the deportation was restricted to the northeastern military operational zones and the southern border areas; lately, however, it has been extended to the country's interior and thereby the assumption that the removal of the Jews was necessitated by military considerations has been invalidated. Also invalidated has been our hope that the masses removed from the country were being taken for labor; one can hardly square this assumption with the circumstance that people have been taken out of the country irrespective of age, sex, or health. According to the data at our disposal, by June 20 427,000 Jews, about half of the Jews of Hungary, suffered the terrible fate of deportation. This figure is divided as follows:

Carpatho-Ruthenia (Kárpátalja)		Rear of the Tisza (Tiszahát)	
Munkács	26,000	Nyíregyháza	20,000
Ungvár	14,000	Kisvárda	12,000
Beregszász	10,000	Szatmárnémeti	24,000
Nagyszőllős	8,000	Mátészalka	17,000
Máramarossziget	12,000		
Huszt	10,000	Upper Province (Felvidék)	
Felsővisó	8,000		
Szeklence	5,000	Kassa	12,000
Iza	3,000	Sátoraljaujhely	15,000
Bárdfalva	3,000	Miskolc	21,000
Técső	10,000	Eger	9,000

Hatvan	12,000	Szabadka	3,500
Balassagyarmat	4,000	Szeged	4,000
Salgotarján	4,000	**Transylvania**	
Léva	4,000		
Komárom	8,000	Kolozsvár	22,000
Érsekujvár	7,000	Dés	10,000
Dunaszerdahely	8,000	Beszterce	8,000
		Nagyvárad	36,000
Transdanubia		Marosvásárhely	6,000
(Dunántul)		Szászrégen	8,000
Győr	5,200	Szilágysomlyó	7,000
Székesfehérvár	4,000	**Concentration Camps**	
Délvidék		Bácstopolya	5,000
Baja	8,200	Sárvár	1,000
Nagykanizsa	9,000	Kistarcsa	2,000
Barcs	2,500	Total	427,400

Although the pertinent Cabinet Decree ordered only that the Jews be placed in separate quarters of the city, in fact these separate city parts (ghettos) became concentration camps from where the provincial Jews were crowded, under even more miserable conditions, into brickyards, deserted mills, etc., located at the outskirts. It was from these internment camps that the physically and spiritually broken people were taken to the deportation trains, in many cases, according to our information, after undergoing severe interrogations and physical abuse, where they were crowded 70 to 80 into a freight car. The cars were sealed and there was no air except for the narrow ventilation slots. These unfortunates travelled for days deprived of everything, and without money. They received a few loaves of bread and two buckets, one full of water and the other for sanitary needs. This is how all of them were taken towards their unknown fate—women, men, infants, the critically sick and the aged.

It was with great shock that we learned that these terrible things are continuing, in Kecskemét, Békéscsaba, Szolnok, Sárvár, Debrecen, Szombathely, Szeged, and several other places, and that tens of thousands of unfortunate people are placed into concentration camps at the city outskirts, obviously in order to be deported.

After all this . . . it is with the greatest anxiety that we received the news that the deportation of the Jews of the capital is also to begin within the next few days, so that the dejewification of all of Hungary will become a reality.

Your Excellency! In the name of humanity and God's command for neighborly love, we raise our voice against the relentless and merciless application of collective responsibility to one million Hungarian citizens, which is rejected and condemned by the Scriptures and the Church alike. We appeal before God and man to the sense of justice of the Hungarian nation which was always manifest and cannot now, in this crucial phase of its history, be denied, and which cannot permit the deportation of close to one million citizens without a hearing or judicial sentence, a cruel judgment such as has not been known in the Hungarian legal system. If there are sinners among us, as there are and can be in every community, let the severity of Hungarian law and the judgment of the Hungarian judge strike them. But every just man, whatever his affiliation, must cry out in pain when innocent children and infants are taken to destruction in their mother's arms, and when helpless invalids, aged, and pregnant women are taken on their fateful journey without food, care, or proper clothing, in airless freightcars, on a journey from which there is hardly any return. The children of the many thousands of Jews who served with honor in World War I are taken away in the same way as the wives, children, and parents of the several tens of thousands of labor servicemen on duty on the battlefield or fulfilling auxiliary military functions in the rear during this war. In some cases, the people exempted on the basis of military or patriotic decorations have also failed to escape deportation.

According to the figures cited above, about half of the Jews of Hungary have already been deported. Now, when we are, so to say, in the last hour, we ask for mercy for those still at home and beg for the lives of innocent children, and refer to the 1,000-year-old history of the Hungarian homeland and to that communality of fate that tied local Jewry to the Hungarian nation through good and bad times, since the founding of its homeland.

May it be permitted for us to quote from the speech by the Minister of Industry, Lajos Szász, in Nyíregyháza, which probably reflects the position of the Royal Hungarian Government:

"The guide in the solution of the Jewish question cannot be an anti-Semitism fueled by hate, but only and exclusively a love-imbued defense of race. No one wants to extirpate the Jews from the world; we only want to save our race from their harmful influence. I believe that all of us who are the fighters and workers for, and the followers of the idea of, race defense will and would be very happy if the unlucky people of Ahasuerus found a home somewhere on this globe."

We believe unflinchingly in the Hungarian nation's love of justice and chivalry, which does not want and could not permit the destruction of hundreds of thousands of defenseless and innocent people. We believe in the holy spirit of humanity and in the rule of the world order of Christian morality. We place our lives, the lives of our parents, children, brothers and sisters, in the hands of the eternal Hungarian nation.

It is with broken soul and imploring hope that we look, in this tragic situation of ours, to the responsible government of the country, and beg it to put an end to the horrors of the deportation with extraordinary urgency, and to use the labor force of Hungarian Jews for production and for building the country.

With respect to the Jews already removed from the country, we appeal to your Excellency to try to assure humane treatment for them and to make it possible for them, like other foreign workers, to support themselves and their families.

Addressing our appeal to save several hundreds of thousands of people entrusted to our care to the good will of your Excellency and the Royal Hungarian Government, and imploring once again for urgent consideration, we remain, with our sincere esteem, the Provisional Executive Committee of the Association of the Jews of Hungary.[77]

The petition was submitted when the government was in the midst of discussing the Jewish question in light of the national and world-wide reaction against the anti-Jewish measures. The government was subjected to severe criticism and covert threats by the representatives of the Christian churches, including the Papal Nuncio. The spokesmen for the neutral governments appealed for a moderation or cessation of the anti-Jewish course while those of the Allies threatened reprisals.[78] Spurred by the neutral representatives in Budapest and by the Jewish organizations in Switzerland, the foreign press in the non-Axis world discussed the Hungarian anti-Jewish measures with increasing frequency and detail and uniformly condemned the inhumanity and barbarism of "the once chivalrous Hungarians." The diplomatic representatives of Hungary in the neutral countries kept the Hungarian Foreign Ministry abreast of these developments by sending summaries or full accounts of the foreign press reports.

It was in the context of these domestic and foreign pressures that the Council of Ministers met in a series of crucial meetings to discuss the Jewish question late in June. Most of them were held while the close to 250,000 Jews of Budapest were in the process of relocating into specially designated "yellow-star houses" in accordance with the provisions of a series of decrees passed under the signature of Ákos Doroghi Farkas, the newly inaugurated mayor.

Although Deputy Foreign Minister Mihály Arnóthy-Jungerth was very eloquent in presenting the case for the cessation of anti-Jewish measures, especially the deportations, as being harmful to the interests and reputation of Hungary, the meetings proved generally indecisive. It was only after Baky attempted a coup early in July that Horthy finally decided to put an end to the deportations. But in the meantime, even while the Council of Ministers met, the Jews of Western Hungary—in Zone V—were being concentrated and readied for deportation. In fact, the deportation plans were so much on schedule that the dejewification squads were already in process of concentrating the Jews in the immediate vicinity of Budapest—the last scheduled phase of the anti-Jewish operations.

Notes

1. The original plan called for the headquarters to be located in Kecskemét. Ferenczy Report of June 12, 1944.

2. Ferenczy Report of June 29, 1944. According to Veesenmayer, the number of Jews

deported from this zone was 41,499. *RLB,* Doc. 182. For details on the entrainment centers from which the Jews were deported, see below.

3. Some of the details relating to these ghettos are taken from a document of the Central Jewish Council, which was reproduced by Lévai in his *Zsidósors Magyarországon,* pp. 414–17. This source cites Jászberény as having been in this zone, though the Jews assembled in this community were eventually transferred for deportation to Monor, which was in Zone I (see chapter 22).

4. Since a considerable number of the local Jews were taken to Strasshof via Szeged, the proportion of survivors was relatively high. In 1946, the community still numbered 605. By 1949, however, when it was led by Béla Deutsch and László Gruber, the community had declined to 430. *Zsidó Világkongresszus,* no. 4 (April 15, 1947), pp. 2–3; no. 13–14, May 1949, pp. 12 and 25.

5. Statement by Eugene Ligeti, YIVO, Archives File 768, Protocol 3555, p. 4. See also *Pinkas ha'kehilot,* pp. 275–78.

6. Jenő Lévai, *Szürke könyv magyar zsidók megmentéséről* (Gray Book on the Rescuing of Hungarian Jews) (Budapest: Officina, n.d.), pp. 75–76; *Pinkas ha'kehilot,* pp. 466–67.

7. *Ibid.,* pp. 474–75.

8. *Ibid.,* pp. 506–7.

9. This is the reason that in 1946 the Jewish community still numbered 1,123 (3.1 percent). In 1949, the Neolog community, numbering 263, was headed by Manó Szemere and Henrik Schulmann, and the Orthodox one, numbering 497 members, was headed by Benő Guttmann and Nándor Lemberger. *Zsidó Világkongresszus,* no. 4 (April 15, 1947), pp. 4–5; no. 13–14 (May 1949), pp. 15, 24, 25. See also *Pinkas ha'kehilot,* pp. 350–52.

10. *Ibid.,* p. 371.

11. *Ibid.,* pp. 414–15.

12. In 1941, Szentes had 510 Jews, representing 1.5 percent of the city's total. For details on the community's background, see László Harsányi, *A szentesi izraelita hitközség története* (The History of the Jewish Community of Szentes) (Budapest: A Magyar Izraeliták Országos Képviselete, 1970), 210 pp. See especially, pp. 118–63. The work also includes some aspects of the history of the Jewish communities of Mindszent and Segvár. See also *Pinkas ha'kehilot,* p. 405.

13. In 1941, there were 934 Jews in the community (3.1 percent). Of these, 212 were men, 254 women, and 187 children. Although the community was revived after the war, it gradually declined as a result of emigration. In the early 1960s, it consisted of only a few families under the leadership of Dr. Pál Józan. By 1969, there were only 16 Jews left; the following year the synagogue was sold. László Harsányi, *Adalékok a hajduvárosok zsidóságának történetéhez* (Contributions to the History of the Jews of the Hajdu Cities) (Budapest: A Magyar Izraeliták Országos Képviselete, 1970), pp. 8–13, 56–57. See also Pál Kardos' *Adalékok a hajduböszörményi zsidóság történetéhez* (Contributions to the History of the Jews of Hajduböszörmény) (Hajdúböszörmény, 1949), and *Pinkas ha'kehilot,* pp. 264–66.

14. In 1941 the community consisted of 321 Jews representing 2.73 percent of the city's total. About 60 of these returned after the war, but by 1970 only two remained. The community's property, including the synagogue, had been sold and demolished. Harsányi, *Adalékok a hajduvárosok zsidóságának történetéhez,* pp. 31–55, 62–64. See also *Pinkas ha'kehilot,* pp. 266–67.

15. In 1941, the town had 1,080 Jews (5.75 percent of the population). Although in 1946 Hajduhadház still had 198 Jews, by 1967 it had only 8 left. Harsányi, *Ibid.,* pp. 25–27, 59–61; *Pinkas ha'kehilot,* p. 267.

16. In 1946, Hajdunánás still had 205 Jews, but because of emigration caused partially by anti-Semitic demonstrations during the Hungarian Uprising of 1956, the community ceased to exist by the early 1960s. The community buildings were sold and the synagogue was demolished. Harsányi, *Adalékok a hajduvárosok zsidóságának történetéhez,* pp. 13–19,

57–58. See also Moshe Élijáhu Gonda, *A debreceni zsidók száz éve* (The Hundred Years of the Jews of Debrecen) (Tel Aviv: A Debreceni Zsidók Emlékbizottsága, n.d.), pp. 296–303, 385–95. The latter pages contain the names of the martyred Jews of Hajdunánás. See further *Pinkas ha'kehilot*, pp. 268–69, and the following personal narratives at the YIVO: Mrs. Lajos Schlüssler (File 773, Protocol 2043) and Lewis Falus (File 774, Protocol 2714).

17. *Uj Élet* (New Life), Budapest, December 4, 1945, p. 5.

18. In 1941, Hajduszoboszló had a Jewish population of 490, representing 2.78 percent of the town's total. Of these, approximately 180 returned after the war. Ármin Katz, the rabbi who also survived, left the community and became the Rabbi of Amsterdam. By 1969, only 25 Jews were still in the town, forcing the liquidation of the communal institutions. Harsányi, *Ibid.*, pp. 19–25, 59.

19. *A karcagi zsidók története* (The History of the Jews of Karcag). (Tel Aviv: Lahav Printers for A karcagi zsidók emlékbizottsága, 1977), 219 pp. plus Hebrew summary. For the list of those who died in Auschwitz, see pp. 160–64. See also *Pinkas ha'kehilot*, pp. 479–80.

20. Gonda, *A debreceni zsidók száz éve*, pp. 306–11, 397–403. These pages also contain the names of the martyred Jews of Hajdusámson, Téglás, and Vámospércs. For further details on Vámospércs, see Harsányi, *Adalékok a hajduvárosok zsidóságának történetéhez*, pp. 28–31, 61–62. See also *Pinkas ha'kehilot*, pp. 270–71, 280–81, 296–97.

21. The Délvidék, or the Bácska and Baranya regions that constitute Yugoslav Voivodina, was occupied by the Hungarians in April 1941. In February 1942, the Hungarian Armed Forces undertook a punitive raid in the Délvidék to comb the area for "partisans." In the course of the raid, over 3,000 Serbs and Jews were killed (see chapter 6). It is also quite likely that the Jews of Voivodina were more aware of the fate that befell their brethren of Serbia, Croatia, and Bosnia shortly after the defeat of Yugoslavia than their Hungarian fellows were.

22. The Bácska Topolya internment camp was established by the Hungarians shortly after the occupation of the Délvidék.

23. Immediately upon their entry into Délvidék, the Germans, acting in concert with the local *Volksdeutsche*, killed 10 Jews: 4 in Parabić, 3 in Török Kanizsa, and 1 each in Szabadka, Ujvidék, and Zenta. In Ujvidék more than 300 "hostages" were arrested and kept at the Szabadság (Freedom) Hotel, where they were abused and maltreated in the course of their investigation. Most of them were freed after 19 or 20 days in prison, only to be placed into ghettos and deported. *The Crimes of the Fascist Occupants and Their Collaborators Against Jews in Yugoslavia*, Zdenko Löwenthal, ed. (Belgrade: Federation of Jewish Communities of the Federative People's Republic of Yugoslavia, 1957), p. 166. (The book is in Serbo-Croatian with the title and summary of chapters in English. Referred to hereafter as *The Crimes of the Fascist Occupants.*)

24. A temporary exception was the case of the Jews of Szabadka who were ordered into the ghetto about a week later. For details, see chapter 17.

25. The text of the ordinances was similar to the one used in Kassa. See p. 546. For the ones used in Ujvidék and Zenta, for example, see *The Crimes of the Fascist Occupants*, pp. 169–70.

26. In Zenta, the anti-Jewish measures, including the ghettoization, were carried out under the immediate command of Mayor György G. Ussáth. For further details on the transfer of the Jewish communities to Szeged, see *Saopštenja o zločinima okupatora i njihovih pomagača u Vojvodini od 1941–1944* (Reports on the Crimes of the Enemy Occupation Forces and Their Collaborators in Vojvodina, 1941–1945), vol. 1. *Bačka i Baranja* (Bácska and Baranya) (Novi Sad: Pokrajinska Komisija za Utvrdjivanje Zločina Okupatora i Njihovih Pomagača u Vojvodini, 1946), *passim*.

27. The ransom, expressed in Yugoslav currency, amounted to appeoximately five

million *Pengős*. During the 1941–42 period, the official value of the *Pengő* was approximately 20 cents. The black market price of the dollar, however, ranged from about 11 to 13 *Pengős*. Sándor Ausch, *Az 1945–46. évi infláció és stabilizáció* (The Inflation and Stabilization of 1945–46) (Budapest: Kossuth, 1958), pp. 30–31.

28. In 1943, when Prime Minister Kállay was searching for a way out of the war, General Bajor was tried and condemned by the Hungarian High Court of Justice (*Magyar Kuria*) to two years, having been found guilty of embezzlement, forgery of official documents, blackmail, and blackmarketeering. After the war he was handed over to the Yugoslavs, who condemned him to death on October 30, 1946. Artúr Geyer, "Az 1942 évi újvidéki 'razzia' " (The Újvidék "Raid" of 1942), in *Új Élet naptár 1959* (New Life Calendar, 1959) (Budapest: A Magyar Izraeliták Országos Képviselete Kiadása, 1959), pp. 41, 50–51.

29. For an historical review of the community, see Imre Radó *and* József Mayor, *A noviszádi zsidók története* (The History of the Jews of Ujvidék) (Noviszád: Uránia Nyomda for the Chevra Kadisa, 1930), 225 pp.

30. *The Crimes of the Fascist Occupants*, p. 170.

31. *Saopstenja o zlicinima okupatora*. For further details on the Jews of Zombor, see E. H. Spitzer, *Kehilat Sombor b'hurbana. Dapei zikkaron l'kedoshei ha'kehila* (The Zombor Community During Its Destruction. Pages of Commemoration to the Martyrs of the Community) (In Hebrew, Jerusalem: The Author, 1970), 29 pp.

32. The transport from Bácska Topolya, like that from Kistarcsa the day before, was put together by the *Honvédség* (Hungarian Armed Forces) rather than by the Eichmann-*Sonderkommando*. The *Honvédség* apparently acted in accordance with the provisions of a Hitler–Horthy deal agreed upon at Klessheim on March 18, 1944. For details see Randolph L. Braham, "The Holocaust in Hungary: An Historical Interpretation of the Role of the Hungarian Radical Right," *Societas*, Summer 1972, pp. 210–15. See also chapter 11.

33. *The Crimes of the Fascist Occupants*, p. 167.

34. Although Baja is not in what used to be called the Délvidék, it is treated in this section because the fate of its Jewish community was intertwined with that of many communities in the Délvidék.

35. *The Crimes of the Fascist Occupants*, pp. 175–76. See also *Pinkas ha'kehilot*, pp. 168–70.

36. József Rosenfeld, "Emlékezés a bajai gettóra" (Reminiscences About the Ghetto of Baja), in *Évkönyv 1973/74* (Yearbook 1973–74), ed. Sándor Scheiber (Budapest: Magyar Izraeliták Országos Képviselete, 1974), pp. 146–54. In 1973, Baja still had close to 70 Jews. *Ibid.*, p. 154. In 1949, the Congressional community consisted of 360 Jews under the leadership of Sándor Rostás, József Rosenfeld, and Rabbi Tibor Klein. *Zsidó Világkongresszus*, no. 13–14 (May 1949), p. 8.

37. *A tizhónapos tragédia* (The Tragedy of Ten Months), ed. Ervin Szerelemhegyi, István Gyenes, Károly Kiss, and Jenő Lévai (Budapest: Müller Károly, 1945), 2:47–48.

38. *The Crimes of the Fascist Occupants*, p. 172. For the list of the martyred Jews of Szabadka see *Imenik Subotickih jevreja zrtava fasisticke okupacije, 1941–1945* (List of the Jews of Szabadka, Victims of the Fascist Occupation) (Szabadka: Jevrejska veroispovedna opstina u Subotici, 1948), 54 pp.

39. Ferenczy Report of June 12, 1944.

40. In 1941, Bácsalmás had a Jewish population of 186 or 1.4 percent of the total of 13,310. *Pinkas ha'kehilot*, p. 178.

41. *The Crimes of the Fascist Occupants*, pp. 172 and 176. According to another source, the separation of the trains took place at Felsőzsolca, just east of Miskolc. Rosenfeld, "Emlékezés a bajai gettóra," p. 149. See also *Pinkas ha'kehilot*, pp. 178–79.

42. The capital of Békés County, Békéscsaba in 1941 had a Jewish population of 2,433 representing about 4.6 percent of the city's total. Before the occupation the community

was under the spiritual leadership of Chief Rabbi Dr. Ödön Szabó. In 1946, the community had 552 members representing but 1 percent of the total. The Congressional and Orthodox factions at the time were led respectively by Dr. Árpád Gottlieb and Fülöp Markovits. While greatly reduced in number, the community was still functioning in 1958, when it was under the leadership of Dr. Andor Vértes. Lévai, *Zsidósors Magyarországon,* pp. 146 and 416; *Zsidó Világkongresszus,* no. 4 (April 15, 1947), pp. 4–5; no. 13–14, (May 1949), pp. 9, 24, and 29; *Uj Élet,* August 1, 1958. See the personal narrative of Katherine Erdős, YIVO, 771/3216.

43. A city in Békés County located northeast of Szeged, Orosháza in 1941 had a Jewish community of 579 representing 2.1 percent of the city's population. Because many of the deportees ended up in Strasshof, where the survival rate was high, the community still had 381 members in 1946. By 1949, the number of Jews was reduced to 328. In that year they were led by Géza Nádas and Lajos Platschek. The community was still in existence in 1957, when it was under the spiritual leadership of Rabbi Zsidmond Guttmann. *Zsidó Világkongresszus,* no. 4 (April 15, 1947), pp. 4–5; no. 13–14 (May 1949), p. 17; *Uj Élet,* June 1957.

44. Lévai, *Szürke könyv,* pp. 105–6.

45. *Pinkas ha'kehilot,* pp. 180–82.

46. In 1941, Debrecen had a Jewish population of 9,142, representing about 7.3 percent of the city's total. Following the Soviet offensive during the fall of 1944, liberated Debrecen became the seat of the Democratic National Provisional Government headed by General Béla Dálnoki Miklós (November 1944), and of the first National Assembly. It was also to Debrecen that the first thousands of liberated Jews flocked. Most of them were former labor servicemen and people returning from hiding or from Romania where they had found refuge. The returning Jews founded here the Association of the Jews of Hungary under the leadership of Jenő Leitner, who was also invited to become a member of the National Assembly. In 1946, the city had a Jewish population of 4,641 representing about 3.6 percent of the total. By 1949 it had a Status Quo and an Orthodox congregation headed respectively by Leó Csengeri and Jakab Schreiber. A memorial to the 6,000 martyrs of Debrecen was unvailed in July 1959 in the Jewish cemetery at Monostorpályi Road. The community at that time numbered fewer than 1,000 and was under the leadership of Dr. Imre Kulcsár. Lévai, *Zsidósors Magyarországon,* pp. 146, 416–17; *Zsidó Világkongresszus,* no. 4 (April 15, 1947), p. 23; no. 13–14 (May 1949), pp. 10, 24, 25; *Uj Élet,* August 1, 1959. For a detailed account on the history of the Jews of Debrecen and of the neighboring communities of Balmazujváros, Derecske, Hajdunánás, Hajdusámson, Konyár, Mikepércs, Téglás, and Vámospércs, see Gonda, *A debreceni zsidók száz éve,* 409 + 264 pp. (Hungarian and Hebrew).

47. After the war, Szabó was condemned by a court in Debrecen to death by hanging. *Mementó. Magyarország 1944* (Memento. Hungary, 1944), eds. Ödön Gáti, et al. (Budapest: Kossuth, 1975), pp. 50–52.

48. Lévai, *Zsidósors Magyarországon,* p. 264. See also *Pinkas ha'kehilot,* pp. 245–51.

49. In 1941, Kecskemét had a Jewish population of 1,346 representing 1.5 percent of the city's total. By 1949, the Congressional community, which was under the leadership of Dr. Gyula Stein, was reduced to 276. Lévai, *Zsidósors Magyarországon,* pp. 146, 415–16; *Zsidó Világkongresszus,* no. 4 (April 15, 1947), pp. 2–3; no. 13–14 (May 1949), pp. 13, 24.

50. Based partially on a communication by Mrs. Malka Weisz.

51. See the personal narrative of Lewis Vidor at the YIVO (File 775, Protocol 3192). See also Moshe Sandberg (Sanbar), *My Longest Year* (Jerusalem: Yad Vashem, 1968), 114 pp. and *Pinkas ha'kehilot,* pp. 475–79.

52. In 1941, Szeged had a Jewish population of 4,161 representing 3.0 percent of the city's total. Following the liberation many surviving Jews from the neighboring rural communities came into the city; in 1946 the community numbered 2,332 or 1.7 percent of

the total. The congressional community was under the leadership of Márton Stern and Rabbi Jenő Frenkel. By the late 1950s, however, the community had shrunk to around 900, led by József Káldor and Rabbi József Schindler. *Zsidó Világkongresszus*, no. 4 (April 15, 1947), pp. 2–3; no. 13–14 (May 1949), pp. 20, 24, 25; *Uj Élet* (June 1957); May 1, 1958.

53. A city in Csongrád County, Csongrád had a Jewish population of 286 in 1941, representing 1.1 percent of the total. In 1946, the number of Jews was 66 and in 1949 only 52. The Status Quo community in the late 1940s was led by Ferenc Régner and Károly Weisz. *Zsidó Világkongresszus*, no. 4 (April 15, 1947), pp. 4–5; no. 13–14 (May 1949), p. 10.

54. For a complete list of the communities from which the Jews were transferred to Szeged for entrainment, see Harsányi, *A szentesi izraelita hitközség története*, p. 122.

55. Statement by the head of the Jewish Council, Dr. Robert Pap (YIVO, 768/3560). See also the personal narratives of Eugene Ligeti (768/3555), Emerich Bálint (768/3575), A. Kármán (768/3576), Anne Engel (768/3577), and Dr. Leopold Löw, the son of the world-renowned Rabbi Immanuel Löw of Szeged (768/3618).

56. The atrocities committed at Szeged were also witnessed by Mrs. István Kovács, the wife of a professor and a personal friend of Admiral Horthy. In the war crimes trials, she testified that she had revealed her observations about the ghetto and the camp to Admiral Horthy. Munkácsi, *Hogyan történt?* pp. 168–70.

57. Statement by Dr. Robert Pap.

58. Lévai, *Zsidósors Magyarországon*, pp. 146–47, 264. See also his *Szürke könyv*, pp. 74–75 and 82.

59. *Pinkas ha'kehilot*, pp. 393–99.

60. Lévai, *Szürke könyv*, p. 108.

61. In 1941, Szolnok had a Jewish population of 2,590 representing 6.2 percent of the city's total. By 1946, this was reduced to 587 or 1.4 percent. In 1949 the congressional community had 577 members under the leadership of Andor Rákos. In the late 1950s the community was under the leadership of Dr. Károly Fodor. Lévai, *Zsidósors Magyarországon*, pp. 146, 264, and 415; *Zsidó Világkongresszus*, no. 4 (April 15, 1947), pp. 4–5; no. 13–14 (May 1949), pp. 21, 24, 25; *Uj Élet*, January 15, 1958.

62. *Pinkas ha'kehilot*, pp. 415–17. For a moving fictionalized account of life in the concentration and entrainment center of Szolnok and in Strasshof, see Mária Ember, *Hajtükanyar* (Hairpin Bent) (Budapest: Szépirodalmi Könyvkiadó, 1974), 384 pp.

63. Gonda, *A debreceni zsidók száz éve*, pp. 312–16, 403–09. The latter pages contain the lists of the martyred Jews of Derecske and Konyár as well as those of Esztár, Monostorpályi, and Pocsaj.

64. For the text of Kasztner's memorandum, see Jenő Lévai, *Eichmann in Hungary* (Budapest: Pannonia, 1961), pp. 195–96. See also chapter 29.

65. Blaschke approached Kaltenbrunner with his labor request on June 7, 1944. In his response to Blaschke, dated June 30, Kaltenbrunner alerted the Mayor of Vienna about the impending arrival of four transports with 12,000 Jews. Of these, he insisted, only 3,600 were ablebodied. *RLB*, Doc. 184.

66. Kasztner had originally suggested that 100,000 Jews be "laid on ice." To prove the readiness of the *Vaada* to pay for the deal, he offered Eichmann about 5 million Swiss Francs worth of jewelry, *Pengős* and foreign exchange. When Eichmann consented to the transfer of the Jews to Austria he demanded that the 5 million Swiss Francs be paid. The bargaining was eventually completed on a per capita basis. Eichmann had originally asked for $200 per capita, but a settlement was apparently reached with the acceptance of Kasztner's offer of $100 "minimum" for every Jew allowed to remain alive. *Der Kastner-Bericht*, pp. 113–14.

67. In this letter to Blaschke cited above, Kaltenbrunner intimated that Jews who were

unable to work as well as women and children were to be kept in a guarded camp and held "in readiness for special action." For the transcript of the interrogation of Kaltenbrunner on this matter in Nuremberg on April 12, 1946, see *IMT*, 11:344–46.

68. See statement of Dr. Leopold Löw, which also includes the names of the prominent Jews taken to Budapest for an eventual deal.

69. *Der Kastner-Bericht*, p. 121.

70. Lévai, *Zsidósors Magyarországon*, p. 264. Lévai does not indicate the source of his data. Kasztner is also inaccurate in the presentation of his figures. At one point he refers to 17,000 and at another point to 18,000 Jews. See *Der Kastner-Bericht*, pp. 115 and 147.

71. Credit for saving the Strasshof Jews is also claimed by Andreas (Andor; Bandi) Biss. He asserts that it was his close relationship with SS-*Hauptsturmführer* Otto Klages that made possible Himmler's cooperation in the transfer. See his *A Million Jews to Save*. (London: Hutchinson, 1973), pp. 74–81. This author interviewed a number of "Strasshof Jews" who survived the war in Austria. Many of them had warm memories about their humane treatment by Austrian farmers and villagers. See also the personal narratives of Eugene Ligeti, Emerich Bálint, and A. Kármán cited earlier. For a fictionalized account of a Hungarian Jewish group's experiences in Strasshof, where they were employed by the Waagner-Biro, A. G. Eisen & Stahlwerk Works under the command of Ernst Weber, see Ember, *Hajtükanyar*.

72. *Der Kastner-Bericht*, pp. 278–79.

73. *Ibid.*, pp. 276–78.

74. Ferenczy Report of June 29, 1944. In his telegram (No. 1838) of June 30, 1944, Veesenmayer reported that 41,499 Jews had been deported from Zone IV and that the total number of Jews deported from Zones I–IV was 381,661. *RLB*, Doc. 182.

75. The "Waldsee" postcard trick was apparently first used in connection with the deportation of the Greek Jews in 1943. The Jews of Greece were "informed" that a Jewish state was being formed around Cracow and that only those with families would be eligible to resettle there; the single men and women would remain in Salonika to do forced labor. Suddenly a large number of Jews got married and "purchased land." The first deportees taken to Auschwitz and Treblinka were compelled just before they were gassed to write back home that "We are at Waldsee and doing well." Lévai, *Eichmann in Hungary*, p. 42.

76. Philip Freudiger, *Five Months* (Manuscript dated November 21, 1972 submitted to this author), pp. 20–21.

77. Munkácsi, *Hogyan történt?*, pp. 124–29.

78. For details on the attitude of the Christian Churches, see chapter 30; for details on the position of the Vatican, the Papal Nuncio and the neutral countries, see chapter 31.

CHAPTER TWENTY-TWO

THE LAST PHASE: ZONES V AND VI AND AUSCHWITZ

Zone V: Western Hungary

AFTER COMPLETION OF the dejewification campaign in Zone IV, there came the turn of the Jews in Gendarmerie Districts III (Szombathely) and IV (Pécs) encompassing the Dunántul (Transdanubia), the area west of the Danube (see map 13.1). The plans for the concentration and deportation of the Jews were completed at a conference late in June at Siófok, the resort town at Lake Balaton, where Endre was vacationing in the company of his fiancée, Countess Katalin.[1] In addition to the dejewification squad members, the conference was also attended by administrative, gendarmerie, and police officials of the two gendarmerie districts.

Aside from the eight major concentration and entrainment centers which had also served as the ghettos for the local and neighboring Jewish communities (see below), ghettos had functioned in the larger towns of the zone for several weeks. These ghettos, which were liquidated through the transfer of the Jews into the deportation centers, included those of Bonyhád, Keszthely, Körmend, Kőszeg, Mohács, Nagyatád, Nagykanizsa, Sárbogárd, and Veszprém.[2]

Bonyhád. The ghetto of Bonyhád, a town in Tolna County situated northeast of Pécs, was in and around the synagogue. It held close to 1,180 Jews, most of whom were from the town itself. Most others were brought in from the neighboring communities of Aparhant, Bátaszék, Kély, Kisveke, Tevel, and Zomba. It also included a part of the Jewish community of Szekszárd. The remainder of the Jews of Szekszárd were taken to Dombóvár, Pincehely, and Tamási, from where they were transferred to the entrainment center at Kaposvár. The Jews assembled in Bonyhád were transferred on July 1–2 to the Lakics military barracks in Pécs.[3]

Keszthely. The ghetto of this town located at the southern tip of Lake Balaton was in the synagogue and the adjacent community buildings. It held the 700-plus local Jews and those from the rural communities in the district. The Jewish Council was headed by Dr. Endre Kovács, a lawyer. Toward the end of June, the ghetto population was transferred for entrainment to Zalaegerszeg.[4]

Körmend. A town in Vas County, Körmend is situated between Szombathely and Zalaegerszeg. The ghetto was set up on May 5 in and around the synagogue and included the close to 300 local Jews, with their Chief Rabbi Jakab Krausz, and a smaller number of Jews from the neighboring rural communities. Early in June, 15 of the Jews were taken to Kőszeg; the others were transferred toward the end of the month to Szombathely.[5]

Kőszeg. The local ghetto was established in the house of Arthur Deutsch at 8 Schey Fülöp Street and the produce warehouses in its immediate vicinity. It held 103 Jews who were ordered into it on May 11. Of these, 80 were from Kőszeg itself, 8 from Perenye, 4 each from Nagycsömöte and Gyöngyösfalu, 3 each from Kőszegszerdahely and Bozsók, and 1 from near Póse. Toward the end of June, the ghetto population was transferred for entrainment and deportation to Szombathely.[6]

Mohács. The site where the Hungarians were defeated by the Turks in 1526, Mohács, located southeast of Pécs, had two ghettos. The larger one was located in and around the synagogue, the other near the Danube harbor in a factory loft. They held the approximately 700 Jews of the town as well as 470 Jews from the neighboring communities of Mágocs, Pécsvárad, and Sásd.[7] On June 29, the Jews were transferred to Pécs. According to one account, some of the Jews of Mohács, including the Rabbi, ended up in the Szeged ghetto.[8]

Nagyatád. Located in the southwestern corner of Hungary, Nagyatád had a Jewish community of around 200. Early in April, when the area adjacent to Croatia was declared a military operational zone, 16 Jews were apprehended and taken to Nagykanizsa's internment camp. From there they were deported to Auschwitz ahead of the other Jews in the town. The local ghetto was established on May 25 in the area around the synagogue. The entrainment took place in Barcs, to where the Nagyatád Jews were transferred toward the end of June.[9]

Nagykanizsa. The town was in the area of Zala County that was declared a military operational zone early in April. The measure was allegedly taken because of the fear of the possible impact of Tito's forces fighting in neighboring Yugoslavia. As one of the "precautionary" measures ordered by the authorities, the Jews of Nagykanizsa and the immediate vicinity were rounded up on April 19 by policemen especially brought in from Szombathely. The emergency roundup, which affected the Muraköz area and the districts of Alsólendva, Csáktornya, Délsomogy, Nagykanizsa, and Perlak netted 8,740 Jews, of which approximately 3,000 were from Nagykanizsa.[10]

Sárbogárd. In this town situated southwest of Budapest, the ghetto held the close to 300 local Jews as well as those of the neighboring communities of Alap, Cece, Hercegfalva, Igal, Kálóz, Sárkeresztur, Sárosd, Sárszentágota, Sárszentmiklós, Szolgaegyháza, and Vajta. The ghetto consisted of a number of Yellow-Star houses. Toward the end of June, the ghetto population was transferred to Kaposvár for entrainment.[11]

Veszprém. Located at the northwestern tip of Lake Balaton, Veszprém had two ghettos, both of which were established on April 15 and closed on May 1. One of them was set up in the military barracks at Komakút for the approximately 500 Jews from the rural communities in Enying and Veszprém districts, including the towns of Enying and Herend. The other was located in Horthy Miklós Street, in the synagogue and the adjacent community buildings, and contained the 650 Jews of Veszprém and 53 Jews from the villages surrounding it. Approximately 170 Jewish men from Veszprém escaped deportation because they had been called up for service in the labor service system.[12]

The Concentration Process

According to the plans worked out by Lieutenant-Colonel Ferenczy, the Jews assembled in the various ghettos of Zone V were concentrated in eight centers having adequate entrainment facilities. Of these, five were located in Gendarmerie District III and three in Gendarmerie District IV (see map 13.1). The transfer of the Jews from the ghettos began at 5:00 A.M. on June 30 and was completed on schedule at 8:00 P.M. on July 3.

The drive resulted in the concentration of 29,405 Jews, of which 17,201 were assembled in the five camps of Gendarmerie District III and 12,204 in the three camps of Gendarmerie District IV, as shown in table 22.1.

As in the other gendarmerie districts, the concentration of the Jews, like their original ghettoization, took place without major incidents. The Jews were as resigned and submissive as the Christian population was passive. The attitude of many clergymen in this as in the other dejewification zones was similar to that of Elek Oberndorf, the Evangel-

TABLE 22.1.
NUMBER OF JEWS IN THE GHETTOS
AND ENTRAINMENT CENTERS
IN GENDARMERIE DISTRICTS
III AND IV

Gendarmerie District III (Szombathely)		Gendarmerie District IV (Pécs)	
Szombathely	3,609	Pécs	5,963
Zalaegerszeg	3,209	Kaposvár	5,159
Pápa	3,557	Paks	1,082
Sopron	3,305	Total	12,204
Sárvár	3,521		
Total	17,201		

SOURCE: Ferenczy Report of June 30, 1944.

ical Minister of Mohács, who found appalling not so much the measures that were taken against the Jews ("a foreign body that had to be removed from the national body") as the methods employed for their deportation. The Minister of Mohács gave vent to these feelings in his letter of June 30, addressed to Albert Radvánszky, the Vice President of the upper house of the Hungarian Parliament and general warden of his denomination, asking for his intervention in behalf of three converts in Mohács. Responding in the name of the warden, Sándor Vargha, the Secretary General, assured Oberndorf that the Church was doing everything in its power to prevent the inhuman treatment of the Jews, but that no radical changes could be achieved.

Although the Jews transferred from the various ghettos in Zone V were held in the entrainment centers for only a few days, they too were subjected to searches for valuables. Again, as elsewhere, the rich and those suspected of hiding valuables were treated in a particularly brutal fashion, though the extent of the maltreatment varied from camp to camp.[13]

Kaposvár. The local ghetto was established early in May and was located in and around Berzsényi and Kanizsai streets, the center of the community which included the synagogue, the Jewish school, and the various communal institutions. The ghetto was administered by a Jewish Council headed by Ödön Antl, who had been elected President of the local Neolog community shortly before the occupation. The Council was composed of 16 members, including József Kardos and Sándor Hajdu. The mayor of the city, György Kaposvári (Véteg), was quite decent in his behavior toward the Jews. Near the end of June, the close to 2,500 local Jews were transferred from the ghetto to the artillery barracks near the railroad lines. The barracks held 5,159 Jews, over half of whom were brought in from the neighboring communities in Somogy County, including Tab.[14]

Paks. The city is located on the west bank of the Danube south of Budapest. The ghetto was established in the Jewish section that included the synagogue and the Jewish school; it contained 1,082 Jews, a number of whom were brought in from Dunaföldvár, Fadd, and Szekszárd. The town clerk, Gergely Tarisznyás, refused to cooperate with the authorities in the establishment of the ghetto and, in a noble act of protest, resigned from his position. Among the deportees was the last rabbi of the community, Simon Altman.[15]

Pápa. The ghetto was located in and around Petőfi, Eötvös, Rákóczi, Szent László, and Bástya Streets and was administered by a five-member Jewish Council acting under the command of a notoriously cruel police officer by the name of Dr. Pál Lotz.[16] A few days before their deportation, the 2,565 local Jews in the ghetto[17] were transferred to a fertilizer plant in the gypsy section of the city where 992 Jews from the neighboring communities in the Devecser, Pápa, and Zirc districts in Veszprém County had already been concentrated.[18] The assembly center was under the command of Gendarmerie Captain Dr. Zoltán Pap.[19] The 3,557 Jews gathered here were deported in two transports that left the city July 4 and 5. They reached Auschwitz via the Budapest-Hatvan-Kassa route on July 8. Of the 2,565 Jews of Pápa only around 300 returned after the war. Among these were most of the 51 from this city included in the so-called Kasztner group.[20]

Pécs. Of the 5,963 Jews concentrated in Pécs, about 3,500 were from the city.[21] The remainder were from the neighboring communities, including Bonyhád, Mohács, and Pécsvárad. The local Jews were ordered into the ghetto on May 9. Located in the area that encompassed Bánffy Dezső, Ispitaalja, Vas Gereben, Kassa, Szilágyi Dezső, and Tompa Mihály Streets, the ghetto was sealed off on May 21. Some Jews were quartered in the local warehouse of the MÁV (Hungarian Railways).

Even before their official ghettoization, 57 Jews had been arrested by the local Gestapo, under the leadership of a certain Auringer. The Jewish Council was headed by Dr. József Greiner assisted by Rabbi Moric Krémer. On June 28–29, the ghetto population was transferred to the so-called Lakics military barracks from which they were entrained five days later for Auschwitz. Among the deportees was a noted professor of medicine, Dr. Géza Mansfeld, and his family; their exemption papers were withheld by the local police.[22]

Ferenc Virág, the Bishop of Pécs, who had already distinguished himself during the 1920s when he was in the forefront of the struggle against the *Numerus Clausus* Act, intervened with Mihály Nikolics, the Prefect of Baranya County, to ease the situation of the Jews concentrated in the ghetto. Because of his stand in behalf of the Jews, Bishop Virág was placed under military guard during the Szálasi era.[23]

Sárvár. Located east of Szombathely, Sárvár was the seat of one of the major internment camps in Hungary. Most of the political prisoners were detained in the local sugar and silk plants. As an entrainment center, Sárvár held 3,521 Jews, of which approximately 750 were from the town itself[24] and the others from the neighboring communities in the Celldömölk and Sárvár districts, including Jánosháza. The ghetto for the local population was set up early in May in the synagogue and the surrounding communal buildings, including the rabbi's house. The Jewish Council was composed of Jenő Fischer (chairman), Sándor Krausz, Imre Rátz, and Albert Löwinger.[25] The Sárvár Jews were transferred to the silk plant just a few days before their scheduled entrainment on July 4 and 6. After the deportation of the Jews, the local authorities discovered a number of infants and children in the camp and handed them over to the Nazis "for labor in Germany."[26]

The internment camp was under the command of a Hungarian named Gribowszky. On August 5, an SS Captain, accompanied by 40 SS men, appeared in the camp and ordered the commander to cooperate in the entrainment and deportation of the inmates in the same manner as was done earlier at Kistarcsa (chapter 25). Surrounded by German tanks, the commander yielded. The deportation used German freight cars; only a few physicians, veterinarians, and engineers the Hungarians needed were left behind.[27]

Sopron. Jews had lived in this city for centuries. (In 1958, a medieval synagogue was unearthed there.) The ghetto of Sopron was established around the middle of May in the Paprét section of the city, in and around the synagogue. It held 3,305 Jews, of whom approximately 1,800 came from the city itself.[28] The others were brought in from the neighboring communities, including Csepreg, Csorna, and Kapuvár. The Jewish Council was composed of Zsigmond Rosenheim (chairman), Emil Steiner, József Rosenberg, Dr. Manó Léderer, Dr. Béla Krausz, Sándor Goldschmied, Géza Krammer, and Béla Hasler.[29] On June 19, the ghetto population was transferred to the half-completed residence halls of the Evangelical Teacher-Training Institute (*Evange-likus Tanitóképző Intézet*), which was located near a railroad line. From here the Jews were entrained on July 5, and deported the following day. Among the survivors of the local community were the 42 Jews that were included in the Kasztner group.

Szombathely. The ghetto-type concentration camp at Szombathely held 3,609 Jews of whom a little over 3,000 came from the city itself.[30] The remainder came from the neighboring communities in the Körmend, Kőszeg, Szentgotthárd, Szombathely, and Vasvár districts of Vas County. Among these were those of Beled, Körmend, Kőszeg, Szentgotthárd, and Vasvár. The ghetto was located at and around the crossing of Thököly and II. Rákóczi Ferenc Streets, where the synagogues of the two major congregations were located. It also included the community buildings on Bátthyány Square and Zrinyi I. Street.[31] The Jewish Council was headed by Dr. Imre (Wesel) Vese and included Dr. Iván Hacker, Zalán (a paper manufacturer), and Dr. Dán (a lawyer). The conditions in the ghetto were a bit more tolerable than in many other ghettos, though the detective team entrusted with the search for valuables, one of whose members, István Fürdős,[32] a local chief detective, was quite strict. Because of the relatively tolerant attitude of the local police, the supervision of the ghetto was subsequently entrusted by the local Gestapo unit (headed by a *Scharführer* named Arndt), to a special unit from the Gendarmerie School of Nagyvárad. The women were searched by a group of students brought especially from the school for midwives at Nagykanizsa. At the end of June the Jews were taken to the rail-loading facilities of the Magyar Motor és Gépgyár Rt. (Hungarian Motor and Machine Works, Inc.), which were connected with the city's freight station. They were entrained on July 4.[33]

Bishop Sándor Kovács, who had just taken office, followed in the footsteps of his predecessors, János Mikes and József Grösz, and vigorously protested the measures instituted at Szombathely. He actually managed to save a few Jews with the cooperation of the local authorities.[34]

Zalaegerszeg. The ghetto was established in two streets in the gypsy section of the city. It held 3,209 Jews, of which approximately 900 came from the city itself.[35] The remainder were brought in from the neighboring communities including Balatonfüred, Keszthely, Lenti, Lesencetomaj, Sümeg, Tapolca, Tűrje, Zalabár, Zalalővő, and Zalaszentgrót. Before their deportation, the Jews underwent particularly cruel treatment at the hand of the investigators searching for valuables. One of the especially brutal sadists, Béla Horvát, was caught after the war and condemned to life imprisonment. In the wake of the "interrogations" 30 Jews had to get medical help, others died, and many more went mad or committed suicide.[36]

Deportation: A Zonal Evaluation. The deportation of the Jews from Gendarmerie Districts III and IV took place during July 4–6, in four trains each during the first two days and two trains during the third day. The first day of deportations saw the departure of the first transports from Pécs and Sárvár and the evacuation of the camps at Szombathely and Kaposvár. The second day was devoted to the evacuation of the camps at Sopron, Zalaegerszeg, Pápa, and Paks. (The 1,082 Jews of Paks were attached to the Kaposvár transport at Pusztaszabolcs.[37]) The second and final transports from Sárvár and Pécs left on July 6. The total number of Jews deported in ten trains from Zone V was 29,556, or 151 more than Ferenczy originally reported. Of these, 17,667 were deported from Gendarmerie District III and 11,889 from Gendarmerie District IV.[38] With the completion of the operation in Zone V, Ferenczy could report that by July 6, 410,223 Jews had been deported from Hungary in 139 trains.[39]

Zone VI: Budapest and Its Environs

The concentration and deportation of the Jews in Zone V took place simultaneously with the anti-Jewish operations in Zone VI, which it was envisioned would end with the liquidation of the Jews from Gendarmerie District I that included Budapest (see map 13.1). While the deportations from Zones V and VI were in progress, an attempt was made by László Baky and the gendarmerie to overthrow the Regent. This challenge, which was successfully met, contributed to the Regent's decision to halt the deportations on July 7 (see chapter 25). By this time, however, the Jews of Budapest and of the neighboring cities around the capital were either relocated within Yellow-Star buildings or placed into ghettos. Although the Jews of Budapest suffered many deprivations while in the special buildings, and a considerable number of casualties during the *Nyilas* era, they escaped the mass deportations. The Jews in the cities ringing the capital, including Budafok, Csepel, Kispest, Pestszenterzsébet, Rákoscsaba, Rákospalota,[40] Sashalom, Soroksár, Szentendre, and Ujpest, were less lucky. They suffered the same fate as the provincial Jews—most of them were deported after

Horthy had decided to halt the deportations. The largest concentrations of Jews in these suburban cities were in Csepel, Kispest, and Ujpest.

Csepel. The approximately 900 Jews of Csepel, the island town in which the giant Weiss-Manfréd Works is located, were first concentrated in a section of the island in accordance with the joint instruction of April 15 of László Koltay of the Hungarian State Security Police and Hermann A. Krumey of the Eichmann-*Sonderkommando.* On May 10, the leaders of the Jewish community were instructed to relocate the Jews—this time into the bicycle storage rooms of the Weiss-Manfréd Works, which had no sanitary or any other facilities. In the days that followed, the ghetto population increased to approximately 3,000 through the addition of the Jews of Dömsöd, Kiskunlacháza, Ráckeve, Szigetszentmiklós, Taksony, and Tököl.[41]

Kispest. The approximately 4,000 Jews of Kispest were crowded into 548 rooms in selected buildings located on 53 different streets in the city. The relocation took place between May 15 and 30. The Jewish Council was composed of Dr. Zoltán Rosenfeld, Dr. Károly Nemes, Dr. Ernő Frank, Dr. Lajos Krausz, János Vas, and Nándor Gergely. The Council after a short while was expanded at the mayor's instruction to also include Henrik Somogyi, Sándor Ungár, József Herskovits, and Dr. Sándor Gergely.[42]

Ujpest. At the time of the anti-Jewish drive, Ujpest had a Jewish population of approximately 14,000.[43] These were ordered into specially designated Yellow-Star houses around the middle of May; they were not allowed to leave their place of residence between 6:00 P.M. and 11:00 A.M. The Jewish Council was composed of Dr. Dénes Friedman, Dr. György Székely, Dr. László Lengyel, and János Szűcs.[44]

Concentration and Entrainment Centers

With a few exceptions, the Jews of the cities surrounding Budapest were placed into ghettos or Yellow-Star-marked buildings between May 22 and June 30.[45] Their relocation into the entrainment centers took place between June 30 and July 3 (table 19.1).

The major concentration centers for the Jews in the Yellow-Star houses and ghettos in the immediate vicinity of Budapest were the brickyards of Budakalász and Monor, located respectively to the northwest and southeast of Budapest.

Budakalász. The local community consisted of 35 Jews (13 families). On May 24 they were placed into the ghetto of Csillaghegy.[46] Following the designation of the local brickyards as a concentration camp, the Jews from the ghettos in the communities north of the municipality of Budapest, including those of Kispest, Pesterzsébet, and Ujpest, were brought into the city.[47] Also brought into Budakalász were the approximately 17,500 Jews held in various camps on Csepel Island, including the lawyers and journalists who had been arrested on the basis of special lists handed over to the Jewish Council (see chapter 17), and the close to 3,000 Jews who had been arrested during a special raid on Üllői Road on July 3. These Jews were brought from the island in boats that landed at the Pünkösfürdő Station.[48] The entrainment of many of those deported from Budakalász took place at Békásmegyer where the Jews were subjected to the customary cruel treatment in search for hidden valuables by the gendarmes, led by Major Andrássy.[49] Some of the richer Jews in Békásmegyer managed to bribe the gendarmes who for a fee of 5,000 *Pengős* were willing to escort them home "to check out their Christian status," and in fact set them free. Since the number of people entrusted to them on these expeditions was carefully noted by the camp leadership, on their return the gendarmes simply picked up an equivalent number of unsuspecting yellow-star-wearing Jews from the streets of Budapest.[50]

Monor. Located southeast of Budapest, Monor served as the concentration and entrainment center not only for the approximately 350 local Jews,[51] but also for those in the communities south and east of the municipality of Budapest. Approximately 7,500 Jews were entrained from the brickyards in Monor.[52] They included the Jews of Jászberény and those of the various communities first assembled there.

Jászberény was the headquarters of Labor Battalion I, from which many labor service companies had been assigned to serve in the Ukraine and in the copper mines of Bor, Serbia (see chapter 10). The local ghetto was established in and around the synagogue. In addition to the approximately 550 local Jews, it held the Jews from the neighboring communities of Alatyán, Jánoshida, Jászalsószentgyörgy, Jászapáti, Jászfelsőszentgyörgy, Jászladány, Jásztelek, Pusztamizse, and Pusztamonostor. These were transferred to the Monor brickyards on June 30. Several other communities in Jász-Nagykun-Szolnok County, including those of Jászárokszállás, Jászfényszaru, and Jászkisér, were also taken there.[53]

The 24,128 Jews concentrated in Budakalász, Monor, and other centers in Zone VI, excluding Budapest proper, were deported in eight trains during July 6–8.[54] The deportation was completed one day after the Regent had ordered a halt to "the transfer of the Jews to Germany" on July 7. With the completion of this phase of the operations in Zone VI, Ferenczy was able to report that 434,351 Jews had been deported between May 15 and July 8 in 147 trains.[55] Within less than four months after the German occupation, the country, with the exception of the Jews of Budapest, the handful of exempted Jews and Jews in hiding, and the Jews in the labor service companies, had become *Judenrein.*

Hungarian Jews in Auschwitz

The ultimate destination of the Jews deported from Hungary was Auschwitz, the largest center of destruction in Nazi-occupied Europe.[56] The SS administration of the camp was well prepared for the anticipated daily arrival of 12,000 to 14,000 Jews from Hungary. The officials of the death camp were alerted about the impending arrival of the Hungarian transports by SS-*Gruppenführer* Richard Glücks, Chief of *Amtsgruppe D* of WVHA (*Wirtschaft- und Verwaltungshauptamt;* Economic and Administration Main Office), the SS unit in charge of the concentration camps, and Inspector General of the SS "Death's Head Formations."[57] He, in turn, had been informed by Kaltenbrunner and Rolf Günther, Eichmann's deputy in Berlin, soon after the Eichmann-*Sonderkommando* in Budapest "agreed to take over the surplus Jews from Hungary" as "requested" by the Baky-Endre group. The extermination machinery, which had lagged for months, was put into peak condition to assure smooth, effective, and continuous operation. The crematoria were renovated, the furnaces relined, the chimneys strengthened with iron bands, and large pits were dug in the immediate vicinity of the crematoria. A new railway branch line was laid between Auschwitz and Birkenau and the debarkation point was advanced to within 200 yards of the crematoria. The strength of the two Jewish special *Kommandos* serving the gas chambers was increased from 224 to 860 and the "Canada" *Kommando,* which was in charge of sorting the loot, was increased to about 2,000.[58]

Although the first deportation train left Hungary from Kistarcsa on April 28, the massive deportation program did not begin until May 15. By the end of June so many convoys were arriving that new camp facilities (BIIb and BIIc in Sector BII) had to be established. Mountains of luggage accumulated in the warehouses and on the ramps. The SS, like the Jewish *Kommandos,* were reduced to a state of complete exhaustion—the former because of their engagement in life and death decisions "classifying" the new arrivals; the latter because they had to work day and night to sort the loot and to carry the gassed bodies to the crematoria and burning pits.

The deportation trains from Hungary reached Auschwitz in three or four days, unmolested by local partisans or by the Alllies. At the urging of Rabbi Michael Dov Weissmandel of the Rescue Committee of Bratislava, the Jewish leaders of the West tried to persuade the Western Powers in June 1944, to destroy the major rail lines and bridges leading to Auschwitz and the instruments of annihilation in Auschwitz itself. This was rejected because it was felt that such an operation would require the diversion of considerable air support from normal combat operations. Not a single act of sabotage was attempted on the rail lines leading to Auschwitz either in Hungary, Slovakia, or Poland in spite of the operation of partisan forces in the areas (see chapter 31). The deportation schedule called for four trains per day with each trainload consisting of approximately 3,000 to 3,500 Jews. The victims were crammed 70 to 90 per freight car, which was supplied with two buckets: one filled with water and the other empty, for excrements. The doors of the freight cars were padlocked and the barred "windows" almost hermetically sealed. The trains were accompanied and guarded by Hungarian gendarmes until their arrival in Kassa, where they were replaced by the SS.

The inhumane overcrowding in the freight cars and the early summer heat were such that many Jews, especially among the ill and elderly, died en route, mostly of suffocation. Upon arrival, the Hungarian Jews, completely exhausted and emaciated, behaved in a lethargic, apathetic, and quiet manner, relieved to be able to breathe a little fresh air. Above all, having traveled for days in brutally hot, sealed freight cars with little or no water, they were invariably plagued by raging thirst. The thought of water so preoccupied them that they could not really pay attention to the realities around them. The reduction of their vital energies by prolonged thirst was part of the carefully planned, preprogrammed suffering prior to their being gassed. The SS aimed to paralyze their ability to notice things and their will to resist. While on the ramp waiting to be processed, their restlessness was usually subdued by promises of water or soup after the "disinfecting showers." They were occasionally addressed in German, but more often in Hungarian by *Unterscharführer* Eckardt, a young SS-man born in Hungary. As was the case with the many transports from other Nazi-occupied countries, the processing of the Hungarian Jews proceeded as follows:

Children up to age of 12 or 14, older people above 50, as well as the sick, or people with criminal records (who were transported in specially marked wagons) were taken immediately on their arrival to the gas chambers. The others passed before an SS-doctor[59] who, on sight, indicated who was fit for work and who was not. Those unfit were sent to the gas chambers while the others were distributed in various labor camps.[60]

The extermination operation was organized on an assembly line basis using the most up-to-date method in mass killing. After the gassings, the bodies were "processed" by the inmates in the Special Commando for the advancement of the economic interests of the Third Reich: their teeth were extracted for the salvaging of gold and silver, the orifices searched for hidden valuables, and the hair of women cut off. After the completion of these operations, the corpses were released for cremation (figs. 22.1–5).[61] The number of Jews waiting their turn outside the crematoria and along the roads between the camps was constantly several thousand strong. Eyewitnesses described the scene as follows:

Even the primitive gas chambers which had been used before the crematoria were constructed had to be brought back into commission. Enormous heaps of corpses were cremated in recently prepared pits. The entire area was wreathed in smoke which at times completely blotted out the sun. A revolting stench of burning human bones and flesh pervaded the camp. Night and day, without a break, the murdering continued—in several shifts. The death factory was at full pressure![62]

To make the burning process more effective, *Oberscharführer* Otto Moll, an unusually cruel and unscrupulous SS-man who was in charge of the crematoria at Auschwitz, ordered that trenches be dug around the piles of corpses inside the pits. These were designed to serve as conduits—the fat which trickled down from the roasting bodies was thus captured and returned to make the bodies burn faster.

As a result of this application of science and technology, about 400,000 Hungarian Jews were killed by this conveyor-belt system of mass murder in Auschwitz during the summer of 1944.[63]

Hungarian Jews in Other Concentration Camps

Of the close to 435,000 Hungarian Jews deported to Auschwitz from May 15 to July 8, 1944, approximately 10 percent were selected as fit for labor (fig. 22.6). Some of these were retained to work in Auschwitz itself; the rest were dispersed to 386 different camps in the Nazi empire. The largest groups were concentrated in the notorious

Figure 22.1.
Arrival in Auschwitz-Birkenau of a Hungarian-Jewish transport from
Carpatho-Ruthenia during the second half of May 1944.

Figure 22.2.
The selection process: The separation of the "fit" and the "unfit" for labor.

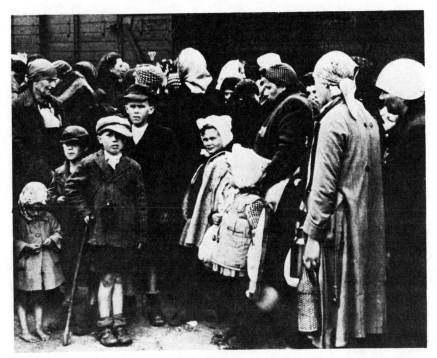
Figure 22.3.
The "unfit" selected for immediate liquidation.

Figure 22.4.
On the way to the crematorium.

Figure 22.5.
Processing of the loot by the so-called "Canada-Commando."

Figure 22.6.
Groups of men and women found "fit" for labor.

camps of Bergen-Belsen, Buchenwald, Dachau, Grossrosen, Günskirchen, Mauthausen, Neuengamme, and Ravensbrück.[64] In the fall of 1944, many of these camps also became the ultimate destination for the many thousands of Jewish labor servicemen withdrawn from the Ukraine and the copper mines at Bor as well as for the thousands of men and women who were marched from Budapest by the *Nyilas*, ostensibly to build the wall for the defense of Vienna (see chapter 26).

The liquidation of the provincial communities of wartime Hungary constituted one of the last drives in the Nazis' Final Solution program. The speed and efficiency with which these communities were destroyed on the eve of Allied victory reflect the zeal of the German and Hungarian Nazis to complete, before their ultimate defeat, at least one of their ideologically defined main objectives. They also highlight the general conspiracy of silence surrounding the implementation of the Final Solution program: the currently available evidence indicates that the leaders of the free world, like some of the leaders of world and Hungarian Jewry, were aware of this program well before the German occupation of Hungary.

Notes

1. Lévai, *Zsidósors Magyarországon*, p. 148.

2. Some of the details relating to these ghettos were culled from a Jewish Council document reproduced by Lévai, *ibid.*, pp. 407–21.

3. In 1941, Bonyhád had a Jewish community of 1,159. By 1946, the community was reduced to 205; it increased, albeit temporarily, in the next few years. In 1949, it had a Neolog congregation with 108 members led by János Eisner and an Orthodox one with 172 members headed by Manó Galandauer. *Zsidó Világkongresszus*, no. 6–7, (August 15, 1947), p. 19; no. 13–14, (May 1949), pp. 9, 24. For further details on Bonyhád, see János Eisner, *A bonyhádi zsidók története* (The History of the Jew of Bonyhád) (Tel Aviv: Migdal, 1965), 190 pp., mimeo. *Uj Élet* (New Life), Budapest, May 1, 1958, and *Pinkas ha'kehilot*, pp. 224–26. On Szekszárd, see pp. 411–13.

4. In 1941, Keszthely had a Jewish population of 755 representing 6.3 percent of the city's total. In 1949, the congressional congregation consisted of 134 members led by Dr. Mihály Lukács and Árpád Frank. By 1958 the community was reduced to about 80 led by Sándor Biró. *Zsidó Világkongresszus*, no. 4 (April 15, 1947), pp. 4–5; no. 13–14 (May 1949), p. 13; *Uj Élet*, August 15, 1958. See also *Pinkas ha'kehilot*, pp. 469–71.

5. For details on the Jewish community of Körmend and the list of the martyred Jews of the community see *A vasi zsidók. Emlékére a mártir-halált szenvedett vasmegyei zsidóságnak* (The Jews of Vas County. In Memory of the Martyred Jews of Vas County), ed. Albert Avraham Löwinger. (Tel Aviv: Izsák Efrájim for the Az Izraelben élő Vasmegyei Zsidók Emlékbizottságának Kiadása, 1974), pp. 47–50, 157–59. See also *Pinkas ha'kehilot*, pp. 494–95.

6. In 1941, Kőszeg had a Jewish community of 101, representing 1.1 percent of the town's total. For further details on the community, see László Harsányi, *A kőszegi zsidók* (The Jews of Kőszeg) (Budapest: A Magyar Izraeliták Országos Képviselete, 1974), pp.

203–8. Pages 205–7 list the entire ghetto population. See also *A vasi zsidók,* pp. 51–59 and 166–67, and *Pinkas ha'kehilot,* pp. 190–93.

7. In 1941, Mohács had 707 Jews (3.9 percent). In 1946, it had only 122, and in 1949, when the community was led by Vilmos Orbán and József Gábor, only 112. *Zsidó Világkongresszus,* no. 4 (April 15, 1947), pp. 2–3; no. 13–14 (May 1949), p. 16. See also *Pinkas ha'kehilot,* pp. 353–54.

8. Statement by Eugene (Jenő) Ligeti, YIVO, File 768, Protocol 3555.

9. *Pinkas ha'kehilot,* pp. 365–66.

10. For details on the "emergency" measures effectuated in the area, see chapter 17. See also *RLB,* Doc. 262; Lévai, *Zsidósors Magyarországon,* p. 103; and *Pinkas ha'kehilot,* pp. 372–74.

According to the census of 1941, Nagykanizsa had a Jewish population of 2,891 representing 6.8 percent of the city's total. In 1946, the congressional congregation had 279 members, including many survivors from the neighboring communities. By 1949, the membership increased to 291 and was under the leadership of László Demeter and Gizella Mádai. *Zsidó Világkongresszus,* no. 4 (April 15, 1947), pp. 2–3; no. 13–14 (May 1949), pp. 16, 28, 29.

11. *Pinkas ha'kehilot,* p. 521.

12. In 1941, Veszprém had a Jewish population of 887, representing 4.1 percent of the city's total. In 1946, there were 106 Jews in the city. The community shrank to 84 by 1949, when it was under the leadership of Ede Lichter. *Zsidó Világkongresszus,* no. 4, (April 15, 1947), pp. 2–3; no. 13–14 (May 1949), p. 23. For some details on the Jewish community of Enying, see *A vasi zsidók,* pp. 167–68. See also *Pinkas ha'kehilot,* pp. 282–84.

13. *Vádirat,* 3:19–23.

14. Statement by Ödön Antl to this author. See also Lévai, *Zsidósors Magyarországon,* p. 148 and *Mementó. Magyarország 1944* (Memento. Hungary 1944) eds. Ödön Gáti *et al.* (Budapest: Kossuth, 1975), pp. 48–49. See further the personal narratives of Anna Kardos (YIVO, 771/3544), Géza Hajdu (771/3543), and Stephen Boskovits (774/2982). In 1941, Kaposvár had a Jewish population of 2,346 representing 7.1 percent of the total. By 1946, this was reduced to 439 or 1.3 percent. During this time, the Neolog congregation was under the leadership of Ödön Antl. In the late 1950s the community, which was reduced to a little over 200, was under the leadership of Pál Fischer. *Zsidó világkongresszus,* no. 4 (April 15, 1947), pp. 2–3; no. 13–14 (May 1949), pp. 13, 26, 28, and 29. See also *Pinkas ha'kehilot,* pp. 472–74.

15. Lévai, *Zsidósors Magyarországon,* p. 418; *Pinkas ha'kehilot* p. 438; *Mementó,* p. 48. For details on the history of the Jewish community of Paks see *Mazkeret Paks* (Paks Memorial Book), ed. D. Sofer. (Jerusalem, 1962), 158 pp. (Hebrew), and Fülöp Grünwald, "Sárospatak—Mátészalka—Paks" in *Évkönyu 1971/72* (Yearbook 1971–72) ed. Sándor Scheiber (Budapest: Magyar Izraeliták Országos Képviselete, 1972), pp. 137–44. See also the personal narrative of R. Weiss (YIVO, 771/3526).

16. The survivors of the community emphasized Lotz's complicity with Dr. János Horváth, another police officer, in the murder of the city's three exempted Jews during the Szálasi era. Lotz escaped after the war, first to Switzerland and after he was unmasked there to Australia where he allegedly lives under an alias. Jehuda-Gyula Láng, *A pápai zsidóság emlékkönyve* (The Memorial Book of the Jews of Pápa). (Tel Aviv: Lahav Printers for the Az Izraelben élő Pápai Zsidók Emlékbizottsága, n.d.), p. 131.

17. In 1941, Pápa had a Jewish population of 2,613 representing 11.0 percent of the total. By 1949, the number of Jews, including those who settled in the city after the war, was 470 or 2.0 percent. In 1949, the orthodox community had 317 members led by Márton Wittmann. *Zsidó Világkongresszus,* no. 4 (April 15, 1947), pp. 2–3; no. 13–14 (May 1949), pp. 18, 28. Lévai, *Zsidósors Magyarországon,* p. 148. For a detailed history of the

Jews of Pápa, see Láng, *A pápai zsidóság emlékkönyve*, 188 + 24 pp. (Hungarian and Hebrew).

18. Among the Jewish communities concentrated in Pápa were those of Ajka, Ajkarendek, Apácatorna, Bódé, Csékut, Csögle, Dabrony, Devecser, Doba, Halimba, Iszkáz, Kerta, Kiscsőz, Kislőd, Kiskamond, Kispirit, Marcaltő, Nagylasony, Nagypirit, Nemesszalók, Öcs, Padrag, Pusztamiske, Somlójenő, Somlószőllős, Somlóvásárhely, Somlóvecse, Tósok, Tüskevár, Ugod, and Zirc. For the lists of the martyrs of these communities and of Pápa, see Láng, *Ibid.*, pp. 135–73.

19. Pap was arrested after the war and condemned to 12 years in prison. *Ibid.*, p. 131.

20. *Ibid.*, pp. 130–32. See also *Pinkas ha'kehilot*, pp. 428–32. Concerning the Kasztner group, see chapter 29.

21. In 1941, Pécs had 3,486 Jews, 4.8 percent of the city's total population. By 1946, the size of the community was reduced to 706 or 0.9 percent of the total population. In 1949, the community numbered 928 Jews under the leadership of László Polgár and Rabbi József Schweitzer. While reduced in number, the community continued to function in the late 1950s under the leadership of Lipót Reich. *Zsidó Világkongresszus*, no. 4 (April 15, 1947), pp. 2–3; no. 13–14 (May 1949), pp. 18 and 25; *Uj Élet*, August 1957.

22. Lévai, *Szürke könyv*, p. 108.

23. Lévai, *Zsidósors Magyarországon*, pp. 148, 418. For a detailed account, see József Schweitzer, *A pécsi izraelita hitközség története* (The History of the Jewish Community of Pécs). (Budapest: A Magyar Izraeliták Országos Képviselete, 1966). See also József Schweitzer, *"A pécsi hitközség a deportáció és a felszabadulás korszakában"* (The Community of Pécs in the Period of Deportation and Liberation) in *Uj Élet naptár 1960–1961, 5720/5721* (New Life Calendar, 1960–1961, 5720/5721) (Budapest: A Magyar Izraeliták Országos Képviselete, 1960), pp. 71–74. See also *Mementó*, pp. 52–53, and *Pinkas ha'kehilot*, pp. 432–35.

24. In 1941, Sárvár had 780 Jews, representing 6.7 percent of the town's population. *Pinkas ha'kehilot*, pp. 522–23.

25. Personal communication by Albert Löwinger. See also Lévai, *Zsidósors Magyarországon*, pp. 418–19, and the personal account of Adolf Baaer at the YIVO (771/3531). For further details and the list of the martyred Jews of Sárvár, consult *A vasi zsidók*, pp. 65–70, 150–54.

26. After the Jewish "political" prisoners were deported on July 4, the commander of the Sárvár Auxiliary Detention Barracks (*Sárvári kisegitő toloncház*) sent notifications to Police Headquarters in Budapest about the individuals "handed over to the Germans." According to one such notification, dated July 14, Mária Ágnes Schrey, 2 years old, and Judit Steiner, 7 years old, were "handed over to the German military for labor in Germany." For samples of such notifications, consult *Vádirat*, 3:178–86.

27. Friedrich Born, *Bericht an das Internationale Komitee vom Roten Kreuz in Genf* (Report to the International Committee of the Red Cross in Geneva) (Geneva, June 1945), p. 28. Born's report identifies the date of the raid as August 5. See also *Notiz über die Situation der Juden in Ungarn* (Note on the Situation of the Jews in Hungary), an International Red Cross document dated November 14, 1944, available in Yad Vashem Archives M-20/47.

28. In 1941, Sopron had a Jewish population of 1,861 representing 4.4 percent of the city's total. By 1946, the size of the community was reduced to 274 or 0.6 percent. As a result of immigration from the neighboring rural communities, the community steadily increased and by 1949 the Neolog congregation had 284 members and the Orthodox one 124 members. The former was led by Dr. Richard Hollós and the latter by Sándor Léderer. By the late 1950s the community was greatly reduced in number, but continued to operate under the leadership of Dr. Hollós. *Zsidó Világkongresszus*, no. 4 (April 15, 1947), pp. 2–3; no. 13–14 (May 1949), pp. 20, 24, 25; *Uj Élet*, March 15, 1958; July 7, 1958.

29. Lévai, *Zsidósors Magyarországon,* p. 418. See also Marton Raab, *Sopronmegye zsidóságának multjából és jelenéből* (From the Past and Present of the Jews of Sopron County) (Sopron: The Author, December 1955), 29 pp. See also Endre Sós, *Zsidók a magyar városokban* (Jews in Hungarian Cities). (Budapest: Libanon Kiadás, n.d.), pp. 153–81; *Pinkas ha'kehilot,* pp. 528–32; and Mária Ember, *Hajtűkanyar* (Hairpin Bent) (Budapest: Szépirodalmi Könyvkiadó, 1974), pp. 188–89.

30. According to another source, the number of Jews in the Szombathely concentration center was 4,228. *A vasi zsidók,* p. 43.

In 1941, Szombathely had a Jewish population of 3,088 representing 7.2 percent of the city's total. By 1946, their number was reduced to 453 or 1.0 percent. In 1949, the Neolog community had 236 members and the Orthodox one had 136. The former was under the leadership of Dr. Iván Hacker, and the latter under that of Dezső Holczer. During the late 1950s, when the community was much smaller; leadership was exercised by Rezső Hirschler. *Zsidó Világkongresszus,* no. 4 (April 15, 1947), pp. 2–3; no. 13–14 (May 1949), pp. 21, 24, 28, 29; *Uj Élet,* July 15, 1958.

31. Harsányi, *A kőszegi zsidók,* p. 208.

32. *Ibid.,* p. 209. According to another source, the name of the detective was Károly Fördös. See *A vasi zsidók,* p. 43.

33. Harsányi, *A kőszegi zsidók,* p. 209. For further details on the Jews of Szombathely and for the list of the martyred Jews of the community, see *A vasi zsidók,* pp. 39–43, 85–87, 129–48, and 180–83. The book also contains the accounts (and lists of martyrs) of the following communities: Jánosháza (pp. 44–47, 154–57); Körmend (pp. 47–50, 157–59), Kőszeg (pp. 51–59, 166–67), Nagysimonyi (pp. 60–61, 157), Celldömölk (pp. 62–65, 159–62), Sárvár (pp. 65–70, 150–54), Vasvár (pp. 70–72, 164–66), Szentgotthárd (pp. 72–73, 162–63), Rohonc (pp. 73–77), Muraszombat (77–78), Németujvár (pp. 78–79), Városszalónak (p. 79), and Enying (pp. 167–68). It also contains the lists of the martyred Jews of many villages in Vas County, including Alsóság, Hegyfalu, Ikervár, Keményegerszeg, Nagysitke, Pósfa, Porpác, and Uraiujfalu. See also *Pinkas ha'kehilot,* pp. 417–19.

34. Lévai, *Zsidósors Magyarországon,* pp. 148–49. See also his *Szürke könyv,* pp. 77–78.

35. In 1941, Zalaegerszeg had a Jewish population of 873, representing 6.2 percent of the city's total.

36. Lévai, *Zsidósors Magyarországon,* pp. 148, 227, 419. See also *Mementó,* p. 48, and *Pinkas ha'kehilot,* pp. 290–92.

37. Ferenczy Report, June 30, 1944, relating to Zone V.

38. *Ibid.,* July 9, 1944.

39. *Ibid.* See also *RLB,* Doc. 189.

40. For details on the background of the Jewish community with emphasis on the family of Mihály Duschinszky, the martyred rabbi of Rákospalota, see Ráchel Áhároni (Duschinszky), *A rákospalotai zsidó hitközség története* (The History of the Jewish Community of Rákospalota) (Tel Aviv: Lahav Printers, 1978), 204 + 50 pp. (Hungarian and Hebrew). For the list of the local martyrs, see pp. 104–14.

41. Munkácsi, *Hogyan történt?,* pp. 69–70. See also *Pinkas ha'kehilot,* pp. 458–59.

42. Lévai, *Zsidósors Magyarországon,* p. 421, and *Pinkas ha'kehilot,* pp. 500–501. See also the following personal narratives at the YIVO: Mrs. Paul Herczeg (771/3241), Mrs. Mór Fényes (771/3275), and S. Rottman and Edith Wetheimer (772/2336).

43. In 1941, Ujpest had a Jewish population of 10,882, representing 14.3 percent of the city's total. *Pinkas ha'kehilot,* pp. 139–41.

44. Statement by Emeric Kepes, YIVO, 768/3588. For further details on the Ujpest community, see László Szilágyi-Windt, *Az ujpesti zsidóság története* (The History of the Jews of Ujpest) (Tel Aviv: Lahav Printers, 1975), 325 + 23 pp. The listing of the community's martyrs is on pp. 54–219. See also Munkácsi, *Hogyan történt?,* pp. 83–84; *Mementó,* pp.

45–47; and the following personal narratives at the YIVO: Mrs. Arnold Schwarcz (768/3589), Julia Vándor (768/3595), László Endre (768/3642), George Hanák (771/3464), Mrs. J. Heinz (771/3542), Dr. Helene László (772/2448), Mrs. Béla Fürst (773/2053), and Helene Antal (773/2069).

45. Lévai, *Zsidósors Magyarországon*, p. 162.

46. *Vádirat*, 3:11.

47. Ferenczy Report of June 30, 1944. See the following personal narratives relating to the camps at Budakalász and to the ghettos from which the Jews were brought in: Emeric Kepes (YIVO, 768/3588), Mrs. Arnold Schwarcz (768/3589), Rose Büchel (769/1126), Mártha Gerő (771/3512), Mrs. J. Heinz (771/3542), Dr. Helene László (772/2448), H. Weisz (773/1989), Mrs. Béla Fürst (773/2053), Stephen Gross (775/3203), and M. Féder et al. (776/63).

48. Lévai, *Fekete könyv*, p. 180.

49. On Békásmegyer and on the Jews from the neighboring communities, including Budafok, Pestszenterzsébet, Rákospalota, Sashalom, Szentendre, and Ujpest, see the following personal narratives: László Endre (YIVO, 768/3642), Lajos Farkas (769/1530), George Hanák (771/3464), and Mrs. Max Rácz (774/2641).

50. Lévai, *Fekete könyv*, p. 181.

51. In 1941, Monor had a Jewish population of 344, representing 2.6 percent of the town's total. *Pinkas ha'kehilot*, pp. 355–57.

52. Ferenczy Report of June 30, 1944. See also Lévai, *Zsidósors Magyarországon*, p. 180.

53. *Ibid.*, p. 415. See also *Pinkas ha'kehilot*, pp. 327–34.

54. Ferenczy Report of July 9, 1944. Israel Police, Bureau 06, Eichmann Trial Doc. 1322. For personal accounts on Monor and some of the Jewish communities transferred there, see the following documents at the YIVO: Mrs. Paul Herczeg (771/3241), Mrs. Mór Fényes (771/3265), Mrs. L. Nádas (771/3548), and S. Rottman and Edith Wertheimer (772/2336).

55. Ferenczy Report of July 9, 1944. In his report of July 11, 1944 (Telegram No. 1927), Veesenmayer claimed that 437,402 Jews had been deported by July 9. *RLB*, Doc. 193.

56. The processes of destruction have been described elsewhere in considerable detail. See, for example, Ota Kraus *and* Erich Kulka, *The Death Factory. Documents on Auschwitz.* (Oxford: Pergamon Press, 1966), 284 pp., and Raul Hilberg, *The Destruction of the European Jews* (Chicago: Quadrangle, 1961), pp. 555–635. For an account by the only survivor of the death-commando in Auschwitz, see Filip Müller, *Auschwitz Inferno. The Testimony of a Sonderkommando*, ed. and translated by Susanne Flatauer (London: Routledge & Kegan Paul, 1979), 180 pp.

For references to other descriptions and analyses of the extermination processes in the various camps, consult the works published in the bibliographical series on the Holocaust by YIVO and the Yad Vashem in Jerusalem. For accounts by Hungarian survivors, see *The Hungarian Jewish Catastrophe. A Selected and Annotated Bibliography*, ed. Randolph L. Braham (New York: YIVO-Yad Vashem, 1962), pp. 29–31.

57. Glücks disappeared during the Red Cross registrations of April 1945, and allegedly committed suicide shortly thereafter. See also Wisliceny's affidavit, *RLB*, Doc. 440.

58. Of the 860 special commandos serving the gas chambers and crematoria at the time, approximately 450 were Hungarian, 200 Polish, 180 Greek, and the remainder Slovak, German, and Soviet POWs. Müller, *Auschwitz Inferno*, pp. 132–33.

59. Among the most infamous of these doctors was Dr. Josef Mengele, the "Angel of Death" in Auschwitz. Mengele spent the first two years of the postwar period undisturbed in his home town in Bavaria. With interest renewed in him, he first fled to Argentina from where, shortly after Eichmann's capture in 1960, he escaped to Paraguay. His Paraguayan citizenship was revoked by the Supreme Court on August 9, 1979, on the

technical ground that he had been out of the country for more than two years. That same day, Simon Wiesenthal, the head of the Vienna Jewish Documentation Center, offered a $50,000 reward for information leading to Mengele's capture. Another "doctor" active at the Auschwitz selection ramp was Victor Capesius, a pharmacist of Transylvanian origin, who spoke both Hungarian and Romanian. Capesius was tried in the "Auschwitz Trial" before the court at Frankfurt-am-Main (1963–1965) and condemned to nine years of hard labor. Bernd Naumann, *Auschwitz. A Report on the Proceedings Against Robert Karl Ludwig Mulka and Others Before the Court at Frankfurt* (New York: Praeger, 1966), 433 pp. See also Miklós Nyiszli, *Dr. Mengele boncolóorvosa voltam az auschwitzi krematóriumban* (I Was Dr. Mengele's Pathologist in the Auschwitz Crematorium) (Debrecen: Debrecen Város és a Tiszántuli Egyházkerület Könyvnyomda Vállalata, 1947), 165 pp., and Gizella Perl, *I Was a Doctor in Auschwitz* (New York: International Universities Press, 1948), 189 pp.

60. *RLB*, Doc. 439

61. Müller, *Auschwitz Inferno*, p. 136.

62. Kraus and Kulka, *The Death Factory*, p. 194. See also the statement by Pery Broad, a member of the Waffen-SS who served in the Political Section in the Auschwitz concentration camp, in Naumann's *Auschwitz*, pp. 162–82.

63. Statement by Rudolf Franz Höss, the former commandant of Auschwitz. 3868-PS as reproduced in *Nazi Conspiracy and Aggression*, 6:787–90. See also Doc. 161-L in *IMT*, 37:626–27.

64. For personal accounts by Hungarian Jews in various German concentration camps, consult Randolph L. Braham, *The Hungarian Jewish Catastrophe*, 86 pp. See also YIVO files 768–783 and Yad Vashem Institute's collections 0–2, 0–3, 0–7, 0–11, 0–15, 0–33, 0–37, and 0–39. See also Nuremberg documents D–258, D–277, NIK–6282 and NIK–13137. Accounts of this type may also be found in *Mementó*, pp. 139–239; Lévai, *Eichmann in Hungary* (Budapest: Pannonia, 1961), pp. 230–43; and *Dapim lecheker tekufat hashoa* (Studies on the Holocaust Period) (Tel Aviv: Hakibbutz Hameuchad, 1978), 1:229–52.

CHAPTER TWENTY-THREE

THE CONSPIRACY OF SILENCE

The Facts and Sources of Information

PERHAPS NO OTHER aspect of the Holocaust has evoked more searching questions or elicited more agonizing debates than the wartime attitude of the Jewish and governmental leaders of the free world and of
the doomed Jewish communities. The attitude of the Hungarian Jewish
leadership has come under special scrutiny because the community
managed to survive until the second quarter of 1944, when many of
the secrets of Auschwitz had already surfaced and the downfall of the
Third Reich was generally considered inevitable. The question of what
the national Hungarian Jewish leaders knew about the realities of the
Nazis' extermination program by the time the mass deportations began
on May 15, 1944, thus acquires a special significance if one is to assess
their attitudes and reactions.

It is generally recognized that:

- The Jews of Hungary, excepting those of Budapest, were destroyed with unprecedented speed in the most ruthless deportation and massacre program of the war.
- The provincial Jews behaved in a resigned and docile manner
  throughout the ghettoization, concentration, and deportation
  process.
- The deportation of the Jews of Budapest, the last surviving
  community, was halted on July 7, 1944, by Admiral Miklós
  Horthy, the Regent of Hungary, after he had been approached
  by President Roosevelt, the King of Sweden, the Vatican, and
  his own son, Miklós Horthy, Jr., who had been informed about
  the realities of Auschwitz by the national Hungarian Jewish
  leaders some time in June.

Given these facts, a number of controversial and bewildering questions arise: What exactly did the national Hungarian Jewish leaders
know about the extermination of the Jews in Nazi-occupied Europe
and when did they learn of it? If they did know exactly how the Nazis
intended to solve the Jewish question, why did they fail to alert the
leaders of the provincial Jewish communities and the Jewish masses in

general? Why did they fail to adopt "illegal" means to enlighten Hungarian public opinion? Why did they wait until the second half of June, when the bulk of the provincial Jews had already been deported, before informing Horthy and other governmental leaders?

Currently available evidence indicates that many of the national leaders of Hungarian Jewry, like the Jewish and governmental leaders of the free world, were fully aware of the realities of the Final Solution program well before the German occupation. While their information about the mass extermination of the Jews was perhaps not totally substantiated during the first two years of the war,[1] hard-core evidence was definitely at hand weeks before the beginning of the mass deportations from Hungary.

The Jewish leaders' sources of information were many:

- Newscasts by "enemy" radio stations, including the BBC, the Voice of America, and Kossuth Radio, the Hungarian-language transmissions from Moscow.
- "Illegal" contacts with Jewish organizations abroad, especially the Zionist and Orthodox units in Switzerland, Palestine, Istanbul, and Bratislava.
- Refugees and camp escapees from Poland, Slovakia, and elsewhere.
- Reports by Hungarian soldiers and officers.
- Contacts with German military, police, and intelligence officers, including those affiliated with the *Wehrmacht*, the SS, and the *Abwehr*.

The First Revelations About the Mass Murders

The decision to bring about the Final Solution was reached at the Wannsee Conference on January 20, 1942,[2] although in reality mass executions began soon after the invasion of the Soviet Union on June 22, 1941. Hundreds of thousands of Polish and Soviet Jews were systematically rounded up and shot by the *Einsatzgruppen*, the mobile killing units which followed the Nazi armies, even before the extermination camps were set up in Poland.[3] Among these were the 14,000 to 16,000 "alien" Jews that had been deported from Hungary in August 1941. Their liquidation near Kamenets-Podolsk, in fact, marked the first Holocaust-period massacre of such dimensions.[4]

In spite of the stringent security measures taken by the SS, the killings were on too massive a scale to be totally concealed. Some of these mass executions were witnessed not only by the local population, but also by members of the Nazi satellite armies, including the Romanians and the Hungarians. Many of the Hungarians were especially appalled by the machine-gunning of innocent men, women, and children. They expressed their shock in letters to their families and gave detailed reports on what they saw when home on furlough. The harsh anti-Jewish laws notwithstanding, the Hungarian Armed Forces in the Ukraine included a limited number of Jewish soldiers—armed and in uniform because of their special expertise as drivers, mechanics, engineers, or doctors—who also witnessed the horrors committed by the *Einsatzgruppen*. Their accounts, like those of the Christian soldiers and officers, were brought to the attention of the communal and Zionist leaders of the country. Reports based on these accounts were even published in the American press.[5]

The accounts of the Hungarian military were fully corroborated by deportees who managed to escape and return to Hungary. Among these were some of the relatives of Sámuel Springmann and Joel Brand, two leading Hungarian Zionists who had good contacts with Hungarian officials.[6] The escapees unfolded a harrowing story of suffering and mass murder. One of the survivors, Lajos Stern, Brand's brother-in-law, accompanied by a delegation from MIPI (*Magyar Izraeliták Országos Irodája;* Welfare Bureau of Hungarian Jews) led by György Polgár, informed Ferenc Keresztes-Fischer, the Minister of the Interior, about the details of the massacres in and around Kamenets-Podolsk. The Minister, an old-fashioned conservative and a very decent individual, was visibly shocked and immediately ordered the halting of all further deportations.[7]

By late summer 1941, the Hungarian Jewish leaders had solid information not only about the extermination of the Jews deported from Hungary, but also about the mass executions carried out by the *Einsatzgruppen* and their local henchmen—Latvians, Lithuanians, Poles, Romanians, and Ukrainians—in the Baltic States, the Ukraine, and Bessarabia and Bukovina—as well as about the first experimental use of gassing vans.[8]

The first public disclosure relating to the mass killings of Jews was made by novelist Thomas Mann, in his BBC broadcasts in December 1941 and January 1942.[9] Though Mann's reports were unverified, the accounts of the Slovak escapees from the camps in the General Government (one of the administrative areas of German-occupied Poland), confirmed the widely held beliefs about the persecution and massacre of Jews. The first transport, composed of 999 Slovakian Jews, left from

Poprad for Auschwitz on March 26, 1942; it was followed by many others. By the end of April a few escapees who had managed to return had provided the earliest evidence about the fate of the deportees. Their accounts were forwarded by the ÚŽ (*Ústredňa Židov;* Central Jewish Office), the Nazi-established central "authority" representing the Jews of Slovakia, to the Jewish organizations in Britain, Palestine, and Switzerland as well as to the leaders of the Slovakian state, including President Josef Tiso.[10]

By this date the Vatican apparently was also aware of the realities in Poland. During the first wave of deportations from Slovakia, the Papal Nuncio in Bratislava, Msgr. Giuseppe Burzio, informed Tiso and his Prime Minister, Vojtech Tuka, that the Jews were being gassed and pleaded for the ending of the deportations. In response, Tuka asked Wisliceny for permission to send a Slovak delegation to the General Government to inspect the situation of the deportees (June 1942).

Wisliceny denied the "rumor" of the gassing, but in order to protect Germany's long-range interests, including the maintenance of good relations with Slovakia and the safeguarding of the Final Solution program elsewhere, he decided in consultation with Hanns Elard Ludin, the German Minister in Bratislava, to recommend to Berlin the temporary suspension of the deportations from Slovakia. But by that time (late in June 1942), approximately 55,000 Jews, or two-thirds of the Slovak Jewish community, had already been deported.[11]

In May 1942, the Jewish Socialist Party of Poland, the "Bund," transmitted a report to London informing the world that the Germans had "embarked on the physical extermination of the Jewish population on Polish soil." The report provided exact data on the places and dates of the executions and the number of Jews involved. It estimated that the Nazis had already annihilated 700,000 Polish Jews. It also provided the first reliable information on the gassing operations that were set up at Chelmno. The Polish Government-in-Exile, which included Szmul Zygielbojm and Dr. Ignacy Schwarzbart as its two Jewish representatives, took the report seriously and was instrumental in having parts of the report broadcast over the BBC on June 2 and June 26, 1942. The details of the report, including the German intentions about exterminating the Jews of Poland and the gassings at Chelmno, were also published by the *Daily Telegraph* on June 25 as well as by the Jewish press, including the *Zionist Review,* the *Jewish Chronicle,* and the *Jewish Telegraphic Agency.* An article based on the report appeared in the *New York Times* of July 2, 1942.[12]

By this time the British press, and presumably even the American one, was privy not only to the fact and extent of the Nazis' Final Solution program, but also to the methods used, including gassing. Moreover it was reportedly also aware of the "existence of a deliberate plan to exterminate *all* the Jews under Nazi rule."[13] In spite of the press revelations and the desperate pleas for retaliations or threats of retaliations advanced by Schwarzbart and Zygielbojm, the world at large remained complacent. The Jewish leaders in the free world "made no visible attempt to put pressure on their governments for any active policy of rescue."[14]

In addition to the BBC reports of June 2 and 26, the Polish Government-in-Exile exerted many other efforts to inform the Allies and the world at large about the Germans' systematic drive to exterminate the Jews. Shortly after its meeting of June 6, when the various secret reports from Poland were discussed, General Wladyslaw Sikorski, the head of the Government-in-Exile, sent a message to the Allies emphasizing that "the extermination of the Jewish population [was] being carried out on an unbelievable scale." On June 9, he warned the world in the course of a BBC broadcast that "the Jewish population of Poland has been doomed to destruction in accordance with the Nazi pronouncements on destroying all the Jews regardless of the outcome of the war." He gave detailed facts about the extent of the slaughter in the various Polish cities and informed the world that he was bringing these atrocities to the attention of the Allies. On June 10, the Polish authorities in exile also published a call to all the parliaments in the free world concerning the anti-Jewish measures in Europe in general and in Poland in particular. These activities of the Polish Government-in-Exile were intensified during July, when the mass deportation of the Jews of Warsaw began.

Reports about the ruthless campaign to extirpate Polish Jewry in 1942 continued to reach the leaders of the free world throughout the year. Aside from the occasional publication of summaries of these reports in the back pages of certain newspapers, no concrete or meaningful measures were taken to alleviate the plight of Polish Jewry. The reports made it clear that the exterminations were taking place in Auschwitz and elsewhere and that the deportations were being disguised as "resettlements."[15] Similar reports with details about the Nazis' Final Solution program and specific recommendations and urgent pleas reached the Jewish leaders in America, Britain, Switzerland, Turkey, and Palestine periodically throughout 1943 and 1944.

The Jewish National Committee, representing the fighting Jews in Poland, wrote to Rabbi Stephen S. Wise, Nahum Goldman, and the AJDC on March 17, 1943, suggesting specific steps to save the remnant of Polish Jewry. On November 15, 1943, six months after the crushing of the Warsaw Ghetto Uprising, the leaders of the Committee wrote to Dr. Ignacy Schwarzbart in London, not only condemning the Nazi barbarians but also berating the Jewish leaders of the free world. They wrote: "The blood of 3,000,000 Polish Jews will take revenge not only against the Nazi murderers, but against those indifferent elements which have contented themselves merely with words but have done nothing to rescue from the hands of the beasts a people doomed to extermination. This we . . . can never forget or forgive."[16]

Frustrated by the silence and apathy of the world in the face of the Nazi murder of the Jews, Zygielbojm committed suicide on May 12, 1943, at the age of 48. In his farewell letter he wrote: "I cannot be silent. I cannot live while the remnants of the Jewish population of Poland, of whom I am a representative, are perishing. My friends in the Warsaw ghetto died with weapons in their hands in the last heroic battle. It was not my destiny to die together with them but I belong to them and in their mass graves. By my death I wish to make my final protest against the passivity with which the world is looking on and permitting the extermination of the Jewish people."[17]

Reports on the Nazi Resolution Relating to the Final Solution

In the summer of 1942, the representatives of leading international Jewish organizations in neutral Switzerland received first-hand information about the Nazi hierarchy's intent to liquidate European Jewry. Information of this sort was also communicated through official channels to the heads of the Western Allies at about the same time. The accounts as to who first informed whom vary.

According to Arthur D. Morse's account, Gerhart Riegner, the representative of the World Jewish Congress in Switzerland, was informed on August 1, 1942, by a leading German industrialist who had access to Hitler's headquarters, that the Führer had ordered the extermination of the Jews of Europe. The informant had overheard the discussion on the order, which also stipulated the use of prussic acid, the lethal ingredient of the Zyklon B gas that was actually used in the extermination camps. By that time, Riegner was presumably already aware of the

Bund report and had ample factual information about the "resettlement" of the 380,000 Jews in the Warsaw Ghetto, which began on July 22, and about the deportation of Jews from occupied Belgium, Holland, and France.

Because of wartime censorship regulations and in order to assure privacy, Riegner dispatched a report in the form of a telegram via the American Consulate in Geneva on August 8. Vice-Consul Howard Elting, Jr., included a covering memorandum to the State Department in which he evaluated Riegner as "a serious and balanced individual" and requested that the message be delivered to Rabbi Stephen S. Wise, the head of the World Jewish Congress. The telegram was at first suppressed by the State Department, but when it was discovered that the British Foreign Office had forwarded its copy to the London branch of the World Jewish Congress, Rabbi Wise was notified on August 28.

It appears that the British had been informed about the existence and implications of the Führer Order just as soon as, if not sooner than, the Americans. In fact, according to the currently available evidence, Riegner's source was the very Jewish source that originally alerted the British—Dr. Chaim Pozner, then Co-Director of the Jewish Agency's Palestine Office in Geneva.[18] The communication about the Führer Order relating to the Final Solution was relayed, according to this version, not by a "German industrialist," but by a fiercely anti-Nazi officer, Lieutenant-Colonel Artur Sommer. A highly esteemed economist, Sommer had been attached in the early 1940s to the Wehrmacht High Command.[19] In this capacity and as a member of a German economic delegation, he often visited Switzerland officially, ostensibly for the advancement of German economic interests. Sommer reestablished and maintained discreet contact with his former instructor, Professor Edgar Salin of Basel University, and became the conduit of invaluable information for the Allies. For example, he tipped off Salin some time in June 1941 about the Nazis' plan for the imminent attack on the Soviet Union. Appalled by the Nazis' intention to exterminate the Jews, Sommer also revealed this information to Salin with the request that it be relayed to Churchill and Roosevelt. His discreetly submitted memo, which also included a specific suggestion for action, noted that:

In the East, camps are being prepared where all the Jews of Europe and a great part of the Russian prisoners of war will be exterminated by gas. Please relay this information immediately to Churchill and Roosevelt personally. If the BBC comes out every day with a warning against lighting the gas ovens, then perhaps they will not be put into operation, for the criminals are doing everything to prevent the German people from finding out what they are planning to do and will certainly carry out.[20]

Salin, an internationally famous economist-sociologist and an equally staunch anti-Nazi, passed on the information received from Sommer to another former student of his, Dr. Chaim Pozner. Pozner, in turn, immediately relayed the information to the British via V. C. Farrell, the head of the British Passport Control Office in Geneva, who also served as the head of the British Intelligence unit in Switzerland.[21] Concurrently, Dr. Pozner informed Dr. Benjamin Segalowitz, the director of the press bureau of the Union of Jewish Communities in Switzerland, who, in turn, alerted Dr. Gerhart Riegner.[22]

The question as to why Sommer's crucial communication, faithfully transmitted by Salin and Pozner, was handled in such a discreet and private fashion remains a mystery. Pozner's freedom of action was limited by his foreign status and commitments to Farrell, from whom he had regularly received information about the Jewish community of Poland. Sagalowitz, however, was a free agent and as press bureau director he could perhaps have brought the information to the attention of the Swiss press. It is also possible that he did so, but in 1942, when Germany was still triumphant, the Swiss, concerned with the protection of their neutrality, may have been reluctant to publish anything that could have been construed as derogatory by the Reich.

In addition to the information received from Sagalowitz, Riegner continued to submit additional corroborative documentation concerning Hitler's resolution to solve the Jewish question. But these, like practically all subsequent communications by Riegner and other Jewish representatives, remained for a long time unheeded. A similar fate befell many of the communications forwarded by American and foreign diplomatic representatives.

Rabbi Wise reportedly requested Sumner Welles, the U.S. Under Secretary of State, to have the Riegner report verified, promising that he would in the interim withhold information about it.[23] In September, Rabbi Wise received another report, this time from Jacob Rosenheim, a European representative of the World Jewish Congress, which contained more specific details about the Nazis' Final Solution program. After the Jewish Telegraphic Agency broke the Riegner story in October and the State Department received additional corroborative reports, Welles informed Rabbi Wise that his deepest fears had been confirmed.

The reports referred to by Welles included one by Anthony J. Drexel

Biddle, Jr., the U.S. Ambassador to the Polish Government-in-Exile, which he forwarded to President Roosevelt on August 26, 1942. It included a report by Ernest Frischer, a leading member of the Czechoslovak State Council, in which he described the massacre of Jews in East Central Europe. Another report, by Dr. Donald A. Lowrie, an American representing the World Alliance of Young Men's Associations, included details about the deportations in France. Leland Harrison, the American Minister in Berne, wrote two personal letters to Welles, bypassing the Department of State. In his first letter, dated October 24, 1942, Harrison provided some additional details about the origin of the news on the Führer Order. (These details differ from those offered by either Morse or Salin and Pozner.) He confirmed that the German industrialist, whose name he already knew, was indeed a member of the inner circle of advisers on the Nazi war economy. In his view it was Dr. Carl J. Burckhardt, a leading figure of the International Committee of the Red Cross, who brought the existence of the Führer Order to the attention of Professor Paul Guggenheim, the distinguished Swiss lawyer and Riegner's friend. In his second letter, dated October 31, Harrison included Guggenheim's sworn affidavit, dated October 29, in which he declared that there was indeed a Hitler Order relating to the extermination of all Jews in the German-controlled areas. Professor Guggenheim further revealed that the Order was brought to the attention of Burckhardt, his informant, by an official of the German Foreign Office and an officer of the German Ministry of War, acting independently of each other.[24]

In desperation, Rabbi Wise contacted President Roosevelt on December 2, 1942, and again on December 8. At that time he submitted a 20-page document titled "Blueprint for Extermination." In it he presented a country-by-country analysis of the Nazis' extermination program. The details on the Final Solution were reinforced by another report by Riegner (dated January 21, 1943), which was included in the dispatch forwarded by Harrison on January 27, 1943.[25] The leaders of British Jewry undertook similar measures with their government and a variety of church and political leaders. The efforts of the Western Jewish leaders were on the whole fruitless, because the Allies were reluctant to divert any of their resources for rescue purposes, arguing that victory offered the most effective remedy. The Jewish leaders were caught in an awkward position. Many of them feared that if they were to press for direct action for the rescuing of Jews, their own patriotism might be impugned.

The Revelations by Polish and Slovak Refugees

The Hungarian Jewish leaders were in a particularly good position to ascertain the veracity of the foreign radio broadcasts, which they, like many ordinary Jews, heard regularly, if at a certain risk. Thousands of Jewish refugees had escaped into Hungary from Poland and Slovakia in the wake of the draconic anti-Jewish measures adopted in those countries. Some of them were smuggled into Hungary with the assistance of the *Vaada* (see chapters 3 and 29). One of the major functions of this organization was to collect and transmit the personal accounts of the escapees, along with its own reports about the realities of the Nazi persecution of the Jews to its Jewish Agency contacts in Istanbul and Switzerland. The Budapest *Vaada* set up a regular underground intelligence unit, where the escapees were closely questioned and the details about the ghettoization, concentration, deportation, and extermination program in Poland, Slovakia, and elsewhere were carefully scrutinized and counterchecked. Hundreds of such accounts were thus authenticated in Budapest and forwarded to the Jewish Agency, *Hehalutz*, and AJDC offices in Istanbul and Switzerland.[26] These contained details about the "mass murders in the East"[27] as well as specific information about gassings and the operation of the crematoria.[28] Ghastly reports of this kind, coupled with desperate appeals for monetary assistance, were also sent along to Saly Mayer both before and after the occupation of Hungary.[29] Many of these reports found their way to England and America. The American Jewish leaders, for example, received news from Geneva on April 4, 1944, that the Germans intended to exterminate Hungarian Jewry within six months. That was almost two weeks before the beginning of the ghettoization in Carpatho-Ruthenia, but the Allies reportedly refused to heed the Jewish leaders' appeals.[30]

The Jewish Agency office in Istanbul was, of course, kept up-to-date about the Nazis' extermination program by other sources as well. Aware of the techniques used in the Final Solution program, the Istanbul office in fact alerted the Budapest *Vaada* about the dangers of cooperating with the Germans in case of an occupation. In letters dated September 25 and October 23, 1943, when speculation was rampant about an imminent German occupation of Hungary, Menachem Bader, a leading member of the Istanbul office, instructed his colleagues in Budapest to desist from cooperating with the Germans even passively. He warned that carrying out such activities as taking a census, submitting to concentration, or wearing the yellow star, were "preparation for destruction."[31]

Reports similar to the ones collected and forwarded by the Budapest *Vaada* were also processed and sent to Istanbul *Vaada* and to the Jewish Agency, *Hehalutz*, and AJDC offices in Switzerland by Gisi Fleischmann, a leading member of the "Working Group" (*Pracovná Skupina*) operating within the framework of the Bratislava Jewish Council.[32] She also regularly kept the Hungarian Jewish leaders, especially those associated with the Kasztner group, abreast of developments in Poland and Slovakia.[33] Moreover, members of the Bratislava and Budapest *Vaada* offices exchanged visits periodically. When the Slovak Jewish community was in trouble, the Bratislava leaders did not always get the kind of assistance they expected from the Hungarian Jewish leaders, who were relatively well off. Fleischmann expressed her disappointment in one of her letters to Nathan Schwalb: "In connection with my stay [in Budapest], I dealt with the leading elements of Jewish life and must note first of all that, in all objectivity, our friends there know neither Jewish solidarity nor social responsibility nor charity."[34] This assessment of the shortsightedness of Hungarian Jewry was corroborated by Ottó Komoly, the President of the Hungarian Zionist Association and of the *Vaada*,[35] as well as by some of the leaders of the *Hehalutz* movement, including Rafi (Friedl) Ben-Shalom. Shortly after his arrival from Slovakia in January 1944, Ben-Shalom, who would become one of the heroes of the Jewish underground later in the fall, observed that he and his refugee colleagues "came to know Hungarian Jewry as a particularly ugly kind."[36]

The Orthodox leadership of Hungarian Jewry was as well informed as the *Vaada* leadership. It was briefed separately by Rabbi Michael Beer-Dov Weissmandel of the Bratislava Committee.[37]

The Bratislava Rescue Committee, for example, had informed the Budapest Committee weeks before the beginning of the deportations that a railway agreement had been signed by Hungary and Slovakia and that the SS were in the process of improving and renovating the gas chambers and crematoria in Auschwitz in anticipation of the arrival of the Hungarian Jews. The report even quoted the words of a *Scharführer* to the effect that the SS "will soon eat fine Hungarian salami."[38]

In addition to informing the Hungarian Jews, Rabbi Weissmandel kept the Jewish leaders of Switzerland abreast of the Nazis' Final Solution program. In 1944, his heartbreaking letters and desperate calls for help were concerned primarily with the plight of Hungarian Jewry. He provided detailed and accurate accounts of the Final Solution program in Hungary and suggested specific steps that the Jewish leaders of the free world could take in order to bring the bloodletting to an end. Like many other Jewish leaders in Nazi-occupied Europe, he was shocked by what he perceived as the inaction, silence, and insensitivity of the free world's Jewish and governmental leaders in the face of mass murders. He gave vent to his anguish in a letter addressed to the *Hehalutz* in Geneva toward the end of May, when the mass deportations from Carpatho-Ruthenia and Northern Transylvania were at their height. After describing the workings of Auschwitz, which was then devouring the Jews of Hungary, Rabbi Weissmandel added:

And you, our Jewish brethren in all the free countries, and you, government leaders in all countries, how can you be silent in the face of these murders in which some six million Jews have been killed up to now and in which thousands are still being killed every day! With devastated hearts the murdered Jews are screaming at you and about you, you cruel ones, you murderers, because of your cruel silence and your folding your hands in inaction, because you have the ability to refuse to allow—and to prevent—these events at this time.[39]

Rabbi Weissmandel had been in the forefront of rescue work since shortly after the deportation of the Slovak Jews began in March 1942. In June of that year, he contacted Dieter Wisliceny, Eichmann's aide in charge of the deportations from Slovakia, and offered him a bribe to cease the anti-Jewish operations. By coincidence, the deportations were halted shortly thereafter, for reasons discussed earlier; Rabbi Weissmandel and his Bratislava colleagues then became convinced of the "vital" role played by Wisliceny. The latter, having "established his credentials," continued to exploit the possibilities of the bargaining process. By October 1942, the bargaining was extended to include, under the so-called "Europa Plan" (see chapter 29), the suspension of deportations from Europe to Poland, but not the killing operations within Poland itself, "which Wisliceny had no jurisdiction over." The negotiations over the plan gained momemtum after May 7, 1943, when Gisi Fleischmann took charge in behalf of the Bratislava *Vaada*.

Using a secret code system, which incidentally was used by the leaders of all the wartime Jewish agencies involved in relief and rescue work,[40] Fleishmann regularly informed the Jewish Agency, *Hehalutz*, and AJDC offices in Switzerland and Turkey about the plan.[41] Her reports also contained detailed and authenticated information about the destruction of the Jews in Poland and Slovakia.

On March 24, 1943, for example, she reported that the communications by all the couriers sent into Poland were negative, for the entire territory of the General Government had become *Judenrein*. She identified the three major centers where Jews were still in existence as Auschwitz, Birkenau, and Lublin, emphasizing that those still alive were basically healthy men and women still able to work.[42] On May 9, 1943, she reported again on the mass murders in Poland. She informed the Jewish leaders in the free world that not only were families being totally destroyed, but those selected for labor in the camps were also eventually subjected to these murders. The inmates' lives in the camps, she stated, were those of prisoners. "As long as the individual continues to be capable of working he justifies his right to exist. Should he become weak, or prevented by illness from carrying out his work, he simply ceases to exist."[43]

A few days after meeting with Wisliceny, on May 10, 1943, Fleischmann wrote an important report which was marked "Top Secret; Destroy Immediately." The report, a copy of which has survived in spite of her instructions, contained not only the conditions worked out by Wisliceny and his superiors for the effectuation of the "Europa Plan," but also further details about the annihilation of the Jews in Poland:

We are under the spell of the couriers [schlichim], who have brought us reports that make one's blood run cold. Over one million comrades [chaverim] have already been resettled from Poland; the location is unknown. Hundreds of thousands more have lost their lives due to starvation, disease, and cold, and uncounted others, numbering many many tens of thousands, have fallen victim to violence. The reports state that the corpses are used as chemical raw materials. The reports also agree with the news of some refugees [plitim] who were fortunate enough to escape in the most daring ways. We have also received written reports to the same effect from the couriers. 120 comrades are crammed into a cattle wagon which would normally hold 40. There is a layer approximately 10 centimeters deep of unslaked lime on the floor, and since the people in the wagons must relieve themselves where they are standing, when the wastes touch the lime gasses are formed which bring about an exceedingly high mortality rate. It is presumed that those who were resettled from Poland are being taken beyond the Bug, but so far no sign of life has reached us from there.[44]

She was even more specific in her report of September 5, 1943, a copy of which was also received by Dr. Adolf Silberschein in Geneva:

We know today that Sobibor, Malkyne-Treblinki, Belzec, and Auschwitz are annihilation camps. In the camps themselves small work parties are being maintained to create the impression that they are [ordinary] camps.[45]

The communications by Fleischmann, like those of the Rescue Committee of Budapest,[46] constitute some of the most convincing evidence that the Jewish leaders of the world, including, of course, the Hungarian ones, were fully acquainted with the Nazis' massacre program.

Among the refugees in Hungary were some who had played an active role in the partisan movement and who after they had been captured had managed to escape, acquire Aryan papers, and live semilegally in the country. One of these was Bruce B. Teicholz, who was captured as a partisan north of Munkács and was brought to Hungary in March 1942.[47] He managed to escape in Budapest and joined a Polish-Jewish underground organization under the code name "Glick." At the same time he was also registered with the KEOKH [*Külföldieket Ellenőrző Országos Központi Hatóság;* National Central Alien Control Office]—the agency with jurisdiction over foreign nationals living in Hungary—as a Polish Christian under the name of Bronislaw Szczepipiorka. In this triple capacity Teicholz maintained close contact with the Polish refugee organizations in Hungary and abroad, with Dr. A. Silberschein of the World Jewish Congress in Geneva, the official leaders of Hungarian Jewry (including Samu Stern and Fülöp Freudiger), and with the members of the Rescue Committee (including Komoly, Kasztner, and Brand). Some time in April 1943, Teicholz had a meeting with the leaders of Hungarian Jewry, including Freudiger, Kasztner, Moshe (Miklós) Krausz of the Palestine Office (*Palesztina Hivatal*), and Dr. József Pásztor of the OMZSA [*Országos Magyar Zsidó Segítő Akció;* National Hungarian Jewish Assistance Campaign], the major Jewish fund-raising organization. At this meeting he explained in detail the Nazis' techniques in Poland. He identified the specific steps employed, and reviewed the techniques utilized to lull the Jews into submission and cooperation in their own destruction. He warned the Hungarian Jewish leaders to take all necessary precautionary measures and to be aware of the Nazi techniques of extermination. These leaders, however, "assured" Teicholz that what happened in Poland could not possibly happen in Hungary.[48]

Teicholz's account and his assessment of the Hungarian Jewish leaders' position before the occupation are corroborated by the young *Halutzim* from Poland and Slovakia[49] and by Hermann Adler, a German-Jewish poet and author. Adler's views were particularly condemnatory. He fled to Budapest in October 1943 after having spent the previous two years in the underground movement in the Vilna, Bialystok, and Warsaw ghettos.[50] As a member of the underground in Poland, Adler was in touch with Anton Schmidt, a legendary *Wehrmacht* sergeant. Schmidt, who had cooperated with the Jewish underground in Vilna and Bialystok by providing its members with false papers and transportation, was eventually detected by the Gestapo and executed.[51]

Adler was also in touch with a number of other Germans involved in the anti-Nazi resistance.[52] By the time of his arrival in Budapest, Adler was fully familiar with the extermination of the Jews at Treblinka and the realities of the Final Solution program in Poland as a whole. He revealed all he knew to Professor Valdemar Langlet, the representative of the Swedish Red Cross in Budapest, and to the leaders of Hungarian Jewry, including those associated with the *Vaada*. These leaders, Adler claims, refused to believe his accounts about Treblinka. Kasztner, for example, wanted to know whether Adler had actually been in Treblinka. "It wasn't easy to convince the Hungarian Jews," Adler complained.

Acknowledgments by Jewish Leaders

Teicholz's and Adler's revelations about the camps were eventually acknowledged by the Hungarian Jewish leaders. Describing the circumstances under which he had emerged as the head of the Jewish Council (*Zsidó Tanács*) of Budapest, the agency entrusted with "power" over all of Jewry, Samu Stern wrote:

I—nor others I suppose—was not taken in by the faked good will, hypocrisy, and treachery of the Gestapo's debut. *I knew what they had done in all German-occupied states of Europe;* I knew their activities to be a long, long sequence of murders and robberies. In the first days mass arrests had already begun, mostly at railway stations, where unsuspecting passengers were picked up under the pretext that they were attempting to flee. Their practices were already clearly running counter to their perfidious declarations. I had heard enough about the methods of the Gestapo's notorious Jewish department to know that they always shunned sensation, disliked creating panic and fear, worked silently, coolly, and in deepest secrecy, so that their listless, ignorant victims would have no inkling of what was ahead of them—even while the freight cars were taking them toward death. I knew the Nazis' habits, deeds, and terrifying reputation, and yet I accepted the chairmanship of the Council. *And the others knew as much as I did when they joined the Council as members.*[53]

Béla Fábián, the former member of the lower house of the Hungarian Parliament and the wartime President of the Jewish Veterans' Committee (*Hadviseltek Bizottsága;* see chapter 10) was also aware of the nature of the Nazis' drive against the Jews in the neighboring countries. He had excellent connections not only with the small and relatively ineffective Hungarian underground, but also with some of the top officers of the Ministry of Defense. Among the latter were Minister Vilmos Nagy and Lieutenant-General Gusztáv Hennyey, who was in charge of the labor service system. After the war, Fábián stated:

We heard a great deal about Auschwitz and the deportation of the Jews from Poland, Czechoslovakia, and Slovakia, where our friends lived. We had been with them at the universities and in the army and we now felt their tragic existence very keenly. We were afraid that the same thing would happen to us.[54]

Kasztner's admissions after the war matched Stern's acknowledgment of his awareness of what the Germans had done in Nazi-occupied Europe, if not Fábián's foreboding about the catastrophe that would befall the Hungarian Jews as well. As a Zionist, Kasztner perhaps was in an even better position than Stern to keep abreast of the anti-Jewish measures in Europe, since he was in constant touch with the representatives of Jewish organizations abroad by a variety of underground channels (see chapter 3).

Shortly after liberation, Kasztner brought out a detailed though self-serving report on the wartime activities of the Budapest Rescue Committee.[55] In it, he provides both direct and indirect evidence that he and his colleagues on the Committee were fully aware of the draconic measures that had been adopted against the Jews in Nazi-occupied Europe. He is basically silent about their failure to inform Hungarian Jewry, but all the more pugnacious and bitter over the passivity and complacency of the Jewish and non-Jewish leaders in the free world. In his endeavor to undercut the position adopted by many leaders of the Grand Alliance both during and after the war that they had been unaware of the "apocalyptic extent of Hitler's anti-Jewish measures," he emphatically declared that there was no dearth of such information. From Budapest alone, he argued, innumerable reports had been sent out by underground channels since the middle of 1942 about what was going on in Poland.[56] Keeping track of the anti-Jewish measures in Nazi-occupied Europe and informing the Jewish and non-Jewish leaders of the free world had, in fact, been among the major functions of the *Vaada*.[57] Among those who provided undercover courier services for the Committee were Josef Winninger and Dr. Schmidt of Admiral Canaris' *Abwehr* (Intelligence) unit in Budapest and Dr. Rudolf Sedlacek of the SS. After the occupation, these agents were chiefly responsible for the establishment of contact between Kasztner and the Eichmann-*Sonderkommando*.

After the war, Kasztner also testified in two major trials that he had been aware of the destruction of European Jewry before the German occupation of Hungary on March 19, 1944. Appearing as a witness for the prosecution in the Veesenmayer Trial on March 19, 1948, Kasztner responded as follows when asked by Mr. Caming, one of the prosecutors, whether he was "in a position to gain a clear picture of the Jewish situation in Hungary."[58]

I was the President of the Zionist Organization of Hungary,[59] and after the arrival of the first Jewish refugees from Slovakia I had a mandate to build up a committee to provide rescue and help for these refugees. In this capacity I was, I think, one of the best informed in Hungary about the situation of the Jews at that time. . . . In addition, I have learned from talking to these refugees that some of them managed to escape from Auschwitz. *We had, as early as 1942, a complete picture of what had happened in the east to the Jews deported to Auschwitz and the other extermination camps.* (Italics supplied)

However, when he was cross-examined by Dr. Doetzer, Veesenmayer's defense counsel, as to why he or his organization had failed to inform Horthy about what they had known about the extermination camps since 1942, Kasztner hedged and gave an evasive reply:

We certainly should have tried this. We ought to have tried it, and we did, but you must visualize the situation in Hungary at the time immediately after the German occupation. It was a state of terror. Many of the friends and acquaintances through whom we could have informed Regent Horthy were already gone. Others were afraid to get in touch with us. It took quite some time before we found the men and the opportunity to inform Horthy about it.[60]

While Kasztner was partially correct in depicting the situation *after* the German occupation, his answer fails to shed light on the national Hungarian Jewish leaders' failure, *before* the occupation, to inform Horthy and the other governmental leaders of Hungary as well as the provincial Jewish community leaders, if not the Jewish masses, about what they had known since 1942. This is particularly important in light of the power demonstrated by Horthy in July 1944 to halt the deportations. One can only speculate, of course, whether Horthy would have acted earlier had he been officially informed about the realities of the Final Solution program before or at least immediately after the German occupation. It must be added that the evidence indicates that Horthy and some of the top Hungarian leaders were in fact aware of at least some aspects of the Final Solution program. Moreover, Horthy halted the deportations not so much because of concern over the exterminations, but primarily for military reasons, including the Normandy invasion and the Baky-led coup attempt (see chapter 25).

Kasztner also admitted to knowledge about the extermination of the Jews in Poland during the trial of the famous Grünwald-Kasztner case in Israel in 1954–1955, in which Judge Benjamin Halevi found him guilty of "having sold his soul to the devil." When questioned by

Shmuel Tamir, Grünwald's defense lawyer, on his dealings with the SS, Kasztner testified:

Toward the end of April 1944, the German military agents informed me that they had finally decided on the total deportation of Hungarian Jews . . . An agreement was made between Hungary and Slovakia for the transfer of deportation trains from Hungary to Auschwitz.

I also received information from Auschwitz that they were preparing there to receive the Hungarian Jews. . . . I was allowed by . . . Krumey to go to Kluj [Cluj, Kolozsvár] and contact . . . Wisliceny. This was approximately the third of May, 1944. . . . A few days later I visited Wisliceny at his home in Budapest. He told me that it had finally been decided—total deportation.[61]

Kasztner's visit to Kolozsvár during the ghettoization of the North Transylvanian Jews early in May 1944, has emerged as the source of one of the greatest controversies concerning the attitude of the Jewish leaders during the Holocaust. By that time, Kasztner was, of course, fully familiar with the Nazis' extermination program,[62] but allegedly had failed to inform the local Jewish Council or the Rescue Committee leadership about the impending disaster. Kasztner's closest friends, including Hillel Danzig and Dezső (David) Hermann, who had played a prominent role in the Zionist movement, denied having been told anything about Auschwitz.[63]

Regardless of specifics, it stands to reason that these leaders must have been informed by Kasztner about certain realities of the deportation of which the masses were kept in the dark. In response to a question by Judge Halevi, Kasztner admitted that he had given his father-in-law certain hints and that "he had to know that there was deportation and that extermination would follow." When asked why the Jews of Kolozsvár had not been informed, he confessed that his colleagues in Kolozsvár, including his father-in-law, "did not do all in their power—did not do all that could have been done—all that they had to do."[64] And, in fact, if Kasztner is correct, his colleagues must have known a lot, because at the time of his visit to Kolozsvár on May 3, Kasztner already was in possession of hard-core "inside" evidence on the extermination of the Jews in Auschwitz.

The Auschwitz Protocols

If the eyewitness accounts collected and distributed by the Bratislava and Budapest Rescue Committees contained first-hand experiences on the ghettoization, concentration, and deportation processes and convincing although not personally observed details on the extermination program within the camps, the revelations by five escapees from Auschwitz in April 1944, weeks before the deportation of the Hungarian Jews, should have dispersed all doubts about what was going on.

Unlike the many individuals who attempted to flee the camp only to save their own lives, these five Jewish inmates, who had actually escaped in April with the aid of the resistance movement, fled with the intent to inform the world of what was happening and to warn the Jewish communities, especially the Hungarian, about the impending disaster.[65]

The first to escape on April 5, 1944, was Siegfried Lederer, whose mission was to alert the Jews in the ghetto of Theresienstadt and the International Red Cross in Geneva. Lederer fled in an SS uniform with the aid and in the company of Viktor Pestek, an SS guard of Romanian-German origin who was in love with Renée Neumann, a Czech Jewish girl. Lederer managed to pass on the information to the Jewish Elders in Theresienstadt and to the International Red Cross in Geneva. The transmission of the news in Theresienstadt was particularly important because most of the Jewish captives there lived under the impression that the Jews taken to Auschwitz were relatively well off. This impression was fostered by the fact that the 9,971 Jews transferred from Theresienstadt to Auschwitz on September 6–7 and December 16–20, 1943, had been kept as intact families separated from the other inmates under relatively good conditions. This was one of the Nazis' propaganda ploys "to show to the visiting German and International Red Cross teams that contrary to enemy propaganda the Jews were not mishandled at Auschwitz." It was reportedly only after Lederer's escape that the Jewish Elders of the Theresienstadt ghetto discovered that these people also were murdered on March 7, 1944, after they had outlived their usefulness as "exhibits."[66]

By far the most important escape was that of Walter Rosenberg (Rudolf Vrba) and Alfred Wetzler (Josef Lanik) on April 7.[67]

Both Rosenberg and Wetzler had held positions in the camp which enabled them to move comparatively freely throughout Auschwitz and collect exact information about the incoming transports, and the selection and extermination of the victims: Rosenberg was a clerk in the quarantine block, while Wetzler had the same position in the main camp of Birkenau.

After a dramatic escape and an adventurous journey of 10 days they reached safety on Slovakian soil on April 21. Four days later, they were telling their story at the Zilina headquarters of the Jewish Council to Dr. Oscar (Yermiyahu) Neumann, Oskar (Karmil) Krasznyansky, Erwin Steiner, and Hexner. The escapees were closely scrutinized, their stories carefully counterchecked and verified, and they were interrogated anew on the 26th. That same day, Krasznyansky, with the assistance of the escapees, prepared a detailed report in German which was typed by Mrs. Steiner.[68]

The report contained a detailed description of the camp facilities, including the barracks in which the prisoners were quartered, the kitchens, and the hospitals, and the processing of the incoming deportees, including the techniques used in their "selection," tattooing, gassing, and cremation. It also described the administrative structure in the camp and gave exact data on the number and origin of the Jews gassed at Birkenau between April 1942 and April 1944. The report included sketches of the building plans prepared by a professional architect. In his introduction to the report, Krasznyansky included biographical notes on the escapees and vouched for the accuracy and authenticity of their account.[69] He also added a supplement in which he urged the Allies to destroy the crematoria and the railroad lines leading to Auschwitz.[70]

The Working Group (*Pracovná Skupina*) of the Jewish Council of Slovakia, including Gisi Fleischmann, Oscar Neumann, Leo Rosenthal, Tibor Kovacz, Rabbi A. Frieder, Rabbi Weissmandel, and of course, Krasznyansky, decided to forward copies of the report to the Jewish Agency unit in Istanbul; Nathan Schwalb of the *Hehalutz* in Geneva; Giuseppe Burzio, the Papal Nuncio in Bratislava (who was expected to deliver it to the Vatican); Kasztner (who was to deliver copies to Horthy and to Jusztinián Cardinal Serédi).[71]

The shocking but factual accounts of Vrba and Wetzler were fully corroborated a few weeks later by two other escapees from Auschwitz—Arnošt Rosin of Snina, Slovakia, and Czezlaw Mordowicz of Mlawa, Poland—who had escaped on April 27. Their account was recorded by Krasznyansky during the first half of June 1944, in Liptovský Mikuláš (Liptószentmiklós) in the home of Boby Reich, a member of the local Jewish community. It provided new and important data on the deportation and extermination of European Jews up to the time of their flight.[72]

The record is vague as to the exact date when the first set of the Auschwitz Protocols was forwarded. Vrba claims that he had been assured by Krasznyansky and Neumann on April 26 that the report had already been sent out to the Hungarians. In his own memoirs, Neumann is vague about the dates and claims that the Protocols were forwarded "shortly" after they were typed. Krasznyansky, on the other hand, claims that Kasztner, who visited Bratislava during those days, had read the original German text there and had him translate the Protocols into Hungarian as well. He recalls that the Hungarian translation was forwarded to Budapest within two weeks.[73]

In his report on the activities of the Budapest *Vaada,* Kasztner is basically silent about the Auschwitz Protocols. He merely alludes to them in connection with the precautionary measures taken upon the arrival of the Germans in the Hungarian capital, mentioning that Josef Winninger, one of the *Abwehr* agents with whom the *Vaada* leaders had good relations, removed for safekeeping some of the suitcases of the *Vaada* that contained valuables, correspondence with Bratislava, Istanbul, and Switzerland, as well as "Protocols of Auschwitz, Treblinka, and Lemberg."[74]

The Protocols are also ignored by Samu Stern, who admits only to having received "in the middle of April" the news about a "railway conference" and the consequent allocation of "rolling stock for some unknown purpose."[75] Ernő Pető, one of the leading members of the Budapest Jewish Council, only alludes to them in his account of how he tried sometime in June to contact Andor Jaross, the Minister of the Interior, and Secretaries of State László Baky and László Endre, "to inform them personally of the already known horrors of Auschwitz." Unable to see any of the three, he managed to reveal his knowledge about Auschwitz to Lajos Reményi-Schneller, the Minister of Finance, and to the Nunciatura.[76] In the "Report on Hungary," which he wrote with co-authors a few months after his arrival in Bucharest on August 10, 1944, Fülöp Freudiger is also silent about them.[77] In a taped interview late in 1972, Freudiger declared that he had received a copy of the Protocols from Rabbi Weissmandel sometime between June 5 and 10, 1944.[78] Confirming this declaration, Freudiger asserted on another occasion that "by the time [they] learned the truth about Auschwitz, the first phase of the deportation, involving some 310,000 Jews, was already over."[79] This assertion, however, appears to contradict his statement made at the Eichmann Trial in 1961. Responding to the question posed by Gabriel Bach, the Assistant State Attorney, as to when it was actually clear to him that the transports were going to Auschwitz, Freudiger stated:

That the people were being sent to Auschwitz, in fact, I perhaps knew even before the trains arrived at Auschwitz because I received a letter from Rabbi Weissmandel. A few days before the 15th of May, on the 10th or 11th, I received a letter wherein he wrote that to our regret and sorrow this is the lot and fate decided upon for those Jews.[80]

While Krasznyansky and Kulka claim that Kasztner had taken along a copy of the Protocols from Bratislava in April 1944,[81] it appears that the "official" leaders of Hungarian Jewry learned about their content from Freudiger's copy. At the time when Freudiger admits having received the Protocols, the dejewification experts were completing the deportations from Northern Transylvania, and were beginning the concentration of the Jews in Northern Hungary. But while the German and Hungarian Nazis were pressing on with their Final Solution program, the Jewish leaders handled the Protocols "confidentially" in order "not to create panic"[82] and wasted invaluable time on translating them. In the middle of June Rabbi Fábián Herskovits, who had studied in Rome, was busy translating the Protocols from German into Italian with the assistance of Dr. Sára Friedländer and Lea Komoly Fürst, Ottó Komoly's daughter, "in order to transmit a copy to the Nuncio and the Pope"—as if the latter did not know German.[83]

It was only during the second half of June that the Hungarian Jewish leaders began to distribute copies of the Protocols among the infuential governmental and church leaders of Hungary and among their friends abroad. A copy was given by Pető to Miklós Horthy, Jr. for transmission to his father. Miklós (Moshe) Krausz of the Palestine Office of Budapest submitted an abbreviated English version of the Protocols, together with a report on the ghettoization, concentration, and deportation processes in Zones I–III, to Switzerland on June 19, 1944. He claimed that he had received the material only the day before from József Reisner, a Jewish employee of the Turkish Legation in Budapest.[84] The material was taken to Switzerland by Florian Manoliu, a member of the Romanian Legation in Berne, who had close, and reputedly lucrative, relations with George (Mandel) Mantello, a Jewish businessman originally from the Transylvanian city of Beszterce, who was then serving as the First Secretary of the General Consulate of El Salvador in Geneva. Manoliu's mission was undertaken at the request of Chaim Pozner, Krausz's counterpart in Switzerland, whose note Manoliu took along to Budapest as his "letter of accreditation."

The material provided by Krausz was duplicated and disseminated in Switzerland thanks to Mantello.[85] It was distributed with a covering letter dated July 4, 1944, and signed by Professor D. Karl Barth of Basel, Professor D. Emil Brunner of Zurich, Dr. W. A. Visser t'Hooft, Geneva, and Pastor Paul Vogt of Zurich.[86] A more nearly complete version of the Protocols was brought to Switzerland about the same time (June 19–20) by a courier of the Czech underground. It was delivered to Dr. Jaromir Kopecky, the Czechoslovak Minister, who immediately made it available to the World Jewish Congress and other international Jewish organizations.

In Switzerland, the leaders of the local Jewish community were as well acquainted with the Final Solution program as the representatives of the international Jewish organizations who operated there. As mentioned earlier, Dr. Segalowitz, the director of the press bureau of the Union of Jewish Communities in Switzerland, was among the first to learn of Hitler's resolve to destroy the Jewish people. The leaders of the *Hehalutz*, Jewish Agency, and AJDC, who were virtually bombarded with accurate reports about the massacres, including the Auschwitz Protocols, by Bratislava, Budapest, and Istanbul, kept the Swiss Jewish leaders accurately informed. The latter were also kept abreast by Mantello and Dr. Mihály Bányai, the head of the *Schweizerisches Hilfskomitee für die Juden in Ungarn* (Swiss Committee of Assistance for the Jews in Hungary; *Comité d'entr'aide Suisse pour les juifs en Hongrie*). The latter sent, among other things, two reports on the destruction of the Jews in Hungary to the president of the Jewish Community of Zurich (*Israelitische Cultusgemeinde Zürich*) on June 24, 1944. These were not even acknowledged until July 31 "due to the president's tour of duty in the army."[87]

The leaders of the domestic and international Jewish organizations in Switzerland kept the representatives of the Allies up to date. The flow of information from Berne to London and Washington was continuous. One of the major conduits was Roswell McClelland, the WRB's representative in Switzerland. Much of this information was shared with the leaders of British and American Jewry.

The leaders of the Western world learned about the details of the Nazis' anti-Jewish drive not only through reports, but also directly from representatives of the underground. One of these was Jan Karski, a lieutenant in the Polish Underground Army, who visited London twice. During the second trip he also visited Washington, where he paid a visit to President Roosevelt in the company of Jan Ciechanowski, the wartime Polish Ambassador, on July 28, 1943. He informed the President that the Nazis had already killed 1.8 million Jews in Poland and that "the Germans are out to exterminate the entire Jewish population of Europe." He relayed the instruction received from both the Polish and Jewish underground to be conveyed to the leaders of American

Jewry and to the Allied governments "that only through direct reprisals, such as mass bombing of German cities, after dropping millions of leaflets telling the Germans that they were being bombed in reprisal for exterminating Jews, could this mass extermination be stopped or at least limited."[88]

The western Jewish and governmental leaders' knowledge about the extermination of the European Jews was also shared by the Vatican. Like several of the major Jewish organizations, it too had received a copy of the Vrba-Wetzler version of the Auschwitz Protocols via Nuncio Burzio shortly after they were completed by the Bratislava *Vaada* late in April 1944.[89] However, the Vatican, like most other governmental and nongovernmental leaders, including those of Hungarian and world Jewry, chose for reasons of its own to remain silent for a long time while the provincial Jews of Hungary were being deported. The first overt reaction of the Vatican came around June 20, presumably after it had received the second set of protocols based upon the escapes of Rosin and Mordowicz. At this time the Vatican's legate, Monsignor Mario, arrived in Bratislava to interview the escapees from Auschwitz and double-check the veracity of their accounts. Krasznyansky, who was contacted for this purpose by Mikulaš (Miklós) Sternfeld of the Rescue Committee of Bratislava, accompanied two of the escapees, Vrba and Mordowicz, to the Svaty Jur monastery, near Bratislava, where they were interviewed in depth for five hours with the aid of a French interpreter.[90]

Apparently, the Papal legate was fully satisfied with the outcome of the interview, because Admiral Horthy was shortly thereafter to be besieged by the entreaties of many world leaders to put an end to the anti-Jewish measures in general and the deportations. The Pope addressed a personal plea to Horthy on June 25, which was followed by the warning of President Roosevelt on June 26, and that of King Gustav of Sweden on June 30.[91]

There is no doubt that these communications played an important, if not determining role in Horthy's decision of July 7 to prohibit further deportations from Hungary.

It cannot be established with any degree of certainty whether these communications were undertaken as a result of Monsignor Mario's interview and the Vatican's consequent positive reaction or the publicity associated with the material Krausz sent out on June 19. If Horthy was indeed induced to halt the deportations partially in response to the reaction of the Vatican and the Western and neutral leaders and their press to the Protocols and partially by his own reaction to them when he received them toward the end of June 1944 (see below), the agonizing question remains: Why did the Jewish leaders in Hungary, Switzerland, and elsewhere not distribute and publicize the Protocols immediately after they received copies of them late in April or early in May 1944? Why did the *Vaada* leaders of Budapest, who continued to maintain contact with the Jewish leaders in Switzerland, including Saly Mayer, even after the German occupation, fail to include copies of the Protocols in their lengthy reports on the conditions in Hungary and the status of their negotiations with the SS? Why did the leaders of the AJDC, Jewish Agency, and *Hehalutz*, for example, fail to publicize the reports they had received from the *Vaada* leaders in Bratislava and Budapest, including the Weissmandel reports? Why was the report on Hitler's resolution to bring about the Final Solution handled as a top secret diplomatic communication? It is fair to assume that the press in the Allied and neutral countries would have published accounts of the slaughter earlier. And even after June 19, the initiative was taken by a nonestablishment Jew, George Mantello, who, because of his contacts, was fortunate enough to have had a chance to look right away at the material Krausz had sent.[92]

In the absence of a concerted publicity effort, when the BBC broadcast some sections from the Protocols they were construed by world public opinion basically as horror propaganda directed by a belligerent power against a mortal enemy. Had the neutral countries, including Sweden and Switzerland, and the Vatican, engaged in a vigorous press and radio campaign as soon as the Protocols had been received from Bratislava, the world most probably would have reacted differently and Horthy would possibly have been induced to act earlier. But the Vatican and the neutral countries were more concerned with maintaining strict neutrality than with publicizing their concern for the Jews of Hungary. Even the Pope's and King Gustav's pleas late in June were forwarded as secret diplomatic messages without any publicity. The United States establishment did not find it possible to publicize the Protocols until November 1944,[93] when in the wake of the inexorably advancing Red Army the Nazis themselves were already eager to demolish the extermination facilities and eradicate all traces of their crimes.

The Protocols appear also to have been ignored by, or perhaps not even brought to the attention of, the Palestine press, including the Hebrew- and Yiddish-language one.[94] Under the dateline of London, July 10, 1944, the Jewish Telegraphic Agency (JTA) brought out an account of the Auschwitz and Birkenau camps based upon the Protocols, which probably emanated from Mantello.[95] The leaders of the Jewish Agency were kept abreast of the Nazis' anti-Jewish program in Hungary by a variety of sources, including the *Vaada* branch offices in Bratislava, Budapest, Istanbul, and Switzerland, and diplomatic channels. By mid-June 1944 they were personally briefed by Joel Brand (see chapter 29). On June 24, 1944, for example, Ignacy Schwarzbart informed the Agency in Jerusalem about an official communication that was received by the Polish Government-in-Exile according to which 100,000 Hungarian Jews were gassed in Auschwitz and urged an "immediate worldwide outcry."[96] A day earlier, Chaim Weizmann informed G. H. Hall of the British Foreign Office of information he had received from the Polish Government-in-Exile (information the Foreign Office must have also received directly) that the Hungarian Jews were being subjected to mass deportation "to the death camps in Poland."[97]

On July 10, 1944, Moshe Shertok (Sharett), who was of course by then fully acquainted with the Nazis' Final Solution program, was informed by Dr. O. Gorka of the Ministry of the Interior of the Polish Government-in-Exile about the text of a coded telegram sent from "somewhere in Poland" on June 27 concerning the deportation and the gassing of Jews from Hungary.[98] This, like the many other earlier communications relating to the destruction of Hungarian Jewry, did not find its way to the Palestine press, and the "worldwide outcry" never really materialized. One of the primary factors underlying this silence was the censorship policy of the British Mandate authorities in Palestine (see chapters 29 and 31). The silence was also due, according to some observers, to errors committed by the Zionist leadership.[99]

The Hungarian Leaders' Awareness of the Catastrophe

There is ample evidence that Horthy and many of the other leaders of Hungary were as fully acquainted with the Nazis' anti-Jewish program as many of the Jewish leaders long before the German occupation of the country, even though Pető did not give a copy of the Protocols to the Regent's son until the second half of June 1944.[100] For example, at his first Schloss Klessheim meeting with Hitler in April 1943, Horthy was advised by the Führer that Hungary should follow the example of Poland, where "the Jews who did not want to work were simply shot." This advice was amplified by Ribbentrop, who suggested that the Jews "should either be killed or sent to concentration camps."[101] Upon his return to Hungary, Horthy decided to defend himself against the Führer, who had reproached him for his alleged "mild treatment of the Jews in Hungary." In the original draft of his letter of May 7, 1943, addressed to the Führer, Horthy attempted to defend himself and the Kállay government against Hitler's reproach, by denying that Hungary had "failed to take as far-reaching an action *in the extirpation of the Jews* as Germany had taken or as would appear desirable in other countries" [italics supplied]. Although this sentence was replaced by one referring to Horthy's well-substantiated claim that he was the first in Europe to raise his voice "against the destructive attitude of the Jews" and that measures were being enacted "for the gradual elimination of the Jews," it clearly reveals that Horthy and the officials of the Ministry of Foreign Affairs who prepared the draft had been informed about what was happening to the Jews of Germany.[102]

Döme Sztójay apparently knew about the Nazi design to "solve the Jewish question in a radical manner during the war" as early as 1942, when he was still Hungary's Minister to Berlin. He revealed his knowledge to György Ottlik, a member of the influential Foreign Affairs Committee of the upper house of the Hungarian Parliament and the editor-in-chief of the German-language *Pester Lloyd* of Budapest, the semi-official organ of the Hungarian government. Ottlik, who had visited Germany in the course of his West European tour of August-September, 1942, transmitted this information to the Hungarian Ministry of Foreign Affairs on October 10.[103] According to Dieter Wisliceny, "both Endre and Baky had been accurately informed as to what the deportations meant."[104] In his report of May 29, 1944, Lieutenant-Colonel László Ferenczy, who had been in charge of the deportations, openly refers to Auschwitz as a place where the deported Jews were subjected to a process of "selection."[105]

The currently available evidence indicates that not only the pro-German and ultra-rightist elements, but also some of the anti-Nazi leaders in Hungary were acquainted with the Nazi extermination program. Kasztner claims, although without providing sufficient evidence, that the leaders of the Social Democratic Party, including Anna Kéthly, Anton Bán, Illés Mónus, József Büchler, Miklós Kertész, and Manó Buchinger, had been kept informed about the destruction of the European Jews and about the Nazis' methods.[106] Angelo Rotta, the Papal Nuncio in Budapest, was also familiar with the realities of the deportations. In his letter of May 15, 1944, protesting the measures that the

Hungarian government took or planned to take against the Jews, Rotta stated that "the whole world knows what the deportation means in practice."[107]

An Attempt at Assessment

The historical record is clear: Although many of the Jewish and Christian leaders of the world, including of course the Hungarian ones, had well-substantiated knowledge about the extermination program starting in the spring of 1942 and irrefutable evidence in April 1944, the deportations that began on May 15 were not halted until July 7, when only the Jews of Budapest and those in some of the labor service companies remained in the country.

It is almost universally assumed that Horthy decided to halt the deportations in response to the worsening military situation and to the interventions made by foreign state and church leaders, who were motivated to act, *inter alia,* by the Auschwitz Protocols. These interventions presumably were reinforced by Horthy's own reaction to the Protocols, which had been shown to him by his son during the second half of June.

These assumptions give rise to a number of bewildering questions. Why were the Protocols not forwarded to these leaders of the world soon after they were completed on April 26? Why were the Hungarian Jewish masses not alerted about their content? What would have been the consequence had they been alerted before the deportations?

These questions are obviously controversial and require a careful differentiation between facts, claims, and presumptions. The *facts* are:

- The escapees from Auschwitz told their story to the Jewish leaders of Slovakia on April 25 and 26, 1944.
- Freudiger admits having received the Protocols between June 5 and 10.
- Kasztner acknowledged his awareness of the mass destruction of the Jews in Nazi-occupied Europe before the German occupation of Hungary.
- The Hungarian Jewish masses were not authoritatively informed about them.
- The deportation of the Jews from Carpatho-Ruthenia and Northern Transylvania began on May 15 and was completed on June 7 and the deportation of the Jews of Northern Hungary did not begin until June 11.
- The Hungarian Jewish leaders were still busy translating and duplicating the Protocols on June 14–16 and did not distribute them till the second half of June.

- The Hungarian Jewish leaders completely ignored the Protocols in their postwar memoirs and statements.

Although the claims advanced in connection with the Protocols are plausible and to a considerable extent convincing, there is no foolproof evidence to substantiate them. Among these statements are:

- Krasznyansky's contention in 1964 that he handed a copy of the Protocols to Kasztner during the latter's visit to Bratislava late in April 1944.
- Neumann's assertion that the Protocols were sent to Hungary, Switzerland, and the Vatican "shortly" after they had been completed.
- Vrba's claim that he was assured by Neumann and Krasznyansky on April 26 that the reports were already in the hands of Kasztner.
- Munkácsi's declaration that the Protocols were handled in Hungary in a "confidential" manner in order "not to create panic" among the remaining Jews.
- The charge that Kasztner deliberately remained silent in accordance with an agreement with Eichmann under which he was allowed to save a few thousand "prominent" Jews, including his own family and friends.

Kasztner and the Auschwitz Protocols. It is safe to assume that Krasznyansky's recollection about Kasztner's visit to Bratislava late in April 1944, and about his receiving a copy of the original German text there is correct. It is also safe to accept Krasznyansky's claim that he himself translated the Protocols into Hungarian and forwarded them to Hungary "within two weeks," which would have been May 10–15. Krasznyansky, after all, played a pivotal role in the preparation and distribution of the Protocols. Moreover, Kasztner was a frequent visitor in Bratislava, especially after he had established contact with the SS early in April. He must obviously have been eager to consult the leaders of the Bratislava Rescue Committee, who had considerable experience in dealing with Wisliceny and other members of the Eichmann-*Sonderkommando.*

Given the evidence that at the time of the German occupation of Hungary both Kasztner and the official leaders of Hungarian Jewry were aware of the Nazis' extermination program, how can one explain their silence?

A case against Kasztner and indirectly against some of his closest associates in the provinces and in Budapest has been made after the war by both Jews and non-Jews using a variety of political-ideological, historical-moral, and judicial arguments.

In his postwar memoirs, Eichmann for example argues that he and Kasztner, the two "idealists" who pursued different and conflicting objectives, reached a "gentleman's agreement," under which Kasztner allegedly offered to remain silent and "help keep the Jews from resisting deportation and even keep order in the collection camps" in exchange for the opportunity to rescue 15,000 to 20,000 "biologically valuable" Jews. For Eichmann this was a good bargain, for he admittedly was not concerned with the escape of small groups of Jews.[108] His primary concern, given the limited forces at his disposal, was the smooth, efficient, and orderly deportation of the close to 800,000 Hungarian Jews without incurring the risk of another Warsaw uprising.

The same conclusion was reached by a number of anti-Zionist or anti-*Mapai* Zionist figures, including Vrba and Ben Hecht. According to them, Kasztner and his associates constituted a group of quislings who sold out Hungarian Jewry to save themselves, their friends, and a few rich Jews. They reject the view of some historians, including Professor J. L. Talmon of the Hebrew University of Jerusalem, that by the time those associated with the Jewish Councils "grasped what the real aim of the Nazis was they were no more than helpless and benumbed hostages."[109] Vrba claims that men like Kasztner were far from "helpless." They were in fact "clever diplomats who knew what their silence was worth."[110] Hecht, with his own "revisionist" axe to grind against the official Zionist leadership, extends this accusation to virtually everyone associated with the *Mapai* or the Jewish Agency.[111]

The Communist historians and propagandists—especially those of the Soviet Union—have also condemned the Jewish leaders' silence. After the launching of the anti-Jewish drive in the Soviet bloc in September 1948 (disguised as a campaign against "Zionism and cosmopolitanism") the Soviet propaganda line called for the identification of Zionism with Nazism. As part of the campaign, which became ever more vitriolic after the Six-Day War, Kasztner's activities have been portrayed as closely synchronized with those of the Gestapo aiming at the destruction of millions of innocent people.[112]

At the judicial level, by far the most damning conclusion concerning Kasztner was reached by Judge Benjamin Halevi of the Jerusalem District Court in 1955. He concluded that Kasztner had "sold his soul to the devil" by collaborating with the Nazis against the interests of Hungarian Jewry for the opportunity to save a few thousand "prominent Jews." In January 1958, the Supreme Court of Israel reversed Halevi's decision. However, in a dissent from this reversal Judge Moshe Silberg reached a conclusion similar to Halevi's. His dissent emphasized that the shocking success of the Nazis in exterminating the Jews easily and peacefully was "the direct result of the concealment of the horrifying truth from the victims."[113]

As to the silence of the leaders of the Jewish Council of Budapest, the interpretations offered after the war naturally also tend to vary. Ilona Benoschofsky,[114] for example, argues that perhaps the Jewish Council members thought that "since Hungarian Jewry could not be saved, it was better that it did not know the fate awaiting it. And since the Germans threatened to execute those who spoke of deportation, the Council did not assist in publicizing the real objective of the deportation, namely the gas chamber and the crematorium."[115] She continues her argument by claiming, in a somewhat neo-Marxist fashion, that if the "Jewish Council thought that there was no way out for the masses, there was one for itself." She attempts to substantiate her thesis by asserting that since the anti-Jewish measures of the Horthy era, including the major anti-Jewish laws, affected primarily the lower civil servants, the small traders, and the artisans, the members of the Jewish Council, "who knew of these restrictive measures largely only by hearsay, obviously had hoped that they would be exempted this time as well."[116]

Ironically, a related conclusion was reached by Chaim Cohen, then Attorney General of Israel, in defending Kasztner against the accusation of collaboration with the SS. He explained Kasztner's predicament and silence as follows:

Kasztner was convinced and believed that there was no ray of hope for the Jews of Hungary, almost for none of them, and since he, as a result of his personal despair, did not disclose the secret of the extermination in order not to endanger or frustrate the rescue of the few—therefore he acted in good faith and should not be accused of collaborating with the Nazis in expediting the extermination of the Jews, even though, in fact, he brought about its result.[117]

Judge Shlomo Chesin of the Supreme Court agreed with this line of reasoning, arguing that Kasztner "didn't warn Hungarian Jewry of the danger facing it because he didn't think it would be useful, and because he thought that any deeds resulting from information given them would damage more than help."[118]

According to the reasoning of Cohen and Chesin, Kasztner followed in the footsteps of Rabbi Leo Baeck, the former Chairman of the Reich Association of the Jews in Germany (*Reichsvereinigung der Juden in Deutschland*). While in Theresienstadt, where he was deported from

Berlin on January 27, 1943, Baeck was fully aware of the realities of the Nazis' extermination program. Nevertheless, he

followed a policy of nonrevelation in view of his judgment that nothing could have been done to change the course of events. It was—in his view—advisable not to let victims know the truth and to spare them the agony and ultimate desperation that comes from knowledge that the end is near and there is absolutely no way out.[119]

Rabbi Baeck had learned about the realities of Auschwitz some time in August 1943, from a fellow inmate named Grünberg. "So it was not just a rumor," Baeck commented, "or, as I had hoped, the illusion of a diseased imagination." He rationalized his decision to remain silent as follows:

I went through a hard struggle debating whether it was my duty to convince Grünberg that he must repeat what he had heard before the Council of Elders, of which I was an honorary member. I finally decided that no one should know it. If the Council of Elders were informed, the whole camp would know within a few hours. Living in the expectation of death by gassing would only be the harder and this death was not certain at all: there was selection for slave labor; perhaps not all transports went to Auschwitz. So I came to the grave decision to tell no one.[120]

Kasztner, like Leo Baeck, apparently also realized that all of the Hungarian Jews could not possibly be saved. He offered the following rationale for "cooperating" with the Moloch in his desperate attempt to save what he thought were the most valuable elements of the community:

Once again we were confronted with the most serious dilemma, the dilemma which we had been faced with throughout our work: Should we leave the selection to blind fate or should we try to influence it? . . . We did, we tried to do it. We convinced ourselves that—as sacred as every human being has always been to the Jews—we nevertheless had to strive to save at least those who all their lives had labored for the Community [Osekim be-tsorche tsibur] and, by the same token those women whose husbands were in the labor camps; we also had to see to it that children, especially orphans, would not be left to destruction. In brief: truly holy principles had to be employed to sustain and guide the frail human hand which, by writing down on paper the name of an unknown person, decided his life or death. Was it the gift of fate [Gnade des Schicksals] if, under these circumstances, we were not always able to prevail in these endeavors?[121]

These views of Kasztner were clearly opposed to the principles of Moses Maimonides, the great Hebrew scholar and codifier of Jewish law. Maimonides addressed himself to a similar problem, which had been raised a thousand years earlier in the Talmud by Rabbi Joshua ben Levi, a third-century rabbi of Lydda. The Rabbi had advised a political fugitive to surrender to the Roman authorities in order to save the city from destruction. Maimonides argued:

If heathens said to Israelites, "Surrender one of your number to us, that we may put him to death, otherwise, we will put all of you to death," they should all suffer death rather than surrender a single Israelite to them. But if they specified an individual, saying "Surrender that particular person to us, or else we will put all of you to death," they may give him up, provided that he was guilty of a capital crime . . . If the individual specified has not incurred capital punishment, they should all suffer death rather than surrender a single Israelite to them.[122]

Kasztner's rationalizations were also condemned as "morally disastrous" by Hannah Arendt, the noted philosopher. In her view, the acceptance of the idea of "exceptions"—of the category of "prominent Jews," which the Nazis introduced in 1942—meant the implicit recognition of the Nazis' rules of the game. The advancement of the view that a "famous Jew had more right to stay alive than an ordinary one" and the assumption of responsibility of participating in the selection of "'famous' people from the anonymous mass" were tantamount to "involuntary complicity," the implicit recognition of the rule that spelled death for the mass of ordinary Jews. The Nazis must have felt, she argues, "that by being asked to make exceptions, and by occasionally granting them, and thus earning gratitude, they had convinced their opponents of the lawfulness of what they were doing."[123]

Kasztner's position and actions, on the other hand, appear to have been in accord with a thesis expressed in the Talmud and the theological views of Abraham Duber Cahana Shapiro, the sage Rabbi of Kaunas (Kovno) during the 1940s.

The Talmud tells us: "He who saves a single life, it is as though he has saved the entire world."[124] Probably inspired by this thesis, Rabbi Shapiro adopted the same position.

When the Nazis demanded of the Kaunas Jewish Council, late in October 1941, that it select a certain number of Jews for deportation and certain destruction, it was advised by Rabbi Shapiro as follows: "If a Jewish community . . . has been condemned to physical destruction, and there are means of rescuing part of it, the leaders of the community should have the courage to assume the responsibility to act and rescue what is possible."[125]

While the many relevant though often conflicting moral-ethical arguments and practical strategical considerations cited above have considerable validity in characterizing the desperate situation of the Hungarian Jews *after* the German occupation, they do not fully explain and much less justify the silence of the Jewish leaders before it.

The Hungarian Jewish leaders, like their co-religionists elsewhere, and the leaders of the world at large, were unwilling or unable to understand both the extent and the speed of the destruction that was taking place in Nazi-dominated Europe. Their false optimism was based on the continued survival of the Hungarian Jewish community in the midst of the cataclysm that was engulfing the neighboring Jewish communities. When coupled with their incapacity to accept the worst, the result was ultimately a disaster. Although many of them continued to nurture the illusions of the past, many others awoke to reality after the German occupation. But by that time it was too late: the fate of Hungarian Jewry had been sealed.

Notes

1. Ernő Munkácsi, the Executive Secretary of the Jewish Community of Pest, asserted that the Hungarian Jewish leaders were "more or less aware of the fate of German Jewry and of the fact that the Jewish population in the Nazi-occupied countries were deported." However, he continued, only "indefinite and vague news was spread about all these." Munkácsi, *Hogyan történt?* p. 11.

2. For an account of the Wannsee Conference consult Raul Hilberg, *The Destruction of the European Jews.* (Chicago: Quandrangle Books, 1961), pp. 264–66. On the "Killing Center Operations," see pp. 555–635.

3. On the *Einsatzgruppen* and their operations, see *ibid.,* pp. 242–56.

4. Randolph L. Braham, "The Kamenets-Podolsk and Délvidék Massacres: Prelude to the Holocaust in Hungary," in *YVS,* 9:133–56. See also chapter 6.

5. See, for example, the January 28, 1958 statement of Sámuel Springmann, a former member of the Hungarian Zionist movement, available at Yad Vashem, Archives File No. 500/41-1; Arthur D. Morse, *While Six Million Died. A Chronicle of American Apathy* (New York: Random House, 1967), pp. 304–5.

6. See Sámuel Springmann's statement cited above, and Alex Weissberg, *Advocate for the Dead. The Story of Joel Brand* (London: André Deutsch, 1958), pp. 21–23.

7. Braham, "The Kamenets-Podolsk and Délvidék Massacres," p. 142.

8. *Der Kastner-Bericht,* p. 37.

9. Henry L. Feingold, *The Politics of Rescue. The Roosevelt Administration and the Holocaust, 1938–1945* (New Brunswick, N.J.: Rutgers University Press, 1970), p. 168.

10. Livia Rothkirchen, *The Destruction of Slovak Jewry. A Documentary History* (Jerusalem: Yad Vashem, 1961), pp. xxiii–xxiv.

11. NG-4407 and NG-4553; *RAH,* p. 6; Rothkirchen, *The Destruction of Slovak Jewry,* p. xxxii. See also *Der Kastner-Bericht,* pp. 15–16. The Vatican's notes to Prime Minister Tuka to the effect that the "resettled" Slovak Jews were in fact being destroyed were also confirmed by Hans Gmelin, the former Counselor to the German Legation in Bratislava. NO-5921.

12. "Allies Are Urged to Execute Nazis." *The New York Times*, July 2, 1942, p. 6.

13. Andrew Scharf, "The British Press and the Holocaust" in *YVS*, 5:186–87.

14. Yehuda Bauer, "When Did They Know?", *Midstream*, New York, April 1968, pp. 51–58. The article also contains the text of the Bund Report in Polish original and in English translation. For a succinct review of how the news of the Final Solution became known and how that news was received by world Jewry and the world at large, see Walter Laqueur, "Jewish Denial and the Holocaust." *Commentary*, New York, 68, no. 6 (December 1979):44–55.

15. See, for example, "Himmler Program Kills Polish Jews," *The New York Times*, November 25, 1942, p. 10; "Slain Polish Jews Put at a Million," *ibid.*, November 26, 1942, p. 16. With the passage of time, the reports became ever more specific and detailed. See, for example, "Report Bares Fate of 8,000,000 Jews" and "Deliberate Nazi Murder Policy Is Bared by Allied Official Body," *ibid.*, August 27, 1943.

16. The letters were signed Ziviah and Yitzhak (Ziviah Lubetkin and Yitzhak Zuckerman), the two heroes of the Warsaw Ghetto Uprising, who miraculously survived and settled after the war in Israel, where they founded the Beit Lohamei Hagetaot (The Ghetto Fighters' House) *Kibbutz*. For references to the letters, see Herbert Druks, *The Failure to Rescue* (New York: Robert Speller and Sons, 1977), pp. 29–31.

17. Lucy S. Dawidowicz, *The War Against the Jews, 1933–1945* (New York: Holt, Rinehart and Winston, 1975), p. 316.

18. The central role of Dr. Pozner in the relaying of this dramatic information is also reviewed by Shlomo Derech, the ideological expert of the *Ha'Kibbutz Ha'Meuchad* in Israel, in his introduction to the Hebrew edition of Morse's work: *Vehaolam shetak. Et nispu shisha milionim*. Beit Lehamei Hagetaot al shem Yitzhak Katzenelson, 1972.

19. For details on Sommer's background and about his revelations, see Edgar Salin, "Über Artur Sommer, den Menschen und List-Forscher" (On Artur Sommer, the Man and List-Researcher). *Mitteilungen der List Gesellschaft* (Communications of the List Society), Basel, no. 4/5, November 30, 1967, pp. 81–90.

20. Salin, *Über Artur Sommer*, pp. 85–86.

21. After the war, Dr. Pozner (Pazner) settled in Israel where he became associated with the Yad Vashem Institute in Jerusalem. His services to the Allies were recognized in a note issued by V. C. Farrell on July 27, 1945. For further details on Dr. Pozner's role during the war, see chapters 29 and 31.

22. Riegner acknowledged that Sagalowitz was his source in a letter to the editors of *Das Neue Israel* (The New Israel) of Zurich. "Brief von Dr. Gerhart Riegner an die Redaktion zu: Arthur D. Morse: 'While Six Million Died' " (Letter of Dr. Gerhart Riegner Relating to Arthur D. Morse's "While Six Million Died"). *Das Neue Israel*, 21, no. 5 (November 1968):359–61.

23. According to several accounts, it was the Department of State that asked Rabbi Wise to repress the news about the report until it was verified by the Department. For a somewhat negative evaluation of the role played by Rabbi Wise and some other Jewish leaders in handling the reports on the extermination of the European Jews, see Druks, *The Failure to Rescue*, pp. 29–44.

24. Arthur D. Morse, "How the Indifference of the U.S. State Department Aided the Nazi Murder Plot." *Look*, 31, no. 23 (November 14, 1967):67 ff. See also his *While Six Million Died*. For further details on the attitude of the Allies and of the international community to the destruction of the Jews of Hungary, see chapters 29 and 31.

25. The report stated that the Nazis were killing Polish Jews at the rate of 6,000 a day. On February 10, 1943, Welles inadvertently signed and sent Harrison a note requesting that he no longer accept reports submitted to him for transmission to private persons in the United States "unless such action is advisable because of extraordinary circumstances." Alerted by the Treasury Department about the message he had inadver-

tently signed, Welles rescinded the order in April and asked Harrison for additional reports from Riegner.

26. The vast correspondence between the *Vaada* offices in Budapest and Istanbul may be found in the archives of Beth Lohamei Hagetaot, the Israel State Archives in Jerusalem, and at Moreshet, Israel. For a catalog of these files, see *Arkhivon lishkat hakesher be'Kushta* (Archives of the Yishuv Rescue Board in Istanbul). Compiled by Frieda Laster (Haifa: The University of Haifa and The Ghetto Fighters' House, November 1977), 117 pp. See also Weissberg, *Advocate for the Dead*, pp. 30–31; and Andre Biss, *A Million Jews to Save* (London: Hutchinson, 1973), pp. 74–75.

27. *Der Kastner-Bericht*, p. 26.

28. Taped interview with Hansi Brand, dated October 10, 1972. Much of the information about gassing and the crematoria came from Herman Adler, a Slovak Jewish refugee. For further details on Adler, see below.

29. Copies of reports like these may be found in the Israel State Archives, Jerusalem, File 31:124/53.

30. Aryeh L. Kubovy, "The Silence of Pope Pius XII and the Beginnings of the 'Jewish Document' " in *YVS*, 6:13.

31. Moreshet, Israel. Archives, D.1.735 as cited in *RAH*, p. 442.

32. Fleischmann was in her mid-forties during this catastrophic period. Because of her involvement in the Rescue Committee and related resistance activities in Slovakia, she was singled out for destruction during the last phase of the deportations from Slovakia in the fall of 1944. She was deported from the camp in Sered on October 17, 1944, and SS-*Sturmbannführer* Anton Brunner, who was in charge of the deportations at this time, identified her transport as R.U. (*Rückkehr unerwünscht;* Return undesirable). Upon arrival in Auschwitz her name was called out at the platform and she was led straight to the gas chamber. Yirmeyahu Oscar Neumann, *Gisi Fleischmann. The Story of a Heroic Woman* (Tel Aviv: The World WIZO Department of Organization and Education, 1970), 35 pp.

33. Kasztner acknowledged that Fleischmann sent authenticated personal accounts about "the mass executions and gassings abroad." *Der Kastner-Bericht*, p. 28. See also Rothkirchen, *The Destruction of Slovak Jewry*, p. xxviii.

34. Letter dated January 14, 1943. Yad Vashem Archives, M-20/93. See also chapters 3 and 29.

35. See Komoly's letter of August 25, 1943, addressed to Chaim Barlas in Istanbul, in The Central Zionist Archives, Jerusalem, File S26/1190 a/b.

36. Rafi (Friedl) Ben-Shalom, . . . *weil wir leben wollten* (Because We Wanted to Live), Moreshet Archives, Doc. D.2.88, p. 6.

37. Rabbi Weissmandel alerted Freudiger and the other leaders of Hungarian Jewry sometime in April 1944, that the railway administrations of Germany, Hungary, and Slovakia had concluded an agreement for the transfer of a large number of freight cars to Hungary for deportation purposes. Weissmandel had received this information from an anti-Nazi official of the Slovak Railways. Weissmandel also sent a copy of the so-called Auschwitz Protocols to Freudiger. Like Fleischmann, Weissmandel was deported with his whole family in the fall of 1944, but jumped from the deportation train. After the end of the war he settled in Brooklyn, where he died of a heart attack in 1957. For his account of the Slovak and Hungarian Jewish catastrophe, his dealings with the Hungarian Jewish leaders, and appeals to the Jewish leaders of the free world, see his *Min Hametzar* (Out of the Depth) (New York: Emunah, 1960), 252 pp. See also Rothkirchen, *The Destruction of Slovak Jewry*, pp. xxvi and xli.

38. *Der Kastner-Bericht*, p. 82.

39. For the complete text of the letter, written in a cave near Lvov on the 39th day after Passover 1944, see Rothkirchen, *The Destruction of Slovak Jewry*, pp. 237–42. For the German text of a similar letter, dated July 16, 1944, see Yad Vashem Archives, M-20/47.

40. In this code system, for example, "Ella" meant Fleischmann or Slovakia; "Miklos" and "Hagar"—Hungary; "Willy"—Wisliceny; "Roshe"—Hitler; "Kuschta"—Turkey; and "Ziwiah"—Poland.

41. Fleischmann wrote her reports and letters in German. Many can be found in the archives of Yad Vashem in Jerusalem under File no. M-20/93.

42. Yad Vashem Archives, M-20/93.

43. Ibid.

44. Ibid.

45. Yad Vashem Archives File no. M-20 as reproduced in Documents of Destruction. Germany and Jewry, 1933–1945, ed. Raul Hilberg (Chicago: Quadrangle Books, 1971), p. 192.

46. See, for example, the following reports dated "Budapest, 23 August 1943" and "September 1943" at the Beit Lohamei Hagetaot, the Yitzhak Katsenelson Institute in Israel, under file no. G1054/5, G1054/8, and G1054/3.

47. Mr. Teicholz stems from the Lvov (Lemberg) area of Poland. He survived the war and eventually settled in New York.

48. Personal communication, June 28, 1971.

49. See, for example, Ben-Shalom, . . . weil wir leben wollten. For an expanded Hebrew version see his Neevaknu le'Maan he'Haim (We Struggled for Our Lives) (Givat Haviva: Moreshet, 1977), 223 pp. See also Zvi Goldfarb, "On 'Hehalutz' Resistance in Hungary," in Extermination and Resistance (Kibbutz Lohamei Hagetaot, 1958), 1:162–72. For further details on the activities of the Hehalutz, see chapter 29.

50. Adler was born on October 2, 1911, near Bratislava, where his mother was visiting from Nuremberg. With the rise of Nazism, he escaped to Czechoslovakia in 1934, and when that country was dismembered early in 1939 he fled to Poland. Following the conquest of Poland, Adler spent a year in Russian-occupied Lvov and then the next two and a half years in the ghettos of Vilna, Bialystok, and Warsaw or in the underground with aryan papers. He is the author of Gesänge aus der Stadt des Todes (Songs From the City of Death), a collection of poems written in Vilna and Warsaw. He was included in the so-called Kasztner group that left Budapest on June 30, 1944, and survived the war. Personal communication, February 10, 1975.

51. Gideon Hausner, Justice in Jerusalem (New York: Harper & Row, 1966), p. 258.

52. One was Franz Fritsch, the manager of a plant manufacturing uniforms. Dismissed by the Gestapo because of his benevolent attitude toward the Jews, Fritsch went underground using Dutch identification papers. He was one of the chief organizers of escape routes to Budapest. Personal communication by Adler cited above.

53. Samu Stern, " 'A Race with Time': A Statement," adapted from HJS 3:56.

54. The Reminiscences of Béla Fábián (New York: Columbia University. Oral History Research Office, no. 79, November 1950–January 1951), p. 439.

55. Rudolph (Rezső) Kasztner, Der Bericht des jüdischen Rettungskomitees aus Budapest, 1942–1945 (The Report of the Jewish Rescue Committee of Budapest, 1942–1945). ([Basel]: Va'ath Ezra Ve'Hazalah beBudapest, [1946]), xiii + 191 pp. (Mimeographed.) An edited version of the report was published under the title Der Kastner-Bericht.

56. Der Kastner-Bericht, p. 21.

57. Ibid., pp. 26 and 37.

58. Ministries Case, Court 4, Case 11, session of March 19, 1948, transcript p. 3622.

59. The de jure head of the Hungarian Zionist Association (Magyar Cionista Szövetség) in 1942–45 was Ottó Komoly. However, Komoly was to a large extent overshadowed by Kasztner, who took over the de facto leadership of the Vaada. For further details see chapter 29.

60. Ministries Case, pp. 3651–52.

61. Ben Hecht, Perfidy (New York: Julian Messner, 1961), pp. 59–60. Hecht's version

of Kasztner's testimony is highly condensed. For Kaztner's complete testimony of February 18, 1954, see District Court, Jerusalem *Criminal Case 124/53*, at the YIVO Institute for Jewish Research, New York, Film 221 M, Roll 2, p. 9. (In Hebrew.)

62. When Kasztner was asked by Tamir whether he knew at the time he was in Kolozsvár "the true significance of the deportation to Auschwitz," he answered laconically "I knew." Hecht, *Perfidy*, p. 112. For the original transcript of Tamir's interrogation of Kasztner on March 1, 1954, see District Court, Jerusalem, *Criminal Case 124/53*, YIVO, Film 221 M, Roll 2, p. 44.

63. For some details on Danzig's and Hermann's position during the trial of the Grünwald-Kasztner case in 1954 in Jerusalem, see chapter 29.

64. Hecht, *Perfidy*, pp. 117–18. In his report on the Kasztner transport dated February 10, 1946, Zoltán Glatz stated that Fischer knew that the Hungarian transports were not going to Kenyérmező as the Jewish masses were being told. He was informed of the real destination of the transports by his son-in-law. Yad Vashem Archives, M-20/95.

65. According to Erich Kulka, who was taken to Auschwitz in October, 1942, after he had lingered in Dachau and Neuengamme since 1940, and who was a member of the Auschwitz underground, 280 attempts at escape were noted during the existence of Auschwitz and about 80 prisoners actually succeeded in escaping. Erich Kulka, "Five Escapes From Auschwitz," in *They Fought Back. The Story of the Jewish Resistance in Nazi Europe*, ed. Yuri Suhl (New York: Crown, 1967), p. 201. See also Laqueur, "Jewish Denial and the Holocaust," p. 47.

66. For details on the fate of the family camp and Lederer's escape, see Kulka, "Five Escapes From Auschwitz," pp. 196–205.

67. After his return to Slovakia, Rosenberg was supplied with false identification papers bearing the name of Rudolf Vrba, which he kept permanently. His arrest and experiences in Auschwitz, his adventurous escape, and disappointment over "the Zionist leaders' failure to heed his warnings about the Hungarian Jews" are described in his *I Cannot Forgive* (New York: Grove Press, 1964), 281 pp., written in cooperation with Alan Bestic. Wetzler, who was given the name of Josef Lanik, continued to use this name as a literary pseudonym. Under this pen-name he published *Oswiecim, hrobka styroch milionov ludi* (Auschwitz, Tomb of Four Million People) (Kosice: Vydalo Poverenictve SNR, 1946), 73 pp.; and *Co Dante nevidel* (What Dante Did Not See) (Bratislava: Osveta—SV SPB, 1964), 269 pp.

68. Statement by Krasznyansky. The Hebrew University. The Institute of Contemporary Jewry. Oral History Division, Catalog no. 3, 1970, p. 120, no. 410 S.E. Protocol in Czech, pp. 10 and 13.

69. The Auschwitz Protocols may be found at the Yad Vashem Institute Archives in Jerusalem under no. M-20/149. For their Hungarian version see Munkácsi, *Hogyan történt?* pp. 88–110. In Nuremberg it was submitted in evidence under NG-2061.

70. Kulka, "Five Escapes From Auschwitz," pp. 206–7.

71. The Protocols were translated into Yiddish by Rabbi Weissmandel. *Ibid.*, p. 207.

72. For further details on the background and flight of Rosin and Mordowicz see *ibid.*, pp. 207–11.

73. Vrba and Bestic, *I Cannot Forgive*, p. 250; Oscar Neumann, *Im Schatten des Todes* (In the Shadow of Death) (Tel Aviv: Olamenu, 1956), pp. 178–82; Neumann, personal communication, November 19, 1972; Krasznyansky, personal communication, February 7, 1973. In his interview in Jerusalem in 1964, Krasznyansky stated that a copy of "the Protocols was handed over to Dr. Kasztner" (*Weiter wurde ein Protokol dem Dr. Kastner überreicht*") Oral History Division, Catalog no. 3, 1970, p. 117, no. 398. Protocol in German, pp. 5–6).

74. *Der Kastner-Bericht*, p. 57.

75. *HJS*, 3:14.

76. *Ibid.*, pp. 52, 56.

77. *Ibid.*, pp. 74–142.

78. Taped interview with this author in B'nei B'rak, Israel, on October 10, 1972. The circumstances under which he received a copy of the Protocols are described in his *Five Months;* manuscript dated November 21, 1972, p. 19. György Gergely, who was for a while one of the Jewish Council's liaisons with the SS, claims that Freudiger received the Protocols at "the beginning of May." See his *Beszámoló a Magyarországi Zsidók Szövetsége Ideiglenes Intéző Bizottsága munkájáról* (Report on the Work of the Provisional Executive Committee of the Jewish Council of Hungary). Manuscript, 1945, p. 24.

79. *HJS,* 3:143–46. The deportation referred to by Freudiger involved the Jews of Carpatho-Ruthenia and Northern Transylvania. For details see chapters 17 and 18.

80. Uncorrected English transcript of the Eichmann Trial, May 25, 1961, session 52, pp. L1-01 (mimeographed).

81. Erich Kulka, "Auschwitz Condoned." *The Wiener Library Bulletin,* (London), 23, no. 1, n.s. 14 (Winter 1968–1969):3. Kulka also claims that "although Dr. Kasztner noted and frequently quoted from these protocols, he never disclosed in any of his reports the source of his information." Vrba claims that one of the reasons the Nazis wanted to capture him at any price was that Kasztner had allegedly shown his copy of the Protocols to Eichmann, who consequently feared that his operation involving Hungarian Jewry would be jeopardized as long as Vrba and Wetzler were alive and at liberty. Vrba and Bestic, *I Cannot Forgive,* p. 252.

82. Munkácsi, *Hogyan történt?,* p. 111.

83. Taped interview with Fábián Herskovits, Tel Aviv, October 9, 1972, and personal communication by Lea Fürst on October 13, 1972, in Ramat Gan, Israel. Whatever the shortcomings of the procedures followed, one must give credit to the courage and heroism of the translators for engaging in this illegal and highly dangerous underground operation.

84. Interview with this author, Jerusalem, October 16, 1972. Krausz, Kasztner's long-time enemy, also claimed, without providing proof, that Kasztner had obtained a copy of the Protocols some time in April 1944.

85. Krausz claims that the material was addressed to Dr. Chaim Pozner, although the copies distributed in Switzerland identify Mantello as the addressee. In a letter addressed to Pozner on July 19, 1971, Krausz confirmed that he had in fact sent the material to him and not to Mantello, whom he "did not know at the time and had not even heard of." He asserted that the version reproduced in several books and in the press, addressed to Mantello, was a "blatant falsification." Moreover, he disclaimed the signature and the handwritten text in Yiddish at the end of the document, claiming that it was "the fruit of someone's imagination." For a sample of the reproduction disclaimed by Krausz, see Jenő Lévai, *Zsidósors Európában* (Jewish Fate in Europe) (Budapest: Magyar Téka, 1948), p. 48. This book includes a highly sympathetic portrayal of Mantello's role in Switzerland. For the text of Krausz's letter and reports of June 19, 1944, see File M-20/95 in the Archives of Yad Vashem, Jerusalem. For further details involving the activities of Krausz, Mantello, and Pozner, see chapters 29 and 31.

86. Yad Vashem Archives M-20/47. A copy of the report circulated by Reverend Vogt, head of the *Flüchtlingshilfe* (Refugee Aid) of Zurich, was the basis of a short article in the *New York Times* of July 6, 1944, p. 6 ("Two Death Camp Places of Horror").

87. Yad Vashem Archives M-20/47.

88. Jan Ciechanowski, *Defeat in Victory* (New York: Doubleday, 1947), pp. 179, 182–83.

89. For details on the attitude of Pope Pius XII and other church leaders toward the destruction of European Jewry in general and Hungarian Jewry in particular, see chapter 31.

90. Vrba allots only a few paragraphs to the Svaty Jur conference, and completely ig-

nores the presence and role of Morodowicz. *I Cannot Forgive*, pp. 256–57. This is not the only questionable section in his account. For example, on p. 257, he claims that the reason the Pope's intervention must have made an impression on Horthy was that "he was a Roman Catholic and his son was married to a Jewess." Neither assertion is correct. Horthy was a Protestant and neither of his two sons, Miklós Jr. and István, was ever married to a Jew. For Krasznyansky's version of the Svaty Jur meeting see Kulka, "Five Escapes From Auschwitz," p. 210.

91. For the text of the Pope's note and Horthy's reply of July 1, 1944, see Lévai, *Szürke könyv magyar zsidók megmentéséről* (Grey Book on the Rescuing of Hungarian Jews), (Budapest: Officina, [1946]), p. 21. For Roosevelt's warning see Lévai, *Fehér könyv. Külföldi akciók zsidók megmentésére* (White Book. Foreign Operations for the Rescuing of Jews) (Budapest: Officina, 1946), pp. 56–57. For the text of King Gustav V's telegram of June 30 and Horthy's reply of July 1, see *ibid.*, pp. 72–73. See also chapter 31.

92. In a letter to Vrba, dated May 18, 1964, Mantello made the following comments on the reports he had received from Budapest: "These reports . . . were short and arrived in Switzerland rather late. . . . If we had received your complete report about six or seven weeks earlier, say about the same time that you had sent it to Budapest, perhaps we could have put a stop to the deportations, since we would have started a big press campaign in Switzerland and abroad." Kulka, "Five Escapes From Auschwitz," pp. 217–18.

93. A brief reference to the Protocols and their contents appeared in the *New York Times* ("Inquiry Confirms Nazi Death Camps") of July 3, 1944.

94. Raphael Vágó, "The Destruction of Hungarian Jewry as Reflected in the Palestine Press" in *HJS*, 3:291–324.

95. For the JTA account ("Mass Murderers of Oswiecim and Birkenau Indicted in Report of Allied Governments: Poison Gas Manufactured in Hamburg Used for Execution"), see Weizmann Files, Israel State Archives, Jerusalem.

96. The Central Zionist Archives, Jerusalem, Doc. S26/1190.

97. Weizmann Archives, Rehovoth, Israel.

98. *Ibid.*

99. Shabetai B. Beit-Zvi, *Ha'Tsiyonut hapost Ugandit ba'mishvar ha'shoa* (Post-Ugandian Zionism in the Crucible of the Holocaust) (Tel Aviv: Bronfman, 1977), 495 pp. For a more extremist view, see Reb Moshe Shonfeld, *The Holocaust Victims Accuse* (Brooklyn, N.Y.: Neturei Karta of USA, 1977), 124 pp.

100. Horthy mistakenly claimed that the secret information about the extermination camps reached him only in August. Admiral Nicholas Horthy, *Memoirs* (New York: Speller and Sons, 1957), p. 219.

101. *RLB*, 1:xv.

102. *The Confidential Papers of Admiral Horthy*, eds. Miklós Szinai and László Szücs (Budapest: Corvina Press, 1965), pp. 248–57.

103. Randolph L. Braham, "The Holocaust in Hungary: An Historical Interpretation of the Role of the Hungarian Radical Right." *Societas*, 2, no. 3 (Summer 1972):202. See also Randolph L. Braham, "The Rightists, Horthy, and the Germans: Factors Underlying the Destruction of Hungarian Jewry" in *Jews and Non-Jews in Eastern Europe, 1918–1945*, eds. Bela Vago and George L. Mosse (New York: John Wiley, 1974), pp. 137–56.

104. *Der Kastner-Bericht*, p. 302.

105. Israel Police, Bureau 06, Eichmann Trial Doc. 1319.

106. *Der Kastner-Bericht*, p. 49. See also the section on Hungarian resistance in chapter 29.

107. *Vádirat*, 1:317.

108. "Eichmann Tells His Own Damning Story." *Life*, 49, no. 23 (December 5, 1960):146.

109. See, for example, Talmon's letter in *The Observer*, London, September 15, 1963.

110. *Ibid.*, September 22, 1963. See also his *I Cannot Forgive*.

111. See his *Perfidy*.

112. For examples of this kind of propagandistic article published in many parts of Communist Eastern Europe and the USSR, consult *Jews in Eastern Europe*, a periodical newsletter edited by Emanuel Litvinoff and published by the European Jewish Publications of London.

113. Hecht, *Perfidy*, p. 272. For the complete text of Judge Silberg's opinion, see *Arar plili 232/55. Beirur shel hamerarer: Hayoets hamishpati lememshala neged hamegir: Malkiel Grünwald* (Appeal Civil Case No. 232/55. Appeal of Appellant: The Government Prosecutor Against Accused: Malkiel Grünwald) (Jerusalem: Mifal Hashichpul shel Histadrut ha' Studentim shel ha'Universita Haivrit, 1957), pp. 130–63. See also chapter 29.

114. Benoschofsky, the postwar Director of the Jewish Museum of Budapest, is co-editor of the first two volumes of the *Vádirat*.

115. *Vádirat*, 2:44.

116. *Ibid.*, pp. 44–45.

117. As quoted by Judge Moshe Silberg in Hecht, *Perfidy*, p. 273. For Judge Silberg's original opinion see *Arar plili 232/55*.

118. Hecht, *Perfidy*, p. 270. For Judge Chesin's original opinion see *Arar plili 232/55*, pp. 174–97.

119. Jacob Robinson, "Introduction: Some Basic Issues That Faced the Jewish Councils," in Isaiah Trunk, *Judenrat* (New York: Macmillan, 1972), p. xxxi.

120. Erich H. Boehm, ed., *We Survived: The Stories of Fourteen of the Hidden and the Hunted of Nazi Germany* (New Haven: Yale University Press, 1949), p. 293.

121. Jacob Robinson, "Some Basic Issues," pp. xxxiii–xxxiv.

122. *Maimonides, Mishneh Torah: The Book of Knowledge*, trans. Moses Hyamson (Jerusalem, 1965), chap. 5; Precepts, p. 40b as quoted by Dawidowicz, *The War Against the Jews*, p. 285. See also Robinson, "Some Basic Issues," p. xxxi.

123. Hannah Arendt, *Eichmann in Jerusalem. A Report on the Banality of Evil.* (New York: Viking, 1963), pp. 117–18.

124. "V'chol ham'kayam nefesh achas mi'Yisrael maaleh olov hakasuv k'ilu kayahm olam molah," *Sanhedrin*, chap. 4, p. 37.

125. Robinson, "Some Basic Issues," pp. xxxi–xxxii.

CHAPTER TWENTY-FOUR

FATE OF THE JEWS
OF BUDAPEST

Concentration of the Jews of Budapest:
The Establishment of Yellow-Star Houses

THE FIRST CONCRETE PLANS for the establishment of one or several ghettos for the Jews of Budapest were formulated shortly after the massive and systematic Allied bombing of the Hungarian capital started on April 2, 1944. However, most of the plans were haphazard and inconsistent with each other. One of the earlier ones called for the establishment of a large ghetto similar to the one operating in Warsaw. The authors of this plan—the SS-*Sonderkommando* and Péter Hain's office—called for the establishment of a large contiguous ghetto encompassing the area between Rákóczi Road and Podmaniczky Street, which was inhabited by a large number of Jews. Some consensus over the general dimensions of this plan must have been reached soon after the German occupation, as the Jewish Council was instructed early in April to order the Jews being removed from their apartments at that time to relocate within this area.[1] While a ghetto similar to the one envisioned by this plan was in fact established toward the end of the year by the Szálasi regime, the proposal was still being rejected in April. The area was inhabited by a relatively large number of Christians whose sensitivities the German and Hungarian police authorities did not wish to offend; more importantly, the authorities feared that if the Jews were segregated, the Allies would then concentrate their bombing exclusively upon the Christian-inhabited territories.

At this stage of the anti-Jewish drive, the German and Hungarian dejewification experts agreed on a number of other plans, which though smaller in scale were deemed to be rational as well as punitive. One of them called for the immediate vacating of hundreds of Jewish apartments for the benefit of Christian victims of Allied bombings. The Jews in the affected apartments were to be relocated by the Jewish Council acting in conjunction with the appropriate municipal housing authorities and agents of the Ministry of the Interior (chapter 15). Another plan called for the arrest of a large number of hostages—

refugees and other "alien" Jews, journalists, lawyers, and other professionals—and for their internment in the immediate neighborhood of military and industrial establishments especially vulnerable to air attacks. Many of these internments, like the vacating of apartments, also came to pass through the forced intermediation of the Council (chapter 17). The internment camps were set up in the dilapidated or bombed-out sections of the Weiss-Manfréd Works, the Danubian Aircraft Plant (*Dunai Repülőgépgyár*), a branch of the German Messerschmitt Works, and the Tsuk furrier plants on Csepel Island and in the Horthyliget, south of Budapest. Most of the internees were brought to these camps after a stay at the "auxiliary jail" (*kisegítő tolonchaz*) at 25 Rökk Szilárd Street.[2]

The effectuation of these plans, coupled with the beginning of the ghettoization drive in Carpatho-Ruthenia, on April 16, gave rise to new, rapidly spreading rumors about the imminent round-up of the Budapest Jews as well. These rumors whetted the greedy appetite of thousands upon thousands of Christians eager to acquire the apartments—along with the belongings—of the Jews.

The order for the identification and registration of apartments and buildings in which Jews lived was issued on May 3. László Endre's plans for the concentration of the Jews in specially designated buildings were informally communicated to the Jewish Council by Counselor József Szentmiklóssy, the head of the Social Policies section (*Szociális Politikai Osztály*) of the Municipality of Budapest. An extremely decent individual who had been of great help during the April relocations, Szentmiklóssy revealed Endre's designs to István Kurzweil, one of the leading officials of the "Housing Department" of the Jewish Council, during a lengthy informal meeting on May 17. Szentmiklóssy disclosed that he was in line to be placed in overall charge of the plan, which he personally abhorred and condemned as both inhuman and illegal. Shortly thereafter, accompanied by some trusted aides, he held a secret meeting with the leaders of the Jewish Council who, convinced of his sincerity and humanity, advised him to stay on, as otherwise execution of the plan might be entrusted to someone less understanding. Szentmiklóssy promised to work first for the rejection of the plan, failing that for its postponement, and finally for its half-hearted implementation. In his discussions with his superiors and with the authors of the draft legislation, he in fact raised a series of objections and outlined the difficulties and hardships that the plan represented for the Christian population. But all his pleading was to no avail. He kept the Jewish

Council informed about the developments in his office and in the Ministry of the Interior, enabling the Jews to make contingency plans and to take precautionary measures.[3]

The identification and registration of the Jewish-inhabited apartments and buildings were completed by Szentmiklóssy's office in May or early June on the basis of data supplied by the National Statistical Office. The results of the inventory were published by the anti-Semitic press with the customary vitriolic commentary. The organs of propaganda ceaselessly emphasized that the Jews, who constituted about 20 percent of the population, occupied 47,978 rooms in 21,250 apartments, while the rest of the population had only 70,197 rooms in 32,224 apartments.

Having rejected the plan for a centralized territorially contiguous ghetto, the dejewification authorities decided to relocate the Jews of Budapest into specially selected buildings throughout the city which were to be identified as Yellow-Star houses (*sárga csillagos házak*). The selection of the buildings was based on a number of criteria, of which the most important was the percentage of Jews residing in them: a building in which close to 50 percent of the tenants were Jewish was to be identified as a Yellow-Star house. Other major criteria were the condition and location of the buildings, and the background and influence of their Christian tenants. By these criteria, 2,681 of the close to 36,000 residential buildings in Budapest were originally designated as Yellow-Star houses to be inhabited exclusively by Jews.[4]

Soon after news of the imminent mass resettlement plans were leaked, and especially after the official announcement to this effect was published, Szentmiklóssy's office was besieged by petitioners requesting changes from the original designations. The overwhelming majority of the pleaders were Christians requesting that their building not be designated as Yellow-Star houses; Jews usually had the opposite request.[5] Most of the complaints were handled by Zsigmond Székely-Molnár, a high-ranking official of the Ministry of the Interior and a close confidant of Endre. His closest associates in this endeavor were Károly Kiss, the municipal attorney (*fővárosi tisztiügyész*), and István Puskás, a Pest County Clerk. As a result of their decisions on individual cases, the Yellow-Star designation was removed from 700 to 800 buildings, further aggravating the situation of the Jews through another drastic reduction in their assigned living space. It also caused great hardship for the Jews who had just moved into these particular buildings, as these unfortunates had to find other quarters after practically all the allocated rooms had already been occupied, and were compelled to move for a second time within a few days.

The adjustments did not and could not, of course, remedy all the complaints advanced by Christians either. In the end, close to 12,000 of them had to remain in Yellow-Star houses. While some took advantage of their privileged position, many were of great assistance to the persecuted Jews. They were especially helpful during the curfew by shopping or doing errands for the Jews, and by hiding or safekeeping their valuables.[6]

The Relocation of the Jews

"Legal" Provisions. The decrees for the relocation and concentration of the Jews of Budapest were issued on June 16 over the signature of Ákos Doroghi Farkas, the newly inaugurated Mayor,[7] and were published the following day. Each of the 14 districts was the subject of a separate decree that identified the Yellow-Star houses by street and number. The general provisions relating to the relocation of the Jews and the specific instructions for their implementation were incorporated in Decree No. 147.501/1944.-IX pertaining to District I of the city.[8]

So that the Yellow-Star houses could easily be identified, the decree stipulated the use of special signs on every entrance to the buildings. The sign was to consist of a canary-yellow Star of David, 30 centimeters in diameter, on a 51 x 36 cm black background. The acquisition and maintenance of these signs were made the responsibility of the landlords. The decree originally stipulated that all relocations had to be accomplished by June 21—i.e., within three days; this was later extended to eight days. After that deadline, no Jew—whether landlord, tenant, guest, or boarder—could live anywhere except in a Yellow-Star house. The decree specified that wherever possible the Jews being relocated were to move within the same building, street, or district; they were to occupy space vacated by Christians moving out of Yellow-Star houses, as well as excess rooms in apartments within these houses already occupied by Jews. Under the decree, a Jewish family was entitled to occupy only one room, except when the room was smaller than 25 square meters, the family consisted of more than four persons, or the living quarters were also used as an office or shop; in these cases, an additional room per family could be authorized. Under no circumtances was a Jewish family, whatever its size or occupation, allowed to have more than two rooms.

The decree did not affect commercial or industrial space held by Jews outside of the Yellow-Star buildings, but the Jews were forbidden to use such areas as residential quarters. In theory, the Jews were permitted to take along all their belongings, except for domestic appliances; if this was impossible for space or other reasons, they were to be allowed to stack up their belongings in one room, leaving all others empty. As the Jewish former occupants vacated an apartment, it was to be locked and sealed, and nobody was to enter it without the joint permission of the housing authorities, the warden of the building, and the owners (or their deputies). Prior to the sealing of the apartment, the representatives of these three parties would inventory whatever appliances and other goods were being left behind in the vacated rooms and certify the readings on the utility meters. The inventory and safekeeping of the stored goods were the responsibility of the Ministry of Finance. Upon completion of the formalities, the Jews were to surrender all keys to their apartments. After departure of the Jewish tenants, the superintendent of every affected building was to prepare and post a list of vacancies, specifying the location, number of rooms, and rental cost of the newly freed apartments. Responsibility for the relocation of the Jews rested with the Jewish Council under the supervision of the authorities.[9] Jews who were able to make private arrangements for exchanges of apartments were urged to do so and to report their new addresses to the Council within 24 hours.

Within the Jewish Council, overall responsibility for the resettlement was exercised by Rezső Müller, the head of the Council's Housing Department.[10] Thanks to Szentmiklóssy's cooperation, Müller's department was ready with operational plans when the decrees were published, and had obtained complete statistical data on the number of vacancies and the number of Jews in each Yellow-Star house. Müller, an extremely able and energetic man, also managed to mobilize the moving and transportation facilities available to the community. Nevertheless, the task of relocating tens of thousands of people within a few days proved a gargantuan one, running into innumerable unanticipated difficulties. The magnitude of the task confronting the Council and the community may be gauged by the following excerpt from a report by the Council:

Altogether, the decree identified only 2,600 buildings as Jewish houses. Inasmuch as Jews were living in 10,000 buildings, they had to be relocated from over 7,000 buildings into the designated 2,600. This meant the emptying of approximately 28,000 apartments; the resettlement decree affected 200,000 people. The above figures serve to give an idea of the magnitude of the relocation. The Housing Department proceeded with this gigantic task by first authorizing agreements between friends, acquaintances, and relatives to move in together. Even after this, however, tens of thousands were left without lodging. The relocation was made more difficult by a shortage of transportation and the fact that most moving men were serving either in the military units or in the labor service system. The Housing Department divided the capital into 216 districts, each with an office, grouped into 23 main districts.[11]

The last day of the relocation, June 24, was a Saturday. Budapest looked like a medieval town at the time of the expulsion, with thousands upon thousands of Jews in all parts of the city moving toward their assigned rooms in the designated Yellow-Star houses, carrying their belongings in horse-drawn wagons, handcarts, wheelbarrows, or even on their backs. Despite strenuous efforts to meet the midnight deadline, some Jews were unable to complete their relocation on time because of last-minute complications. The only "concession" by Andor Jaross, the Minister of the Interior, was a promise that no raids would be made in the newly vacated houses on the 25th.

Immediately after the relocation was completed, a new regulation was passed which drastically restricted the Jews' freedom of movement. The regulation, which was posted all over the city on June 25, read as follows:

1. Jews who, under the provisions of Decree No. 1.240/1944. M.E., are compelled to wear the Yellow Star are only allowed to leave the houses where the Mayor of the City of Budapest has assigned them living quarters between the hours of 2 P.M. and 5 P.M., and exclusively for medical treatment, cleaning, and shopping.
2. Jews may not entertain guests in their homes. They may not carry on conversations with persons across the street through the windows.
3. The owner or building superintendent of every Jewish house together with the air-raid defense warden or his deputy will prepare, within 24 hours, a list in triplicate of the Jews living on the various floors; the list is to be signed by both [warden and owner or superintendent]. The list must include all Jews living in the house, giving the apartment, name, age, and sex of each. One copy is to be posted near the main entrance or in another suitable and easily visible location, and is to be protected from deterioration. The other copies are to be kept by the owner or building superintendent, and are to be shown or submitted to the authorities on request. The building superintendent must check daily . . . that the complement of Jews in the building accords with the list, and must report any that might be missing to the nearest precinct.
4. The Jews must keep their apartments in sanitary condition in accordance with public health requirements. In apartments tenanted by several Jews, the residents will select an apartment superintendent who will be responsible for

the fulfillment of the preceding provisions and for the maintenance of order and cleanliness in the apartment. The building superintendent must post a list of the apartment superintendents by the front entrance, and replace it if it is destroyed or damaged.

5. In the houses assigned to Jews, the commander of the air-raid shelter or his deputy must identify and secure a section of the shelter, preferably physically separate, for the non-Jewish tenants of the house. Jews that cannot be accommodated in the shelters are to be assigned to other deep underground areas of the building during air raids.

6. Jews may travel in the last car of streetcars consisting of several cars.

7. Jews may not go to parks and promenades.

8. Throughout the area under the jurisdiction of the Chief of Police, it is strictly forbidden under penalty of internment to hide Jews or to admit them for no matter how brief a period into either Christian houses or the Christian-tenanted portions of Jewish houses.

If the act is not part of a more serious infraction, anyone violating the provisions of Articles 1 through 8 commits a violation punishable by a fine of 100 *Pengős*. Arrest [internment] may also follow, in addition to criminal responsibility.[12]

A few days later the restrictions on the Jews' freedom of movement were eased when they were given permission to leave their Yellow-Star houses between 11 A.M. and 5 P.M. The apprehension of the Budapest Jews nevertheless grew from day to day, not only because of the growing frequency of police raids but also because of their fear that the concentration was but a prelude to eventual deportation. To protect themselves against surprise attacks or raids, the male inhabitants of the Yellow-Star houses took turns guarding the major entrances and warning their fellow Jews of any impending disaster. The Jews of Budapest, who until that time had hardly been touched by the draconic anti-Jewish measures enacted against their brethren in the provinces, now began to feel the brunt of the Nazi program directly. Many of them were so apprehensive that they went to bed fully clothed and with their bags or knapsacks packed for every eventuality.

Shortly after the completion of the relocations,[13] the Jewish Council issued an appeal to all the Jews in the Yellow-Star houses. It implored them to be considerate to each other and to solve all problems arising from their overcrowded condition in an amicable fashion. In a ten-point program, it specified measures for the management of collective householding and for the assistance of orphans, the sick, and the destitute. It also provided for the selection of representatives by apartment, floor, and house, to deal with problems and complaints. In addition, each Yellow-Star house was requested to select an individual to serve as liaison with the central Jewish Council, whose Housing Department's Pacification Committee (*Lakáshivatal Békéltető Bizottsága*) was to be the final arbiter of all disputes.[14] The central Jewish organizations were also in charge of the maintenance of updated address files for all Jews and the organization of social welfare services. For the latter purpose, each Yellow-Star house was to select a representative to deal with the Social Division of the Jewish Council.[15]

The Separation of the Converts

As a result of the intervention of the Christian churches and of the leaders of the Association of the Christian Jews of Hungary, a plan was devised to separate the converts from the members of the Jewish faith. In conformity with this plan, the Mayor of Budapest issued an appeal on July 11 asking all persons who had converted before August 1, 1941, to register with the appropriate denominational authorities between July 12 and 17. The appeal specified that the registration applied only to persons who had converted within Hungary but outside of Budapest and who were living in the capital at the time of the requested registration.[16] Under the plan authorized by the Minister of the Interior, all those who had converted before August 1, 1941, were to be relocated into separate Yellow-Star houses that would be additionally marked with a cross. The relocation was to be completed by August 6. Meetings on the plan were held on July 31 and August 1, with the participation of György Auer, Sándor Török, and Dezső Strasser as representatives of the Christian Jews, Ernő Pető and Károly Wilhelm as delegates of the Jewish Council, and Zsigmond Székely-Molnár and Lieutenant-Colonel László Ferenczy as spokesmen for the Hungarian authorities. While the representatives of the Jewish Council argued against the separation, which would have involved the relocation of 40,000 to 50,000 people and would cause renewed panic and a new wave of suicides, Auer was quite eager to effectuate it, requesting merely that the Christian Jews be allowed more time for the relocation and that families not be broken up because of the date-of-conversion stipulations of the laws. Török was more apprehensive about the plan, and inquired whether the separation did not in fact denote a wish for a temporary delay in considering the question of the Christian converts and the beginning of deportations for the nonconverts.[17]

Although some of the Jews and converts did change their living quarters, the mass relocations did not take place. The leaders of the

Jewish Council as well as of the Association of the Christian Jews, especially Török, became involved, in the months before the Szálasi coup, in various schemes to prevent the threatened deportations of the Jews of Budapest. They acted in collusion with Ferenczy, who by this time was eager, for a while at least, to earn some goodwill to counterbalance his role in the earlier deportations, and with the leaders of the Hungarian anti-Nazi forces.

The Administration of Jewish Apartments. The government appointed a Government Housing Commissioner for Budapest and Environs (*Budapest és Környéke Lakásügyi Kormánybiztos*), acting under the Minister of the Interior, for the administration of the vacated Jewish apartments and their allocation to Christian bombing victims and other applicants.[18] Naturally, there were many violations of the procedures relating to the transfer of apartments, as well as outright plundering of the furniture, bedding, and valuables left behind by the Jews. Some of these excesses even aroused the ire of the agencies responsible to the Ministry of Finance who were nominally responsible for the inventorized property of the Jews. According to a complaint filed by one of these agencies with Doroghi Farkas, many alleged bombing victims, "ordinary workers" who previously had lived in very modest two-room apartments, were assigned fully furnished four-room luxury apartments complete with Persian carpets and crystal chandeliers.[19]

Aside from the hundreds of buildings that had originally been identified as Yellow-Star houses but later reclassified as non-Jewish, the authorities periodically ordered the dejewification of additional buildings, either at the request of influential Hungarians or on instructions from the Germans. For example, on September 15—during the relatively more relaxed Lakatos era—the Mayor was requested by the Ministry of the Interior to vacate 14 specified Yellow-Star houses in various districts of the capital and to place them at the disposal of the German military command.[20]

No sooner was the relocation of the Jews completed than rumors about the imminent deportation of the Budapest community began to spread, as by this time practically everyone realized that in the provinces ghettoization and concentration had been the first steps leading to the deportations. These rumors had some basis in fact, for the German and Hungarian dejewification experts were indeed planning to begin the deportations on July 10. Their sinister designs were frustrated only by the decision of Admiral Horthy on July 7 to put an end to the deportations. The decision of the Regent was based on a number of considerations including the successful landing of the Allies in Normandy, Baky's attempt to overthrow the regime, and rising domestic and foreign pressures against the anti-Jewish measures. The decision was finalized as the culmination of a series of meetings of the Council of Ministers held during the second half of June.

Notes

1. Munkácsi, *Hogyan történt?*, pp. 129–30.

2. The auxiliary jail at this address consisted of the premises of the National Theological Institute, which had been sequestered for this purpose by the Gestapo. For further details, see chapter 15.

3. In recognition of Szentmiklóssy's valuable services, on July 1 a grateful Council sent him a memo acknowledging that all the concessions which had been wrested during the requisitions of apartments in April and during the June relocations were due to his understanding, good will, and tireless efforts, Munkácsi, *Hogyan történt?*, pp. 133–34.

4. Lévai, *Zsidósors Magyarországon*, p. 166. In 1944 the Jewish population of Budapest was close to 250,000. According to the census of 1930, 204,371 (20.3 percent) of the 1,006,184 persons in Budapest were Jewish. Stefan Barta, *Die Judenfrage in Ungarn* (The Jewish Question in Hungary) (Budapest: Stadium, n.d.), table XIV.

5. One of the most prominent of the non-Jewish petitioners was Ferenc Rajniss, a notorious anti-Semitic journalist and politician, who was upset by the designation of his building at 18 Kossuth Lajos Square as a "Jewish house."

6. Lévai, *Zsidósors Magyarországon*, p. 167.

7. Doroghi Farkas was inaugurated on June 14. In a speech at his inauguration, Andor Jaross, the Minister of the Interior, touched on the Jewish question by ominously referring to the possible deportation of the Jews of Budapest: "We shall see to it that all the infecting elements who were the natural propagators of cosmopolitanism in the capital will be extricated from the city's life." *Ibid.*, p. 172.

8. "Budapest székesfőváros polgármestere 147.501/1944.–IX. számu rendelete zsidók által lakható épületek kijelölése a székesfőváros I. közigazgatási területében" (Decree No. 147.501/1944.–IX of the Mayor of the Municipality of Budapest Concerning the Identification of Buildings in Administrative District No. I of the Municipality in Which Jews May Live). *Budapesti Közlöny* (The Gazette of Budapest), no. 135 (June 17, 1944), pp. 3–4. The same issue of the gazette (pp. 4–8) includes the decrees which identify the streets and buildings in the city's other districts in which Jews could live, i.e., Decrees No. 147.502/1944.–IX through 147.514/1944.–IX for Districts II through XIV. In the wake of the complaints lodged after the initial designation of the buildings, two additional decrees were issued for the reclassification of buildings, mostly in favor of non-Jews. See Decrees No. 148.451/1944.–IX and 148/452/1944.–IX, *Ibid.*, no. 141 (June 24, 1944), pp. 6–9.

The Mayor's authority in this sphere was based on Decree No. 1.610/1944. M.E. of the Council of Ministers relating to the establishment of ghettos and on Ordinance No. 523.926/1944.–XXI of the Minister of the Interior pertaining to the same subject.

9. During and after the war, the Council members were subjected to severe criticism for the role they played in the concentration of the Jews. Those who were evicted from their apartments naturally blamed the Council—as if it had had exclusive power over the resettlement program. While many inequities inevitably occurred, considering the awesome restrictions placed on it, the Council acted with considerable skill in effectuating the

relocations with as little pain as was possible under the circumstances. It also provided cash and movers to help the needy with relocation. For the Council's position, see the statement of Samu Stern in *HJS*, 3:23–24.

10. For a description and evaluation of the functional-operational units of the Jewish Council, see chapter 14.

11. Lévai, *Zsidósors Magyarországon*, p. 167.

12. *Ibid.*, pp. 170–71.

13. At the Council of Ministers meeting of August 2, 1944, Jaross estimated the number of Jews in Budapest at 280,000, of whom 170,000 were identified as living in the Yellow-Star houses and the others "illegally" in Christian buildings. *Vádirat*, 3:329.

14. *Magyarországi Zsidók Lapja* (Journal of the Jews of Hungary), 6, no. 27 (July 6, 1944):3. The same issue contains an informative note (p. 5) about the legal obligations of the Jews for rent payments on the apartments they had been compelled to leave. Their responsibilities as tenants were stated to end on the last day of the month in which they vacated the apartments—i.e., they were responsible for rent through June 30.

15. See, for example, the appeal of the Jewish Community of Buda for updated addresses of all those who had "changed apartments" since March 1. While the appeal was probably made at the request of the authorities, it is difficult to believe that the Jewish leaders were not yet aware of the importance of such lists in the Nazis' deportation programs. *Ibid.*, 6, no. 28 (July 13, 1944):2, 4.

16. For a facsimile of the appeal see *Vádirat*, 3, opposite p. 160.

17. *Ibid.*, 3:305–10. At the August 2 meeting of the Council of Ministers, Jaross estimated the number of converts in Budapest at 20,000. *Ibid.*, p. 329.

18. Decree no. 2510/1944. M.E. of July 5, 1944. *Ibid.*, 3:121–24. The Commissioner's jurisdiction covered Budapest and the following neighboring cities and towns: Albertfalva, Békásmegyer, Budafok, Csepel, Kispest, Mátyásföld, Pesthidegkut, Pestszenterzsébet, Pestszentlörinc, Pestujhely, Rákoshegy, Rákoskeresztur, Ráskospalota, Rákosszentmihály, Sashalom, and Ujpest. The position of Commissioner was filled by the notoriously anti-Semitic Major-General Alajos Haynal. Lévai, *Fekete könyv*, p. 186.

19. *Vádirat*, 3:599–600.

20. The instructions were signed by István Puskás. *Ibid.*, pp. 549–50.

CHAPTER TWENTY-FIVE

FROM THE END OF THE DEPORTATIONS TO THE SZÁLASI COUP

IN LATE June 1944 the deportations from the provinces were virtually complete. The attention of the dejewification squads turned next to the Jews of Budapest, the largest Jewish community still relatively intact in Nazi-dominated Europe. The SS and their Hungarian hirelings, dedicated of course to the Final Solution of the Jewish question in Hungary, proceeded with their plans for the liquidation of this last surviving Jewish community. The relocation of the Jews within specially designated Yellow-Star houses was to have been the first step. Their design, however, was frustrated primarily because of the rapidly deteriorating military position of the Axis and the concurrent rise of domestic and foreign opposition to the continuation of the deportation program. The opposition, which grew louder and more widespread with each passing day, compelled the Hungarian Council of Ministers to place the Jewish question on its agenda almost continuously.

Meetings of the Council of Ministers

One of the Germans' primary objectives throughout the occupation period was to retain the façade of Hungarian sovereignty—a goal also shared by their Hungarian supporters. Consequently, in the adoption of anti-Jewish measures, they were particularly careful to pay heed to the legislative formalities engendered by the country's constitutional system. Within this system, the source of most major anti-Jewish laws and decrees—and the main forum for the discussion of various facets of the Jewish question—was the Council of Ministers. The main spokesman on these questions was normally Andor Jaross, the Minister of the Interior. Although he was ultimately responsible for all acts adopted by his Ministry, on Jewish matters he usually acted in accordance with the recommendations of László Endre, his rabidly anti-Semitic Secretary of State. As Minister of the Interior, Jaross periodically informed the Council about the progress of the anti-Jewish drive, usually disguising the deportations as "transports of Jews for labor in Germany." His reports were formally acknowledged and approved by the Council and recorded in its minutes. With respect to the Jewish question, Jaross and his ministerial colleagues received a free hand from the Council, just as the Council was given a free hand by Horthy. The attitude of the Hungarian Head of State was revealed at the fateful March 29, 1944, meeting of the Council, when the first batch of major anti-Jewish decrees was adopted. The minutes of that Council meeting (item 66) record Horthy's position as follows: "His Highness has granted full powers to the government under his leadership in respect to all anti-Jewish regulations, and in this matter he wishes to exercise no influence whatever."[1]

The reports by Jaross and his subordinates were usually approved, if not always applauded, by the Council members—at least during the first three months of the occupation. However, questions about the possible negative impact of the anti-Jewish drive began to be raised in the Council early in June when the deportations from the countryside were at their peak.

The one member who tried to focus attention on the counterproductive aspects of the Final Solution program was Deputy Foreign Minister Mihály Arnóthy-Jungerth.[2] His stance against the continuation of the deportations became firmer as the domestic and foreign pressures became stronger. Arnóthy-Jungerth revealed his position as early as May 17, when Jaross routinely informed the Council about the beginning of the deportations two days earlier, identifying them as operations "made necessary by military considerations." The Deputy Foreign Minister warned the Council about foreign reactions, pointing out that he had seen a letter addressed by Pope Pius XII to Angelo Rotta, the Nuncio in Hungary, in which the pontiff referred to "Hungary, the country of the Virgin Mary and Saint Stephen, whose treatment of Jewry will become a permanent blemish on its honor."[3]

The Council remained unpersuaded. On June 1, it heard another report from Jaross concerning the imminent completion of the drive in northeastern Hungary, including Northern Transylvania, and about the operations scheduled in Zones III and IV. The report aimed, among other things, to enlighten Sztójay, who was scheduled to meet Hitler on June 6.

The meeting with the Führer was designed not only to enable Sztójay to introduce himself as Prime Minister, but also to convey Horthy's expressed wish to have the German forces, and above all the Gestapo and the SS units, recalled. The request was also included in Horthy's June 6 letter addressed to Hitler, in which he reminded the German leader of his Schloss Klessheim promises concerning the retention of Hungary's sovereignty and the recall of the occupation forces after the establishment of a "suitable" government.[4] Sztójay met Hitler in the company of János Vörös, the Hungarian Chief of Staff. Although the meeting was brief and formal, the Führer's message was clear: he would not recall the German forces until the Jewish question was totally solved in Hungary.[5]

Perhaps it was in reaction to the Führer's position that Horthy began to rethink his attitude toward the handling of the Jewish question. By that time he was undoubtedly fully and accurately informed about the realities of the anti-Jewish drive in all their dimensions (see chapter 23). He had in his possession many reports about the measures enacted against the Jews, including the ghettoization, concentration, and deportation process and the active involvement of the Hungarian authorities. Some of these reports emanated from the Jewish Council. Among these was a memorandum dated May 25, 1944, which provided gruesome details about the operations in the northeastern parts of the country. It emphasized that the measures adopted against the Jews in Hungary far exceeded those employed against the Jewish communities of the other European countries in terms of their severity and the manner and speed of their implementation.[6] In fact, Horthy apparently referred to this memo indirectly, when he approached Sztójay early in June, requesting that certain categories of Jews, including converts and those valuable for the national economy (engineers, doctors, and technicians) be exempted from the anti-Jewish measures. In his letter to the Prime Minister, Horthy obviously aimed at justifying his position since the occupation and at denying any responsibility for the anti-Jewish drive. He reminded Sztójay that the Jewish question had been handled contrary to Hungarian conceptions or interests and that "according to his latest information" the measures adopted against the Jews of Hungary had exceeded those taken in Germany itself, including the brutal and inhuman way they were implemented. Nevertheless, while he demanded the exemption of certain categories of Jews and the dismissal of Endre and Baky, he was not yet ready to request Sztójay to urge, nor did he order himself, the suspension of the deportations.[7] The large-scale deportations from the countryside continued for almost another month. As was the case with practically everything else, Horthy's letter to Sztójay came to the attention of Veesenmayer. The

German envoy was not far off the mark when he informed his Foreign Minister that Horthy's probable motives were to shift the blame for the handling of the Jewish question entirely to the government, and to get into the good graces of the "English and the Americans in case the war ends badly."[8]

Sztójay took up the questions raised by Horthy at the June 10 meeting of the Council of Ministers, which was convened to hear his report on the visit to Hitler. The Prime Minister, obviously as aware of the atrocities committed against the Jews as Horthy, warned about their possible countereffects. He emphasized that they would merely lead to the development of a philo-Semitic trend. Like Horthy, Sztójay stopped short of ordering the suspension of the deportations; he merely suggested that they be carried out more humanely.

The government continued to be subjected to great pressure on the Jewish question, especially from the representatives of the neutral countries and the Christian churches. The Council of Ministers took up the issue again at its meeting of June 21. Arnóthy-Jungerth, well-armed with facts and figures, reviewed the foreign reaction to the persecution and deportation of the Jews. He had at his disposal not only the dispatches of the Hungarian ministers abroad, but also copies of the foreign radio communications relating to Hungary as well as the memoranda submitted by the representatives of the neutral countries in Budapest. He informed the Council that according to the materials in his possession the Jews were being taken to Auschwitz where they were gassed and burned. Arnóthy-Jungerth warned the Council about the vulnerability of Hungary as a small nation which would need the sympathy and help of the great powers in a postwar settlement. He called on the Council to put an end to the deportations and atrocities.[9]

It is possible that men like Arnóthy-Jungerth first learned about the realities of the deportation only from the dispatches from abroad or the memoranda submitted by the Jewish leaders. The Hungarian press and radio were completely silent about the deportations. They merely talked about the relocation of the Jews for purposes of labor. The Jews themselves were told when the deportations began in the East that they were being relocated to Kenyérmező and other areas of the Dunántul (Transdanubia) "to work in the fields."

Arnóthy-Jungerth's appeal went unheeded. All the Ministers present tended to believe Jaross, who informed the Council that the "rumors" about the atrocities were untrue, for the "laborers" were being sent to Germany in a planned and orderly fashion. Jaross denigrated the importance attached by the Foreign Ministry to "world public opinion" by arguing that "all miracles last only three days" and that the world would soon forget about the anti-Jewish measures in Hungary. Similar positions were also taken by Imrédy, Jurcsek, Kunder, and Szász. It was at this meeting that Jurcsek asserted publicly for the first time that "the infants and the aged are being taken along because Jewish workers work better when their families are around." Arnóthy-Jungerth was urged to give the same explanation to the neutral countries.[10] His reaction allegedly was that the "representatives of neutral countries will not understand this, for they know that the Jew works best when he knows that his family and relatives are at home."[11] The Council decided to adjourn and to request Baky and Endre, the two Under Secretaries in the Ministry of the Interior immediately in charge of Jewish affairs, to report directly at the next session.

The "Explanations" of Baky and Endre. The Council of Ministers met again on June 23 and heard the statements of the two secretaries. Baky assured the Council that all the phases of the deportation were being carried out in an orderly manner on the basis of prior planning with the Eichmann-Sonderkommando:

Everything is taking place as a result of precise planning and preparations; there is nothing to worry about, the complaints are unfounded. The Jews are going to work in Germany under normal circumstances. The Hungarians, the gendarmes, accompany the Jews only until they reach the camps; within the ghetto and in the trains along the route only Germans are in contact with the Jews.[12]

In his written statement, dated June 20, which he read at the Council meeting, Endre was even more brazen in "explaining" the whole ghettoization and deportation process. While the statement was designed to assuage the more moderate members of the Council, it also revealed the politics and mechanics of the anti-Jewish drive and Endre's pathological anti-Semitism:

The cleaning out of Jews from the country's territory began on May 3 and is continuing to date. In accordance with governmental decrees, ghettos have been set aside throughout the entire country for those Jews compelled to wear distinguishing markings; with the exception of Budapest, the transfer of the Jews into these separated areas was completed by May 31. In the capital, the segregation is now in progress and is to be completed by midnight of June 21.

The segregation was carried out by my public administrative authorities with the cooperation of my public security organs. As a general principle, I determined that the concentration should be carried out with the least possible violation of Christian interests. While minor violations took place, especially in the countryside, they have since been remedied. Where it was not possible to find suitable detached city areas, my administrative organs designated certain buildings as places where the Jews could be moved in together. Where the implementation of this segregation caused difficulties, the needed guidance and information was provided on the spot partially by me and partially by my expert advisory organs. In general, every person who is required to wear the Yellow Star is also required to enter the ghetto. Most of the difficulties and individual violations were caused by the complicated problem of mixed marriages. This question really revealed Jewry's tremendous intermixing of blood, and because of the above reason, it was necessary as a matter of principle to work by the theory that families should not be broken apart. Because of mixed marriages, it was necessary in many cases to take measures that conflicted with the spirit of the law. In the case of those mixed marriages where one of the parties was Christian and the other racially and denominationally Jewish, only the one compelled to wear the Yellow Star was forced to go into the ghetto; in such cases, it often happened that the Christian partner voluntarily also entered the ghetto with the Jewish spouse.

In connection with the concentration, the question of the country's housing shortage appears to be solved for the time being. Although one cannot yet show statistically how many apartments were vacated, reports received so far show that this question seems to be solved as a result of the concentration.

No restrictions were imposed on the property that those compelled to enter a ghetto could take with them. In practice, not much could be taken, so that most of the property of these Jews was left behind in their original homes. The Minister of Finance was authorized to collect, inventory, and store this property. The collection and inventory is currently underway throughout the entire country and, on the basis of my instructions, my security organs assist the Minister of Finance in this work. Moreover, a government commissioner has been appointed for the liquidation of Jewish wealth.

Following the order for the concentration into ghettos, . . . Jews endeavored to use all their connections, influence, and economic power to escape from the order. My security organs have uncovered document-falsifying factories producing fake documents for Jews. Unfortunately, and I must say this honestly, clergymen of all kinds and ranks in the Christian denominations are in the forefront of the efforts to save Jews. Never before have protection and intervention reached such heights as today. The clergymen carry out their rescue activities by referring to Christian and brotherly love.

The Executive Committee of the Association of the Jews of Hungary was set up as the only central organ representing the interest of the Jews; it serves as a liaison organ between Jewry and governmental institutions. We saw to it that this committee shall also suitably represent the interest of those belonging to Christian denominations. To avoid the ghettoization, Jews have begun to escape abroad, especially to Romania. Of all the neighboring states, it was Romania that, because of weak border control, made possible the infiltration of our Jews. Apparently it wanted thereby to advance its secret foreign policy objectives toward the Anglo-Saxons. In this connection, I asked the Minister of Foreign Affairs to instruct his foreign representative organs to take the necessary diplomatic steps.

Hand in hand with the declaration and sequestration of Jewish wealth, there appeared, as a natural accompanying phenomenon, a number of abuses such as the hiding of property, bribery, abuses by public officials, etc. In the cases that were brought to my attention I took the needed measures, and I emphasized at every meeting the need for the merciless crushing of abuses with an iron hand. At the start of ghettoization, the defense authorities called up 80,000 Jews for labor service, either by individual notification or by announcement; these men are currently not being included in the Jewish worker transports being directed abroad. In accordance with my instructions, the clergymen of the Jews concentrated into ghettos as well as those serving the Jews belonging to Christian denominations may visit their members without hindrance and provide them with religious-moral instruction.

Health services in the ghettos are provided by the Jewish physicians residing there. I have placed great emphasis on making sure that the Jews, who are not too inclined toward cleanliness, be under continuing medical supervision, and that the spread of contagious diseases be suppressed. I have facilitated the hospitalization of those seriously ill and of women due to give birth. The feeding of the Jews in the ghettos can be considered satisfactory since, in accordance with the ghetto-related provisions of the lower authorities, they are allowed to leave during specified hours. I have assured the ghettos of order and discipline by all means at my disposal, partially through my security organs and partially through the Jewish police organized by them. The mood and disposition of the ghettos are generally quiet and satisfactory. There have been only a few suicides, and most of these took place in the camps during preparation for departure.

Ever since the rumor spread among the Jews that the transports going abroad were in connection with an exchange of English war prisoners and the return of Hungarians marooned in America, their attitude tends increasingly to reflect the same lack of concern that characterized their mood during the liberal peacetime years.

The second phase of the cleaning out campaign was the placement of the Jews from the ghettos into concentration camps, from which the entrainment and transport actually take place. Even before the start of ghettoization, on May 14, the Jews living in the territory of Army Corps VIII and IX of Kassa and Kolozsvár, respectively, as well as those from the country's southern border area—all military operational territories—began to be transported for labor abroad. These swift and nondelayable measures were made absolutely necessary by the ever-increasing danger of partisans and the war's coming nearer to the country's borders. It was especially in Carpatho-Ruthenia and in Transylvania that the Jews hid and aided the activities of Soviet paratroopers and partisans. Consequently the immediate clearing out of these territories became an unpostponable duty. In the areas of these two Army Corps, concentration camps were established into which the Jews were assembled, and from which their removal began according to a schedule and in a previously determined manner. Jews could take along into these camps only 50 kg of luggage and food for 14 days. The supervision and feeding of the camp inmates was the responsibility of the German Security Police acting in cooperation with the Hungarian administrative authorities. The removal of the Jews concentrated in the camps in the areas of Army Corps VIII and IX was completed by June 7 and consisted of the transport of 275,416 Jews. From the southern border area, 340,162 Jews were removed. In other words, 615,416 [sic] Jews were removed from the three war-operational zones.

There followed the placement into concentration camps of the Jews concentrated in the ghettos in the areas of Army Corps II and VII, Székesfehérvár, and Miskolc respectively. Their resettlement from these areas was ended on June 15 and consisted of the removal of 50,805 Jews for labor abroad. In other words, we removed 662,382 [sic] Jews from the territories of Army Corps II, VII, VIII, and IX and from the southern border areas.[13]

At present we are in the process of concentrating and removing the Jews gathered in the ghettos in the areas of Army Corps V and VI, Szeged and Debrecen respectively.

The removal from the various Army Corps areas was preceded by conferences attended by the appropriate Army Corps commanders, the prefects of the Army Corps areas in question, and the organs of the police and gendarmerie. At these conferences, the necessary detailed instructions were issued, in part by me and in part by Secretary of State Baky. These conferences were also always attended by the representative of the German Security Police.

The transport from the entrainment stations generally took place in a calm and orderly manner. In one case, in Carpatho-Ruthenia, such a transport was attacked by a small partisan group but it was dispersed by the accompanying forces.[14]

Despite the strict supervision, escapes naturally took place from both the camps and the freight cars; the search for the escapees is underway.

Except for one or two sporadic instances, there was no use of weapons by the gendarmerie in the course of the cleaning out operation. We are currently investigating the justification for using weapons in the cases where it happened. In the camps Jews slated for entrainment are subjected to rigorous body searches and luggage inspection; in this manner, valuable objects have been found in the most impossible places. Following the transfer of the Jews from the ghettos into the camps and from the camps into the trains, my administrative authorities order immediate disinfection to the greatest possible extent. The ghettos and camps revert to their original function. Unmarried Jewish physicians, engineers, and veterinarians are taken from the camps and removed to Army Corps headquarters where they are assigned to military medical and war-production-plant services.

In accordance with the decision of the Minister of Justice, Jews compelled to wear the Yellow Star who are in jails and reform institutions are also being removed. Mental institutions, hospitals, sanatoria, rest homes and other similar places in which Jews might hide are also being cleared of them.

In the transfer to the camps and during the resettlement in general, the prevailing principle is that they are to take place in a humane and humanitarian manner in accord with the Christian spirit. Wherever I experienced the slightest abuses, I ordered the strictest investigations and harsh retaliation. I also saw to it that so-called "refreshment" services be organized at the railway stations to assure as far as possible the comfort of the Jews.[15] I entrusted their organization to the Jewish Council which is setting up this charitable service through Jews not required to wear the Yellow Star. The cleaning out campaign is continuing at this time. In the parts of the country cleared of Jews, the economic, political, public safety, and nationality questions have taken on a completely different tone. It is as if the cleared parts of the country had been liberated from a thousand-year-old nightmare; even the air has changed.

The uncertainty of the first days, perhaps weeks, has ceased, the healthy strong circulation of a tree cleared of the blood louse has started. In the economic sphere, the black market has disappeared and black-market prices have fallen sharply. The markets show almost an abundance of goods, supplies are at maximal price levels, and buyers are often sought even below these prices. Usury and its accompanying manifestations have ceased. The will for enterprise is very buoyant, despite the lack of capital. Industry and commerce are awaiting with great interest the earliest possible reentry into the country's circulation of the sequestered stock of Jewish plants and businesses. In these areas one need no longer fear the oppressive economic superiority of the Jews; in other words, courageous initiatives have slowly started. One no longer sees on the streets whispering Jewish heads leaning toward each other, sly looks as they evaluate the non-Jews approaching them. In restaurants and cafés, in places of entertainment, and all the places where one can enjoy the goodness of life and where they dominated until now, one no longer sees Jews. The horror stories, the whispering propaganda, the destruction and corruption of the civilian population, the blood-sucking by Jewish lawyers, and the avalanche of civil suits, have all ceased. In the military operation zones, the supplying of partisans, the hiding of Soviet paratroopers, intelligence gathering, sabotage, and the organization of leftist politics has ceased. Conditions of public safety have been strengthened and the typical and characteristic Jewish intellectual crimes have ceased. There is no longer anybody to incite the nationalities to restlessness. Following the resettlement of the Jews, the Christian population is trying to put its life on a new basis and one can notice everywhere the feeling of liberation which, after decades of long and pressing fear, carries within it the conditions for a cleaner and better prosperity.[16]

After hearing Baky's and Endre's reports, Arnóthy-Jungerth, who was visibly shocked by the brazen lies of the two officials of the Ministry of the Interior, remarked sarcastically that in light of what he had just heard "one can be really sorry not to be Jewish and unable to take part in these excursions."[17]

Lieutenant-General Gábor Faraghó, the Commander of the Gendarmerie, next reported that about 20,000 gendarmes had taken part in the anti-Jewish operations and that disciplinary measures had to be taken against only three of them. At this juncture Endre remarked cynically that no one molested the Jews except the Jewish police within the ghettos. Miklós Mester, the political Secretary of State in the Ministry of Cults and Public Education, reviewed the domestic ramifications of the anti-Jewish measures. Mester, a former ultra-rightist, who was taking a more moderate position on the Jewish question and an increasingly anti-German stand during the summer of 1944, reviewed the petitions of the Christian churches and warned about the consequences of the deportation of many internationally known scientists and scholars. He complained that the exemptions granted to many Jews were being ignored by the local authorities who would insist on getting instructions to this effect from either Baky or Endre. Mester suggested that the handling of the Jewish question be transferred from the jurisdiction of the Ministry of the Interior to another department. Former Prime Minister Imrédy inquired whether there was a written agreement with Eichmann on the solution of the Jewish question and suggested that responsibility over its handling be shared with the Hungarian Parliament.

Arnóthy-Jungerth, supplementing the statement he had made on the Jewish question on June 21, drew the attention of the Council of Ministers to the following facts:

- The Foreign Affairs Committee of the U.S. House of Representatives (Chairman: Congressman Bloom) had issued a warning at its meeting of June 21 that Hungary end the persecution of the Jews.
- The Romanians promised the Americans that they would allow the entry of Hungarian Jewish refugees and that they would ease the anti-Jewish restrictions in their country.
- The Hungarian representative in Madrid suggested that the Spanish Foreign Ministry's request for the emigration of Kálmán Zala's family be authorized.[18]

The June 23 session of the Council of Ministers ended by instructing Baky and Endre to put an end to the atrocities. Sztójay allegedly also suggested that Márton Zöldi be expelled from the country once again[19] and that the Ministry of the Interior settle the exemption applications submitted to it. However, the Council took no action on terminating the deportations.[20]

Pressure on Horthy. The domestic and foreign elements opposed to the cruel anti-Jewish measures were obviously dissatisfied and disheartened by the indecisive and inconclusive nature of the Council's actions. They kept up a relentless pressure on Horthy, by now well acquainted with the realities of the deportation programs and Auschwitz, to halt the deportations. He had been told of the horrors by his son, Miklós Jr., who had learned of them from Ernő Pető, one of the leading members of the Central Jewish Council. Pető's connection with the Horthys was through his son-in-law who, although Jewish, had served as secretary to young Horthy in the 1930s. Sometime in June 1944 Pető was introduced to Horthy Jr. by Dr. Dezső Onódy, who was then serving as his secretary. At the Fort, which he visited in secret, Pető revealed in great detail the horrors of the deportations from the provinces and the realities of Auschwitz as described in the Auschwitz Protocols (a copy of which had been in his possession since the previous month). Horthy Jr. promised to reveal all he heard to his father and gave Pető his secret telephone number. Pető was one of the few leading Jewish figures who maintained close contacts with the Governor's son until October 15, 1944, when Horthy Jr. too became a prisoner of the Germans.[21]

Aside from Pető and the leaders of the churches, Horthy was also induced to act by Count Móric Esterházy[22] and by Count István Bethlen, his confidant and friend who was in hiding at the time. Toward the end of June 1944, Bethlen submitted a long memorandum to Horthy in which he reviewed the necessity for the replacement of the Sztójay government and the means for achieving it. One of the major tasks of the new government, Bethlen argued, was

to put an end to the inhuman, stupid, and cruel persecution of the Jews, which does not behoove the Hungarian character, but with which the current government has besmirched the Hungarian name before the eyes of the world and which has given rise to the most loathsome corruption, robberies, and thieveries, into which, unfortunately, a considerable part of the Hungarian intelligentsia was also drawn. Unfortunately it will hardly be possible to erase this stain from our good reputation, but these barbarities must be put to an end, because otherwise Hungarian Christian society itself will become incurably infected.[23]

Concurrently with the ever-increasing pressure at home, Horthy was subjected to ever-louder protests against the deportations and to specific demands for the cessation of all anti-Jewish measures from abroad. These protests and demands acquired a new dimension in July. Whereas until that date as a rule only the leaders of foreign states were acquainted with the realities of the anti-Jewish persecutions through their diplomatic representatives in Hungary, in July the foreign public in general also found out about the barbarities associated with the ghettoization and deportation. Until that time the world press, including that of the Western Powers and the neutral countries, had provided only occasional references to the persecutions in Hungary. Although the leaders of these countries as well as many other individuals both in and out of governmental service were by then fully acquainted with the realities of Auschwitz (chapter 23) they prevented the news from being widely publicized. The breakthrough came late in June, when an abbreviated version of the so-called Auschwitz Protocols together with a summary of the ghettoization and deportation activities in the provinces were sent by Moshe (Miklós) Krausz of the Budapest Palestine Office (*Palesztina Hivatal*) to Switzerland (chapter 23).

Copies of these materials were distributed to a number of influential church and political leaders of Switzerland as well as its leading newspaper publishers and editors. Practically overnight a press campaign was launched against the barbarous persecutions, ridiculing the so-called "chivalrous" character of the Hungarians. The newspapers provided gruesome details about the ghettoization and deportation processes and about Auschwitz and other concentration camps. They emphasized the incompatibility of the anti-Jewish measures not only with the previous reputation of Hungary, but also with the fundamental laws of humanity and of Christianity.[24] The details provided by the Swiss press were picked up by newspapers in the Allied and neutral countries, providing additional momentum for action.

The Pope was finally induced to act and addressed a personal plea to Horthy on June 25. President Roosevelt followed suit on June 26, and the King of Sweden on June 30. The President of the United States demanded an immediate end to the deportations and a cessation of all anti-Jewish measures, threatening further armed reprisals in case of refusal. Roosevelt's ultimatum threatened that "Hungary's fate will not be like that of any other civilized nation . . . unless the deportations are stopped." Shortly thereafter, the President's message was reinforced by an unusually heavy air raid on Budapest on July 2.[25]

Seriously perturbed as Horthy must have been over this reaction, perhaps the most important reason for his decision to do something about mitigating if not entirely ceasing the anti-Jewish persecutions was the swiftly deteriorating military situation, which threatened the collapse of Hungary together with its Nazi allies. The expeditionary forces of the Western Allies, after their successful invasion of June 6, had occupied Cherbourg; the Soviet forces, maintaining their relentless offensive, had occupied Vitebsk on the Dvina River and were about to cross the Dnieper; the Japanese fleet had suffered a defeat at the Marianas Islands.

The Crown Council Meeting of June 26. In response to all of these factors, including the inconclusive character of the Council of Ministers meetings of June 21 and 23, Horthy convened a Crown Council meeting for June 26 under his chairmanship. The draft statement that was prepared for him by Gyula Ambrózy, the head of the Governor's Cabinet Office (*Kormányzói kabinetiroda*), included the following points on the Jewish question:

- A review of the domestic and international protest against the Jewish persecutions to be summarized by Arnóthy-Jungerth.
- An expression of desire to halt the deportations, or at least if the Germans insisted on their continuation to have them handled by the German units themselves without the participation of the gendarmerie. This was to be reviewed by Lieutenant-General Faraghó.
- A request that the Jewish labor forces, which were needed by Hungary, be left in the country together with their families. This was to be reviewed by Lieutenant-General Gusztáv Hennyey, the chief of the labor service unit in the Ministry of Defense.
- A wish that the exempted Jews as well as those to be exempted in the future not be taken illegally into the ghettos or deported.
- An expression of desire that Endre be relieved of the handling of the Jewish question and that Baky be relieved as Secretary of State.[26]

At the Crown Council meeting of June 26, Horthy reviewed the domestic and international protests against the Jewish persecutions and specifically referred to some of the excesses that had taken place in the course of the deportations, including those at Komárom and Kiskunhalas. These were subsequently elaborated upon by Arnóthy-Jungerth. Faraghó maintained that the atrocities were the consequence of German actions. Sztójay, Imrédy, and Reményi-Schneller spoke up in support of the Germans. Horthy, according to Arnóthy-Jungerth's recollection of the meeting, was quite annoyed and ended the discussion by stating:

I shall not tolerate this any further! I shall not permit the deportations to bring further shame on the Hungarians! Let the Government take measures for the removal of Baky and Endre! The deportation of the Jews of Budapest must cease! The Government must take the necessary steps![27]

However, one of the first steps Sztójay took that same day was to advise the Hungarian representatives in the friendly and neutral capitals (Ankara, Bucharest, Sofia, Zagreb, Berne, Vichy, Madrid, Lisbon, Copenhagen, Helsinki, and Bratislava) how to respond to the "allegations that appeared in the enemy and neutral press about the deportation of Hungarian Jews to Germany." They were instructed to give the following explanation:

In view of the position of the labor market in Hungary as well as of the full share this country takes in the war, the government has not been able to raise the contingent of Hungarian workers for Germany but has wished to comply with the requests of the Germans by placing Jews at their disposal. It was on the grounds of this agreement that Jews were sent to Germany for work. Experience having proved that in foreign countries the Jews' willingness to work diminishes when they are separated from their families, the members of their families were sent along with them.[28]

This telegram appears to be the only available official document proving that the deportation of the Jews was the consequence of an *agreement* between the Germans and the Hungarians.[29]

The following day, June 27, the Council of Ministers met again to follow up on the Crown Council meeting and on the recommendations of the Governor. Arnóthy-Jungerth gave a report on the American warning note of June 26 (which had been delivered via Maximilian Jäger, the Swiss Minister in Budapest) and on the petition from the Vatican. He further reviewed the offers by the Swedish Red Cross on behalf of 300 to 400 Jews, by the Swiss for the emigration to Palestine of about 7,000 Jews, and by the American War Refugee Board to help the Jews in the ghettos and camps. Acting in the name of the Foreign Ministry, Arnóthy-Jungerth recommended that the Council accept the foreign offers in principle and reproached the Council for the haste with which the Jewish question was being solved in Hungary. He pointed out that though Slovakia, Romania, and Bulgaria had been invaded by the Germans respectively in 1939, 1940, and 1941, those countries still had relatively large numbers of Jews—Slovakia 18,000 to 20,000, Romania 250,000 to 300,000, Bulgaria 40,000.

In spite of the opposition of Imrédy, Jaross, Jurcsek, and Reményi-Schneller, the Council of Ministers approved the recommendations of the Foreign Ministry concerning the Swedish and Swiss emigration schemes but rejected the offer of the U.S. War Refugee Board.[30] However, the Council of Ministers, like the Crown Council meeting the day before, took no action to halt the deportations.

That same day, in accordance with the resolutions of the Council of Ministers, Sztójay personally handed Veesenmayer a note which incorporated the details of the Swedish and Swiss offers; Sztójay realized that with all the good will of the Hungarians, they could not fulfill their assumed obligations without the cooperation of the Germans. The note (322/res. pol. 1944), dated June 27, summarizes the Hungarian government's conception of the foreign schemes for rescuing or assisting Hungarian Jews at the time:

Recently several international welfare and humanitarian organizations have applied to the Hungarian government for permission to carry out welfare activities in the country.

They are pursuing humanitarian goals and thus want to extend aid to the Jews as well.

Among them are the following activities:

1. On June 11, 1944, the Swedish Minister in Budapest requested of the Royal Hungarian Ministry of Foreign Affairs that the Hungarian government take a position on the activities planned by the Swedish Red Cross, whose objectives include:

(a) The placement, feeding, and clothing of orphaned and abandoned children in children's homes to be established through the Hungarian Red Cross.

(b) Aid for persons who were bombed out and left homeless and without means.

(c) Facilitating emigration to Sweden of Jews who will receive Swedish citizenship from the King of Sweden.

(d) Facilitating the emigration to Sweden and Palestine of Jews who have relatives in Sweden or have had business relations with Sweden over a longer period.

About 300 to 400 Jews are involved.

2. The emigration of Jews to Palestine. The emigration to Palestine, initiated by the Palestine Immigration Committee, of persons for whom the English government offered entry permits. Entry permits that are issued will be forwarded to the Swiss Legation in Budapest by the Swiss government. On April 26, 1944, the Legation requested the Hungarian government to issue exit permits for the following Jews who are already in possession of immigration certificates to Palestine:

(a) One thousand children under 16 years of age, and 10 percent adults as accompanying personnel.

(b) Nine families per week (approximately 30 to 40 persons).

(c) Six hundred persons by ship from Constanţa.

(d) One thousand four hundred and fifty families.

A total of approximately 7,000 people are involved.

Accordingly, so far there has been a regular emigration from Hungary such that about 400 to 500 people left the country for Palestine each month. Now the Swiss Legation is inquiring whether the Hungarian authorities would permit this activity to continue.

The Turkish Minister in Budapest communicated that he was authorized to issue transit visas to a large number of Jews passing through on the way to Palestine.

3. The American War Refugee Board, through the intermediation of a third party, has approached the Hungarian Legation in Berne for the transmission of the following proposals:

(a) It wishes to send clothing, food, and other articles via the Red Cross to the Jews and other (English, American) internees and political prisoners in ghettos and camps.

(b) It recommends financial assistance to the Jews combined with the repayment in *Pengős* of Hungary's indebtedness in dollars.

(c) It proposes the removal to Palestine of Jewish children under 10 years of age.

According to reliable sources Romania is in contact with the Americans in this connection. It envisions the transfer of 40,000 Jews, of which 5,000 have already left Constanța for Istanbul. According to the communication of the Turkish Minister in Budapest, the transit visas for travel to Palestine of these Jews have already been issued.

The Hungarian government investigated the activities listed under 1, 2, and 3 from the following points of view:

1. (a) The Swedish Red Cross rendered great service during World War I by caring for the wounded and by its protection of Hungarian prisoners of war.

1. (b) This was also the situation during World War I in the exchange of prisoners of war.

1. (c) After the current war, the same type of positive services by the Swedish Red Cross will presumably again prove of great importance.

1. (d) On the basis of these activities, the Swedish Red Cross enjoys great prestige in Hungary.

1. (e) In all the enemy countries Sweden is the power representing Hungary.

2. (a) In the British Empire and especially in the U.S.A. there are large numbers of people of Hungarian origin.

2. (b) In these countries there are also large numbers of Hungarian citizens of considerable wealth.

2. (c) In these countries there are Hungarian citizens in internment camps, and the rejection of the above proposals might influence their treatment.

All these considerations induced the Hungarian government to deal with these proposals and, after a thorough investigation, to take a positive stand up to the limit where they might affect the use of the Hungarian labor force.

In view of the fact that the Hungarian government wants to act on these questions in agreement with the government of the German Reich, it respectfully requests the German Legation to inquire regarding the position of the Reich government on the above proposals. In this connection, it also respectfully requests that in the evaluation of this issue attention be paid as well to the considerations that have induced the Hungarian government to deal with the proposals.[31]

As a direct result of the Crown Council and Council of Ministers meetings, Baky and Endre were nominally "relieved" of certain of their positions in the Ministry of the Interior. On June 30, Jaross requested that they give up their functions relating to the handling of the Jewish question while continuing to serve as Secretaries of State in the Ministry.[32] However, they both in fact continued to be actively involved in the anti-Jewish drive until they were removed by the Lakatos government.[33]

While Horthy and the Council of Ministers were discussing the desirability of putting an end to the atrocities and deportations, the dejewification squads were completing the entrainment and deportation operations in Zone IV and were preparing to launch the Final Solution program in Zone V.

Horthy himself had not yet taken a definite stand in favor of halting the deportations; at the meetings in June, he merely expressed a wish to prevent the deportation of the Jews of Budapest. The wavering position of Horthy was noted by Veesenmayer in his telegram of June 30 to the German Foreign Office. According to Veesenmayer, who was always accurately informed about the deliberations of the Council by some of its ultra-rightist, pro-Nazi members, Horthy had withdrawn his objections to the deportations after Jaross's energetic appeal. Horthy allegedly changed his position following a compromise under which the Jews of Budapest would, temporarily at least, be exempted from the deportations. The Regent was promised that the *Aktion* in Budapest would "not be carried out immediately, but somewhat later, after the completion of the campaign in the last provincial Zone." Veesenmayer assured his superiors that as a result of these maneuvers the *Aktion* in the Hungarian capital would only be postponed by about ten days, and that in order to facilitate it the evacuation of the Jews in the immediate vicinity of Budapest had already begun.[34]

The expectations of the Germans and of their Hungarian accomplices were frustrated a few days later, when Horthy finally decided to put an end to all deportations. Although, as we have seen, the pleas of the allied and neutral powers, the massive air raids on Budapest, and the deteriorating military situation all played a role in his decision, it is almost universally believed that one of the decisive factors was the attempt by Baky and his supporters to overthrow Horthy.

The Baky Coup Attempt and the Scheme to Deport the Jews of Budapest

During the first three months after the German occupation Horthy abstained from exercising many of his duties as head of state. The Germans and the Hungarian Nazis took full advantage of the Regent's passivity, and under the aegis of his sovereignty they implemented many features of their joint program, including the Final Solution. The power vacuum created by the Regent's abstention from state affairs—a grandiose but, in retrospect, futile and counterproductive display of passive resistance—was to a large extent filled by Baky, Endre, and Jaross, the ultra-rightist elements in control of the Ministry of the Interior who had at their disposal the major instrumentalities of coercion (the civil service, the police, and the gendarmerie). By late June this trio, and especially Baky who had immediate control of the gendarmerie, became most eager to overthrow the ruling elite and acquire power for Szálasi and his National Socialists.[35] Baky's ambition was fueled not only by the desire for absolute power and the intention to establish a true Nazi regime, but also by his resolve to complete the liquidation of Hungarian Jewry. This last aspect acquired special importance in light of the meetings of the Council of Ministers discussing the possible termination of the atrocities and deportations.

Baky's scenario involved the simultaneous achievement of both objectives. One of his first plans, which failed, was as bizarre as it was unsuccessful. It called for gaining access to Horthy's private residence in the Palace and arresting him. In furtherance of this plan, on the night of June 29 Vince Görgey, one of Baky's close associates on the staff of the *Nyilas* daily *Uj Magyarság* (New Magyardom) and a leader of the Organization for the Rescuing of the Nation (*Nemzetmentő Szervezet*), which had been newly organized by Deputy Premier Jenő Rátz, attempted to assassinate the ministerial secretary of the Council of Ministers, István Bárczy. Acting in collusion with Kornél Láng, a *Nyilas* Air Force captain, Görgey then tried to obtain the key to the gate of a tunnel linking the offices of the Council of Ministers with the private living quarters of the Regent in the Palace.

Following the failure of this quixotic plan, Baky worked out a more realistic approach, the major outlines of which were discussed in late June in the context of the conference on the deportations of the Jews from the Budapest area. According to Ferenczy, the conference was attended by the usual dejewification experts, including Eichmann and Endre, and reportedly by Gábor Faraghó, the Commander of the Gendarmerie.[36] The participants at the meeting devised a covert plan which took into consideration not only the special conditions in Budapest, but also the changing political climate. They took cognizance of the fact that the Jews of Budapest were scattered throughout the 14 districts rather than in a compact ghetto. They were also mindful of the fact that the Regent as well as several members of the Council of Ministers were showing increasingly overt opposition to the continuation of deportations.

Under the plan, thousands of experienced gendarmes were to be concentrated in Budapest and its environs without attracting suspicion, on the pretext of participating in a flag-award ceremony honoring the gendarmerie unit of Galánta. The ceremony was scheduled for July 2 at Heroes' Square (Hősök-tere); Mrs. Horthy was to serve as matron of honor. During the three days following the ceremony, the gendarmes were to spend their "furlough" in Budapest getting acquainted with the size and location of the Yellow-Star houses and working out plans to prevent the Jews from escaping. The preparations for the deportations were to be completed within a few days and the trains were expected to begin rolling on the 10th of July. The details of the deportation and entrainment operations were worked out by Colonel Jenő Péterffy with the assistance of Colonel Tibor Paksy-Kiss, presumably on the basis of their experience in Nagyvárad and other Northern Transylvanian cities. Overall command of the deportations from Budapest proper was to be exercised by Paksy-Kiss, and Győző Tölgyessy was to be in command in the adjacent cities. Gendarmes from the Galánta battalion were to be used in both areas; a special unit of the Nagyvárad battalion was to assist in Budapest proper. Details of the operational decisions were communicated to Ferenczy on June 28.

During the last days of June and on July 1, thousands of cock-feathered gendarmes with bayonetted rifles in fact appeared on the streets of Budapest. According to one of the "official" explanations, the gendarmes were brought in to supervise the relocation of the Jews in the Yellow-Star houses.

The sudden appearance of the gendarmes, reinforcing the intelligence reports about the impending coup, induced the Regent to take firm countermeasures. As a first step, he called off the ceremonies scheduled for July 2, citing the danger of air raids. Three days later, when he learned the details of the planned coup, he summoned Faraghó and the leading officers of the two gendarmerie battalions and instructed them to return to their base stations. That same night[37] Tölgyessy and Paksy-Kiss, who were staying at the Pannónia Hotel not far from the headquarters of the Jewish Council, were brought to the Palace where Major General Károly Lázár, the Commander of the Palace Guards, informed each of them separately that he had assumed supreme command in Budapest at the request of the Regent. At the same time Lázár, in cooperation with General Szilárd Bakay, another officer trusted by the Regent, and General Géza Lakatos, who was later named Premier, brought into Budapest an armored regiment from Esztergom and an infantry regiment from Szeged to be at hand during the move against the gendarmerie. The following day, under the cloak of a long "air-raid alarm," the pro-Baky officers of the gendarmerie units were replaced and many of the approximately 3,000 gendarmes, including all those deemed disloyal by Lázár and Bakay, were ordered to leave the city.[38]

The Halting of the Deportations

The evidence is not conclusive as to whether the ultimate objective of the massed gendarmes was the coup or the roundup and deportation of the Budapest Jews. Baky's show of force, and above all the constantly deteriorating military situation, induced the Regent to act. He must have made up his mind while the gendarmes were still in the capital, for on July 5 he intimated to János Vörös, his Chief of Staff, that he intended to "prevent the further removal of the Jews in order to retain at least those living in Budapest."[39] He made his resolution public on July 7, when he ordered the halting of "the transfer of Jews to Germany." With this declaration, Horthy finally carried out the intentions he outlined at the Crown Council meeting of June 26.

Thus, the danger of the coup and of the deportations was over, for the time being at least (except, of course, for the Jews in the communities around the capital, who were hastily entrained and deported during the two days after Horthy made his decision public; see chapter 22). What was perhaps just as important for the Jews of Budapest was that, for the first time since the German occupation, the Regent had begun to reassert his authority and to reestablish Hungarian sovereignty over domestic affairs. His decisive intervention showed the Germans and their Hungarian accomplices that they could not proceed with their deportation plans without the cooperation of the Hungarian authorities.

Horthy's final decision was preceded by a Council of Ministers meeting on July 5. Arnóthy-Jungerth again reviewed the negative reaction to the deportations abroad, especially in the neutral countries, as well as the tone and substance of the protests lodged with the Hungarian government. Sztójay emphasized the reaction in the Anglo-Saxon countries and the fact that the reports of the British and American representatives in Switzerland had stressed the cruelty of the deportations from Hungary. He also stated that according to the Anglo-Saxons the deportations were in fact identical with extermination and involved the gassing of 6,000 Jews daily. He suggested that since no Jews had been killed in Hungary and the deportations involved merely the supply of labor for Germany, the "rumors" about the atrocities should be adequately countered and foreign public opinion properly enlightened. Jaross gave a report on the status of the deportations and, undeterred by Arnóthy-Jungerth's pleas, urged the necessity of completing the process in the following few days with the deportation of the Jews of Budapest, "for otherwise the opinion about the government would deteriorate a great deal."[40]

Acting in concert with Baky and Endre, his two henchmen in the Ministry of the Interior, Jaross made determined efforts to frustrate the Regent's anti-deportation plans. He was partially successful; it was due almost exclusively to his efforts that the dejewification squads continued with their deportation operations on July 8, completing the entrainment of the Jews from the communities surrounding Budapest at the Békásmegyer and Monor stations (see chapter 22). Jaross actually boasted about his ability to contravene the Regent's order during his secret talks with Veesenmayer on July 9. On that occasion he also promised the Reich Plenipotentiary that he would manage to complete the deportation of the Jews of Budapest. His plan was to concentrate them into the camps just vacated by the Jews of Zone V and to deport them in batches whenever 30,000 to 40,000 were concentrated.[41]

The Germans were naturally kept informed by the likes of Jaross and Reményi-Schneller about the stand of the Regent on the Jewish question as well as on all other matters of national concern. Officially, however, the Hungarian government was at first very hesitant in explaining the decision to halt the deportations. Sztójay tried to hedge by citing the pressing manpower needs of Hungarian industry, which was working primarily for German interests, and by referring to the great pressures being exerted on Hungary by the leaders of the Christian churches, the International Red Cross, the Vatican, and the neutral countries.

Germany and the Deportation of the Budapest Jews

Predictably, the Germans were furious that the deportations from Hungary had been halted. They were compelled, however, to subordinate their ideological drive to the concrete requirements of the continually deteriorating military situation of the Axis. The retention of Hungary in the Alliance and the full exploitation of its military and natural resources were vital considerations in the strategy of the Germans.

In the plans of the SS and their Hungarian counterparts, the deportation of the Jews of Budapest was of primary importance. In fact, they had originally thought to start the deportations in Budapest; only fears of mass escape into the countryside and especially of the approaching Soviet forces had compelled them to leave the dejewification of the capital for last. Some of the details of the Budapest operation were communicated to Eberhard von Thadden, the specialist on Jewish affairs in the Inland II Section of the German Foreign Office late in May. Reporting on his mission to Budapest, Thadden noted that the deportation, a large-scale one-day action, would take place about the middle of July and would involve the cooperation of such state employees as the police, the gendarmerie, the mailmen, and the chimney-sweepers; it would be a day when all traffic in the capital would be halted.[42] Paul K. Schmidt, Chief of the Information and Press Division, suggested on May 27 that the *Aktion* be camouflaged to assuage public opinion. He advised that it should be preceded by the "discovery" of plots against the government and of "explosives in Jewish clubs and synagogues," and by "the unearthing of sabotage organizations." These suggestions were promptly forwarded by Thadden to Veesenmayer.[43]

On June 6, the experts of the Foreign Office urged that the deportations from Budapest be undertaken immediately to take advantage of the attention the world press was giving to the military operations on the beaches of Normandy.[44] What is more, the plans for the *Aktion* in Budapest had become so well known that on that same day the *Völkischer Beobachter* of Vienna published an informative article about the imminent "removal of Jews from Budapest." Veesenmayer was annoyed at this because the leak violated the basic secrecy about the deportations and was bound to disquiet the Jews scheduled to be removed. He also rejected Schmidt's and Thadden's suggestions on the grounds that world opinion would be no more shocked about anti-Jewish measures in Budapest than it had been about the "evacuation measures" in the provinces. Moreover, he thought that their suggested cover stories would be found "incredible" in light of the close surveillance under which the Jews were being held.[45]

The German-Hungarian crisis over the deportation of the Budapest

Jews came to a climax during Baky's coup attempt. Disgusted by the machinations against him, the Regent on July 4 had a two-hour talk with Veesenmayer in which he not only requested the recall of the Gestapo in order to reestablish Hungarian sovereignty, but also expressed his dissatisfaction with Sztójay and his contempt for Baky and Endre. With respect to the Jewish question, he said that while he was not a friend of the Jews he was being bombarded by appeals from abroad to ease the pressure against them. For political reasons, therefore, he was ready to intervene on behalf of Christian Jews, and for the retention in Hungary of physicians and of the labor service companies engaged in important war-related work.[46] While Horthy was not yet ready to announce his resolution to halt the deportations entirely, Veesenmayer had a chance to learn something about that decision two days later when he had a lengthy conversation with Sztójay.

The Prime Minister finally corroborated the Regent's and the government's decision to stop the further deportation of the Jews by citing the following principal considerations:

- The more lenient treatment of the Jews in neighboring Romania and Slovakia, both pro-Axis countries.[47]
- The consternation caused by the deal that permitted the escape of the Manfred Weiss family.[48]
- The great pressures brought upon the Regent and the Hungarian government both domestically and abroad to end the deportations.
- The revelations being received about what was really happening to the deported Jews.

The last of these arguments was obviously a result of the Auschwitz Protocols, which the leaders of the Jewish Council had earlier submitted to the Regent and to some members of the government.

Sztójay mentioned that, according to his information, the communications forwarded to American and British authorities requested the initiation of retaliatory measures including the pinpoint bombing of the death camps and all transportation facilities leading there, the German and Hungarian establishments in Hungary, and Budapest itself. Sztójay added that he himself did not believe the "horror stories" and that, moreover, they left him cold, since if the Axis side won the matter would be of no interest, and if the opposite were true his life would come to an end in any case.[49]

The details of Horthy's and Sztójay's communications to Veesenmayer were also forwarded to Himmler, via the Higher SS and

Police Leader in Hungary, Otto Winkelmann. The latter, who was a rival of Veesenmayer, suggested to the *Reichsführer*-SS that the Führer in order to "express his views in all clarity," summon Horthy to a meeting and that Veesenmayer, who in his view had become ineffective, be given new firm instructions.[50]

On July 8, Veesenmayer was summoned by Horthy and informed about the actions taken against the gendarmerie in view of Baky's attempted coup. With respect to the Jewish question, Horthy tried to soften the impact of his earlier stand on stopping the deportations; he informed the Reich Plenipotentiary that he had ordered the segregation of the converted Jews and that he would "soon" allow the deportation of more nonconverted Jews from Budapest. He insisted, however, that the Jews must be treated better since their ill-treatment "went against the grain." Veesenmayer pressured Horthy for permission to resume the *Aktion* against the Jews immediately, emphasizing "the danger presented by hundreds of thousands of Jews to the capital of a country in its fifth year of war." Veesenmayer had a similar meeting with Sztójay that same day, as a result of which he decided to recommend to Ribbentrop that the Hungarian-supported requests on behalf of a limited number of Jews by the Swiss, Swedes, and Americans be heeded because "then the entire Jewish question could be solved quickly."[51] Although Horst Wagner, the head of *Inland II*, advised Ribbentrop to reject the requests, Hitler, following Veesenmayer's recommendations, decided on July 10 to accept them "provided that Horthy is willing to allow the speedy resumption of the deportations."[52]

Sztójay reviewed Hitler's decision at the Council of Ministers meeting of July 12 emphasizing that the Führer, like the other German officials, merely objected to the emigration of the Jews to Palestine "since this would violate the interests of the Arabs."[53] With respect to the proposed resumption of the deportations, the Prime Minister suggested that they should take place more "humanely" and that every deportee should have a seat on the trains. He also reported that he had asked Veesenmayer to have the Germans urgently refute the allegations that the deported Jews were being gassed and cremated. Arnóthy-Jungerth inquired why Hungary should not allow emigration to Palestine when Hungarian Jews in Romania were being helped by the Romanian government to do so. He also urged that the decisions of the Council of Ministers concerning the Jews be made public and communicated to Hungary's representatives abroad so that they could counteract propaganda attacks against the country.[54]

Following Arnóthy-Jungerth's suggestion, explanatory notes were sent to the Hungarian legations in Axis and neutral countries on July 14 to communicate Hungary's decision not to send any more Jews "for labor abroad" until the American, Swedish, and Swiss requests were taken care of.[55] A more detailed note was sent on July 15 to Sándor Hoffmann, the Hungarian Minister in Berlin, together with a copy of Sztójay's June 27 note to Veesenmayer.[56]

On July 18, the government forwarded a comprehensive note to its representatives abroad explaining the status of the Jewish question in the country:

The current status of the measures adopted by the Hungarian government with respect to the Jews is as follows:

I

1. The dispatch of Jews abroad for the purpose of labor is temporarily suspended.

2. On the basis of proposals submitted by the Swedish Red Cross, the War Refugee Board, and the Jewish Agency, we have authorized the emigration of Jews to Sweden, Switzerland, Palestine, and other countries.

(a) Within the framework of the activities of the Swedish Red Cross, those Jews who have acquired Swedish citizenship from the King of Sweden are permitted to emigrate. Those Jews who have relatives in Sweden or who have had commercial relations with this country for some time may emigrate to Sweden or Palestine. There are approximately 400 to 500 persons in this group.

(b) Through the intermediation of the Swiss Legation [in Budapest], the Jewish Agency for Palestine is authorized to make possible the emigration to Palestine of 7,000 Jews. These individuals may emigrate to Palestine when they are in possession of immigration certificates issued by the British authorities.

(c) On the basis of the abovementioned proposal by the War Refugee Board, the Hungarian government has empowered the International Red Cross to send children under the age of 10 years to Palestine. The same committee [Board] has been authorized to give material help to the Jews interned in Hungary.

II

In addition to the allowances cited above, the following concessions have been authorized with reference to the handling of the Jews:

1. The dispatch of converted Jews for labor abroad shall henceforth cease.

2. A special representative organization, the Council of Converted Jews, has been established on July 6 and all converted Jews shall belong to it.

(a) Jews who converted prior to August 1, 1941, shall remain in the country but shall be separated from non-Jews.

(b) They shall be given every opportunity to freely exercise their religion.

3. These concessions relating to converted Jews pertain not only to Budapest residents but also to converted Jews living outside the capital.

(a) A review is under consideration about the matter of converted Jews sent to Germany for labor service.

4. A determination will be made in the shortest possible time as to who is to

be considered a converted Jew; this applies not only to those between the ages of 16 and 60 but to all age groups.

5. The following persons have been exempted from wearing the Yellow Star:

(a) Members of the immediate families of Christian clergymen (parents, sisters and brothers, and, in the case of Protestant clergymen, children);

(b) Holders of Church [Papal] Orders;

(c) Members of the Order of the Holy Grave [*Szent Sír*].

III

1. (a) The Governor has been given the right to exempt a certain number of Jews. Further, the following are exempted:

(b) Jews married to Christians.

(c) Holders of war decorations.

(d) Jews who earned special awards.

(e) Clergymen of Christian churches.

2. The dispatch of Jews for labor service abroad shall in the future accord with humanitarian requirements, and the Hungarian Red Cross will be assured the right of inspection.

3. With the intermediation of the Red Cross, it will be permitted to send food parcels to internees in the concentration camps.[57]

Horthy's unhappiness with his inability to exercise complete control over the government and to effectuate the removal of Baky and Endre was matched by his resolution to institute a military-dominated government. Influenced by Bethlen, his personal confidant,[58] and moved by the personal appeals of world dignitaries, including the Kings of Sweden and Britain, he even decided to write a personal letter to Hitler on the various problems confronting Hungary as he saw them. In a draft letter dated July 17, he demanded the recall of the occupation forces and especially of the SS and the Gestapo, and informed Hitler of his resolution to dissolve all political parties and to replace the conflict-ridden Sztójay government with one headed by a lieutenant-general. With respect to the Jewish question, Horthy assured Hitler that its solution would be pursued, but "without the often unnecessary brutal and inhuman methods." He emphasized in this context that the Sztójay government had "used methods which have been used by no other nation, and which have provoked the disapproving criticism even of the German authorities in the country."[59] Although apparently Horthy did not send the letter, its contents were communicated to Veesenmayer that same day. Hitler's response was prompt and resolute, as expected. Veesenmayer was instructed to prevent the dismissal of the Sztójay government by warning the appropriate Hungarian authorities that such a move, directed against those who were carrying out the anti-Jewish measures, would be considered treason. Furthermore, Horthy was to be informed of the Führer's desire that the contemplated measures against the Budapest Jews be carried out without further delay. Veesenmayer was also instructed to warn the Regent that if the "treasonable" activities in Hungary continued, Hitler would act without scruples and without regard for Horthy's personal safety.[60]

Veesenmayer had an almost two-hour discussion with Horthy on July 17. According to his telegram to Ribbentrop that same day, Veesenmayer not only carried out his instructions faithfully but also warned the Regent that he was being misled by his close advisers, including Bethlen, and that Germany and the Führer had enough supporters and power in Hungary to assure a "correct" course for the country. Horthy told Veesenmayer that Hungary's position would be explained by General Béla Miklós during his visit to the Führer.[61] He also complained that Germany was not meeting her commitments relating to the modernization of the Hungarian forces.[62]

In contrast to his position on June 8, when he had rejected the idea of camouflaging the actions against the Jews, Veesenmayer, reacting to Sztójay's request, was now ready to counteract the foreign "propaganda." On July 17 he proposed that a communiqué intended for use abroad be issued explaining the nature of the deportations. Following the standard Hungarian explanations, Veesenmayer's draft communiqué emphasized that the deportations merely involved the supply of surplus Hungarian labor to Germany, and that the Jews were given everything they needed during their "journey." However, Ribbentrop remained adamantly opposed to the issuance of any communiqués relating to the Jewish question.[63]

In the meantime, the German Foreign Office was becoming increasingly impatient with the dilatory tactics of the Hungarians. Veesenmayer was once again requested to report on his negotiations with Sztójay with respect to the date of the deportations from Budapest and the number of Jews involved, as well as on the status of Baky and Endre. He was also informed that according to a communication from Himmler to Ribbentrop the failure to provide sufficient manpower was jeopardizing the progress of the *Jägerstab* project.[64] The latter argument was in line with one of the "military considerations" that had induced Horthy to concur to the deportation of "Jewish laborers." Veesenmayer was in a somewhat difficult position, as Sztójay had become sick and Arnóthy-Jungerth was quite slow in responding. Nevertheless, Veesenmayer insisted that at least 50,000 Jews be made available to the

Reich immediately and that Endre and Baky not be deprived of their titles or functions.[65]

Subjected to constant and relentless pressure both by the Germans who demanded the immediate resumption of the deportations and by some of the most influential political and ecclesiastical leaders of Hungary who, apprised by the Jewish Council of the plight of the Jewish community in a lengthy memorandum dated July 24,[66] demanded the definitive suspension of draconic measures against the Jews, the Hungarian Council of Ministers again reviewed the Jewish question on August 2. In line with his secret commitments to Veesenmayer, Jaross was bent on solving the Jewish question in defiance of Horthy's orders. Citing national security and the military danger presented by the large number of Jews in the capital in light of the approaching battlefront, Jaross suggested that the deportations resume immediately, preceded by a segregation of the approximately 20,000 converted Jews. By his estimate there were 280,000 Jews in the capital, of whom 170,000 were registered as occupants of Yellow-Star houses and about 100,000 [sic] were in hiding in Christian homes or elsewhere. Jaross recommended that the deportations begin in Districts VI, VII, and VIII, those most densely inhabited by Jews. The Prime Minister agreed that the capital could not tolerate the presence of such a large number of Jews, and estimated that the deportations would resume in one or two weeks. He added that he had no objections to the deportations per se; he only wanted them to be carried out "humanely."[67]

Horthy was becoming increasingly impatient with the most outspokenly pro-German elements in his Cabinet. He decided to reshuffle the government as a first step toward the establishment of a military-dominated Cabinet more to his liking. On August 7, he relieved Jaross, Imrédy, and Kunder "at their own request," and appointed Miklós Bonczos, the Secretary of State in the Ministry of Justice, to serve as Minister of the Interior, while empowering Lajos Szász, the Minister of Industry, to take over the Ministry of Trade and Transportation on a provisional basis.[68]

The replacement of Jaross did not, of course, put an immediate end to the plans for the deportation of the Jews of Budapest. However, these plans now acquired a new dimension, as a strange coalition was formed to exploit the various schemes for the concentration of the Jews as a possible means of "rescuing" them. This coalition for a while included Lieutenant-Colonel László Ferenczy, the gendarmerie officer in charge of the deportations from the provinces, who was eager to earn some good points in the rapidly changing domestic and international climate.

Horthy's resolve to replace Jaross was motivated to a large extent by evidence that the Minister was in collusion with both Veesenmayer and the Eichmann-*Sonderkommando*. Eichmann was personally informed about the suspension of deportations by Endre. Without the continued cooperation of the Hungarian gendarmerie, Eichmann was helpless. On Himmler's advice, he consequently scaled down his requests and demanded only a "partial" removal of the Jews of Budapest. Largely returning to Jaross' deportation program advanced at the August 2 meeting of the Council of Ministers, Eichmann requested permission for the deportation of only the Jews in Districts VII, VIII, and IX. When this request was refused, he asked for "a mere 10,000."[69]

Frustrated in his attempts to get the cooperation of the Hungarian authorities, Eichmann decided to continue to challenge the Hungarians. A few weeks earlier, in an act of arrogant defiance directed against Horthy personally, he had arranged to deport the helpless Jews in the Kistarcsa concentration camp.

The Kistarcsa Tragedy

Even before the German occupation, Hungary had a number of concentration camps for the detention of political prisoners, refugees, and Jews who could not prove their citizenship. The most infamous of these camps were those of Csörgő, Garany, Kistarcsa, Nagykanizsa, and Ricse. The camp at Kistarcsa, about 15 miles northeast of Budapest, was perhaps the largest and certainly the best known. The Jewish inmates of the camps were assisted by the Welfare Bureau of Hungarian Jews (MIPI—*Magyar Izraeliták Pártfogó Irodája*) and by the Orthodox Jewish community through its Public Kitchen (*Orthodox Népasztal*) services.

Shortly after the occupation the camps were expanded to accommodate the large number of hostages and Jews arrested in so-called "individual operations" (*Einzelaktionen*) by both the German and the Hungarian authorities. At Kistarcsa, the number of internees was usually somewhere between 1,500 and 2,000. They were housed in five multistorey buildings. One of these was reserved for *Wehrmacht* and SS personnel that had been found guilty of various infractions, and was guarded by Germans directly responsible to their appropriate military units. Another housed the political prisoners, mostly Socialists and

Communists, as well as some vagrants and prostitutes. The center building, "Pavilion-B," was reserved for the approximately 280 prominent persons being held as hostages—industrialists, politicians, physicians, and lawyers—who had been taken there at the end of March 1944 from the National Theological Institute (*Országos Rabbiképző Intézet*) at 26 Rökk Szilárd Street in Budapest, which was then in use as an internment camp. The hostages enjoyed certain privileges denied to other camp inmates: they did not have to work, they slept on straw mattresses, and they were attended by the ten rabbinical students who had been assigned to this duty at the Institute.

The remaining buildings at Kistarcsa housed the inmates in the far larger remaining categories. The largest group, usually 800 to 1,000, consisted of those arrested by the Gestapo, who were referred to as the "Gestapo internees" (*gestaposok*). As a rule these unfortunates had first spent some time at the Pest County jail and were brought to Kistarcsa by a Gestapo unit headed by an SS warrant officer named Lemke. Among them were a number of Jews accused of conspiracy or of sabotage.[70] The last group of inmates consisted of those arrested by the Hungarian authorities during the first few days after the occupation at various rail and streetcar stations or for having made "illegal" telephone calls.

It was from Kistarcsa that the first transport of 1,800 "Jewish laborers" was shipped to Auschwitz on April 28.[71] After the departure of this transport, the number of Jewish inmates was temporarily reduced to about 350 to 400. The camp population, however, was soon replenished by new victims arrested on a variety of flimsy charges, including failure to wear the yellow star or to attach it properly.

Fortunately for the Jews of Kistarcsa, the camp was under the command of a very decent police inspector, István Vasdényei. Some of his men were also willing to cooperate with the representative of the Jewish welfare organization.[72]

A tragic episode for Kistarcsa internees, however, began on July 12, when Vasdényei tipped off MIPI representative Sándor Bródy[73] that the dejewification squad was planning another transport despite Horthy's ban. The plan called for the deportation of 1,500 Jews—1,000 from Kistarcsa and 500 from the National Theological Institute—who were to be put on trains at the Budapest jailhouse. About 1,450 Jews were indeed brought in from the two camps, and to complete the planned number an additional 50, including some journalists and lawyers, were taken to the jailhouse from Horthyliget. However, the Jewish Council, having been informed by Bródy of the planned transport, notified the Regent and informed Jusztinián Cardinal Serédi, the Primate of Hungary; Vilmos Apor, the Bishop of Győr; and the diplomatic representatives of the neutral powers, who all also approached the Regent on the matter. As a result of the massive intervention, Horthy summoned Jaross and ordered him to prevent the deportation. Consequently Captain Leó Lullay, Ferenczy's deputy, caught up with the train near Hatvan and brought it back to Kistarcsa.

Eichmann was furious. In order to uphold his authority and reputation, and to put something over on the Regent and the Jewish Council who had thwarted one of his plans, he devised a scheme to reinstate the deportation of the Kistarcsa group. Being fully informed about the Council's activities and connections, he ordered all the members of the Jewish Council to appear in his office in the Majestic Hotel on the Svábhegy in Buda at 8 A.M. on July 19. There they were held incommunicado all day; after waiting for a few hours they were kept busy by SS-*Hauptsturmführer* Otto Hunsche, one of Eichmann's deputies, who made small talk about such topics as ways to improve the mood of the Jewish community and the reasons why Jews did not go to the movies. The objective, of course, was to keep the Council leadership from communicating with Hungarian officials during the day. In the meantime, a Gestapo unit headed by SS-*Hauptsturmführer* Franz Novak went to Kistarcsa and, in conjunction with the Hungarian dejewification squad, especially Baky and Pál Ubrizsi, the police officer in charge of the auxiliary jail at Rökk Szilárd Street, managed to round up the remaining 1,220 members of the earlier transport[74] and to start their deportation at full speed that same day. The victims were first taken by truck to Rákoscsaba; there they were loaded into small freight cars, 80 to 90 to a car, amid brutal beatings by the guards to speed things up, and the rail deportation was started. By 7:30 P.M., when the members of the Jewish Council were finally allowed to go home, the train was already well on the way to Auschwitz.

MIPI representative Bródy, who had been at Kistarcsa as usual that day, had also been arrested by the Gestapo and was scheduled to be deported with the others. However, he managed to escape with the aid of camp commander Vasdényei, who had been neutralized by the Gestapo during the raid. As soon as the Council members were released, they were informed by Bródy about the operation; the details were also

confirmed by some anti-Nazi Hungarian officials and by Sámuel Pol-
láck who had managed a near-miraculous escape from the deportation
train.

The illegal deportation of the Jews from Kistarcsa aroused the ire of
the Regent. It also elicited a strong reaction abroad. The representatives of Hungary in the neutral countries, in particular, were besieged
with complaints about this apparent breach of faith. For example,
Baron Károly Bothmer, the Hungarian Minister in Berne, reported the
concern expressed by the head of the International Red Cross and
warned that many of the comments about the "incident" included comments about Horthy personally. Minister of Finance Lajos Reményi-
Schneller, who was doubling as Acting Prime Minister during Sztójay's
illness, assured Bothmer and through him the International Red Cross
that the deportation from Kistarcsa had been carried out by lower-
ranking German authorities without the knowledge or consent of the
Hungarian government. He further stated that the Hungarians had
lodged a protest with the German government and that the incident
would not be repeated because "the handling and implementation of
the Jewish question will in the future become the exclusive responsibility of the Hungarian government and of its organs."[75]

In spite of Reményi-Schneller's assurances, a similar "incident" took
place on July 24, when approximately 1,500 internees were deported
from the Sárvár camp in the same manner as in Kistarcsa.[76]

The Jewish Community of Budapest in the Summer of 1944

Horthy's decision to stop the deportations early in July eased but did
not totally dissipate the anxiety of the Jews of Budapest. While they felt
relieved that the immediate threat of deportation had been averted,
they continued to suffer from the discriminatory measures that were
constantly being adopted, even after the completion of the deportations from the provinces. They were also aware that the dejewification
squads were capable of making the cities surrounding Budapest Judenrein in spite of the Regent's decision. This feeling of uneasiness was
later reinforced by Eichmann's actions in Kistarcsa.

Nevertheless, Horthy's decision rekindled in them the illusions that
had sustained them before the entry of the German troops and even
during the deportations from the provinces. Like the Hungarian Jews
in general, they were not fully informed about the realities of the anti-
Jewish persecutions elsewhere in Nazi-controlled Europe. Guided by a

basically decent, hardworking, but anti-Zionist and assimilationist leadership, they considered what information they did have to be horror stories spread by anti-Nazi propaganda. They consequently adopted an ostrich-like posture under the shortsighted policies pursued by their leaders: They did not publicly protest the brutal anti-Jewish measures in Poland and elsewhere; they did not provide any meaningful assistance to their brethren abroad;[77] they did not even take any precautionary measures in anticipation of a possible disaster. Fully convinced of the protection afforded by the Horthy regime, they tended to rationalize their "special" status, arguing that what had happened in Poland could not possibly happen in Hungary. When the deportations began in the northeastern parts of Hungary, those in the "assimilated" western parts and in Budapest argued that only the "Galician" Jews were being resettled from the "military operational zones"; finally, when the Jews of the Dunántul were being deported, the Jews of Budapest argued that what had happened in the provinces could not possibly happen in the supposedly civilized capital, in full view of foreign diplomats. They awoke to reality only when the Jews were being deported from the suburban communities and when the first cock-feathered gendarmes appeared on the streets of Budapest early in July.

The fears of the Budapest Jews grew in intensity during Baky's attempted coup. They were eased after Horthy's announcement of July 7, but again grew intense just before August 5 and August 25–26, the two other deportation target dates before the Horthy regime itself came to an end.

In addition to constantly having to live with the Damoclean fear of deportation, the Jews of Budapest were exposed to a steady barrage of discriminatory "legal" actions affecting all aspects of their lives. Even the passage of these decrees was rationalized by the Budapest Jews: they considered them to be proof that they were destined to remain alive. "Why else would the government adopt them?" they would argue.

Cultural-Educational Status. In the cultural-educational sphere, the Jews were subjected to a vicious drive aimed at their humiliation and degradation. In the wake of the "cultural purification" drive, launched late in April and culminating in the elimination from the libraries of all books written by Jewish authors (both Hungarian and foreign),[78] large numbers of books written by Jews were actually burned in the public squares of many cities, during the course of carefully staged political rallies. Speaker after speaker would emphasize that the burning of the books represented the purge from traditional Magyar national-Christian culture of the domination and subversion caused by the rootless cosmopolitanism and decadence of the Jews.

The lot of Jewish students, already deplorable, became wholly intolerable. Jewish college students, subjected to harsh discriminatory practices since the adoption of the *Numerus Clausus Act* in 1920, were now excluded from the institutions of higher learning. The public schools as well as the various non-Jewish denominational schools severely restricted the admission of Jewish children. Following the German occupation, they were, by decree after decree, gradually excluded.[79] The education of the Jewish children consequently remained the exclusive responsibility of the Jewish communities. By the summer of 1944, the problem of education was reduced to those under 18 years of age still alive in Budapest, as most Jewish males of college age were serving in the labor service system.

During the second half of August 1944—and especially after the crisis of August 25–26 had passed—the Jewish lay and religious leaders devoted considerable attention to the educational needs of the children crammed into the Yellow-Star houses. Lakatos' reform measures notwithstanding, the institutions of higher learning, including the prestigious Pázmány Péter University, continued to bar the admission of Jews.[80] The state-run and the non-Jewish denominational elementary and secondary schools had equally exclusionary policies, but were willing to admit the children of converts and of exempted Jews who were themselves converted or covered by the exemption ruling.[81]

The Rabbinate (which was often quite critical of the policies of the Jewish Council and especially bitter over the Council's failure to consult it) and the Educational and Cultural Section (*Oktatási és Kulturalis Osztály*) of the Council adopted contingency measures for the education of the surviving children.[82] Their decisions concerning registration and the identification of the institutions where instruction would be provided were periodically published in the *Magyarországi Zsidók Lapja,* a journal which, though censored by the authorities, was their only means of communication at the time. In addition to instruction at the primary levels, the Rabbinate organized a series of classes for religious instruction. Interested children were also offered refresher or regular courses at the secondary school level. Indicative of the leaders' dedication to education and learning was the decision to reopen a number of professional institutions for the advancement of the career objectives of interested students. Among these were the Károly Goldmárk School of

Music (*Goldmárk Károly Zeneiskola*), the National Theological Institute, and the National Jewish Teacher Training Institute (*Az Országos Izrae-lita Tanítóképző Intézet*).[83]

Concerned as the Jews of Budapest were with the protection of their cultural heritage and their rapidly dwindling possessions and property rights, their primary preoccupation was with the constantly threatening problem of survival. While Horthy's decision to halt the deportations relieved, however temporarily, all the Jews, two categories of Jews managed to acquire special protection and virtual immunity from further persecution. These were the converted and the exempted Jews.

Conversions and the Converts. Following its emancipation in 1867, Hungarian Jewry became one of the most assimilated communities of Central Europe. Nevertheless, although the Hungarian Jews managed during the half century before World War I to make phenomenal strides in advancing their political and legal rights and in achieving success in the professions, business, and industry, they could not fully eliminate the stigma associated with their religion and customs. Although they tried to integrate themselves into the larger national community, Hungarian society was not yet ready to alter its traditional prejudiced attitudes. The legal and political emancipation of the Jews was consequently not followed by their social emancipation. During the *Ausgleich* (Compromise) period, some Jews had decided to pursue the process of assimilation and acculturation, which had begun with Magyarization, to its logical conclusion: conversion. During this era, the converts tended to come primarily from the assimilated families of the upper bourgeoisie in Western Hungary and especially in Budapest.

During the counterrevolutionary period after World War I, when the principles of Liberalism were gradually replaced by those of proto-Fascism and clerical anti-Semitism, the most important social motivation behind many conversions was opportunism. (This, of course, is not to deny that many of the conversions were from conviction.) It was during the counterrevolutionary years of 1919 and 1920 that many of the outstanding Jewish writers, artists, and leaders of the country's economic and political life decided to abandon their faith. Although the rate of conversions declined considerably during the Bethlenite era of consolidation (chapter 2), it began to rise again with the inauguration of the Gömbös regime, and rose precipitously following the adoption of the first major anti-Jewish acts in 1938 and 1939. The number of Jews standing in line in front of the rabbinical offices on Wesselényi Street waiting to declare their conversion grew from year to year in spite of the strenuous efforts of the Jewish communal leaders to dissuade them. One of the tragic ironies of this era was that while the anti-Jewish laws were intended to curtail the influence and reduce the percentage of Jews in the professions and in business and industry, they affected primarily the "little Jews" who played no such role in Hungarian society—many of those against whom the acts were ostensibly designed were in fact those who had converted and subsequently became immune to the discriminatory measures. The desire to convert was enhanced by the attitude of the Christian church leaders, who generally approved the first two major anti-Jewish laws and intervened primarily on behalf of the converts (see chapter 30).

For example, while in 1936, Gömbös's last year in office, the Jewish Community of Pest (*Pesti Izraelita Hitközség*) lost only 871 Jews to conversion, during the first five months of 1938 the Community lost 1,170. In 1938 as a whole, 2,716 Jews converted in the capital and about 8,000, or approximately 2 percent of the entire Jewish population, in the country. Within the framework of the Jewish Community of Pest, the country's largest, the number of Jews who declared their conversion to Christianity was 2,260 in 1940, 1,463 in 1941, 1,858 in 1942, and 994 by the end of September 1943.[84]

The number of converts in the early 1940s was so large that they felt compelled to form their own organizations under the auspices of the various churches. One of their primary objectives was the promotion of social welfare among the converts. In the summer of 1942, "The Good Shepherd Mission" (*Jó Pásztor Misszió*) was established under the leadership of József Éliás to serve the needs of those converted to Protestantism. The Holy Cross Society (*Szent Kereszt Egyesület*) was established under the leadership of József Cavallier for those converted to Catholicism.[85]

The somewhat privileged position enjoyed by the converts became a matter of life and death following Hungary's entry into the war in June 1941. Between this time and the German occupation in March 1944, most new converts were persons who were subject to the military-related labor service laws. As converts they were usually placed in special labor service companies (although some served in mixed companies with Jews) and wore white armbands in contrast to the yellow of the Jews. As members of these special white armband companies, they were very unlikely to be sent to the front lines in Galicia and the Ukraine, which in many cases meant certain death (see chapter 10).

Following the German occupation, conversion took on a new dimension. Since the Christian churches had launched a fairly well organized drive to have the converts exempted from the brutal measures adopted against the Jews, many decided to find protection under the umbrella of Christianity and were ready to convert to whichever Christian denomination proved receptive to their pleas.[86] In the provinces, where the masses were not really aware of the impending disaster, the ghettoization-deportation process was so swift that there was little if any time for escape by conversion. Moreover, the Jews first subjected to this process lived in the northeastern parts of the country and were among those most devoted to Judaism. Also, during this phase of the Holocaust in Hungary, when the Hungarian institutions of coercion were wholeheartedly cooperating with the Germans under the convenient silence of Horthy, conversion offered no real means of rescue. The converts, like all the others who were identified as Jews under the Nuremberg-type racial Third Law of 1941 (see chapter 6) were treated just like those who clung to their ancient religion.

Conversion emerged as a means of escaping further persecution only after Horthy's decision to halt the deportations on July 7 and the consequent establishment of the Association of the Christian Jews of Hungary. In response to vociferous demands by the Christian churches, the converts received a number of governmental guarantees, including the suspension of their "dispatch for labor abroad" and their separation from the Jews. But by this time only the Jews of Budapest and those in labor service companies were still in the country. Although the government stipulated that the privileges were to apply only to those who had converted before August 1, 1941, many of the capital's Jews decided to escape the burdens of Judaism by embracing Christianity. The lines of would-be converts waiting outside the rabbinical offices on Wesselényi Street and the parishes of the Christian churches on Nagymező and Proféta Streets surpassed those of 1938 and 1939.[87] They were often so long that they aroused the interest of the Germans, who threatened appropriate countermeasures.

According to various reports, the "conversion fever" was triggered by a rumor that those converted up to July 11 would be immune to further persecutions.[88] The rumor had a basis in fact, for, as Veesenmayer reported in his telegram of July 8 (the day after the deportations were halted) Horthy had assured him that after the separation of the converts he would "soon" permit the deportation of the Jews of Budapest.[89] The telegram was obviously based on the agreement between the Sztójay government and Cardinal Serédi. In response to an intensive pressure campaign by the Christian churches (unfortunately it was a campaign among officials, not the public) culminating in the Cardinal's threat to issue a pastoral letter to be read in all the Catholic churches of the country, Sztójay clarified the position of the government in line with Horthy's decision. In his note to the Cardinal dated July 7, Sztójay emphasized that the converts would be allowed to form their own organization and above all that in case of the deportations' resumption the converts would be exempted.[90] As the news of this governmental decision leaked out, however distortedly, the number of Jews eager to convert increased precipitously.

The German and Hungarian dejewification experts opposed this decision and launched a campaign to disseminate the Nazi view concerning the racial identity of the converts and those clinging to their faith. Their intention, of course, was to include the converts too in the Final Solution program. In this drive, they also managed, via Bosnyák, to maneuver one of the members of the Jewish Council into giving an interview in the July 29, 1944, issue of the *Harc* (Battle), the Hungarian anti-Semitic journal (see chapter 14).

The natural tendency of many Jews to avoid persecution by conversion aroused great controversy in both the Jewish and non-Jewish communities. Many of the Jews eager to convert were, of course, keenly aware of the realities of the deportations from the provinces and had lost faith in the ability of their lay and religious leaders to assure their survival. Like the Marranos during the Spanish Inquisition, many of the "converted" Jews clung secretly to their ethnic identity, if not religious faith, and merely professed to accept Christianity in order to escape persecution. Nevertheless, their behavior disturbed both the leaders and the devout section of the community. The leaders appealed to them to retain their loyalty to Judaism and to avoid the disruption and disharmony they might cause within the community by their conversion.[91] The devout condemned them for their cowardice and opportunism.

Ironically, the anti-conversion position of devout Jews was as vociferous as that of the anti-Semites, if for different reasons. Whereas the former wanted to retain the unity of the Jewish community, the anti-Semites agitated against conversions in order to assure the total success of the Final Solution program. They were vehemently opposed to the churches' offering any help or any means of rescue to the Jews. They were eager to prove that a Jew remained a Jew even after conversion and as such subject to the draconic anti-Jewish measures. As the anti-conversion campaign took on an ominous tone, ordinary Christians often denounced Jews for their attempt to circumvent the anti-Jewish laws through an "insincere" conversion.[92]

With the easing of the deportation threat after July 9, the churches themselves adopted a more restrictive position. The hierarchies of the various churches reminded their subordinate parishes to abide by the traditional rules and regulations relating to conversions, including the determination of the attitude and sincerity of the applicants and their completion of religious studies. In most cases, the churches required an approximately six-month preparatory program of study and training in the faith.[93]

The tougher position adopted by the churches and the easing of pressure during the Lakatos era brought about a significant decline in the number of conversions. Following the Szálasi coup on October 15, the *Nyilas* went on a rampage without distinguishing between devout, converted, exempted, or protected Jews. The embracement of Christianity now took on a new, informal form. Many of the Jews managed to acquire falsified Christian (not conversion) certificates or identity papers with which they survived the ordeal. It was one of the many forms of resistance at the time against the Nazi design to effectuate the Final Solution program.

In contrast to the *Nyilas* mobs which contained large numbers of armed adolescents, many among the official leadership continued to differentiate between various categories of Jews. The "protected" categories included most of those who were originally covered by the special exemption system introduced by the Horthy regime.

The Exemption System. The system of exempting certain categories of Jews from the general anti-Jewish measures was originally introduced during the late 1930s, when the first major anti-Jewish laws were adopted with the ostensible aim to drastically reduce the Jews' influence and proportion in the professions and in business and industry. These laws exempted, for example, war invalids, and those who had converted to Christianity before August 1, 1919.

The German occupation and the consequent almost immediate adoption of a large number of ever harsher anti-Jewish measures placed the exempted Jews in a privileged category. The exempted Jews, including certain categories of decorated war heroes, did not have to wear the yellow star and were immune to official persecution and harassment. Many of these privileged Jews took advantage of their position to help their beleagured coreligionists. Among these, for example, was Ottó

Komoly, the head of the Hungarian Zionist Association. In addition to those exempted under Hungarian law, there were a limited number of Jews who enjoyed *de facto* exemption by virtue of favors granted them by the SS with whom they dealt. Perhaps the most prominent among these was Rezső Kasztner. In addition a limited number of Jewish leaders, although not formally or totally exempted, enjoyed certain privileges not shared by others. Among the most coveted of these privileges during the early phase of the occupation was the ownership of an SS-issued Immunity Certificate that gave the bearer greater freedom of movement. (The granting of favors to the Jewish leaders, and especially to those associated with the Jewish Councils, was one of the Nazis' tactics for the more effective implementation of their anti-Jewish programs.)

Most of the major anti-Jewish decrees issued by the Sztójay government made some provision for the exemption of a limited number or categories of Jews.[94] The most frequently exempted category was that of highly decorated war heroes. Most of the exemption provisions were consistent but some led to minor discrepancies, which induced István Antal, the Minister of Justice, to propose at the April 26, 1944, meeting of the Council of Ministers the adoption of a general decree relating exclusively to exemptions.[95] Such a decree was adopted on May 10, providing for the following five major exemption categories:

- Heroes of World War I decorated either with a gold medal or two first-class silver medals or medals of similar value.
- 75 percent war invalids of World War I or of action undertaken since the adoption of Law no. II of 1939, excepting those serving in "auxiliary labor service companies."
- Those exempted under Article 2 of Law no. IV of 1939; Article 66 of Decree no. 7.720/1939. M.E.; Article 3 of Decree no. 2.220/1941. M.E.; and Article 2 of Decree no. 8.550/1941. M.E.
- The widows and orphans of those who had died a hero's death during World Wars I and II, excepting those who had served in the "auxiliary labor service companies."
- Foreign Jews registered with the National Central Alien Control Office (*Külföldieket Ellenőrző Országos Központi Hatóság—* KEOKH) if Hungary had relations of reciprocity with the particular foreign country.[96]

Jews, especially veterans, who felt that they were covered by the exemption provisions of the various decrees would normally apply for verification of their status to the National Valiants' Bench (*Országos Vitézi Szék*).[97] After April 30, 1944, the power of verification and determination of exemptions was transferred to the Ministry of the Interior dominated by the Baky-Endre-Jaross group.[98] Nevertheless, between late March and July 31, 1944, Jaross approved 550 exemption applications, which covered approximately 1,000 Jews. Within the Ministry, the processing of these applications was the immediate responsibility of László Szilágyi, a Ministerial Counselor.[99]

Aside from the relatively few highly decorated war heroes, the most frequently exempted Jews were those who were classified as *bona fide* Christians under existing legislation. These were even entitled to have their confiscated apartments and property returned.[100]

Following Horthy's decision to halt the deportations on July 7, a question was raised about the Governor's granting of special exemptions to certain Jews not covered by existing legislation. At the Council of Ministers meeting of July 12, Antal Kunder, the Minister of Trade and Communication, proposed that the Jews exempted by the Governor should not be subject to removal from the country.[101] The Germanophile Minister was probably not so much interested in protecting the exempted Jews as in undercutting the Governor's general anti-deportation decision. However, the idea of special exemptions was not acted upon until August 21, when Horthy, reasserting his role as Governor, was instrumental in the adoption of a new decree providing such exemptions for certain groups of Jews not covered by previous legislation. Issued on August 21 over the signature of Lajos Reményi-Schneller, then Acting Prime Minister, Decree 2.040/1944. M.E. authorized the Governor to provide, on the recommendation of the Council of Ministers, special exemption to persons who had made great contributions to the nation in various fields, including the arts, the sciences, and the economy. The decree stipulated that the Jews so exempted would still be subject to the provisions of the racial Third Anti-Jewish Act of 1941 and that their property rights would be spelled out in the individual exemption certificates.[102] The decree was well received by most of the Jews, but vehemently denounced by the extreme Right, especially by some elements of the Hungarian National Socialist Party.[103]

The idea of special exemptions was developed by Miklós Mester acting in cooperation with Gyula Ambrózy, the head of the Governor's Cabinet Office. Its adoption was assured only after the governmental changes of August 7 that saw the replacement of Imrédy, Jaross, and Kunder by men more loyal to the Governor. Before the adoption of Decree no. 2.040, Ambrózy would issue special "provisional" exemption certificates entitling the holders to remain in their apartments and to remove the yellow star from their garments. It was in this manner that the three leading figures of the Jewish Council—Stern, Pető, and Wilhelm—appeared, to the shock and consternation of several of their colleagues, without their telltale badges for the Council meeting of August 17.

Although the Jews filed their applications for exemption with various ministries, these were normally forwarded to the offices of the Council of Ministers, where lists were prepared for submission to and approval by the Governor. The center for the transmission of the exemption applications was Mester's office in the Ministry of Cults and Public Education, which included a number of officials who were sympathetic to his views on exemptions.[104] Through Ambrózy's and Mester's activities, some of the most outstanding Jewish writers, artists, scientists, and academicians were granted special exemption status.[105] The technical aspects of the exemptions were handled by the office of Counselor István Balla on Úri Street, near the Royal Palace. The system naturally led to some abuse and corruption. Although many thousands of Jews in the categories specified by the decree were exempted only after they had furnished voluminous documentation, others with connections and money received theirs without any special effort.[106]

A few Jews who were eligible for exemption refused to accept that status, preferring to demonstrate their solidarity with the Jewish masses (among these was Lajos Stöckler, a member and later head of the Jewish Council), but most of those who had an opportunity eagerly sought their exemption. They had no moral scruples about dissociating themselves from the rest of the beleaguered community; under the extraordinary conditions of stress, few, if any, questioned their right to stay alive when so many "ordinary" Jews were being threatened with death. It presumably never occurred to them that by accepting the categories of "exempted" or "special" Jews they were in fact pursuing a morally disastrous course by implicitly recognizing, as Hannah Arendt pointed out, the Nazis' rule "which spelled death for all non-special cases."[107]

Most eligible Jews naturally considered their exemption as a means of survival for themselves and their families; others viewed it as a means by which they could better help the community's survivors. Among the latter were some of the top leaders of the Jewish community. The Jewish Council's petition for exemptions included 26 names. Some of them, including Stern, Pető, and Wilhelm, also applied to have their property interests exempted—to the embarrassment of Hungarian officials and many Jewish leaders, including Ottó Komoly.[108]

The exempted Jews were freed from practically all of the harshest anti-Jewish restrictions. They could remove the yellow star from their garments, regain their apartments (and often even their jobs), and their children were frequently readmitted to the public schools.[109] In the midst of the great and ever-recurring crises, many of the exempted Jews, including the members of the Council, took full advantage of their exemption to help their less fortunate brethren. However, some of them also created considerable intracommunal tension when they tried to reacquire their old apartments, which had been assigned to nonexempted Jews during the June relocations.[110] The only collective rejection of exemptions came from the Rabbinate, which adopted a resolution on August 30 to the effect that its members would not accept exemption status until all the Jews were exempted, excluding those occasions "when they have to appear before a governmental authority in behalf of a fellow Jew or the community."[111]

The system of exemptions employed both by the Ministry of the Interior and by the Governor's office engendered a flurry of activity in behalf of individual Jews. Many Hungarian clergymen and intellectuals would petition for exemption status for their Jewish friends.[112] But not all of the exempted Jews fared equally well. Some of them were in fact deported before the receipt of the exemption certificate. One such was Dr. Géza Mansfeld, a noted physician, who, with his family, was deported from Pécs. The local police had intentionally delayed the forwarding of the issued exemption certificate.[113] Others were taken to Germany together with many other "illegally" deported individuals.[114] During the summer of 1944, the Ministry of Foreign Affairs submitted several official notes to the Germans requesting the return both of the exempted Jews and of those who had been deported "illegally" or "by mistake" due to the overzealousness of the gendarmerie in the provinces. Each diplomatic note normally included a list of the individuals involved together with detailed personal data. As expected, the efforts of the Ministry were of no avail. The Germans either did not respond or adopted dilatory tactics, forwarding the Hungarians' notes from one ministerial office to another.[115] The Germans could not, of course, satisfy the request of the Hungarians, for most of the people involved had already either been killed at Auschwitz or deployed without trace to one of the many German concentration camps. Theodor Horst Grell, the *Referent* on Jewish affairs in the German Legation in Budapest, tried to "explain" Germany's dilemma in his July 21 discussion with Sándor Nékám of the Hungarian Ministry of Foreign Affairs. Grell noted that the return of the Jews previously handed over to the Germans was impossible, and would violate the German-Hungarian agreement concerning "the dispatch of Jews for labor in Germany." Under the agreement, Grell reminded Nékám, the Hungarians were to determine the groups of Jews to be handed over to the Germans, but once delivered the Hungarians would no longer have any jurisdiction over them. Moreover, he argued, these Jews had already been assigned to various branches of the German economy from which they could not be removed, and even if they could, their transportation would present insurmountable technical problems.[116]

While thousands of exemption certificates were being processed or about to be delivered, the Horthy regime was toppled on October 15 by a coup engineered by the Germans in concert with the *Nyilas*. On October 23 the new Szálasi government decided to revise the exemption system by rescinding the exemption certificates issued by the Ministry of Defense and upholding only those granted by Jaross. It also decided to reexamine the certificates issued by Horthy and to limit the number in this category to 800. The revisions were to be completed by November 15 under the supervision of Gábor Vajna, the new Minister of the Interior.[117] As a result of these measures, many Jews lost their exempt status and became once again subject to all the anti-Jewish decrees. Vajna issued only 501 exemption certificates, and even that small number irked Gábor Kemény, the new Minister of Foreign Affairs. Of the many thousands of "Horthy-exempted Jews," only 70 managed to obtain exemption certificates from Szálasi.[118]

In contrast to the viciously hostile attitude manifested by the leaders of the new Szálasi government and by the masses instigated by *Nyilas* agitators, during the months before the coup the Jews enjoyed the support of many governmental leaders and of many decent ordinary Hungarians, who intervened in their behalf, often in support of petitions for exemption certificates. During this period, the Jewish leaders also acquired an unexpected "ally" for the possible rescue of the entire surviving Jewish community. The individual involved was none other than Lieutenant-Colonel László Ferenczy of the Gendarmerie, the commander of the deportation squads in the provinces.

Ferenczy "to the Rescue"

Horthy's decision to end the deportations early in July and the domestic and foreign diplomatic and military pressures underlying it made a tremendous impression on Hungarian officials, including some who had been actively involved in the deportation of the Jews from the provinces. Drawing the logical conclusion from the untenable military position of the Axis, they began to see the handwriting on the wall. With the Red Army moving inexorably toward the Carpathians and with the Western Allies fanning out from their beachheads in Normandy, many Hungarian officials finally became convinced that Germany would inevitably lose. They no longer believed in the Führer's assertions about the inevitability of final victory for the Reich, or in German reassurances about the deployment of new "wonder weapons." Thus, by adopting an opportunistic anti-German posture, the Hungarians hoped to mask the despicable crimes they had committed only a few months earlier.

One of the most prominent among such officials was Lieutenant-Colonel László Ferenczy, the liaison between the Eichmann-*Sonderkommando* and the Hungarian authorities and the gendarmerie officer in charge of the deportations from the provinces.[119] Shortly after the completion of the deportations from the communities surrounding Budapest, Ferenczy, reassessing the domestic and international situation, decided to ingratiate himself with the Regent and with the leadership of the Jewish Council. Ferenczy hoped to persuade the Regent that he was a nationalist eager to protect Hungarian national interests against encroachment by the Germans, and to persuade the Jewish Council he was the savior of the Jews of Budapest; he was thus most eager to meet with the Regent and the leaders of the Council. Since he could not approach the Regent directly, he decided to first inform his immediate superiors in the government—the Minister of the Interior and the Prime Minister[120]—about the Germans' apparent intention to expand the scope of the occupation if the Final Solution program was not completed: the Germans seemed so eager for the deportation of the Jews of Budapest that they were ready to transform Hungary into a protectorate to achieve it. He outlined the details of the Germans' designs in a lengthy memorandum he first submitted to Jaross. (It was around this time, incidentally, that Ferenczy claimed to have become convinced that the Jews "deemed unsuitable for work" were indeed being exterminated in crematoria at Auschwitz; he based his new-found conviction on Eichmann's response to his request to visit Auschwitz "to see for himself how the Hungarian Jews were being screened and assigned to labor." Eichmann had agreed to the request, but with the proviso that the visit could only take place 30 days after the departure of the last transport of Jews from Hungary.)

Ferenczy's appeal to Jaross and Sztójay for permission to see Horthy was unheeded.[121] He therefore decided to exploit the connections of the Jewish Council with the Palace, and to take the opportunity to persuade the Council leaders of his readiness to save the Jews of Budapest. He found a chance to get in touch with the leaders of the Council around the middle of July, about the time when Eichmann and his SS associates were planning the deportation of the Jews from the Kistarcsa camp. Earlier in the month Raoul Wallenberg, one of the heroes of the Holocaust period, had arrived in Budapest (see chapter 31). Wallenberg had brought with him a list of 630 Hungarian Jews whose immigration into Sweden was being sponsored by friends, relatives, or business associates there and for whom the Swedes had issued the necessary visas. When this list was given to Ferenczy for handling, along with the Swiss list of 2,000 Jews approved for emigration to Palestine, he had a good pretext for approaching the Council. Accordingly, sometime during the middle of July he telephoned the Council and requested that one of its members come to see him. Unaware of the details of his plans but fully conscious of his criminal role in the earlier deportations, the members of the Council were understandably apprehensive about Ferenczy's intentions. István Kurzweil, a leading member of the Council's Housing Department, volunteered to see him.[122] Ferenczy told the astonished Kurzweil about the opportunity for 2,630 Jews to leave the country with the approval of the German authorities and the cooperation of the neutral countries. Ferenczy also assured him that arrangements had already been made by his office to allow the emigration in the very near future. He requested that "for reasons of security" the Council make available a number of modern Yellow-Star houses exclusively for these Jews.

The Council received Kurzweil's report with ambivalent feelings. The members did not want to jeopardize the possible emigration of a relatively large number of Jews, but they were nevertheless fearful that Ferenczy's plan was just a ruse, which would lead only to the renewal of the deportations. They decided to proceed very cautiously to ascertain the true character and implications of Ferenczy's request. They insisted on first receiving the lists of individuals involved, claiming that without personal data they could not make arrangements for relocation. To their great surprise, Ferenczy immediately handed over the Swedish list. A few days later, under pressure from Ferenczy's office, the Council leaders set aside a number of Yellow-Star houses on Pozsonyi Road for the Jews slated for emigration to Sweden. These would become the first so-called "protected" (*védett*) houses, which later served as the nucleus of the "international ghetto" (*nemzetközi gettó*) during the Szálasi era (see chapter 26). They were also the source of a major conflict among the Jewish leaders.

A short time later, Kurzweil and Ferenczy had a second meeting, this time with several other members and officials of the Council (including Pető, Béla Berend, and Gábor) and with Captain Leó Lullay, Ferenczy's deputy. Ferenczy told the Jewish leaders about the changed situation, the dominant role the Germans had played in the deportations, and the "life-and-death struggle" he and his close associates were waging against the Gestapo. To camouflage his own criminal role in the Final Solution program, he inquired, feigning naïveté and innocence, about the realities of Auschwitz inasmuch as he was unable to travel there to obtain first-hand information.

Speaking for the group, Pető enlightened him about the German extermination camps and reminded him of the tenuous military position of the Axis, intimating that Hungary might suffer at any peace conference because of its cruel treatment of the Jews.

After this meeting, Ferenczy's contacts were restricted mostly to the three leading figures of the Council (Pető, Stern, and Wilhelm), although on some occasions he also met Rezső Kasztner, Lajos Stöckler, and the Zionist leader Ottó Komoly.[123] Some of the talks were held at Stern's home, in the greatest secrecy. Ferenczy again tried to persuade the Jewish leaders of his own innocence by "proving" that the deportations and all the horrors associated with them were the exclusive responsibility of the Germans.[124] Taking advantage of his changed position and bolstering his ego by singling him out as the possible savior of the Jews of Budapest, the Jewish leaders worked out with Ferenczy a secret plan for preventing further deportations. According to the plan the Hungarian authorities, including of course the gendarmerie, would simulate continued cooperation with the Germans, but when it came to the actual deportation of the Budapest Jews the combined gendarmerie-military forces of Hungary would in fact intervene to prevent their removal.

Since neither the Jewish masses nor the other members of the Jewish Council had any idea of the secret understanding between Ferenczy and the top Jewish leaders, the appearance of gendarmes on the streets of Budapest, coupled with rumors about impending deportations, caused near-panic among the Jews of the capital. Lajos Stöckler, who was appointed to the Council on July 22, was particularly upset by the failure of the leadership to call an Executive Committee meeting on the issues confronting the remaining Jewish community. He gave public expression to his feelings on several occasions.[125]

In the meantime, Stern and his close associates continued to work out the details of their clandestine deal with Ferenczy. On one occasion they also discussed the possibility of active resistance against the Germans and their Hungarian hirelings, the *Nyilas,* with the collaboration of organized labor. The support of the latter was promised by two prominent trade union leaders of Hungary—Lajos Kabók, the Social Democratic member of the lower house, and Sándor Karácsonyi, the head of the Iron Workers (*Vasasok*)—who also met Ferenczy at the behest of the Jewish leaders. (Both were killed by the *Nyilas* in the fall of 1944).

Ferenczy and Lullay prudently insisted that all the plans be kept secret even from the members of the Sztójay government, as otherwise they might be jeopardized. Pető, who had already established close personal relations with Horthy Jr., kept the Regent's son fully informed about all developments.

In the course of one of the meetings with the Jewish leaders, Ferenczy requested their help in obtaining an audience with the Regent. Through the good offices of Horthy Jr. a meeting was set up for early in August; Ferenczy also saw the Regent three more times that month. He brought him up to date on the activities of the Gestapo in Hungary and the troop strength of the various German units in the country.[126] During his first meeting with the Regent Ferenczy also submitted the text of a protest note, in German, which he had prepared with the cooperation of the Council and planned to transmit to Veesenmayer. Designed to crystallize the new position of the Hungarian government on the Jewish question, the note made five major points:

- The Hungarian government would remove the Jews from Budapest to various camps in the provinces, but would not hand them over to the Germans for removal from the country.
- The Eichmann-*Sonderkommando* was to be recalled from Hungary.
- All political and legislative leaders in German custody were to be surrendered to the Hungarian judicial authorities.

- The Pest County Jail was to be transferred to Hungarian control.
- The Germans were to surrender all Jewish wealth and warehouses confiscated since the occupation.

The note was edited into a diplomatically more acceptable form by Dénes Csopey, the head of the Political Department of the Ministry of Foreign affairs, but was not handed to Veesenmayer until late in August.[127]

Some of the Jewish leaders' suspicions about Ferenczy's double-dealings were fully corroborated shortly after the coup. With Szálasi in power, Ferenczy once again assumed an openly active role in the anti-Jewish drive. The leading members of the Jewish Council, who knew too much about Ferenczy's revelations to the Regent, had to run for their lives, for the gendarmerie officer did not want to become the subject of blackmail or have any potentially "dangerous" witnesses around. The prevailing evidence clearly indicates that Ferenczy never really intended to switch sides. His primary objective in getting access to Horthy was his desire to obtain details about the Regent's plans for a *volte face* and transmit them to the Germans, whose trusted informer he always was.

New Deportation Threats

The Eichmann-initiated deportation of the Jews in the Kistarcsa camp in defiance of Horthy's orders emboldened the dejewification experts to resume their preparations for the deportation of the Jews of Budapest, which they rescheduled for August 5. The Kistarcsa incident, coupled with the preparatory work taking place in Békásmegyer (the camp from which the Jews of the Budapest suburbs had been deported earlier in the month) created a very depressing atmosphere among the Jews of the capital. As rumors ran rampant about the imminence of the deportation, they prepared themselves physically and psychologically for the worst. Their fears proved unfounded at this time, though, mostly because the Hungarian gendarmerie was no longer as readily available to the Germans as it had been before July 8. Moreover, Baky and Endre had by this time been relieved of jurisdiction over Jewish affairs and Ferenczy was visibly searching for an alibi.

The passing of the August 5 deadline and the replacement of Minister of the Interior Jaross by Miklós Bonczos two days later were greeted with great relief. This was, however, temporary; on the night of August

9, Freudiger, along with his family and some friends, escaped to Romania, and the news spread rapidly through the Jewish community on the following day. Freudiger had managed to leave with the aid of Wisliceny, with whom he had been on reasonably good terms since shortly after the German occupation thanks to the intermediation of Rabbi Weissmandel of Bratislava (see chapter 14). Because of his close contact with Jewish leaders abroad and with Wisliceny, Freudiger was widely believed to be one of the best-informed members of the Jewish community. Accordingly, his sudden departure was construed as a harbinger of imminent deportation. Aside from the panic that it created among the uninformed Jewish masses, Freudiger's escape resulted in the arrest of some leaders of the Council. János Gábor was arrested almost immediately after Freudiger's escape became known; by coincidence, he had been visiting Eichmann's office at the time. On August 18 the Gestapo also arrested Pető, Stern, and Wilhelm, who only the day before had been exempted from wearing the yellow star. The latter two were freed the following day after the resolute intervention of Governor Horthy, but Pető was mistreated and kept in custody until August 21.

Notwithstanding the governmental reorganization of August 7, the Jewish question continued to preoccupy the Hungarian authorities both internally and in their dealings with the Germans. At the August 10 meeting of the reorganized Council of Ministers, Arnóthy-Jungerth again took the initiative in outlining the position worked out by the Ministry of Foreign Affairs.[128] He argued for the adoption of a policy that would put the Jewish question to rest. In his view, this was required for domestic political reasons, for reasons connected with German-Hungarian relations, and to enable Hungary to meet its commitments to the neutral countries and the International Red Cross with respect to the possible emigration of the Jews on the Swedish and Swiss lists.

In Arnóthy-Jungerth's view, the Jewish question could be put to rest if the Governor were to issue a declaration specifying the measures he would be ready to adopt in return for certain commitments on the part of the Germans. According to Arnóthy-Jungerth, there were 164,000 Jews registered in Budapest's Yellow-Star houses, of whom 20,000 were converts and 10,000 were scheduled for emigration. He suggested that the problem of the remaining 134,000 could be solved as follows:

- Approximately 50,000 to 60,000 Jews, identified as "Galician and infiltrated," were to be offered to the Germans.

- The Jews in the labor service units and their families (wives, children, and possibly parents) were to be retained, but those not actively employed were to be placed into ghettos in the countryside "like the 45,000 German Jews in Theresienstadt."
- Jews legally exempted from the anti-Jewish laws as well as those, up to a given number, exempted by Horthy's special dispensation, were to be retained in the country.

As a *quid pro quo*, the Germans were to issue a declaration stating that:

- As a result of these measures, the Jewish question would be considered solved and the *Sonderkommando* would be recalled.
- All direct contacts by the Germans with the Jewish Council would be severed and no unilateral deportations like those of Kistarcsa and Sárvár would be undertaken.
- Direct negotiations with Jews relating to various emigration schemes not involving the Hungarian authorities would be discontinued.[129]
- The emigration of the specified Jews covered by the initiatives taken by the International Red Cross, the Swedish Red Cross, and the Swiss government would be permitted.
- The deported Jews would remain alive.
- The property of the deported Jews would be recognized as part of the Hungarian national wealth.

In addition to the position paper, the Ministry of Foreign Affairs prepared the draft letters for submission to the Germans. According to these drafts, "the Jewish labor force needed for the German war effort" was to be placed at the disposal of the Germans beginning on August 28.[130]

In the meantime, the German-Hungarian discussions on the possible resumption of the deportations were continuing at the diplomatic level within the framework of the Ferenczy scheme. Twice postponed, the deportation of the Jews of Budapest was rescheduled for August 25.[131] Shortly after the governmental reorganization of August 7, Sztójay assured Veesenmayer that the deportations would be resumed "within eight to 14 days." A similar promise was made by Bonczos to Eichmann on August 13. The August 25 date was selected on the basis that by then the exit visas for the Swiss and Swedish groups would be available.

Excluded from the deportation would be all Jews with foreign citizenship (they were to be interned on August 26) and about 3,000 "exempted" Jews in whom Horthy had shown a special interest.[132]

Even those Jewish leaders aware of the secret understanding with Ferenczy again feared imminent disaster when Pető, upon his release from jail, was ordered to prepare a list of the leaders, officials, and employees of the Council, and to submit it to the Eichmann-*Sonderkommando* headquarters on the Svábhegy. To stall for time, the Council prepared such a list, containing over 1,000 names, but did not include anyone's address. A request for the missing information was not received until the day before the scheduled deportation.

The *Sonderkommando* in Hungary seems to have been in a vengeful mood. Practically everywhere else in Nazi-dominated Europe, including the Hungarian provinces, the SS tried to gain cooperation from Council members. They would be among the last to be taken into the ghetto, and were usually deported with the last transport. In Budapest, however, the Jewish leaders had continuously tried to strengthen their ties to Hungarian political, military, and governmental leaders in hopes of keeping their community alive until the end of the war. Specifically, their objective was to enlist the Hungarian authorities' aid to prevent the deportation of the remaining Jews. The SS recognized the increasing influence of the Jewish leaders, as reflected in Horthy's decision to halt the deportations and in the Kistarcsa incident. It therefore concluded that in Budapest, the successful deportation of the Jews required the prior elimination of the Jewish leadership.

Some of the details of the Germans' plans were revealed by Ferenczy when he met with Pető and Wilhelm on August 24. He confirmed that the SS had decided to give priority to the deportation of the Council members and their families and gave them other details of the planned operation, including the order in which the districts were to be evacuated and where the camps surrounding Budapest, from which the deportations were to take place, would be established. The entire process was scheduled to be completed by September 18.[133]

The Jewish Council leaders became extremely apprehensive. While they recognized that Ferenczy had legitimate reasons to collaborate with them, they were not absolutely convinced, given his prior record, that he would carry out his commitment. They were also plagued by the nightmarish feeling that Ferenczy might in fact be an *agent provocateur* working for the SS in a bizarre plot to doublecross Horthy and his allies. Their great apprehension was paralleled by the frustration and anger of those other leaders of Jewry who were not privy to the secret arrangements and by the panic of the Jewish masses, which grew day by day as the deportation deadline approached.[134] Accordingly, the Jewish Council leaders decided to take all possible precautionary measures in addition to the scheme worked out with Ferenczy. They pleaded with their friends among the Hungarian officialdom and the representatives of the neutral countries and of the Vatican to intercede against the resumption of the deportations. The latter obliged. An unusually blunt note, signed by Apostolic Nuncio Angelo Rotta, Minister of Sweden Carl Ivan Danielsson, representative of Portugal Carlos de Liz-Texeira Branquinho, representative of Spain Angel Sanz-Briz, and representative of Switzerland Antoine J. Kilchmann, was sent to the Hungarian government. It emphasized that the world was aware of the realities behind the deportations, euphemistically referred to by the Hungarians as "supplying labor for Germany." Dated August 21, it read as follows:

The undersigned representatives of the neutral powers accredited to Budapest have learned with painful surprise that the deportation of all the Jews of Hungary is to be started soon. We also know, and from an absolutely reliable source, what deportation means in most cases, even when it is masked as labor service abroad.

Aside from the sad fact that the new deportations in your country will deal a death blow to the reputation of your country, which is already seriously damaged by the deportations effectuated so far, the representatives of the neutral powers, motivated by feelings of human solidarity and Christian love, feel duty-bound to lodge a strong protest against the unjustly motivated and inhumanely implemented process, as it is absolutely impermissible that people should be persecuted and sent to their death simply for their racial origin. We demand that the Royal Hungarian Government put a definitive end to this process, which for the honor of humanity should not have been permitted in the first place. We express the hope that Hungary, pursuing its ancient traditions, will return to the chivalrous and deeply Christian principles and methods that have secured it such a high place among the civilized nations.[135]

The anxiety of the Jews was heightened by plans for the relocation of the "protected" Jews into special Yellow-Star houses on Pozsonyi Road with the concurrent transfer of the "unprotected" occupants to the apartments thus vacated. This exchange was viewed as still another ominous sign of the impending disaster. The relocation issue became the source of a vehement dispute among the Council members. One of the leaders who was particularly upset about the selection of the buildings on Pozsonyi Road was Lajos Stöckler. Emerging as the champion of the "unprotected" Jews, Stöckler thought it would be a great injustice to the inhabitants of the affected houses, who had been assigned there just a few weeks earlier, to be relocated once again for the benefit of a relatively small number of newly privileged Jews, many of whom had good personal relations with leading members of the Council.

Heeding Ferenczy's warning, however, the Jewish Council proceeded with its relocation plans. According to its resolution of August 23, overall responsibility for the relocation was entrusted to Jenő Bleier. He was to be assisted by Ernő Szalkai and Vilmos Vasadi, who would act as liaison men with the Swedish Legation. Overall administrative responsibility for the "protected houses" on Pozsonyi Road was entrusted to György Bognár. Only Jews in possession of the Council's relocation certificate and of the Protective Pass (Schutzpass) issued by the Swedish Legation were to be permitted entry into the selected houses.[136]

In the meantime, the German-Hungarian discussions relating to the planned deportations of the Jews of Budapest were continuing in the midst of mutual suspicion. While the Germans, in accordance with the Führer's directive, insisted that the bulk of Budapest Jews be deported before they would issue exit visas for the few thousand Jews on the Swiss and Swedish lists (or at least that both operations occur simultaneously), the Hungarians were eager to ensure the emigration of these few thousand Jews in order to acquire some international good will, but wanted to stall on the issue of mass deportations. One of the reasons that Hungary resolutely refused to start the deportations as scheduled on August 25 was that Romania had extricated itself from the Axis Alliance only two days earlier. Indeed, Hungary's historical enemy had not merely asked for an armistice, but had actually joined the Allied powers and had shortly thereafter declared war on both Germany and Hungary.

Horthy had a lengthy talk with Veesenmayer on August 24 during which he pointed out that he had often warned the Führer about the unreliability of the Romanians. He also discussed with him the possibility of a governmental reorganization.[137] With respect to the Jews of Budapest, the Regent told him that he would "shortly" have them transferred from the capital to the interior, but that his conscience forbade him to allow their deportation to Germany. The message from the other spokesmen of the Hungarian government was the same. The Ministry of Foreign Affairs apparently informed all its representatives abroad that "there will be no more deportations."[138] Bonczos informed Eichmann on August 24 that in accord with Horthy's instructions and "in contrast to his earlier position" the Jews of Budapest would be transferred from the capital into five large camps yet to be built somewhere outside the city, but would not be deported to Germany. Eichmann, obviously shocked, requested the RSHA to recall the Sonderkommando, as it had become superfluous.[139]

Himmler's response was a telegram addressed to Otto Winkelmann, the Higher SS and Police Leader in Hungary—it was delivered at 3:00 A.M. on August 24—by which further deportations from Hungary were forbidden.[140] Following Romania's change of sides, the *Reichsführer*-SS had become especially eager not to offend the Hungarians and, despite Hitler's more intense ideological position on the Jewish question, had decided to safeguard Hungary's alliance in the Axis camp even at the expense of a partial failure of the Final Solution program. Himmler's decision did not, of course, denote a fundamental change in his attitude toward the Jews; it merely reflected a tactical retreat, based upon military considerations, with the aim of safeguarding the position of German troops in Romania and elsewhere in the Balkans by assuring that their supply lines and avenue of escape via Hungary were not cut off. The Final Solution program was to be resumed after the expected stabilization of the military situation.

The decision of the Hungarian government to prevent the further deportation of the Jews was officially communicated to Veesenmayer on August 25 by Lajos Reményi-Schneller, who had been serving as Acting Prime Minister.[141] At practically the same time, Ferenczy was given almost exclusive jurisdiction over the handling of the Jewish question in Hungary. He so informed the Jewish Council in a note dated August 28, emphasizing that from that date forward no other representative of any Hungarian or "allied" (i.e., German) organ or organization could negotiate with the Council or issue orders or instructions to it. These functions were thenceforth to be carried out exclusively by him as the representative of the Ministry of the Interior.[142] The following day Bonczos notified all the prefects and requested that they cooperate fully with Ferenczy in the implementation of his duties.[143] The actions of Reményi-Schneller, Ferenczy, and Bonczos were already a clear reflection of the spirit and policies of the new government Horthy was about to formally appoint.

The Lakatos Government

When he had consented to the establishment of the Sztójay government in March 1944, Horthy presumably believed that its members, although ultra-reactionary and pro-Axis in their ideological orientation, would pursue policies that would advance the national interests of Hungary as he understood them. Under the control and direction of the openly pro-Nazi elements, however, the government very quickly became a servile tool of the Germans, who consequently exercised *de facto* sovereignty during the first months of the occupation. To a large extent this was also due to Horthy's failure to exercise his powers and exert his leadership; he conveniently decided to abstain from "involvement in certain questionable acts." The disastrous consequences of his abstentions and his government's servile policies became clearly visible by June. Undoubtedly Horthy's awareness of his country's deplorable condition was also advanced by the spectacular successes of the Allies on both the western and eastern fronts.

Around the middle of June Horthy, convinced that for all practical purposes the Axis had already lost the war, began to toy more seriously than ever before with the idea of changing the government and thereby assuring a new course for the country's policies. His resolution to act on the matter was reinforced by a lengthy memorandum he received later that month from his trusted adviser, Count István Bethlen. Bethlen reviewed the disastrous policies pursued by the Sztójay government, often on the initiative of Imrédy, Jaross, Reményi-Schneller, Kunder, or Endre. He suggested that the government be replaced and that "conscientious and strong men" should be appointed who would:

- Place "honest and energetic men, irrespective of party politics" into leading positions.
- Liquidate the war "in an honorable manner."
- Put an end to the "inhuman, foolish, cruel persecution of the Jews."

The memorandum also described the difficulties underlying the anticipated transfer of power and the measures required to overcome them. Bethlen went so far as to make concrete suggestions regarding appointees for various positions in the government.[144]

Horthy first intended to replace the Sztójay government early in July, following Baky's coup attempt; he considered it again on July 17. Hitler's stern warnings and the fear of a possible total occupation of the country, however, dissuaded him from carrying out his intentions that month. As a result of Bethlen's realistic counsel, Horthy decided to approach his goal cautiously, by first partially reorganizing the government through the replacement of outspoken pro-Nazi elements—including Imrédy, Jaross, and Kunder (August 17)—and then sending Sztójay on a two-week "medical furlough." The German reaction to these preliminary moves was, unexpectedly, quite subdued. Presumably

Hitler was preoccupied with domestic problems following the unsuccessful attempt on his life on July 20, as well as being increasingly concerned over the constantly deteriorating military situation. By August 29, Horthy decided that the time was propitious for the formal appointment of General Géza Lakatos, the former commander of the First Hungarian Army, as Prime Minister.

In recognition of Hungary's delicate position as a member of the Axis Alliance eager to find an honorable way out of the war, the Lakatos government was a well-balanced one. To pacify the Germans, Horthy retained Reményi-Schneller and Jurcsek; however, to advance his own objectives, he also appointed some new members whose sympathies were clearly anti-Nazi, including Iván Rakovszky and Gusztáv Hennyey.[145]

An immediate and far-reaching consequence of the Lakatos appointment was the purging of many high ministerial officers who had served as supporters or agents of the Nazis, including Baky, Endre, and Mihály Kolosváry-Borcsa. Among the new appointees replacing them were more trusted men like Béla Horváth, Baron Péter Schell, and Endre Hlatky. Schell, a close friend of Lakatos who had for many years been the Prefect of Kassa, became Secretary of State in the Ministry of the Interior;[146] Hlatky, the former Prefect of Bihar County, became Secretary of State for the Press.[147] Of equal if not greater importance was the concomitant replacement of most right-wing municipal and county prefects who had sympathized with or openly supported Imrédy, or the Nyilas, or the Right extremists within the MÉP.

Upon his appointment, Lakatos summarized his program as follows:

- Continuation, as honorable Hungarians, of the struggle in defense of the frontiers.
- Absolute preservation of peace and order.
- Increase of production.[148]

Lakatos' declarations were obviously primarily for foreign, especially German, consumption. The tasks with which he had actually been entrusted by Horthy could not be publicized. They included:

- The reestablishment of Hungarian sovereignty.
- Preparations for Hungary's extrication from the war.
- The immediate cessation of the Jewish persecutions.[149]

With the inauguration of the Lakatos government, the anti-Jewish pressure in Budapest eased. With the removal of Baky and Endre, Jewish matters in the Ministry of the Interior became the responsibility of

Gyula Perlaky, a Ministerial Counselor. In accordance with the policies of the new government, Perlaky arranged to free the Jews being held at Horthyliget[150] as well as the 220 hostages from Kistarcsa.[151] A delegation headed by Lajos Stöckler paid a visit to Gusztáv Hennyey, the new Foreign Minister, requesting that the government find a way to help the deported Jews.[152] Through the cooperation of various Red Cross organizations, Hennyey was instrumental in inducing the Swedish authorities to send parcels to various concentration camps. Although the gifts were stolen by the Germans on arrival, the Jews were grateful: in a statement to Hennyey Stöckler declared that "after a long time, this has been the first benevolent gesture of the Hungarian government toward the Jews, who know how to appreciate it."[153]

Another sign reflecting the new trend in the government's Jewish policy was the decision to permit the Jews greater freedom of movement during the upcoming High Holy Days and in connection with their work.[154]

Lakatos summarized the position of his government on the Jewish question in his inaugural speech of September 21 before a joint session of the Hungarian Parliament:

With regard to the regulation of the Jewish question, we are in the process of implementing a procedure that will assure, through the strict application of legal means, the gradual employment for useful work of the most harmful elements and of the unemployed.[155]

During the debate that followed the inaugural speech the Jewish question was raised by Tibor Koródy, a member of the lower house. Koródy, who had been elected as a *Nyilas* deputy, had changed his position over the summer and maintained close relations with Komoly in an attempt to ease the lot of the Budapest Jews.[156] He startled the lower house by demanding the repeal of the "illegal measures" adopted by the government and a review of the entire Jewish question. The following excerpt from the parliamentary minutes reflects the scope of his statement and its reception:

During the past six months we have seen the adoption of a large number of decrees from which the nation received no benefit. (A voice from the extreme left [the side of the hall where the *Nyilas* were seated]: "But you did!") and whose only aim was to harm others, namely Jewry. (Loud interruptions from the extreme left).

We all know that the innumerable Jewish decrees that were adopted and implemented during these six months brought no improvement in the war situation either. (Continuous noise. The President uses his bell.) On the contrary, they denote the sabotaging of our total effort, for in this country, here in Budapest, during the greatest manpower shortage, there still live 250,000 Jews whose labor force could be exploited; these were compelled during the past six months merely to consume, because in the absence of freedom of movement they could not engage in production. (Noise from the extreme left. Ferenc Rajniss: "Return them to bank directors! That's the wisest thing!" Lajos Csoór: "Surely not that!") To reestablish a balance, immediate repeal is needed of all the above mentioned decrees that were issued without any base in law or legality, and it is absolutely necessary at least to submit them to Parliament for its evaluation. (László Budinszky: "This is destructiveness!" Ferenc Rajniss: "Where is your green shirt?" A voice from the extreme left: "It turned yellow!" Laughter.)

I therefore respectfully request the acceptance of my proposal in order that Parliament may declare whether it agrees with the government's program or not. (A voice from the extreme left: "What do you earn from the Jews?" Noise.)[157] As expected, the lower house rejected Koródy's motion.

The Jewish question took on a new dimension under the agreement between the Germans and the Hungarians at the end of August. Following the Hungarians' resolute intervention to prevent the deportations that had been scheduled for August 25, the Germans reluctantly agreed to yield jurisdiction over the handling of Jewish affairs to the Hungarian authorities, to terminate direct contacts between the *Sicherheitspolizei* and the Jewish Council, and to gradually liquidate the internment camps. The Hungarians, for their part, agreed to the removal of the Jews from Budapest and to their useful employment.[158]

Mobilization for Labor

During the few weeks immediately before and after the formation of the Lakatos government, what remained of the Jewish community was torn between two conflicting feelings: fear that the gendarmes and Ferenczy were in fact acting in collusion with the Germans and that the agreement relating to the concentration of the Jews of Budapest in the countryside was but the prelude to their eventual deportation; hope that in view of the rapidly changing military situation Horthy would stand by his resolution and prevent any further deportations. With the easing of the pressure following the original decision to halt the deportation early in July, the Jewish leaders devoted increasing attention to improving the living conditions of the people they led. With the material and monetary resources of the community almost exhausted, they tried to use the intercession of political, governmental, and church leaders to obtain more freedom of movement for the Jews and above all to obtain permission for the gainful employment of the physically and mentally able Jews. A plea to this effect was included in their lengthy memorandum addressed to the government on July 24.

The military successes of the Allies coupled with the systematic bombing of Budapest provided a propitious climate for the political and church leaders who intervened on the Jews' behalf. Late in July, the Council of Ministers instructed the Ministry of Defense to recruit through the Budapest municipal authorities 2,000 yellow-star-wearing laborers and skilled workers for rubble-clearing operations.[159] Within the Jewish Council, the recruitment and administration of the labor service became the responsibility of the Veteran's Committee (*Hadviseltek Bizottsága*). The recruited Jews received a daily meal and a per diem monetary allowance, and their services were generally equivalent to those rendered in the labor service companies. By the first half of August, the headquarters of the Jewish Council at 12 Síp Street had become an official "labor service recruitment center" operating under the jurisdiction of Section XI of the Ministry of Defense.[160] Toward the end of the month, the rubble-clearing operations became intertwined with the general mobilization of the Jewish labor force for possible use in defense and related projects.

The Germans were, of course, still in pursuit of their ultimate objective relating to the Jewish question, and were becoming increasingly impatient with the lack of movement on the implementation of the agreement to resettle the Budapest Jews. They tried to exploit the issue of Jewish emigration under the Swedish and Swiss schemes as a lever to pressure the Hungarians into beginning the resettlement program. In view of their considerably weakened state by the end of August, however, they were no longer in a position to impose their will. Nevertheless, for tactical reasons, they first insisted on at least a token resettlement of 1,000 Jews.[161] Their tactics apparently aimed at establishing the principle of resettlement *per se;* if their test case proved successful, they expected to follow it up first by mass resettlement into the Hungarian countryside and then with deportation.

The Jewish leaders were aware of the agreement regarding resettlement and of its possible pitfalls. Since they had to take some risks by cooperating with Ferenczy, but at the same time wanted to take precautionary measures, they decided to pay lip service to the agreement by appearing to be busily implementing it. They took full advantage of one of the provisions, which called for the establishment of camps that were to be up to "European standards." (They had the full cooperation of the Ministry of Defense, which had been the source of rescue for many thousands of Jews during the deportations from the provinces.) They consequently decided to work toward the assignment at first of only a small number of Jewish units to build the concentration camps. The members of these units were to be selected on the same basis as those of the rubble-clearing detachments. The concentration of the Budapest Jews was to be initiated only after the completion of the camps and their verification by the Red Cross as being up to "European standards."

The first authoritative news about the nature and dimension of the Jews' mobilization for labor was published on September 7. The newspapers emphasized the difficult position of Hungary and the intolerable situation under which thousands of Jews had been living for months without work or income, while the country was suffering from an acute shortage of labor. They reported that henceforth all Jews between the ages of 14 and 70, irrespective of sex or exemption status, would be employed "for defense work within the country" after undergoing an examination of their fitness.[162]

The following day, the newspapers gave additional details about the recruitment procedures. Special examination commissions were to evaluate the Jews and assign them to various defense work projects in accordance with their skills. Those selected for labor were to receive the remuneration normally accruing to labor servicemen. Those unfit for defense work were to be concentrated in camps in the countryside under the supervision of the Red Cross and possibly employed in local enterprises requiring no special skills. Skilled workers were expected to be employed in defense-related industries and to be housed in Yellow-Star buildings. Unemployable Jews, including children and the aged, were to be housed under the supervision of the Red Cross.[163]

Supervision over the organization and implementation of the plan for the Jews' mobilization for labor was entrusted to Colonel János Heinrich of the Ministry of Defense. This very decent and well-meaning officer, who was under the command of Major-General Ernő Horny,[164] worked in close collaboration with Captain Ede Gobbi. The latter worked out the details of the mobilization program, including the specification of the recruitment center's activities. The medical evaluation of the labor recruits was the responsibility of Dr. József Doby, a military physician. The Jewish Council was represented on the recruitment board by Ferenc Schalk, who did everything in his power to drag out the recruitment proceedings.

The registration of all Jews born between 1874 and 1930 was to be the responsibility of the air-raid wardens. It was also their responsibility to take the registered Jews under their jurisdiction to the recruitment stations and to present them to the recruiting officers along with lists they had prepared. The following categories of Jews were not required to serve:

- Exempted military personnel.
- War invalids (at least 50 percent invalidated).
- Retired military personnel.
- Persons with foreign citizenship.
- Self-employed artisans working for defense industries.
- Members of the Rubble-Clearing Organization (*Romeltakarító Szervezet*).
- The members and employees of the Jewish Council and of the Association of the Christian Jews of Hungary.
- Workers in the service of the Demographic Statistical Office (*Népmozgalmi Nyilvántartó Hivatal*).
- Workers employed by various state agencies, including the railways.
- Workers employed by the Germans if supplied with certificates from Wilhelm Neyer of the *Todt* Organization.
- Workers employed in war industries.
- Persons performing religious functions.
- Engineers, pharmacists, physicians, veterinarians, rabbis, teachers, and professors.
- Persons exempted by the Governor.[165]

Concurrently with the mobilization activities under the jurisdiction of Colonel Heinrich, an intensive campaign for the "successful" implementation of the concentration program was being pursued by Ferenczy. He showed his special eagerness to fulfill the Hungarian commitment to the Germans by pressing the initiation of the concentration of those under 14 and over 70 in camps outside of Budapest. These were to be followed by the "unemployable" Jews of working age. He suggested an abandoned estate near Tura, northeast of Budapest, as a possible area of concentration for the first few thousand Jews from Budapest. Ferenczy's zealousness induced the Jewish leaders to do everything in their power to delay and possibly prevent the concentration of the Jews, rightfully fearing that once concentrated the Jews would become an easier prey for deportation. Since the Hungarian declarations relating to the German-Hungarian agreement stipulated that an important role would be played by the Hungarian Red Cross, the Jewish leaders decided to approach Dr. Lajos Langman, the chief physician of the organization, to make sure he understood the background and possible implications of the concentration and to propose specific recommendations for its delay or avoidance. Their memorandum read as follows:

The idea of placing the unemployable Jews into provincial camps in connection with the mobilization of Budapest's Jewry for labor has a long historical antecedent. Originally, following the entry of German troops, the Hungarian government agreed with the Germans that the solution of the Jewish question would fall under German jurisdiction. It was on this basis that the Hungarian and German authorities effectuated the deportation of the provincial Jews. After that only the Jews of Budapest remained, and systematic deportation was therefore halted on July 10, and deportations thereafter took place only occasionally, without the knowledge or permission of the Hungarian authorities, and in fact against their will. Thus, at the end of July 1,400 people were taken from Kistarcsa, and early in August 1,500 people from Sárvár by the Germans, who appeared suddenly, surrounded the camps with their forces, cut telephone lines and, notwithstanding the protestations of the camp commanders, placed the prisoners into prepared freight-cars and took them immediately out of the country.

Following protests and pressures by leading domestic personalities and by the whole outside world, the Hungarian government reached another agreement with the Germans toward the end of August under which the Jewish question was placed under the jurisdiction of the Hungarian government. In this connection the government, interested in utilizing the Jewish labor force to the country's advantage, undertook to remove the Jews from Budapest and place them in the provincial camps.

On September 3, Lieutenant-Colonel Ferenczy informed us officially that the mobilization for labor would take place, but that the concentration in the provinces would not. On the fourth, he instructed us that the recruitment would begin, but on the fifth he stated that the unemployable persons would be transferred into provincial camps after all and that the recruitment would begin on the seventh. The recruitment has been going on ever since. On the basis of the well-known communiqué, the Hungarian Red Cross is also involved in the concentration. As the communiqué reveals, the role of the Red Cross revolves around the establishment of the provincial camps. It is also the responsibility of the Red Cross to "care for, supervise, feed, and provide health services to" children under working age. One may thus conclude that the Red Cross will play a decisive role in (1) the selection of campsites; (2) the supply and furnishing of the camps; (3) the accommodation of those transferred there; (4) the feeding of the inmates; (5) the provision of health services; and (6) general social welfare services.

Inasmuch as the entire operation was undertaken under increasing German pressure and presumably not in accordance with the preferences of the Hungarian government or the interest of all Hungarians, it would be desirable to be thorough in its implementation and thereby assure the concurrent delay of camp construction. In this connection, the activities of the Red Cross offer many opportunities.

Referring to the points above,

(1) The sites must be selected so that they are located in larger provincial centers in order to avoid a possible repetition of a Kistarcsa-type event;

(2) The camps must satisfy all humane and hygenic requirements, including the availability of sufficient drinking water, satisfactory kitchens, and adequate sanitary facilities. If these facilities are not available then work toward their establishment should be performed at the selected sites whatever the length of time required;

(3) At the time of the relocation emphasis must be placed on the avoidance of overcrowding and of the breakup of families;

(4) One of the most important tasks of the Red Cross involves the food supply; it can help improve the lot of the "resettled Jews" through the organization and effective operation of a supply system that would permit the Jews to acquire food supplies themselves;

(5) Health services could be provided by the physicians transferred to the camps, with the Red Cross merely providing general supervision. Hospitals and suitable health-related equipment are absolutely essential;

(6) With reference to social services we are thinking primarily about the employment of the resettled Jews, i.e., about providing employment for every person in accordance with his work capacity. Related to this are the supervision of the working period and provisions to ensure that children, the sick, and the aged shall not work beyond their physical capacity and at the expense of their health. Also related to this are visiting rules and the establishment of mail service between the camps as well as between workers and their families.[166]

In addition to the Red Cross, the Jewish leaders also got in touch with many political, church, and governmental leaders, including Horthy.[167] Through the intermediation of Miklós Mester and Gyula Ambrózy, Samu Stern paid Horthy another visit, incognito, around the middle of September to warn him of the great danger that the concentration of the Jews would present. He pointed out that once the Jews were concentrated, the Hungarian government, "with all its good will," might not be able to prevent their deportation. It was also possible, he argued, that the Germans might bomb the camps using disguised aircraft markings as they had done in Kassa in June 1941.[168] The arguments advanced by Stern must have made an impact upon the Governor, for the head of the Jewish Council left with assurances that there would be no more deportations or concentrations.[169]

In the meantime, the Germans became increasingly annoyed with the obvious procrastination of the Hungarian government and pressed on relentlessly with their demand for the total evacuation of the Jews from Budapest. In a telegram to the German Foreign Office on September 15, Veesenmayer complained not only about the failure of the government to carry out its commitments, but also about the activities of the representatives of neutral countries in behalf of the Jews.[170]

The Germans continued to rely on Ferenczy for information. While dealing with Horthy and the Jewish leaders (with whom he opportunistically displayed an ostensibly fierce anti-German position) Ferenczy was in fact in close contact with the Germans. In a memorandum of September 26, Theodor Horst Grell, the expert on Jewish affairs in the German Legation, emphasized Ferenczy's assurance that the Jewish leaders themselves were now ready to cooperate in the removal of the Jews from Budapest because otherwise, they feared, their problem might be "solved" by the Germans following the return of the Eichmann-*Sonderkommando*.[171] Ferenczy also assured Grell that he was committed to the relocation of the Jews and demanded "symbolic German support" for his efforts.[172]

In another secret memorandum, dated September 28, Grell was even more optimistic about the final outcome, having been told by Ferenczy that a new drive was planned against the Jews of Budapest in which 14 so-called "flying commissions" (*fliegende Kommissionen*), each able to seize between 400 and 500 Jews a day, would systematically search every house. The first transport of around 5,000 Jews was expected to depart within four to five days. An addendum to the memorandum listed the assembly centers in Budapest as well as the "evacuation centers"—i.e., concentration camps—in the provinces.

According to the memo, the Jews of Budapest were to be assembled at eight strategic locations and removed shortly thereafter to camps located near Alsónémedi, Gálpuszta, Maglód, Üllő, Dunaharaszti, and Tura.[173] Grell assured his superiors that the operation had in fact already begun that very day with the removal of an unspecified number of Jews by truck. He envisioned the daily removal of between 250 and 350 Jews.[174] Reporting on still another meeting with Ferenczy on September 30, Grell appeared somewhat more pessimistic. He requested guidance because he felt that Ferenczy was using an excuse to postpone the promised deportations. Grell must have misinterpreted Ferenczy's intentions, which were basically identical with his own. While at first Ferenczy had indeed complained that he was unable to begin the relocation of the Jews of Budapest because the camp at Tura had been taken over by a *Wehrmacht* unit, a week later, on October 7, he suggested that the Jews be instead placed in a ghetto similar to that of Warsaw.[175]

Grell's various memoranda were submitted to the German Foreign Office by Veesenmayer on October 10, with a cover letter in which he complained that in spite of the various assurances given by the Hungarian authorities "not one single district has been properly cleared of Jews." He noted that at least a beginning could have been made in the evacuation of Jews from Budapest "if more energy and fewer humanitarian considerations . . . had prevailed." Veesenmayer suggested that the German attitude be changed and that new measures be initiated "in order to carry out the evacuation of the remaining Jews from Hungary or Budapest either through German forces themselves or through pressure on the Hungarian government."[176] Relaying Veesenmayer's messages to Ribbentrop, Horst Wagner, the head of *Inland II,* attributed the Hungarians' reluctance to carry out the anti-Jewish program to their desire "to establish an alibi . . . for future eventualities." Wagner presumed that the solution of the Jewish question in Hungary required the involvement of SS troops and inquired whether Himmler should not be consulted in this matter.[177]

The Germans' annoyance and frustrations over the failure to complete the Final Solution program were matched by their anger over the Hungarians' almost overt attempts to extricate themselves from the war. They were fully informed about all the discussions under the chairmanship of the Regent[178] and of all the decisions of the Council of Ministers in this respect. The Hungarians began to consider the idea of cutting their losses in the middle of the summer, when they became fully convinced that the Axis had lost the war. The drive acquired special momentum after the Romanians, acting more discreetly and more resolutely, anticipated the Hungarians with their dramatic move of August 23. This added a new and unexpected dimension to the problem, for the Hungarians now had to be concerned not only with their possible extrication from the war but also with the fate of Transylvania. These two concerns were among the most difficult problems confronting the new Lakatos government.

Owing to German pressure and to the desire to advance its national security interests (including at least the retention of Northern Transylvania, if not the reacquisition of the rest) Hungary decided early in September to move into Southern Transylvania. It was a desperate attempt, doomed to failure. The ill-equipped Hungarian forces were no match for the combined Soviet-Romanian troops, who were not only well supplied with armor and other equipment but were also enjoying the momentum of a long string of victories.

During their brief occupation of some parts of Southern Transylvania some Hungarian units, led by ultra-rightist officers, engaged in anti-Jewish excesses reminiscent of the barbarities of the Iron Guard era. Their brutality was particularly evident at Sármás, which was occupied by Hungarian troops on September 5. Three days later the local Jews were required to post a yellow star on their front doors. On September 9 a group of local anti-Semites meeting in the home of Iuliu (Gyula) and Ecaterina (Katalin) Varga, the town's pharmacist, decided to eliminate the Jewish community. The town's 126 Jews were first concentrated in the barns of Ion Pop, where they were held for about eight days; during this time, their homes were assigned to non-Jews by Alexandru (Sándor) Szallay, the town's Mayor. On the night of September 16–17 the Jews were taken to the nearby Suscut Hill, where they were massacred by a gendarmerie unit from Zilah under the immediate command of Captain László Lancz.[179]

Threatened by the approaching Red Army, and with Budapest and other strategic Hungarian cities under almost constant bombardment, the Hungarian government spent virtually the entire Lakatos era "finding an honorable way out of the war." The Germans, who were fully aware of all the supposedly secret moves, made all necessary preparations not only to forestall the "stab in the back" but also to replace the Lakatos government by an exclusively *Nyilas* one. The ill-fated attempt by Horthy for a *volte-face* on October 15, which was as naïve politically as it was unprepared militarily (Horthy, out of a misplaced sense of honor, told Veesenmayer of his intentions without taking any viable military contingency measures), put an end to an important chapter in Hungarian history. It not only brought about the downfall of the Lakatos regime[180] and the abandonment of Hungary's traditional social and political system, but it also began a new tragic chapter in the history of Hungarian Jewry.[181]

Notes

1. *Horthy Miklós titkos iratai* (The Confidential Papers of Miklós Horthy), eds. Miklós Szinai and László Szücs (Budapest: Kossuth, 1963), p. 450.

2. Prime Minister Sztójay also served as the *de jure* Foreign Minister. However, Arnóthy-Jungerth acted as the *de facto* Minister, having received a free hand in the operation of the Ministry of Foreign Affairs.

3. Lévai, *Zsidósors Magyarországon*, p. 213.

4. For the complete text of the letter, see *Horthy Miklós titkos iratai*, pp. 454–56.

5. Lévai, *Zsidósors Magyarországon*, p. 214.

6. *Horthy Miklós titkos iratai*, pp. 444–49. The document was found, without identification, in the offices of the Regent's Cabinet Bureau.

7. *Ibid.*, pp. 450–54.

8. *RLB*, Doc. 180.

9. For the text of Arnóthy-Jungerth's statement see, Jenő Lévai, *Fehér könyv. Külföldi akciók zsidók megmentésére* (White Book. Foreign Campaigns for the Rescuing of Jews) (Budapest: Officina, 1946), pp. 48–49. In his *Zsidósors Magyarországon* (p. 214), Lévai identifies the meeting of June 21 as having taken place on June 19 and that of June 23 as having taken place on June 21.

10. Lévai, *Fehér könyv*, pp. 50–51.

11. Munkácsi, *Hogyan történt?*, p. 164. See also Elek Karsai, *Itél a nép* (The People Judge) (Budapest: Kossuth, 1977), pp. 204–8.

12. Lévai, *Zsidósors Magyarországon*, p. 214.

13. These statistical data are in error. The number of those deported from the territories of the Army Corps cited in the text was around 362,000. The total number of Jews deported from Hungary until July 9, when the deportations were halted, was a little under 440,000. For a review of the figures relating to ghettoization and deportation, see table 19.1.

14. There is no evidence that a partisan group ever intervened to block either the ghettoization or deportation process. Endre probably twisted the incident that took place in Sátoraljaújhely, where a number of distraught Jews refused to enter the freight cars and laid down on the tracks. They were all shot by the gendarmes in charge of the entrainment. Lévai, *Zsidósors Magyarországon*, p. 142.

15. This reference in Endre's statement is probably due to pressures in this connection from the Hungarian Red Cross (*Magyar Vöröskereszt*), which, on June 20, 1944, applied to Prime Minister Sztójay for permission to set up refreshment and first aid stations at the major railway hubs along the deportation routes. The letter, signed by Elemér Simon, the national head of the Hungarian Red Cross, and Mrs. István Horthy, the Governor's daughter-in-law in her capacity as the chief volunteer nurse of Pest-Pilis-Solt-Kiskun County, stated that the Association of the Jews of Hungary did not have sufficient means to set up such facilities and that the International Red Cross Committee might one day question the Hungarian Red Cross about whether it had done everything possible to help the suffering human beings applying for such help. The application was supported by the Hungarian Ministry of Foreign Affairs, but by the time the Prime Minister's Office forwarded the request to the Foreign Ministry on July 14, the deportation of the provincial Jews had already been completed. *Vádirat*, 3:186–88.

16. Lévai, *Zsidósors Magyarországon*, pp. 214–18.

17. Munkácsi, *Hogyan történt?*, p. 164.

18. Lévai, *Fehér könyv*, pp. 52–53.

19. Zöldi fled Hungary on January 15, 1944, after he had been condemned to 11 years' imprisonment for his role in the Délvidék massacres. He returned to Hungary with the German occupants as a member of the Waffen SS. See chapter 6.

20. During their trials in 1946, Jaross and Sztójay gave conflicting versions of the Council's decision of June 23. Sztójay claimed the Council decided to end further deportations and permit the emigration of Jews to neutral countries, whereas Jaross claimed that while Sztójay expressed an opposition to further deportations at that meeting, no decision was then taken to terminate them. Munkácsi, *Hogyan történt?*, pp. 166–67. See also Lévai, *Zsidósors Magyarországon*, pp. 219–21.

21. Statement by Ernő Pető in *HJS*, 3:54–56.

22. Count Esterházy prepared a number of memoranda on the Jewish persecutions and personally submitted them to Horthy. He was also influential in inducing the Nuncio, who lived on an estate at Csákvár, to mobilize the representatives of the neutral countries to exert pressure on Horthy and the Hungarian government and to inform their own governments and the world about the persecutions in Hungary. Munkácsi, *Hogyan történt?*, pp. 171–72.

23. *Horthy Miklós titkos iratai*, p. 460.

24. For example, see the following articles: Georges Rigassi, "Les Juifs persécutés" (The Persecuted Jews), *Gazette de Lausanne* (Journal of Lausanne), July 8, 1944; "Darf man schweigen?" (Can One Remain Silent?), *Neue Zürcher Nachrichten* (News of Zurich), July 5, 1944; "Die Ritter" (The Knights), *St. Gallener Tagblatt* (St. Gallen Daily), July 20, 1944.

25. On the attitude of the USA and the other members of the Grand Alliance toward the persecution of Hungarian Jewry, see chapter 31.

26. *Vádirat*, 3:3–6.

27. Lévai, *Zsidósors Magyarországon*, p. 221.

28. Lévai, *Eichmann in Hungary* (Budapest: Pannonia Press, 1961), p. 119. See also Lévai's *Fehér könyv*, pp. 54–55. On June 27, one day after Sztójay's telegram was sent, the Radio Monitoring Service of the Hungarian Telegraphic Agency (*A Magyar Távirati Iroda Rádiófigyelő Szolgálata*) reported that a group of former Hungarian ministers abroad had made a joint declaration condemning the measures being taken against the Jews and other opponents of Nazism. The declaration, which was read in the Hungarian-language broadcast of the Voice of America of July 17, was sponsored by György Barcza, Baron György Bakács-Bessenyei, Count Gábor Apor, Antal Ullein-Reviczky, Ferenc Ambró, György Szabó, Andor Wodianer, and László Velics, the pre-occupation Hungarian ministers to London, Berne, the Vatican, Stockholm, Madrid, Helsinki, Lisbon, and Athens. The declaration was also sponsored by I. Bogdán, a Counselor of the Hungarian Legation in Athens. For text of the declaration, see *Vádirat*, 3:270.

29. Whereas Veesenmayer had rejected the suggestion of Paul Karl Schmidt, the Chief of the Information and Press Division of the German Foreign Office, to provide "external causes and reasons" for the deportations as unnecessary (chapter 19) in early June, by the middle of July he too was ready to "explain" the deportations in order to counteract the "vicious propaganda directed against Hungary." Like Sztójay, Veesenmayer also planned to explain that the "surplus labor" created by the anti-Jewish measures in Hungary was being shipped to Germany on the basis of an "agreement." Veesenmayer's planned communiqué would have explained how well supplied the Jews were and how humanely they were treated during their transportation to Germany. Ribbentrop, however, vetoed the publication of any communiqués at all on this matter. *RLB*, Docs. 200 and 202.

30. Lévai, *Fehér könyv*, pp. 56–71. This negative position on the War Refugee Board offer was subsequently altered. In his July 18 communication to Hungary's representatives abroad, Sztójay claimed that the Hungarian government had authorized the International Red Cross to enact some of the proposals advanced by the Board, including the sending of children under 10 years of age to Palestine. For further details, see below and chapter 31.

31. Lévai, *Zsidósors Magyarországon*, pp. 222–24; *Vádirat*, 3:199–204. Veesenmayer relayed the communication to the German Foreign Office on June 29. For the reaction of the German Foreign Office and of the *Führer*, see below. For further details on Horthy's decision to halt the deportations, see below; on the Swedish and Swiss offers, see chapter 31.

32. *Vádirat*, 3:5. Endre stated that after his removal, the handling of the Jewish question was entrusted to László Szilágyi, a ministerial counselor in the Ministry of the Interior. See Endre's statement of December 17, 1945, in connection with the trials in Kolozs-

vár of László Gyapai, László Vásárhelyi, and László Csóka, the mayors of Nagyvárad, Kolozsvár, and Szatmárnémeti. The original of the statement is in this author's possession. Other sources, however, claim that the handling of the Jewish question after Endre's removal was entrusted to Gyula Perlaky, another ministerial counselor in the Ministry of the Interior. For further details, see below.

33. Following the ouster of the Lakatos government and the overthrow of Horthy on October 15, 1944, both secretaries returned to power under the auspices of the new Szálasi regime. See chapter 26.

34. *RLB*, Doc. 183.

35. *Ibid.*, Docs. 187–88.

36. Ferenczy's statement to police authorities after the war. Faraghó denied having attended the meeting, claiming that he never dealt with either Eichmann or Endre on the deportation of the Jews. Concerning Faraghó's actual involvement in the plot see C. A. Macartney, 2:304.

37. While Munkácsi (*Hogyan történt?*, p. 177) places these events on July 5–6, Lévai claims (*Zsidósors Magyarországon*, p. 228) that they took place on July 7 and 8.

38. Munkácsi, *Hogyan történt?*, pp. 175–79; Lévai, *Zsidósors Magyarországon*, pp. 227–30; *Mementó. Magyarország 1944* (Memento. Hungary, 1944), eds. Ödön Gáti et al. (Budapest: Kossuth, 1975), pp. 63–65.

39. György Ránki, *1944. március 19* (March 19, 1944). 2nd. ed. (Budapest: Kossuth, 1978), p. 273.

40. *Vádirat*, 3:63–64.

41. *RLB*, Doc. 192. Veesenmayer assured Jaross that there were no plans to deploy additional SS troops to Hungary, since the deportation of the Jews of Budapest was the responsibility of the Hungarians themselves.

42. *Ibid.*, Doc. 166. The timing was corroborated by Veesenmayer in a telegram of June 13 in which he gave a detailed accounting of the deportations until that time. *Ibid.*, Doc. 174.

43. *Ibid.*, Docs. 168–69.

44. *Ibid.*, Doc. 171.

45. *Ibid.*, Docs. 172–73. For further details, see chapter 19.

46. *Ibid.*, Doc. 186.

47. The more lenient treatment of the Jews in these countries became the subject of an intensive diplomatic campaign in the summer of 1944. *Ibid.*, Docs. 194, 196–197. See also chapter 28.

48. For details on the deal between the SS and the Weiss-Manfréd Works, see chapter 16.

49. *RLB*, Doc. 187.

50. Memorandum by Winkelmann dated July 7, 1944. *Ibid.*, Doc. 188.

51. *Ibid.*, Docs. 190–91.

52. *Ibid.*, Docs. 324–26.

53. The Grand Mufti of Jerusalem had requested the Hungarian government on June 22, 1944, to prevent the emigration of Jews to Palestine. On July 14, the Hungarians assured the Mufti via Sándor Hoffmann, the Hungarian Minister in Berlin, that they would carefully consider the request. *Vádirat*, 3:159.

54. *Ibid.*, pp. 158–60.

55. *Ibid.*, pp. 189–90.

56. *Ibid.*, pp. 197–204.

57. Lévai, *Zsidósors Magyarországon*, pp. 233–34.

58. For information on Bethlen's memorandum to Horthy submitted at the end of June, see below.

59. *The Confidential Papers of Admiral Horthy*, pp. 316–19.

60. *RLB*, Docs. 198–99.

61. Miklós was received by Hitler on July 21, the day after the dictator escaped an assassination attempt. According to Horthy, the General informed the Germans that "if Hungary was not given the aid that had been promised her, she would have to withdraw from the war." Horthy, *Memoirs*, p. 222.

62. *NA*, Microcopy T-120, Roll 4203, Frames K209133-134.

63. *RLB*, Docs. 200 and 202.

64. See Schulenburg's telegram of July 27. *Ibid.*, Doc. 203. For details on the *Jägerstab* Project, see chapter 11.

65. *Ibid.*, Doc. 204.

66. In their memorandum of July 24, the Jewish leaders outlined the desperate physical and psychological state of the Jews of Budapest following the deportation of the Jews from the provinces. They also mentioned the desirability of allowing the able-bodied Jews to work to the benefit of the community and the country, and pointed out that they were ready to emigrate if this would avert the danger of deportation. For text see Munkácsi, *Hogyan történt?*, pp. 203–6.

67. *Vádirat*, 3:329–30.

68. *Budapesti Közlöny*, no. 178, August 8, 1944, p. 1. The Germans were, of course, fully informed about the impending governmental changes. Veesenmayer was particularly eager to retain Imrédy in the government. See Kaltenbrunner' note of August 4, 1944, addressed to Ribbentrop. *NA*, Microcopy T-120, Roll 4203, Frames K209118-120.

69. Lévai, *Zsidósors Magyarországon*, p. 236; Munkácsi, *Hogyan történt?*, p. 189.

70. For example, the technicians and physicians of the X-ray department of the Jewish Hospital at Szabolcs Street in Budapest were accused of hiding a radio transmitter among their equipment, and a number of engineers and officials at the General Hungarian Hard Coal Mines (*Magyar Általános Kőszénbánya*—MÁK) were accused of having engaged in sabotage activities.

71. *RLB*, Doc. 150.

72. Among the camp officials who showed an understanding for the plight of the Jews were Flórián Szemző, the camp administrator, and his assistant Kenyér, as well as the chief detective assigned to the camp, Varga, who was in close touch with Miklós Gál, the MIPI representative, until they were both arrested in June 1944. Béla Jámborfy, Vasdényei's deputy, showed a less understanding attitude.

73. Bródy took over as the MIPI representative at Kistarcsa after the arrest of his predecessor Miklós Gál, who was deported from Sárvár earlier in the summer and never returned.

74. On July 17, 280 of the 1,500 Jews who had been returned to Kistarcsa on July 14 were transferred to the camp at Sárvár.

75. Lévai, *Zsidósors Magyarországon*, pp. 235–39; *Fekete könyv*, pp. 182–85; Munkácsi, *Hogyan történt?*, pp. 194–97; *Mementó. Magyarország 1944*, pp. 62–75; *Vádirat*, 3:422–23; Statement by Imre Reiner, Israel Police, Bureau 06, Eichmann Trial Doc. 347, pp. 23–27.

76. Friedrich Born, *Bericht an das Internationale Komitee vom Roten Kreuz in Genf* (Report to the International Committee of the Red Cross in Geneva) (Geneva, June 1945), p. 28. See also *Notiz über die Situation der Juden in Ungarn* (Note on the Situation of the Jews in Hungary), an International Red Cross document dated November 14, 1944, available in Yad Vashem Archives M-20/47.

77. An exception, of course, was the activity in support of the refugees who had fled to Hungary, and the operations of the *Vaada*. For further details on the attitudes of Hungarian Jewry before and after the German occupation, see chapter 3.

78. For a listing of the Jewish authors purged in the spring of 1944, see Appendix 4. See also *Vádirat*, 1:276–81, and 2:102–5, 195–96, 323–25.

79. See list of anti-Jewish decrees in Appendix 3.

80. *Vádirat*, 3:380–81.

81. *Ibid.*, pp. 447, 449–50, 501, 508–9, 561–62, and 563.

82. *Ibid.*, pp. 446–47.

83. *Magyarországi Zsidók Lapja*, 6, no. 34 (August 24, 1944), p. 3; no. 35 (August 31, 1944), p. 3; no. 36 (September 7, 1944), p. 3; no. 39 (September 28, 1944), p. 2; no. 40 (October 5, 1944), p. 1; no. 41 (October 12, 1944), pp. 2, 3.

84. Lévai, *Fekete könyv*, pp. 33, 37, 74–75. In the other larger Neolog communities, the rate of conversions was about the same. Aside from conversions, the demographic status of Hungarian Jewry was worsened by negative changes in the death-birth ratio and by emigration following World War I. For pertinent demographic data see *ibid.*, pp. 74–75, *Zsidó Világkongresszus*, no. 10, 1948, 10 pp., and Zeev Rotics, "Beshule hanetunim hastatistiim al hamarot hadat bekerev yehudei Hungaria beshanim 1900–1941" (Jewish Conversion in Hungary. Remarks on the Statistical Data for 1900–1941) in *Dapim lecheker tekufat hashoa* (Studies on the Holocaust Period) (Tel Aviv: Hakibbutz Hameuchad, 1978), 1:222–28.

85. The Good Shepherd Mission is frequently also identified as the Good Shepherd Committee (*Jó Pásztor Bizottság*). For details on these organizations, see chapter 30.

86. Whereas only 176 Jews converted in Budapest between January and March 19, 1944, the day of the German occupation, 788 converted within one month after the occupation. See declaration by Rabbi Zsigmond Groszmann in *Magyar Zsidók Lapja*, 6, no. 16 (April 20, 1944): 5.

87. Officially there were 4,770 conversions registered in Budapest; however, approximately 80,000 Jews were in possession of various types of "conversion certificates," of which most were forgeries. Lévai, *Fekete könyv*, p. 190.

88. "'Tauffieber' der Budapester Juden" ("Conversion Fever" of the Jews of Budapest). *NA*, Microcopy T-120, Roll 4664, Frame No..K1509/350353. See also "Miért?" (Why?), an editorial in *Magyarországi Zsidók Lapja*, 6, no. 28 (July 13, 1944): 1.

89. *RLB*, Doc. 190.

90. For the text of Sztójay's note, see Jenő Lévai, *Szürke könyv magyar zsidók megmentéséről* (Gray Book on the Rescuing of Hungarian Jews) (Budapest: Officina, n.d.), pp. 52–53.

91. See, for example, the editorial in *Magyarországi Zsidók Lapja* cited above as well as that published in no. 32 (August 10, 1944): 1.

92. For samples of such denunciations, see *Vádirat*, 3:215–18, 257–58.

93. *Ibid.*, pp. 195–96, 211–14, 459, 593–97. See also Lévai, *Fekete könyv*, pp. 190–91.

94. See, for example, Article 4 of Decree no. 1.200/1944. M.E.; 9 of 1.210/1944. M.E.; 5 of 1.220/1944. M.E.; 3 of 1.240/1944. M.E.; 6 of 1.300/1944. M.E.; 9 of 1.370/1944. M.E.; 1.450/1944. M.E.; 6 of 1.490/1944. M.E.; 14 of 1.600/1944. M.E.; 6 of 1.530/1944. M.E.; 13 of 1.540/1944. M.E.; 7 of 1.580/1944. M.E.; 7 of 108.500/1944. K.M. For the subject matter of these decrees, see Appendix 3.

95. *Vádirat*, 1:250.

96. Decree No. 1.730/1944. M.E. *Budapesti Közlöny*, no. 108, May 13, 1944.

97. An order of ex-servicemen who were awarded the "valiant" title during the Horthy era. Some Jews applied for exemption on grounds other than those specified by the law. Most frequent were elderly Jews who applied on the ground that their sons were serving in the military or labor service system. See, for example, the application of Márkusz Boskovitz addressed to Lajos Csatay in August 1944, in *Vádirat*, 3:408–10.

98. The review of the eligibility and status of exemptions was the responsibility of a committee appointed by the Minister of the Interior. It was composed of a chairman, four regular, and four alternate members. Only one regular and one alternate were appointed at the recommendation of the military-dominated National Valiants' Bench. Before granting a final exemption, the Minister of the Interior normally requested the prefect of the county or municipality for a statement relating to the applicant's moral and patriotic attitudes since the receipt of the decorations or medals. See Decree no.

1.530/1944. M.E. of April 26 in *Budapesti Közlöny*, no. 97, April 30, 1944. See also *Vádirat*, 1:274–76, and 3:10–19, 42–49.

99. *Ibid.*, 3:556–57; Munkácsi, *Hogyan történt?*, p. 232.

100. *Vádirat*, 3:110–11.

101. *Ibid.*, pp. 158–60.

102. For the text of Decree 2.040/1944. M.E. see *Budapesti Közlöny*, no. 189, August 22, 1944. This decree did not specifically or automatically cover the exempted persons' immediate family. These were covered by Decree no. 3.670/1944. M.E. of October 11, which went into effect four days later, the last day of the Horthy regime. *Ibid.*, no. 235, October 15, 1944.

103. *Vádirat*, 3:426–27.

104. Among Mester's most loyal collaborators in the handling of exemption cases in the Ministry were Gusztáv Csomor, András Molnár, Szabolcs Lörinczy, Endre Giday, and László Simon. Lévai, *Szürke könyv*, p. 111.

105. Among these were academicians and scientists like Károly Goldzieher, Pál Oravecz, Béla Purjesz, Frigyes Riesz, and István Rusznyák. Among the writers and artists were such well-known figures as Iván Boldizsár, Jenő Heltai, Ernő Ligeti, and Kálmán Rózsahegyi. Some, including Purjesz and Rusznyák, were actually brought back from Strasshof after their deportation from Szeged. Others, like Károly Marót and Rozsahegyi, were even allowed to resume their professional activities. For additional names of artists, writers, and scientists exempted in 1944, see *ibid.*, pp. 108–9.

106. By October 15, 1944, when the Horthy regime was toppled by the Szálasi coup, 6,998 exemption certificates had been issued. Lévai, *Zsidósors Magyarországon*, p. 257.

107. Hannah Arendt, *Eichmann in Jerusalem* (New York: Viking, 1963), pp. 117–18.

108. See, for example, Komoly's comments on this issue in *HJS*, 3:209, 212.

109. *Vádirat*, 3:563.

110. These Jews were reminded that the exemption system did not obviate the provisions of the Third Anti-Jewish Act and of measures dealing with property relations. *Magyarországi Zsidók Lapja*, 6, no. 36, (September 7, 1944): 2.

111. *Vádirat*, 3:490–91.

112. See, for example, the appeal by Bishop Sándor Raffay, which was addressed to Horthy on September 8 in behalf of a group of converted Jews. *Ibid.*, p. 527.

113. Lévai, *Zsidósors Magyarországon*, p. 256.

114. Ferenc Herczeg, a noted writer of rightist-nationalist inclination, intervened in behalf of his publisher, István Farkas, the owner of the Singer & Wolfner Publishing House. He was shocked to learn that the Germans would try to have him returned if "Mr. Farkas has not yet gotten into the crematorium." *Ibid.*, pp. 270–71.

115. *Ibid.*, pp. 257–58. See also *RLB*, Doc. 207, and *Vádirat*, 3:528.

116. Lévai, *Zsidósors Magyarországon*, p. 258.

117. Decree 3,780/1944. M.E. of October 25, 1944. *Budapesti Közlöny*, no. 247, October 29, 1944, p. 1.

118. Lévai, *Zsidósors Magyarországon*, pp. 310, 332.

119. For some biographical details on Ferenczy, see chapter 13.

120. Sztójay in fact received Ferenczy twice, once in the company of István Antal and the second time in the presence of Béla Imrédy, Bálint Hóman, and Lajos Reményi-Schneller. On both occasions Ferenczy tried to place all blame for the deportations and the associated atrocities on the Germans and on his superiors Baky and Endre, by then already removed from power. Lévai, *Zsidósors Magyarországon*, p. 268.

121. This account is based on his testimony at his postwar trial as reproduced in Munkácsi, *Hogyan történt?*, pp. 190–91.

122. *Ibid.*, p. 191. In his postwar memoirs, Pető claims that Ferenczy was visited by a delegation consisting of himself, Kurzweil, and János Gábor. *HJS*, 3:60.

123. Komoly first met Ferenczy on August 23 through the good offices of Lullay. For

Komoly's account, see *HJS*, 3:156 ff. For further details on Komoly's role in 1944 see chapter 29. On Stöckler's account of his dealings with Ferenczy, see his "Gettó elött— gettó alatt" (Before the Ghetto—During the Ghetto). *Uj Élet* (New Life), Budapest, January 22–April 17, 1947.

124. For Stern's and Pető's accounts of their dealings with Ferenczy, see *HJS* 3:33–41, 60–67.

125. Stöckler expressed his disappointment in a letter to Stern dated August 14, and in several notes and memoranda, including those dated August 22 and 28, emphasizing that he was not ready to assume collective responsibility for decisions in which he was not involved. See his "Gettó elött—gettó alatt." For text of his August 28 memorandum, see *Vádirat*, 3:485–87.

126. By the summer of 1944, German troop strength in Hungary was greatly diminished, and no longer represented a real threat. On one occasion in the summer, the Germans, eager to dissuade the Hungarians from attempting to extricate themselves from the war and to prove their strength for possible unilateral deportations, had staged an impressive military parade in Budapest involving columns of tanks, armored vehicles, and cannons. In actual fact the Germans were bluffing, and the parade consisted of a limited number of units going around in circles to give the appearance of great strength.

127. Munkácsi, *Hogyan történt?*, pp. 180–94, 192–200, 216–18. According to Munkácsi, a copy of the note was left with the Council. I have been unable to locate the document in any source book or archive. A draft of a proposed governmental position paper on the treatment of the Jewish question, incorporating some of the points made in Ferenczy's draft, was indeed prepared by the Ministry of Foreign Affairs (*Vádirat*, 3:451–53). According to the documentation submitted during the Veesenmayer trial in 1948, a similar five-point demand was submitted to Veesenmayer on August 24, by Reményi-Schneller, then Acting Prime Minister. C. A. Macartney, 2:321.

128. The position paper was prepared by the Political Department headed by Csopey. Following the decision by the Council of Ministers, the details were to be communicated to the Governor by the Minister of Finance and the Minister of the Interior. *Vádirat*, 3:373–75.

129. Reference here is clearly to the Kasztner negotiations with the SS. For details on these, see chapter 29.

130. *Vádirat*, 3:375–80. According to another draft, prepared around August 23, the government was to offer the Germans 55,000 to 60,000 labor servicemen "whose families were already in Germany" as well as Jews who had a criminal record or who in the judgment of the Hungarian authorities represented a danger to public safety. *Ibid.*, pp. 451–53.

131. Most official German and Hungarian sources identify August 25 as the date scheduled for the resumption of the deportations (*RLB*, Doc. 209); Jewish sources refer to August 26.

132. *RLB*, Docs. 208–10.

133. Munkácsi, *Hogyan történt?*, pp. 219–20.

134. On the scheduled deportation date, the panic was especially severe. A rumor, originating with Jenő Bauer, one of the officials of the Council, claimed that every Yellow-Star house would be occupied by two gendarmes. *Vádirat*, 3:485–86. Stöckler claims that the deportation plan was devised by Ferenczy in order to make his pet project—the concentration of the Jews of Budapest in specially designated provincial camps—more palatable to the Jews. See his "Gettó elött—gettó alatt."

135. Lévai, *Zsidósors Magyarországon*, p. 274.

136. *Vádirat*, 3:427–31. See also Stöckler, "Gettó elött—gettó alatt." For further details, see chapters 29 and 31.

137. Probably to distract Veesenmayer's attention from his plans to establish a military-dominated government, Horthy told him that he planned to appoint Jurcsek, an outspoken Germanophile, as Deputy Premier. Apparently Veesenmayer took Horthy's statement at face value, since on that same day he contacted Jurcsek to work out with him the composition of the proposed new government. RLB, Doc. 212.

138. Vádirat, 3:433.

139. RLB, Doc. 213. According to a hand-pencilled note on the document, Rolf Günther, Eichmann's deputy in Berlin, reassured the Foreign Office that "a part of the Kommando would, in any case, remain [in Hungary] as observers."

140. Ibid., Doc. 214. In his telegram of August 25, Veesenmayer requested Ribbentrop to verify Himmler's instructions to Winkelmann and to issue directives with respect to "the other Führer orders."

141. In an attempt to facilitate the replacement of the Sztójay government, the Regent had authorized a two-week vacation for the Prime Minister "to enable him to recover from his illness." Reményi-Schneller's appointment was made on August 12. Budapesti Közlöny, no. 183, August 13, 1944, p. 1.

142. Lévai, Zsidósors Magyarországon, p. 278.

143. Vádirat, 3:489.

144. Horthy Miklós titkos iratai, pp. 457–66.

145. The proposed changes had been discussed with Veesenmayer, who insisted on the inclusion of Bárdossy, Endre, Ruszkay, and Szálasi as well as on the retention of Sztójay in some capacity. He did not get his way. The government decided upon by the Hungarians consisted of: Lajos Reményi-Schneller, Minister of Finance; Lajos Csatay, Minister of Defense; Béla Jurcsek, Minister of Agriculture as well as Minister of Supplies; Miklós Bonczos, Minister of the Interior; Iván Rakovszky, the Bethlenite former President of the Administrative Court, Minister of Cults and Education; Gábor Vladár, Minister of Justice; Lieutenant-General Gusztáv Hennyey, Minister of Foreign Affairs; Olivér Markos, Minister of Trade and Transportation; and Tibor Gyulay, the Secretary General of the Budapest Chamber of Commerce, Minister of Industry. Budapesti Közlöny, no. 197, August 30, 1944, pp. 1–2.

146. On October 12, Schell succeeded Bonczos as Minister of the Interior.

147. Budapesti Közlöny, no. 206 (September 10, 1944), p. 1.

148. C. A. Macartney, 2:324–27.

149. Ibid., p. 320.

150. Among those freed from Horthyliget were 11 of the 55 journalists and lawyers who had originally been interned at Csepel through the involuntary intermediation of the Jewish Council. Lévai, Zsidósors Magyarországon, p. 284.

151. A petition for the freeing of all the hostages and all those "illegally" arrested and interned since the German occupation was submitted by the Jewish Council on July 28. For text see Lévai, Fekete könyv, pp. 207–8.

152. The delegation included Andor Balog, István Földes, Albert Geyer, Sándor Groszmann, Dezső Sándor, József Sebestyén, Miklós Szegő, and Miklós Vida. Lévai, Zsidósors Magyarországon, p. 284.

153. Ibid. See also Lajos Stöckler, "Gettó elött—gettó alatt."

154. During the two days of Rosh Hashana (September 18 and 19) and on Yom Kippur (September 27) the Jews of Budapest were allowed outside their homes from 9:00 A.M. to 7:00 P.M., and on the eve of the Holy Days from 5:30 P.M. to 7:00 P.M. Vádirat, 3:545. Gainfully employed Jews were issued special certificates by Police Headquarters after July 27, which allowed them more freedom of movement. (On that date it was also announced that all personal identification cards issued after March 20, 1944, would become invalid on August 1.) Similar arrangements were made by István Kultsár, the Govermnemt Commissioner for Matters Relating to White-Collar Unemployment

(*Értelmiségi Munkanélküliség Ügyeinek Kormánybiztosa*) on behalf of employed Jews, through Decree 188.358/1944 EMK. *Budapesti Közlöny,* no. 174, August 3, 1944, p. 15.

155. *Vádirat,* 3:563. By that time the Parliament had been transformed into a docile instrumentality of the regime, inasmuch as the parties had been dissolved on August 24.

156. Koródy, a journalist by profession, represented Szabolcs and Ung Counties. For some details on Koródy's dealings with Komoly, see chapter 29.

157. *Vádirat,* 3:564–65.

158. Most sources claim that the agreement was signed by the Lakatos government soon after its inauguration. (Cf. Lévai, *Zsidósors Magyarországon,* p. 277, and Munkácsi, *Hogyan történt?,* p. 224.) Lakatos, on the other hand, claims that the agreement was signed by the outgoing Sztójay government (NG-1848). No German documents have so far been found to substantiate this agreement. In his telegram of August 30, Veesenmayer informed Ribbentrop—probably on the basis of Reményi-Schneller's or Jurcsek's statement—that the new Hungarian government had decided to begin the concentration of the Jews on September 1 and their removal on September 2. *RLB,* Doc. 215. See also C. A. Macartney, 2:327.

159. *Magyarországi Zsidók Lapja,* 6, no. 31 (August 3, 1944):3.

160. *Ibid.,* no. 32 (August 10, 1944), p. 3. While the Jewish labor squads had originally been slated exclusively for rubble-clearing in Budapest, they gradually came to be employed for other purposes and in other localities as well. See, for example, *FAA,* 2:618–25 and 641–43.

161. *Vádirat,* 3:499.

162. *Magyarországi Zsidók Lapja,* 6 no. 36 (September 7, 1944):3. It should be noted in this context that most of the able-bodied males of 18 to 48 were already in the regular labor service companies.

163. Munkácsi, *Hogyan történt?,* p. 226.

164. For details on Horny's role in the labor service system, see chapter 10.

165. Munkácsi, *Hogyan történt?,* pp. 227–29.

166. *Ibid.,* pp. 230–32. In another memorandum, the Jewish leaders provided Dr. Langman with capsule background information on the various Hungarian and German officials involved in the ghettoization and deportation process, including Ferenczy, Lullay, Eichmann, and Krumey. *Ibid.*

167. Much of the ground work for the mobilization of the Hungarian political governmental, and church leaders was done by Ottó Komoly. Acting as the representative of the International Red Cross, Komoly, in contrast to Kasztner who pursued the SS line, followed the Hungarian line, which proved much more productive. He maintained close and effective relations with Miklós Mester, Reverend Albert Bereczky of the Reformed Church, Mrs. Zoltán Tildy, and many other leaders. Among his close associates were Sándor Török, the head of the Christian Jews, and the members of the *Vaada,* which he also headed. It was often the position that was worked out by the various groups headed by Komoly that Samu Stern presented to the Regent. See Komoly's diary covering August 21 through September 16, 1944, in *HJS,* 3:147–250. See also Béla Vágó, "Budapest Jewry in the Summer of 1944. Ottó Komoly's Diaries," in *YVS,* 8:81–105. For further details see chapter 29.

168. Reference is to the alleged German bombing of Kassa in June 1941 by aircraft with Soviet markings, to provide an alibi for Hungary's entry into the war against the USSR. For further details, see chapter 6.

169. Munkácsi, *Hogyan történt?,* p. 236. See also Stern's statement in *HJS,* 3:39–41.

170. *RLB,* Doc. 217.

171. The Eichmann-*Sonderkommando,* though recalled, was only formally but not actually dissolved. Wisliceny was reassigned to his original post in Bratislava; Dannecker was ordered to remain in Budapest to carry out some unspecified functions; even those who

were recalled to the RSHA headquarters in Berlin were advised to stay in Budapest another week "in anticipation of a political change in the country." See Grell's memorandum of September 29, 1944. *Ibid.,* Doc. 220.

172. *Ibid.,* Doc. 218.

173. The eight assembly centers were identified as follows: 5 Csáky Street; the synagogue on Öntőház Street; the synagogue at 55 Aréna Road; 4 Jókai Road; 32 Akácfa Street; the synagogue at 2 Bethlen Square; the former internment camp at 39 Páva Street; and 46 Columbus Street. The camp at Tura was expected to be used after its evacuation by the *Honvédség. Ibid.,* Doc. 219.

174. *Ibid.*

175. *Ibid.,* Docs. 221, 381.

176. *Ibid.,* Doc. 224.

177. *Ibid.,* Doc. 225.

178. Horthy held many of his secret meetings in the company of his closest advisors, including Bethlen, Count Móric Esterházy, Count Gyula Károlyi, Baron Zsigmond Perényi, and Kálmán Kánya. Among the military he especially trusted Csatay, Hennyey, Lakatos, Szilárd Bakay, and retired Generals Vilmos Rőder, István Náday, and Hugó Sónyi.

179. For details on the Sármás massacres, see Matatias Carp, *Sărmaş. Una din cele mai oribile crime fasciste* (Sármás. One of the Most Horrible Fascist Crimes) (Bucharest: Socec, 1945), 47 pp., illus.

180. For Lakatos' account see his statement of June 10, 1947, issued in connection with Veesenmayer's trial in 1948 by the Nuremberg Military Tribunal (NG-1848). For his statement on the background of his premiership and on his six-week tenure, which was written for his *Nyilas* captors at Tihany on October 28, 1944, see Péter Gosztonyi, "Lakatos Géza beszámolója miniszterelnöki tevékenységéről" (The Account of Géza Lakatos on his Activities as Prime Minister), *Uj Látóhatár* (New Horizon), Munich, no. 5, 1970, pp. 440–458. Lakatos died in exile in Adelaide, Australia, on May 21, 1967, at 77 years of age.

181. For a fascinating and detailed account of the negotiations involved in Hungary's attempt to extricate itself from the Axis Alliance, see C. A. Macartney, 2:319–443.

CHAPTER TWENTY-SIX

THE SZÁLASI ERA

Toward the Denouement

HORTHY'S DECISION to suspend the deportations on July 7 and to dismiss Prime Minister Döme Sztójay the following month convinced the Germans that the Hungarian head of state was indeed resolved to remove Hungary from the Axis. The Germans were, of course, fully aware of every move of the Regent and the Hungarian government, thanks to their agents, among whom were many high-ranking governmental officials. They consequently lost no time in taking the necessary measures to safeguard the interests of the Third Reich.

Although convinced of the Regent's "treacherous" activities, Edmund Veesenmayer—an ideologically firmly committed but politically pragmatic Nazi diplomat—continued to believe, as he had in March, that the interests of the Reich required the presence of Horthy. He quite correctly realized that the Regent not only represented the sovereignty of the Hungarian nation, but also provided legitimacy for the actions of the government. Therefore, in his attempt not to alienate Horthy further, Veesenmayer was willing to countenance the new military-dominated government of General Géza Lakatos. In fact, he even received Lakatos at the German Legation late in August, although at the same time he and his assistant Kurt Haller were also engaged in intensive discussions with the representatives of the *Nyilas* concerning the possible establishment of a Szálasi government. At a meeting with Baron Gábor Kemény, the *Nyilas* spokesman for foreign affairs, Haller went so far as to discuss the possibility of arresting Lakatos and of using pressure on Horthy by threatening to publicize a false rumor—his wife's alleged Jewish origin. Veesenmayer, eager to reconcile the appearance of legitimacy provided by Horthy with the servile loyalty to be expected from Szálasi, managed to arrange a meeting between the two Hungarian leaders on August 29. However, as in the case of the earlier encounters between these representatives of the irreconcilable aristocratic-conservative and ultra-radical wings of the Hungarian Right, this meeting, too, was fruitless. In fact it extinguished the hope of any possible future cooperation between them.

Shortly after the inauguration of the Lakatos government on August

29, Horthy proceeded with his plans for the honorable withdrawal of Hungary from the war. Acting in his capacity as Supreme War Commander (*Legfelsőbb Hadúr*) and enjoying at least the ostensible support of all the members of the government, Horthy decided to sue for an armistice on September 8.[1] However, the decision ended up not being carried out because Horthy felt honor-bound, in accordance with his earlier pledges to Hitler and Veesenmayer, to inform the Germans of his plans. As a way around this quixotic position, Lajos Csatay, his trusted Minister of Defense, had suggested that the Germans be warned that unless they provided five armored divisions for the defense of Hungary within 24 hours, the Hungarians would have no alternative but to surrender.[2] This seemingly ingenious plan failed. To the great surprise of the Hungarians (who of course expected the Germans would not or could not comply), the Germans managed to deploy some forces to Hungary within the time limit of the ultimatum. While less than the strength stipulated by the Hungarians, the forces were large enough to frustrate the intentions of the Regent and to threaten the possibility of a civil war. In the view of the government, the Germans were bound to support the struggle of the Right extremists against the increasingly visible anti-Nazi forces, whose potential members included the Jewish labor service companies, which were expected to be aided by the advancing Red Army.

As Horthy's intentions became clear, the political-military battle lines between the extreme rightists (with their German supporters) and the moderate-conservative forces (with their new leftist allies) became clearly drawn. Each camp began actively to prepare for the expected final showdown.

Aware of the machinations of the top *Nyilas* leaders, Horthy ordered their arrest on September 16. However, Colonel G. Királyi, the officer in charge of the gendarmerie at the Palace, who had been entrusted with the operation, reported that they could not be arrested because they were under the protection of the SS. Kemény was protected by Haller; Emil Kovarcz, who three days earlier had been appointed by Szálasi as Supreme Commander of all Arrow Cross forces, was under SS protection in a villa on Pasaréti Road in Buda where he worked on the master plan for the *Nyilas* takeover; Károly Ney and Imre Bolhóy, the leaders of the ultra-rightist veterans' association Comradely League of the Eastern Front (*A Keleti Arcvonal Bajtársi Szövetsége*—KABSz) were protected by their mentor Otto Winkelmann, the Higher SS and Police Leader of Hungary, who apparently found them more effective and reliable than Kovarcz; Szálasi himself had been placed by Veesenmayer in the care of SS-*Obergruppenführer* Karl Pfeffer-Wildenbruch, the Commander of the SS forces and of those slated to defend Budapest, and devoted his time to the preparation of a series of documents in anticipation of a Hungarist regime.

Szálasi's grandiose plans, which in the context of the military situation at the time were not only unrealistic but downright quixotic, even included a solution of the Jewish question. The Jews, by that time consisting merely of those still alive in Budapest and in the labor service companies and defined in strictly racial terms, were to be employed on domestic public-works projects until the end of the war, when by virtue of an international agreement they were to be transferred to some place still to be specified.[3] Szálasi's program for the solution of the Jewish question was summarized as follows:

Jews shall perform labor service for the Nation inside the country; their treatment shall be determined by their behavior; their legal status shall be regulated by law; no difference shall be made between one Jew and another. When the war is over, all Jews shall be removed from Hungary to a place to be determined by international agreement. The Jews shall never be allowed to return to Hungarian soil [*Lebensraum*]. Mixed marriages shall be annulled and everyone may enforce application of this right. Those who fail to do so shall fall into the same category as the Jewish spouse; in such cases the children shall count as Jews.[4]

This policy statement was used as a guideline by László Budinszky, the *Nyilas* Minister of Justice first entrusted with the handling of Jewish affairs, shortly after the inauguration of the Szálasi government.

While the *Nyilas* were biding their time, Horthy and his trusted advisers proceeded with their poorly concealed plans for the conclusion of an armistice. The Regent now realized that the Anglo-Saxons would indeed allow the Soviet domination of Eastern Europe. Convinced at last that the Western Allies were contemplating neither the invasion of Europe from the Balkans nor the deployment of airborne troops to Hungary "to forestall the advance of Bolshevism" (this had previously been a Hungarian fantasy), Horthy finally authorized the conclusion of an armistice agreement with the Soviet Union.[5] On September 27, he empowered General Szilárd Bakay, one of the few high-ranking military officers he still trusted, to take command of the forces that were to protect the capital during the *volte-face*. However, on October 8 he was abducted by the Gestapo as he was returning to his headquarters at the

Duna Palota Hotel. With him the Germans also acquired the secret plans for the defense of Budapest.[6]

The armistice plan, like the military precautionary measures, was ill-conceived and inadequately prepared.[7] Not only were the Germans aware of them, they had effective countermeasures to frustrate them. By September 16, Hitler had personally entrusted Major Otto Skorzeny, the leader of the commandos who had temporarily rescued Mussolini, with a number of specific tasks designed to frustrate Horthy's plans. Skorzeny, in cooperation with General Friesner, the new commander of the German forces in Budapest, and Winkelmann, was expected to take care of the occupation of Buda Hill and the elimination of Miklós Horthy Jr., who was correctly perceived as a major anti-Nazi leader at the time.[8] Also alerted for possible military action was SS-*Obergruppenführer* Erich von dem Bach-Zelewski, the chief of the anti-partisan units, who was then stationed in Warsaw. He arrived in Budapest on October 13 with the specific mission of taking command of all local police and SS units in order to implement *Operation Panzerfaust* (Armored Fist Operation) in case Horthy's "maneuvers" led to "warlike complications."[9] To provide additional political support for Veesenmayer's efforts, Rudolf Rahn, the German Ambassador to Mussolini's Italy, was summoned from Gargagno on the Lago di Garda where he had been vacationing with the Duce.

In addition to these measures taken at the initiative of Berlin, a number of further precautionary measures were taken by Veesenmayer and his Hungarian allies at the local level. Toward the end of September, Veesenmayer entered into an agreement with Szálasi concerning the procedures to be used for the transfer of power[10] as well as the composition of the envisioned new *Nyilas*-dominated government.[11] The rightist deputies who were opposed to Horthy's plans were organized into a separate parliamentary group known as the Legislators' National Alliance (*Törvényhozók Nemzeti Szövetsége*), under the leadership of Ferenc Rajniss. Designed to provide a "constitutional" basis for the transfer of power to the *Nyilas* and the consequent blocking of the armistice, the Alliance, having been joined by 138 deputies, was activated early in October. Veesenmayer pinned high hopes on the Alliance and its Executive Committee[12] as a means of putting pressure on both Horthy and the government. In spite of the frequent interventions initiated by the Alliance, he still believed that the interests of the Reich would be better served with Horthy in power. As late as October 12,

Veesenmayer still expressed a preference for the retention of the Lakatos government provided that it was ready to join Horthy in issuing
a proclamation relating to the continuation of the struggle on the side
of Germany; "solve" the Jewish question on a definitive basis; and stop
the "persecution" of the Right.[13]

This was obviously not the response Lakatos had expected when he
submitted a note on September 27 requesting that all political prisoners
held by the Gestapo be transferred to the Hungarian authorities; that
the Hungarian Chief of Staff be informed in advance of all German
military operations in Hungary; and that no Hungarian troops be
transferred without the consent of the Hungarian Chief of Staff.[14]

Ever more clearly aware of each other's ultimate intentions, both
sides made final preparations for the decisive showdown which appeared increasingly imminent and inevitable.[15]

The Armistice Attempt and the Coup of October 15

Although the plans for the *volte-face* were carefully laid during the
first half of October, their implementation on October 15 had all the
ingredients of a tragicomedy. The original plans were worked out by
Horthy in close cooperation with members of his immediate family,
especially Horthy Jr. and the Regent's daughter-in-law Ilona; Gyula
Ambrózy, the head of his Cabinet Office (*Kabinetiroda*); Lieutenant Colonel Gyula Tóst, his aide-de-camp; and a few of his most trusted officers, including General Antal Vattay and General Károly Lázár, the
Commander of the Palace Guard.

The plans called for a coordinated effort involving both the loyal
military units stationed in and around Budapest and the forces allegedly at the disposal of the gradually emerging resistance movement.
On several occasions General Lázár held discussions with György
Gergely and János Beér, representing the Jewish Council, about the possible arming and deployment of Jewish labor service companies. Some
of the details of the plan were communicated by General Vattay to
General Béla Miklós and General Lajos Veress, the commanders respectively of the front-line First and Second Hungarian Armies, who
were instructed to join the Soviet forces on receipt of an agreed-upon
coded order.[16] The text of an Armistice Proclamation was completed
and a copy prepared for delivery to Secretary of State Endre Hlatky,
who was to handle its broadcasting.

The carefully laid plans collapsed. One important reason was the sudden and unforeseen change of the execution date from October 18 to October 15. Horthy had decided to move up the date for a number of reasons, of which by far the most important were the pressures exercised upon him both by the *Nyilas* and their Nazi allies and by the Soviets. He was persuaded that the *Nyilas*, now openly supported by Veesenmayer and the *Wehrmacht* and SS units stationed in Budapest, were on direct orders from Berlin, ready to proceed with their coup. (The *Nyilas* were in fact planning to launch their coup at Esztergom.) At the same time Moscow, annoyed with the Hungarians' apparently dilatory tactics, called for immediate action in accordance with the prearmistice conditions that Horthy had already accepted on October 11.

While Horthy's sudden October 14 decision to carry out the *volte-face* the following day undoubtedly upset the plans of the *Nyilas*, it also inevitably undermined the success of his own designs, since it caught off guard most of his closest political and military associates—and his potential supporters as well. The troops deemed loyal to him could not be brought to the capital, the Jewish labor servicemen did not have arms, and the workers promised by the resistance leaders were not mobilized. Horthy apparently gambled on the advantages of surprise and on the expected loyalty of the Hungarian Army, the many Germanophile officers notwithstanding. Once his decision was made, he called a Crown Council meeting for 10:00 A.M. on October 15 and invited Veesenmayer to see him at noon the same day, to inform them of his proposed action.

October 15, 1944, will undoubtedly go down in history as one of Hungary's darkest days. By its end, the Horthy era had ended—along with the "historical" Hungary, with its mixed feudal-bourgeois socioeconomic structure. The day began with a tragedy that may have been decisive in Horthy's decision to yield power to the *Nyilas*: Miklós, Jr. was captured by the Gestapo early in the morning, before the scheduled Crown Council meeting. A leader of the anti-Nazi opposition— he was the head of the so-called "extrication office" (*kiugrási iroda*)— Miklós had maintained close contact with the leaders of the resistance, several members of the Jewish Council, and reportedly also with some representatives of Tito's partisan movement. The Germans were fully aware of these activities. On that morning he had been scheduled to meet with Yugoslav emissaries at the offices of Felix Bornemissza, the director of the Hungarian Danube Shipping Company. The house was staked out by Skorzeny's men, who proceeded to arrest Miklós together with Bornemissza. Rolled up in carpets, they were whisked out of Budapest; Miklós eventually ended up at the Mauthausen concentration camp. One of the casualties of the raid was SS-*Hauptsturmführer* Otto Klages, the chief of the Budapest SD, who was shot in the stomach and died shortly afterwards.[17]

The Crown Council meeting, which did not actually begin until 10:45, heard a visibly broken Horthy announce his decision to accept the Soviet armistice terms. His decision was substantiated by a report on the untenable military situation, given by General János Vörös. The Hungarian Chief of the General Staff emphasized that the Red Army was already fighting along the Szeged–Csongrád line, forcing a passage across the Tisza, and that a major tank battle was going on south of Debrecen, the outcome of which was surely predictable. He warned that the Soviet forces might reach Budapest itself in two days' time. The hopelessness of the political and military situation was also confirmed by Lakatos and by Foreign Minister Gusztáv Hennyey.

The meeting was interrupted at noon to enable Horthy, accompanied by Lakatos and Hennyey, to keep his appointment with Veesenmayer. Unnerved by his personal tragedy, Horthy first accused the German envoy of having had his son abducted, and threatened to hold him as hostage until his son's safe return. He then revealed his decision to accept the armistice, citing the arguments incorporated in his Proclamation. Veesenmayer asked for an opportunity to consult the Führer, and to Horthy's great surprise announced that Rudolf Rahn, Hitler's special envoy, had just arrived on a special mission "to ease the tension. . . . and to find a compromise." Although Horthy, probably out of politeness, agreed to see Rahn, he also decided at the urging of Ilona to proceed with his original plans, including the broadcasting of the Proclamation. This latter mission was successfully set in motion thanks to the efforts of Endre Hlatky, as agreed.[18]

While the Proclamation was being read over the Hungarian State Radio at around 1:00 P.M., Horthy met with Rahn. Although impressed with the German special envoy's "reasonableness," Horthy reaffirmed his decision and expressed the hope that there would be no military confrontation between the former comrades-in-arms, and that the Germans would be enabled to withdraw peacefully. The meeting ended amicably, although there was a misunderstanding on future communications. Rahn had no further meetings with Horthy but remained in constant communication with the officials of the Hungarian government, especially Lakatos, until the situation was cleared with the assumption of power by Szálasi the following day.[19]

In his Proclamation, the Regent informed the nation that the war, into which Hungary had been dragged because of its geographic position and under German pressure, was lost, and that the Third Reich was confronted with inevitable defeat. He then catalogued the crimes Germany had committed against Hungary, including the deployment of Hungarian troops against his wishes and the many excesses of the Gestapo and SS after the occupation. He also emphasized the Germans' collusion in the abduction of General Bakay and the preparations for the *Nyilas* coup. With respect to the Jewish question, Horthy had the following to say: "Under the protection of the German occupation, the Gestapo took the handling of the Jewish question into its hands, employing the means used elsewhere in this sphere and using the well-known methods that contrast with the requirements of humanitarianism."

Following the reading of the Proclamation, the broadcast continued with Horthy's Order of the Day addressed to the Hungarian Armed Forces. He called upon the soldiers to remain loyal to their oaths and to carry out his instructions, "upon which the survival of the nation depends."[20] But in the course of the early afternoon, the coded order that Vörös was supposed to send to the commanders of the frontline armies was replaced by another one. Issued in Vörös's name and with his consent, the new order stated that the Regent's Proclamation, as issued, did not apply to the troops and that they would shortly be getting special instructions on what to do. Until then they were to continue to fight.[21] Later in the afternoon, when the broadcasting station was occupied by *Nyilas* elements aided by the Germans, Vörös's new orders to continue to fight were broadcast a number of times together with an appeal for General Károly Beregfy, a pro-*Nyilas* officer, to come to Budapest.

The contradictory news and instructions filling the airwaves that afternoon left the armed forces and the civilian population confused and bewildered. Since the loyal Army commanders and the resistance leaders had expected "zero hour" to come three days later, they were unprepared for resolute action. The workers, like the masses in general, remained passive and kept their ears glued to their radio receivers in hopes that the situation would be clarified. As on March 19 during the occupation, the people were overcome by a collective sense of helplessness, compounded by apprehension about the impending changes engendered by years of vicious anti-Communist and anti-Jewish propaganda. The passivity was heightened by the fact that it was a Sunday and the factories were closed.

The only visible jubilation, however short-lived, came from the Jew-

ish community and from some of the traditionally anti-Horthy and
anti-*Nyilas* elements. Some of the Jews tore off their yellow badges and
left the Yellow-Star buildings in a state of euphoria. Many members of
the Jewish labor service companies removed their yellow armbands and
threw away their shovels and pickaxes. But by late afternoon their ec-
stasy was replaced by a feeling of doom. When in the wake of Vörös's
order most of the armed forces, the gendarmerie, and the police sided
with those advocating "the continuation of the struggle against Bolshevism," the Jews began to realize that their jubilation had been prema-
ture. Instead of facing liberation, they were about to enter one of the
most horrible phases of the war.

Having lost control over the instrumentalities of power and with the
Nyilas firmly in possession of the radio station, Horthy and the political-
military figures around him were ready to concede that their gamble
had failed and that the assumption of power by the radical Right had
become a *fait accompli*. They therefore concentrated on a means of
yielding power "without unnecessary bloodshed." As a matter of fact,
Szálasi and his prearranged government—the only one still enjoying
the confidence of the Germans—were waiting impatiently under the
protection of the SS, ready to take over power, preferably with the blessings of Horthy. They obtained Horthy's reluctant concurrence the following day under conditions that were both bloodless and anticlimactic.

The *Nyilas* coup finally enabled the radical Right to assume power
and to enjoy the glory of the Hungarist State, though under constant
military pressure, until almost the end of the war. Their success was
primarily due to the mistakes of their opposition and to a number of
unanticipated favorable developments. The treachery of some high-
ranking officers,[22] the wavering and incompetent political leadership,
the insufficiency of the military contingency measures, the apathy of
the masses—all helped the cause of the *Nyilas*, who also were assisted by
the diplomatic skills of Veesenmayer and Rahn, by Skorzeny and the
SS, and by the show of force put on by the few dozen Tiger tanks
under the command of Von dem Bach-Zelewski.

Although the *Nyilas* coup became a *fait accompli* by late afternoon of
October 15, the diplomatic maneuvering continued through the night.
The Germans and their *Nyilas* allies were preoccupied with the transi-
tion of power to Szálasi, peacefully if possible.[23] Lakatos and his
aides,[24] including Vattay and Tóst, were primarily concerned with the
safety of Horthy and his immediate family. The situation was solved
the next day, when Horthy was maneuvered into signing two docu-

ments: one nullifying his proclamation and reaffirming Vörös's order "for the devoted continuation of the fight"; the other entrusting his nemesis, Ferenc Szálasi, with the formation of a "Cabinet of national concentration."[25] The following day Horthy and his immediate family, escorted by Skorzeny, were allowed to leave for exile in Germany. They were taken to Schloss Hirschberg, near Waldheim in Bavaria, where they were eventually liberated by the Americans. Miklós Jr., contrary to Veesenmayer's specific promise, was never allowed to join them; he was eventually liberated by the Americans in Dachau, where he had been taken from Mauthausen. Lakatos, after having carried out his role in the transfer of power, was arrested by the Nyilas and taken to Tihany.[26]

Unleashing of the Nyilas Terror

No sooner was the radio broadcasting station in the hands of the ultra-rightists than it began a vicious campaign against the "Judeo-Bolshevik menace," inciting the mob to anti-Jewish violence. The vitriolic propaganda, which was also directed against "the coalition of interests of the internal enemy," was interrupted only for martial music and "official" Nyilas pronouncements. These included Szálasi's Order of the Day and the proclamations of the "Arrow Cross Party, Hungarist Movement" and of KABSz. The latter included especially strident diatribes against the Jews, and declarations of allegiance to the new regime by the police, gendarmerie, and army. The radio campaign was coupled with the distribution of leaflets directed against Horthy, who was denounced as "a hireling of the Jews and a traitor to his country."

By the time of the Nyilas coup, the Hungarian Jewish community was reduced to one-third of what it had been at the beginning of the year. An estimated 150,000 Jews were serving in the various labor service companies, and from 150,000 to 160,000 were either concentrated in Budapest in the Yellow-Star houses or living under relatively unrestricted conditions because of their protected or exempt status.[27]

Intoxicated by years of anti-Semitic propaganda and incited by their leaders, almost immediately after the coup frenzied gangs of Arrow Cross youths, many in their early teens, began an anarchic spree of murder and looting. The stunned and helpless Jews who were the object of their fury cowered in their Yellow-Star houses or in their labor service units. Armed with various types of weapons, including automatic rifles and grenades, the Nyilas gangs slaughtered several hundred Jews in the Yellow-Star houses and labor service units during the night of October 15–16. One of their excuses was that some labor servicemen in possession of arms had shown resistance a few hours earlier, at 31 Népszinház Street and 4 Teleki Square. Most of the victims were taken from Yellow-Star houses after the inhabitants were first ordered to gather in the cellar shelters by the invading gangs. Another relatively large group were labor servicemen caught in Óbuda. They were herded barbarically toward Pest and shot into the Danube from the Margit Bridge and the Chain (*Lánc*) Bridge.

The atrocities in Budapest were matched by those perpetrated in the countryside, where many of the labor service companies were stationed. Like the Jews in the capital, the labor servicemen were still dazed by the swiftly moving events. Just a few hours earlier most of them had been celebrating "the end of the war" and the less prudent among them had torn off their yellow or white armbands and thrown away their shovels and pickaxes.

The revenge of the *Nyilas* was quick. On that first night, for example, the Jólsva company—a company of 160 labor servicemen composed almost exclusively of physicians, engineers, and other professionals, which was in the process of redeployment to Western Hungary—was slaughtered at Pusztavám, a small community northwest of Székesfehérvár.[28]

The news of the coup and the anti-Jewish excesses that followed it triggered a series of suicides among the Jews. On October 16, the Yellow-Star houses of Budapest were sealed off for about 10 days. Jews were not permitted to leave their own buildings whatever the emergency. Women in labor could receive no help; the dead could not be buried; the ill and disabled could not be treated unless there happened to be a doctor in that particular building; and all had to rely on whatever food was still at hand, since shopping was impossible.

During this period the Jewish Council was completely impotent, since its members shared the common predicament. On October 16 all the top leaders of the Council were either in hiding or were forced to stay in their Yellow-Star building by *Nyilas* gangs.

The only one who managed to reach the Council headquarters that morning was Miksa Domonkos, a leading official who headed the Technical Services Department. Confronted by an armed *Nyilas* unit that ostensibly wanted to search the facilities of the Council—in reality they were trying to plunder—Domonkos got in touch with Lieutenant-Colonel László Ferenczy. It was to no avail: the double-dealing gendarmerie officer had again changed his position. After having tried to establish an alibi for himself by ostensibly cooperating with the anti-German forces, including some of the Jewish leaders, during the Lakatos era, Ferenczy was now realigning himself with the *Nyilas,* with whom he had been secretly associated all along. Instead of fulfilling his earlier commitments, Ferenczy told Domonkos that "the Jews finally got what they were asking for." Nevertheless, Domonkos took a gamble and informed the *Nyilas* thugs in his office that Ferenczy had warned that unless they departed immediately he would come over and reestablish order. The trick worked and the office was, at least temporarily, freed.

During the days that followed, several Hungarian and German "search" parties appeared at the Council's headquarters, all eager to lay their hands on the keys to the safe. When Domonkos called Ferenczy a second time he was equally adamant, but expressed eagerness to get in touch with the three leading members of the Council—Samu Stern, Ernő Pető, and Károly Wilhelm—who had been privy to his dealings during the Lakatos era.

With the aid of Imre Reiner, the former legal adviser of the Orthodox community, who had managed to get to Council headquarters around 11:00 A.M. on October 16, and of Miklós Gelléri, a secretary, Domonkos tried to handle the many emergency problems confronting the Council, including the phone calls from desperate Jews—the hunted, wounded, or dying victims or their friends and relatives all over Budapest. Many such desperate calls also came from the ambulance, police, and first-aid units in the city, manned by decent Hungarians who were outraged by the anti-Jewish excesses. During these difficult days Domonkos was also greatly assisted by Zoltán Rónai, his subordinate in the Council, who acted as "police liaison." The bold and self-assured manner of this courageous man (he even refused to wear his yellow star) deceived the police officers and *Nyilas* functionaries with whom he dealt into believing that he was one of their men.

In addition to the emergency problems, Domonkos also had to handle the normal responsibilities of the Council, including the feeding of the Jews in the internment camps and the supply of provisions to the public kitchens. During this period, he managed to accomplish the impossible by illegally wearing his captain's uniform and claiming to be issuing instructions in the name of Ferenczy.[29] His air of authority and commanding manner were such that the *Nyilas* who periodically appeared at Council headquarters thought that he was in fact a representative of the Hungarian Armed Forces. Through this daring ruse and with the cooperation of a number of Christian couriers, he managed within a few days to free some of the Council members, including Ist-ván Földes, József Nagy, and Lajos Stöckler. Among his couriers were several guards of Labor Service Company No. 101/359—the so-called clothes-collecting (*ruhagyüjtő*) company, commanded by Captain László Ocskay, a particularly decent officer—which was stationed at Council headquarters.

In retaliation for the resistance shown during the coup by the armed labor servicemen, the *Nyilas* rounded up several thousand Jews, mostly from District VIII of Budapest, and herded them into two large syna-gogues, on Rumbach Sebestyén and Dohány Streets, which had been preselected for the purpose a short while earlier by local *Nyilas* leaders including Márton Homonnay. Among those taken to the Great Syna-gogue at Dohány Street were Ferenc Hevesi, the Chief Rabbi, and Ernő Bródy, a leading member of the Jewish community. Following the en-ergetic intervention of the representatives of the neutral countries and of many outraged Hungarians, the synagogues were vacated and the Jews were returned to their homes under cover of darkness.

For the first few days, the public reaction of the new Szálasi govern-ment to the murderous frenzy of the *Nyilas* gangs was one of indiffer-ence.[30] It probably looked upon the atrocities as a convenient way of deterring the attention of the masses from the country's tragic situa-tion, and as a warning to all would-be resisters to the new regime. When informed of the atrocities Szálasi insisted that he did not want to discuss these issues with anyone, since he considered the Jewish ques-tion as definitively settled.[31] When Angelo Rotta, the Papal Nuncio, approached him on October 21, Szálasi assured him that the Jews would be neither deported nor exterminated, but that they "would be made to work for Hungary."[32] He failed to mention that Germany had not been stricken from the list of places where they might be "made to work."

The government soon realized, however, that the plundering and murdering by the *Nyilas* gangs represented a danger to the stability of the nation. To avoid a breakdown of law and order, Gábor Vajna, the notoriously anti-Semitic Minister of the Interior, felt it necessary to issue a statement that not only clarified the Arrow Cross Party's attitude toward the Jewish question but also included a thinly veiled warning to the anarchy-bent thugs. Vajna's statement, issued on October 18, read as follows:

I have taken steps officially to ensure that the officers and executors of public administration, state security, and public order, knowing the present requirements, will do everything to preserve public order, calm, and state security. The summary decrees which will appear on posters are the commanding words of life and contain necessary measures. In connection with the Jewish question, which in recent months has given rise to so much excitement among both the Jews and certain circles of their friends, I declare that we shall solve it. This solution—even if ruthless—will be what the Jews deserve by reason of their previous and present conduct. To solve the Jewish question, detailed regulations will be published and carried out. Let no one be an arbitrary or self-appointed judge of the Jews, because the solution of this question is the task of the state. And this question—everyone may rest assured—we shall solve. Let me emphatically warn the Jews and those serving their interests that all the organs of state power are vigilantly watching their conduct, and that I shall execute with particular severity the regulations in effect and still to be issued, in view of the war. In this connection I do not recognize Jews as belonging to the Roman Catholic, Lutheran, or Israelite denominations but only as persons of the Jewish race. I recognize no letter of safe-conduct of any kind, nor any foreign passport which a Jew of Hungarian nationality may have received from whatever source or person. Jews living in Hungary at this moment are under the control and guidance of the Hungarian state, and no one may interfere in this question either from home or from abroad. Let not a single person of the Jewish race, then, believe that with the help of aliens he can circumvent the lawful measures of the Hungarian state. If any Jew should nevertheless try to commit an outrage or any other criminal act against the army or civilian population of the Hungarian nation or its allies, then we shall adopt coercive measures against Jewry here which will satisfy our nation and our allies.[33]

In accord with his statement and the new governmental policy, Vajna issued an order extending the scope of the existing anti-Jewish legislation to all Jews—even those formerly exempt and those under foreign protection. Moreover, following an allegedly secret directive by Szálasi, members of the Arrow Cross Party were exempted from all criminal liability for acts committed in pursuit of their objectives, including, of course, their anti-Jewish drive.[34] Vajna's order, however, was rescinded a few days later, when the representatives of the Vatican, the International Red Cross,[35] and the neutral states lodged a vigorous protest with Gábor Kemény, the Foreign Minister, threatening the complete severance of relations with Hungary.

The German Dimension in the Renewed Anti-Jewish Drive

The Germans realized that the new government provided a new opportunity to complete the Final Solution program. At the urging of Winkelmann in Budapest and in response to the orders of Kaltenbrunner in Berlin, Eichmann returned to Hungary on October 17. He immediately reestablished contact with his former Hungarian associates and demanded that, as a matter of the highest priority, 50,000 able-bodied Jews be marched on foot to Germany for labor; all other able-bodied Jewish men be immediately employed for the construction of defense fortification lines around Budapest; the remaining Jews be concentrated in ghetto-like camps near the capital; the Jews in the labor service companies be placed under stricter supervision; the exempted and protected Jews be treated like all other Jews; and a campaign be launched in the provinces for the apprehension of Jews in hiding and the formerly protected ones.[36]

On October 18, Eighmann had a lengthy meeting with Vajna and reportedly reached an agreement under which:

- The Hungarian Minister of the Interior, despite Szálasi's earlier decision in principle no longer to permit the deployment of Hungarian Jews to the Third Reich, consented to the transfer of 50,000 Jews "to replace the worn-out Russian and other POW's" in German plants.
- The Jews were to be dispatched on foot under the supervision of German commandos.
- The remaining able-bodied Jews would be placed into four camps near the capital and employed on various domestic projects.
- The Jews not suited for labor would be placed into ghetto-like camps.
- The Eichmann-*Sonderkommando* would escort the foot marches and act as advisers, but the action itself would be carried out by the Hungarian gendarmerie under the command of Ferenczy.[37]

As Veesenmayer informed Ribbentrop, Eichmann's intentions went beyond these scaled-down demands. After the successful completion of this first phase of the new anti-Jewish drive, the chief deporter was ready to repeatedly ask for additional groups of 50,000 Jews, until none were left.

The following day Theodor Grell, the expert on Jewish affairs in the German Legation in Budapest, prepared a lengthy memorandum on the status of the Jewish question in Hungary, which was submitted to the Hungarian Foreign Office on October 20. The comprehensive note reviewed the agreement under which the provincial Jews had been "taken to Germany for labor." It emphasized Germany's dissatisfaction with the manner in which the Jewish question had been handled since the early part of July, when Horthy decided to halt the deportations. It reminded the Hungarian authorities about their obligations with respect to the Final Solution program and reiterated that Germany, on its part, was ready to abide by its commitments and grant visas to the 8,412 Jews holding either foreign citizenship or immigration visas. Of these, 400 were eligible to go to Sweden; the 7,000 holding certificates for Palestine would be permitted to go to Switzerland inasmuch as the Third Reich was opposed in principle to the emigration of Jews to Palestine. In addition, nine could go to Portugal, three to Spain, and 1,000 children might be permitted to go to Palestine or other enemy territories if the negotiations were successfully completed.[38] The objective of the note, of course, was to induce the Szálasi government to agree speedily to the other part of the agreement originally suggested by Hitler—the extension of the Final Solution program to all other Jews.[39]

That same day Veesenmayer reported to the Foreign Office that he had held a lengthy discussion with the new Hungarian Foreign Minister on the Jewish question, emphasizing anew that Germany would permit the emigration of a number of Hungarian Jews if the remainder were deported. He conveyed his belief that the Hungarians would soon initiate measures to implement this position.[40] Ribbentrop reinforced this view, urging that the application of the severest methods against the remaining Jews would be in the best interests of the Reich.[41]

The Drive Against the Jews

In accordance with the provisions of the Eichmann–Vajna agreement, the systematic drive against the Jews began on October 20 at 5:00 A.M. *Nyilas* elements accompanied by policemen entered the Yellow-Star buildings and ordered all Jewish males to gather in the courtyards. There they were told that those between 16 and 60 years of age had to be ready for departure within one hour, taking along three days' provisions. Later that morning the Jews selected by the combined police–*Nyilas* flying squads were taken to either the race track (*Ügető Versenypálya*) at Kerepes Street or the KISOK sport field.[42] The health and fitness criteria and age limitations specified by the authorities were often ignored by the "recruiting officers": many of the recruited Jews were physically handicapped or well beyond the specified maximum age. Some of them were close to eighty and a few were even older. Jews holding foreign protection passes or exemption or medical certificates did not necessarily fare better than the rest: many of them were simply lumped together with the other Jews, often after their documents were destroyed. On the other hand, a number of "qualified" Jews managed to escape recruitment by bribing the *Nyilas* or police, since corruption was rampant.

Following their concentration, the many thousands of Jewish men were hastily organized into labor companies. The companies formed at the race track were first ordered to the Ferihegyi airport; those organized at the KISOK sport field were first transferred to the sports arena at Ujpest. From these assembly centers the newly formed slave-labor companies were deployed for the digging of trenches and the building of defense fortifications along the southern and southeastern periphery of Budapest.

Since the mobilization and recruitment drive had been initiated so suddenly, many of the Jews were exceedingly ill-equipped for the hardships that awaited them. Some died on the way to their work assignment; others were tortured to death by the *Nyilas;* still others died within a few days of exhaustion or starvation. The surviving Jews had to work very long hours with almost no food, under the constant pressure of their *Nyilas* tormentors. Many were quartered under the open sky, without protection from the chill of the late autumn nights.

On October 22, a new announcement appeared on the streets of the capital, calling on all Jewish males between 16 and 60 years of age who had not been recruited two days earlier, and on all Jewish women between 18 and 40 years of age, to report for "recruitment." By October 26, an estimated 25,000 Jewish males and 10,000 Jewish females were taken. Among those exempted, wherever the *Nyilas* were cooperative, were Jews married to Christians, the immediate relatives of labor servicemen on active duty, those working in war industries, and mothers with large numbers of children.[43]

The Jewish Council[44] was besieged by the desperate relatives of the mobilized men and women. Urgent appeals for aid also came from the more compassionate Christian company commanders, who requested clothing and provisions. In fact, when the *Nyilas* guards were not around, some of these commanders permitted a number of old and disabled Jews to return to their homes. Although the Jewish Council leaders were given a hard time by the officials they contacted, they managed, together with the representatives of the International Red Cross and of the neutral powers, to bring about the release of many Jews who were totally unfit for labor or who held foreign safe-conduct passes.[45] A large role in the release of debilitated Jews was played by the leaders of the Christian churches, including the Papal Nuncio, who lodged many protests with the authorities (see chapter 30). Unfortunately, the interventions came too late for many of the affected Jews. A large number died on the way back to Budapest or shortly after their arrival at the headquarters of the Council.

The plight of the Jewish trench-digging companies worsened considerably after the Soviet forces launched a new offensive against the Hungarian capital on November 2. Shortly thereafter Soviet armored columns reached Gyálpuszta and Kispest, just 13 kilometers (8.1 miles) from Budapest, and the German and Hungarian armies began to withdraw in panic toward Budapest and Transdanubia. The Jewish companies suffered through two weeks of privations, murders, and atrocities while digging the defense lines; they were herded along the road beds and trenches by the accompanying *Nyilas* and gendarmes, who mercilessly shot those who could not keep pace. Some companies were subjected to particularly brutal treatment while crossing Budapest or when stationed temporarily in nearby communities. The Jews were constantly mistreated by the *Nyilas* guards, who often also stole their meager provisions. Many of the Jews, including Jewish "foremen commanders," were shot whimsically on flimsy pretexts; this happened, for example, in Dunaharaszti, Pestszentimre, Pécel, and Domony. The number of Jewish casualties was especially high when the companies were marched over the Horthy Miklós bridge in Budapest: the *Nyilas* soldiers and guards would amuse themselves by shooting straggling Jews into the Danube. The slaughter assumed such dimensions that special police units had to be called out to protect the Jews from the maddened *Nyilas*.[46]

The plight of the Jews in the trench-digging companies was aggravated by the total pauperization of the Jewish community. On November 3, the Szálasi government issued a sweeping decree under which the remaining Jewish property was confiscated "for the benefit of the State." Theoretically, it was to be used for financing war-related expenditures and the implementation of the anti-Jewish laws. Exempted from confiscation were only a few strictly personal items such as wedding bands, religious artifacts, textbooks, and drugs, plus a two-week supply of food and fuel, and a nominal amount of cash.[47]

Later in November, after the Soviet offensive stalled for a short while, many of the trench-digging companies were returned to the left side of the Danube to build additional fortifications. When the offensive resumed, most of the surviving trench diggers were taken to

Óbuda and quartered in the local Ujlaki Brickyards. After a few days, they were made to march on the "death road" to Hegyeshalom, where they were transferred to the Germans to build the "East Wall" for the defense of Vienna.

The Death-Marches to Hegyeshalom

A few days after the Eichmann–Vajna agreement, Szálasi reneged on his promise to forbid the deployment of Hungarian Jews in the Third Reich. On October 23, Veesenmayer gleefully informed his superiors that he had succeeded in persuading Szálasi to allow the transfer of 25,000 able-bodied Jewish males "for labor in the Reich for half a year." Details of the agreement were to be worked out between Winkelmann and Kovarcz.[48] Veesenmayer's zeal in wresting the agreement from Szálasi was motivated by a number of factors, including his eagerness to complete the Final Solution program in Hungary, to make Budapest *Judenrein* (allegedly in order to protect the German forces from the disaffected Jews while the capital was under direct threat by the advancing Soviet Army), and to provide Jewish manpower for the construction of the "East Wall" for the defense of Vienna. In contrast to the original agreement, the practical details relating to the mobilization and transfer of the Jews were mostly worked out between Kovarcz and Jury, the *Gauleiter* of Western Austria.[49]

On October 26 Beregfy issued Decree 975/M. 42-1944 authorizing the transfer to the Germans of 70 labor service companies between October 27 and November 11.[50] The companies were ordered to proceed to Mosonmagyaróvár via Tata and Győr; from there they were directed to Hegyeshalom, the Hungarian checkpoint on the road to Vienna.[51] The transfer began on November 2.

Jewish women were the subject of two special call-up orders issued on November 2 and 3. The former ordered the call-up of women between 16 and 50 years of age who knew how to sew;[52] the other repeated the order of October 26 and ordered the registration of all Jewish women between 16 and 40 years of age for "labor service related to the national defense."[53]

For the implementation of these decrees, the Ministry of Defense acted in close cooperation with the police authorities in Budapest. On November 7, the Chief of the Budapest Police instructed all building superintendents and air-raid wardens to make doubly certain that no Jews were hiding in buildings under their supervision. The superintendents and wardens were also instructed to search the "Christian houses" to find whether any Jews not wearing the yellow star were hiding there, and to immediately report any suspected fugitives to the police precincts.[54]

The Jewish men and women apprehended in Budapest and those already employed in trenchdigging operations were later officially classified as a distinct category of Jews—those "to be lent to the Germans for work in behalf of Hungary." Among those privy to the decision to send them abroad was Count Miklós Serényi, the head of the Dejewification Division (*Zsidótlanitó osztály*) of the Arrow Cross Party. Serényi's successor, István Kelecsényi, communicated this decision to Kurt Rettmann, who headed the Dejewification Section of Budapest and Environs (*Budapest és környéke zsidótlanitási osztálya*), the party unit directly involved in the anti-Jewish drive in the capital.[55]

The marches toward Hegyeshalom—the checkpoint for the transfer of the "loaned" Jews—began on November 8 (at least officially; some over-eager *Nyilas* began the march two days earlier). Each day, 2,000 Jews were deployed. After the advance of the Red Army toward Budapest, the Jews were first removed from their trench-digging locations, amid many horrors and atrocities, to various transit centers in Transdanubia (Dunántul) such as Albertfalva, Budafok, and Pünkösdfürdő. From these centers, as well as directly from Budapest itself, most of the Jews were first taken to the Ujlaki brickyards camp at Óbuda, which was under the command of András Szentandrássy.

The Jews were kept in the brickyards for two to three days under conditions reminiscent of those that prevailed in the provinces at the height of the concentrations and deportations. Thousands were kept in the brick-drying barns (which had roofs but no walls) and many others were compelled to stay in the rain in the courtyard. They were not given any food and the *Nyilas*, who exercised real power although nominally the police were entrusted with keeping order, robbed them of their valuables, clothing, blankets, and whatever supplies they had.[56]

Because of the terrible conditions in the brickyards, many of the Jews fell ill. They had little, if any, hope for proper medical attention or drugs. With the resources of the Jewish community almost totally exhausted, the International Red Cross was able to provide some help through the generous cooperation of a number of Christian physicians who volunteered their services. These doctors, including Ferenczy, Boldizsár Horváth, and Tibor Verebély, organized daily visits to the yards, often bringing along desperately needed drugs.

In spite of the tight security in the yards, several hundred Jews were successfully freed from there. Many of these were rescued "legally" through the interventions of the neutral states: Raoul Wallenberg and Charles Lutz paid frequent visits to the yards to reclaim their wards and to distribute protective passes. Many others were smuggled out in daring rescue operations undertaken by young *Halutzim* disguised in SS or *Nyilas* uniforms. Still others were saved by being provided with Christian identification papers, often with the cooperation of sympathetic police officers.

Most of the Jews taken to the Óbuda brickyards, however, fared less well. Usually after a few days the Jews, regardless of age or sex, were started on the march to Hegyeshalom. The route toward the Reich led through Piliscsaba, Dorog, Süttő, Szőny, Gönyű, Dunaszeg, and Mosonmagyaróvár.

The escorting of the Jews and their feeding and housing en route were to be handled by the Ministry of Defense in conjunction with the Ministry of the Interior, which was in charge of the police and gendarmerie forces. Theoretically, the Jews were to be housed and fed along the route in accordance with a schedule prepared by the Ministry of the Interior.[57] In reality, however, the marches, which involved tens of thousands of men, women, and children, were so horribly barbaric that the route became a highway of death.[58]

A vivid account of the suffering was given by Nándor Batizfalvy at a meeting held on November 22 at the Swedish Legation in Budapest. The meeting, attended by Raoul Wallenberg, Miklós Krausz,[59] Dr. Koerner, and Dr. Farkas (representing respectively the Swedish, Swiss, Portuguese, and Spanish Legations) was convened to synchronize the actions of the neutral powers in support of the persecuted Jews. Batizfalvy was a KEOKH police officer who had provided the legislative framework for the expulsion of the "alien" Jews from Hungary in 1941 (see chapter 6). Just returned from an inspection trip to Hegyeshalom and the major scheduled stopover points on the way from Budapest, Batizfalvy presented a grim picture of the condition of the marchers, providing statistical data about those already in Hegyeshalom, those en route, and those who had either been murdered or committed suicide. At the urging of Krausz and Charles Lutz, the Swiss Consul, Batizfalvy obtained from Ferenczy four "open order" (*offene Befehle; nyilt parancs*) forms. Each of the four neutral legations planned to send two delegates to the German border with the forms, where they would issue safe-conduct passes to as many "foreign-protected" Jews as possible. The campaign of the neutral powers was also embraced by the representatives of the Vatican and the International Red Cross.

The following morning Leopold Breszlauer and Ladislaus Kluger, representing the Swiss Legation, left for Hegyeshalom. Their report of November 28, covering their inspection trip of November 23 to 27, fully corroborated Batizfalvy's grim account. From their intensive interviews with the victims as well as with some of the officers, the Swiss representatives were able to reconstruct the horrid details of the marches and the conditions at the various checkpoints in their report:

The first groups traveled along the main transport routes [highways], but the later ones used side roads [alternate routes]; they usually covered the 200–220 kilometers to Hegyeshalom in 7 to 8 days. Those who became sick on the way were often shot dead by the escort personnel, or they were left behind in abandoned agricultural sheds where they stayed without medical help; only in rare cases were arrangements made for feeding them, and even then they got at most a portion of watery soup every day. The start-off of the marching groups was always staged in such a way that they would arrive at Hegyeshalom between 11 A.M. and 12:00 noon. We emphasize that the groups of people marching on foot received at most 3 to 4 portions of soup throughout the entire duration of the foot march, but usually went several days without receiving any food at all.

The delegates of the International Red Cross submitted a similar report. The delegation, which was set up with the cooperation of the Papal Nuncio included Sándor Ujváry, a writer; Géza Kiss, a textile merchant; and István Biró, a parliamentarian from Transylvania. The report corroborated the picture portrayed by Batizfalvy and Breszlauer and Kluger, and reported the heroic activities of a Lazarist priest named Köhler, who dared the *Nyilas* to shoot him for his "crime" of aiding the Jews.[60]

The inhumanity with which the marchers were treated even shocked some elements of the SS. *SS-Obergruppenführer* and General of the *Waffen-SS* Hans Jüttner described these marches as follows:

In November 1944 I made an official tour of inspection of the *Waffen-SS* Divisions fighting in the Hungarian area. In preparation for this tour I had ordered *Obersturmbannführer* [Kurt] Becher to meet me in Vienna. . . . On the evening of my arrival Becher told me that on his journey from Budapest to Vienna he had met columns of Jews marching to the Reich frontier. The march had made a strong impression on him, since the terrible exhaustion of these people was apparent at first sight. At first I would not believe his description, since these things appeared to me almost impossible.

The next morning I drove to Budapest accompanied by Becher and my adjutant. About halfway to Budapest or a little later we met the first columns. Further columns followed at intervals of between 25 and 30 kilometers. As far as I can remember they consisted mainly of women. Unless my memory fails me, all ages up to 60 were represented. The columns were accompanied by *Honvéd* soldiers. The first columns, which had been on the march already for several days, made a truly terrifying impression and confirmed Becher's statement of the day before. Between the individual columns we met stragglers who had been unable to march on and lay in the road ditch. It was at once apparent that they would never be able to march as far as the frontier. These scenes upset me so much that I at once told Becher that immediately after our arrival in Budapest I was going to the Higher SS and Police Leader [Otto Winkelmann] in order to protest sharply against what I had seen on the road. . . .[61]

Upon their arrival in Hegyeshalom, the surviving remnants of the ragged columns of Jews were taken over by a Captain Péterfy, whose closest collaborators were Captains Kalotay and Csepelka. Breszlauer and Kluger described the conditions in Hegyeshalom as follows:

At Hegyeshalom we found the deportees in the worst imaginable condition. The endless labor of the foot march, the almost total lack of food, made worse by the torturing steady fear that they were being taken to the extermination chambers in Germany, have brought these pitiful deportees to such a state that all human appearances and all human dignity have completely left them. Their condition cannot be compared with that of any others who were brought down by physical privations and suffering. The denial of the most elementary human rights, the fact that they were usually totally at the mercy of the brutally behaving escorts, who in practice could do whatever they wanted with them—from spitting in their face through slapping and beating to shooting—left the mark of these horrors on the unfortunate victims. Human dignity can be preserved even among the poverty-stricken and the suffering, as long as there are legal rights; but this dignity is lost when one is totally deprived of one's rights and at the mercy of someone else. We emphasize this because one can feel the beginning of an aversion to the unhappy victims under these circumstances, even among otherwise well-inclined persons. All social conventions, results of civilization and progress, cease completely among these people. The people—women as well as men—satisfy their bodily needs in front of each other and of strangers, feelings of shame having totally left them. The feeding of the deportees in Hegyeshalom was more satisfactory. They were fed twice daily, and as a result of our visit and our intervention has apparently improved even more. Their accommodations, however, were very poor even in Hegyeshalom, since even there the people were put up in sheds on straw bedding. But the straw was already so worn from several preceding transports that it was filthy and unquestionably infected.[62]

Usually the Jews were taken to the German border one day after their arrival in Hegyeshalom, and were transferred to a German commission headed by Dieter Wisliceny, the man who had previously headed the ghettoization and deportation drive in the provinces. The Hungarian commission in charge of the transfers was headed by Lieutenant-Colonel László Bartha. The transfers usually took place between 7 and 9 A.M. The minutes merely identified the number of Jews involved; as was the case during the mass deportations, no attempt was made to identify the Jews by name or even to give a breakdown by sex or age. The German commission tended to be selective, since it was primarily interested in receiving relatively able-bodied Jews; at times it rejected totally debilitated people or women in an advanced state of pregnancy.[63] On the other hand, the Hungarian officers were usually most eager to clear Hungary of all Jews, regardless of their physical condition.[64]

The representatives of the neutral powers managed to arrange for the return from Hegyeshalom and from the checkpoints along the route of several hundred Jews holding genuine or recently issued safe-conduct passes.

The Fate of the Labor Servicemen in the Military

In addition to "mobilizing" thousands of Jewish men and women during the second half of October, the Hungarian authorities decided to deploy the remaining regular labor service companies in the building of fortifications in Western Hungary along the line going through Hegyeshalom, Sopron, and Kőszeg. Among these were many newly formed "protected" (*védett*) companies—companies enjoying the protection of the neutral powers. (They had been formed after rigorous protests by the neutral countries over the failure of the *Nyilas* authorities to honor protective passes when they mobilized Jews for the trench-digging operations.) Eager for recognition by these countries, Szálasi on November 2 again agreed to recognize protective passes and to grant extraterritoriality to the buildings in which their holders lived. As a result of this agreement the military authorities returned those mobilized Jews who held protective passes to Budapest, where they were put into a special "foreign assembly" (*idegen-gyüjtő*) company stationed at Benczur Street. This company soon included several thousand "recruits" and had to be broken into subcompanies. The lot of the people in those units not transferred to the Germans was quite tolerable, since Adorján Stella, a writer and a highly decorated reserve officer serving as liaison between the Jewish Council and the military authorities, managed to establish close cooperative relations between Colonel József

Herbeck of the Ministry of Defense and the two leading members of the Jewish Council at the time, Földes and Stöckler.[65]

Some of the labor companies, especially the protected ones, were helped somewhat thanks to the activities of Captain Ede Gobbi, then acting as commander of all labor servicemen stationed in Budapest. It was Gobbi, for example, who alerted the representatives of the neutral countries about the imminent danger confronting the protected companies. The companies protected by the Swedes were in a somewhat better position than the others, primarily due to the greater zeal of Wallenberg.

While many of the labor servicemen were taken on foot toward the border (as were the men and women from the Óbuda brickyards), most were entrained at the Józsefvárosi railway station in Budapest, under conditions reminiscent of the deportations from the provinces. The number of Jewish labor servicemen eventually handed over to the Germans was estimated at 50,000.[66] The lot of these servicemen was not very different from that of the Jews in the most notorious concentration camps.[67]

The *Nyilas* and their SS allies went on a rampage as the Red Army approached, and hundreds upon hundreds of labor servicemen were killed in cold blood.[68] The surviving ones were herded toward the Third Reich. Many of them ended up first in the Mauthausen concentration camp and later in the Günskirchen camp.

The fate of the labor servicemen was shared by the thousands of other Jewish men and women who had been force-marched from the Óbuda brickyards. Many of them perished while building the "East Wall"; many were transferred to various concentration camps in the spring of 1945 when the Soviet troops were approaching the Austrian border. The luckier ones, mostly those holding genuine or falsified protective passes, were taken back to Budapest where they were placed in the so-called international ghetto.

The International Ghetto

The barbarous treatment of the surviving Jews after October 15 brought forth a large number of ever harsher protest notes from the representatives of the neutral states and the Vatican. The atrocities committed at Hegyeshalom and on the way there, coupled with the fear that the Hungarian government was in fact resolved to deport all remaining Jews, induced the representatives of these powers to issue a vigorous joint protest note on November 17. In it, they reproached the government for failing to honor its commitment to avoid further deportations and intimated that they were aware of the realities of the Final Solution program. They pleaded for the Hungarian government to rescind its deportation decision.[69]

In response to similar earlier pressures and pleas by leaders of the Hungarian Christian churches, on November 17 Szálasi issued a new "final plan" for the solution of the Jewish question in Hungary. Shortly afterward Gábor Kemény communicated it to all interested parties, including the Germans. Szálasi divided the remaining Jews of Hungary into six categories:

(1) *Jews Holding Foreign Protective Passes.* These Jews were to be relocated to the so-called Palatinus buildings in the Szent István district of Budapest by 4:00 P.M. of November 20. They were to be allowed out of doors for one hour in the morning, from 8:00 to 9:00 A.M. Their departure from Hungary was to be made subject to the development of diplomatic relations between Hungary and the respective neutral states and to the settling of transportation problems between these states and Germany.

(2) *Jews to Be Lent to the German Government.* These "loan Jews" (*kölcsönzsidók*) would be "employed by the German government for the advancement of the common war effort." They were to work abroad for the Hungarian nation under the supervision of a Hungarian Commission to be named by the Minister of the Interior. The Commission, which was also to include a delegate representing the International Red Cross and the interested foreign legations, would keep track of all Jews transferred to Germany after October 16. The fate of these Jews was to be determined jointly with that of all other European Jews; in the meantime, their treatment would depend on their behavior.

(3) *Jews Awaiting Departure from Hungary.* These Jews were to be placed into ghettos. The following were included:

a) Jews lent to Germany whose departure was delayed;

b) Children, the aged, pregnant women, the sick, and others unable to march or unsuited for transport;

c) Children under the protection of the International Red Cross;

d) Christian Jews, who were to be put into separate buildings in the ghetto marked by crosses.

(4) *Jews Holding Exemption Certificates.* These fell into three categories:

a) Jews holding exemption certificates issued by Horthy that had been reviewed and accepted by the Minister of the Interior;

b) Jews holding exemption certificates issued by the previous Minister of the Interior that had been certified by the current Minister of the Interior;

c) Some highly decorated or war-wounded Jews recognized as worthy of special treatment by the Minister of the Interior.

These Jews were still subject to many restrictive racial laws.

(5) *Clerics.* This category included priests and nuns of Jewish origin who were to be placed in special buildings and eventually relocated abroad.

(6) *Jews of Foreign Citizenship.* These Jews, together with Hungarian-Jewish nationals with valid exit papers who had registered their passports with the KEOKH authorities by 2:00 P.M. of November 17, were expected to leave the country by December 1, 1944.[70]

Grell forwarded the memorandum to the German Foreign Office on November 20, emphasizing in his cover letter that the document was designed primarily for foreign use.[71]

Szálasi's document undoubtedly aimed at counteracting the protest notes of the neutral states; it also endeavored to provide a political framework for the planned or already implemented actions against the remaining Jews of Budapest, such as the placement of the "protected" Jews awaiting immigration into the "international ghetto" in the Szent István section of the city.

The government's decision about the "protected" Jews had been informally transmitted to the Jewish Council by Ferenczy on November 7. He emphasized that Jews in possession of valid foreign protective or safe-conduct passes who failed to relocate to the protected buildings by November 15 would be arrested and placed in labor camps. Representatives of the neutral states, the Vatican, and the International Red Cross were informed of this decision by Gábor Kemény at a meeting on November 10. The Hungarian Foreign Minister took advantage of the opportunity to review the position of his government and of the German authorities concerning the number of Jews authorized to leave the country under the aegis of the various foreign states.

Official instructions for the relocation of the "protected" Jews were issued on November 12, 1944, over the signature of János Solymossy, the Deputy Chief of Police. They were addressed to the superintendents and air-raid wardens of the Yellow-Star houses:

In accordance with the agreement between the Royal Hungarian Government and the legations of the neutral states, all Jews under the protection of a neutral state who can prove this by a provisional passport, safe-conduct pass, or protective certificate stamped by the appropriate legation must be relocated by November 15 to the Yellow-Star buildings allocated to them in the Fifth District near Pozsonyi Road and Szent István Park. The Jews under the protection of the various legations may inquire about their newly assigned apartments directly at the Jewish Council, 12 Síp Street, telephone 423-930.

On the basis of the orders of the Royal Hungarian Government, I call upon the air-raid wardens and building superintendents to remove from their buildings Jews in possession of provisional passports, safe-conduct passes, or protective certificates issued by the various neutral states so that they will occupy the apartments designated for them. For these Jews, the Chief of Police has rescinded the restrictions relating to freedom of movement in the capital for the period of their relocation, namely November 13, 14, and 15. These individuals may move freely in the streets during these days from 8:00 A.M. to 4:00 P.M.[72]

A similar plan had been devised by Ferenczy late in August (see chapter 25), but under the more liberal conditions of the Lakatos era the leaders of the Jewish Council, especially Stöckler, had been able to countermand it. These leaders championed the cause of the "little Jews" who would have to vacate the buildings in the Szent István district in favor of the more "privileged" protected Jews. This time, however, there was no alternative. Ineligible Jews were simply removed from the buildings designated as protected houses. Males between 16 and 60 years of age, and females between 18 and 40, were taken to the Óbuda brickyards, from where most of them were shortly marched to Hegyeshalom; the others were moved to other Yellow-Star buildings, mostly in the area which later became the Ghetto of Budapest.

Under the agreement between the Hungarian government and the legations of the neutral states and the Papal representative, slightly more than 15,000 Jews were identified as officially eligible for relocation in the protected houses. Of these, 7,800 were under the protection of Switzerland; 4,500 of Sweden; 2,500 of the Vatican; 698 of Portugal; and 100 of Spain.[73]

Although the relocation deadline was extended by 48 hours, the mass movement in opposite directions of "evicted" and "protected" Jews—all carrying the few possessions they still had—recalled the scenes of the previous June when the Jews of Budapest had first been compelled to move into the Yellow-Star buildings. Actually, conditions were even worse this time since the *Nyilas* were on a rampage, plundering and killing the helpless Jews. Ironically, the "protected" Jews were often subjected to greater abuse than the "unprotected" ones, since the *Nyilas* gangs believed they were wealthier. Many of these Jews were apprehended and taken to the *Nyilas* Party Houses at 41 Andrássy Road or 2 Szent István Boulevard, where *Nyilas* interrogators not only robbed them but often tore up their safe-conduct or protective passes when they invoked their "protected" status.[74]

The Jewish Council was virtually helpless to improve the situation. On November 13 it sent a telegram to Szálasi and all his ministers begging for an opportunity to discuss the plight of the Jewish community. Those ministers who bothered to respond were cynical and condemnatory. For example, László Budinszky, the Minister of Justice, stated that the planned removal of the Jews from Budapest was in the interest of the Jews themselves, to protect them from dangers associated with the possible transformation of the capital into a battleground. He warned that the treatment of the Jews would depend on their behavior, for it was imperative that the interests of the Hungarian nation be protected against the treacherous activities of the Jews. He requested the Jews to use their influence with their friends—the neutral and enemy states—to bring about a cessation of attacks against the Hungarian nation. Baron Gábor Kemény chastised the Jewish leaders for their alleged failure to prepare a list of the remaining Jews of Budapest "as requested by the Minister of the Interior"—a request that the Interior Minister had never made—but promised to look into the matters raised in the telegram. Nevertheless, the status of the Jews continued to deteriorate.[75]

While the "protected" Jews may have felt a greater sense of personal physical security than the "unprotected" ones, basically both groups were in the same situation. This was reflected in the living conditions in the "international ghetto," where close to 15,600 Jews holding genuine protective passes were assigned to apartments that had previously housed only 3,969 persons. Even these apartments were not really fully available, since many of them were occupied by Jews with forged protective documents. The 7,800 Jews holding Swiss protective passes, for example, were at first assigned only 60 buildings. Upon the intervention of the Swiss Legation, 12 additional buildings were added. Since many were already fully or partially occupied, the newcomers in many cases had to find accommodations in areas other than the apartments assigned to them, i.e., in the attic, the cellar, or even the staircase. It was not unusual for a two-room apartment to contain 50 to 60 persons.[76]

After the transfers were completed, many of the buildings of the "little" or international ghetto were systematically raided by the *Nyilas* on various pretexts, bypassing the authority of Zoltán Tarpataky, the police officer in charge of protecting law and order in the area.[77] The most often invoked reason was a check of the protective passes.[78] At 8 Abonyi Street, 260 Jews who had just been rescued by Swiss Consul Charles Lutz from the Óbuda brickyards were robbed by the *Nyilas* on November 16. Ten days later the building at 35 Pozsonyi Road was raided, allegedly because of shots fired by Jews there. Those who were merely robbed were relatively lucky; many of the Jews were taken to the banks of the Danube and shot into the river. Most of those apprehended with falsified passes in one of the investigative raids were ordered into Yellow-Star buildings in the area which subsequently became the "large ghetto." [79]

The international ghetto remained in existence for only a short time. Early in December, when the Red Army was approaching Budapest and the Szálasi government had given up all hope of establishing normal relations with the neutral states, the ghetto population was subjected to particularly great pressure. Many of the "protected" Jews were arbitrarily removed from their crowded shelters and forcibly taken to the banks of the Danube for sorting by *Nyilas* gangs. Those considered physically fit—and this was decided quite capriciously—were placed into columns to be marched to the Reich; most of the children and the elderly Jews were directed into the just established large ghetto. The luckier among these were allowed to find shelter in the buildings owned by, or administered under the jurisdiction of, the neutral states. In particular, the Swiss House, the so-called "glass house" at 29 Vadász Street, which was under the *de facto* control of the Zionists, provided a haven for a few thousand persecuted Jews. According to Szöllősi, approximately 18,000 Jews were transferred from the international ghetto to the Ghetto of Budapest (the "large ghetto").[80]

The lot of the protected Jews, like that of the ghetto dwellers in general, became particularly harsh during the last weeks before liberation. The situation became so critical early in January 1945 that Raoul Wallenberg decided to have the Swedish-protected Jews transferred into the large ghetto, where their survival was presumed to have a better chance. An order to this effect was in fact sent on January 4 to the commanders of the buildings housing these Jews.[81] The following day, the Swedish-protected Jews in the even-numbered buildings on Pozsonyi Road were transferred into the large ghetto. The approximately 5,000 Jews involved in this transfer were followed the next day by an approximately equal number of Jews who were under the protection of Portugal, Switzerland, and the Vatican.

The *Nyilas* had intended to liquidate the international ghetto, allegedly because the neutral states had reneged on their promise to recognize the Szálasi government. Wallenberg's skilled diplomacy, however, headed this off. During the relocations of January 5–6, Wallenberg struck a bargain with the *Nyilas* under which the latter were to receive some of the provisions designed for the protected Jews. As a result, the Swedish-protected Jews who lived on the odd-numbered side of Pozsonyi Road were allowed to stay in their dwellings.

Those ordered into the large ghetto were robbed of all their possessions on the way to the ghetto or at Klauzál Square within it.[82]

The Ghetto of Budapest

On November 18, one day before the completion of the relocation of the "protected" Jews, the government informed the Jewish Council of its decision to set up a ghetto for the remaining Jews of Budapest. The Jewish leaders were summoned to Police Headquarters at 5 Mosonyi Street where János Solymossy, the Deputy Police Chief, had just been appointed by Gábor Vajna as "Ministerial Commissioner in Charge of the Concentration of the Jews" (*A zsidók összeköltöztetésére kirendelt miniszteri biztos*). The Commissioner, who was previously noted for his tough behavior at the Óbuda brickyards, informed them that the ghetto would be situated in the 7th ("Jewish") District of the capital. He also discussed with them some of the major problems associated with the planned concentration of the Jews.[83]

In the next few days the leaders of the Council, especially Stöckler, Földes, Nagy, and Szegő, had almost daily discussions with Solymossy on a variety of subjects related to the proposed ghetto. The number of buildings to be assigned to the Jews and the number of Jews and Christians affected by the relocations were discussed on November 23. According to Solymossy, the area designated as the ghetto had 162 Yellow-Star buildings, of which 18 were inhabited exclusively by Jews and the rest by a mixture of Jews and Christians. In these there were 2,393 Jewish apartments with 4,725 rooms inhabited by 3,556 people, 974 Christian apartments with 1,997 rooms inhabited by 4,019 people, and 133 Christian buildings comprising 2,346 apartments with 3,162 rooms inhabited by 7,916 people. The master plan called for the relocation of 11,935 Christians from the proposed ghetto area into the Yellow-Star buildings elsewhere. These were to be vacated by Jews, who would be transferred to the ghetto. About 63,000 Jews were to be transferred—an average density of 14 Jews per room.

The Jews were to vacate almost immediately 6,000 apartments outside the ghetto area to provide apartments for the Christians affected by the relocations. According to Solymossy's plans, they were to be allowed to take along all their movable belongings with the exception of furniture. They were to assemble in Klauzál Square, a large area in the proposed ghetto. From there, they could take along to their assigned ghetto apartments only as much of their belongings as they could carry themselves.

In the few days before the establishment of the ghetto, the Jewish leaders attempted to devise solutions to the many problems relating to the feeding and housing of the ghetto population, as well as to sanitation and health care. Their most important contact was, of course, Solymossy, to whom they frequently addressed petitions of various kinds. In Solymossy's absence they often dealt with his deputy, Szinyei-Merse. They also dealt routinely with János Rosta, Albert Kállai, and Hegedüs, the municipal officials in charge respectively of food supplies, fuel and heating materials, and sanitation. The foreign representatives most often approached on such matters were those of the neutral states and of the International Red Cross.[84] Jewish doctors were mobilized by the Council to deal with health-related matters, including the setting up of makeshift hospitals. Among the physicians most actively involved were Dezső Acél, László Benedek, Ferenc Groszmann, and László Tauber. On November 27, the Council formally requested Solymossy to assure an adequate supply of electricity, gas, and water, as well as transportation, bathing and disinfection facilities, and drugs.

The decree (no. 8935/1944. BM.) on the establishment of the ghetto, signed by Vajna, was made public on November 29. The most important sections of the decree, which also included the ghetto map (map 26.1), read as follows:

The Royal Hungarian Government orders all Jews compelled to wear the Yellow Star to relocate into the area bounded by Dohány, Nagyatádi Szabó István, Király, Csányi (no. 3–6), and Rumbach Sebestyén (No. 15–19) Streets, Madách Imre Road, Madách Imre Square, and Károly Király Streets in District VII of Budapest, and the separation of the territory assigned to the Jews (the ghetto) from the territory inhabited by non-Jews. The buildings facing the streets and roads specified as boundaries are not included in the area assigned to the Jews.

Non-Jews may not live in the areas assigned to Jews and may not work there, and authorities and public institutions may not have offices in these areas.

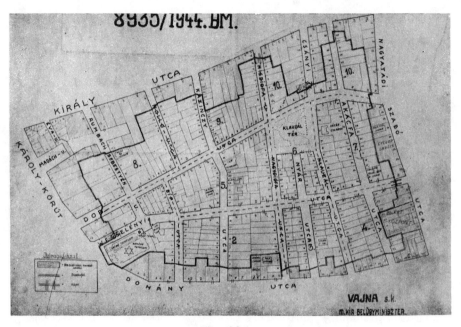

Map 26.1.
Contour map of the ghetto of Budapest.

In this life-and-death struggle, which may decide the fate of the Hungarians for centuries to come, all of us must make sacrifices. The government is aware of the extraordinary difficulties that are bound to be experienced by the non-Jewish population scheduled for resettlement. With a firm belief in a better future and as a pledge for victory, we must bear this sacrifice.

I shall see to it that the resettled non-Jewish residents (owners, tenants, beneficiaries, Christian custodians or superintendents, etc.) shall receive apartments equivalent to those they were compelled to leave, on the Pest side of the city.

If possible, non-Jewish lodgers of resettled tenants will be resettled along with them into the same apartments. Non-Jewish lodgers in the apartments of Jews being resettled may remain in the apartments for the time being; in accordance with the rule in effect, they must enter into new agreements with the new tenants of the apartments. However, the new tenants shall have the right to cancel the agreement within 10 days. Lodgers entitled to leases may be assigned apartments after completion of the resettlement. . . .

Non-Jews must leave the area assigned to Jews between December 2 and December 7.[85]

Most of the provisions of the decree dealt with the rights and privileges of the Christian population to be removed from the ghetto area. The relocation of the Christians began after most of the Jews had already been brought into the ghetto. The property left behind by the relocated Jews was theoretically inventoried and stored before the Christian tenants moved in. In reality, however, there was little if any attempt to comply with this provision of the decree. During the six days in which the Christians were to leave the ghetto area, Jews were allowed outdoors only two hours daily, from 9:00 to 11:00 A.M.[86] Members of the Jewish Council were unrestricted from 8:00 A.M. to 6:00 P.M. The exempted Jews who were associated with or worked for the Jewish Council had, of course, complete freedom of movement at all times. In addition a number of Council officials received special "travel permits" (közlekedési engedélyek) to enable them to maintain contact with the authorities, the representatives of the neutral states and the International Red Cross, as well as with the "protected" Jews in the international ghetto.[87]

The relocation of the Jews began toward the end of November and was virtually completed by December 2. The Christian Jews, including those under Papal protection—about 3,000 in all—were originally envisaged to be housed in separate buildings in the area bounded by Csányi, Dob, and Nagyatádi Szabó Streets.[88] The many hundreds of Jews arriving during the last days of the relocation period were temporarily quartered at the Council headquarters. Many unattached aged or ill Jews with no families were placed in makeshift centers and synagogues on Rumbach Sebestyén and Wesselényi Streets.

The Christian professional and auxiliary personnel of the Volunteer Ambulance Service (Önkéntes Mentőegyesület) were very helpful in the transfer of the ill and aged, often performing their humanitarian tasks despite the interference or attacks of the Nyilas. One of the leaders of the organization, Dr. László Bisits, was especially helpful to the Jews. Working closely with Raoul Wallenberg, Dr. Bisits brought back to Budapest a number of deported "protected" Jews from Hegyeshalom and Balf.[89]

As was the case during the relocation of the "protected" Jews, the Nyilas preyed on the Jews straggling toward the ghetto. Many were attacked, robbed, and massacred near the Feld Theater in the Városliget area of the city. Like many other crimes committed by the Nyilas after the coup of October 15, these were perpetrated by a gang of ultra-Rightists with headquarters at 80 Thököly Road in the Zugló section (District XIV) of the city.[90] The Nyilas also attacked Jews awaiting relocation. On December 3, for example, they attacked the special camp (Sonderlager) on Columbus Street where a large number of Jews were "awaiting emigration." Although the camp was under the territorial jurisdiction of the International Red Cross, the *Nyilas* invaded it and killed several Jews including the camp physician Dr. Rafael and the camp commander Moskovits as well as the latter's family.[91] According to one report, the aged Jews from the camp were taken to the ghetto and the others were eventually entrained at the Józsefvárosi Station and deported to Bergen-Belsen.[92]

The Budapest Ghetto encompassed an area of 0.3 square kilometers (0.1 sq. mi.) (a small fraction of the city's 207 square kilometers [80 sq. mi.]). Like the Warsaw Ghetto, it was surrounded by a tall wooden fence, with gates facing in each direction, through which, according to Szálasi, Jews were to be brought in but no longer permitted to leave. The erection of the fence was entrusted to a construction firm headed by József Auguszt; as in Warsaw, the fence was built at Jewish expense and with Jewish manpower.[93]

After the ghetto was officially sealed on December 10, the four main entrances were the gates located at the beginning of Wesselényi Street, at the corner of Wesselényi and Nagyatádi Szabó Streets, at the end of Nagydiófa Street near Dohány Street, and at Kisdiófa Street near Király Street (see map 26.1). Each gate was guarded by well-armed *Nyilas* cadres and regular policemen.

The ghetto population increased rapidly all through December. Early in the month, before the relocation deadline, the area contained approximately 33,000 Jews. By the end of the month the ghetto population had increased to 55,000 and when its population reached its peak, in January 1945, the ghetto held close to 70,000 Jews. Most of them were children under 16, the ill, and men and women over 50 years of age.

The precipitous increase in the ghetto population was caused by a variety of reasons. Among these was the transfer of a large number of protected Jews from the international ghetto and of many children from homes protected by various religious and charity organizations and the International Red Cross.

In accordance with Szálasi's resolution of November 17 relating to the classification of Jews, the approximately 6,000 children who had been placed by their parents under the care and protection of the Red Cross were to be relocated into the ghetto beginning on December 6. Acting in consultation with Friedrich Born and Hans Weyermann, the Jewish Council declared itself willing to accept the children if the government placed at its disposal the municipally owned educational establishments within the ghetto. The Council adopted dilatory tactics, first requesting the transfer of the buildings and then pointing out the desirability of having them cleaned, disinfected, and furnished. The objective was, of course, to gain time, for the Council members were convinced that the children were better off under the protection of the Red Cross outside the ghetto. The children's protection division of the Red Cross was at the time under the leadership of Ottó Komoly, a Zionist leader who enjoyed exempt status. In December, the Red Cross had six children's homes under its jurisdiction, with approximately 500 children in each. During the siege and in the wake of the *Nyilas* excesses, the supervisory personnel and counselors of some of the homes escaped, leaving the children to their fate. The situation of the children's homes at Teleki Pál, Perczel Mór, and Nagyfuvaros Streets was particularly depressing.

Despite the Council's efforts to stall, a police unit commanded by Police Counselors Szinyei-Merse and Koppány brought the first contingent of 500 children to the ghetto on December 12. They were placed in the halls of an abandoned market at Klauzál Square. Another group of children was housed at 23 Síp Street, after the occupants of the building—the local branch office of the internal revenue bureau— were relocated at the expense of the Council. The transfer of children into the ghetto continued throughout the month, to the great dismay of the Red Cross. By December 24, most of the 6,000 children had been removed from the homes and shelters despite the valiant efforts of Dr. Gábor Sztehló, an Evangelical minister associated with the Red Cross who was particularly active in protecting the interests of the children.[94] On that date, the representatives of the neutral powers, acting on Lutz's and Wallenberg's initiative, submitted a vigorous protest note demanding the suspension of the transfer of children into the ghetto and permission for them to remain in their homes with their mothers.[95] The note arrived only after the 6,000 children had already been relocated and the Hungarian authorities were of course neither willing nor interested in reversing their decision.

In addition to the transfer of the children, the increase in the ghetto population was also due to the constant relocation by the *Nyilas* of Jews apprehended in hiding. There was also a small voluntary influx of Jews no longer able to survive in hiding on their own after their resources were exhausted. To many, the ghetto seemed a last refuge. However miserable the conditions there, it offered the comfort of shared sorrow as well as occasional free meals, however meager. Moreover, many of the Jews were drawn to the ghetto by the hope that the Russians would vent their fury against the rest of the capital but safeguard the integrity of the ghetto.

Administration of the Ghetto

Although the ghetto of Budapest was in existence for only about seven weeks, it had a well-developed administrative apparatus and a network of communal services. Overall responsibility for its administration rested with the Jewish Council, which was of course accountable to the authorities for all its actions. The Minister of the Interior had authorized a Council staff of 800, but the number of persons associated officially or unofficially with its various activities was much larger.[96]

The ghetto was divided into ten districts (*körzetek*), each headed by a district leader (*körzeti elöljáró*) assisted by two deputies; each district consisted of a number of buildings in contiguous streets. The district leaders were appointed by and directly responsible to the Council. Acting as the executive organs of the Council, they were responsible for the implementation of all the instructions of the authorities as transmitted by the Council. The district leaders maintained close contact with the Council, whose directives normally served as their guidelines. However, they enjoyed a degree of autonomy (which proved particularly useful during the Soviet siege, when contact with the Council leaders was all but impossible). By exercising their autonomy, the district leaders were able to offer some relief to the Council members who were besieged at their headquarters by masses of Jews requesting desperately needed help.

The functions and responsibilities of the district leaders were many and crucially important. It was they who had to provide utilities, food, and firemen. They were entrusted with keeping records on all inhabitants under their supervision, exercised considerable judiciary powers in their areas, and were responsible for the children. For a while, the Hungarian authorities permitted the operation of an internal ghetto postal service run from the offices of the district leaders. However, this mail service was never well established and only a few sackfuls of mail were distributed during the lifetime of the ghetto.

The ten districts of the ghetto were drawn so as to assure the best possible service for the inhabitants and to provide the most effective liaison and communication with Council headquarters (table 26.1).[97] Within the districts, each building had a "building commander" (*házparancsnok*) appointed by the Council. This person was responsible

TABLE 26.1.
THE BUDAPEST GHETTO DISTRICTS
AND THEIR LEADERS

District No.	District Headquarters	District Leader	Deputy Leaders
I.	6 Wesselényi Street	Tivadar Gárdony	Ferenc Schiffer Miklós Horváth
II.	8 Kazinczy Street	Zoltán Balassa	Gyula Breuer Manó Stern
III.	11 Nyár Street	Ármin Bergmann	Jenő Mangold Lajos Vásárhelyi
IV.	27 Akácfa Street	Gyula Berger	István Faludi Ármin Rejtő
V.	18 Wesselényi Street	Sándor Ungár	Ferenc Grünwald Jenő Hermann
VI.	26 Wesselényi Street	István Havas	Ignác Engel Lajos Szőke
VII.	37–39 Akácfa Street	Lajos Kolos	Jenő Weiner
VIII.	16 Dob Street	László Stein	Albert Glück Vilmos Kohn
IX.	1 Holló Street	Dezső Hausner	Sándor Földes József Márton
X.	46/b Dob Street	Dániel Brüll	Endre Weisz Vilmos Gorodi

for the upkeep of the building, and had to keep a list of all the "apartment commanders" (lakásparancsnokok) in the building and to transmit to them all instructions from the authorities or the Council.

The inhabitants of each apartment were directly subordinated to these apartment commanders. Although appointed by the building commanders, they were accountable to and removable by the district leaders at the recommendation of the building commanders. They were directly responsible for cleanliness in the apartments, for the care of children and the aged, and for reporting all changes in apartment population to both the district leader and the Council.

The Council also appealed directly to each ghetto dweller:

1. Let us see to it that the apartment, the building, and the sidewalks are clean! Let us not litter! The apartment commander is responsible for the cleanliness of the apartment, and the building commander is responsible for the cleanliness of the building and the sidewalk. Everybody must follow their instructions.
2. Let us care increasingly about the cleanliness of the children. Every contagious disease must be reported to the building commander.

3. Let us behave modestly and quietly in the apartments and the buildings. The instructions of the authorities must be accepted obediently.
4. It is strictly forbidden to form groups in the street. We must unconditionally avoid any intervention by the authorities. The instructions of the police authorities must be carried out without any discussion.
5. The regulations relating to the blackout of the buildings must be carried out in accordance with the instructions of the air-raid wardens and under the supervision of the building commander.
6. Let us be increasingly careful about fire, water pipes, gas, etc., because in light of the overcrowded conditions they may lead to mass accidents.
7. Let us behave with the greatest understanding toward our fellow tenants and avoid all disputes, for these may lead to disadvantages for all.
8. Nutrition is one of our greatest problems. Let us help the community by our disciplined behavior and by lowering our claims.
9. Let us bring our petty disputes to the district representatives, who will settle them as best they can.
10. Let us help and support the aged, the ill, and the children, as well as the pregnant mothers. Let us help all those who need help. This is our human responsibility.[98]

The System of Public Safety

The apartment, building, and district leaders worked closely with the Jewish "ghetto police" (gettórendészet). This police organization—which of course was unrelated to Budapest's regular police—was under the overall command of Miksa Domonkos. Immediate command over the policemen (whose average age was 60) was exercised first by Miklós Szirt and later by Ernő Szalkay. Each ghetto district had its own police precinct.[99]

The policemen wore their own civilian clothes with the Yellow Star badge. Their only uniform was a black cap distributed by the Council; each carried a rubber truncheon. However, the truncheons were frequently confiscated by the Nyilas or the SS, who often "visited" the ghetto.

A Jewish policeman was stationed at nearly every ghetto street corner. Although no mass riots or disturbances took place during the life of the ghetto—and this is quite a tribute to the discipline of the Jews during the most adverse period in their history—some looting took place, especially after bombardments by the Red Army, which became ever more frequent in December. As in the Nazi concentration camps, most of the crimes committed by Jews against Jews involved the theft of food; during the harsh winter weeks in the ghetto, the emaciated and half-frozen Jews were also desperate to obtain anything that could be used as fuel (coal, wood, lumber, furniture). A special problem was presented by the Jewish inmates in the prisons of Budapest who had been brought into the ghetto, where there were no special facilities for their incarceration.

Ghetto police power had to be used with increasing frequency to induce Jews to render essential social and communal services. Under the conditions of famine and combat, fewer and fewer Jews volunteered to help the communal organs in supplying the kitchens with water and wood, caring for the children or the ill, and burying the dead.[100]

Under the extraordinary conditions of the Soviet siege, the ghetto often became the target of "visits" by a variety of uniformed groups— *Wehrmacht, SS, Nyilas,* and *Honvéd*—hoping to find hidden treasures within the ghetto or among the Jews, or simply aiming to vent their murderous instincts against the helpless.

The ghetto policemen of Budapest and, by the same token, those of the other ghettos of Hungary—unlike their counterparts in many ghettos in Nazi-occupied Europe—never faced the unpleasant task of having to select Jews for deportation and extermination. Since the ghettos of Hungary were short-lived and the Nazis acted in great haste (with the full and often enthusiastic collaboration of the Hungarian authorities), the Jewish Councils were also spared this agony.

The primary function of the ghetto police—and it performed this function quite successfully—was to maintain law and order among the Jews and to assure the performance of vital services within the ghetto. It was, of course, almost totally helpless in dealing with armed outsiders and had to rely upon the Jewish Council to cope with the marauding gangs.[101] The leaders of the Council were of course themselves powerless, but they at least had formal access to the authorities. When the ghetto was invaded, they often lodged their complaint with, or requested the help of, the appropriate authorities. After December 15, when Solymossy was appointed Police Chief by Gyula (Mohaupt) Mohay, Budapest's new mayor (his predecessor, József [Vogel] Forgács, had fled), their major contact was Police Major István Lőcsey, the newly appointed ministerial counselor in charge of Jewish affairs. Lőcsey did in fact take a number of measures to halt entry into the ghetto by unauthorized personnel. Among other things he issued new blue-colored permits for Christians authorized to enter the ghetto. However, this regulation was not heeded by the *Nyilas* bent on harming the Jews.

The maintenance of order within the ghetto was also the responsibility of a regular police precinct located at Nyár Street. To prevent or minimize the *Nyilas* excesses, Löcsey decided on December 17 to have the ghetto area supervised by mixed patrols of policemen and *Nyilas*.[102] By the middle of January 1945, there were 15 *Nyilas* guards and about 100 regular policemen within the ghetto. While they contributed to the maintenance of order, they were also a source of problems, for they had to be fed by the Jewish community. Their meals had to include generous portions of bread and meat, curtailing the supplies available for the Jews.

Food and Supplies

The feeding of the ghetto population presented an especially difficult problem for the Jewish leadership. Toward the end of November, the Jewish Council established a Division of Public Feeding (*Népélelmezési Osztály*) under the leadership of Stöckler. Immediate control rested with Szidonia Feldman and her assistant, József Halpern. Their responsibilities included the establishment of public kitchens, the acquisition of fuel and food, and the supply of water. The problems, of course, increased with the expansion of the ghetto population.

By far the largest public kitchen facility was that originally established by the Orthodox Jewish Community to help feed the poor of the capital. During the early phase of World War II, the Orthodox Public Table (*Orthodox Népasztal*) as the facility was called, had expanded to serve many of the refugees from Austria, Poland, and Slovakia, as well as the Jews interned at Kistarcsa, Garany, and Csepel. Following the establishment of the ghetto, the kitchen's facilities were further expanded through the addition of five 700-liter kettles.[103]

Next in size was the so-called Stern kitchen, which used the facilities of the former Stern Restaurant at 10 Rumbach Sebestyén Street. Then came the Skreck kitchen and a number of smaller ones located at 5, 12, and 22 Síp Street. In theory, ghetto dwellers were to receive 100 to 150 grams of bread a day. The bread was at first supplied by the Communal Food Works (*Községi Élelmiszerüzem*); later, it was baked by smaller bakeries within the ghetto (1 Holló Street, 9 Síp Street, and 25 Nagydiófa Street) whenever the International Red Cross was able to provide the necessary flour.

With coke and coal almost nonexistent, the fuel problem was largely "solved" by the Soviet bombardments:[104] the buildings destroyed by the raids would be stripped of their wood. The kitchen employees had, of course, to compete with the other dwellers of the ghetto, who were equally eager for some fuel.

Under the siege, many of the utilities were damaged or totally destroyed. Water for cooking and dishwashing was taken from the relatively few buildings that still had running water, or from the natural wells in the ritual-bath facilities in the ghetto (16 Kazinczy Street). A number of artesian wells, which had been abandoned after the installation of the water system in Budapest, were reactivated. They supplied many buildings, including those containing public kitchens.

By far the greatest difficulty was caused by the lack of food. Its acquisition was financed by the municipality, the International Red Cross, and the internal reserves of the community.

On December 2, Rosta informed the Jewish leaders that the daily ration specified for the Jews was 150 grams of bread, 40 grams of flour, 10 grams of oil, and 30 grams of legumes. Jews were also to receive 600 grams of salt per month and 100 grams of meat per week "if available." The food allocated to the Jews contained 690 to 790 calories—prison inmates received 1,500. (This calorie level was allegedly determined by Vajna.) However, even this limited quantity of food was not always made available to the ghetto population, which would have starved had it not been for the food deliveries arranged by the neutral powers' representatives.[105] The International Red Cross was particularly concerned with the feeding of the children, many of whom had been relocated into the ghetto from its protected children's homes. The main warehouses of the Red Cross were often the target of *Nyilas* raids.

Some of the supplies were purchased by exempted Jews or Jews who had special permits to leave the confines of the ghetto. With the cooperation of the Red Cross, a special committee was formed on December 8 to supervise purchases and the allocation of supplies from the warehouses. Its members included Ottó Komoly (then acting as a leading Red Cross official), Mrs. Joel Brand, Wilhelm, Bauer, Vas, Stöckler, and Faragó. Also active in these endeavors were Pál Graber, István Kurzweil, József Pásztor, Jenő Váradi, and Miklós Vida. On December 18, the Red Cross decided to establish an office within the ghetto (at 17 Wesselényi Street) with about 50 employees.

Delivery of food shipments was frequently prevented by the *Nyilas* who manned the main gates of the ghetto. When called upon by Lőcsey to halt this interference, János Bata, the local *Nyilas* leader, expressed anger over the "seditious" activities of the Jews. Bata was particularly upset that the Red Cross had supplied some cheese and eggs for the ghetto's children when these items were no longer available in Budapest itself. Occasionally some food found its way into the black market, both within and outside the ghetto, but the price was prohibitive for almost all the Jews. The official price of bread, for example, was 1.5 *Pengős*. The black market price outside of the ghetto was 10 to 12 *Pengős*, while within the ghetto it was 500.

After the Soviet encirclement of Budapest on December 25, the supplying of the ghetto, like that of the capital as a whole, became all but impossible. With the dwindling of local reserves, the number of meals became fewer and the portions became ever smaller and the soups ever thinner. Nutritional problems were aggravated by the fact that many ghetto dwellers were older people requiring special diets. In addition, close to 6,000 children and about the same number of sick Jews in the 18 makeshift infirmaries or hospitals also required special attention, or special diets.[106] The meals were normally distributed in the buildings from large cauldrons, theoretically containing as many portions as there were Jews in the respective buildings.[107] However, the distribution was not always equitable, in part because the cauldron-bearing kitchen employees were occasionally attacked by other hungry ghetto inhabitants bent on getting more than their rightful share. The public kitchens did not, of course, have the resources to make up the losses, and as a result a number of Jews occasionally had to do without food for longer periods of time.

During the few weeks before the liberation, the situation within the ghetto became ever more critical. The number of Jews dying of starvation increased daily.

Health Problems

Hunger was but one of the many critical problems that confronted the ghetto population. Coupled with overcrowding and the inadequacy of sanitary facilities, it contributed to a major health problem with which the Jewish leadership could hardly cope. This was aggravated by the atrocities of the *Nyilas* whose ferocity increased with the tightening of the Soviet ring around the capital and by the intensity of the Soviet rocket and mortar attacks which did not spare the ghetto.

The ghetto suffered from many health-related problems, of which the most important ones were the absence of soap and disinfectants, inadequate hospital care, and no place to bury the dead.

Bathing was virtually impossible. Those fortunate enough to have had apartments with bathrooms were no better off than those without them: there was not enough water or fuel. Moreover, the tubs were normally used to store water. Through the good offices of Solymossy the Jewish Council acquired a large laundry at 9 Kazinczy Street and the use of the "Hungaria" bathing facilities for two days a week. But by the time these facilities were put into operation, the ghetto was about to be freed.

Huge piles of garbage accumulated throughout the ghetto's existence; in spite of the Council's oft-repeated appeals, the sanitation department (*Köztisztasági Hivatal*) failed to remove it. (In all fairness, at the time of the siege the department lacked the equipment and manpower to remove garbage from the city itself, let alone the ghetto.) By the time of the liberation, the garbage accumulated during the seven weeks of the ghetto's life lay in heaps in the squares, street corners, and behind the gates and fences of the ghetto buildings. The danger of epidemics the piled-up garbage posed was averted only because of the cold winter.

The health and hospital situation of the ghetto dwellers was desperate. The well-equipped modern Jewish Hospital on Szabolcs Street had been taken over by the Germans shortly after the occupation, after which the Jewish Council, with the cooperation of the displaced physicians and nurses had established two makeshift hospitals—one at a converted Jewish parochial school at 44 Wesselényi Street, the other at 2 Bethlen Square (in a section of the OMZSA building). Since both of these institutions were outside the ghetto limits, special permission had to be obtained for their use by the ghetto population. In an effort to protect them from the onslaught of the *Nyilas,* they were renamed "Central Emergency Hospital of the International Red Cross" (*Nemzetközi Vöröskereszt Központi Szükségkórháza*). The small auxiliary units within the ghetto were identified as "Red Cross Hospital" (*Vöröskeresztes kórház*). The *Nyilas,* however, attacked all the same.

The facilities of the central hospitals, like those of the auxiliary units within the ghetto, were taxed to the limit. They were overcrowded not only because of an excessive number of legitimate patients, but also because of the large number of other Jews who sought refuge there. The problem persisted even after the "unauthorized" Jews were removed into the ghetto following Szegő's resolute actions on December 21. In fact, it became more aggravated after that period due to the increased intensity of the Soviet attacks and the growing brutality of the *Nyilas.*

The scenes at the makeshift hospitals evoked images of Dante's inferno. The number of emergency cases increased daily and the hospital beds were soon filled. Patients had to be laid all over the floor. Soon even the nurses' and the doctors' quarters were filled with patients. Drugs were in short supply, and sanitary and toilet facilities were inadequate. Water declined in availability, as did food. And during the last weeks of the siege, it was impossible to bury the dead.

Most of the patients arrived in critical condition. There were hundreds of suicide cases, mostly among the converted and highly assimilated Jews—those who suddenly found their world in shambles; others were brought in with serious injuries following armed attacks by the *Nyilas*—some of them after having been shot into the Danube, or in the wake of Soviet bombardments; still others suffered from a variety of chronic illnesses associated with old age, malnutrition, or infection. Emergency surgery was frequently performed on kitchen tables covered by sheets and often without anesthetics. The surgical team composed of Drs. György Frank, József Róth, and László Tauber worked near miracles. After Christmas day, electricity was no longer available; many of the emergency operations had to be performed by the light of home-made candles or flashlights. The hospitals had a maternity section as well as other specialized services under the competent care and guidance of a number of self-sacrificing physicians and assistants.[108]

A major health problem for the community was the difficulty of coping with the increasing number of dead. The Jewish Council was responsible for the burial of the Jews who died in the ghetto as well as those who were killed outside it. Originally the Jewish Council had agreed with the Funeral Enterprise (*Temetkezési Vállalat*) of Budapest that the Jewish dead would continue to be buried in the community's large cemeteries. However, a complication arose when the Jewish employees of both large cemeteries were suddenly arrested and deported to Auschwitz, even before the *Nyilas* coup. After the coup, the leaders and most officials of the Jewish Burial Society (*Chevra Kadisha*) of Pest were also arrested, compounding the problem. The emergency was handled with remarkable effectiveness thanks primarily to the tireless efforts of Márkus Trebitsch, the Secretary General of the Burial Society.[109] With the help of Solymossy and the appropriate municipal authorities, the Burial Society was permitted to continue its operations using the facilities of the Communal Funeral Society (*Községi Temetkezési Egylet*). As a result of Trebitsch's efforts, offices were established in both ghettos for record-keeping, though often this was all but impossible because the *Nyilas* destroyed the victims' documents.

Before the encirclement of Budapest by Soviet troops on December 24, burial was relatively orderly. The ritual services were held within the ghetto at a makeshift funeral home at 44 Kazinczy Street. The coffins were escorted to the ghetto gate, where they were handed over to Christian drivers who took them for burial, mostly in the large Rákoskereszturi Cemetery. The services were usually officiated by Dr. Béla Berend, the Rabbi of the ghetto. The services for those who died in the international ghetto were usually held at 32 Pozsonyi Road.

The bodies of Jews who died outside the two ghettos were collected in the facilities of the Institute of Anatomy (*Bonctani Intézet*). Thanks to the cooperation of Dr. József Juhász, a police counselor, the bodies were not subjected to autopsies, as these were prohibited under Jewish law.

Not all the bodies transferred to the main cemetery could be immediately interred, for there was an acute shortage of manpower. Since the Jewish gravediggers had been removed, only 10 to 12 Christian gravediggers were available to bury between 80 and 120 bodies daily. The burial was supervised by János Nyíri, the Christian chief gardener of the cemetery, who not only continued to perform his traditional functions, but took on most duties of the traditional *Chevra Kadisha* representative. He kept accurate records of the graves, including, in the case of the approximately 100 double graves, the names of those who were buried underneath and of those who were buried on top.

After December 24, the intensity of the fighting made the transfer of the bodies to the Rákoskereszturi Cemetery all but impossible. For a while the corpses were collected at the old cemetery near Kerepesi Road, where they eventually were buried after the liberation. After January 3, 1945, bodies could no longer be removed from the ghetto. While a few were buried in Klauzál Square and some other parts of the ghetto, most corpses were first collected in the community's ritual-bath building at 40 Kazinczy Street. After the tubs and halls were filled, the corpses were stored in the courtyard of the buildings, as well as in the courtyards of hospitals and of the Council's headquarters. Corpses were also stacked like lumber in a number of emptied commercial establishments, in Klauzál Square, and in the courtyard of the Dohány Street Synagogue.

When the ghetto was liberated on January 17, approximately 3,000 bodies awaited burial. Since no facilities existed for taking the bodies to the Jewish cemeteries for ritual interring, 2,218 were buried in several mass graves in the garden surrounding the Heroes' Temple (*Hősök*

Temploma) adjacent to the Great Synagogue on Dohány Street. The number of Jews who died in Budapest in 1944 and 1945—many as a result of the excesses of the *Nyilas*—came close to 17,000.[110]

Education and Religious Life

In such dark days religion offered a degree of solace to the persecuted Jews of Budapest. Religious life in the capital remained relatively normal until the middle of June 1944, when the Jews were ordered into the Yellow-Star houses. Afterward, religious services were organized in the adjacent synagogues and in the air-raid shelters of most Yellow-Star buildings. Often even nonbelievers partook in the services, to provide a *minyan*. Children, especially those of *Bar Mitzvah* age, were given religious instruction by rabbis and teachers who volunteered their services. In addition lectures were given on a variety of themes drawn from the Bible or from Jewish history.

The establishment of the ghetto brought about a further intensification of religious life not only because of the greater spiritual needs of the Jews but also because of their greater concentration. A meeting held on December 4 by some leaders of the Jewish Council and a few interested rabbis and teachers, including Rabbi Ödön Kálmán, led to the systematic organization of religious services and instruction. Of the three major synagogues within the ghetto, one—the Orthodox Synagogue at Kazinczy Street—had been closed down by the Germans. The two others—the Great Synagogue at Dohány Street and the synagogue at Rumbach Sebestyén Street—had been used as internment camps for Jews apprehended by the *Nyilas*. They were gradually cleared and opened for services, which were scheduled for the hours when the Jews were permitted to leave their homes. Attendance was naturally highest on Friday nights and Saturday mornings. At other times most Jews held their prayer sessions in the shelters of their buildings.

Special services and social welfare programs were organized for the various denominations of converted Jews. Especially active in this sphere were Jakab Raile of the Catholic Church, Gyula Nagy[111] and Sándor Borsos of the Reformed Church, and Ferenc Sréter of the Lutheran Church. A number of missionary priests and ministers offered salvation through conversion.

In addition to ministering to the spiritual needs of the ghetto dwellers, many rabbis consoled the sick and the disabled.

The religious education of children was the responsibility of teachers and rabbis who had responded to the appeal of the Jewish Council. Classes were normally held in empty commercial establishments near air-raid shelters, where the children were also fed. As in the Yellow-Star buildings earlier in the year, the emphasis was on preparing children for their *Bar Mitzvah*.[112] The elders of the community made a special effort to celebrate *Hanukkah*. The lighting of the candles in commemoration of the Temple's rededication in 165 B.C. had a welcome though short-lived uplifting effect upon the dejected population of the ghetto.

Governmental Quixotism and Unchecked Terror

On December 9, 1944, the Red Army, having broken through the "Friesner Line," launched a massive offensive that reached the Danube at Vác, just north of Budapest. On December 22, Soviet forces led by Marshal Fyodor I. Tolbukhin attacked in force between the Balaton and the Danube; they reached Buda two days later. The last two roads out of Buda, leading to Esztergom and Szentendre, were cut on December 26. On December 27 the Soviets finally encircled Budapest.[113] The collapse of the Szálasi regime, and the long-awaited liberation of the country from the Nazi yoke was now inevitable. Nevertheless, the *Nyilas* government, members of Parliament, and party officials, who had earlier moved to Sopron (and partly to Kőszeg) in Western Hungary, continued to operate as if all were well. Completely oblivious to the realities of the Soviet siege, the government continued to issue decrees and hold meaningless parliamentary sessions; it did so until the country's liberation on April 4, 1945. As part of the charade, Szálasi, Kemény, and Beregfy paid a visit to Hitler on December 4. The question of the possible abandonment of Budapest was discussed at the Hungarians' request. The Germans were adamant in their decision to defend the Hungarian capital, at whatever cost.[114]

A few days before fleeing Budapest, Gábor Vajna had found the time to order that all Hungarian streets, roads, and squares named after Jews, or whose names had any connection with Jews, should immediately be renamed.[115] On December 23, Vajna capped his legislative madness by issuing a decree calling on all Jews in hiding to report within 24 hours to the Jewish Council for assignment to the ghetto. The decree read as follows:

In my Decree of December 2 made public by posted announcements, I instructed all Jews required to wear the Yellow Star living in the municipality of

Budapest to move into the territory assigned to them [the ghetto] within a specified period of time.

I have been informed that a large number of the Jews required to move into the ghetto are hiding in the capital and are avoiding their obligation to relocate, often by using false identification papers.

Because of its importance for public order and security, I call upon those Jewish persons who have not yet abided by the decrees in force and have not yet moved into the ghetto to report within 24 hours after publication of this Decree to the Jewish Council, 12 Síp Street, for relocation.

The obligation to report is also extended to those who have thus far held exempt status as labor servicemen or employees of war industries.

They may take along to 12 Síp Street:

a) The clothes they are wearing;
b) Two sets of underwear and shirts;
c) Bedding;
d) Their entire stock of food;
e) All their money and smaller items of value (rings, jewelry, etc.).

The 24-hour deadline does not apply to:

1) Very sick Jews in hospitals who are unable to walk, regardless of whether or not the hospital holds exemption status;
2) Jewish children in children's homes;
3) The Jewish personnel assigned to the care and treatment of the persons mentioned under (1) and (2) (physicians, nurses, children's supervisors, servants, cleaners). However, the number of such persons may not exceed 10% of the number of persons under their care or treatment. The exempt persons listed above must also report to the ghetto by noon of December 31 at the latest.

II

All Jewish patients and persons receiving care in hospitals, whether Christian or Jewish ones, must be transferred to the temporary hospitals established in the ghetto or to the hospitals at 44 Wesselényi Street and 2 Bethlen Square which are temporarily allowed to operate outside the ghetto. The transfer is the responsibility of the director or chief physician of the hospital where the patient is confined at the time of publication of this decree. The superintendents of the Jewish buildings in the so-called International Ghetto must prepare an exact list of their protected tenants and prevent, under threat of internment, the hiding of Jews who do not belong there.

The superintendents and air-raid wardens as well as the heads of war industries, enterprises, plants, and institutions (hospitals, sanatoria, welfare establishments, schools, etc.) must instruct the Jews compelled to wear the Yellow Star living in the buildings or employed in the plants or enterprises to move immediately into the ghetto; if the instructions are not followed, then within 48 hours after the publication of this decree they must report these Jews in writing to their police precincts and obtain a receipt for their report.

All persons hiding Jews as well as those listed in the above paragraph who do not abide by the obligations specified therein, and those who by virtue of their employment, assignment, or circumstances know or should know about Jews in hiding and the hiding of Jews (for example, foremen, personnel supervisors, household or industrial custodians, neighbors, etc.), and fail to report them, are subject to the penalties specified in Article 18 of Decree 8.935/1944.B.M. of December 2 [deportation of family heads to labor camps and internment of all members of the immediate family].

Military personnel violating this decree will be considered deserters according to the martial decrees, and will be handed over to the Royal Hungarian Armed Forces for punishment.[116]

The manhunt for Jews in hiding, which had been feverish enough since the establishment of the ghetto, was further intensified after the issuance of Vajna's decree. In their zeal to fulfill what they imagined was their patriotic duty, the *Nyilas* brought into the ghetto not only Jews caught in hiding places or denounced by their neighbors, but also Jews of foreign citizenship, "protected" Jews, and even a few non-Jews. The day after the issuance of the decree, for example, the *Nyilas* brought in 19 persons of Swedish citizenship. Among these were Asta Nielson, King Gustav's cousin, and a Miss Bauer, the Swedish Minister's secretary.[117]

Early in 1945, the *Nyilas* Parliament authorized Christians married to Jews to divorce their partners without incurring any responsibility toward them. The act also stipulated that Christians in mixed marriages who were unwilling to divorce their spouses would be subjected to the anti-Jewish provisions in effect.[118]

During the last few months of the war, when the liberated part of Hungary was gradually returning to normality under the leadership of a new Soviet-backed Hungarian government seated in Debrecen,[119] the *Nyilas* exploited the chaos and anarchic conditions in the areas still under their control to continue their excesses against the Jews. Their looting and murder had a devastating effect upon the Jews, and also a negative effect on Hungary's contribution to the war effort. While the Germans were not, of course, concerned with the former, they were quite angered over the latter. Constant pressures for the protection of the interests of the Reich were exerted by all German agencies in Hungary, including the SS.[120] Most of the *Nyilas*, however, paid little heed and continued to pursue their own murderous instincts, creating a climate of unchecked terror.

The reign of terror that had begun with Szálasi's assumption of power on October 15 went almost completely out of control after the beginning of the Soviet siege. Gangs of armed *Nyilas* roamed Budapest and the other territories under their control, looting and killing defenseless victims and above all Jews. The situation was aptly described by Ferenc Fiala, the noted anti-Semitic journalist and Szálasi's Press Chief, in his postwar memoirs: "Order broke down in the capital and anyone who carried a machine-gun . . . could act as judge and executioner."[121]

The gangs, consisting mostly of teenagers, roamed around the city hunting for Jews "in hiding." They attacked Jews huddled in their shelters, cellars, and homes outside the ghetto, in the international ghetto, and in the large ghetto. Their attacks became increasingly daring and ever larger in scale.

The number of Jews "executed" by the *Nyilas,* who often tortured their victims first, usually varied between 50 and 60 a night. Among the victims were a number of exempted Jews whose preferential status the *Nyilas* chose to ignore. The bodies of the Jews killed outside the ghetto were usually removed to the morgue of the Institute of Forensic Medicine. After the storage areas were filled to capacity, the Institute's head, Dr. Ferenc Orsos, himself a *Nyilas* or *Nyilas*-sympathizer, reportedly urged that the bodies be thrown into the Danube "to avoid another Katyn."

In the last few weeks before the liberation *Nyilas* gangs invaded a large number of Jewish-inhabited buildings, including those at 30 Pozsonyi Road, 39 and 48/b Legrády Károly Street, 30 Eötvös Street, 45 Sziget Street, 49 Damjanich Street, 36 Visegrádi Street, 1 Jókai Street, 21 Katona József Street, and 27 Wesselényi Street.[122] Usually, the Jews were first robbed of their last remaining valuables. Many were shot on the spot; others were taken to the banks of the Danube and shot into the river. The method of execution was to tie three people together, place them at the edge of the Danube, and shoot the middle one in the back of his head at close range so that the weight of his body would pull the other two living victims into the river. Some of the most horrible atrocities were committed by a gang led by András Kun, a vitriolically anti-Semitic Catholic priest. The luckier among the Jews, mostly women and children, were allowed to stay alive and were transferred into the large ghetto.

On December 28, a mixed gang of *Nyilas* and Swabian SS attacked the Jewish Hospital on Bethlen Square. The patients and the hospital personnel were terrorized for 24 hours and robbed of their possessions. Before leaving the invaders selected 28 younger-looking males whom they took to a commercial school building on Wesselényi Street, where they were murdered two days later. On December 31, late in the afternoon, another gang consisting of 40 to 50 *Nyilas* invaded the so-called Glass House at 29 Vadász Street, which was under the protection of the Swiss. They used a grenade to blast the door open and entered firing their automatic rifles, instantly killing three Jews, including the wife of Rabbi Lajos Scheiber, and wounding 20 others. Their original objective was apparently to loot what they suspected were Swiss warehouses; instead they discovered the hiding place of several thousand protected and unprotected Jews. Miklós Krausz, one of the leading figures in the Swiss protection scheme, then got in touch with the authorities in a desperate attempt to secure assistance. Acting through the Swiss Legation at Szabadság Square, he sought help from Pál Szalai,[123] the *Nyilas* Party's liaison to the Police; Colonel Csipkés, the military commander of the city; and Police Chief Béla Kubissy. Arthúr Weisz, the former owner and commander of the building, tried to gain time by engaging in dilatory negotiations with the *Nyilas* gang leaders. In the meantime the *Nyilas* ordered about 800 Jews into the street for "relocation." These Jews escaped the fate of many of their brethren thanks to the resolute intervention of two squad cars of police and a military unit commanded by First Lieutenant Pál Fábry and Ensign Attila Horváth. They had been ordered to the scene by Szalai. The following day, however, a group of *Nyilas* returned and lured building-owner Weisz into a trap. He was invited to negotiate with the *Nyilas* district leader about "matters of mutual interest," a negotiation session from which he never returned.

That same day, another *Nyilas* gang invaded the Ritz Hotel and found Ottó Komoly, the noted Zionist leader and Jewish Council member, who had moved there from his home on 52 Baross Street a short while earlier for security reasons. He was removed to the *Nyilas* House at 14 Városház Street, where the notoriously savage leadership group composed of Kurt Rettmann, Mihály Balog, and Imre Nidosi killed him. On January 5, another member of the Jewish Council, Miklós Szegő, the former head of the Jewish community of Székesfehérvár, was picked up by the *Nyilas* on his way home from the ghetto near Pannonia Street and killed. He thus became the third member of the Council (János Gábor had been the first) to die violently at the hands of the *Nyilas*. The President of the Council, Lajos Stöckler, was luckier. On January 8, he and the members of his family, together with 154 other Jews, were removed by the *Nyilas* from their shelter at 4 Üllői Road. They were first taken to the Mária Terezia military barracks and transferred shortly afterward to the *Nyilas* House at 41 Ferenc Boulevard. They were rescued by Szalai and Captain of Police Gyulay on orders of Lőcsey, who had been alerted about their arrest by Council member József Nagy.

The atrocities on the Pest side of the capital were matched by those perpetrated in Buda. Here too there were large numbers of individual actions.[124] By far the most shocking crimes, however, were those against the patients and staff of two Jewish hospitals located at Maros and Városmajor streets.

The Maros Street Hospital had been established by the Jewish Holy Society of Buda (*Buda Szentegylet*). During the German occupation it operated under the auspices and protection of the International Red Cross. On January 11, 1945, it was surrounded by a number of *Nyilas* belonging to party chapters headquartered in Districts XII and XIII of the capital. Having blocked off the streets leading to the hospital, the *Nyilas* entered the hospital and began the wanton destruction of equipment and the torture and massacre of the 92 patients, doctors, and nurses who were there at the time. They threw the patients out of their beds, trampled upon their bodies, and shot anyone who could not walk. Those who were still able to walk were ordered to remove the bodies and bury them in a large pit they were first made to dig. When this task was completed, they too were shot into the mass grave. Only one nurse, named Joli, was able to escape; having survived the execution she moved out of the mass grave under the cover of night.

On January 14, the Orthodox Hospital in Városmajor Street was subjected to the same treatment. At the time of the attack it held close to 150 patients, doctors, and nurses, among them a number of Jewish patients who had been transferred from the János Sanatorium six days earlier on the basis of a list prepared by Dénes Rady, the Sanatorium's warden. On January 19, another group of *Nyilas* invaded the almshouse maintained by the Orthodox Holy Society at 2 Alma Road. They removed 90 inmates who were massacred shortly thereafter at Városmajor.

The manhunts, raids, executions, murders, and massacres continued without interruption until the liberation of the capital.[125]

Plans for the Destruction of the Ghetto

The *Nyilas* and the SS also directed their rage against the Jews trapped in the large ghetto. Lootings and mass murders took place daily. Some of these were catalogued by Stöckler and Domonkos in their appeals for help addressed to the *Nyilas* authorities, especially

Lőcsey. In response to their appeal of January 8, 1945, in which they detailed how the ghetto was periodically invaded by members of various uniformed and armed units, Lőcsey persuaded Ernő Vajna, the representative of the Arrow Cross Party assigned to the defense of Budapest (*Budapest védelmére rendelt pártmegbizott*), to issue an order prohibiting entry into the ghetto by unauthorized personnel.[126] The order, dated January 10, stipulated that entrance into the ghetto was to be only through two gates located at the ends of Wesselényi Street, and restricted to persons holding permits issued by Kurt Rettmann, the main district leader of the Hungarist Movement of the Arrow Cross Party; Lieutenant-Colonel Imre Nidosi, the leader of the party organization in District VII; or the Ministerial Counselor in Charge of Jewish Affairs, Lőcsey.

The order notwithstanding, the *Nyilas* continued for a few days at least to invade the ghetto and commit some of the most heinous crimes, including the massacre of the 43 Jews at 27 Wesselényi Street. In response to this crime, on January 12 Szalai had 100 policemen under the command of two officers assigned to the ghetto. These were quartered in the air-raid shelters of the Jewish Council's headquarters. Also assigned to the ghetto was a specially selected 15-member *Nyilas* unit that cooperated with the police in patrolling the streets of the ghetto and guarding its gates. Szalai took it upon himself to personally supervise these police–*Nyilas* forces and assigned his deputy Perjési, who was also respected by the *Nyilas,* to serve in close cooperation with the Council. From that time on, the number of violent incidents declined dramatically.

But the calm that enveloped the ghetto was the calm before the storm. Rumors began to circulate about alleged plans of the SS and the *Nyilas* to destroy the ghetto in a combined lightning operation before the entry of the Soviet troops. According to some of these rumors, the Germans planned to bomb the ghetto from the air. According to another source, the Germans and the *Nyilas* in the Royal Hotel were planning an invasion of the ghetto by an SS force of 500 under the command of Captain Mummi, a *Nyilas* force under the leadership of Vilmos Lucska, and 200 policemen under the command of Commissioner of Police Kubissy. The rumors were reinforced by the continued presence in the Royal Palace—the Fort—of SS-General of Police Hitschler and SS-Major Gottstein, the head of the political section.

Stöckler and Domonkos kept Szalai fully informed. Szalai tried to persuade Ernő Vajna to cancel the sinister plans, but to no avail. He then contacted General Schmidthuber, the commander of the SS-*Feldherrenhalle* armored division, whose political views appeared to differ from those held by the other German generals in Hungary. This is how Szalai described his efforts to save the ghetto of Budapest before a postwar People's Tribunal:

Two days before the liberation of the ghetto, in the late afternoon, one of the police officers ran into my office in the City Hall shelter and informed me that there was in readiness at the Royal Hotel a force consisting of approximately 500 German soldiers and 22 *Nyilas* Party members who were planning to mobilize 200 policemen to join them in a mass murder to be committed by machine guns that same evening. They also informed me that if I did not act within the next few minutes the units in the hotel would start their operation.

Károly Szabó, the liaison between Wallenberg, the Swedish Legation Secretary, and myself, was also in the City Hall shelter at the time. I discussed with him the plan for the prevention of this hideous mass-murder plan. I went to Dr. Ernő Vajna, who told me that he was aware of the operation, but would not prevent it.

Also in the City Hall shelter at the time was the German General Schmidthuber, the commander of the so-called SS-*Feldherrenhalle* Division, who, it was my impression, kept himself aloof from the political German generals here.

I asked for an immediate meeting with him through a German First Lieutenant named Fritz, who was his interpreter. I asked him whether he was aware of the operation planned for the ghetto, and I also informed him that members of his unit were among those mobilized in the Royal Hotel. I warned him that according to Wallenberg's communication, if he did not prevent this crime he would be held responsible and would be called to account not as a soldier but as a murderer. Thereupon he summoned *Nyilas* Party member Vilmos Lucska, a barber's assistant, who would have commanded the entire operation in his position as *Nyilas* leader of District VII. He also summoned a German captain by the name of Mummi who was headquartered in the Royal Hotel and would have led the Germans. He further summoned Dr. Ernő Vajna and Police Commissioner Kubissy, whom he ordered to prevent this crime as a result of my personal protest.

Instead of Mummi, a German sergeant appeared with Vilmos Lucska. While Schmidthuber immediately arrested the German sergeant, Dr. Ernő Vajna permitted Vilmos Lucska to escape. The happiest moment of my life came when I was able to prevent this awful crime. I believe I must state for the historical record that the approximately 120,000 people belonging to the Jewish Community of Budapest can attribute their survival to those who struggled for the life of their fellow men and who did not shrink in the face of mortar fire, constantly placing their own life in jeopardy.[127]

In the last analysis, the rapid advance of the Soviet forces was the major factor in the liberation of the ghetto and of the Jews in the rest of the capital. In spite of last-minute reinforcements, the German and

SS troops under the overall command of General Pfeffer-Wildenbruch and the remnants of the Hungarian army under the immediate command of General Iván Hindy proved no match for the victorious Red Army.[128] The Soviet forces liberated Pest on January 17–18, 1945 and Buda, after a bitter struggle, on February 13.[129]

The liberation of the Jews of Budapest did not put an end to the suffering of Hungarian Jews in Nazi-*Nyilas* hands. There were still thousands of trenchdiggers and labor servicemen in Western Hungary building the East Wall for the defense of Vienna. Many of these were freed by April 4, when all of Hungary was finally liberated. Others were removed to various German concentration camps in which they shared the fate of other victims of Nazism until the end of the war on May 9.

Notes

1. Even Lajos Reményi-Schneller and Béla Jurcsek, the two most vocally Germanophile members of the government, went along with the pro-surrender vote at the Crown Council Meeting of September 7. C. A. Macartney, 2:338. The unanimity was apparently achieved only after the following unrealistic armistice conditions were agreed upon: the Allies would occupy only the main strategic positions; no Romanian or Yugoslav troops would participate in the occupation; the Hungarian police and civil service would be left in their positions; and the Allies would permit the withdrawal of the German forces from Hungary. Ágnes Rozsnyói, *A Szálasi puccs* (The Szálasi Coup) (Budapest: Kossuth, 1962), p. 29.

2. The Germans were informed of this decision at both the civilian and military levels. Lakatos communicated with Veesenmayer; General János Vörös, the Chief of the General Staff, informed Hans Greiffenberg, the German Military Attaché in Budapest. C. A. Macartney, 2:338.

3. *Ibid.,* p. 367.

4. *Eichmann in Hungary. Documents,* ed. Jenő Lévai (Budapest: Pannonia, 1961), p. 146.

5. The Hungarian armistice delegation was led by General Gábor Faraghó, who was the administrative head of the gendarmerie and as such had been directly or indirectly involved in the deportations. His selection was presumably based on his "good connections" in Moscow where he had served as Hungarian Military Attaché in 1940–1941.

6. C. A. Macartney, 2:363, 376.

7. For an identification and evaluation of the forces assigned to the defense of the capital see *ibid.,* pp. 362 ff.

8. Skorzeny arrived in Hungary on September 21, equipped with a map of the underground labyrinth that honeycombed the Royal Palace area. For Skorzeny's account see his *Skorzeny's Secret Missions* (New York: Dutton, 1950), pp. 193–218. The account is rendered in a somewhat different version in the British edition: *Skorzeny's Special Missions* (London: Robert Hale, 1957), pp. 126–46.

9. For further details on the role of Skorzeny and Bach-Zelewski see *Criminals at Large,* eds. István Pintér and László Szabó (Budapest: Pannonia, 1961), pp. 242–70.

10. In spite of his unsuccessful meeting with Horthy on August 29, Szálasi continued the drive for the acquisition of power, preferably with the blessing of Horthy and the

consent of the Germans. This point was emphasized, for example, in SS-*Obergruppenführer* Gottlob Berger's note of September 11, 1944, addressed to Himmler via Karl Brandt. *NA,* Microcopy T-175, Roll 59. (Archives of the *Reichsführer*-SS.)

11. The agreement called for the Szálasi government to be composed of eight Arrow Cross and three MÉP representatives, one National Socialist, one ex-Imrédist, and two generals. The Arrow Cross was to be represented by Szálasi (Prime Minister and Acting Head of State), Jenő Szőllősi (Deputy Prime Minister), Gábor Kemény (Foreign Affairs), Gábor Vajna (Interior), László Budinszky (Justice), Emil Szakváry (Industry), Ferenc Kassay (Propaganda and National Protection; *Nemzetvédelmi és propaganda*), and Emil Kovarcz (The Nation's Total Mobilization and War Readiness; *A nemzet totális mozgósitására és harcbaállitásá*ra); the MÉP was to be represented by Lajos Reményi-Schneller (Finance), Béla Jurcsek (Supply), and Lajos Szász (Trade and Communications); Fidél Pálffy, the National Socialist, was to become Minister of Agriculture, and Ferenc Rajniss, a former associate of Imrédy in the Party of Hungarian Renewal, was to become Minister of Cults and Public Education. The two generals, both members of the Hungarian Generals' Corps (*Tábornoki kar*), were Károly Beregfy, slated for the Ministry of Defense, and Vilmos Hellebronth, to be in charge of "continuity of production" (*a termelés folyamatos vezetése*). C. A. Macartney, 2:370. When the Szálasi government was inaugurated on October 16 its composition was exactly as agreed. The only addition was Sándor Csía, Szálasi's longtime friend and *Nyilas* party leader, who was appointed minister without portfolio. *Budapesti Közlöny,* no. 236, October 17, 1944, p. 1.

12. The Executive Committee consisted of Lajos Szász, President; Rajniss and Jenő Szőllősi, Vice-Presidents; Ödön Andréka, László Baky, László Bárdossy, Kálmán Bocsáry, Ferenc Hamm, Bálint Hóman, Lajos Huszovszky, Andor Jaross, Mihály Kolosváry-Borcsa, Béla Marton, István Milótay, József Nyirő, Jenő Rátz, Count Mihály Teleki, and Gábor Vajna, members. Iván Nagy, a deputy from the Délvidék area, was added later. C. A. Macartney, 2:386.

13. *Ibid.*

14. Lévai, *Zsidósors Magyarországon,* p. 288.

15. For a well-documented account of the *Nyilas* drive for power, see Teleki, *Nyilas uralom Magyarországon,* pp. 9–27.

16. General József Heszlényi, the Germanophile Commander of the Third Army, was not informed of the plan. The code message for the alignment with the Red Army was: "Order of March 1, 1920, to be executed." For further details on Heszlényi, see chapter 9.

17. For details on "Operation Mickey Mouse," as the operation against Horthy Jr. is often referred to, see C. A. Macartney, 2:355, 399–401. For the German version of the background of the operation, see Wilhelm Hoettl, *The Secret Front* (New York: Praeger, 1954), pp. 211–14.

18. Hlatky was lured back to the Royal Palace while the Proclamation was being read, and placed under arrest. He was subsequently deported.

19. For Rahn's account of his encounter with the Hungarians, see his *Ruheloses Leben. Aufzeichnungen und Erinnerungen* (Restless Life. Notes and Recollections) (Düsseldorf: Diederichs Verlag, 1949), pp. 262–74. See also C. A. Macartney, 2:406–7.

20. For the complete text of the Proclamation and of the Order of the Day, see Lévai, *Zsidósors Magyarországon,* pp. 295–96. For the English version, see *The New York Times,* October 17, 1944.

21. According to the evidence gathered by Macartney, Vörös consented to the dispatch of the substitute order. The original one had come into the hands of a rabidly Germanophile officer, General Dezső László. László had been shown the original by Captain Albin Kapitánffy, Vörös's adjutant, who had received it from Vattay for transmission to the frontline commanders. During a brief meeting involving László, Kapitánffy, General

Jenő Major, Colonel Lajos Nádas (the head of the Operational Section of the Ministry of Defense), and Veesenmayer, Vörös—described by Macartney as "a despicable creature" and as "a coward and double-dealer"—lost his nerve and agreed to the substitution of orders. C. A. Macartney, 2:413–18. Two days after the coup Vörös fled to the Soviet side after having been held briefly by the Gestapo. He insisted, apparently falsely, that the original order had been faked by disloyal subordinates before it reached him.

22. Vilmos Nagy, the former Minister of Defense, claims that many of the top-ranking officers who played an important role in assuring the victory of the *Nyilas* were of German-Swabian background. He identifies the following officers in this category (their original German name is within parentheses): Major Abonyi (Nareddi); Colonel Mihály Bán (Friebert); Captain Pál Darnóy (Danzinger); Major Károly Demjén (Kirchlechner); Captain Jenő Dénes (Dotzauer); Major Dienes (Turcsin); Captain Lajos Hajdu (Rösler); Colonel János Henkey (Hering); Captain József Ijjas (Freiler); Major Albin Kapitánfy (Kratzner); Colonel Nádas (Nadler); Lieutenant-Colonel Jenő Németh (Popovics); Lieutenant-Colonel Valér Porzezsinszky; Captain Antal Radnóczy (Riedl); Captain Artur Rády-Péntek (Freitag); Major-General Sándor Szávay (Szlávits); and Captain Emil Szörényi (Reischl). Almost all of these officers had been associated with the General Staff. Vilmos Nagy, *Végzetes esztendők, 1938–1945* (Fateful Years, 1938–1945) (Budapest: Körmendy, n.d.), p. 258.

23. The German version of the coup and of its antecedents are detailed in Winkelmann's memorandum to Himmler dated October 25, 1944. In it, the Higher SS and Police Leader in Hungary reveals not only the specific roles played by the SS officers, including the role of Skorzeny and SS-*Hauptsturmführer* Otto Klages in the abduction of Horthy Jr., of SS-*Untersturmführer* Kernmayr in the occupation of the radio broadcasting station, and of Bach-Zelewski and SS-*Standartenführer* Zehender in the storming of the Fort, but also the rivalries with the Foreign Office and its representative, Veesenmayer. The memorandum, hand-delivered by Kurt Becher, was acknowledged by Himmler "with thanks for a job well done" on October 30. *NA*, Microcopy T-175, Roll 59.

24. For Lakatos's version of the events leading to the coup, see NG-1848.

25. For Horthy's account of the coup see his *Memoirs* (New York: Robert Speller and Sons, 1957), pp. 227–41.

26. For further details on the coup see C. A. Macartney, 2:391–443; Teleki, *Nyilas uralom Magyarországon*, pp. 28–51; and Nagy, *Végzetes esztendők*, pp. 229–72. See also Rozsnyói, *A Szálasi-puccs*, 105 pp.

27. Teleki, *Nyilas uralom Magyarországon*, pp. 134–35. In his telegram to the German Foreign Office dated October 28, 1944, Veesenmayer gave the following statistical breakdown: On March 19, there were 800,000 Jews. Of these, 430,000 were transferred to the territory of the Reich; 150,000 were serving in the labor service companies, and 200,000 were in Budapest. *A Wilhelmstrasse és Magyarország. Német diplomáciai iratok Magyarországról, 1933–1944* (The Wilhelmstrasse and Hungary. German Diplomatic Papers on Hungary, 1933–1944), eds. György Ránki et al. (Budapest: Kossuth, 1968), p. 907. See also *RLB*, Doc. 236.

28. Lévai, *Zsidósors Magyarországon*, p. 301.

29. It was such an instruction, issued on October 17, for example, that enabled Sándor Boros to continue his services on behalf of the Jewish inmates at Kistarcsa and elsewhere. For the text of the instructions see Lévai, *A pesti gettó* (The Ghetto of Pest) (Budapest: Officina, n.d.), p. 21.

30. The government, inaugurated on October 16, was composed in accordance with the earlier Veesenmayer-Szálasi agreement (see above). Among the major officials associated with the Ministry of the Interior were István Láday, a gendarmerie colonel who was made a Secretary of State in charge of the Political Police; Péter Hain, the notorious Hungarian secret security chief, who was reappointed to head the state security agency;

and László Baky, who was put in charge of public safety in the military operational territories. For well-documented details on the organization, structure, and personnel of the *Nyilas* party and governmental institutions, see Teleki, *Nyilas uralom Magyarországon,* pp. 112–23, 221–48.

31. During his trial in 1945–46, Szálasi tried to place all the blame for the atrocities on the KABSz members and on the Germans. *Ibid.,* pp. 136–37.

32. Lévai, *Zsidósors Magyarországon,* p. 319.

33. *Eichmann in Hungary,* pp. 145–46. A summary of Vajna's views coupled with a memorandum relating to the handling of the Jewish question in Hungary, which was submitted by the German Legation in Budapest to the Swiss Legation on October 19, 1944, were forwarded to the British Legation in Berne on November 29. *PRO,* Fo.371/42824, pp. 87–92.

34. This detail was revealed by Ferenczy in his testimony in the Vajna trial in 1946. Elek Karsai, *Itél a nép* (The People Judge) (Budapest: Kossuth, 1977), pp. 263–65.

35. For details on the activities of the IRC during the first month of the Szálasi era, containing accounts of the anti-Jewish persecutions, see *Notiz über die Situation der Juden in Ungarn* . . . (Note on the Situation of the Jews in Hungary . . .). Geneva, November 20, 1944, 8 pp. Gruesome details about the excesses committed against the Jews are also included in *Bericht über die Lage der Juden seit der Machtübernahme seitens der Szálasi Regierung* (Report on the Situation of the Jews Since the Acquisition of Power by the Szálasi Government), November 26, 1944. Both documents are available at Yad Vashem, Jerusalem, Archives M-20/47.

36. *RLB,* Doc. 226.

37. *Ibid.,* Doc. 227.

38. *Ibid.,* Doc. 234. A copy of the note was transmitted to Ribbentrop on October 24.

39. See chapter 25. In view of the changed political climate in Hungary, Horst Wagner, the head of Inland II, suggested that Veesenmayer make no further "concessions" beyond those agreed to by the Führer. *RLB,* Doc. 238.

40. *Ibid.,* Doc. 231.

41. *Ibid.,* Doc. 230.

42. Orders for this were only issued the following day, October 21. For text see *FAA,* 2:643–44.

43. *RLB,* Doc. 235.

44. The Council was reorganized shortly after the *Nyilas* coup. Although Ferenczy objected to the inclusion of Stern, Pető, and Wilhelm—the three who were intimately familiar with his dealings during the Lakatos era—he finally consented to Stern continuing as chairman. The reorganized Council included Berend, Földes, Ottó Komoly, Nagy, Stöckler, Miklós Szegő, and Lajos Vas. The actual leadership of the reorganized Council, which was never legally appointed, was exercised by Stöckler. It ceased to be an effective organization after its meeting of October 28, at which the SS suddenly appeared and took Stern and Stöckler to the Aschner Villa, on 13 Apostol Street, which was occupied by the Eichmann-*Sonderkommando.* Although he was released after one and a half hours, Stern, convinced that Ferenczy was after his life, decided to go into hiding. Most of the other members also decided to avoid Council headquarters from then on. Their fears were well-founded: a number of the leading officials of the Jewish community and Council, including Zoltán Kohn, Hugó Csergő, and Rezső Müller, were arrested and many of them were subsequently killed.

45. For example, when Stöckler tried to get in touch with Szálasi via First Lieutenant Ernő Gömbös, Szálasi's aide, he was informed that "the Leader of the Nation does not receive people on Jewish matters." When he attempted to see Vajna the latter's secretary, Kutassy, informed him that the Minister of the Interior would only see him on the recommendation of Ferenczy, "the person in charge of Jewish affairs." Lévai, *Zsidósors*

Magyarországon, p. 309. See also Stöckler's testimony in the trial of Vajna and Ferenczy in 1946 in Karsai's *Itél a nép,* pp. 265–68.

46. Lévai, *Zsidósors Magyarországon,* p. 318. For additional details on the atrocities committed against the Jews, see *Bericht über die Lage der Juden seit der Machtübernahme seitens der Szálasi Regierung.*

47. Decree 3.840/1944. M.E. *Budapesti Közlöny,* no. 250 (November 3, 1944), pp. 2–4.

48. Veesenmayer pointed out that in contrast to Winkelmann, who had asked for 50,000 Jews immediately, he had requested "only 25,000." The scaled-down request was designed to elicit prompt approval and was to be followed up by requests for additional installments of 25,000 Jews until the Final Solution of the Jewish question was achieved. On behalf of Ribbentrop, Brenner, on October 29, encouraged Veesenmayer to follow this approach. The tactics proved successful: Veesenmayer was able to report on November 1 that Szálasi had authorized the "loan" of an additional group of 25,000 Jews. Later in the month several informal agreements were reached by lower ranking officials for additional transfers of Jews. For example, at the Belvedere Hotel in Budapest the local Gestapo chief, SS- *Brigadeführer* Hans Geschke, reached an agreement with officials of the Ministry of Defense (Colonel József Herbeck) and the Ministry of the Interior (Colonel István Láday and Lieutenant-Colonel László Ferenczy) for the transfer of an additional 17,000 labor servicemen. *RLB,* Docs. 232, 233, 237, and 239. See also Lévai, *Zsidósors Magyarországon,* p. 358. and ———, *A pesti gettó,* p. 59.

49. The "East Wall," approved by Hitler, was to be built along the Vág Valley to Styria following the Austro-Hungarian border. Szálasi's original reluctance to "lend" the requested Jews for the project was apparently overcome through the direct intervention of Hitler and Martin Bormann at Jury's urging. C. A. Macartney, 2:450.

50. For text of the order and a list of the labor companies involved showing their number, location, and date of transfer, see *FAA,* 2:651–57. See also Appendix 2.

51. *Ibid.*

52. Order 171 005 Eln. 45.-1944. *Ibid.,* p. 658.

53. *Ibid.,* p. 659.

54. Police Order 10 690/Fk. Eln. 1944. *Ibid.,* pp. 662–63.

55. Kelecsényi was also associated with the anthropological section of the Arrow Cross Party headed by Csaba Gaál. In this capacity, he was primarily concerned with preserving the racial purity of the *Nyilas.* Lévai, *Zsidósors Magyarországon,* pp. 331–32.

56. *Protokoll einer Sitzung in der Swedischen Gesandschaft Budapest* (Minutes of a Meeting at the Swedish Legation in Budapest) (Jerusalem: Police d'Israel, 6-eme Bureau; document supplied for use in the Eichmann Trial.)

57. Decree 17 874. 1944/VII. res. of the Ministry of the Interior signed by László Hajnácskőy of the Gendarmerie. *FAA,* 2:660–61.

58. In his telegram of November 13, only five days after the start of the marches, Veesenmayer reported that according to Eichmann 27,000 Jews were already en route to Germany and that 40,000 more were expected for delivery in batches of 2,000 to 4,000 per day. *RLB,* Doc. 240.

59. Krausz, the head of the Budapest branch of the Palestine Office, had been co-opted as an officer of the Swiss Legation in the summer of 1944. For further details on his activities, see chapters 29 and 31.

60. For Ujváry's account see his "Szabálytalan önéletrajz" (An Irregular Autobiography) in *Menora* (Toronto), February 17, 1979. The report is in *Protokoll einer Sitzung in der Schwedischen Gesandschaft Budapest.* The Breszlauer-Kluger report may be found at Yad Vashem, Jerusalem, Archives M-20/47. For personal narratives by women who survived the marches and the subsequent deportations, see *FAA,* 2:647–48, 648–49, and 649–51.

61. NG-5216.

62. *Protokoll einer Sitzung in der Schwedischen Gesandschaft Budapest.*

63. SS-*Sturmbannführer* Rudolf Franz Ferdinand Hoess, the former commandant of Auschwitz, who was then in charge of the Jews employed in trench-digging operations in the Lower Danube area, in fact insisted that he wanted only able-bodied Jewish males, preferably under 40 years of age. *RLB,* Doc. 242. (Veesenmayer telegram no. 3353 of November 20, 1944.)

64. The position of the officers at Hegyeshalom was shared by practically every member of the Szálasi government. The one notable exception was Gábor Kemény, the Foreign Minister, who wanted the Jews employed in Hungary on projects of interest to the Hungarian nation. The position of the other members of the government was reflected in a report by the *Wehrmacht* Command in Hungary of November 21, a copy of which was sent to Himmler two days later. According to this report, the gendarmerie officer (presumably Ferenczy) appointed by the Hungarian government on October 30 to "solve" the Jewish question was authorized to hand over all the remaining Jews to the Germans. To make Hungary permanently *Judenrein,* the Hungarians allegedly insisted that the Jews marched to the frontier be employed only within the borders of the Reich. In pursuit of this objective, they were even willing to employ Christian civilians to build fortifications within Hungary. A resolution to this effect was in fact adopted by the National Manpower Committee (*Országos Munkaerő Bizottság*), when a German unit wanted to deploy Jews for the construction of some defense lines on Hungarian soil. *RLB,* Doc. 245. See also Teleki, *Nyilas uralom Magyarországon,* pp. 147–48.

65. Lévai, *A pesti gettó,* pp. 31–32.

66. Lévai, *Fekete könyv,* p. 275.

67. László Harsányi, *A kőszegi zsidók* (The Jews of Kőszeg) (Budapest: A Magyar Izraeliták Országos Képviselete, 1974), pp. 211–17. For further details see chapter 10.

68. For statistical data relating to the atrocities committed against the labor servicemen along the Austrian border, consult Lévai, *Fekete könyv,* pp. 275–76; Harsányi, *A kőszegi zsidók.* See also chapter 10.

69. For the text of the joint memorandum, see Lévai, *Zsidósors Magyarországon,* pp. 327–28. For further details see chapter 31.

70. *RLB,* Doc. 241.

71. *Ibid.* The cover letter and memorandum were forwarded by Eberhard von Thadden to Rolf Günther, Eichmann's deputy in Berlin, with a request that a position be taken concerning "the second category of Jews." *NA,* Microcopy T-120, Roll 4664. The Jewish Council was informed officially of the new classification of Jews and the imminent establishment of a ghetto by Jenő Szőllősi, the Deputy Prime Minister. Lévai, *A pesti gettó,* pp. 35–37.

72. Lévai, *Zsidósors Magyarországon,* pp. 322–23.

73. *Ibid.*

74. The "protected" Jews were subjected to particularly brutal treatment at the 2 Szent István Boulevard headquarters of the *Nyilas,* where Dénes Győri, the *Nyilas* leader of District V, and Sándor Straub, the *Nyilas* judge, were active. Lévai, "A pesti gettó végnapjai és felszabadulása" (The Last Days and the Liberation of the Ghetto of Pest), *Uj Élet* (New Life), Budapest, January 15, 1975.

75. For the text of Budinsky's and Kemény's responses, see Lévai, *A pesti gettó,* pp. 40–41.

76. Lévai, *Zsidósors Magyarországon,* pp. 323–24.

77. Lévai, *A pesti gettó,* p. 42.

78. The investigative raids became more frequent and severe after November 27, when Vajna declared that there were about 27,000 forged protective passes in circulation. Many of the raids were carried out in conjunction with an SS unit under the command of *Obersturmbannführer* Theodor Dannecker. Lévai, *Zsidósors Magyarországon,* p. 333.

79. *Ibid.*, pp. 332–34, 357. Those holding falsified Swiss passes were especially vulnerable; many of these passes were stamped "Susse" instead of "Suisse." For further details on the atrocities committed by the *Nyilas* in the international ghetto, see *Bericht über die Lage der Juden seit der Machtübernahme seitens der Szálasi Regierung* (Report on the Situation of the Jews Since the Acquisition of Power by the Szálasi Government) (Budapest, November 26, 1944). Yad Vashem, Archives M-20/47.

80. Teleki, *Nyilas uralom Magyarországon*, p. 143.

81. Upon receiving this news, Endre Milkó, the Swedes' representative in Tátra Street, attempted suicide, together with the members of his family. He succeeded, but his wife and two children were rescued.

82. Lévai, *A pesti gettó*, pp. 115–17.

83. For text of Solymossy's note, see *ibid.*, p. 43.

84. The head of the International Red Cross at the time was Friedrich Born; on December 9, 1944, Hans Weyermann was sent to Budapest to assist him. For further details on their role in Hungary see chapter 31.

85. For the complete text, see Lévai, *A pesti gettó*, pp. 53–57.

86. After the completion of the mass relocations on December 2, the freedom of movement within the ghetto was extended to four hours. The Jews were allowed also to leave their buildings between 2:00 and 4:00 P.M.

87. The permits held by Jews were green. Theoretically, Christians could enter the ghetto only with special blue permits issued by the Ministerial Commissioner in Charge of Jewish Affairs.

88. Lévai, *A pesti gettó*, p. 68.

89. Lévai, *Zsidósors Magyarországon*, p. 364.

90. The crimes committed by the "Zugló *Nyilas*" were revealed in great detail during their June 1967 trial in Budapest. For details on the trial, see József Solyom and László Szabó, *A zuglói nyilasper* (The Trial of the Zugló *Nyilas*) (Budapest: Kossuth, 1967), 384 pp. See also Lévai, "The War Crimes Trials Relating to Hungary: A Follow-up," in *HJS*, 3:251–90 and chapter 32.

91. The *Sonderlager*, in the facilities of the Institute for the Deaf and Dumb (*Siketnéma Intézet*) of the Jewish Community of Pest, served as a transit camp for the Jews awaiting emigration under the Kasztner–Eichmann deal reached earlier in the year. Until Eichmann's departure during the Lakatos era, the camp was under the protection of the SS. Because of its reputation as a haven, many Jews sought refuge there after the Szálasi coup; at one time it harbored 3,600 Jews, including several hundred deserters from the labor service companies. For further details on the Eichmann–Kasztner deal and the camp, see chapter 29.

92. Lévai, *A pesti gettó*, p. 69; Lévai, *Zsidósors Magyarországon*, p. 364.

93. When the Red Army began its attack on Budapest a few days later, Auguszt was among the first to flee the capital. He left behind his deputy Novak to complete the construction of the fence.

94. Dr. Sztehló's heroism and humanitarianism were recognized by the Special Commission for the Designation of the Righteous of Yad Vashem, Jerusalem, which awarded him its highest honor: a medal, a certificate of honor, and the right to plant a tree on the Avenue of the Righteous at Yad Vashem. For details on Sztehló's activities see "The Good Shepherd Committee" in chapter 30.

95. The note was signed by Angelo Rotta for the Vatican and by Carl Ivan Danielsson, Harald Feller, Jorge Perlasca, and Count Pongrácz for the Swedish, Swiss, Spanish, and Portuguese governments, respectively. For text see Lévai, *Zsidósors Magyarországon*, pp. 374–75. See also pp. 372–73.

96. Communication to the Council leaders by Solymossy on November 22. Lévai, *A pesti gettó*, p. 44.

97. *Ibid.*, pp. 143–45. The source also identifies the buildings included in each district.

98. *Ibid.*, pp. 142–43.

99. For the location of the police precincts, see *ibid.*, pp. 147–48.

100. In January 1945, at the height of the Soviet siege, the situation got so out of hand that the Jewish Council was compelled to issue an order requesting compliance with all demands of the ghetto police. For the text of the order, see *ibid.*, p. 110.

101. On December 16, for example, armed *Nyilas* gangs invaded the buildings at 10 Rumbach Sebestyén Street, 5 Klauzál Square, and 30 Klauzál Street. The raids were "justified" by their allegation that the Jews had hidden arms. *Ibid.*, pp. 84–85.

102. *Ibid.*, pp. 85, 155–56.

103. At the time of the occupation, the *Népasztal* was headed by Mór Weisz. The effectiveness with which the internees of the various camps were served was to a large extent due to the activities of Sándor Boros. During the *Nyilas* era, the *Népasztal* continued to function thanks to the heroic efforts of men and women like Mór and Sámuel Löwinger, József Friedmann, and Aranka Katz, the kitchen head. Boros, who settled some time after the war in Givat Mordechay in Israel, outlined his wartime activities in a memorandum addressed to Miksa Domonkos. A copy of this memorandum is in this author's possession.

104. The headquarters of the Jewish Council was hit by a mortar shell in the afternoon of December 10. Several buildings were bombarded on December 20 and 21 and many more after the encirclement of Budapest by Soviet forces on December 25. Among those who died on December 10 were Mrs. Endre Szebényi, Klári Ormai, and Lici Müller—all employees of the Council.

105. Testimony of Stöckler in the case against Vajna in 1946. Karsai, *Itél a nép*, p. 267.

106. On December 30, 1944, when the ghetto's population was approximately 50,000, there were 5,644 children, 5,957 patients, and over 10,000 old people who needed special diets.

107. The public kitchens played a vital role during the ghetto's life. Their effective operation in the midst of great adversity is due not only to the devotion and sense of duty of the managers, cooks, and kitchen personnel, but also to the heroic endeavors of the leaders and officials of the Jewish Council. The kitchens' capacity increased with the passage of time. On January 10, 1945, for example, the public kitchens distributed 58,845 portions. Of these, the Orthodox Public Table was responsible for 23,000, the Stern Kitchen for 15,131, the Skreck Kitchen for 12,757, and the kitchens at 5 and 22 Síp Street, for 2,836 and 5,121 portions, respectively.

108. Among the most prominent of the physicians active in the ghetto, in addition to the surgical team cited above, were Drs. Dezső Acél, the ghetto's chief physician, Jenő Bársony, Zoltán Barta, László Benedek, Glancz, Ferenc Groszman, Lajos Lévy, Német, and Hugó Richter. Drs. Acél and Barta were killed shortly after the liberation during a grenade attack that hit the hospital. Among the nurses and administrative personnel special mention must be made of Magda Clausius, Ibi Gál, Ilonka Grüngold, Vera Kolchner, Mrs. Samu Löwenstein, and Mrs. Tibor Reiner.

109. The head of the Budapest Burial Society was Pál Lunzer, who was arrested shortly after the German occupation and kept as a hostage in Kistarcsa. From there he was deported to Auschwitz on July 19, 1944, in the transport smuggled out of Hungary by Eichmann. For further details surrounding the arrest and deportation of Lunzer, see *Az Ember* (The Man), New York, July 1, 1961. On the extraordinary deportations from Kistarcsa, see chapter 25.

110. Lévai, *A pesti gettó*, pp. 139, 164–67.

111. In the 1970s, Reverend Nagy served as the pastor of the First Hungarian Reformed Church of New York. For his recollections of the ghetto period, see his "Képek a szomorúemlékű budapesti gettóból" (Reflections on the Sorrowful Days of the Budapest Ghetto). *Megújhodás* (Revival), Budapest, February 15, 1947, p. 4.

112. Lévai, *A pesti gettó*, pp. 168–74.

113. C. A. Macartney, 2:463. See also Teleki, *Nyilas uralom Magyarországon*, pp. 200–17.

114. The meeting was also attended by András Mecsér, the Hungarian Minister in Berlin since November 2, and by Keitel, Guderian, and Veesenmayer. C. A. Macartney, 2:461. See also Teleki, *Nyilas uralom Magyarországon*, pp. 172–80, and Péter Gosztonyi, "Szálasi látogatása Hitlernél" (Szálasi's Visit to Hitler). *Menora*, Toronto, December 14, 1974, p. 3.

115. Decree 960/1944. B.M. dated December 5, 1944. *Budapesti Közlöny*, no. 279, December 6, 1944, p. 5.

116. Lévai, *A pesti gettó*, pp. 94–95.

117. These two Swedish women were released the same day, following the resolute intervention of Born. The others were placed in the Swedish hospital within the ghetto. *Ibid.*, p. 97. In his *Fehér könyv* (White Book), pp. 172–74, Lévai asserts that Nielson (spelled Nilsson) and Bauer were freed through the intervention of Raoul Wallenberg.

118. The draft legislation was championed in the lower house by Róbert Haála, a *Nyilas* deputy. The representatives of the Christian churches opposed the law because, among other things, it violated the prerogatives of the ecclesiastical authorities. C. A. Macartney, 2:468. Teleki, *Nyilas uralom Magyarországon*, pp. 141–42.

119. On December 23, 1944, the Soviet government announced the formation in Debrecen of a "Provisional National Government of Hungary" headed by General Béla Miklós and a 230-member Hungarian Provisional National Assembly composed of 72 Communists, 57 Independent Smallholders, 35 Social Democrats, 12 National Peasants, 1 Peasant Unionist, 19 trade union representatives, 8 bourgeois party representatives, and 26 deputies representing various smaller parties and organizations. In his policy declaration of the following day, General Miklós promised the repeal of all antidemocratic laws, including the anti-Jewish laws, and the punishment of traitors and war criminals. C. A. Macartney, 2:464.

120. Otto Winkelmann, the Higher SS and Police Leader in Hungary, was also concerned about protecting the long-range economic interests of the Reich. In a lengthy note addressed to Himmler on December 26, he requested that all agencies dealing with Hungarians on all matters, including the possible transfer of Hungarian enterprises and industries to Germany, be subordinated to him. *NA*, Microcopy T-175, Roll 59.

121. Ferenc Fiala, *Zavaros évek* (Troubled Years) (London: Arányi Mária, 1965), p. 92.

122. The exact details of the 27 Wesselényi Street massacre have been recorded in a memorandum prepared at that time by Rabbi Béla Berend. Around 10:40 P.M. on January 11 a gang of six to eight individuals dressed in German, *Nyilas*, and *Honvéd* uniforms entered the cellar where they first robbed and then killed 26 women, 15 men, and a child. They also killed a couple in another apartment. For Berend's memorandum, see Lévai, *A pesti gettó*, pp. 129–30. Several statements on the Wesselényi Street massacres, including the one by Ernő Szalkay, the former head of the ghetto police, are included in the files of Berend's postwar trial. Fővárosi Biróság (Court of the Capital), Budapest, NB. 2600/1946, pp. 42–81.

123. Szalai, a long-time member of the Party, had been won over by the Jewish leadership toward the end of the war. He performed a number of valuable services for the Jews, including possibly the saving of the ghetto. (In recognition of his merits, the postwar People's Tribunal exonerated him in spite of his *Nyilas* past.))

124. The Jews arrested in various raids in Buda were normally taken to the *Nyilas* House at 46 Kapás Street or to the Radetzky Armory at Pálffy Square. Their treatment was no different from that suffered by Jews in the *Nyilas* houses in Pest. Among those who were tortured to death at Kapás Street were Géza Steinhardt, a noted comedian, and Béla Elek, an official of the Swedish Legation who had saved hundreds of Jews during the death-marches to Hegyeshalom.

125. For further details on the crimes committed by the *Nyilas* and Nazi elements in

Hungary during the Szálasi era, see Lévai, *A pesti gettó,* pp. 102–5, 112–13, 117–21, and 129; ——, *Zsidósors Magyarországon,* pp. 384–99.

126. For the complete text, see Lévai, *A pesti gettó,* pp. 117–19.

127. *Ibid.,* pp. 133–34.

128. For an identification of the German and Hungarian forces fighting in Budapest, see C. A. Macartney, 2:463. For an account of the battle for Budapest, see *Ibid.,* pp. 465–70.

129. For further details on the liberation of the ghetto, see Lévai, *A pesti gettó,* pp. 123–25, 132–35; ——, *Zsidósors Magyarországon,* pp. 394–99. See also Frigyes Bramer, "A budapesti gettó utolsó két hete" (The Last Two Weeks of the Ghetto of Budapest) in *Évkönyv 1975/76* (Yearbook 1975–76), ed. Sándor Scheiber (Budapest: A Magyar Izraeliták Országos Képviselete, 1976), pp. 9–17.

*

CHAPTER TWENTY-SEVEN

TREATMENT OF FOREIGN JEWS IN HUNGARY

The Foreign Jewish Nationals in Hungary Before the German Occupation

UNTIL THE German occupation of Hungary on March 19, 1944, the Jews of foreign citizenship in Hungary, whether refugees, visitors, or residents, enjoyed—with one tragic exception—the effective though often unenthusiastic protection of the Hungarian state and the support of the Hungarian Jewish community. Some of the foreign Jews managed to become successfully assimilated within the country's economy and the Jewish community's social and religious life.

The one exception was the campaign against the "alien" Jews in the summer of 1941. Acting on the recommendation of Germanophile politicians and officers, the Bárdossy government had consented to the relocation to eastern Galicia of "Polish and Russian Jews" and those of dubious citizenship. The round-up and relocation was entrusted to the National Central Alien Control Office (*Külföldieket Ellenőrző Országos Központi Hatóság*—KEOKH). As a result of this campaign, from 16,000 to 18,000 "alien" Jews, including a number of Hungarian Jews who were in the way of the local authorities or whose citizenship papers were not immediately available, were deported to the then Hungarian-occupied part of Galicia. Late in August 1941, most of them were slaughtered near Kamenets-Podolsk, providing the first five-figure massacre in the Nazis' Final Solution program (see chapter 6).

According to various estimates, the number of foreign Jews in Hungary at the time of occupation was anywhere from 15,000 to 35,000.[1] Most were refugees from the Third Reich, Poland, and Slovakia. Some of them managed to acquire false identification papers and lived in Hungary as "aryans"; others had obtained official residence permits or were classified as transients en route to Palestine, a status they acquired through the efforts of the Palestine Office (*Palesztina Hivatal*) of Budapest.[2] A considerable number of refugees were interned in camps where they were cared for by Hungarian Jewish welfare organizations.

In addition to the refugees, there were a few hundred foreign Jews visiting or residing in Hungary at the time of the German occupation. In the course of the summer and fall of 1944, foreign citizenship or foreign protection was granted to a few thousand Budapest Jews by a number of neutral states, especially Sweden and Switzerland (see chapter 31).

The Anti-Jewish Measures and the Foreign Jewish Nationals

The introduction of the draconic anti-Jewish measures shortly after the occupation confronted the German and Hungarian authorities with a dilemma in regard to the treatment of foreign Jews. The problem concerned primarily the Jewish citizens of enemy and neutral states. The authorities feared that the inclusion of these Jews in the ghettoization and deportation measures might provoke reprisals on the part of the enemy states and grave political complications in connection with the neutral states. The initiative for the solution of this problem was taken by the Germans, who persuaded the Hungarians to follow the approach that had been used in the Third Reich. The enemy and neutral states were to be informed that unless they repatriated their Jewish nationals by a certain date these would be interned in special camps.

Jewish nationals of the Third Reich or of states in the Nazis' sphere of influence (Serbia, Greece, Norway, Denmark, the Netherlands, Belgium, the Protectorate of Bohemia and Moravia, the Baltic States, and the General Government) were simply included in the measures directed against the indigenous Jews. The situation of the Jewish nationals of Axis-allied states (including Croatia, Slovakia, Romania, Italy, Bulgaria, and France) varied from country to country (see below).

Early in April, 1944, when the Final Solution program was about to be implemented, the problem of the foreign Jews became acute. Eberhard von Thadden, the specialist on Jewish affairs in the *Inland II* Section of the German Foreign Office, was particularly concerned about the possible political and economic implications if the Jews of enemy and neutral states were included in the ghettoization and deportation program. To assist Veesenmayer in the solution of this problem, he offered to send Adolf Hezinger from his own office[3] and von Saucken, an official in the Personnel Division of the Foreign Office, to Budapest for six to eight weeks.[4]

Veesenmayer reacted favorably to Thadden's suggestion and on April 12 requested that Hezinger be sent to Budapest for four weeks to serve as his liaison with the German and Hungarian authorities entrusted with the solution of the Jewish question.[5] Two days later, Thadden asked Ribbentrop to approve the transfer.[6] Hezinger arrived toward the end of April, when the "illegal" ghettoization of the Jews in Carpatho-Ruthenia and northeastern Hungary was already in full swing.[7]

The Sztójay government appointed Pál Sebestyén, a legal expert in the Ministry of Foreign Affairs, to deal with the questions relating to foreign Jewish nationals and citizens of enemy states. In the Ministry of the Interior, the same functions were exercised by Károly Halász, an appointee of Andor Jaross, and Colonel Gyula Király, the head of KEOKH.[8]

The first meeting between Veesenmayer and Sebestyén took place on April 27. Sebestyén disclosed that the position of the Sztójay government on these issues was based on the suggestions received from SS-Sturmbannführer Otto Hunsche, a leading member of the Eichmann-Sonderkommando.[9] Accordingly, Sztójay had agreed that the representatives of the neutral states should be requested to repatriate their Jews within a specific period of time, and that those of enemy states should be interned, although non-Jews of these states should be treated according to the principle of reciprocity.[10]

Veesenmayer took advantage of this opportunity to remind Sebestyén of the German position concerning the handling of enemy property and the Reich's opposition to continued emigration of Jews to Palestine; in his view, any Jews allowed to emigrate were carriers of horror "propaganda."[11]

Two days later Veesenmayer, accompanied by Hezinger, had another meeting with Sebestyén in which the position of the Hungarian government was further crystallized. According to Sebestyén, the Hungarians were resolved to:

- Inform within a week the representatives of the neutral states (Portugal, Spain, Sweden, Switzerland, and Turkey) to repatriate their Jewish nationals by the end of four to six weeks. After that period, the Jewish nationals of these states would become subject to the anti-Jewish laws in effect in Hungary. (Veesenmayer suggested that the repatriation formula be applied only to those Jews who had been citizens of these countries before March 19 or March 22, 1944.)
- Apply the same formula to French Jewish nationals, since diplomatic relations between France and Hungary had never been severed.

- Request the Romanians to repatriate their Jewish nationals.
- Inquire in Bulgaria whether the Hungarians could deal with Bulgarian Jewish nationals the same way the Third Reich did.
- Request the Slovakian authorities to submit a list of those Slovak Jewish nationals legally in Hungary in whose repatriation they were interested.
- Treat Yugoslav Jews according to the current status of their home states in the former Yugoslav Kingdom. (At the time, Croatia was an allied state and Serbia an occupied state.)
- Intern the Jewish and non-Jewish nationals of certain enemy states in special buildings in Budapest. (Argentinian nationals, both Jewish and non-Jewish, were to be spared from any action temporarily, at Veesenmayer's suggestion).[12]
- Entrust the handling of the property of Jews to be repatriated to neutral states to the representatives or trustees of these states. The property of enemy Jewish nationals would be handled in accordance with prevailing general principles.

Veesenmayer and Hezinger once again reminded Sebestyén about the German opposition to the emigration of Jews to Palestine. Citing the German attitude toward the Arabs, they asked that such emigration of Jews to Palestine be delayed and eventually be halted altogether. They also asked Sebestyén to see to it that all interventions in behalf of Hungarian Jews in the German sphere of influence be withdrawn.[13] Their intention, of course, was to enable the Nazi authorities in the various German-controlled countries to include the Hungarian Jews still under their jurisdiction in the Final Solution operations.

The Governmental Decisions

At its meeting of May 3, the day the official ghettoization began in many parts of Hungary, the Council of Ministers devoted a special session to the treatment of foreign nationals in Hungary. The problem had become urgent, since in their eagerness, dejewification squads had arrested a number of foreign nationals, which had brought about a strong and immediate reaction from states whose nationals were affected. Sztójay, acting in his dual capacity as Prime Minister and Minister of Foreign Affairs, revealed the details of the model suggested by Hunsche during his visit to the Ministry of the Interior early in April and summarized by Sebestyén in his discussions with Veesenmayer. He provided further details concerning the handling of the property issues. The land holdings of foreign nationals were to be placed under Hungarian trusteeships; all other properties were to be handled on the basis of reciprocity, depending upon the treatment by the respective states of Hungarian nationals, both Jewish and non-Jewish.[14]

The same day, acting under the authorization of the Council of Ministers, Andor Jaross issued a highly confidential order to the Chief of Police of Budapest relating to the implementation of the decision. Jaross classified the foreign Jews in Hungary into five categories:

1. Those of enemy states.
2. Those of neutral states (Portugal, Spain, Sweden, Switzerland, and Turkey).
3. Those of states in the Axis sphere of influence (Slovakia, Croatia, Serbia, Greece, Bulgaria, Fascist Italy, France, Belgium, Holland, Denmark, Norway, Poland, Latvia, Estonia, and Lithuania).
4. Those of Finland and Romania, who were to be treated like the nationals of the neutral states.
5. Stateless Jews and Jews of doubtful citizenship.

The Jews in category 1 were to be treated like the non-Jewish nationals of enemy states. They were to be interned in specially selected buildings in Budapest and allowed to have certain amenities, including their own clothes, linen, and bedding. Those who had rendered great service to Hungary or who suffered from certain disabilities were not to be interned. The Jewish citizens of the neutral countries and of Finland and Romania were to be interned in Budapest until the question of their repatriation was settled. The Jewish nationals of states in the Axis sphere of influence were to be subjected to the same treatment as the Hungarian Jews, but interned in separate police-controlled jail-houses. Stateless Jews were to be treated like the Hungarian Jews.[15]

On May 5, the Hungarian Foreign Ministry, acting in cooperation with the Ministry of the Interior, requested the representatives of the neutral states in Budapest to repatriate their Jewish nationals within four to six weeks.[16] However, the measures outlined in Jaross's confidential order appeared unreasonable to several officials of the Ministry and above all to Mihály Arnóthy-Jungerth, the *de facto* Foreign Minister. They summarized their suggested policy as follows:

- The Jewish nationals of neutral states should neither be interned nor compelled to do labor service.
- The Jewish nationals of enemy states should be interned only if they represented a threat to national security.
- The property of Jewish nationals of neutral and enemy states should not fall under the provisions of the Hungarian anti-Jewish laws.

• The Hungarian Jewish employees of foreign legations or missions in Hungary should be exempted from the general anti-Jewish laws in effect.[17]

In response to pressure by the Foreign Ministry, Jaross was compelled to repeal his order of May 3. On May 31, he issued a new highly confidential order, following the general directives outlined by the Foreign Ministry. Accordingly, the Jewish nationals of enemy states who were deemed security risks were to be interned together with non-Jewish nationals of these states. The other non-Jewish nationals of these states were to be left in their homes, providing they reported to the authorities once a week. The Jewish nationals of the neutral states were to be left in their homes until the expiration of the repatriation deadline. (An exception was made for those deemed dangerous to national security.)[18] Until then they were to report once a week to the authorities and were prohibited from engaging in gainful employment. After the deadline, they were to be interned.

The Jews of countries in the Axis sphere of influence were to be treated in the same way as those of the neutral states. The provisions of the earlier order relating to stateless Jews and those whose citizenship was in doubt were left intact.[19]

By the time Jaross issued his amended order the ghettoization had already been carried out everywhere except Budapest, and the deportations were in full swing. A fair number of foreign Jewish nationals found themselves in ghettos. Hezinger toured some of the major ghettos shortly after the beginning of the mass deportations on May 15 and actually picked out about 50 Jewish foreign nationals.[20] He disclosed this on May 26, when he visited Sebestyén in the company of Franz Adamovic, an expert on Jewish questions in the German Legation in Budapest.[21] The Jewish foreign nationals picked out from the ghettos were taken to the Institute for the Deaf and Mute in Budapest.[22] Sebestyén reported on the responses received by that time from neutral and allied states to the Foreign Ministry's request for the repatriation of their Jewish nationals.

The discussions between Hezinger, Adamovic, and Sebestyén took place shortly after the visit to Budapest by Eberhard von Thadden, who had come to double-check the effectiveness of the anti-Jewish operations then in effect, as well as to solve the problem of "German and Hungarian Jewish property within a European-wide framework."[23]

The responses of the neutral and enemy states, while differing in nuances, was of course that of consistent opposition to the measures enacted against the Jews in general and the foreign Jews in particular. The attitude of the states in the Axis alliance, on the other hand, fluctuated in the course of the year not only in terms of the states' relationship with the Third Reich, but also with the changing international political climate and military situation.

The Axis-Allied States

As long as the Hungarian authorities cooperated fully with the Eichmann-*Sonderkommando* in the implementation of the Final Solution program, the representatives of most of the pro-Axis or Axis-occupied countries showed little interest in protecting their Jewish nationals. Indeed, some of them showed so little interest that they consented to the inclusion of their nationals in the general anti-Jewish measures directed against the Hungarian Jews. Others voiced their intentions to defend their nationals' interests, then quietly consented to their ghettoization and deportation. Still others, their eyes on the political and military situation, sought to delay a decision.

After the Western Allies' landing in Normandy on June 6, 1944, and the inexorable advance of the Red Army during the summer, and especially after Horthy's decision early in July to halt the deportations, attitudes began to change. The fate of their Jews caught in Hungary varied accordingly.

Bulgaria. There were few Bulgarian Jews in Hungary. The Bulgarian regime, which protected most of its Jewish nationals at home,[24] was reluctant to respond to the Hungarian Foreign Ministry's appeal for repatriation. It expressed no interest in its few nationals in Hungary and consented to their treatment along the Nazi lines.[25]

Croatia. A creation of the Third Reich following the dismemberment of Yugoslavia in 1941, Croatia had officially consented to the repatriation of the few Jewish Croatian, mostly Hungarian-speaking, nationals "if they were to cross the borders legally and their property were transferred to the Croatian State." Actually, the Croatians, like the Bulgarians, allowed their Jewish nationals to be subjected to the same treatment as the Hungarian Jews.[26]

Finland. Finland, like Bulgaria, was an Axis-allied country that refused to cooperate in the liquidation of the few thousand Jews within its borders. The exact number of Jews of Finnish nationality in Hungary in 1944–45 is not known; by virtue of a decision of the Hungarian Ministry of the Interior, they were to be treated like the Jewish nationals of neutral states.[27]

France. The few French Jewish nationals in Hungary represented more of a problem than was the case with other European countries under German occupation: Hungary and France were not legally at war. Furthermore, the German authorities in Hungary operated under the directive of the *Reichsführer*-SS that no French Jews be allowed to return to their homeland.

The Vichy government expressed its readiness to readmit those Jews who voluntarily submitted themselves to repatriation and to consent to the treatment of the others as POW's. This position angered von Thadden and the other officials associated with the Final Solution program, especially since by that time Hungary had already expressed its lack of interest in its own Jews living abroad. The RSHA naturally insisted that French Jewish nationals in Hungary be "transferred to the Reich for labor."

According to the French Minister in Budapest, no French Jewish nationals applied for repatriation, although a few from Lebanon and Syria wanted to return to the Levant. This request was rejected by the Germans because the area was under Allied control. The French Jews, like the Jewish nationals of other West European neutral states, feared repatriation at the time because the route went through the Third Reich.

On July 17, Grell had still another discussion with Sebestyén. Sebestyén revealed that the Hungarians had decided on the internment of those Jewish foreign nationals who were not repatriated by July 31. Thadden continued his intrigues, advocating the internment of the French Jews in Bergen-Belsen "until their situation could be cleared through direct German–French negotiations." But by that time the deportations from Hungary had been already halted and the Germans themselves were more eager to assure the continued contribution of Hungary to the Axis war effort than to antagonize Horthy over a few foreign Jews. At the end even the RSHA consented to the internment of the French Jewish nationals in Hungary.[28]

The question of the nine French Jewish nationals (one man, four women, and four children) was the subject of a discussion on July 22 between the Hungarian Foreign Ministry officials and the representatives of the French Legation in Budapest. It was agreed that since the nine Jews (of whom seven were converted) feared repatriation because of the transit through the Third Reich, they would be interned in a villa and allowed certain privileges, including exemption from wearing the Yellow Star. The citizens of Syria and Lebanon would be accorded the same privileges pending receipt of their Turkish transit visas.[29] The July 31 deadline was allowed to pass, and the Hungarian authorities decided late in August to intern only the two nonconverted Jews, a Mrs. Remoussin and her daughter (apparently, primarily because their villa had been confiscated by the Gestapo). The others were allowed to stay in their homes.[30]

The Third Reich. In this context, the term includes the territories of the Third Reich and also the German-occupied territories—the Protectorates, Serbia, Greece, Norway, Denmark, the Netherlands, Belgium, the Baltic States, and Poland (Government General). While there are no statistics on how many Jews of these foreign nationalities were in Hungary at the time of the German occupation, it is known that the bulk of the 15,000 to 35,000 Jewish refugees in Hungary late in the fall of 1943 came from Germany, Austria, Poland, and Slovakia.

Most of the Jewish nationals of these countries were included in the measures directed against the Hungarian Jews, placed into ghettos, and deported to Auschwitz. With their deportation, a major aspect of Hungary's refugee problem, especially relating to German and Polish Jews, was "solved."[31]

Italy. After a short period of hesitation, the representatives of Mussolini's Fascist government adopted the same position as Bulgaria.[32] While the Italians protected, relatively speaking, their Jewish nationals at home, they expressed disinterest in the few Jewish-Italians in Hungary. As a result, these were included in the general anti-Jewish measures applied against Hungarian Jews.[33]

Romania. Though still a German ally, Romania at the time of the mass deportation of the Hungarian Jews was already toying with the idea of a *volte face.* Moreover, although Romanian Iron Guardists committed many horrible crimes in January 1941, the Antonescu regime resisted German pressures for the application of the Final Solution program against the Romanian Jews. In 1944, the Jews of Romania proper, including those of Southern Transylvania, survived relatively unscathed, as did the survivors from Transnistria who had returned home.[34]

Although it was an Axis ally alongside Hungary, Romania formulated many of its political and military policies with an eye on their possible impact upon the traditionally troubled relations with Hungary. The alliance and Hitler's "solution" of the Transylvanian problem in

1940 could not overcome the age-old animosity between the countries over that land. Because of the fragility of these relations, the German and Hungarian authorities could not proceed against the relatively large number of Romanian Jewish nationals in Hungary as easily as against the Jewish nationals of some other allies. The Hungarian decision to treat Romanian Jews on an equal footing with those of the neutral powers—after the failure of an appeal to Romania to express lack of interest in its Jewish nationals—was a direct result of these considerations. A differentiation, however, was made between Romanian Jewish nationals who had entered Hungary legally, and those who had arrived illegally when the situation in Hungary was relatively better than in Romania. The latter were treated as stateless Jews.

Romania permitted the repatriation of several groups of Jews, all the while paying lip-service to anti-Jewish measures. On May 29, 1944, for example, the Romanians adopted a law imposing the death penalty for crossing the borders illegally. This law seems to have been designed merely to assuage the Germans who were pressing Romania to adopt stricter measures against the Jews; there is no evidence that it was ever applied.[35] It made the life of the indigenous Jews more tolerable and showed great understanding and leniency toward the Hungarian Jews who managed to escape into the country. To the great annoyance of the Nazis, the Romanians also permitted a number of ships loaded with Romanian, Hungarian, and other Jewish refugees to leave for Turkey en route to Palestine.[36] On August 23, 1944, Romania left the Axis.

Slovakia. Approximately half of the 15,000 Jewish foreign nationals in Hungary in the fall of 1943 were, according to the *Vaada* of Budapest, of Slovakian origin.[37] The influx of Slovakian Jews began in the spring of 1942, when mass deportations started there. Ironically, at the time of the ghettoization and deportation of the Jews of Hungary, the situation in Slovakia was relatively stabilized. Although in labor camps, the remnant of the Jewish community that had escaped the deportation waves of 1942 managed to survive until the fall of 1944.[38] Because of the differences in the conditions in the two countries in the spring and summer of 1944, many Slovakian Jewish refugees tried to return to their homeland. There is no record of how many managed to do so, illegally, before the beginning of the mass deportations from Hungary.

Following the advice of the Germans, the Hungarian Foreign Ministry approached the Slovak Legation in Budapest, requesting that the Slovak authorities prepare a list of their Jewish nationals in whose repatriation they were interested, and allow the remainder to share the fate of the Hungarian Jews.

Slovakia expressed an interest in the repatriation of those few of its Jews who were legally in Hungary and were deemed of great usefulness to the national economy. It also expressed a general, though detached, interest in the Slovak Jewish nationals still at liberty in Hungary—among them a relatively large number of children whose parents had been deported in 1942—not so much to assure their protection, but to uphold the principle of Slovak sovereignty vis-à-vis Hungary.

The German and Hungarian authorities were somewhat disappointed in the initial Slovak reaction, which seemed to indicate that the Slovak authorities wanted to exert a negative influence on the Hungarian operations against the Jews. On June 13, when some regions of Hungary were already *Judenrein,* Veesenmayer urged the Foreign Office to exert pressure upon the Slovak government to allow the inclusion in the Final Solution program of their Jewish nationals in Hungary. Following up on the immediate reaction of the Foreign Office, Hanns Elard Ludin, the German Minister in Bratislava, approached Alexander (Šano) Mach, the Slovak Deputy Prime Minister and Minister of the Interior, on June 24. On July 1, Mach assured Ludin that Slovakia was interested only in the few Jews who were living in Hungary legally. He reminded Ludin about his own anti-Jewish stance and about Slovakia's decision to close its borders with Hungary on March 20 (the day after the German occupation) specifically to prevent the escape of Jews from Hungary. The attitude of the Slovak authorities was crystallized on July 17 in Sebestyén's discussions with Grell. While the diplomatic exchanges were taking place, the German and Hungarian dejewification squads quietly included all Slovakian Jews they apprehended in the general anti-Jewish measures.[39]

Enemy and Neutral States

The enemy states (whose interests were represented primarily by Switzerland) and the neutral states did not have many Jewish nationals in Hungary during the German occupation. Their response to the Hungarians' appeal to repatriate these Jews was positive. By July 24, applications were filed with the German authorities (who controlled travel) for permission to repatriate a number of foreign Jewish nationals. Nine were Portuguese, four Swiss, four Liechtensteiner, four Swedish, and one was Spanish. The Germans had a stranglehold over all travel; those wishing to leave the country needed a permit to do so.

Probably anticipating that Argentina would become a haven for Nazis escaping from Europe, the Germans themselves were attentive to Argentinian nationals in Hungary, both Jewish and non-Jewish. On July 28, Wagner requested Veesenmayer to get Eichmann's agreement to have a group of Argentinian Jews in Hungary transferred to Sweden "without stop-over in the Reich" in order to effect an exchange of diplomats.[40]

The Anglo-American nationals were less lucky. Those picked up in the various ghettos were brought to Budapest and first housed in the Institute for the Deaf and Mute. Later they were removed to the outskirts of the city and housed at 3 through 7 Pálma Street. Early in the summer of 1944, these five buildings contained 140 persons; only one, at number 5 had a well-built air-raid shelter, and a smaller shelter was located in the cellar of number 7. Although they were not in an industrial or militarily strategic area, the buildings at 4 and 5 Pálma Street suffered direct hits during the massive raid on Budapest on July 2, which took place around 10:00 A.M. At the time of the raid, the shelter of 5 Pálma Street held 110 persons, and that of 7 held 25. The casualty figures were revealed two days later: 98 Jews dead; 33 wounded, and 8 unaccounted for.[41]

As the representative of Anglo-American interests in Hungary, the Swiss intervened a number of times with respect to the property interests of British and American Jewish and non-Jewish subjects.[42]

The representatives of Switzerland, like those of Sweden and to a lesser extent of the other neutral states, also undertook a series of measures to naturalize a limited number of Jews or grant them the status of "protected" (*védett*) persons (the Vatican also cooperated). They began to issue various types of *Schutzpässe* (Protective Passes), which provided a modicum of protection, if not total safety, to the Jews holding them. Under great pressure from opposition leaders at home and from leaders of the enemy and neutral states as well as the Vatican, Horthy consented to the emigration of these few thousand Jews when he halted the deportations on July 7. Hitler, persuaded by Veesenmayer and Ribbentrop, went along with the idea of emigration "provided that Horthy [was] willing to allow the speedy resumption of the deportations" (see chapters 25 and 31).

With the easing of the anti-Jewish pressures during the Lakatos era and Hungary's desperate search for a way out of the war, the question of emigration was relegated to secondary importance. It came into focus again following the Szálasi coup of October 15. The status of the foreign Jews (by this time predominantly those of the enemy and neutral states were still alive) was regulated under the new Szálasi edict which provided for the establishment of an International Ghetto. There the relatively few *bona fide* foreign Jews continued to enjoy a degree of security, but many of the "protected" Hungarian Jews shared the fate of their brethren in the main ghetto of Budapest.

Notes

1. In their postwar memoirs, some of the former Hungarian government officials tend to exaggerate the number of Jewish refugees who enjoyed the protection of the Hungarian state during the war. Some of them place the number at 70,000. The *Vaada* of Budapest, however, established their number at approximately 15,000 on November 22, 1943. *Der Kastner-Bericht*, p. 45. See also chapters 3 and 6.

2. Livia Rothkirchen, "Hungary—an Asylum for the Refugees of Europe," in *YVS*, 7:131.

3. For biographical details on Hezinger and for his account on his activities in Hungary, see NG-4457.

4. *RLB*, Doc. 132.

5. NG-5630.

6. *NA*, Microcopy T-120, Roll 4355, Frame K213634.

7. Although the ghettoization decree was not issued until late in April, the Jews of Carpatho-Ruthenia and northeastern Hungary were being rounded up and placed into ghettos as of April 16. For details, see chapter 17.

8. *RLB*, Doc. 297.

9. Hunsche outlined the German model for the solution of the question of foreign nationals in general and of foreign Jewish nationals in particular during a visit to the Ministry of the Interior early in April 1944.

10. Sebestyén reminded Veesenmayer, for example, that in contrast to the internment of German nationals in the United States, none of the close to 10,000 Hungarian nationals were interned. There were only a few hundred American nationals in Hungary, most of whom were returned naturalized Hungarian-Americans. *RLB*, Doc. 296.

11. *Ibid.*, Doc. 297. See especially appendix 2 to the document.

12. The Germans deferred to the Argentinians for two reasons. For one thing, many of them looked at Argentina as a future haven. The immediate reason was the planned exchange of diplomats in Sweden. Such an exchange took place during August 15–20, 1944, for which purpose the Germans allowed six Hungarian Jews identified as Argentinian nationals to go to Sweden. For further background information on the exchange and the identity of the six Jews, see *NA*, Microcopy T-120, Roll 4355, Frames K213530-536. See also *RLB*, Docs. 297, 312.

13. *Ibid.*, Doc. 297. Veesenmayer submitted the memoranda of his two discussions with Sebestyén to the Foreign Office on May 2. Copies were forwarded to Eichmann by Thadden on May 5. *NA*, Microcopy T-120, Roll 4665, Serial K1509/K350109–.

14. For the minutes of the Council of Ministers' meeting of May 3, see *Vádirat*, 1:286–89.

15. For the text of Jaross's confidential Order No. 7.233 1944/VII. res. B.M., see *ibid.*, 1:290–93.

16. Veesenmayer telegram 1241 of May 6, 1944. *NA*, Microcopy T-120, Roll 4665, Serial K1509/K350109–.

17. Jenő Lévai, *Fehér könyv. Külföldi akciók zsidók megmentésére* (White Book. Foreign Actions for the Rescuing of Jews) (Budapest: Officina, 1946), p. 37.

18. The deadline was originally set as July 1 but subsequently extended to August 1 and then to August 26, the day after the third scheduled deportation of the Jews of Budapest; by that time, however, Sztójay was about to be replaced by Lakatos. During the Lakatos era the anti-Jewish measures were relaxed, and the deadline was extended to September 30, 1944. The treatment of foreign Jewish nationals remained in limbo until shortly after the Szálasi coup. See chapters 25 and 26. See also *RLB*, Docs. 209 and 311, and *Vádirat*, 3:343–44.

19. Order 9.999/1944. VII. res. B.M. Lévai, *Fehér könyv*, pp. 36–39.

20. Hezinger claims that by the time Theodor Horst Grell replaced him around the middle of June 1944, between 100 and 200 Jews of foreign nationality had been removed from the ghettos. NG-4457. See also *RLB*, Doc. 153.

21. Adamovic's report was forwarded by Veesenmayer to the German Foreign Office on May 30. *RLB*, Doc. 299.

22. This was the special camp into which the Hungarians had promised to put all Jewish nationals of enemy and neutral states the day the "legal" ghettoization began on May 3. See Veesenmayer's telegram no. 150 of May 3 addressed to Ritter. *Ibid.*, Doc. 261.

23. *Ibid.*, Doc. 298.

24. Frederick B. Chary, *The Bulgarian Jews and the Final Solution, 1940–1944* (Pittsburgh: University of Pittsburgh Press, 1972), 246 pp.

25. *RLB*, Docs. 299, 311.

26. *Ibid.*, Docs. 299, 306, 311, and 315.

27. See Orders 7233 1944/VII and 9.999/1944.VII cited above and *RLB*, Doc. 311.

28. *Ibid.*, Docs. 302, 303, 307, 308, 309, 311, 313, 314.

29. The Hungarian participants in the discussion were Sebestyén, Ervin Morlin and Jenő Miske-Gerstenberger, two experts on international law in the Ministry of Foreign Affairs, and Gyula Perlaky, representing the Ministry of the Interior. The French were represented by Christian de Charmasse, the Legation Counselor, and an official called Adere. *Vádirat*, 3:257.

30. See the *Pro domo* by Count Miklós Zay of the Foreign Ministry dated August 22, 1944. *Ibid.*, p. 424.

31. Hungary had wanted to get rid of 300 German Jews as early as May 1940. See Weizsaecker's note of May 3, 1940 concerning the request advanced by Sztójay. NG-2709 According to a statement made on November 1, 1947 by SS-*Obergruppenführer* Gottlob Berger, Walter Schellenberg, the former head of the RSHA's Counterintelligence Section had promised former Swiss President Jean-Mary Musy that 5,000 older German Jews would be allowed to leave Hungary for Switzerland. The plan, allegedly approved by Himmler, was vetoed by Martin Bormann. NO-5762. See also *RLB*, Doc. 311. The Hungarians differentiated between the Jewish and non-Jewish Polish refugees in the country, especially after the German occupation. Polish Jews apprehended by the authorities were subjected to the ghettoization and deportation program like all other Jewish nationals of countries under Nazi domination. *RLB*, Docs. 268 and 305. See also NG-2709, and chapters 3 and 6.

32. After the signing of the Italian Armistice Treaty of September 3, 1943, Hungary recognized the pro-Badoglio members of the Italian Legation staff in Budapest as accredited representatives of their country. However, after great German pressure following the Reich's recognition of the newly established Mussolini government in Northern

Italy as "the only legitimate Italian government," Jenő Ghyczy, the anti-Nazi Foreign Minister, recognized Mussolini. Following the German occupation of Hungary on March 19, 1944, the representatives of the Badoglio government were arrested together with many other anti-Nazi political figures. Mussolini's representative in Hungary at this time was Antonio Casertano. For further details, see Stephen D. Kertész, *Diplomacy in a Whirlpool. Hungary Between Nazi Germany and Soviet Russia* (Notre Dame, Indiana: University of Notre Dame Press, 1953), pp. 66–67.

33. *RLB*, Docs. 299 and 311.

34. Shortly after joining Germany in the war against the Soviet Union on June 22, 1941, Romanian units participated in several operations against Jews in the "liberated" areas—Bukovina, Bessarabia, and the Ukraine. These areas were within the jurisdiction of *Einsatzgruppe D*. Later in the year, the Romanians deported to Transnistria, the occupied area between the Dniester and the Bug, close to 185,000 Jews, mostly from Bukovina and Bessarabia. Approximately one-third of these survived and, following the advance of the Red Army and the changing Romanian attitude, were allowed to return late in 1943. For further details, see Raul Hilberg, *The Destruction of the European Jews* (Chicago: Quadrangle, 1961), pp. 485–509.

35. *RLB*, Doc. 196.

36. *Ibid.*, Docs. 299, 311. See also NG-5630, and chapter 28.

37. *Der Kastner-Bericht*, p. 45.

38. For details on the tragedy of the Slovakian Jews, see Livia Rothkirchen, *The Destruction of Slovak Jewry* (Jerusalem: Yad Vashem, 1961), lxxv, 257 pp. (Hebrew and English); Yeshayahu Jelinek, "The 'Final Solution'—The Slovak Version." *East European Quarterly*, 4, no. 4 (1971):431–41.

39. *RLB*, Docs. 297, 299, 300–302, 308, 310, 311; NG-5630.

40. *RLB*, Docs. 209, 299, 311, 312.

41. At the initiative of the Hungarian Ministry of Foreign Affairs, a commission of inquiry prepared a memorandum about the details and consequences of the raid of July 2. Dated July 4, the memorandum was signed by Charles Lutz and Hans Steiner of the Swiss Legation; Friedrich Born, the delegate of the International Red Cross; Per Anger, Secretary of the Swedish Legation; Kemal Sayit, Counselor of the Turkish Legation; Gyula Perlaky of the Hungarian Ministry of the Interior; and Sándor Nékám and Baron Iván Rubidó-Zichy of the Ministry of Foreign Affairs. The memorandum included two depositions by survivors (Ignace Schiller and Eric S. Satan) about the raid. *NA*, Microcopy T-120, Roll 4664, Serial K1509/K350354–.

42. See, for example, the memo of István Gombó, an official of the Foreign Ministry, about his discussions with Hans Steiner on August 19 concerning these matters in *Vádirat*, 3:411–12.

CHAPTER TWENTY-EIGHT

TREATMENT OF HUNGARIAN JEWS ABROAD

The Pre-Occupation Era: An Overview

DURING THE Kállay era, Jewish Hungarian nationals abroad enjoyed the effective if not always wholehearted protection of the Hungarian state even if they lived in the sphere of influence of the two main Axis partners. This was quite remarkable, since the Jewish nationals of many other states were included in the anti-Jewish measures directed against the local Jews.

The German authorities in Nazi-occupied Europe did not always respect their obligations under international law. In many cases, they simply ignored the official position of the Hungarian government and clandestinely included Hungarian Jews in the transports directed "to the East for labor." This was especially true in September–October 1942, when the West European Jewish communities were being liquidated. At the time (almost half a year before the crushing defeat of the Hungarian and German armies at Voronezh and Stalingrad) the Hungarian authorities themselves were not yet protecting their Jewish nationals abroad with much energy.

The first, rather timid, demands on behalf of Hungarian Jews abroad were made soon after the news of the inclusion of Hungarian Jews in the deportations from Western Europe in September–October 1942 reached Hungary; however the campaign that really annoyed the Germans was not launched until 1943. The German policy toward the Jewish nationals of allied and neutral states was to include them in the general anti-Jewish measures unless their governments agreed to repatriate them by a certain deadline. These deadlines were extended a number of times. Hungary complied to a certain extent, allowing the repatriation of smaller groups of Jews whose Hungarian citizenship was fully established. Most of the Hungarian Jews awaiting clearance or repatriation from Nazi-dominated Western Europe were in camps such as Drancy in France and Westerbork in the Netherlands. With the expiration of the final repatriation deadline in October 1943, most of them were sent to either Buchenwald or Ravensbrück, but not as *Strafjuden*. They were to be kept in these camps until the Nazis had an opportunity to "transport them to the East."

In Italy and the Italian-held areas, the Hungarian Jews had an even better chance of protection because of the greater humanity of the Italians as well as the closer relations enjoyed by Hungary and Italy—both of which feared German expansionism. During his April 1–3, 1943, visit to Rome, Kállay was reportedly assured by Mussolini that the Hungarian Jews in Italy would not be discriminated against and would enjoy the same treatment as other Hungarian subjects.

The situation changed radically soon after the German occupation of Hungary. Shortly after the beginning of the mass deportations on May 15, 1944, the Sztójay government yielded to the Germans and stated that it was no longer interested in its Jewish nationals in Nazi-dominated Western Europe. After their "evacuation to the East," the only sizable number of Hungarian Jewish nationals living in the Axis world were those residing in Romania, Slovakia, and to a lesser extent Croatia.[1] At the time of the mass deportations from Hungary, the situation of the Jews in Romania and Slovakia was quite tolerable. In fact, many of the Jews who had previously escaped from those countries during the anti-Jewish drives of 1940–1943 were now returning there (mostly illegally) together with a number of Jews from Hungary.

The relatively lenient treatment of the Jews in these countries became a source of embarrassment to the Germans. When Horthy decided to halt the deportations early in July, the Hungarians used the treatment of the Jews in Romania and Slovakia as one of the excuses for their action. On July 6, when Sztójay confirmed to Veesenmayer that Horthy and the Hungarian government had decided to halt the deportations, he in fact emphasized that the step was motivated, among other things, by the more lenient treatment of the Jews in Romania and Slovakia.[2] Five days later, Vessenmayer sent an urgent telegram to the Foreign Office complaining about the difficulty of carrying out the Final Solution program in Hungary. He was particularly bitter that the Germans demanded of the Hungarians "a most ruthless proceeding against the Jews," while the Romanians and Slovaks were allowed to treat Jews more humanely. *Inland II* reacted immediately and approached the German legations in Bucharest and Bratislava, but to no avail. The Romanians, shrewdly preparing to change sides, became even more tolerant. The Slovaks also became more cautious, though at the end the Jews, like many of the Slovak patriots captured after the unsuccessful uprising at Banská Bystrica and elsewhere in Slovakia late in August 1944, were once again subjected to deportation.

Romania: From Adoption to Rejection of the Final Solution

It is one of the ironies of history that Romania, a country with a long tradition of official anti-Semitism, emerged as a haven both for its indigenous Jews and for many refugees. Following the rise of Nazi influence in the Balkans in the mid-1930s, Romania adopted an anti-Jewish program which was particularly vicious during the shortlived Goga-Cuza regime. Sizeable losses of Jewish lives, however, did not occur until after September 1940, when Romania had suffered considerable territorial losses to the Soviet Union (Bessarabia and Northern Bukovina), Hungary (Northern Transylvania), and Bulgaria (Southern Dobrudja). The fury and frustration engendered by the territorial losses were channeled by the ultra-Right radical elements against the Jews, who were labeled, as was fashionable at the time, "agents of Bolshevism."

On September 6, 1940, the royal dictatorship of King Carol II was replaced by a new National Legionnaire State (*Statul Național Legionar*) headed by General (later Marshal) Ion Antonescu, who soon acquired the title *Conducător* (Leader).[3] The drive for the Romanianization of the economy and the aryanization of Jewish property was soon accompanied by small pogroms in various parts of the country. A major pogrom took place late in January 1941, before Romania's entry into the war, when the Iron Guard (*Garda de Fier*)—the Romanian Nazi elements led by Horia Sima—rose in an attempt to overthrow Antonescu. Hundreds of Jews were massacred most brutally in Bucharest, Jassy, and elsewhere.

In the interim between the unsuccessful coup and Romania's involvement in the war against the Soviet Union on June 22, 1941, the anti-Semitic drive was restricted to the economic sphere. One of the most important measures enacted against the Jews was the decree of March 27 under which their real estate was expropriated. The instigator of many of the anti-Jewish measures was Radu Lecca, the General Commissar for Jewish Questions; he collaborated closely with *SS-Sturmbannführer* Gustav Richter, the SS expert in the German Legation in Bucharest on the Jewish question.

The situation changed drastically after Romania joined the Third Reich in the war against the Soviet Union. Flushed by their early military successes and driven by feelings of revenge, many Romanian units vented their hatred of the Jews and in some cases even outdid the Germans in brutality. The Jews were subjected to barbarous treatment in the recaptured areas of Northern Bukovina and Bessarabia and in the conquered territories in the Ukraine. Like the *Einsatzgruppen,* and sometimes in cooperation with them, the Romanians were also significantly involved in the mobile killing operations, "disinguishing" themselves in Bălți, Cernăuți, and Odessa. In the latter city, Romanian units massacred from 60,000 to 80,000 Jews.[4] During the early phase of the war, atrocities were also committed in some of the communities in Old (i.e., pre-1918) Romania. In Jassy, for example, thousands of Jews were killed during the pogroms of June 29–30, the estimates ranging from 4,000 to 8,000.[5] The killings by the German and Romanian military units continued all along the invasion routes, decimating if not completely annihilating the Jewish populations of the "liberated" cities and villages.

To rid itself of the "alien" Jews, the Antonescu government selected Transnistria, the Romanian-occupied part of the Ukraine between the Dniester and the Bug, as a major dumping ground. The first expulsions of Jews took place in August 1941. The well-planned and effectively organized mass deportations began in the fall of that year, and continued through the spring and summer of 1942. At their peak, the various concentration camps of Transnistria—most of which were established before the German extermination camps became operational—contained approximately 185,000 Jews.[6] Except for slightly over 10,000 who were "mistakenly" picked up in Dorohoi County in Old Romania, almost all the deportees were from Bukovina, Bessarabia, and the Herta region—the areas formerly ceded to the USSR.

The Jews of Old Romania (Muntenia, Oltenia, and Moldavia), Southern Transylvania, and Southern Bukovina fared much better. Although they were subjected to great economic hardship and the men in many places were compelled to do forced labor in specially organized labor companies, they were never forced to wear yellow stars and they were never ordered into ghettos. At war's end, nearly all of the Jewish communities in these areas had survived almost intact.[7]

Following the adoption of the Final Solution program late in January 1942, the Germans of course began to pressure Romania to institute stern measures. Unlike most of the other countries in the German sphere of influence, however, Romania decided to retain its sovereignty even on the Jewish question, pursuing its own "Romanian" approach to the problem. In mid-1942 the Germans briefly had the impression that the Romanians were ready to go along with the German approach. According to a communication from Luther to Ribbentrop, Weizsaecker, and Wormann, dated August 17, 1942, deportations were to begin in the Transylvanian towns of Arad, Timişoara, and Turda. However, the Romanian government changed its position shortly after Lecca's return later that month from Berlin, where he was allegedly snubbed by German officials. It is all but impossible to determine how Lecca's treatment in Berlin influenced the Romanian decision-making process; nevertheless, the Antonescu government did not retain its enthusiasm for the German version of the Final Solution program. Indeed, the Romanians became determined to retain their authority in this matter. From the autumn of 1942 on, the Romanians continued (and in some cases even intensified) their expropriation program, but they no longer showed interest in anything more drastic. On December 12, 1942, Manfred von Killinger, the German Minister in Bucharest, reported to the German Foreign Office that according to Lecca Marshal Antonescu was ready to allow 75,000 to 80,000 Jews to emigrate to Palestine in return for a payment by the Jews of 200,000 *lei* (approximately $1,336) per emigrant. According to Killinger, the Marshal was eager to collect 16 billion *lei* ($107 million) for the Romanian State, and get rid of a large number of Jews "in a comfortable manner."

The German Foreign Office and RSHA did everything in their power to bring about a reversal of the new Romanian position on the Jewish question, but to no avail. On January 14, 1943, Heinrich Müller, the head of the Gestapo, assessed the situation in Romania very pessimistically. Six days later, Himmler himself concluded that nothing else could be done in Romania and suggested the recall of the Jewish expert from Bucharest. The German Foreign Office, however, continued its strenuous efforts to induce the Romanians to change their minds and "recognize the importance of the Jewish menace."[8]

Müller and Himmler had assessed the situation correctly, as the further actions of the Romanians soon revealed. The situation of the surviving Jews of Transnistria gradually improved and toward the end of 1943, following the Red Army's crossing of the Dnieper and advance toward the Bug, the camps were dissolved and the one-third of the deportees who had survived the ordeal were repatriated. The Romanian authorities became increasingly interested in schemes for Jewish emigration to Palestine and became even more tolerant toward their own Jews. In 1944, when various Romanian political and military elements were actively engaged in finding an effective and reasonably quick way out of the Axis, Romania also became a haven for thousands of Jewish refugees from neighboring countries, including Hungary.[9]

Romania as a Haven for Hungarian-Jewish Refugees

According to a report by G. Bertrand Jacobson (the HICEM-HIAS representative in Bucharest) dated December 28, 1944, approximately 1,500 Hungarian Jews had clandestinely crossed the Romanian border from the beginning of the mass deportations in Hungary to that date. Most lived at the time in Bucharest, Arad, and Timişoara. In addition to these escapees, there were 11,200 other Hungarian Jews in Romania: approximately 3,200 Jewish labor servicemen, who had been employed at the copper mines in Bor,[10] had been allowed to cross into Romania following their liberation by Tito's forces in late summer–early fall 1944; and about 8,000 labor servicemen had been liberated by the Soviet-Romanian troops. Jacobson also claimed that in addition to the 12,700 Hungarian Jews in Romania there were approximately 4,000 to 8,000 liberated Hungarian Jewish labor servicemen in Northern Transylvania at that time. The number of the latter continued to increase with the victorious advance of the troops.

When draconic anti-Jewish measures were introduced in Hungary, after March 1944, Romania naturally emerged as a potential place of refuge. The Germans, of course, were also aware of this and on March 30 they alerted all their agencies about the possible illegal flight of Hungarian Jews to neighboring Bulgaria, Romania, and Slovakia.[11] They also began an intensive campaign aimed at persuading Romania to take effective countermeasures.

The Romanian government ostensibly complied on May 29, when it enacted a stiff law that mandated the death penalty for Jews entering Romania fraudulently and for those who aided them.[12] The Romanians, with a few exceptions, nevertheless continued to treat incoming refugees with a considerable degree of indulgence. They had in fact issued confidential instructions to their border control authorities to facilitate the admission of Jewish refugees from Hungary.[13] On June 2, 1944, the Prime Minister of Romania advised the Romanian delegate to the International Red Cross that he might give formal assurances that Jewish refugees from Hungary would be allowed to enter Romania notwithstanding formal declarations to the contrary, and that "their safety would be looked out for by the Romanians."[14] The Romanians' level of tolerance continued to increase until August 23, when Romania finally took the decisive step and extricated itself from the Axis alliance. From that time on, of course, the status of the Jews, both indigenous and foreign, became radically different. The new anti-Nazi government headed by General Constantin Sănătescu undertook not only to abolish the anti-Jewish measures, but also to protect its North-Transylvanian Jewish nationals under German-Hungarian domination.

In the interim between the German occupation of Hungary and Romania's extrication from the Axis alliance, the initiative for the rescuing of Hungarian Jews was taken by the Hungarian-speaking Jews of Southern Transylvania and the Hungarian-Jewish refugees in Bucharest. The latter acted in close cooperation with the International Red Cross as well as the Zionist and official leaders of the Jewish community of Romania.

During the early phase of the Jewish persecutions in Hungary (March–June 1944), the rescue effort was carried out mainly by the leaders of the Jewish communities of Southern Transylvania bordering Hungary. Some of the largest ghettos in Hungarian-held Northern Transylvania, for instance those of Nagyvárad, Kolozsvár, and Marosvásárhely, were very close to the Romanian border. Nevertheless, only a few thousand Jews availed themselves of the opportunity to escape into Romania. Among the reasons for this were the absence of most able-bodied males (who were in the labor service companies), the reluctance of the physically fit to leave behind the very young and the older members of their families, the risks associated with the illegal border crossing, and the failure of the Jewish leaders of Hungary to keep the masses informed (see chapters 23 and 29).

The few thousand Hungarian Jews who did manage to escape successfully into Romania used various means. Some were well off and bribed the guards; others had good contacts with Romanian diplomatic officials; still others followed the leadership of Zionist couriers (*shlichim*). A considerable percentage of those who dared cross the borders illegally were Jews of Southern Transylvanian background.

The main crossing points to the rescue centers in Romania were Arad, Beiuş, Braşov, Ginta, Sighişoara, Timişoara, and Turda. Of these, Arad and Turda were the busiest ones. The major problems confronting those involved in the rescue operations were the lodging

and protection of the refugees at the crossing points, and their subsequent successful transfer to Bucharest.

These problems were largely solved through Jewish officials' well-es-
tablished contacts with local Romanian authorities and through skillful
illegal activities, including the production of forged documents.[15]

Romanian peasants, many of whom were also oppressed by the Hungarians, often helped Jews crossing the border. The Romanian consular officials in Kolozsvár and Nagyvárad, who had good friends
among the border patrol officers in Romania, were also of great help.
In many cases, it was due to the benevolence of the Romanian officials
that the Hungarian Jewish escapees could go through unchecked by
the border guards. Mihai Marina, the Romanian Consul in Nagyvárad,
and his staff members also followed closely the ghettoization and deportation process in Northern Transylvania.[16] When Professor Vespasian V. Pella, the Romanian Ambassador to Switzerland, stopped over
in Nagyvárad, they made sure he received a lengthy report about the
Jewish persecutions in Hungary. The report included the observations
of the Romanian officials and a statement by Dr. Miksa Kupfer, a
physician in the ghetto of Nagyvárad, about the horrible conditions in
the ghetto. Upon his return to Berne, Pella forwarded the report to the
International Red Cross, which made use of it when it appealed to
Hungary. Presumably Horthy took the report into account when he
halted the deportations.

Despite the Romanians' benevolence, crossing the border was a risky
affair. For one thing, not all of the officials were sympathetic to the
Jewish refugees. Moreover, Romania was still a member of the Axis;
occasionally, Romanian officials, acting on their own or under pressure
from the German commando units, extradited Jewish refugees. Some
of the Jews were caught while still on Hungarian territory. However,
the risks associated with crossing the border were far less than those associated with the deportation. But, as was intimated earlier, the masses
were not aware of this.[17]

While the rescue committees along the border were busy helping the
escapees during their first few days and providing them with documents, a Committee for the Aid of Jewish Refugees from Northern
Transylvania (*Comitetul de asistenţă a refugiaţilor evrei din Ardealul de
Nord*) was organized in Bucharest under the aegis of the Zionist *Aliyah*
Office. The Committee was headed by Ernő (Ernest) Marton, the
former editor-in-chief of *Uj Kelet* (New East—the Hungarian-language

Jewish daily of Kolozsvár that had been shut down by the Hungarian authorities, and a former member of the Romanian parliament. Marton himself had escaped to Romania in May 1944 with the aid of a Romanian consular official shortly after Kasztner had visited Kolozsvár and informed the city's Jewish leaders about the realities of the Nazis' anti-Jewish measures.

The Committee acted in close cooperation with the leaders of Romanian Jewry, including A. L. Zissu and W. Fildermann.[18] During the pre-armistice period, its primary functions were to look after the personal safety of the escapees, ensure the departure of many of them for Palestine, and establish and maintain contact with major Jewish organizations abroad for the acquisition of funds and other material support.

Although by the time the Committee was formed the Romanian government had already repatriated most of the survivors of Transnistria and was showing considerable tolerance toward the Jews, the operations of the Committee had to be very circumspect. The government was under great pressure by the Germans, who were reluctantly reconciled to the Marshal's opposition to the Final Solution program but were seriously upset about the government's plans concerning the emigration of Jews to Palestine and the impact of Romania's policies on the deportations from Hungary.

By late spring 1944, the Romanian leaders had become convinced that allowing the emigration of the Jews was the wisest policy from both domestic and international points of view. Mihai Antonescu, the Deputy Prime Minister and Foreign Minister, was a leading exponent of this view. Under his initiative and chairmanship a Ministerial Conference was held on June 9 to discuss the Jewish question with emphasis on the possible emigration of the Jews. Among the participants were General Dumitru Popescu, Minister of the Interior; General Constantin Vasiliu, Undersecretary for Police and Public Security; General Sova, Undersecretary for the Navy; and Radu Lecca. The outcome of the meeting was revealed in a letter by Mihai Antonescu to Zissu dated June 17:

- The Ministerial Commission for the Regulation of General Emigration, which was established under a directive of Marshal Antonescu, acted positively on the issue of emigration.
- An emigration office was to be established under the chairmanship of Zissu with advisers and officials to be selected by him.[19]

- The transport contracts were to be handled by the Romanian Maritime Service (*Serviciul Maritim Român*—SMR).
- The departure of four foreign-flag ships then stationed in Constanţa was approved in principle, on the condition that they be used for the transport of the orphans from Transnistria, Jewish political refugees from abroad who could not stay in Romania, and other refugees.[20]

The new Romanian policy on emigration angered the Germans not only because it went counter to the Final Solution program, but also because it was in conflict with their policy toward the Arabs. Moreover, the Germans were upset over the relatively tolerant treatment of the indigenous and foreign Jews in Romania, which the Hungarians had used as one of their excuses to halt the deportations early in July. German Foreign Office officials in Berlin and Budapest, alarmed over Romania's changed position on the Jewish question, waged an intensive campaign in June and July to correct the situation.[21] Their hectic diplomatic maneuvers of the period also reflected the reports sent to Berlin by *Volksgruppen* leader Andreas Schmidt and his colleagues about the deteriorating situation in Romania and especially about the activities of Mihai Antonescu.[22]

On June 30, Thadden, following Veesenmayer's frequent communications, approached Killinger, requesting confirmation of the news allegedly emanating from the Romanian General Consulate in Kolozsvár that the Hungarian Jewish escapees in Romania were being treated as political refugees and allowed to leave for Palestine.[23] Killinger confirmed this on July 14.[24] The day before, Wagner had approached both Killinger and SS-*Gruppenführer* Heinrich Müller, the Gestapo chief, complaining that the Romanian government condoned the emigration of Hungarian Jews to Palestine.[25] On July 26, Killinger had no alternative but to verify that Jews were indeed being allowed to leave Romania with the consent of Marshal Antonescu, that Hungarian Jews were moving around freely in the country, and that tolerance toward the Jews was generally on the increase.[26] On August 8, Wagner approached Ribbentrop, proposing to forward through Killinger a request to the Marshal for the full application of the anti-Jewish laws enacted in Romania.[27] Wagner received Ribbentrop's consent on August 14,[28] but by that time Romania was on the verge of quitting the Axis.

The Antonescu government's position toward the Jews during the last few months before the *volte-face* was summarized in a statement given to the Romanian Committee in Geneva through Grigore Gafencu and Vespasian V. Pella.[29] According to the highly confidential statement:

- The Romanian government was according the greatest possible kindness to the Jewish refugees from Hungary and was allowing 2,500 of them to leave the country that year.
- It had made a number of strong and repeated representations to the Hungarian government on behalf of Romanian Jewish nationals in Hungary and Northern Transylvania; it had also repatriated several thousand Romanian Jewish nationals from France, who otherwise would have been deported to Germany.
- It welcomed the Jewish refugees from territories occupied by the Red Army and was permitting the transfer to Turkey of 3,000 Jewish children.
- It had been allowing the Jews in Transnistria to receive large quantities of food and drugs since 1943.
- It had taken measures to avoid all incidents between German soldiers and Jews in the Romanian sector of the Eastern front.
- It was allowing the Jews of Romania to continue working in their professions; some even worked for the state.
- It required the Jews, who were exempted from military service, to make a monetary contribution proportionate to their wealth. Part of the money so collected by the Jewish national organization was used for aid to the Jews. Jews who could not contribute were allowed to render socially useful labor.
- It had violated some of the property rights of the Jews under the impact of certain pressures, but such properties were not transferred to other private individuals, but to the state.
- It was permitting the emigration of Jews as organized by the Jews themselves and had placed a number of ships at their disposal.

Given the attitude of the Sztójay government in Hungary, the position of the Romanian government toward the Jews was quite extraordinary. Naturally, the Romanian position reflected a degree of opportunism along with its relative humanitarianism. Realizing comparatively early that the Axis had lost the war, the responsible Romanian leaders, including Mihai Antonescu,[30] decided quite logically to acquire some good will for their country by changing, among other things, their anti-Jewish stance. In this they were actively encouraged by the highly respected leaders of the opposition, the heads of the historical parties of Romania, including Iuliu Maniu, Dinu Brătianu, and Emil Hațieganu.

Just before Romania changed sides, Zissu and Fildermann separately were asked by Mihai Antonescu to render a service to the Romanian nation. Zissu was requested by Under Secretary of State Ovid Vlădescu, acting in behalf of Antonescu, to contact the Jewish organizations in Britain and America and convince them to induce the Western Allies to pressure the Soviet Union into easing the armistice conditions.[31] When Zissu decided to consult Fildermann, he was informed that the President of the Jewish Community had already acted upon a separate request by Antonescu and that in fact a letter of his addressed to Reuben B. Resnik, the AJDC representative in Istanbul, had been picked up by a courier of the government at 5:00 A.M. In his letter, Fildermann urged "in the interest of the Jewish people" that Romania be occupied and administered after the armistice not only by the Russians, but also by the British and Americans "as in Italy."[32]

Following the anti-German coup of August 23, the Committee for Refugee Affairs acquired legal status. From that time, it concentrated its efforts on legalizing the status of the refugees and providing them with monetary and material assistance through the AJDC. Late in October, when almost all of Transylvania had been liberated by the combined Soviet-Romanian forces, the Committee was consolidated in a General Jewish Committee of Northern Transylvania (*Curatoriu general evreesc al Ardealului de Nord*), known in Hungarian as the *Északerdélyi Zsidó Kuratórium*. Designed to represent all the Jews of the region, the Committee's sphere of activities encompassed administrative, legal, and economic functions. It also claimed to represent the social and political interests of the liberated Jews.[33] One of the primary concerns of the Committee, which was also headed by Marton, was to help bring about the liberation or at least the easing of the lot of the North Transylvanian Jews still in German and Hungarian hands. Toward this end it worked closely with Romulus Pop, the new Minister of Minorities, and Ionel Pop, the newly appointed High Commissioner for the Administration of Liberated Transylvania (*Înalt Comisar pentru administrarea Transilvaniei eliberate*). On November 4, 1944, the High Commissioner approved the establishment of a Special Department on Jewish Questions in the Liberated Territories (*Serviciu special pentru problemele evreești din teritoriile eliberate*).

The main functions of the Special Department, as specified in the High Commissioner's Decision no. 5, were to organize the relief work for the Jews in Northern Transylvania, inventory the property of the Jews in the liberated areas (with an eye toward preserving and returning the confiscated goods to their legitimate owners), submit proposals for the redressing of wrongs caused by the Hungarian anti-Jewish laws, collect data relating to the Jews deported by the Hungarian authorities, and study the means for the return and aid of the deportees.

The Special Department, like the Committee, was placed under the leadership of Marton, acting as Technical Counselor (*Consilier tehnic*).[34] These two new forums of North Transylvanian Jewry undertook an intensive campaign, including the submission of memoranda, designed to help the North Transylvanian Jews still in German camps or under the control of the Szálasi government. Viewing these Jews as Romanian citizens, one memorandum called for the exchange of Romanian Swabians or Saxons—most of whom had sympathized, if not actively collaborated, with the Nazis—for the Jewish deportees. Another called for identifying the Germans in Romania as well as the Jews in German and Hungarian hands as POWs; a third suggested the possibility of holding the Germans in Romania as hostages to pressure the Nazi authorities into yielding on the North Transylvanian Jews. These memoranda were submitted to Grigore Niculescu-Buzeşti, the new Romanian Minister of Foreign Affairs. Appeals were also addressed to the Vatican, the International Red Cross, and the Great Powers. The latter were requested to adopt retaliatory measures against the Germans and the Hungarians and possibly to exchange German POWs under their control for North Transylvanian Jews.

These efforts proved essentially fruitless, although the Sănătescu government approached both Germany and Hungary on these matters through Switzerland. In their note of November 7 addressed to the Hungarian government, for example, the Romanians stated that:

- They had information to the effect that the German and Hungarian governments intended to liquidate the Jews deported from Northern Transylvania and that the survival of the Romanians who were taken to Germany for labor was greatly endangered.
- They had requested the International Red Cross to investigate this matter urgently.
- The Swiss were requested to induce the Hungarian government to consent to these investigations.
- They regarded the Hungarian and German minorities in Romania as co-responsible for the fate of the persons mentioned in the first point and were ready to take just reprisals.[35]

The Germans ignored the Romanian note, but the Hungarians responded almost immediately. In its reply of November 15, the Szálasi government cynically denied the allegations of the Romanians. At the time, when the *Nyilas* terror was at its height in Budapest, the Hungarians brazenly asserted that the North Transylvanian Jews were not being deported but were merely being mobilized for labor; that their lives, like the lives of Hungarian Jews still in Hungary, were not in danger; and that in fact their lot was much better than that of the Hungarians, for they were working at a great distance from the front, while the Hungarians had to endure great sacrifices on the battlefield. The *Nyilas* claimed that they had on their own invited the International Red Cross to investigate the situation of the Romanians and Jews in Germany, and that Hungary would welcome such an invitation on the part of the Romanians (presumably to investigate the status of the Hungarians in Romania). The *Nyilas* claimed that the veiled threat of reprisals was intended merely to justify in advance the Romanians' planned actions against the Hungarian minority in Romania.[36]

The Committee achieved no tangible success along these diplomatic lines. It became increasingly apparent that the fate of the North Transylvanian Jews, like that of all other victims in Nazi–*Nyilas* hands, depended on the military successes of the Allies. The Committee therefore concentrated its attention on helping the refugees in Romania and the Jews in the liberated areas. It was assisted by the AJDC, the International Red Cross, and the Romanian government. Following the liberation by the combined Soviet–Romanian forces of large parts of Hungary, Czechoslovakia, and Poland, the Romanian government placed a special train at the disposal of the Committee to help in the repatriation of the Jews liberated from the Nazi camps.[37] In the spring and summer of 1945, the Committee also aided the liberated Jewish communities of Hungary, Poland, and Czechoslovakia.[38]

Slovakia: A Pioneer of Anti-Jewish Measures

For a while at least, the only other possible refuge beside Romania for Hungarian Jews was Slovakia. A creation and loyal ally of the Third Reich, Slovakia was one of the first countries to emulate the Nazis' anti-Jewish policies.[39] In fact, soon after the establishment of the "independent" Slovak State in March 1939, Dr. Ferdinand Ďurčanský, the new Foreign Minister, assured Hermann Göring that the Jews of Slovakia would be treated in the same way as the German Jews. Indeed, the "solution of the Jewish question" became one of the main preoccupations of the new government.[40] The policies of the government, in this as in all other respects, were influenced if not determined by the German Legation in Bratislava, which was first headed by Manfred von Killinger (March 1939–January 1941) and then by Hanns Elard Ludin. The Legation's special advisor on the Jewish question was SS-*Hauptsturm-führer* Dieter Wisliceny, who arrived in Bratislava on September 1, 1940. A leading member of the Eichmann-*Sonderkommando*, Wisliceny played an important role in the liquidation of the Jews of Slovakia, Greece and Hungary.

The Slovak anti-Jewish drive began soon after the establishment of the new state by the enactment of a decree relating to the definition of Jews (April 18, 1939). This definition, which reflected the views of Dr. Bernhard Lösener as incorporated in the Nuremberg Laws of 1935, was subsequently adopted as part of the so-called Jewish Code (*Zidovsky kodex; Judenkodex*), which was promulgated as Law no. 198/1941 on September 9, 1941.[41]

During the first phase of the anti-Jewish campaign, the Jews of Slovakia were subjected to a ruthless Aryanization program spearheaded by the Central Economy Office (*Ústredný Hospodárský Úrad-ÚHÚ*).[42] About two-thirds of the 15,000 Jews of Bratislava were expelled in October 1941 and forced, together with thousands of others left unemployed in the wake of the Aryanization process, to "do productive work" in labor camps. The largest of these camps—established in the fall of 1941 and originally designed as entrainment-deportation centers—were located in Sered, Novaky, and Vyhne. Smaller camps were at Ilava, Žilina, Degeš, Nitra, Svätý Jur, Láb, and Zohor.

The second and more radical phase began shortly after the adoption of the Final Solution program at Wannsee in January 1942. Slovakia had the distinction of being the first country to deport masses of Jews to Auschwitz. Between March 26 and June 1942 the Slovak authorities deported approximately 52,000 Jews.[43] Most of the remaining Jews eventually received special legitimation, "protective letters" (*Schutzbriefe*) certifying that they were essential to the nation's economy. In spite of German pressure, the mass deportations were not resumed. Smaller transports were "smuggled" out, but the total number of deportees between June 1942 and March 1943 was under 6,000.[44]

By 1943, deportation of the Jews had become somewhat unpopular. The economy was under great strain, the war was not going very well for the Axis, and news had begun to filter in after July 1942 that the deported Jews were in fact being liquidated rather than resettled. The source of this news was none other than the Vatican; this made a tremendous impression on this overwhelmingly Catholic country. Pressed by the Catholic bishops, Prime Minister Tuka expressed to the Germans his desire that a mixed commission inspect one of the camps in which the Jews were "resettled." Embarrassed by the request, the Germans decided to ease, for a while at least, their pressure on Slovakia. In December 1943, however, Edmund Veesenmayer, Ribbentrop's troubleshooter and later Reich Plenipotentiary in Hungary, managed to persuade Tiso to have the 16,000 to 18,000 Jews placed in special camps by April 1, 1944; the approximately 10,000 converted Jews were to be placed in a separate camp.

During this turbulent period in Slovakian history, the status of the Jews in Hungary was quite good despite the many anti-Jewish measures in effect at the time. Following the adoption of the Aryanization program and especially after the beginning of the deportations in March 1942, a relatively large number of (mostly Hungarian-speaking) Slovak Jews sought and found refuge in Hungary. By November 1943, their number reached approximately 8,000 (close to 10 percent of the total Jewish population of Slovakia).

Until the German occupation of Hungary the situation of the Slovak Jews in the country was quite tolerable. They enjoyed the protection of the Hungarian state, the sympathy of Ferenc Keresztes-Fischer, the enlightened Minister of the Interior, and the support of the Hungarian Jewish community. Following the occupation, their fate became intertwined with that of the Hungarian Jews. Although the Slovak government gave lip service to their protection, it was in fact only interested in protecting some of the "valuable" Jews (see chapter 27). Ironically, when the situation in Slovakia stabilized following the suspension of the deportations, the country emerged as a refuge not only for those who had originally escaped from there, but also for many Hungarian Jews.

Slovakia: The Temporary Haven

Aware of the switch in the anti-Jewish postures of the two countries, the RSHA lost no time after the occupation of Hungary in informing the authorities in Bratislava about the "danger" of possible illegal crossings by Jews along the Hungarian border. Similar warnings were sent to Bucharest and Sofia.[45]

Since the Slovak government showed no interest in its Jews abroad, many of the Slovak Jewish refugees in Hungary were included in the Final Solution program. Some of the refugees, however, together with a number of Hungarian Jews, managed to cross the borders illegally, especially along the eastern parts of Slovakia. This alarmed the German authorities in Hungary. On June 14, at the height of the mass deportations from Hungary, Veesenmayer approached the German Foreign Office, requesting a meeting with Ludin to bring about the simultaneous liquidation of both Jewish communities.[46] The positive answer of Ribbentrop arrived the same day.[47] However, the unavailability of Wisliceny and Eichmann, who at the time were busy with the deportation of the Jews of Hungary, necessitated a postponement of the proposed meeting. It was rescheduled, only to be postponed once again because of unexpected developments in both Hungary and Slovakia. Horthy had decided to halt the deportations; in Slovakia the military situation of the Axis had deteriorated to such an extent, with the fast approach of the Soviet forces coupled with the increasingly daring forays of the Slovak partisan units, that the Germans became extremely apprehensive.[48]

Veesenmayer's eagerness to meet with Ludin was motivated by his chagrin over the handling of the Jewish question in Slovakia, and especially over the flight of some Hungarian Jews. He bombarded the Foreign Office with complaints about the alleged difficulty of carrying out the anti-Jewish measures in Hungary because of the leniency manifested toward the Jews by both Romania and Slovakia.[49] The Slovaks, pressured by the German Foreign Office, made one major concession. They showed no interest in most of their Jewish nationals in Hungary, and allowed them to be included in the general deportation measures.[50] As to the Hungarian Jews who managed to escape to Slovakia, Alexander (Šano) Mach, the Deputy Prime Minister, assured Ludin that their number was small, inasmuch as the Slovak borders with Hungary were under heavy guard. As a further concession, Ludin requested the reassignment of Wisliceny to Bratislava to help him with the solution of the Jewish question.[51] Veesenmayer, however, remained adamant in his position, disputing the contentions about the treatment of Slovakian Jews in Hungary and Hungarian Jewish refugees in Slovakia. He continued to insist that the implementation of the anti-Jewish program in Hungary was being made difficult by the leniency with which the Jews were being treated in Slovakia and Romania.[52]

The changing attitude of the Hungarian government six weeks after the halting of the deportations was reflected, among others things, in its renewed interest in the few *bona fide* Jewish Hungarian nationals abroad. On August 25, 1944, for example, the Council of Ministers, which was then headed by Lajos Reményi-Schneller acting in behalf of the ailing Sztójay, decided to extend the validity of the passports held by Hungarian Jews living in Slovakia.[53]

Ironically, by that time, when the situation of the Jews in Hungary was gradually improving under the policies of General Géza Lakatos, the conditions in Slovakia were taking a sharp turn for the worse. Unexpected developments played into the hands of Ludin and Veesenmayer, enabling them to see the attainment of their cherished objective: the liquidation of the remaining Jewish community of Slovakia together with most of the Hungarian Jewish escapees.

Slovakia: The Tragedy Completed

The dilatory way in which the Slovak authorities handled the German pressures was to a large extent grounded in a realistic assessment of the military situation at the time. By June 1944, the Red Army was fast approaching the eastern borders of the country, revitalizing the Slovak underground forces. Acts of resistance and sabotage became ever more frequent and daring. The underground forces, numbering from 12,000 to 15,000 at their peak, included in addition to the Slovak patriots a considerable number of French and Soviet escapees from various concentration and POW camps, and volunteers from several other national groups. Among these were a few thousand able-bodied Jews from the remaining community of Slovakia, mostly escapees from the work camps.[54] As the movement expanded, Soviet and British commandos were parachuted into Slovak territories to help train the fighters. To assist in Jewish rescue operations, a special commando of four Palestinian parachutists from a British unit arrived toward the middle of September.[55] The partisan forces were also joined by thousands of soldiers who had deserted the regular Slovak Army.

The partisan struggle acquired a momentum of its own, compelling the Slovak government, then headed by Stephan Tiso, to declare martial law on August 11 and finally appeal to Hitler (August 25) for urgent military assistance to help quell the uprising. On August 29, SS units under the command of SS-*Obergruppenführer* Gottlob Berger arrived in Slovakia to cope with the situation. That same day the uprising became general, with the insurgents' radio station in Banská Bystrica, the center of the resistance movement, calling on the people to join in the fight against the Germans. In his capacity as *Wehrmachtbefehlshaber* in Slovakia, Gottlob Berger[56] was assisted by two SS officers especially concerned with the solution of the Jewish question: SS-*Obersturmbann-*

HUNGARIAN JEWS ABROAD

führer Vitezka (Dr. Witiska), the SIPO and SD boss of Slovakia and the chief of *Einsatzgruppe* H; and SS-*Hauptsturmführer* Anton Alois Brunner, a leading member of Eichmann's dejewification squad. While Vitezka's units participated in the struggle against the partisans, they were particularly concerned with the round-up of Jews in the areas under their control.

With the fall of Banská Bystrica on October 28 and the collapse of the uprising, the anti-Jewish measures acquired an ominous tone. The Jews not rounded up earlier were now picked up by Brunner's forces assisted by Hlinka Guards. Most of them were taken to Sered and from there were gradually deported to Auschwitz and other German concentration camps.[57] Between October 1944 and March 1945, approximately 13,500 Jews were deported. Among these were the several thousand Jews the Germans had captured during the uprising and an undetermined number of Hungarian Jewish refugees.[58]

Notes

1. The number of Hungarian Jews in Croatia in 1944 is unknown. At a meeting of August 25, 1944, the Hungarian government decided to revalidate the passports of the Hungarian Jews in Croatia. *Vádirat,* 3:477.

2. *RLB,* Doc. 187.

3. Antonescu's official position was Chief of State (*Şeful de Stat*). His rule is often referred to as the "regime of the legionnaires" (*regimul legionarilor*).

4. For a detailed account of the Romanian involvement in the massacre of the Jews of Odessa, see Dora Litani, "The Destruction of the Jews of Odessa in the Light of Romanian Documents" in *YVS,* 6:135–54.

5. For details, see Matatias Carp, *Pogromul dela Iaşi* (The Jassy Pogrom) (Bucharest: Socec, 1947), 162 pp., Aurel Karetki and Maria Covaci, *Zile însîngerate la Iaşi* (Bloody Days at Jassy) (Bucharest: Editura Politică, 1978), 127 pp.

6. Matatias Carp, *Transnistria* (Bucharest: Socec, 1948), 476 pp.

7. According to a statistical study showing the demographic evolution of Romanian Jewry, no more than approximately 15,000 of the 312,972 Jews (1930 census) of Old Romania, Southern Transylvania, and Southern Bukovina (i.e., the Romania ruled by Marshal Antonescu) perished during the war. See Sabin Manuilă and W. Filderman, *Regional Development of the Jewish Population in Romania* (Rome: Stabilimento Tipografico F. Failli, 1957), 15 pp. The authors, the former General Director of the Central Statistical Institute of Romania and the former President of the Jewish Community of Romania, respectively, conclude that "no other country . . . [under] . . . Nazi domination can show so large a proportion of survivors as does Romania."

8. See, for example, the telegram of February 10, 1943, by Fritz Gebhard Hahn, Secretary of Legation in the German Foreign Office, addressed to the German Legation in Bucharest. *RLB,* Doc. 95.

9. For details on the treatment of the Jews in Romania, see Matatias Carp, *Cartea neagră. Fapte şi documente. Suferinţele evreilor din România, 1940–1944* (Black Book. Facts and Documents. The Suffering of the Jews of Romania, 1940–1944) (Bucharest: Socec,

1946), 380 pp.; Raul Hilberg, *The Destruction of the European Jews* (Chicago: Quadrangle, 1961), pp. 485–509; Gerald Reitlinger, *The Final Solution* (New York: The Beechhurst Press, 1953), pp. 394–411. See also Th. Lavi, "The Background to the Rescue of Romanian Jewry During the Period of the Holocaust," in *Jews and Non-Jews in Eastern Europe*, eds. Béla Vágó and George L. Mosse (New York: Wiley, 1974), pp. 177–86.

10. Jacobson's report was forwarded to the State Department by Burton Y. Berry, the U. S. Representative in Romania. The Germans apparently managed to intercept or copy it, since it was placed in the Richter Files (in the author's possession).

11. Documents, dated April 20, 1944, from the Richter Files (Roll 3, Vol. 18), in possession of the author. At this time, ghettoization was already in full swing in Carpatho-Ruthenia.

12. *Monitorul Oficial* (Official Gazette), Bucharest, May 29, 1944. On June 6, Richter informed the SIPO and SD leader in Berlin about the new law. Richter Files.

13. Telegram no. 3867 of June 17, 1944, from Leland Harrison, the American Minister in Berne, to the U.S. Secretary of State.

14. *Summary Report of the Activities of the War Refugee Board with Respect to the Jews of Hungary* (Washington, October 9, 1944), p. 14. (Typescript). The report was prepared by Lawrence S. Lesser, the assistant of John W. Pehle, the head of the WRB. Reports on the increasingly benevolent position of Romania toward the Jews were periodically reported in *The New York Times*. See, for example, the issues of April 1 ("40,000 Refugees Escape to Rumania") and April 11, 1944 ("Steinhardt Helps 245 More Exiles").

15. For a detailed, though not fully documented, account of the activities of the rescue committee of Turda, see Arnold David Finkelstein, *Fénysugár a borzalmak éjszakájában* (A Ray of Light in the Night of Horrors) (Tel Aviv: P. Solar and J. Nadiv, 1958), 400 pp. The author, the former secretary of the Jewish community of Turda, shared the leadership of the committee with Ari (Ernest) Hirsch and Majsi (Carol) Moskovits. He expresses disdain for the leaders of the Kolozsvár Rescue Committee (*Mentési Bizottság*), including Rabbi Mózes Weinberger, Ernő Hátszegi, and Ernő Marton who, he claims, "exploited the material means and available escape routes almost exclusively for their own rescue" (p. 294). The book also contains an account of the nearly miraculous escape of Rabbi József Paneth of Nagyilonda from the ghetto of Dés together with nine members of his family (pp. 302–23).

16. Among the consular officials who visited the various counties of Northern Transylvania to acquaint themselves with the ghettoization and deportation process were Mihai Bologa, Vasile Hossu, Ion Işaiu, Alexandru Olteanu, and Ion Romaşcan. Mihai Marina, "Nu puteam rămîne impasibili!" (We Could Not Remain Impassive!"), *Magazin Istoric* (Historical Magazine), Bucharest, no. 6, June 1976, pp. 39–41. See also pp. 37–38.

17. For incidents of this kind, see Finkelstein, *Fénysugár a borzalmak éjszakájában*, pp. 20–23. See also *RLB*, Doc. 284.

18. Among the members were Martin Hirsch, J. Schmetterer, Leon Goldenberg, Paul Benedek, and D. Lampel. Béla Vágó, "Political and Diplomatic Activities for the Rescue of the Jews of Northern Transylvania," in *YVS*, 6:155. In addition to Zissu and Fildermann, the heads respectively of the Zionist and communal organizations, an active role was played by Jean Cohen and Leon Itzcar.

19. Shortly after the emigration scheme began, a number of technical and jurisdictional difficulties arose, especially with respect to deciding who would be chosen to make the voyage to safe havens. On July 21, Zissu was approached by Ira A. Hirschmann, the Special Attaché of the USA associated with the War Refugee Board, who expressed his concern for the quick movement of the vessels agreed to by the government. For the text of Hirschmann's letter, see The Jewish National and University Library, Jerusalem, Heb. 4o 1253/30. For further details on the War Refugee Board's involvement, see chapter 31.

20. The Germans were fully aware of the Romanians' involvement in the emigration

schemes. A set of documents relating to the meeting of June 9 was forwarded by Killinger to the Foreign Office on July 17. *NA,* Microcopy T-120, Roll 4203, Frames K789/K209065-099; *RLB,* Doc. 317. Wagner briefed Ribbentrop on these matters on July 28. *NA,* Frames K789/K209100-101.

21. *RLB,* Docs. 194, 196, 197, 282, 284.

22. *NA,* Microcopy T-120, Roll 4203, Frames K789/K209100-117. Soon after Romania's turn-about of August 23, the *Volksgruppen* leaders were arrested and placed in special detention camps. *Ibid.,* Frame K209217.

23. *RLB,* Doc. 316. Thadden sent a copy of his communication to Eichmann that same day. *NA,* Microcopy T-120, Roll 4355, Frame K213558.

24. *RLB,* Doc. 317.

25. *Ibid.,* Doc. 196; *NA,* Microcopy T-120, Roll 4355, Frame K213505.

26. *RLB,* Doc. 318.

27. *Ibid.,* Doc. 319.

28. *NA,* Roll 4355, Frame K213510. The note was signed by Reinebeck, a leading official in the Foreign Minister's office.

29. Copies of the statement were forwarded by Josef Mandl, the brother of Georges Mandel-Mantello, then diplomatic representative of El Salvador in Switzerland, to the *Schweizer Hilfscomité für die ungarischen Juden* (Swiss Committee for the Aid of Hungarian Jews) in Zurich and to the International Red Cross. Yad Vashem, Jerusalem, Archives, M-20/47.

30. For an evaluation of the various leaders of wartime Romania, see Alexandre Safran (Former Chief Rabbi of Romania), "The Rulers of Fascist Romania Whom I Had to Deal With" in *YVS,* 6:175–80.

31. Minutes of Zissu's discussion with Antonescu and Vlădescu as taken and signed on August 23, 1944, by Ernő Marton and Leon Itzcar. Available at The Jewish National and University Library, Jerusalem, Heb. 4o 1253/30.

32. *Ibid.*

33. *Renaşterea Noastră* (Our Rebirth), Bucharest, October 20, 1944, p. 1.

34. *Ibid.,* November 10, 1944, p. 4.

35. *RLB,* Doc. 354.

36. *Ibid.,* Doc. 355.

37. The first train for the repatriation of concentration camp inmates left Romania under the leadership of Jacob Schmetterer on April 12, 1945, and returned to Nagyvárad eight days later with 202 deportees. The second train, to Birkenau-Auschwitz and Kattowicz, left on April 25 and returned 18 days later with 405 deportees; the third train left on May 15. Marton's report on the activities of the Committee, dated May 22, 1945, Yad Vashem, Jerusalem, Archives Film JM/2625/1.

38. *Ibid.*

39. According to the census of December 15, 1940, 88,951 of the approximately 2,500,000 inhabitants were Jewish. About 12,300 Jews were identified as entrepreneurs and shopkeepers, 22,000 as private employees, and a few thousand as government employees and professionals. Hilberg, *Destruction of the European Jews,* p. 460.

40. Among the state and government officials most concerned with the Jewish question were President Josef Tiso, Prime Minister Vojtech (Béla) Tuka, and Foreign Minister Ferdinand Ďurčanský. Special roles were played by Šano Mach, the Minister of the Interior; Dr. Geiza Konka and later Dr. Anton Vasek, the heads of the Jewish Division of the Ministry of the Interior; and Augustin Morávek, the chairman of the Central Economy Office.

41. For details on the provisions of the Jewish Code, see Livia Rothkirchen, *The Destruction of Slovak Jewry* (Jerusalem: Yad Vashem, 1961), pp. xviii–xix.

42. *Ibid.*, pp. xiv–xv. For details on the Aryanization program, see also Hilberg, *Destruction of the European Jews*, pp. 460–62.

43. Hilberg, *Destruction of the European Jews*, p. 467.

44. According to Korherr, the SS-statistician, the number of deportees from Slovakia reached 56,691 by the end of 1942 and 57,545 by March 31, 1943. *Ibid.*, p. 468.

45. Secret RSHA (IV B 4 b-2314/43g (82)) note dated March 30, 1944. Richter files.

46. *RLB*, Doc. 175.

47. NG-2829. Also in *NA*, Microcopy T-120, Roll 4355, Frame K213983.

48. For references to the correspondence relating to the scheduled meetings of Foreign Office representatives see *RLB*, 1:lxxix.

49. *Ibid.*, Docs. 194, 197, 320, and 321.

50. *Ibid.*, Doc. 310 (Ludin note dated July 21, 1944). See also chapter 27.

51. *Ibid.*, Doc. 322 (Ludin telegram of August 4, 1944). On August 8, Wagner suggested that Ludin and Veesenmayer meet with Wisliceny to settle the question of the Hungarian Jewish escapees in Slovakia. *Ibid.*, Doc. 319.

52. *Ibid.*, Doc. 323 (Veesenmayer's note to the Foreign Office, dated August 10, 1944).

53. The decision also extended to Hungarian Jews living in Croatia. There are no data relating to the number of Hungarian Jewish nationals living "legally" in these countries. For the minutes of the Council's meeting, see *Vádirat*, 3:477.

54. Rothkirchen, *The Destruction of Slovak Jewry*, pp. xliii–xlvi.

55. The four parachutists were Jews of Slovak origin: Chaviva Reik, Zvi Ben Ya'acov, Rafael Reiss, and Chaim Chermesh. After the resistance was crushed late in October 1944, they were executed together with a group of local Jewish fighters. *Ibid.*, pp. xliv–xlv.

56. After approximately four weeks in Slovakia, Berger, having played a crucial role in the suppression of the uprising, was replaced by SS-General Hermann Höffle.

57. When the camp was evacuated in January 1945, a few thousand deportees were sent to Ravensbrück, Sachsenhausen, Bergen-Belsen, and Theresienstadt. Some had been sent to these camps as early as November 1944, when the gassing facilities of Auschwitz were destroyed.

58. According to Vitezka's report of December 9, 1944, 4,653 of the 18,937 prisoners captured were Jewish and of these 2,257 were immediately subjected to "special treatment" (*Sonderbehandlung*). Rothkirchen, *Destruction of Slovak Jewry*, pp. xlvi–xlvii. According to a source cited by Reitlinger (in *The Final Solution*, p. 392) of the 18,937 prisoners reported by Vitezka, 9,653 were identified as Jews and of these 8,975 were transferred to concentration camps and the remainder subjected to "special handling."

CHAPTER TWENTY-NINE

RESCUE AND RESISTANCE

The Domestic Climate for Rescue and Resistance

THE WARTIME LEADERSHIP of Hungarian Jewry has often been censured for failing to do anything meaningful to forestall or at least to minimize the catastrophe. Though aware of the dimensions of the Nazis' Final Solution program, it failed to prepare any contingency plans of rescue or possible resistance. The attitudes and perceptions of these leaders, like those of Hungarian Jewry as a whole, continued to be shaped by a myopic view of the community's position in Hungary since 1867. As a result, when the Hungarian community still remained relatively intact and well-off while the neighboring communities were being systematically destroyed, the Hungarian Jews were developing a false sense of security. To the very end they deluded themselves —constantly rationalizing that they would somehow survive the war (although under less favorable economic conditions).

When disaster struck with the German occupation of Hungary on March 19, 1944, the Jews soon discovered that they were no less vulnerable than their brethren elsewhere in Nazi-dominated Europe. One by one, the major pillars upon which they based their hope collapsed. The conservative-aristocratic ruling faction of the Hungarian Right on which they counted so heavily for their continued protection was eliminated; the leftist and progressive opposition which they expected would take a stand against the Nazis remained (postwar Hungarian historiography notwithstanding) an impotent shell. Finally, the Christian neighbors with whom they thought they had shared a common destiny for over a thousand years remained basically passive. This was especially true in the provincial communities, where the ghettoization, concentration, and deportation of the Jews were carried out extremely rapidly.

Attitude of the Hungarian Christians

The generally passive, if not openly hostile, attitude of the Christian population was shaped by many factors. Subjected for over two decades to a vicious anti-Semitic propaganda campaign, a large percentage of the unenlightened population developed a distorted picture of the Jews' historical role in Hungary. In the course of time, many Christians came to accept the ultra-rightist image of the Jews and blamed them for all the failures and shortcomings of Hungary. As in Germany, they viewed the Jews both as harbingers of Communism and as champions of plutocratic capitalism. They tended to blame all Jews for the abortive proletarian dictatorship of Béla Kun, even though the overwhelming majority of Hungarian Jewry sided with the Magyars in condemning the Bolshevik adventure.

Conversely, although the great majority of the Jews lived on the edge of poverty, the general public tended to equate all Jews with the small percentage that played a conspicuous role in the professions and in banking, industry, and commerce. The distorted image also included the notion that Jews shunned manual labor, preferring to exploit the work of others.

In the years before the Holocaust, this anti-Jewish bias was reinforced by the vicious campaign of the German-financed ultra-rightist press, the constant preoccupation of the state radio stations with the Jewish question, the agitation of the representatives of the extremist parties and movements, and the policy declarations of anti-Semitic parliamentarians. The preoccupation with the Jewish question and the demands for its effective solution reached fever pitch following the *Anschluss* and especially after the declaration of war against the Soviet Union late in June 1941. An Axis partner, Hungary closely observed Nazi Germany's approach to the solution of the Jewish question and at first showed great eagerness to adopt at least some of its features. Anxious to prove its acceptance of Hitler's New Order for Europe, Hungary adopted a Nuremberg-type law (the so-called Third Anti-Jewish Law) and resettled a large number of "alien" Jews. These draconic measures, like the many others that preceded and followed them, came to be accepted by the Hungarian people as necessary and desirable for the advancement of Hungary's national interests.

The avalanche of ever harsher anti-Jewish decrees adopted almost immediately after the German occupation did not catch the Hungarians totally unprepared. Even the ultimate objective of the Germans—the deportation of the Jews—was not all that surprising, for such steps had been called for in the Hungarian Parliament several years earlier.[1] Having been psychologically and politically prepared, many segments of the Hungarian population in fact looked forward to some of the anti-Jewish measures. Those with more rapacious instincts applauded the ghettoization-deportation program, hoping to take over the homes, professional offices, and businesses of Jews.

A segment of the population viewed the measures enacted against the Jews with helpless disgust; but feeling helpless to prevent them, they usually internalized their indignation. A few officials, however, including some prefects, protested the measures by resigning from their positions.[2] The passivity of the majority was not necessarily because of a lack of concern for the Jews; quite often, it resulted from fear inspired by the quisling government. As part of the anti-Jewish drive, the Christian population was threatened with heavy fines and penalties, including internment, for hiding or protecting Jews or their property. Furthermore, most Christians, like most Jews, had no inkling about the ultimate scope of the Final Solution program. The press and radio were silent on the deportations. Most Hungarians who witnessed the ghettoization, concentration, and entrainment of the Jews were convinced that their removal from their homes involved their eventual relocation "to some distant places where they would be finally made to do physical labor."

In contrast to such German-occupied countries as Denmark and The Netherlands (with their long tradition of democracy, pluralism, and toleration) and even to such Axis-allied states as Bulgaria, Italy, and Romania (where the persecuted Jews received considerable aid from both the people and the indigenous authorities),[3] in Hungary the Sztójay government exceeded the Germans' expectations in its anti-Jewish initiatives and zeal. Ironically, the once-dreaded labor service system emerged as a source of rescue for Jewish men 20 to 48 years of age. Many of them, and in some places even those younger and older, were called to duty at the time of the ghettoizations, saving them from deportation.

A rather large segment of the Christian population openly collaborated with the Nazis. Only a comparatively small number dared to publicly criticize the inhumanity of the measures enacted against the Jewish neighbors with whom they had lived in harmony and friendship for many generations. But there were also a few who risked their freedom, and some even their lives, by hiding Jews[4] or bringing food to their former neighbors, friends, or employers in the ghettos and entrainment centers. In some cases, these Christians were beaten savagely and some were actually forced to join the Jews on the journey to Auschwitz.[5]

However, those who denounced the Jews for ideological, pseudo-patriotic or opportunistic reasons far outnumbered the good samaritans. During the occupation alone, the German and Hungarian dejewification authorities received from 30,000 to 35,000 denunciations against Jews from all parts of the country. The Hungarian Political Police (*Magyar Politikai Rendőrség*), headed by Péter Hain, investigated approximately 7,000 of the denunciations and arrested 1,950 Jews. Of these, 940 of the richer ones were handed over to the Gestapo, which promptly confiscated their property.[6]

The wave of denunciations followed László Baky's appeal of April 15, 1944:

It is in the national interest that the anti-Jewish decrees be carried out one hundred percent. I therefore request every honest Hungarian's cooperation in the implementation of the decrees. Those who become aware that the decrees issued in connection with the Jewish question are being violated, circumvented, or evaded must, as their patriotic responsibility, report these to the nearest security (gendarmerie, police) organ.[7]

Those with rapacious instincts, among whom were many *Volksdeutsche*, received an additional boost from the Führer who suggested that Hungarians engaged in anti-Jewish activities be rewarded with confiscated Jewish capital.[8] The enthusiasm and extent to which the Hungarians responded to the appeals for "cooperation" astonished the Germans. They confessed that in no other country had they encountered so large a number of denunciations.[9] During one of his encounters with Freudiger, Wisliceny reportedly remarked: "The Hungarians really seem to be the offspring of the Huns; we never would have succeeded like this without them."[10]

A similar sentiment was voiced by the representative of the German Security Police in Marosvásárhely. In describing the mood of the Székelyföld population, he emphasized that the local Hungarians demanded, in view of the rapidly approaching front, a "quick and radical solution of the Jewish question since the fear of the Jews' revenge is greater than that of Russian brutality."[11]

A generally favorable assessment of the population's reaction to the escalating anti-Jewish measures was also provided by the Hungarian Right radicals: "The majority and better strata of Hungarian society have received the announcement of the decrees with joy and feel that the long years of struggle waged against Hungarian Jewry socially, culturally, and politically have not been in vain."[12] This assessment became even more positive after the launching of the ghettoization drive. Upon his return from an inspection tour of the ghettos of Northern Transylvania, László Endre declared: "The population in all cities and communities has hailed the government measures with genuine delight . . . ; the population has rejoiced and has frequently supplied means of transportation to speed resettlement and get rid of the Jews."[13]

Those Hungarians who were actively involved in the anti-Jewish drive, although they made up a larger segment of the population than did those actively or openly associated with the defense or rescue of Jews, nevertheless constituted but a small minority. Aside from those who were obviously motivated by greed and envy, there were those who were driven by personal feuds; still others were misguided by perverted patriotic or ideological considerations.[14]

When the Jews were forcibly removed from their homes in the early morning hours and driven to the local ghettos or concentration centers carrying their bundles packed with essential clothing and food, they were often jeered by Christians lining the streets. Expressions of sympathy were relatively rare. The more decent Hungarians simply drew the curtains over their windows.

The general lethargy and passivity of the masses, like the hostility of the rabble-rousers, reflected to some extent the absence of any meaningful underground anti-Nazi leadership. The leaders of the minute leftist parties were themselves under arrest or in hiding, and no effective plans were made or implemented for resisting the Nazis. Effective discussions for some kind of resistance or rescue began only after Horthy had halted the deportations in July 1944. Even these discussions, initiated mostly by Zionist leaders, were rather limited in scope and involved primarily sympathetic church leaders, some disenchanted rightist figures, and Social Democrats. Several statesmen and church leaders took a courageous stand against the Jewish persecutions. But most of these, including Jusztinián Cardinal Serédi, and Count István Bethlen, chose to communicate their opposition in confidential notes to Horthy or the Sztójay government. Only a few, mostly churchmen and statesmen in exile (for whom it did not take too much courage), dared to publicly criticize the inhumanity against the Jews.[15]

With public opinion thus neutralized or openly sympathetic to the Nazi-imposed regime, the Sztójay government found it easy to place the instrumentalities of power at the disposal of the German-Hungarian dejewification experts. Enjoying the support and cooperation of the civil service, police, and gendarmerie, these experts had no difficulty in carrying out the Final Solution program at lightning speed. Without this Hungarian support, the Eichmann-*Sonderkommando* could not possibly have carried out its sinister mission in Hungary.

Lévai, one of the experts on the Holocaust in Hungary, summarized the interplay of these factors as follows:

Owing to their insignificant numbers, the Nazis were practically unable even to supervise the deportations, let alone to carry them out. The marking of the Jews with the Star of David, their roundup into ghettos and concentration camps, were made possible only by the fact that the gendarmerie—although well-acquainted with the situation and numbering some 20,000 men—could everywhere be sure of the aid of the local police. Even then the procedure could not have been carried through if the Christian population had shown resistance. Thus it must be assumed that—quite apart from the part played by the Regent and the Sztójay government—the chief causes for the complete sell-out of the Jews were the anti-Semitic propaganda, with which the Hungarian population had been inundated for scores of years, the stirring up of their hatred and, last but not least, the rousing of the rabble's rapacious instincts.[16]

This assessment was corroborated by both Otto Winkelmann and Edmund Veesenmayer in their testimonies as witnesses in the postwar trial of Hungarian war criminals. Winkelmann testified on December 22, 1945, at the trial of the Jaross-Endre-Baky trio:

It was very important for Germany that Hungary become a transit territory, especially with regard to the oil fields in Romania and the maintenance of contact with the German troops fighting in the Balkans. For this reason, I believe that the anti-Jewish measures would not have been carried out had the Hungarian government opposed them.[17]

Veesenmayer testified in a similar vein the day before:

Eichmann immediately communicated to the Hungarian government the German desire that the Jews be removed from Hungary. [I] could not say whether the influence of Hungarian personalities was involved in this; however, I had learned from Winkelmann that Endre had already been in Berlin earlier, that is, before the despatch of Eichmann. In any case, the setting up of the concentration camps was not a German demand but merely a wish, and there would not have been any further consequences if the Hungarians had not met this wish. This is sufficiently proved by the fact that when Horthy took a vigorous stand the deportation of the Jews of Budapest did not occur, which allows one to conclude that if the Hungarian government had intervened earlier with the same amount of energy the Germans would have desisted from the deportations. While the deportations were in fact a German demand, the center of gravity was with the Hungarian gendarmerie and the Hungarian authorities, inasmuch as 1944 was already a critical year for the Germans, and by that time Germany no longer had sufficient forces at its disposal to be able to enforce its demand. The Germans would surely have continued to exert pressure on the Hungarian government, but without the latter's consent they would have been unable to do anything. Or even if they had attempted to undertake something, the operation would surely not have been so smooth and especially not so quick, since as previously mentioned, the Germans did not have sufficient forces for it at their disposal. This is because the implementation of the deportations required not military but police personnel, and the Germans would have been unable to contribute these. The removal of the Jewish population from the border regions might indeed have been a German wish, but that could only have come from the military.[18]

While the German witnesses were obviously attempting to cover up their own roles in Hungary by placing almost all the responsibility for the deportations on the Hungarian authorities, the currently available evidence indeed shows that without the wholehearted cooperation of the quisling Sztójay government and the passivity of the Christians the Eichmann-*Sonderkommando* would not have been in a position to achieve its anti-Jewish objectives in Hungary.

Jewish Self-Help

The Jews' attempts to help themselves in the struggle for survival took various forms—both individual and collective. The former was more common in the countryside, the latter in the capital. In Budapest, the rescue efforts were, for a variety of reasons, relatively better organized and more effectively directed. In the first place, the opportunities for successfully surviving with Aryan identification papers were much greater in the city than in the countryside, where everyone knew the Jews. Moreover, by the time the organized rescue campaign was launched in the capital, Horthy had already halted the deportations and the country returned, albeit only for a short time, to a semblance of normality. Following the Szálasi coup of October 15, 1944, the rescue campaign entered an acute phase. The rescuing of Jews from the clutches of the *Nyilas* murder squads that terrorized the city became the responsibility of young *Halutzim*. Their acts of heroism provided by far the finest hours of the resistance.

In the provincial communities, the opportunities for rescue were far fewer. For one thing, many of the large Jewish communities were in the Great Plains, where the terrain was not conducive to hiding. Moreover, the ghettoization and concentration of the Jews in the provinces started less than a month after the German occupation, with the leaders of most communities unaware of the meaning and ultimate scope of the anti-Jewish measures. Even among those who had been alerted about the possible danger awaiting them by courageous young Zionists from Budapest, most chose to heed the reassuring messages conveyed by the traditional central leadership of Hungarian Jewry.

They were understandably less inclined to believe the apocalyptic warnings of the young *Halutzim* they did not know than the comforting messages of their trusted leaders with whom they had dealt for many years. They were, of course, unaware of the fact that the organ through which they received the official communications—*A Magyar Zsidók Lapja* (The Journal of Hungarian Jews)—was in fact a much-censored paper primarily serving the interests of the Nazis.

A few provincial Jews took the warning of the *Halutzim* seriously and escaped from the ghettos or entrainment centers. Most but by no means all were relatively young men from the villages who had trusted friends among the peasants or were familiar with the surrounding mountainous terrain; the largest number of escapees were from the ghettos close to the borders with Romania and Slovakia. A number of provincial Jews tried to escape the deportations by building hiding places within the ghettos,[19] and an indeterminate number managed to escape to Budapest and melt into the crowds, usually by means of forged Christian identification papers. A handful of daring Jews succeeded in escaping to Switzerland by hiding in produce-laden freight cars.[20]

The total number of escapees was relatively small. Most of the men between 20 and 48 years of age had been in labor service companies stationed within the country, along the fronts in the Ukraine, or in the copper mines of Bor, Yugoslavia. Within the ghettos, the families were usually resolved to stay together come what may. A number of families in fact managed to escape across the border intact;[21] their number would undoubtedly have been larger had the leaders of the ghettos along the borders, including those of Kolozsvár, clearly informed the masses about the fate the Nazis really were planning for them. While many of these lay and spiritual leaders of these ghettos managed to save themselves by various schemes, the ghetto dwellers were reassured, partly through a rumor intentionally spread by the gendarmerie that they were being relocated to either Mezőtúr or a place called Kenyérmező, where they would be employed as agricultural workers for the duration of the war.

Under the extraordinary conditions of the time, most Jews were psychologically ready to accept without question the Nazis' reassuring lies. The persecution-wise Polish and Slovak refugees, however (many of whom tried unsuccessfully to warn the Hungarian Jews what was really in store for them) energetically attempted to save themselves. Some built bunkers in and around Budapest and stocked them with food and weapons; others returned to their former homelands, where the anti-Jewish drive was by then at a standstill.

A number of well-to-do Jews tried to save themselves and their families by buying off the SS or top-ranking Hungarian police or gendarmerie officers. By far the most spectacularly successful of such deals involved the rescue of 47 members of the Chorin, Mauthner, Kornfeld, and Weiss families, many of them converted Jews, in exchange for the transfer of the Weiss-Manfréd Works to the SS. Some other rich Jewish families were less successful. After they had paid large sums of money to be flown by a Gestapo plane purportedly to Palermo and then on to Egypt, they were arrested on the way to the airport, robbed of their valuables, and eventually deported. Some of them were eventually killed at Auschwitz.[22]

The Jewish Council

Created by and generally construed as an instrumentality of the SS and of their Hungarian hirelings, the Jewish Council (*Zsidó Tanács*) also emerged as a major source of relief and rescue—especially for the Budapest Jews after the completion of the deportations from the provinces.[23] During the first crucial period of the German occupation, the members of the Council were preoccupied with fulfilling the incessant and increasingly exorbitant demands of the Germans. The Hungarian authorities flatly refused to deal with them, claiming that the handling of the Jewish question had become the responsibility of the SS alone. Deprived of their rights as citizens and subordinated to the Eichmann-*Sonderkommando*, the Council members nevertheless tried to do what they could. They became involved in a desperate, and generally futile, attempt to prevent or at least delay or minimize the ultimate catastrophe they feared. Like many people in Hungary at the time, the Council members at first believed that with the inexorable advance of the Red Army the country might be liberated before the Germans had a chance to carry out their sinister designs. But when they realized the zeal with which the German and Hungarian dejewification squads were going about their work they tried to save those who still could be saved. It was a Sysiphean task, for, with Horthy in self-isolation, the conservative-aristocratic wing of the Right eliminated, and the new Hungarian authorities fully collaborationist, the Council leaders had to rely on their own constantly dwindling resources. They tried to get into the good graces of the Germans by fulfilling with servility the Nazis' exorbitant demands for goods and money. As in some ghettos in Poland, they also tried to persuade the Germans that the Jews would be economically valuable if retained within the country. The Germans were reminded of the crucial role the Jews were playing in the economy of a country whose industrial and agricultural production was to a large extent subordinated to the German war effort.

The Germans were of course eager both to further expand their economic and military exploitation of Hungary and to achieve their racist objectives. The Council members found themselves in an increasingly unenviable position: many of the instructions they had to carry out were clearly related to the Nazis' sinister designs. While they were spared the agonizing tasks imposed upon their counterparts in Poland and elsewhere with regard to the selection of Jews for deportation and certain death, they were often used indirectly for this purpose. They were used to lull the Jewish masses into a false sense of security; they were used as a conduit for the distribution of hundreds of summonses to Jews selected by the dejewification squads for "special treatment." Though many of these Jews—lawyers, journalists, and businessmen— ended up in Auschwitz, the Council members rationalized their involuntary involvement as relatively beneficial. They argued that since the summonses were distributed promptly by Jewish couriers, the victims had some time to settle their affairs, prepare some food and clothing, and make arrangements for escape. The dejewification units, on the other hand, would have picked them up without any prior notice.

One of the Council members, Fülöp Freudiger, the representative of the Orthodox Jews in the Council, was particularly active in rescue work during the deportations from the provinces. In addition to his involvement in the Zionist-oriented rescue effort, Freudiger managed through his contacts with Dieter Wisliceny to save close to 80 prominent, mostly Orthodox, Jews—rabbis and communal leaders—from the ghettos of Debrecen, Kassa, Nagyvárad, Nyíregyháza, Pápa, Sopron, and Székesfehérvár just before their scheduled deportation.[24]

During the *Nyilas* era, the most indefatigable members of the Council were Domonkos, Stöckler, and Berend. The latter, pursuing a rather unorthodox course, was particularly active through his dealings with József Sarlosi, the local *Nyilas* leader in the ghetto area. Pető, Stern, and Wilhelm, who had dominated the Council before the coup, were in hiding.

The Council's relief and rescue operations were carried out mostly through its specialized committees. While primarily responsible for the implementation of the various Nazi-imposed demands, they tried to do everything in their power to minimize the suffering of the Jews. With the passage of time, their functions acquired ever greater importance. They faced a gargantuan task during the relocation of the Jews into Yellow-Star houses and especially during the Szálasi era, when the ghetto of Budapest was established. The officials associated with MIPI were particularly active in helping the internees in various camps and, like the *Halutzim*, managed to free a number of Jews by providing them with forged identification papers.[25] The physicians in Council-supported makeshift hospitals worked tirelessly to save the lives of disease-ridden and starving ghetto dwellers and the countless Jews brutalized by the *Nyilas*.[26]

While the central Jewish Council's role had a questionable, if not generally harmful, effect upon the provincial Jewish communities,[27] its efforts on behalf of the Jewish community of Budapest were much more successful. However, the claim of several of its members that by its actions (including the reestablishment of contact with the Regent) the Council played a crucial role in halting the deportations cannot be substantiated. While the Auschwitz Protocols, which the Council members submitted to Horthy after an unforgivable delay, must have influenced his decision, the main impact was from the copy that Miklós Krausz sent to Switzerland on June 19, 1944, which brought responses from the Pope, President Roosevelt, and the King of Sweden. These responses were much more influential in Horthy's decision.

The Relief and Rescue Committee: The Kasztner Line

The Budapest branch of the Relief and Rescue Committee (*Vaadat Ezra ve'Hatzalah*)—the *Vaada*—was established in January 1943. Until the German occupation, the *Vaada*'s work revolved mainly around the persecuted Jews of the neighboring countries (see chapter 3). It maintained close contact with the "Working Group" (*Pracovná Skupina*), the illegal body which operated within the framework of the Bratislava Jewish Council, and with several Jewish underground leaders in Poland, as well as with the representatives of various Jewish organizations in Palestine, Turkey, and Switzerland. It exchanged and disseminated documents, eyewitness accounts, reports, and memoranda relating to the destruction of Jews in Nazi-occupied Europe. It also helped smuggle Polish, Slovak, and other Jewish refugees into Hungary, and provided the refugees with food, shelter, and identification papers. It used its influence with the "progressive" forces within Hungary to ease the lot of Hungarian Jews, including those serving in the labor service system. In addition, it maintained a well-developed communications and courier network that included members of the German and Hungarian intelligence services in Budapest.

The *Vaada* had contacts with foreign Jewish organizations and with agents of the German and Hungarian intelligence services, and consequently its leaders were among the best informed persons in Budapest. They were acquainted not only with the details of the Final Solution program, but also with the complexities of the national and international political and military situation. They kept the representatives of the major Jewish organizations in Istanbul and in Switzerland fully informed about developments throughout Nazi-dominated Europe. Among the recipients of their periodic reports were the Jewish Agency leaders in Istanbul, Saly Mayer of the AJDC, and Nathan Schwalb of the *Hehalutz* in Switzerland.[28]

Provided as they were with such information, the German occupation did not catch the Budapest *Vaada* leaders by surprise. They were in fact alerted about it five days earlier by Josef Winninger, a converted Jew in the service of the German Military Intelligence Service in Budapest.[29]

At the beginning of 1944, the *Vaada* leadership was composed of Ottó Komoly (President), Rezső Kasztner (Executive Officer), Dov Weiss (Secretary), Jenő Fränkel, Moshe Rosenberg, Siegfried Roth, Uziel Lichtenberg, Josko Baumer, Joel Brand, Moshe Schweiger, and Sámuel Springmann.[30] They represented the major Zionist parties in operation in Hungary, each of which, though limited in membership, had its own distinct views and tactics. As a result cooperation within the *Vaada* and between the Budapest and the Istanbul branches of the *Vaada*[31] was not always harmonious. The conflict inherent in interparty political differences was usually exacerbated by sharp personality conflicts among the leaders. Because of these difficulties, the effectiveness of the Budapest *Vaada* often suffered, eliciting critical and reproachful notes from Istanbul.[32]

The German occupation compelled the *Vaada* leaders to subordinate their internecine fights to the immediate problems of rescuing Hungary's Jews. One of the first steps they took was to institute a system whereby each leader was assigned specific functions and responsibilities, determined according to his expertise and domestic and international contacts. Komoly, for example, was entrusted with the pursuit of the "Magyar line"—establishing contact with, and soliciting support from, Hungarian governmental, political, and church leaders. Although he was not formally in the leadership of the *Vaada,* Miklós (Moshe) Krausz, the Executive Secretary of the Palestine Office—the Budapest branch of the Jewish Agency's *Aliyah* (Emigration) unit—was asked, according to Kasztner, to get in touch with the representatives of the neutral countries.[33] Kasztner and Brand were assigned—or perhaps arrogated to themselves—the most controversial task: the establishment of contact with the occupiers. In the course of time, this SS or Kasztner line was also adopted by Hansi Brand and Andor (Andreas, André or Bandi) Biss.

After the occupation, the work of the *Vaada* was overshadowed by the activities of Kasztner and Brand. Friends and yet rivals, these two relatively ordinary individuals, upon whom history bestowed such fateful roles, differed in background and personality. In terms of education, erudition, and political expertise, Kasztner was superior to Brand. Born in Kolozsvár in 1906, Kasztner was a lawyer and journalist by profession, having worked for 15 years (1925–1940) for the *Uj Kelet* (New East), the Hungarian-Jewish daily of his home town. Shortly after the Hungarian annexation of Northern Transylvania in September 1940, Kasztner moved to Budapest. An ardent Zionist by conviction, and an idealistic but opportunistic politician by inclination, he soon acquired a pivotal role in reinvigorating the relatively weak Zionist movement. His standing in the community was enhanced by his marriage to the daughter of Dr. József Fischer, the President of the Jewish community of Kolozsvár and a former member of the Romanian Parliament. A man of unbounded political ambitions with some inclinations toward a bohemian lifestyle, Kasztner had a large number of faithful friends, as well as many bitter enemies who conspired against him. Dictatorial and jealous by nature (he could not gracefully acknowledge the success of others) Kasztner unwisely monopolized the negotiations with the SS. He may have been guided by an SS-imposed directive for secrecy "in order not to jeopardize the success of the deal," and therefore contacted the traditional leaders of Hungarian Jewry only when he needed their financial assistance. It is likely that, motivated by a strong subconscious drive for grandeur, he hoped to emerge as virtually the sole rescuer of close to one million Jews.

Brand, who was one of Kasztner's closest friends and associates in the rescue operations, claimed that he was not an easy man to work with, tending to be slapdash, and that he seemed to many people "the prototype of the snobbish intellectual who lacks the common touch." In social gatherings he was a poor mixer and, according to Brand, also quite unpopular with the young *Halutzim*.[34] He had a sharp analytic mind but, gifted as he was, he did not possess that strength of character which ultimately distinguishes the great from the average man. Nevertheless, in his dealings with the SS, and especially with the leaders of the *Sonderkommando*, he often displayed great skill and courage in championing the cause of rescue.

Brand was born in April 1907 in Naszód, Transylvania, then under Hungarian jurisdiction. Although quite bright, he never completed his studies; in his youth, he was reportedly more interested in adventure and politics. He embraced Zionism after a stint in the leftist movement in Weimar Germany. He joined the Communist Party before the Nazis' seizure of power and soon achieved a leadership position in Thuringia.[35] According to one source, he even served for a while as a Comintern agent.[36] Presumably in this capacity, he visited many parts of the globe, including the United States, the USSR, Japan, and the South Sea Islands. He returned to his native Transylvania shortly after Hitler's seizure of power. According to Biss, Brand was expelled from Romania because of his Communist background. He moved to Budapest, where together with his wife, Hansi Hartmann Brand, he operated a medium-sized glove-manufacturing plant. Although the success of their enterprise had diverted them from their original plan of emigrating to Palestine, the Brands remained actively involved in Zionist affairs.

After the *Anschluss* and the defeat of Poland, they became particularly interested in refugee affairs, organizing a variety of rescue and relief activities. Their concern for the refugees acquired a personal tone in the summer of 1941, when approximately 16,000 to 18,000 "alien" Jews were being resettled by the Hungarian authorities in the then occupied parts of Galicia. Among these were Hansi's sister and brother-in-law, whom they managed to rescue just before the massacre near Kamenets-Podolsk (see chapter 6).

Joel Brand's contact for this rescue operation was József Krem, a member of the Hungarian Counterespionage Service, who became interested in human smuggling operations after having been paid handsomely for his first exploits. This underground operation, initiated by Brand, dovetailed with one organized by Sámuel Springmann that involved the *Abwehr* representatives in Budapest. Consequently, when the *Tiyul* ("Trip") section of the *Vaada* was established in January 1943, Brand became the logical individual to head it.

Until the German occupation, *Tiyul* was primarily concerned with the

smuggling of Jews out of Poland and Slovakia; shortly after the occupation, its foremost concern became the rescuing of Jews within Hungary.
Under Menachem Klein, a Hungarian-speaking Slovak refugee who
succeeded Brand after he left for Istanbul, it became one of the centers
for the production and distribution of Aryan personal documents, including identification cards, marriage certificates, and military dis-
charge papers. It was also engaged in a *Re-Tiyul* program which enabled a number of Polish and Slovak refugees to return to their former
homelands, where the situation of the remaining Jews was, temporarily
at least, much better.

The *Vaada's* negotiations with the SS are quite controversial. This
rescue attempt was based on perfectly logical assumptions at the time.
During the first phase of the occupation, when the Hungarian authorities categorically refused to see or to deal with the representatives of
Jewry, pointing out that the Jewish question fell under the jurisdiction
of the Germans, the *Vaada* leaders concluded that their best chance was
to deal directly with those who seemed to wield real power in the country. At the start of the negotiations on April 5, the *Vaada* leaders were
not yet fully aware that the German forces directly under the control of
the Eichmann-*Sonderkommando* numbered less than 200; that without
the support of the Hungarian instrumentalities of power, the SS could
not possibly carry out the ghettoization and deportation program; that
Wisliceny, Eichmann, and the other representatives of Himmler's
agency had no independent decision-making power over the anti-
Jewish drive, but were authorized only to make relatively minor concessions in order to assure the ultimate success of the Final Solution program; and that negotiations with the SS would help lull Jewish masses
into a false state of optimism, deterring them from other possible avenues of escape.

The first contact with the SS was established two days after the occupation. Freudiger approached Wisliceny at the Astoria Hotel, the
headquarters of the *Sonderkommando*, on behalf of his brother Sámuel
who had been arrested the day before. Freudiger's bold move was
based on his knowledge that Wisliceny had been successfully bribed by
the leaders of the Bratislava "Working Group."[37] In negotiations conducted with Wisliceny by Gisi Fleischmann and Rabbi Michael Dov-
Beer Weissmandel of the Working Group and initiated by Weissmandel, Wisliceny—then in charge of the deportations from Slovakia—had
been approached in an attempt to spare the remaining Jews. Sometime
in June 1942, when approximately 52,000 Slovak Jews (two-thirds of

the community) had already been deported, Wisliceny informed Fleischmann and Weissmandel that the Germans were not interested in the deportation of any more Jews, provided they received certain payments from abroad. The deportations in fact stopped shortly after part of the money demanded by Wisliceny was paid.

The Jewish leaders, now convinced that the catastrophe of the Jews could be avoided or at least mitigated, did not know that the halting of the deportations in Slovakia had little to do with the bribing of Wisliceny. What had actually brought it about was the following: By June 1942, the leaders of the Slovak state had been informed by various sources, including Giuseppe Burzio, the Papal Nuncio, that the deported Jews were in fact being liquidated rather than merely resettled. When Prime Minister Vojtech Tuka, pressed by the Catholic bishops, suggested that a mixed commission inspect one of the camps in which the Slovak Jews were supposedly being resettled, the Germans—to avoid embarrassment and, above all, so as not to jeopardize the Final Solution program then in progress elsewhere in Europe—decided to suspend the deportations in Slovakia until a more auspicious time. A communication to this effect was sent to Berlin on June 26, following a meeting one day earlier between Tuka, Wisliceny, and Hanns Elard Ludin, the German Minister in Bratislava. It emphasized the suspension of the deportations due to the Slovak leaders' opposition.[38]

Weissmandel and Fleischmann, convinced that the deportations had been halted because of the bribing of Wisliceny, extended the frame of their negotiations in October 1942 to include the other persecuted Jewish communities of Europe. The "Europa Plan," as this scheme came to be known, called for the suspension of the deportations of Jews to Poland from all over Europe in exchange for the payment of two million dollars. The Plan did not cover Poland, where the Final Solution program was to continue. In their quest for the first installment of $200,000 and other assistance for Slovak Jewry, the leaders of the Working Group, including Fleischmann, came to Budapest a number of times in 1942–43. Although the Hungarian Jewish leaders were not as generous and understanding as the Slovak Jewish leaders had expected them to be (see chapter 23) they became fully acquainted with the plight of the Jews in Nazi-occupied Europe and with the details of the negotiations with Wisliceny.

During the first week of the occupation, Wisliceny returned briefly to Bratislava to pick up a "letter of recommendation" from Rabbi Weissmandel. Writing in Hebrew, Weissmandel lamented that it was Hungarian Jewry's turn to suffer the fate that had earlier befallen many other Jewish communities in Europe. He nevertheless counseled the Hungarian Jewish leaders to negotiate with Wisliceny within the framework of the "Europa Plan," emphasizing that Wisliceny could be trusted. Weissmandel offered his advice even as the destruction of the European Jewish communities continued.[39] A righteous and courageous man, Rabbi Weissmandel was, of course, motivated by the noblest of intentions. Like most of those who dealt with Wisliceny in Slovakia and Hungary, he too was convinced that this sly colleague of Eichmann could be trusted and that the Germans would fulfill their obligations under the "Europa Plan" if only the Jewish leaders of the free world would deliver the necessary sums. He wrote heartbreaking letters to the Jewish leaders in Switzerland, practically accusing them of complicity in the mass murders for failure to heed his desperate appeals.[40] He and his colleagues who lived in the midst of the bloodletting failed—with much justification—to understand the failure of the free world's Jewish leaders to covertly forward large sums of money and above all to publicize the Nazis' Final Solution program, about which they were receiving detailed and accurate reports. Rabbi Weissmandel and the other champions of the Europa Plan were not and could not be aware that Wisliceny was untrustworthy, and was merely acting in collusion with the other members of the Eichmann-*Sonderkommando* and his superiors in the RSHA in a monstrous scheme designed to mislead, exploit, and finally liquidate the Jews.

Wisliceny's arrival in Budapest also excited the *Vaada* leaders, who were as familiar with his "public record"—though equally unaware of the real background of the halting of the deportations in Slovakia—as Freudiger was. Kasztner and his colleagues approached Wisliceny via Schmidt and Winninger, inquiring whether the *Sonderkommando* was ready to deal on economic terms with the illegal *Vaada* for an alleviation of the anti-Jewish measures.

The offer was promptly discussed by the *Sonderkommando* leaders, who immediately saw in the inquiry another opportunity to smooth the way for an orderly and revolt-free implementation of the Final Solution program, including of course exploitation of Jewish economic resources (one of the reasons why the SS tried desperately to keep the Hungarians in the dark about the negotiations with the Jewish leaders). The Germans also valued the international contacts and foreign currency sources of the Zionists more highly than they did the limited resources of the domestically oriented Council leaders. Therefore, they were happy to enter into negotiations.

The first contact between the SS and the Zionists took place on April 5, the day the Jews were first required to wear the Star of David. Kasztner and Brand met Wisliceny, Schmidt, and Winninger in the latter's apartment. Also present was SS-*Hauptsturmführer* Erich Klausnitzer, a Gestapo agent presumably assigned to safeguard the general interests of the SS. Kasztner inquired about the conditions under which the *Sonderkommando* might abstain from carrying out its plans. Wisliceny assured him that while the Jews could not avoid wearing the Star of David and that their influence would have to be eliminated in all spheres of life, they would be neither placed into ghettos nor deported "unless the Hungarians appealed directly to Berlin over the head of the *Sonderkommando*." [41]

As in Bratislava, Wisliceny played his despicable role well. He of course gave no hint that only the day before the Hungarian authorities in the Ministry of the Interior, who were acting in collusion with him and the other members of the *Sonderkommando,* had already taken the first concrete measure toward this very end: they instructed the local police and gendarmerie units to bring about the registration of the Jews, as a preliminary to ghettoization. Secret instructions for the latter were issued three days later (see chapter 17).

As part of the bargain, Wisliceny demanded $2 million, the same amount as was involved in the Europa Plan. Of this sum he wanted $200,000 in *Pengős* within a very short time as proof of the Zionists' goodwill and financial liquidity. Schmidt and Winninger also demanded 10 percent of the amount for the *Wehrmacht* and a commission for themselves. Wisliceny insisted that they be paid at the blackmarket rate; the total came to approximately 6.5 million *Pengős*. Shortly after his first encounter with Wisliceny, Kasztner met with Samu Stern, the President of the Jewish Council, and with Károly Wilhelm and Ernő (Zvi) Szilágyi to discuss the merits of the proposals. Stern took it upon himself to collect the money, but managed, after a few weeks' effort, to raise only 5 million *Pengős;* the remainder was covered by the *Vaada* from its own resources. The first installment, 3 million *Pengős,* was delivered to Hermann A. Krumey and Otto Hunsche, Eichmann's close associates, along with Kasztner's pleas that the agreement with Wisliceny be upheld. At that time Wisliceny was already in Munkács, the headquarters for the dejewification drive in Carpatho-Ruthenia and northeastern Hungary, directing the campaign for the round-up and internment of the Jews.

One immediate upshot of the negotiations was that the *Vaada* leaders, like the members of the Jewish Council, were supplied by the SS with

Immunity Certificates (*Immunitäts-Ausweise*). While these represented a great personal privilege for their possessors, they also afforded an opportunity for more effective rescue and relief work, which would have been inconceivable without the freedom of movement the certificates assured.

By April 21, when Kasztner met the SS for the third time to deliver to Krumey and Hunsche the second installment, 2.5 million *Pengős*,[42] the ghettoization of the Jews of Carpatho-Ruthenia, which had begun on April 16, was already in full swing. Schmidt himself informed Kasztner, if he needed any further corroboration, that the ghettoization was a *fait accompli*.

Clearly, the SS could not, or would not, keep its side of the bargain. To ease the impact of the ghettoization on Kasztner and his colleagues, the SS freed a number of prominent Jews, including Rose Binet and Miklós Krausz, respectively the secretary and executive officer of the Palestine Office. During the April 21 meeting, Krumey, pursuing the same objective, conveyed the offer of the *Sonderkommando* which emerged as a central theme in the further negotiations between the *Vaada* and the SS. Krumey asserted that the Germans were ready to permit the emigration of a certain number of Jews either to America or any neutral state that was willing to admit them. Kasztner was in a position to respond immediately, for he was aware of the March 16, 1944, telegram from Barlas, the head of the Istanbul *Vaada*, addressed to the Budapest Palestine Office to the effect that a ship was in Constanța ready to pick up 600 holders of Palestine immigration certificates. (The Germans also knew of it because Charles Lutz of the Swiss Legation had approached them earlier at Krausz's behest to obtain the necessary exit permit.)[43]

While some *Sonderkommando* leaders were bargaining, others were busy completing the ghettoization program and finalizing the deportation schedules. In fact, the first transports filled with able-bodied Jews were directed from Kistarcsa to Auschwitz at the end of April. Shortly after the first deportations, Krumey tried to distract Kasztner from the catastrophe by triumphantly announcing Berlin's concurrence with the emigration of the 600 certificate holders. Krumey also offered to permit an additional 100 Jews to emigrate, providing he received a *per capita* payment of 100,000 *Pengős*.

The preparation of the list of 600 emigrants started a major dispute within the Zionist community. The Palestine immigration certificates were normally sent to, and distributed by, the Palestine Office, which was managed by Krausz, a *Mizrachi* leader, under the guidance of a Board of Governors consisting of representatives of the major Zionist parties.[44] Conveniently ignoring that the *Vaada* leadership had a similar composition, Kasztner, fearing that party factionalism would render the Palestine Office impotent, decided to entrust Komoly and Szilágyi—the leaders of both organizations—with the allocation of the certificates. The animosity that had characterized Kasztner's earlier relations with Krausz, reflecting clashing ambitions and deep-seated intra-Zionist party conflicts, took on venomous overtones which made any kind of truly coordinated work impossible.[45] In preparing the list, Komoly and Szilágyi had to consider a number of points. In particular, approximately half of the certificates had to be assigned to Jews still in the provinces, and account had to be taken of the Polish and Slovak refugees as well as of those spiritual and lay leaders, scientists and artists, and Zionists who played an especially important role in the life of the Jewish communities.

While the Zionist leaders wrangled over the preparation of the list, Eichmann, working with his headquarters in Berlin and with the full cooperation of Himmler, came forth with a grandiose new plan that, going beyond the scope of Hungarian Jewry, had clearly discernible international political and military overtones.

The Brand Mission

With Wisliceny in the countryside directing the ghettoization process, Eichmann took over as chief negotiator for the SS. On April 25, 1944, he sent for Brand (via Winninger) and offered him a deal under which the Nazis would "sell" one million Jews in exchange for certain goods to be obtained outside of Hungary. He was ready to allow Brand to go abroad to establish contact with the representatives of world Jewry and of the Allied Powers.

Why Brand was selected remains shrouded in mystery. He claims he met with the *Vaada* shortly after his encounter with Eichmann. At that meeting with the *Vaada*, Kasztner allegedly proposed that either József Fischer (his father-in-law and a well-known lawyer and former parliamentarian) or Ernő Marton (the former editor-in-chief of the *Uj Kelet,* the then outlawed Zionist daily of Kolozsvár) be sent. Brand contends that Komoly and the *Halutzim* within the *Vaada* (including Szilágyi and Révész) insisted that he be the one—as the most qualified and the most trustworthy. On the other hand, Kasztner (whose account differs from

Brand's in many details)[46] maintains that neither the *Vaada* nor any other Jewish forum had any influence in the selection of the delegate representing the Jewish community in these negotiations.

Brand's cousin Biss, a Transylvanian who became active in *Vaada* affairs after Brand's departure, offers still a different version. Biss claims that the SS chose Brand on the recommendation of a shady character named Andor ("Bandi") Grosz, who also used the aliases of Andreas or André György and Andreas Greiner on various occasions.

Born in Hungary in 1905, Grosz was a converted Jew who in January 1942 had joined the *Abwehr*, the German Counterespionage Service then under the command of the anti-Hitlerite Admiral Wilhelm Canaris, partially as protection from the Hungarian authorities, who were looking into his underworld and smuggling operations. By September of the same year, Grosz was also recruited by the Hungarian Military Intelligence, many of whose officers were not only anti-Nazi but also anti-German. Among these were Lieutenant-Colonel Antal Merkly and Ferenc Bágyoni. The latter also served as a courier for the *Vaada*, a function he shared with Grosz, who was recruited for this purpose by Sámuel Springmann, his former classmate. Grosz eventually emerged as a very successful multiple agent. In addition to the *Abwehr*, the Hungarians, and the *Vaada*, he also served or had close contacts with Japanese, Polish, and British and American agents and officers stationed in various places in the Balkans, especially Istanbul.

He carried out his missions as an official of the Hungarian Danube Navigation Company, using a Hungarian service passport. In working for the *Vaada*, Grosz had established close contacts with the *Vaada* representatives in Istanbul, including Venya Pomerantz, Menachem Bader, and Teddy Kollek. It was allegedly through Kollek (who would later become the Mayor of Jerusalem) that Grosz met a number of British and American intelligence officers. By April 1943, when Grosz arrived in Istanbul for his second mission, he formed a link between German, Hungarian, and Anglo-American agents, allegedly all opposed to Hitler.[47]

The *Vaada* was generally satisfied with Grosz's performance. When he went to Istanbul he usually took along correspondence as well as documents and reports about the Final Solution program that had come into Budapest; from Istanbul he would normally bring back correspondence and messages to be forwarded to Poland and Slovakia; he would also bring back money. He was obviously not an ideologically motivated individual and usually received a percentage of the smuggled funds as reward for his services.

Grosz realized immediately after the German occupation of Hungary that power had shifted into the hands of the SS. He prudently transferred his allegiance from the *Abwehr* to the Security Service (*Sicherheitsdienst*), the Budapest unit of which (Special Task Commando F) was under the command of SS-*Haupsturmführer* Otto Klages (Clages, in many sources). After he established his credentials with Klages, who was presumably already familiar with his activities, Grosz was able not only to unmask the *Abwehr* agents who had collaborated with the *Vaada*, but also to undertake a mission allegedly authorized by the highest SS authorities in Berlin. As allegedly instructed by Klages and his aide Fritz Laufer (alias Direktor Schroeder, alias Ludwig Mayer, alias Karl Heinz), Grosz's mission was to arrange through his contacts in Istanbul, especially the American Intelligence Officer Schwarz, a meeting between a number of high-ranking German security officers "except Himmler who was unable to leave Germany" and an equal number of Anglo-American officers to discuss the possibility of a separate peace between the *Sicherheitsdienst* (*sic*) and the Allies. Schwarz was to be contacted first, not only because Grosz knew him through earlier meetings, but also because he, like his personal friend Laufer, was a Czech emigrant.[48] According to several sources, including Grosz's own statement to the British, the mission was in fact initiated with the knowledge of Himmler, who reportedly was at that time already privy to the impending coup against Hitler.[49] Himmler, aware the collapse of the Third Reich was inevitable, allegedly tried to make use of the major Jewish organizations in the West for his peace feelers and also to acquire some merit in the eyes of the world by making some humane gestures relating to the possible freeing of a large number of Jews.[50] Like most Nazis, Himmler was convinced that American Jewry and its international organizations strongly, if not decisively, influenced President Roosevelt's policies. Himmler probably saw the establishment of the War Refugee Board on January 22, 1944, as a signal of America's change of policy and as a new resolve to play a more active role in the rescue of the remnant of European Jewry.[51] Himmler's role was in fact acknowledged by Veesenmayer in his July 22, 1944, telegram to the Foreign Office, forwarded shortly after a discussion with Winkelmann in which he asserted that the Brand-Grosz mission was undertaken "as a result of a secret order of the *Reichsführer*-SS."[52]

The Nazis' selection of Grosz as their intermediary was logical. If the Western Powers had reacted positively, the negotiations would have most probably been continued (without Grosz) at a higher official level; but if the Anglo-Americans rejected the peace feelers, the Nazis could always disavow Grosz as the shady multiple agent that he was.

Grosz also undertook an assignment for the Hungarians. Lieutenant-Colonel Merkly, who wanted a meeting between himself, another Hungarian officer, and the British somewhere in Istanbul, sent Grosz to arrange it. He was instructed to inform the British that the sympathies of the Hungarian General Staff lay with the Allies and that certain Hungarian elements were ready "to go over to the Allies on condition that Russia was not allowed to enter Hungary." [53]

Having been entrusted with this important mission, which the SS allegedly attempted to camouflage with the "blood for trucks" offer, Grosz presumably introduced Brand to Klages. He also told Klages that Brand (the immediate link in his dealings with the *Vaada*), was "the most important executive individual in the *Vaada*." [54] He presumably did this either because he was unaware that the *Vaada* members, according to Biss, "declared unanimously that Brand himself was by no means the man likely to succeed in so difficult a task" [55] or because he thought that Brand was the person he could most conveniently exploit for his own closely concealed personal objective: to escape to the free or neutral world. (His wife was already in Istanbul.) [56]

Finally, there is an unreliable unwritten report that Brand's selection was actually suggested by Kasztner, who supposedly wanted Brand out of his way for personal reasons.

Whatever the reasons, Brand was entrusted with the mission. Once the SS made up their mind about Brand, they wanted to make certain that neither the *Abwehr* nor the Hungarians learned of their plans. On May 10, they arrested Kasztner and interrogated him about his connections with the Hungarian General Staff, especially Lieutenant-Colonel József Garzoly. [57] The following day, the agents of the *Abwehr* with whom the *Vaada* had usually dealt, including Dr. Schmidt, Winninger, and Rudi Scholz, were also arrested. Kasztner was freed after two days; some of the *Abwehr* agents were co-opted into the SS intelligence network. [58]

In his discussions with Brand, Eichmann never gave any inkling of Grosz's mission. As outlined in the "blood for trucks" scheme, Jews were not to be allowed to remain in Hungary, for he had promised Endre and his friends that he would help make the country *Judenrein*.

The one million Jews were to be delivered via Germany after the receipt of the specified goods. According to Kasztner, those goods were 200 tons of tea, 800 tons of coffee, 2 million cases of soap, an unspecified quantity of tungsten and other military-related materials, and 10,000 trucks. The latter, the Germans claimed, were to be used for civilian purposes or only along the Eastern front.[59] The proposal further stipulated that the first installment of 100,000 Jews would be released and the Auschwitz gas chambers blown up soon after the receipt of the Allies' positive response. The Jews were to be allowed to leave Germany for any Allied-controlled part of the world except Palestine, for the Nazis had promised Amin el-Husseini, the Arab nationalist leader, not to permit this.

Almost immediately after the receipt of the offer, the Budapest *Vaada* communicated its contents in coded telegrams to Istanbul and Switzerland, including Pozner's office in Geneva.[60] In a separate telegram, dated May 2, the Budapest *Vaada* leaders also asked Istanbul to urgently provide Turkish visas for Brand and Winninger, the *Abwehr* agent they then expected to accompany Brand.[61] Istanbul's response was swift and positive: "Chaim" was ready to receive the delegate of the Hungarian Jews. Practically all the *Vaada* leaders in Budapest believed that "Chaim" was none other than Chaim Weizmann, the head of the World Zionist Organization, and they informed Eichmann accordingly. Only later did they and Brand discover to their great disappointment that the Chaim mentioned by Istanbul was merely Chaim Barlas, the head of the local *Vaada*.

On May 15, when the mass deportation of the Hungarian Jews began, Eichmann summoned Brand for the last time. He informed him that all the travel arrangements were completed and that he could leave the following day. After a final session with the *Vaada* leaders— they gave him advice for his forthcoming discussions with Weizmann and other world Jewish leaders and urged him to get in touch with Laurence A. Steinhardt, the American Ambassador in Ankara, who was Jewish—Brand was taken to Vienna by Krumey on May 17.

Brand and Krumey were accompanied by Grosz. While his presence was a source of anxiety for the *Vaada* leaders, Brand felt that Grosz was a lesser evil than the alternative, an unknown Nazi companion assigned by the SS.

Brand's documents included three letters of recommendation: one signed on May 16, 1944, by Samu Stern and Fülöp Freudiger, the leaders of the Neolog and Orthodox Jewish communities then serving

Figure 29.1.
Joel Brand's Gestapo-issued German passport bearing the name of Eugen Band.

in the Jewish Council; [62] one from the *Vaada;* and one from the United Youth (*Hehalutz*) Movement. He also carried $2,000 to $2,500 and a German passport. The passport, identifying him as Eugen Band, an engineer residing at Erfurt (see fig. 29.1), was handed to him in Vienna, where he was lodged for two nights in the Hotel Metropole, the Gestapo Headquarters. Brand and Grosz left Vienna on May 19 and, after two intermediate stops in the Balkans, arrived in Istanbul the same day.

The Reaction of the Free World. Brand's string of disappointments began immediately after his landing. To his great dismay, the "Chaim" he had expected was not there to meet him. Worse yet, he was not even permitted to leave the airport because he did not have a Turkish entry visa—apparently the Istanbul *Vaada* leaders had either neglected or been unable to obtain it. After his problem with the Turkish authorities was temporarily solved through Grosz's and the *Vaada*'s connections, Brand was taken to the Hotel Pera, where the Istanbul branch of the *Vaada* had its headquarters. There he was met by the local representatives of the various Zionist groups and parties [63] to whom he revealed the details of the measures adopted against the Hungarian Jews as well as the specific objectives of his mission. Brand claims that he also provided the leaders with a map of Auschwitz and demanded the bombing of both the extermination facilities and the railway junctions at points leading to the death camp.[64] Brand, who conceived of himself as the spokesman for and potential savior of the doomed Jews of Hungary, was disappointed by his encounter with the Zionist leaders, who, he claimed somewhat unjustly, were not only at odds with each other over policy, but also so preoccupied with Palestine that they did not notice the massacre of their followers in Europe.[65]

The Turkish authorities continued to harass Brand, holding him in protective custody for lack of a visa between May 25 and 31. As a result, he was unable to go to Ankara to report to Ambassador Steinhardt; this part of his mission was carried out by Barlas. Steinhardt notified the U.S. State Department about the essence of Eichmann's offer in a telegram dated May 25.[66]

Thanks to the activities of the Istanbul *Vaada,* the Jewish leaders in Jerusalem and London received detailed though somewhat delayed reports about the "bizarre" Brand-Grosz mission. The Barlas group was urged to act swiftly and decisively not only by Brand and the Budapest *Vaada,* but also by the Bratislava Jewish leaders. Shortly after Brand's arrival, they sent two cables confirming the mass deportations from Hungary and demanding the bombing of the railroads leading to Auschwitz. They further urged that the proposals brought along by Brand be given serious consideration.[67]

The Jewish leaders in Jerusalem and London were in the meantime deciding what action to take. Moshe Shertok (later Sharett), the head of the Political Department of the Jewish Agency, and David Ben-Gurion, who were briefed in Jerusalem about the Brand mission by Wenia Pomerantz on May 25, got in touch with Sir Harold MacMichael, the British High Commissioner for Palestine. Sir Harold, who had dismissed the mission as a "Nazi intrigue based on far other motives than the apparent ones," nevertheless immediately notified the Foreign Office about the Jewish leaders' communication.[68] Shertok's attempt to see Brand immediately was frustrated by the British, but he was finally allowed to meet him in Aleppo, Syria, receiving the additional assurance that the British would have no objection to Brand's return to Hungary from there. The British Intelligence Service, which kept a close eye on Brand and Grosz, was obviously anxious for a chance to interrogate both "agents of the SS."

Before his departure, Brand managed to persuade the Istanbul *Vaada* leaders to prepare some kind of protocol or memorandum of agreement to be forwarded to Budapest as "evidence of progress" designed to mislead the *Sonderkommando.* A protocol, signed on May 29,

1944, was prepared. It stated that negotiations were under way to overcome the legal and political difficulties associated with the Eichmann offer, but in the meantime the Germans were urged, as part of the interim agreement, to halt the anti-Jewish drive and permit the emigration of Jews.[69] (Probably because of courier difficulties, the text of the "agreement" was not forwarded to Budapest until July 5.[70]) A letter incorporating the same basic ideas was sent to the Jewish Council on May 28.[71]

Pursuing his own interests and separate "diplomatic" mission, Grosz left Istanbul on June 1 only to be picked up by the British shortly after having crossed into Syria.[72] Brand, equipped with a British visa, left for Aleppo four days later in the company of Echud Avriel of the Jewish Agency. While the train stopped in Ankara, Brand claims that he was confidentially warned by Joseph Klarman and Yaakov Griffel, the representatives of the Revisionist and Agudat Yisrael Zionist groups respectively, that he was being lured into a trap. Brand was in fact taken into custody upon arrival in Aleppo on June 7. He was not even allowed to meet Shertok and two other Jewish Agency officials until June 10. On that day, in the presence of the British, the Jewish officials heard the same account about the plight of Hungarian Jewry and the nature of his mission that Brand had given the Istanbul *Vaada* leaders the month before.

Brand was soon informed by Shertok that he would have to remain in British custody and be taken to Cairo for further debriefing.[73] (The British had reneged on their earlier promise to Shertok, citing reasons of war.) He was not consoled by Shertok's promise to immediately fly on to London to take up the matter with the Jewish and governmental leaders of the Western world. He insisted on being allowed to return home both for the sake of his family and for what he believed to be the best interests of Hungarian Jewry.

Shertok was favorably impressed with Brand, identifying him as a "very solid type . . . [who] . . . breathes honesty." He characterized Grosz, however, as "an irresponsible fellow who would sell his own mother for money." Having completed a report on his discussions with Brand, Shertok returned to Jerusalem on June 13 and reviewed the case before the Executive Committee of the Jewish Agency the following day. On June 15, he and Ben-Gurion saw the High Commissioner for Palestine again and insisted that Jewish lives might be saved if the Germans were given the impression that important negotiations were impending. Recognizing that they would have to find someone without a government connection, Shertok suggested that the Germans might be met by a representative of the War Refugee Board of the United States, the Intergovernmental Committee, or the International Red Cross. Shertok also requested that Brand be allowed to return home and he be permitted to fly to London on a priority basis. Having received the permission a week later, Shertok left Cairo on the 25th, arriving in London on the 27th.[74]

In the meantime the deportations from Hungary were proceeding at the rate of 10,000 to 12,000 a day. The *Vaada* leaders in Budapest were in despair over the apparent failure of the Jewish and governmental leaders of the free world to respond quickly to what they thought was a "serious" German offer. While it is quite probable that the Germans would not have stopped their anti-Jewish drive even if they had received a prompt and positive reply, in the absence of any answer and with their emissaries apparently either unwilling or unable to return, they had no incentive at all to cease their operations. Long weeks were allowed to pass before the Jewish and the Western leaders agreed on a basically noncommittal line of action designed to save some Jewish lives by gaining time—a transparent technique the Germans recognized immediately.

During this period, an agonizingly long time was consumed in seemingly endless communications. Messages from Budapest were sent to the *Hehalutz* or Palestine Office in Geneva or to the *Vaada* in Istanbul, which usually forwarded them to headquarters in Jerusalem. In important cases, such as the Brand mission, the central *Vaada* leader (Gruenbaum) transferred responsibility to the Executive Committee of the Jewish Agency. After a line of action was agreed on, clearance had to be obtained from the High Commissioner for Palestine, who would communicate it to the Foreign Office in London; the Foreign Office, in turn, after appropriate consultations with other agencies, including the War Cabinet, informed Chaim Weizmann. Once a decision was reached at the top, the same procedure would be followed in reverse sequence. In the Brand case, moreover, policy had to be synchronized with that of the Jewish leaders in America and of the governments of the United States and the Soviet Union.

The *Vaada* leaders in Budapest, witnessing the staggering daily toll in Jewish lives, were of course not fully aware of these bureaucratic and diplomatic difficulties, which were compounded by the dilatory tactics of the Allies. Kasztner and Hansi Brand continued to bombard the Istanbul *Vaada* with telegrams desperately requesting the return of the two emissaries "for otherwise everything would be in vain."[75] Istanbul tried to console them by emphasizing that the messages and pleas communicated by Joel Brand were being forwarded to and carefully evaluated by the Allies.[76] Brand had of course no inkling that in spite of the considerable though not always very forceful efforts of the Jewish leaders of the free world, the governmental leaders of the Grand Alliance had adopted a negative position toward his cause.[77] He blamed his frustrations less on the British who had detained him, than on the leaders of the Jewish Agency.

Brand's Perception of the Yishuv Leaders. Brand, of course, was not aware of the worldwide publicity his case aroused. He was held by the British until early in October, when he was finally allowed to go to Palestine. For a while he kept himself busy writing reports[78] and visiting the leaders of the *Yishuv* and world Zionism, including Teddy Kollek, Eliyahu Dobkin, Yitzhak Gruenbaum, David Ben-Gurion, and Chaim Weizmann.[79] A bitter and disappointed man, Brand felt (and continued to feel until shortly before his death in 1964)[80] that because of the failure and shortcomings of these Jewish leaders and the passivity and insensitivity of the Allies the chance to save a million people had been missed. Rabbi Weissmandel shared this view, as he did the opinion that the proposals of the SS had been genuine and serious.[81] Brand was particularly disappointed by the operations of the Jerusalem *Vaada*, the Jewish Agency's central office for relief and rescue work, and the man who headed it—Yitzhak Gruenbaum, a former member of the Polish *Sejm*. He was chagrined that in the midst of the mortal danger confronting Hungarian Jewry, Gruenbaum had allegedly been preoccupied with and wrathfully indignant over the failure of the Budapest *Vaada* to rescue his son in Poland. This attitude induced Brand to conclude that Gruenbaum "had never really appreciated what had happened . . . in Hungary."[82]

Brand's singling out of Gruenbaum for special criticism is somewhat unfair, for unlike many other Jewish leaders he occasionally made public statements about the plight of the Hungarian Jews. For example, shortly after the beginning of the mass deportations from Hungary on May 15, Gruenbaum declared that swift action by the Allies could still save approximately 1.5 million Jews in Hungary and Romania.[83] He regularly forwarded the communications received from Istanbul or Switzerland about the tragedy of Hungarian Jewry to the Jewish leaders of the United States and Britain, requesting urgent intervention possibly including the bombing of Auschwitz and of the rail lines leading to the camp.[84] He also urged that Brand and Grosz be allowed to return to Hungary.[85] Following the Szálasi coup, Gruenbaum in fact bypassed the world Jewish leaders and appealed directly to Churchill and Stalin.[86]

Brand's suspicions and conclusions about the Jerusalem *Vaada* as a whole, however, are not his alone. The benign neglect and resigned fatalism with which the *Vaada* treated the plight of Hungarian Jewry before and after the German occupation was documented during the postwar period.[87] The Budapest *Vaada* leaders were as unaware of the routine, bureaucratic way the free world treated the events in Hungary as they were of the motivations of the SS. They proved to be mistaken in their belief in the power and influence of the international Jewish organizations (a belief shared by the SS), in the Allies' interest in the Jewish cause, and in their assumptions about the "Europa Plan" of the SS. These faulty assumptions underlay the mistakes that characterized their dealing with the members of the Eichmann-*Sonderkommando* and other SS leaders in their desperate effort to save Jewish lives.

The SS Line and Its Achievements

Brand's failure to return and the terse communications from Istanbul convinced the Budapest *Vaada* leaders that the mission was an almost total failure. True, the mission had certainly afforded Brand an opportunity to provide the free world with a first-hand account of the destruction of Hungarian Jewry; however, it failed in its basic objective. The Allies, who were understandably opposed to providing the enemy with war-related materials and to becoming trapped into weakening or even splitting the Grand Alliance, neglected or refused to engage in any meaningful diplomatic maneuvers to save the Jews "offered for sale" by the SS. Neither they nor the Jewish leaders of the free world did anything tangible to arouse world public opinion until late in June. And even then, it was basically the Swiss press that took the lead under the initiative of a nonestablishment Transylvanian Jew, Georges M. Mantello (see chapter 31).

Kasztner and Hansi Brand had the unenviable task of trying to explain to Eichmann the "difficulties" associated with Joel Brand's mission. They also encountered problems with the Hungarian police, who were eager to learn details about the mission and, above all, about the monies and valuables the *Vaada* gave to the Germans, for by that time Jewish property had already been confiscated by and for the Hungarian state. On May 27, they were arrested together with Mrs. Kasztner and Sholem (Sándor) Offenbach, the *Vaada*'s treasurer, and his wife. Agents of the Hungarian police picked them up at the apartment of Biss (who had begun to play a more active role after Brand's departure) which was presumably under German protection. That same day the Hungarians also arrested Menachem Klein, head of the *Tiyul* department. The police acquired the necessary incriminating evidence: a considerable amount of foreign currency in Biss's apartment and a variety of blank false papers in Klein's room. The latter find was particularly painful, for a few days earlier the Hungarians had picked up 18 Polish and Slovak Jews attempting to flee across the Romanian border with similar papers. The Hungarian Political Police, often referred to as the Hungarian Gestapo, headed by Péter Hain, was especially eager to learn details about Brand's mission. Toward this end, they beat Hansi Brand so savagely that she could not stand for weeks. On the sixth day after their arrest, when the police began the interrogation of Kasztner, the whole group was suddenly freed through the interventions of the SS, who were of course eager to protect those who shared with them certain "Reich secrets."[88]

The Kasztner Transport. Upon their release, Kasztner and Hansi Brand resumed their negotiations with Eichmann. Since they could not persuade Eichmann to suspend the mass deportations on the basis of the cryptic "assurances" they had received from Istanbul (and chances are that nothing would have dissuaded him from making Hungary *Judenrein*) they proceeded with their efforts to save at least part of the Jewish community. The negotiations were based on the Germans' "consolation prize," revealed by Krumey on April 21, under which 600 holders of Palestine immigration certificates would be allowed to leave for any neutral country or Allied-controlled territory except Palestine. The offer was confirmed or renewed by Eichmann on May 22. Some of the specifics were ironed out on June 3, when Eichmann, following the scenario previously worked out with Wisliceny, agreed to permit the "prominent" provincial Jews, representing half of the Palestine immigration certificate holders, to be brought to Budapest. Eichmann promised that he would also allow a special Jewish group from Kolozsvár to come to the capital.[89] Was this one of Eichmann's devices to buy off or perhaps compensate Kasztner for his "services"? Was it his expression of gratitude for the smooth way he was able to carry out the anti-Jewish drive, avoiding another Warsaw-type uprising? Did Kasztner fail to see through Eichmann's intentions? Since the opportunity for informing the Jewish masses, both before and after the German occupation, about the realities of the Nazis' Final Solution program was missed and the deportations were already in progress, did he feel that it was his responsibility to save at least those few Eichmann was willing to spare?

In the midst of the despair over the continuing liquidation of the Jewish communities, Kasztner must naturally have been pleased by the opportunity to save at least a few Jews who otherwise would certainly have shared the fate of the others. And who can blame him for the understandable inclination to include in this group his own family and friends?

The original agreement called for the transfer of "approximately two hundred" Jews from Kolozsvár. Kasztner must have been prepared for this eventuality, for he immediately handed Eichmann a list. The *Scharführer* entrusted by Eichmann with the mission suggested to Kasztner, in the expectation of a bribe, that since the agreement was rather vague the final figure could be augmented.

Eventually 388 of the 18,000 Jews in the ghetto of Kolozsvár were brought to Budapest in a special train on June 10. They were placed in barracks specially built in the courtyard and gardens of the Wechselmann Institute for the Deaf on Columbus Street. The Columbus Street Camp, or the "privileged camp" as it came to be known, emerged as one of the safest spots for Jews in Hungary, for it was protected by five SS guards. The original list was prepared by the *Vaada* leaders with the cooperation of Zsigmond Léb, the former president of the Orthodox community of Kolozsvár and a member of the local Jewish Council, who was in Budapest at the time. Priority was allegedly given to those who had distinguished themselves in Jewish public life; those who were in the service of the Jewish community or had made sacrifices for the advancement of Jewish welfare; and the widows and orphans of labor servicemen. The original Budapest list was partially altered and supplemented in Kolozsvár by the local Jewish leaders and by German and Hungarian officials who for a variety of reasons (especially bribes) wanted to save their favorite Jews. Changes to the list were also needed because many on the original list had already been deported. As a result many of the Jews who were finally selected did not meet any of the selection criteria originally agreed upon. This gave rise to embarrassing and often incriminating insinuations both during and after the war. The most often voiced complaint was that those who were in charge of putting together the transport in Kolozsvár favored their friends and families, who were neither Zionist nor prominent in Jewish life.[90]

Shortly after the arrival of the Kolozsvár group in Budapest, Kasztner expanded his negotiations to save some additional Jews from the threat of deportation. He offered Eichmann jewelry, foreign currency, and *Pengős* worth five million Swiss francs (the total the *Vaada* thought it could raise at the time) in exchange for 100,000 lives. Eichmann, who was already playing the Brand card, had another ace up his sleeve. Kaltenbrunner had just requested him to provide a few thousand slave laborers for the agricultural and industrial enterprises in and around Vienna, which suffered from a terrible labor shortage.[91] Eichmann consequently jumped at the opportunity offered by Kasztner. To show his "good will" in connection with the Brand mission and the five million Swiss francs, he informed Kasztner on June 14 that he would allow the transfer of 30,000 Jews (half from Budapest and half from the provinces) to Austria, where they would be "laid on ice" in special family work camps "pending the outcome of the negotiations." In late June, 18,000 to 20,000 Jews, mostly from the Baja, Debrecen, Szeged, and Szolnok areas, were transferred to Strasshof and other places near Vienna, where approximately 75 percent of them, including the children and many of the aged, survived the war (see chapter 21).

During the two weeks following Eichmann's offer, the *Vaada* leaders worked on preparations for the transport of the "prominent Jews" and tried to raise the necessary funds. This proved quite a problem; in addition to the 5 million Swiss francs, they had undertaken to pay $1,000 for each individual in the special transport. To raise funds, a committee of the *Vaada* composed of Komoly, Offenbach, Hansi Brand, and Ernő Reichard, an engineer, sold approximately 150 places to wealthy Jews and converts who had managed to hide part of their valuables in spite of the confiscatory measures enacted by the Hungarians.

Many wealthy Jews struggled over the few seats put up for sale. (The pandemonium at the committee's offices attracted the Hungarian police; yellow-star-wearing plainclothesmen were ordered to infiltrate the building.) In spite of the great risks for all parties concerned, the transactions continued until the quota was filled. The lucky ones were taken to the Columbus Street camp, where they were joined by other nominally prominent Jews from those provincial ghettos not yet liquidated. Their selection was based mostly on lists submitted by the *Vaada* and the Jewish Council; however Wisliceny, who was in charge of the deportations, occasionally altered the lists. Bought off by Freudiger, he included among those to be brought to Budapest approximately 80 prominent Orthodox Jews from various ghettos. In addition, the close relatives of several Jewish Council members found themselves in Budapest; SS escorts had seen them safely there. To accommodate all those destined to be included in the transport, two additional camps were set up in the Arena Street and Bocskay Street synagogues.

The valuables collected by the *Vaada* were delivered to the SS in three suitcases on June 20. One of those accepting the delivery was SS-*Obersturmbannführer* Kurt Becher, whom Kasztner later identified as the person really responsible for Eichmann's "concessions."

The exact value of the treasures handed over to the SS was never determined. Biss, who was entrusted with the settling of accounts with Becher, tried to persuade the SS to accept the currencies and jewelry as full payment. Becher, however, insisted on receiving additional goods. The Jewish leaders provided Becher with documents from their foreign contacts concerning the availability for delivery of thirty tractors in Switzerland and two freightcars of sheep hide in Bratislava. Neither was ever delivered, although Becher was given 15,000 kilograms of coffee, which were in storage in Budapest.[92] Following the delivery of the goods and valuables, Kasztner developed a mutually beneficial relationship with Becher that lasted until the end of the war. The relationship was particularly valuable since Becher had a direct link to Himmler. However, it ultimately proved fateful for Kasztner. Shortly after the war, it emerged as a chief cause of his ruin and tragic death.

The transport, which was originally supposed to consist of the 600 holders of Palestine immigration certificates, gradually swelled to close to 1,700 persons. First Eichmann permitted the addition of the Kolozsvár group; then he consented to the inclusion of the nearly 200 prominent Jews retrieved from other ghettos. On June 30, the day of the scheduled departure, the transport was officially to consist of approximately 1,300 Jews. However, during a delay caused by an air-raid, 450 Jews in the Bocskay Street synagogue climbed into the train under the cover of darkness (only 150 had been authorized to leave from there), as did a few dozen other Budapest Jews who heard about the special transport.

In the end, 1,684 Jews left Hungary for the neutral or Allied world. Each "official" passenger was allowed to take along 50 to 80 kilograms of luggage. Aside from the skillful passengers who had managed to stow away, the transport carried Orthodox Jews on Freudiger's list;

Neolog Jews on Stern's list; Polish, Slovak and other refugees on separate lists; Palestine certificate holders; young Zionists selected by their respective groups; "paying passengers" whose contributions largely financed the transport; those rescued from the provincial ghettos, including the Kolozsvár group; outstanding intellectuals, scientists, and artists based on a list prepared by Komoly and Szilágyi; and orphans, including 17 from Poland. The various lists included many of the family members, relatives, and friends of the Vaada and Jewish Council leaders, including those of Biss, Brand, Kasztner, Komoly, Offenbach, and Stern. (However, Eichmann allowed none of the Council members to join the group.) Among the nationally known figures were Nison Kahan, György Polgár, and Rabbi Joel Teitelbaum, the fiercely anti-Zionist leader of the Szatmár Hasidic sect. Among the stowaways were two labor servicemen. Their freight train had been awaiting clearance for departure to the copper mines at Bor; they seized the opportunity to jump to safety.[93]

The open-ended destination as well as the route of the special transport gave rise to considerable anxiety among both passengers and organizers. The Vaada leaders had suggested that the transport be directed to Palestine via Romania and Turkey, but Eichmann, claiming Germany's obligations to the Arabs and the Hungarians, rejected this plan. The special train, he emphasized, had ostensibly to be part of the deportation program. Consequently, he insisted that the transport be directed to West Africa via Germany, Occupied France, Spain, and Portugal. Upon learning of these conditions, and above all of the idea of an "Aliya in the form of a deportation," several prospective passengers (especially some of the persecution-wise Polish and Slovak refugees) changed their minds. However, their places were quickly filled.

The transport left late in the night of June 30. It was held up for three days at Mosonmagyaróvár, near the Austrian border, where it received new route directions. For a while it appeared that instead of going through Strasshof as originally planned, the train was to pass by Auspitz in the Protectorate of Bohemia and Moravia, which also had a camp for prominent people (Bevorzugtenlager). This caused considerable panic among the passengers, who confused Auspitz with Auschwitz.[94] Their alarm was soon allayed, for the Germans had their own interest in ensuring the safety and well-being of the group. In the end, the passengers were taken along the original route, and given warm food in Vienna and a hot bath in Linz.[95] On July 8, they arrived in Bergen-Belsen, where they were placed in a Bevorzugtenlager not far from the notorious camp that contained a large number of Hungarian Jewish deportees. There, for a while at least, they were quite well off. They were never subjected to any physical labor and received cigarettes and daily rations of bread, margarine, marmalade, and occasionally sausages. Children and the ill also received milk and adequate medical care. They also had ample opportunities for cultural activities and even entertainment.[96] The internal administration of the camp was in the hands of a self-appointed Council, headed by József Fischer, whose closest associates were primarily from among the leaders of the Kolozsvár group.[97]

Kasztner's Negotiations with Becher. The fate of the Bergen-Belsen group became intertwined with Kasztner's further dealings with Becher. When the Budapest Jews became threatened with the danger of deportation, both shortly before and after Horthy's decision to halt the further removal of Jews to Germany, Kasztner approached Becher at Stern's urging and gave him $20,000 to intercede with Himmler. Kasztner also showed Becher the text of the "interim agreement" he had received from Istanbul on July 7, in an attempt to continue the negotiations along the original Europa Plan. Kasztner kept the Jewish leaders in Istanbul and Switzerland fully informed about the new developments and together with Weissmandel[98] implored them urgently to raise the funds required to "assure the success" of the plan.[99]

Since Brand was not permitted to return, the *Vaada*, acting in conjunction with the Istanbul leaders, worked out a plan for Becher and Kasztner to pursue the negotiations in Portugal with Dr. Joseph J. Schwartz, the American AJDC representative in Europe, and Eliyahu Dobkin, a Palestinian-British national who served on the Executive Committee of the Jewish Agency. On July 18, however, Kasztner was again arrested and kept incommunicado for about nine days. This time he was in the hands of the Hungarian gendarmerie leaders in charge of the deportations: Lieutenant-Colonel László Ferenczy and his aide, Captain Leó Lullay. They wanted both to find out details of his dealings with the Germans in general and the "special transport" in particular, and to convince him of their prior unawareness of Auschwitz and their readiness to prevent the further anti-Jewish operations of the Germans, who, they claimed, bore full responsibility for the deportations.[100]

The sudden lengthy disappearance of Kasztner left his Budapest Jewish colleagues dumbfounded, but not totally helpless. Komoly decided to take over the negotiations and made plans to go to Lisbon in

his stead;[101] on July 22, Biss submitted a long memorandum to
Klages—presumably for transmission to Himmler—in which he outlined the measures the SS would have to take urgently in order to assure the "success of the negotiations";[102] Freudiger involuntarily became involved in a new "offer" of trucks, which caused considerable
friction between the *Vaada* and the Orthodox group in Budapest as
well as between the HIJEF and AJDC representatives in Switzerland.

The new ploy was initiated by Rabbi Weissmandel, who was eager to
calm the Germans' apprehension about the "monstrous deal" the British had unmasked on July 20 (chapter 31). Rabbi Weissmandel interpreted the British revelations about the Brand-Grosz mission to Wisliceny as designed merely for public opinion and pointed out that in
reality the Allies were ready to comply, as indicated by the "fact" that
Freudiger already had 250 trucks ready for delivery in Switzerland. To
assure the continuation of the possible rescue operations, Freudiger
felt compelled to corroborate the story and was promptly asked by
Eichmann to discuss the delivery of the trucks with Becher. Freudiger
and his friends, Gyula Link and Sándor Abeles, thought it might be
possible to buy 250 used trucks in Switzerland through the HIJEF
rather than the AJDC. They preferred to work with the Sternbuch
brothers, who were less concerned with legalistic formalities and more
convinced about the chances of dealing with the Germans than was Saly
Mayer, a Swiss national and the local head of the AJDC. The Sternbuch
brothers submitted the essentials of the so-called Freudiger plan to
Roswell D. McClelland, the WRB's representative in Switzerland, calling among other things for the opening of a credit of 700,000 Swiss
francs through the Schweizerische Kreditanstalt. The plan encountered
stiff resistance not only because the Americans, like the other Allies,
had refused to participate in any "ransom" deals, but also because
Mayer had rejected "action along the lines proposed."[103]

In Budapest, the *Vaada* leaders became suspicious of Freudiger's initiatives, fearing that he was in fact interested in taking over the leadership of the negotiations with Becher, and insisted that Biss should accompany him or, preferably, go alone to complete the deal.[104] The
crisis was solved with the sudden reappearance of Kasztner, who resumed his leadership position in the negotiations.

However, the original plans had to be altered when late in July the
Western powers prohibited their nationals from getting involved in any
talks with the Germans. The new chief negotiating partner, selected
with the cooperation of McClelland, was Saly Mayer. His freedom of

action was limited not only by the AJDC, an American-based organization, but also by the WRB and the Swiss authorities. His basic task was to drag out the negotiations and to make no firm commitments relating to the delivery of goods or money. He fully agreed with this policy of delay, and carried out his task faithfully. Saly Mayer was temperamentally a loner and highly suspicious. He did not get along very well with the representatives of the various Jewish national and international organizations in Switzerland, with the possible exception of Nathan Schwalb. He was scrupulous and highly conservative in the handling of AJDC funds—which in the view of many Jewish leaders, especially those living in the Nazi inferno, made effective rescue work all but impossible. He was as fully informed, and as silent, about the Nazis' Final Solution program as the other leaders of the free world.

With the negotiations back on track, Kasztner urged Becher to allow the Bergen-Belsen group to travel to a neutral country as an expression of the good intentions of the SS. Mayer concurred with this request, viewing this as a test case. Becher, who returned from Berlin on August 2, informed Kasztner that Himmler was ready to permit the emigration of Jews from Europe upon delivery of goods and that the first group of 500 Jews from Bergen-Belsen was authorized to travel to a neutral country. When Mayer learned of this development, he got in touch with Heinrich Rothmund, the head of the Swiss Alien Police, on August 8, requesting permission for the group to enter Switzerland.[105]

The first meeting was scheduled to take place on August 21, to coincide with the arrival of the first group from Bergen-Belsen.[106] Since Mayer could not obtain Swiss visas for Becher and his colleagues, the negotiations took place on a bridge linking Austria and Switzerland between Höchst and St. Margrethen, about 20 miles east of St. Gallen. Becher was accompanied by his trusted aide SS-*Haupsturmführer* Max Grüson, Wilhelm Billitz (one of the directors of the Weiss-Manfréd Works which Becher had acquired in May) and Kasztner. He spoke as the personal representative of Himmler regarding the offer given to Brand. Mayer, in turn, emphasized that he was speaking only as the representative of the *Schweizerische Unterstüzungsfonds für Flüchtlinge* (Swiss Support Fund for Refugees), the welfare organization that handled the distribution of money for refugees in Switzerland. His closest advisers were Pierre Bigar, a leader in the *Schweizerischer Israelitischer Gemeindebund* (Swiss Jewish Community Council), and Marcus Wyler, his lawyer. In accordance with his mandate, Mayer adopted a noncommittal posture, berating Becher for the atrocities committed by the

Nazis and demanding that the "Germans finally put an end to their damned gassings." Becher outlined the German position along the original offer given Brand, suggesting that the 10,000 trucks be shipped from America. He added that on their return trip the ships could take along the Jews freed by the Germans. Mayer tested Becher to see whether he might be interested in money instead. The meeting ended on a basically negative tone, with Billitz having to save the situation by proposing that the meeting be postponed to give both parties time for further reflection.

Becher returned to Budapest annoyed by the humiliation of having to negotiate on a bridge. He asked Kasztner how the "leaders of world Jewry" could be expected to deliver any goods when they could not even provide a Swiss entry visa. Nevertheless, he maintained a tone of optimism in his report to Himmler. Writing on August 25, Becher pointed out that the skepticism of the Jewish leaders about the seriousness of the German offer had been dissipated by the freeing of the first group of Jews from Bergen-Belsen. He suggested that in light of the practical impossibility of obtaining trucks, other goods needed by Germany (chromium, nickel, aluminum, ball-bearings, etc.) be accepted through such neutral countries as Sweden, Switzerland, and Portugal. He relayed the Jewish leaders' contention that should further "evacuations" take place the negotiations would not be taken seriously and would be considered pointless. The following day Himmler approved Becher's line of action.[107]

The second series of meetings took place at the same spot on September 3–5, but without Becher, who refused to be "humiliated" a second time. Mayer was joined in the negotiations alternately by Wyler and Bigar. Although the basic position of the Jewish leaders was once again noncommittal, it was, for two reasons, somewhat less intransigent. First, on September 1, McClelland had informed Mayer that the WRB was ready to allocate $2 million for the negotiations. (The license for the actual use of these funds was never forwarded.) Second, following the national uprising in Slovakia on August 28, the Nazis, using the excuse of Jewish participation in the revolt, had renewed their drive against the remnant of the Slovak Jewish community. In light of these factors, Mayer declared that he was ready in principle to deposit five million Swiss francs in the account of his Swiss organization and would try to convince the Swiss authorities to permit the SS to buy whatever goods they wanted in Switzerland. Although no deal was completed, the Germans got the impression that the Jewish leaders, and possibly their Western mentors, were interested in the Nazi offer and were ready to continue the negotiations.

The third meeting took place on Mayer's initiative. On September 26, he cabled Budapest that he was ready to open an account for the Nazis in a Swiss bank. Three days later, he met the Budapest group, which this time was led by Herbert Kettlitz. (Grüson had been transferred from Budapest, allegedly because in Bratislava on September 24 he had associated himself with Kasztner in intervening on behalf of the Slovak Jews.) This meeting appeared to be more productive. At least, something specific was offered the Germans. Becher was informed that funds would be placed at his disposal for the purchase of goods in Switzerland on the condition that the deportation of the Slovak Jews be discontinued; the Germans abandon their plan to deport the Jews of Budapest; the remainder of the Bergen-Belsen group be allowed to leave for Switzerland.[108]

The optimism associated with the discussions and with the internal developments in Hungary was of course dispelled by the *Nyilas* coup. Eichmann, who had been recalled late in August, returned to Budapest to complete his "mission." The urgency of the situation in Slovakia and Hungary compelled McClelland and Mayer to readjust their tactics, but not their ultimate objective. On October 25, Mayer cabled Kasztner that he was ready for a new round of discussions—this time inside Switzerland. (The entry visas for Becher, Kettlitz, Billitz and Kasztner had been obtained thanks to McClelland.) Billitz and Kasztner arrived on October 29, Becher and Kettlitz on November 2. As during his first encounter with Mayer late in August, Becher again had good news: Himmler had authorized the departure of the remnant of the Bergen-Belsen group.

The first round of discussions was held in St. Gallen on November 4. Becher explained that the Slovak Jews had been "liquidated for military reasons" and summarized Himmler's views regarding the Jews of Budapest and the possible freeing of certain Jews upon the delivery of goods. In line with his August 25 note to Himmler, he no longer referred specifically to trucks. A far more important meeting from Becher's point of view was held the following day in Zurich. There he met McClelland, the "personal representative of President Roosevelt," in the company of Mayer. Becher was subjected to great psychological pressure, McClelland and Mayer emphasizing the good will he could acquire by cooperating in the rescue of Jews in view of the inevitable defeat of the Third Reich. He was also given a basis to believe that his mission was not in vain: Mayer showed him the text of Cordell Hull's telegram of October 29, in which the American Secretary of State had indicated that 20 million Swiss francs would be placed at the disposal of Mayer. Becher was of course never informed about the conditions attached by the American government concerning the actual expenditure of the funds. McClelland and Mayer outlined their own demands, stressing the absolute necessity of putting an end to the exterminations and the persecution of people irrespective of their race or creed. Becher promised to convey these demands to Himmler and left Switzerland in the company of Kasztner. Kettlitz was left behind to shop around for goods, only to discover that the money mentioned by Mayer and McClelland was not in fact available. In response to McClelland's telegram of November 16, in which he summarized the discussions with Becher, the State Department and the WRB vetoed the deal (on November 21), stressing that "no (repeat no) funds from any source should be used to carry out such proposal."[109] Becher, who was not yet aware of these "difficulties" was quite content with the meeting with McClelland, which he thought might lead to deals transcending the Jewish question. However Kettlitz, who was soon asked by the Swiss to leave, realized the hopelessness of his mission and so informed Becher.

In the meantime the Soviet troops were swiftly approaching Budapest and Becher became more concerned with his own record than with the acquisition of goods. As a realist, he had no difficulty in seeing through Mayer's tactics though, wisely, he never revealed these to Himmler. He intervened with the SS and *Nyilas* authorities to ease and eventually halt the foot-marches from Budapest.[110] On November 26, following his return from a visit to Himmler, he announced triumphantly that he had convinced the *Reichsführer*-SS about the necessity to suspend the Final Solution program. He told Kasztner that Himmler in fact had authorized the dismantling of the gas chambers.[111] Of course, by that time the SS were desperately trying to eliminate all traces of their extermination machinery not only in Auschwitz but everywhere else, too.[112]

In response to Kettlitz's cables informing Becher that he had not received any funds and could not even get in touch with Mayer, Kasztner and Billitz tried to persuade Becher and Eichmann, who once again became actively involved in the negotiations, that the difficulties were probably due to "certain misunderstandings," which could perhaps be eliminated by another visit to Switzerland. Eichmann demanded a positive answer by December 2, stating that otherwise he would proceed against the Jews of Budapest. On November 28, Billitz and Kasztner, this time accompanied by SS-*Hauptsturmführer* Krell, again went to Switzerland. Kasztner would never again return to Budapest. Upon arrival the next day, they were met at the border by Kettlitz and Rubinfeld, a representative of HIJEF. (Saly Mayer had returned to St. Gallen after having waited at the border for two hours.) Rubinfeld was allegedly brought along by Kettlitz, who not only complained about Mayer's involvement in his ouster but also suggested that better progress could be made by negotiating with the Orthodox; Rubinfeld generally agreed with him.[113] Kasztner and Billitz next met Mayer as well as Schwalb and some representatives of the Sternbuch group (HIJEF), the Orthodox relief and rescue committee of Switzerland. Though Mayer had informed Kasztner on December 1 about the true state of affairs, Kasztner induced Krell and Kettlitz to tell Becher that some funds were in fact available and that the difficulties were due primarily to the failure of the Germans to keep their side of the bargain, including the transfer of the Bergen-Belsen group.[114] Mayer sent the same message to Krell on December 5. The situation was somewhat eased when the remaining Jews in the Kasztner transport were allowed to enter Switzerland on December 7, despite Kettlitz's original opposition. After the Germans again showed their "serious intentions," the Jewish leaders, including Joseph J. Schwartz,[115] who was in Switzerland for a visit, convinced McClelland to pursue a new line under which the AJDC would transfer $5 million dollars through the Red Cross for "board and lodging" for Jews under Nazi rule. The State Department's positive reply to McClelland's request of December 13 did not arrive until January 7, 1945. The reply reiterated the earlier restrictive conditions, emphasizing that the transfer of the AJDC funds was authorized "solely in order that Saly Mayer may have something tangible with which to hold open the negotiations and for the gaining of more precious time."[116] By the time Mayer found out about the restrictive conditions, the Soviet troops, after a month-long siege, had liberated Budapest. To appease Becher in the wake of the dilatory cables from Switzerland and to acquire his good will toward protecting the Jews in the ghetto, Biss "bought" for him 30 trucks in Slovakia from a German-Slovak import-export dealer named Alois Steger. These were German trucks that had been given to Slovakia; Becher never acquired them, though, because they were in the meantime confiscated by the retreating *Wehrmacht*.[117]

Although he could have remained in Switzerland after the arrival of the second Bergen-Belsen group, Kasztner chose to return to the Nazi sphere. After the freeing of the Bergen-Belsen groups and the liberation of Budapest, his efforts were concentrated on rescuing the Jews still in Nazi hands, including those in the concentration camps. At first he spent much time in Vienna, from where he often went to Bratislava on behalf of the Slovak Jews. Late in January 1945, he returned to St. Margrethen for a series of discussions with Mayer, Krell, and Becher, which lasted almost till mid-February.

After Becher was appointed by Himmler to serve as Special Reich Commissioner for All Concentration Camps (*Reichssonderkommissar für sämtliche Konzentrationslager*) on April 6, 1945, much effort was exerted to prevent the destruction of the camps, so that their inmates might be safely transferred to allied hands. Kasztner, who had a German passport that made no reference to his race, pursued this objective by travelling with Becher in the enclave still under Nazi control. Between April 8 and April 18, they visited Berlin, Hamburg, Bergen-Belsen, Neuengamme, and Theresienstadt. As a personal favor to Kasztner, Becher went alone to Mauthausen to free Dr. Moshe Schweiger, a *Vaada* leader who had been one of the first to be arrested by the Gestapo after the occupation, allegedly because of his anti-Hitler stand.

Becher's intention was to enter Switzerland in the company of Schweiger with the valuables received from the *Vaada* leaders. The swift advance of the Americans made this impossible. At the end, the valuables, "worth several hundreds of thousands of dollars," were handed over by Schweiger to a representative of the American OSS.[118]

Others also made attempts to save Jews. The Sternbuch brothers, representing the HIJEF; Curt Trümpy, one of Messerschmidt's representatives in Switzerland; Dr. Jean-Marie Musy, the former President of Switzerland; Felix Kersten, an Estonian of German origin and Himmler's personal doctor; and Count Folke Bernadotte of Sweden all claimed credit for Himmler's decision not to destroy the concentration camps.[119]

The Freeing of the Kasztner Transport. The arrival in Switzerland of the second Bergen-Belsen group on December 7, 1944, meant that the safety of the entire Kasztner transport was assured. It also put an end to the flurry of diplomatic exchanges between the Third Reich and Switzerland, and between the RSHA and the German Foreign Office, that the arrival of the first group had engendered.

Although Hitler was aware of the transfer of Jews to Switzerland (presumably he was informed by Kaltenbrunner) he apparently was under the impression that this was part of the bargain he had suggested to Horthy on July 10, under which close to 8,000 Jews under the protection of Sweden, Switzerland, and other neutral countries would be allowed to leave Hungary in exchange for the resumption of the deportations that had been halted three days earlier.[120] The German Foreign Office was, for a while at least, kept in the dark by the RSHA. Interestingly enough, it received the first official notification about the transfer of the first Kasztner group from the Swiss. Notwithstanding the fact that Saly Mayer had obtained the consent of the Swiss authorities via Heinrich Rothmund (August 8) for the entry of both groups, the Swiss, probably to protect their neutral status, formally complained to the Germans of not having been informed in advance of the transfer date, of the lack of personal data on the refugees (they had no identification papers), and of not having been told of their ultimate destination. The note led to a series of interagency and intradepartmental communications, with the RSHA officials trying to explain the transports as part of the bargain for the acquisition of war materiel for the SS.[121]

The first group consisted not of 500 Jews, as Becher had originally informed Kasztner on August 2, but only of 318, allegedly because Eichmann had sabotaged Himmler's orders. The criteria for selection of Jews to make up the first group were suggested to Fischer in a letter from Kasztner on August 3.[122] The second group, consisting of 1,368 Jews and headed by Fischer, arrived in Switzerland under the command of Krumey.

While in Bergen-Belsen, three members of the group died of natural causes and there were eight births. Only a few from the original transport were retained in the camp. In his pique over Brand's failure to return, Eichmann ordered the retention of his mother and two sisters. One Jew, Dr. Andreas Kassowitz, was held back because he identified himself as Romanian and the Germans wanted to use him as an exchange for a *Volksdeutsche* from Transylvania. The fate of Jenő Kertész and Sándor Weiss, two lawyers from Kolozsvár, was particularly tragic. Their daughters, who lived in Budapest, had been among the first to be deported from Kistarcsa (April 29, 1944) and eventually ended up at Bergen-Belsen.[123] As punishment for their attempt to have their daughters transferred to them at the *Bevorzugtenlager*, they were shifted to the extermination camp, but separated from their daughters. Both died before or shortly after the end of the war.[124]

The first group, which included Dr. Tivadar Fischer, a former member of the Romanian Parliament, was taken to the Military Internment Camp (*Militärisches Internierungslager*) in the Hotel Belmont at Montreux.[125] After the second group arrived, the Jews were placed into two camps in Caux, near Montreux. One "collection camp" (*Auffangslager*) was in the Hotel Esplanade and Regina, under the leadership of Dezső Hermann, a lawyer from Kolozsvár;[126] the other camp, known as Les Rochers, was headed by Ignátz Klein. Following the group's arrival in Switzerland, some of its leaders, including Hillel Danzig, got in touch with the representatives of the major Jewish organizations and through them with the leaders of the Istanbul *Vaada*. Danzig, aided by the effective cooperation in Switzerland of Chaim Pozner, reestablished contact with Brand and exerted special efforts on behalf of 250 Zionist comrades—"the best from Transylvania and Hungary."[127]

In April 1945 the Swiss authorities decided to move the Kasztner group, first to an UNRRA camp in Philippeville, Algeria, and then to Bari, Italy, allegedly to free the camps for other expected refugees. This decision was made in concert with the Americans, who had assumed certain responsibilities in connection with the group. Hermann and Klein, acting for their respective camps, began to bombard the Swiss and above all the local Jewish organizations with petitions and memoranda, outlining the injustices of the proposed measure and threatening to stage a hunger strike and inform the Swiss press.[128] The campaign was successful, for shortly after the end of the war in Europe, the members of the group were allowed to proceed to their freely chosen destination. Many opted to go back to their former homelands; approximately 700 certificate holders led by József Fischer left for Palestine via Bari, in August 1945.

Kasztner returned to Switzerland on April 19, and the following day—one of his happiest—he was honored at a banquet at which he was hailed as a savior.[129] After the group's departure, he remained in Europe for a while, helping the Allies in the prosecution of war crimes trial cases. On September 13, 1945, he signed a long affidavit concerning the destruction of Hungarian Jewry, emphasizing his role in the rescue work.[130] In the months that followed, he devoted much time to detailing his achievements, in a controversial and understandably self-serving report.[131]

Competing Claims for Credit. Kasztner claimed credit for himself and the Budapest *Vaada* not only for rescuing the close to 1,700 "prominent" Jews and a large percentage of the approximately 18,000 Strasshof Jews, but also for the survival of the Jews of Budapest and many of those in German concentration camps. Credit for the latter achievements is also claimed by several other Jewish and non-Jewish leaders. The leaders of the World Jewish Congress, for example, claimed that "no other Jewish organization had a greater share in rescue work during the war than the World Jewish Congress." This claim .was vehemently disputed by Yitzhak Sternbuch, who insisted that the HIJEF committee, including Hugo Donnebaum, Dr. Ruben Hecht, and Dr. Julius Kühl, acting through Musy had managed to persuade Himmler to allow all the Jews in the concentration camps to leave for America via Switzerland. Citing a March 6, 1945 statement by Musy, Sternbuch claims that the only reason why the estimated 750,000 Jews were not allowed to leave (at a rate of 1,800 every two weeks) was that the plan was sabotaged by the AJDC, Saly Mayer, Nathan Schwalb, Kasztner, and Becher, bringing about the consequent opposition of Hitler and Kaltenbrunner.[132]

Credit for the rescue of the Jews of Budapest is claimed not only by most of the organizational leaders cited above, but also by Horthy, the leaders of the Jewish Council, and even some of the *Nyilas* leaders. A highly unlikely person also credited with this achievement is Saly Mayer. In a press release issued on October 4, 1945 by the AJDC headquarters in New York, Mayer was credited, among other things, with having persuaded Becher to cancel the order for the deportation of the 200,000 Jews of Budapest to Auschwitz and with having secured the entry of the close to 1,700 Jews in the Kasztner group to Switzerland. Mayer was also identified as a hero: "At one point," the release claimed, "at the risk of his life, Mayer entered Nazi Germany to carry on the discussions."[133]

A similar conclusion was reached by Yehuda Bauer, who gives the lion's share of the credit for all the achievements claimed by others—including Kasztner, Kersten, and Musy—to Mayer, the very person who, ironically, is identified by many wartime Jewish leaders as one of the chief obstacles to the rescuing of the surviving Jews of Europe.[134]

Although it would be an exaggeration to call Mayer a "savior," the harsh criticism leveled against him is clearly unfair. His abrasive personality was probably the principal reason for his being regarded so negatively. Furthermore, his critics were not fully aware of the limitations and restrictions under which Mayer had to work during the war; afterward, they tended to ignore or underestimate them.

Mayer, the free citizen of a neutral country, had adopted a "tough" position toward the SS officers he negotiated with, often lecturing, moralizing, and admonishing them with an air of arrogance that was not appreciated by Kasztner and the other leaders who had witnessed the Holocaust and were themselves constantly operating in the shadow of death. Could additional Jewish lives have been saved had Mayer been more flexible and, like many other Jewish leaders operating under the Nazi yoke, more amenable to the "illegal" transfer of goods and money to SS negotiators? The question cannot be answered. It is clear, however, that such behavior would have been completely out of character for Mayer, the old-fashioned Germanic Jew—a stickler for formal, legalistic conduct.[135]

The Kasztner Case in Israel

In 1946, Kasztner and his family moved to Israel, where he resumed his journalistic-political career. His postwar ambitions were interlinked with the *Mapai* party, which dominated Israeli politics at the time and would continue to do so for several decades afterward. This link, ironically, indirectly became the source of his downfall and tragic death.

The celebrations associated with Kasztner's rescue activities were short-lived. The congratulatory messages conveyed at Caux and elsewhere in Western Europe gradually gave way to gnawing questions about the propriety of his dealings with the SS. Survivors of concentration and labor service camps began to wonder how it was possible that some "prominent" Jews had survived with their families and friends almost intact, while they had lost most of theirs. As envy gradually turned to hatred, the whispers about possible treachery and collaboration became ever louder.

Questions about the propriety of Kasztner's and the Jewish Council's activities were raised not only in Israel, but also in Hungary and parts of the Successor States from which the Jews were deported in 1944. In the anti-Nazi atmosphere of the immediate post-liberation period, the Hungarian authorities, feverishly involved in the preparation of war crimes trial cases, seriously considered the indictment of *Vaada* and Jewish Council leaders for collaboration with the enemy. The Political and Police Division of the Budapest Police Headquarters of the Hungarian State Police (*Magyar Államrendőrség Budapesti Főkapitányságának Politikai és Rendészeti Osztálya*), in fact, collected a number of depositions and other evidence toward this end in 1945–46.[136] A similar plan was also under way in Transylvania, where there was considerable bitterness, especially in Kolozsvár, against Kasztner and his friends.[137]

In Israel, Kasztner resumed his active public life. He was active in a Hungarian Jewish organization, was appointed head of the Hungarian section of the radio station of the Jewish Agency, and reestablished his affiliation with the *Uj Kelet* (New East), the Hungarian-language daily with which he had already been associated in Kolozsvár. The main vehicle through which he aimed to advance his political ambitions was the *Mapai*, but although the party listed him as one of its candidates in the general elections, he was never elected to the *Knesset*. His main source of income was his job as public relations officer in the Ministry of Commerce and Industry, then headed by Dr. Dov Joseph, an Israeli of Canadian background.

Despite his power and influence, the whispers about Kasztner's alleged wartime collaborationist activities did not end. The fact that courts of honor of the Zionist movement and of the *Mapai* investigated the accusations on several occasions and on each occasion rejected them as without substance or unproven did not seem to help. The campaign came to a climax in 1953, when Malkiel Grünwald (Greenwald in many sources), a *Mizrachi* Zionist who sympathized with the terrorist Irgun Zvai Leumi, published a highly derogatory statement about him. Grünwald, who was over 70 years of age, had come to Palestine before the war. Like most Jews, he had lost many relatives, including six brothers and their entire families. He helped support himself by publishing a Hebrew mimeographed newsletter—*Letters to the Members of Mizrachi*. In issue number 17 of 1953, he wrote:

Beloved friends! I smell rotting carrion! What a first-rate burial we're going to have! This Dr. Rudolf Kastner has to be finished off! For three years I have been waiting for the moment to unmask this careerist who grew fat on Hitler's plunder and murders. Because of his criminal machinations and his collaboration with the Nazis I consider him implicated in the murder of our beloved brothers.[138]

Responding to his Minister's insistence that he be cleared of all accusations, Kasztner, acting in concert with Chaim Cohen, the Attorney General, filed a libel suit against Grünwald in May 1953. The trial began on January 1, 1954 in the Jerusalem District Court presided over by Judge Benjamin Halevi. It was almost immediately adjourned to enable Grünwald to retain counsel. The trial resumed the following month after Grünwald had retained Shmuel Tamir, a bright young lawyer whose sympathies lay with the *Herut*, the Revisionist Party of Menachem Begin.

In the course of the trial it became clear that Tamir's target was not exclusively Kasztner. He tried consistently to demonstrate a correlation between Kasztner's dealings with the Nazis and the *Mapai*'s and the Jewish Agency's alleged "collaboration" with the British. One of his objectives was to show that in contrast to their cowardly behavior, Kasztner and the *Vaada* ought to have emulated the resistance leaders in the Warsaw Ghetto, while the *Mapai* leaders ought to have adopted the tactics of the *Irgun* against the British. The ultimate goal, according to Tamir's critics, was to topple the Sharett government and enable the *Herut* to acquire power.

The first witness called to the stand was Kasztner, who was at least as eager as the public prosecutor to clear his name once and for all. During the first three days on the stand, Kasztner reviewed his and the Budapest *Vaada*'s work during the war, seemingly scoring points for his case. However, he committed blunder after blunder in the course of the cross-examination by Tamir. A stupid lie and subsequent statements to cover it up were as disastrous as the reluctance of the "friends" whom he had saved from the Kolozsvár ghetto to testify in his support (see below). His downfall was the patently false and unexplainable statement that he had not testified in Nuremberg in support of Becher. Tamir, of course, had no difficulty in obtaining a certified copy of a sworn declaration Kasztner had made on August 4, 1947, before Benno H. Selcke, Jr., an interrogator associated with the American Evidence Division of the International Military Tribunal in Nuremberg. In it Kasztner declared, among other things:

There can be no doubt about it that Becher belongs to the very few SS leaders having the courage to oppose the program of annihilation of the Jews, and trying to rescue human lives. . . . I never doubted for one moment the good intentions of Kurt Becher. . . . In my opinion, when his case is judged by Allied or German authorities, Kurt Becher deserves the fullest possible consideration. . . . I make this statement not only in my name but also in behalf of the Jewish Agency and the Jewish World Congress.[139]

He signed it in a boastful manner as "Former Chairman of Zionist Organization in Hungary, 1943–45. Representative of Joint Distribution Committee in Budapest," neither of which was formally correct. It also turned out that he was authorized neither by the Jewish Agency nor by the World Jewish Congress to support Becher. To his great later regret, he also boasted in a letter dated July 26, 1948 to Eliezer Kaplan, Israel's first Minister of Finance, that Becher had been released from prison in Nuremberg by the occupation forces of the Allies owing to his personal intervention.[140] His determining role in the release of Becher was confirmed by Walter H. Rapp, the former head of the Evidence Division of the Chief of Counsel of War Crimes at Nuremberg and Deputy Chief of Counsel to Brigadier-General Telford Taylor. In his affidavit given in Tel Aviv on February 6, 1957, Rapp stated that Kasztner appeared as a voluntary witness on behalf of Becher, emphasizing that "Becher's ultimate release . . . was solely the result of Kasztner's pleadings and the contents of his sworn testimony."[141]

While Kasztner's testimony in support of Becher led to his downfall, the defense demonstrated that Kasztner had also interceded on behalf of Krumey. In another affidavit witnessed by Selcke (May 5, 1948), Kasztner swore that Krumey "performed his duties in a laudable spirit of good will, at a time when the life and death of many depended on him." A little more than a year before, Kasztner had assured Krumey personally that in his report to the Zionist Congress he had "officially clarified and identified the work done by those who were of help to the Jews. . . ." and expressed the hope that his efforts would enable Krumey to regain his freedom and to start a new life.[142]

Kasztner's testimony in support of Becher was quite understandable in view of his personal experiences with this high-ranking SS officer. However it was obviously unmindful of Becher's alleged anti-Jewish activities during the first four years of the war, for which he was presumably looking for an alibi in 1944–45.[143] Kasztner's attempt to cover up his testimony was a fatal mistake, inducing Tamir to conclude that he was capable of any infamy. Caught in a web of boasts and lies, Kasztner was subsequently portrayed by Tamir as a "collaborator," "a Nazi agent in Europe," and a "war criminal." He was accused of preventing the formation of an underground resistance organization, contributing to the lulling of the masses into a false sense of security during the ghettoization-deportation period, withholding news about the Nazis' Final Solution program, persuading the Jewish-Palestinian parachutists to surrender to the Gestapo (see below), and sharing the loot Becher had received as ransom. Perhaps the most damning accusation leveled against Kasztner was that he helped send hundreds of thousands of Hungarian Jews to their death by remaining silent about the Nazis' designs in exchange for the opportunity to save a few thousand "prominent" Jews, including his family and friends.[144]

Among the 18 witnesses lined up by Kasztner were Echud Avriel and Menachem Bader (formerly associated with the Istanbul *Vaada*), Joel (Nussbecher) Palgi (one of the Palestinian parachutists), Joel Brand, and Hillel Danzig and Dezső Hermann (old friends from Kolozsvár).

One of the most controversial points raised during the trial was whether Kasztner, who was fully aware of the Final Solution program (see chapter 23), informed the leaders of the Jewish community of Kolozsvár about the impending disaster when he visited that city early in May 1944 (just a few weeks before the beginning of the mass deportations) and whether they, in turn, relayed this information to the masses. Kasztner claimed that he did; his friends, however, did not corroborate his claim.[145]

When Danzig was asked by Tamir whether he had received any "news from Fischer [Kasztner's father-in-law] that the trains were being led to extermination," he answered that he first learned about the realities of Auschwitz after he got to the Columbus Street camp in Budapest together with the other 387 Jews from Kolozsvár.[146] Hermann, who was the secretary of the Kolozsvár Jewish Council, claimed that he did not meet Kasztner during his May visit and had no knowledge about the exterminations, except the "horror stories" he had heard from the Polish and Slovak Jewish refugees, and that he was convinced, like most Jews, that the Jews were merely being removed for labor.[147]

According to some of the witnesses rounded up by Tamir in Grünwald's defense (among them Jacob Freifeld and Yechiel Shmueli of Kolozsvár), several of the Transylvanian Zionist leaders had inadvertently lent credence to the rumor planted by the Nazis that the Jews were being transferred to Kenyérmező for labor for the duration of the war.[148] Perhaps these leaders were as genuinely convinced about this plan as most of the Jews deported from Northern Transylvania had been. But then the question arises: why did they decide to abandon the flock during a time of great peril? Instead of going with the masses to Kenyérmező to provide continued leadership, most of them (including Danzig, Hermann, Lajos Marton, and Fischer) eagerly joined the Kasztner group that was taken to Budapest with the aid of the SS. Some of the other lay and religious leaders of the Kolozsvár community found other ways of escaping deportation. Rabbi Moshe Weinberger (later Carmilly), the Chief Rabbi of the Neolog congregation, escaped by going with his wife on a "mission on behalf of Hungarian Jewry" to Romania.[149] Ernő Marton, the noted Zionist and former Romanian parliamentarian and editor-in-chief of the *Uj Kelet*, escaped to Romania shortly after Kasztner's visit in such hurry and secrecy that, according to some eyewitness accounts, he kept even his own wife and child in the dark.[150] The only "news" the masses of Jewry received was that they would be transferred to Kenyérmező or some other area in Transdanubia to perform labor.

One can only speculate as to how the masses would have reacted had they been told the truth at that late hour. Isolated in ghettos, with most of the males aged 20 to 48 years in labor service, having been kept in ignorance for so many years about the bloodletting in the neighboring countries, they would most probably have reacted with disbelief. It seems evident that, in fact, very few were ready to admit that the Jews and other "undesirable" peoples were being subjected to a mass extermination program. This attitude was eloquently reflected by the statement of a Hungarian Jew who was among those who boarded the Auschwitz-bound freight train in 1944:

Had I known what Auschwitz was, no power on earth could have made me get on that train. But there was no power on earth that could then have made me believe in the existence of an Auschwitz. Even when I was already inside the camp and a Polish Jew approached us, on arrival, pointing to the high chimneys and saying we would all go up there shortly, I was sure the man was demented.[151]

The trial proceedings, including a brief adjournment, lasted until August 9, when Kasztner began his final statement. This was followed by the statement of Chaim Cohen, counsel for the government, that supported Kasztner as an honorable man, emphasizing that while Kasztner "may have made mistakes . . . there is no reason at all to assume any criminal intent on his part."[152] Tamir, in a final statement that took 30 hours, summarized his earlier accusations and the evidence for them. Claiming that through his dealings with the Nazis Kasztner had become a traitor, Tamir demanded that his client be acquitted of the libel charges and that the accusations against Kasztner and his associates be investigated by the court.

It took Judge Halevi nine months to write his opinion. In the meantime, the political parties of Israel became embroiled in a heated political campaign. The former members and sympathizers of the *Irgun* rallied around the *Herut* in a desperate attempt to topple the "establishment" *Mapai*, Kasztner's party. Perhaps unconcerned with this political battle, Judge Halevi read his 300-page opinion on June 22, 1955, approximately four weeks before the scheduled elections. It was dramatic. Judge Halevi accepted Tamir's line of reasoning and determined that three of Grünwald's charges (collaborating with the Nazis, preparing the ground for the mass murder of Hungarian Jews, and saving Becher from punishment) had been proved. However, he found that Grünwald had not substantiated his claim that Kasztner had shared in the ransom money given to Becher. For this he sentenced Grünwald to pay a token fine of one Israeli pound. In his wrathful judgment, Judge

Halevi asserted that Kasztner and his associates, whom the Jewish masses had trusted in Kolozsvár and elsewhere, had allowed themselves to be used by the SS in a calculated plan to mislead the Jews by spreading false information about Kenyérmező; that these leaders did everything in their power to soothe the Jews in the ghettos and prevent resistance, so that the masses of Jews boarded the deportation trains confident that they were simply being transferred to Kenyérmező; that in return the Nazis allowed Kasztner to rescue close to 2,000 prominent Jews, and that when Kasztner received this present from the Nazis, he sacrificed the vital interests of the Jews: *Timeo Danaos et dona ferentes* (I fear the Greeks, even when bringing gifts).[153] By receiving this present, Judge Halevi concluded, "Kasztner sold his soul to the Devil."[154] In order not to jeopardize the rescue of the "select few," Kasztner and his associates, according to the judgment, gave up all thought of organizing mass resistance or flight and induced the parachutists to give themselves up to the Nazi authorities.

Stunned by the verdict, Kasztner and the Attorney General immediately filed an appeal with the Supreme Court of Israel, requesting the reversal of Judge Halevi's findings. The judgment proved as devastating to Kasztner as it was embarrassing to the government and the *Mapai*. The opposition demanded that Kasztner be prosecuted for collaboration with the Nazis, an offense that was still punishable by death. The government's refusal on the ground that the case was being appealed to the Supreme Court led to its downfall. On June 29, Prime Minister Moshe Sharett's cabinet fell after the General Zionist Party, a coalition partner with four ministers, abstained in a vote of confidence on the government's action in the case.

Because of the historic importance of the case, the Chief Justice designated the five senior justices on the bench to form a panel to study the appeal. The findings of the panel were not revealed until January 1958. In the meantime two countersuits were initiated by the parties. Acting in behalf of Grünwald, Tamir initiated a private criminal complaint against Kasztner, charging that Kasztner had perjured himself in the Jerusalem District Court when he denied having given evidence or having submitted any sworn declaration on Becher's behalf. Kasztner, in turn, initiated a civil libel suit against Grünwald asking for 50,000 Israeli pounds ($28,000) in compensation. On March 15, 1956, Chief Magistrate Moshe Peretz dismissed the perjury charges against Kasztner, accepting his contention that his affidavit in support of Becher had been prepared for a German denazification court. This was the first step toward his eventual rehabilitation. Kasztner, however, did not survive to see his ultimate vindication. He died on March 15, 1957, eleven days after he was shot by an assassin outside his home in Tel Aviv.[155]

The opinions of the five justices on the special Supreme Court panel were read on January 15–17, 1958. The majority opinion was written by Shimon Agranat. It cleared Kasztner of the stigma of "collaboration," rejecting the findings of Judge Halevi. Two justices concurred with Justice Agranat, holding that Kasztner actually had tried to save as many Jews as possible and had risked his own life in so doing. One justice voted with the majority to reverse the lower court's decision but refused to exonerate Kasztner. The fifth one, Justice Moshe Silberg, wrote a dissenting opinion. The panel of justices unanimously upheld the lower court's finding that Kasztner had testified in behalf of Becher.[156]

In his dissenting opinion, Justice Silberg emphasized that the Nazis' ability to carry out the Final Solution program in Hungary as easily and peacefully as they did was "the direct result of the concealment of the horrifying truth from the victims." Referring specifically to the situation in Kolozsvár, Judge Silberg argued:[157]

And the main question is did Kasztner participate in the concealment of this truth? . . . Did he inform while there, any of the leaders of the facts known to him? We have seen earlier that the inmates of this ghetto did not know, boarding the trains, that their last stop was Auschwitz, and therefore one of the two answers is a *must*. Either Kasztner did not disclose to the local leaders the secret of Auschwitz or the leaders did not inform the masses of the secret known to them from Kasztner. A third possibility is nonexistent. . . .

Grünwald was convicted of libel. In view of his advanced age, however, he received only a one-year sentence, which was suspended. This dramatic chapter in Jewish history did not end here; attempts to reopen the case continued for several more years.[158] It caused a political upheaval in Israel, and also led to a debate within the Jewish community about the wartime role of their leaders. It aroused an especially bitter reaction among the leaders of the Hungarian Jewish community in Israel, who feared that their own reputation, like that of Hungarian Jewry's as a whole, was being tarnished. Therefore, the former leaders of Hungarian Jewry and of the Hungarian Zionist Association issued a declaration outlining the achievements of the community before and during the German occupation.[159]

Kasztner's controversial role during the last phase of the war is still debated by historians, theologians, and laymen. To some he is one of the authentic heroes of the war—the savior of thousands of Jews who otherwise would certainly have perished at the hand of the Nazis; to others, especially leftists both in and out of power, he is basically a villain—a collaborator par excellence, who sacrificed the interests of the many to safeguard those of the few. Some, including Hannah Arendt, condemned the attitude of Kasztner and of others like him as "morally disastrous," for by having accepted the categories of "privileged" or "famous" Jews as worthy of "exceptional" treatment, they "implicitly recognized the [Nazis'] rule . . . which spelled death for all non-special cases." The acceptance of special categories, Ms. Arendt argues, must also have induced the Nazis to believe "that by being asked to make exceptions, and by occasionally granting them, and thus earning gratitude, they had convinced their opponents of the lawfulness of what they were doing."[160]

Whatever characterization of Kasztner one wishes to believe—and most appear quite understandably exaggerated—it seems that Kasztner's role cannot possibly be evaluated with any degree of objectivity without assessing the wartime attitudes of both belligerent parties toward the Jews: the Nazis' decision to bring about the Final Solution of the Jewish question and the intensity with which they pursued this goal; the Allies' passivity toward the Jews and their failure to undertake any military measures to frustrate the Nazis' designs (see chapter 31). In this context, Kasztner, like the six million other Jews, was also a victim.

Other Lines of Rescue

Within a week after the departure of the Kasztner group on June 30, Horthy put an end to the further deportation of the Jews. Although Kasztner continued to deal with Becher, rescue via the SS had become largely discredited. The hope associated with the Brand mission and Kenyérmező gave way to apprehension, tempered by Horthy's reemergence on the political scene. The advocates of new rescue approaches became more articulate and persuasive. Some argued for the pursuit of a "Hungarian line," involving the mobilization of leading Hungarian church, political, and governmental figures in the rescue effort; others preferred to involve the International Red Cross and the neutral powers along with the Hungarians; still others suggested an alignment with the emerging resistance forces as the best possible hope. During the six months that preceded the liberation of Budapest—a period almost evenly divided into three months of relative tranquillity and three months of terror—these three proposals became largely intertwined. The most important relief and rescue efforts undertaken during this period were those initiated by Miklós Krausz and Ottó Komoly.

The Rescue Activities of Miklós Krausz. Krausz was the executive secretary of the Budapest branch of the Palestine Office. Complementing the work of the *Vaada*, the Palestine Office was primarily concerned with the practical aspects of emigration to Palestine, including the selection and registration of candidates, the organization of emigrant groups, the distribution of Palestine immigration certificates, the procurement of passports and visas, and the arrangement of transportation. The policies of the office were determined by a commission consisting of 11 representatives of the major Zionist parties[161] while the executive responsibilities were exercised by a three-member presidium. In 1937, the office came under the leadership of Lipót Osztern, who also doubled as the president of the Hungarian Zionist Association. Because of his poor health, the day-to-day operations of the office were gradually taken over by Krausz. After Hungary's entry into the war on the side of the Axis in June 1941, and the subsequent withdrawal of the British diplomatic personnel with whom the office had dealt on matters of immigration, Osztern formally "dissolved" the office and dismissed its employees, including Krausz. Krausz and the presidium, however, refused to acknowledge this action and continued to keep the office in operation. For a while the leadership position was held by Mózes Bisseliches, a former president of the Hungarian Zionist Association, who was appointed to head the office by Osztern. Since the legality of the appointment was in question, Bisseliches refused to play an active leadership role. In the summer of 1943, when Krausz planned to emigrate to Palestine, Brand suggested to Barlas that Komoly and Ernő Marton be entrusted with the leadership.[162] However, Krausz apparently changed his mind and the difficulties continued. New plans for the reorganization of the office and the election of a president were overtaken by the German occupation.[163] During the crucial wartime period, consequently, the office had no appointed leader. Krausz filled the leadership vacuum in his capacity as executive secretary.

According to most contemporaries, Krausz was a rather capable man who established good and useful relations with the Hungarian authorities, including the KEOKH (especially Batizfalvy), and with the British consular officials. After the departure of the British, he developed similar relations with the Swiss, who represented the interests of the Allies in Budapest. A leader of the *Mizrachi,* Krausz did not get along with either the commission and presidium members or the representatives of the *Hehalutz,* many of whom were young Polish and Slovak refugees. The conflict was due not so much to ideological differences, though these were real, as to personality difficulties. Krausz was basically a loner, jealously guarding the secrets of his position. He was eager to monopolize all aspects of the office's work, including the technical matters relating to travel. He tended to exclude his colleagues from decision-making and to keep them in the dark about his dealings with the Hungarian and foreign officials involved in the emigration plans. The problems were compounded during the war, when the office inherited part of the responsibilities of its counterparts in occupied Central Europe and more and more refugees entered Hungary. The competition by the refugees as well as by an increasing number of Hungarian Zionists for the limited number of Palestine immigration certificates became ever fiercer. Krausz's questionable work habits further aggravated the problems.[164]

After the occupation Krausz was entrusted with establishing contact with the neutral powers. Like many other prominent Jews, he was soon arrested by the Gestapo, as was his secretary, Rose Binet. Although they were freed after a short while through the interventions of the *Vaada,* Krausz and his wife decided to seek refuge in the Swiss Legation. As an employee of the legation in charge of emigration matters, Krausz received from the Hungarian authorities the documents exempting him from wearing the yellow star. Taking advantage of his close relations with Consul Charles Lutz, who was primarily concerned with the representation of foreign interests (the representation of Swiss interests was the concern of Maximilian Jäger, the Minister), Krausz initiated two actions that proved highly beneficial to Budapest's Jewry. While at first he was not opposed to Kasztner's negotiations with the SS, by early June he realized that they were not yielding the expected results. On June 8, he so informed the Zionist leaders at a meeting to which he did not invite Kasztner, his rival. Krausz suggested other possible avenues of rescue, based on cooperation with anti-Nazi and anti-Sztójay Hungarian politicians, and with those of the neutral states.[165]

The initiative for Krausz's first positive action came from Switzerland. In response to a contact established through Chaim Pozner and Georges M. Mantello, he forwarded to Switzerland (June 19, 1944) an abridged version of the Auschwitz Protocols together with a report on the operations against the Hungarian Jews up to that date. Although Kasztner and the other *Vaada* leaders in both Budapest and Bratislava had sent similar reports to the *Hehalutz*, AJDC, and World Jewish Congress leaders in Switzerland several months earlier, it was Krausz's report that was publicized in the Swiss press. This was due largely to the efforts of Mantello (see chapter 23). Though Krausz does not explain why he had not used his excellent contacts with the Swiss authorities in Budapest or the *Vaada*'s communication channels to forward for publication similar reports in April and May, he emphasizes with some justification the link between his June 19 report and the actions undertaken by President Roosevelt, the Vatican, and the Swiss and Swedish governments in pressuring Horthy to halt the deportations.[166]

The second major achievement of Krausz is interlinked with the first. As a result of foreign pressures, the Hungarian Council of Ministers decided at its meeting of June 26, 1944, to approve the emigration of around 7,800 Jews. Of these, approximately 7,000 were sponsored by the Swiss, 300 to 400 by the Swedes, and the remainder by the War Refugee Board. The decision was communicated to Veesenmayer by Sztójay the following day. A few days later Horthy decided to halt the deportations. On July 10, Hitler, heeding the advice of Veesenmayer and Ribbentrop, decided to cooperate in the emigration of the 7,800 Jews, provided the Hungarians allowed the speedy resumption of the deportations.[167] Sztójay informed the Council about Hitler's decision on July 12.

Having received the official communication from the Hungarian government, Lutz and Krausz worked out a plan for the registration of 7,000 Jews.[168] Although the agreement called for 7,000 individuals, Krausz and the other Jewish leaders acted in terms of 7,000 family heads, which in effect meant 7,000 families. Following Lutz's advice that the registration take place in a separate place not far from the Swiss Legation, the building at 29 Vadász Street was acquired for this purpose through the cooperation of its owner, Arthúr Weisz, who was also destined to play a leading role in its administration. Because Weisz had previously used it for his wholesale glass business, the building became known as "the Glass House" (*üvegház*). The office was opened on July 24, when the situation in Budapest, though still serious, seemed less critical. It enjoyed exterritorial status and was identified on the outside as: *Svájci Követség Idegenérdekek Képviselete Kivándorlási Osztálya* (Swiss Legation Representation of Foreign Interests. Department of

Emigration). Placed under the overall leadership of Krausz and the immediate administration of Weisz, the Office operated with a staff of a few hundred, mostly young Zionists, who were supplied with Swiss and Hungarian identification papers. As "Swiss employees" they were exempted from wearing the Yellow Star, which gave them many privileges. They could move freely at any time of the day, travel, and even live in "non-Jewish houses."

As the news spread about the new emigration opportunities, thousands of Jews appeared for registration at the Glass House (figs. 29.2–29.3). By the end of the month or early August, a Swiss collective passport including approximately 2,200 names was completed and supplied with a Hungarian exit and a Romanian transit visa. In Krausz's view these people were to be the first batch of the 7,000 families (40,000 Jews) the Germans and Hungarians were willing to let go. He so informed the Jewish leaders in Geneva and Istanbul, who, in turn, began a concentrated drive to induce the British and the Americans to

Figure 29.2.
Thousands of Jews lining up in front of the "Glass House," the annex of the Swiss Legation at 29 Vadász Street, trying to obtain "protective passes."

Figure 29.3.
The lines of Jews in front of the "Glass House" spilled out into the street.

make possible the immigration of these Jews into Palestine. With neither Krausz nor the Jewish leaders of the free world nor the Allies aware of the conditions imposed by Hitler, they became involved in a long and often heated controversy over what came to be known as the "Horthy offer" on the emigration of certain categories of Hungarian Jews.[169]

When the Germans realized that the Hungarians would not permit the resumption of the deportations, they demanded the removal of the Jews of Budapest to camps in the countryside as a precondition to their cooperation in the emigration scheme. Although the plan was seriously considered, it was not carried out. Around this time, Ferenczy and Lullay were trying to convince Krausz, as they had tried to convince Kasztner and others, about their change of heart, and they became quite interested in the emigration program. They even cooperated in setting aside a number of buildings on Pozsonyi Road to house the prospective emigrants in accordance with a memo from Dénes Csopey, the head of the Political Division of the Hungarian Ministry of Foreign Affairs on July 23.[170] This was in fact the origin of the idea of protected buildings housing foreign nationals that eventually constituted the international ghetto during the Szálasi era (chapter 26).

Because of the cover and protection it offered, the Glass House became the center of rescue operations by the *Hehalutz* youth. The young pioneers used the building for a series of illegal activities, including the production and distribution of a variety of forged documents, the rescue of their comrades from internment camps, and the transfer of Jews into Romania, Slovakia, and Yugoslavia. These activities were not condoned by the established leaders of the Glass House and occasionally led to open conflicts with both Krausz and Weisz. These exacerbated the long-standing conflict between Krausz and the *Vaada*, which neither Barlas nor Komoly could bridge in spite of their efforts.[171] The *Hehalutz* continued to use the Glass House as one of their centers for relief and rescue operations, which acquired considerable dimensions during the Szálasi era (see below).

The Rescue Activities of Ottó Komoly. One of the few truly outstanding leaders of Hungarian Jewry, Komoly was born in Budapest in 1892. An engineer of middle-class background, he embraced Zionism under the influence of his father, who had attended the First Zionist Congress in Basel in 1897. A man of irreproachable character, Komoly played a prominent, though unfortunately not a decisively important, role during the catastrophe of Hungarian Jewry. Although he was the President of the Hungarian Zionist Association and of the *Vaada*, he was overshadowed in these organizations by Kasztner. He was practically the only person that all Zionist factional leaders looked upon without rancor or malice. He was a pacifier and unifier by nature, and did everything possible to put an end to the perennial conflicts within and among the various Zionist groups and organizations. As a captain decorated for heroism in World War I, Komoly was exempted from the anti-Jewish laws and retained his freedom of movement. He devoted all his energies to the relief and possible rescue of the beleaguered Jewish community, acting closely with Kasztner.

Komoly played a leading role in the preparation of the Kasztner transport. (It also included his only daughter.) He assumed a more active role after the departure of the transport and the subsequent halting of the deportations by Horthy. By that time the military situation, following the Normandy landings, took a decisive turn in favor of the

Allies and many Hungarians intensified their search for an urgent way out of the war. Among these were not only Horthy and his military and conservative political advisers, but also noted church leaders and rightists, who ceased believing in German invincibility. Their voices began to coalesce with those of the progressive intellectuals and illegal opposition elements, including the representatives of the Smallholder, Social Democratic, and Communist parties. This increasingly discernible reaffirmation of Hungarian national will emboldened some of the Jewish leaders to undertake new rescue attempts, without abandoning Kasztner's dealings with the SS.

The pursuit of the Hungarian line was assumed by Komoly. His background, temperament, and prestige made him the natural and logical choice for dealing with leading Hungarian figures, many of whom were not only anti-Nazi but also anti-German. Some of them, including Miklós Horthy, Jr., Miklós Mester, and Reverend Albert Bereczky, were in fact directly or indirectly associated with the emerging resistance movement (see below). Komoly's position as the leading Zionist spokesman for the surviving Jewish community was buttressed by his association with the International Red Cross (IRC) and later with the reorganized Jewish Council.

Immediately after the occupation, Hungarian officials had refused to deal with the Jewish leaders and referred them to the SS. However, when Horthy halted the deportations many of these same officials became eager to show their anti-Nazi sympathies. Perhaps no other Jewish leader was as keenly aware of these changing attitudes as Komoly. Imrédy, for example, had declined to see him in late March and in May even though some of the country's influential politicians, including Count Ferenc Károlyi, Tibor Koródy, and Mester, interceded in his behalf. After July, however, Komoly was beseeched by several leading rightists and even officials involved in the anti-Jewish measures, including Ferenczy and Lullay, to offer various schemes of rescue; and he had no difficulty in seeing either Rajniss or Baky.

In July and August, Komoly tried his best to prevent the concentration of the Jews of Budapest in camps outside the capital as demanded by the Germans and as suggested by the Hungarian gendarmerie "as a means to protect them." He was afraid that despite the good will of many of the plan's proponents, the Jews, once concentrated, could easily be deported. During these months, he had almost daily contacts with Mester, the Imrédy-oriented rightist Under Secretary in the Ministry of Cults and Public Education who turned anti-German after the occupation; Reverend Bereczky, a courageous minister of the Reformed Church who had some links to the emerging Hungarian resistance;[172] and Koródy, a journalist and Arrow Cross member of the lower house, who, like Mester, turned against the Germans in the summer of 1944. Komoly's dealings with Hungarian political figures involved not only the Jewish question, but also military and political issues, including the possible composition and program of the envisioned post-armistice government.[173]

At this time special measures for the protection of children became an important consideration in view of the lingering threat of deportation, the continuous dwindling of supplies, and the dangers associated with the rapidly approaching front. It was suggested that the children be placed under the protection of the IRC. Friedrich Born, the IRC delegate in Hungary since the middle of May 1944, was approached about this matter early in August. Since under international law the IRC's functions were primarily concerned with POW issues, a legal framework had to be found by which the agency could undertake the tasks suggested by the Jewish leaders. The solution was provided by the Spanish government, which declared its readiness to accept 500 children for resettlement in Tangier. The Swiss government also agreed to permit the entry of 500 children. The IRC was thereupon requested to take these now-"foreign" children under its protection and care for them until their departure. On August 29, Born informed Komoly of his readiness to place at his disposal a room in the IRC office at 4 Mérleg Street for this purpose. Shortly after the offer was renewed on September 7,[174] a special office ("Department A") for the protection of children was opened under the leadership of Komoly. A number of buildings were bought or rented to house the children and store supplies. The buildings and all the employees associated with them enjoyed the protection of the IRC. The financing of Komoly's Department A was the responsibility of the Jewish Council, which relied on AJDC funds.[175]

The value of the children's homes became apparent during the *Nyilas* era, when they emerged as a source of refuge for thousands of children, and adults too. At one time, Department A was in charge of 35 buildings, 550 employees, and 5,000 to 6,000 children. Its facilities were also used by Sholem Offenbach and his colleagues, who were concerned with the welfare of the approximately 1,000 Jewish refugees (700 to 800 Polish, 70 to 80 Yugoslav, and a few hundred Slovak) still in the country, and by Dr. Osterweil, a Polish-Jewish refugee physician who was in charge of approximately 100 orphans, mostly from Poland.[176]

After Komoly was co-opted into the Jewish Council, the work of Department A was greatly expanded and closely coordinated with that of the Council in the administration and supplying of a large number of homes for children and orphans, hospitals, and public kitchens. The expansion of the department's work required its decentralization. The central office, which was under the overall direction of Komoly and staffed primarily by Zionists, had to be shifted to 52 Baross Street. Economic matters, including the supply of the children's homes and later of the ghetto, were handled at 2 Perczel Mór, 3 Békés, and 6 Mérleg Streets. The department was also in charge of the 24 makeshift Jewish hospitals within and outside the ghetto.[177]

At the height of the *Nyilas* terror, many of the buildings protected by the IRC were used by the young *Halutzim*, who enjoyed virtual immunity as employees of Department A, for their underground rescue activities. They also served as places of refuge for many escapees from internment camps and labor service companies.

Following the Soviet encirclement of Budapest, most of the Jewish leaders either went into hiding or moved to safer living quarters. On December 28, Komoly moved to the Ritz Hotel, where Hans Weyermann, the IRC delegate, had his residence, in order to assure constant access at a time when telephone contact was no longer possible and other means of communication and transportation were no longer available. He was not destined to see the liberation that came a little less than three weeks later. On January 1, 1945, he was picked up by three *Nyilas* plainclothes detectives and taken to the *Nyilas* House in Városház Street. In spite of assurances given to Weyermann, he was never seen alive again. His murder by the *Nyilas* marked the end of one of the most illustrious and heroic figures of Hungarian Jewry.

Non-Jewish Rescue Efforts

Except for a few comparatively isolated attempts to save individual Jews from the provincial ghettos, the rescue efforts of Christians were concentrated in Budapest. Among the reasons for this were the speed with which the ghettoization and deportation were carried out in the countryside, coupled with general ignorance about the ultimate fate of the deported Jews, and the fear instilled in both the Jewish and Christian populations of dire consequences for failure to abide by the draconic anti-Jewish laws. These stipulated severe penalties, including internment, for hiding Jews or their property. While there were not many Christian Hungarians who dared hide Jews, a somewhat large number directly or indirectly criticized the actions taken against the Jews. Among the influential Hungarians who expressed their opposition to or intervened on behalf of Jews were such nationally known political figures as Bajcsy-Zsilinszky and Gyula Szekfű, and representatives of the arts and sciences, such as Imre Waldbauer of the Academy of Music.[178]

The institutional approach, though also somewhat limited, was more effective in saving Jewish lives. Among the agencies of the government that contributed toward this end were the Ministry of Defense, which recruited able-bodied Jewish males into the labor service system,[179] and the Cabinet Office of the Regent, which issued exemption certificates to Jews who contributed to the advancement of the arts, the sciences, or the economy (chapter 25).

With the approach of the Soviet forces, the number of those offering assistance to the Jews increased. Among these were policemen and even *Nyilas* leaders who hoped their past deeds would be overlooked. Pál Szalai, the *Nyilas* liaison to the police, for example, emerged as one of the protectors of the Budapest ghetto, a service which was recognized by both the Jewish community and the postwar People's Tribunal.[180]

One of the capital's agencies that not only rescued many Jews from certain death but actually had a considerable number of Jews on its staff was the Volunteer Ambulance Service of Budapest (*Budapesti Önkéntes Mentőegyesület*—BÖME). The ambulance units of BÖME, several of them manned by Jewish physicians and technical personnel, became particularly active during the *Nyilas* era, when they saved many of the Jews gunned down by armed gangs as well as Jews who attempted to commit suicide in the wake of the anti-Jewish measures. Among the officials who distinguished themselves in BÖME's rescue work were Dr. László Bisits, Károly Harkány, and Dr. László Szennik.[181]

In Budapest, hundreds of Jews—especially children—were rescued by courageous members of Christian religious orders: the Jews were hidden, fed, and protected in the convents, monasteries, missions, schools, and institutes of the various denominations. Among these were the Collegium Marianum, the Collegium Theresianum, the Lazarist Fathers (*Lazarista atyák*), the Merciful Sisters (*Irgalmas nővérek*), the Sophianum Institute (*Sophianum intézet*), and the Scottish Mission (*Skót Misszió*).[182] The priests, ministers, and nuns acted in cooperation with many lay Christians who were eager to help the persecuted Jews. Some acted with great bravery, exposing themselves to danger and even deportation. This was the case, for example, with Jane Haining, the Scottish matron of the Girls' Home sponsored by the Scottish Mission. She was arrested on April 25 and following her deportation died in Auschwitz sometime in the summer of 1944.[183]

Unfortunately the heroism of the many men and women involved in individual rescue activities could not compensate for the absence of collective resistance in support of the beleaguered and persecuted Jews.

Resistance

The efficiency and speed with which the Final Solution was carried out in the provinces and the impunity with which the *Nyilas* perpetrated their crimes against the Jews of Budapest were greatly aided by the absence of meaningful resistance on the part of either the Jewish or the Christian population. This was due not so much to a lack of organization—although this too was wanting—as to the neglect of psychological and physical preparedness and the lethargy and general passivity of the population. In a sense the Jews were too well organized, enabling the dejewification authorities to easily identify, separate, and concentrate them.

The non-Jewish Hungarians, whose freedom of action was of course incomparably greater, were generally passive. Although increasingly fewer Hungarians supported the Axis as it became ever more apparent its cause was lost, a formidable segment of the population still clung to Nazism's vicious anti-Semitism in 1944. In contrast, for example, to Poland and Yugoslavia, conditions for the development of a resistance movement in Hungary were unfavorable: the terrain, at least within Trianon Hungary proper, was less conducive to partisan warfare; Hungary was an Axis-allied country, and benefited from that alliance in that some of the "injustices" of Trianon had been redressed; and the democratic and leftist forces were weak, disunited, disorganized, and conflict-ridden. As a result the Germans and their Hungarian underlings had little difficulty in acting as they pleased. No resistance operation was ever undertaken specifically to save Jews. While there were individual acts of heroism by the *Halutzim* toward this end, no collective armed attempt was ever made to free Jews from the ghettos or entrainment centers or to sabotage the loading facilities or rail lines leading to Auschwitz.

Hungarian Resistance. Postwar Hungarian historiography would have us believe that resistance, especially in 1944–45, was both widespread and effective.[184] Without disparaging those brave Hungarians who risked or actually gave their lives in the anti-Fascist struggle, one must conclude on the basis of the available evidence that the Hungarian resistance movement was almost nonexistent, late in formation, and basically ineffective.

The Social Democratic Party, which had operated legally until the German occupation and had its own organ, the *Népszava* (The People's Voice), was as ineffective as the outlawed Communist Party. Its leaders, including Árpád Szakasits, Anna Kéthly, Károly Peyer, Illés Mónus, and Manó Buchinger, were periodically informed by the socialist Zionist leaders about the plight of European Jewry. They even offered concrete suggestions for cooperative efforts for both the wartime and postwar periods. As early as 1941 they submitted to the Social Democrats a "Memorandum on the Jewish Question" in which they made concrete proposals for cooperation and possible joint action in the struggle against Hungarian reaction and anti-Semitism and for the postwar solution of the Jewish question along social-democratic lines.[185]

Before the German occupation, the small group of democratic and leftist leaders sought and received the protection of the Kállay government, though a relatively small number of Communist activists was jailed or placed in internment camps. These leaders tended, however unobtrusively, to support the policies of the government, rationalizing their position by pointing to their limited options and the predicament of the country. Their position was in fact quite sensible; not only were the democratic and leftist forces deplorably weak, but much of the opposition to the Reich (especially on the Jewish question) and to the *Nyilas* came from Kállay and his group, which included Count István Bethlen and Ferenc Keresztes-Fischer, the Minister of the Interior.[186] As a result, the anti-Fascist demonstrations of the leftist forces before the occupation were sporadic, local, and woefully ineffective. On occasion, depending upon the foreign policy interests of the government, they were in fact staged with the consent, if not at the outright request, of Kállay himself.[187]

The Germans were, of course, aware of the impotence of the opposition forces, which emboldened them in their plans to occupy the country. The bombast of the numerous postwar "heroes" and "resistance fighters" notwithstanding, the fact remains that the Germans succeeded in occupying the country without encountering any resistance anywhere. As Gyula Kádár, the former head of the Hungarian Military Intelligence Service, stated "If [Hungary] had as many 'resistance fighters' before March 19, 1944, as it had in May 1945 and later, Hitler would not have risked the occupation of the country, because he would have feared the paralysis in production and deliveries of goods and the necessity to resort to arms.[188]

A more serious though almost equally ineffective drive to organize an anti-Fascist resistance movement was launched after the occupation. In May 1944, a Hungarian Front (*Magyar Front*) was established by the representatives of the then illegal Smallholders', Social-Democratic, and National Peasant[189] parties as well as by delegates representing various anti-Nazi legitimist, conservative, and student groups. The Communist Party, which experienced several organizational changes during the year,[190] was reportedly admitted only after it assured the Front leaders, including Endre Bajcsy-Zsilinszky, that it had no Soviet-appointed delegates and that Moscow did not aim at the Bolshevization of Hungary.[191]

The Hungarian Front, headed by Zoltán Tildy, a Smallholder, adopted an anti-Nazi program based on the principle of national unity. It maintained contact and frequently synchronized its policies with the so-called "extrication bureau" (*Kiugrási iroda*), which was headed by Miklós Horthy, Jr. The bureau, which operated with the tacit consent of the Regent, was the nerve-center of the preparation for Hungary's disentanglement from the war. Closely associated with the bureau were Domokos Szentiványi and Géza Soós, a former confidant of Pál Teleki in the Ministry of Foreign Affairs, who also headed a small group called the Hungarian Independence Movement (*Magyar Függetlenségi Mozgalom*).[192]

The activities of the Hungarian Front were basically inconsequential. It prepared and submitted to the Regent a number of memoranda suggesting specific steps toward the *volte face*.[193] In an attempt to pursue the same objective, the Communist Party leadership established early in September 1944 a Military Committee (*Katonai Bizottság*) under the command of Captain György Pálffy. Its avowed plan was to organize an armed uprising against the Germans, acting in close cooperation with the "progressive political forces" in the country. Nothing of substance came of it.

The same can be said of the military plans worked out by representatives of the amorphous resistance group, including Horthy Jr., Tildy,
Árpád Szakasits and Imre Kovács, in conjunction with General István
Ujszászy, the former head of the Military Intelligence, and Lieutenant-
General Károly Lázár, the Commander of the Regent's Personal
Guard. Lázár, who claimed to have been placed in charge of all troops,
promised to issue arms and munitions sufficient for 15,000 men. He
also discussed with János Beér and György Gergely of the Jewish Council the possibility of arming the 26,000 Jewish labor servicemen stationed in and around Budapest. The plans collapsed in the midst of
crossed signals and blunders befitting a comic opera.[194] The troops that
Lázár was supposed to use "to throw the Germans out of Hungary"
were never assembled, let alone armed, and the Germans continued to
live in Hungary unmolested until they were driven out by the Red
Army. Veesenmayer's postwar remark about the status of the Germans
in Hungary, both before and after the coup of October 15, was quite to
the point: "A day in Yugoslavia," he said, "was more dangerous than a
year in Hungary."[195] The army and the workers, like the population at
large, accepted the *Nyilas* coup with the same tranquillity they had
displayed toward the occupation seven months earlier. As Professor
Macartney observed, the supposedly class-conscious workers in the surviving Csepel factories continued the production of munitions and armaments "almost up to the hour when the Red Army reached their
factories."[196]

Shortly after Horthy's bungled attempt to extricate Hungary from
the Axis, a new organization having the same objective was established.
The initiative came from Endre Bajcsy-Zsilinszky, a Smallholder deputy
who had been in hiding since his release from prison on October 15. It
had both a political and a military arm. Overall political direction was
assumed by the Liberating Committee of the Hungarian National Uprising (*A Magyar Nemzeti Felkelés Felszabadító Bizottsága*); the military arm
was under the command of Lieutenant-General János Kiss and included a number of anti-German officers, including Vilmos Tartsay,
Jenő Nagy, and Kálmán Révay. The plan called for an uprising to be
spearheaded by certain anti-German military units and detachments of
armed workers. The objective was twofold: to help in the liberation of
Budapest and to form the nucleus of a new army fighting the Reich.
Like the György Pálffy plan, this too came to naught. Betrayed by an
agent provocateur, the leaders of the conspiracy were arrested by the
Nyilas on November 23 as they were meeting in Tartsay's apartment for

a strategy session. A *Nyilas* kangaroo court condemned them to death.[197]

The resistance activities of the leftist-progressive forces in Hungary were largely symbolic. They destroyed a statue of Gömbös, engaged in a few skirmishes, sabotaged production in a few plants, managed to fly one of their representatives to the Allies in Italy,[198] participated in the production and distribution of false documents, supported and participated in a few Yugoslav- and Soviet-initiated partisan operations, and distributed some flyers calling on the population to resist the German invaders and their Hungarian friends.[199] However, none was ever directed toward the rescuing of Jews. The attitude of the Peace (Communist) Party and the contents of the flyers distributed by its followers were poignantly summarized by Péter Gosztonyi:

Just as the question of the deportation left the Peace Party totally unmoved, the question simply did not exist in the many Communist flyers distributed in 1944. They called on and encouraged the "Hungarian people" to do many things, but they never said a word about giving refuge to the persecuted Jews or about preventing or delaying the deportation trains by damaging the rail system through sabotage operations.[200]

The same lack of interest in the plight of the Jews characterizes the several underground papers, including the *Szabadságharc* (Liberation Struggle), *Magyar Front* (Hungarian Front), *Szabad Nép* (The Free People), and *Harcoló Bányász* (The Fighting Miner). In the absence of meaningful support from the non-Jewish world, the Jews were compelled to rely upon their own meager and constantly dwindling resources to help themselves.[201]

Jewish Resistance. As in several other countries under Nazi occupation, Jewish resistance in Hungary consisted mostly of individual and collective actions of rescue. In terms of armed rebellion, sabotage, or subversion, the Jewish record of resistance is not fundamentally different from that of the leftist and progressive forces of Hungary. Admittedly, the comparison is a bit unfair to the Jews—while they too were persecuted and many of their leaders were interned, the actual and potential Hungarian anti-Nazi forces never suffered from the extreme oppression under which the Jews had to live. In fact, many of them continued to enjoy freedom of movement with relatively easy access to food and arms practically up to their liberation by the Soviet troops.

Resistance by Hungarian Jews was practically impossible during the German occupation. Herded into ghettos, forced to wear yellow stars, limited in their travel, they were physically and psychologically totally unprepared to fight back. Unaware of the Final Solution, they cherished illusions about their physical safety; the warnings and recommendations of the Polish and Slovak refugees, who knew better, were left unheeded or even ridiculed. The leaders of the Jewish community, confident in the ability of Horthy's government to safeguard the sovereignty of Hungary and to provide protection to the community, failed to take any precautions. After the occupation, mass resistance was all but impossible—especially in the provincial communities.

The quick succession of anti-Jewish measures; the total isolation of the Jewish communities from one another and from the non-Jewish society; the absence of resistance on the part of Hungarian Christians; the passivity, if not hostility, of the Christian masses; the overwhelming power of the Germans (enjoying the wholehearted cooperation of the Hungarian authorities); the almost conspiratorial silence of the free world—these were but a few of the factors that militated against Jewish armed uprising.

To all this one must add the conditions in the ghettos: Isolated and hermetically sealed off within walls, guarded by gendarmes and policemen with guns, automatic weapons, and often attack dogs, the Jews were utterly powerless. In most ghettos, the overwhelming majority of the population consisted of children, women, and the aged, many of whom suffered from various handicaps; most of the men between 20 and 48 were in labor service companies stationed in various parts of Hungary, along the front lines in the Ukraine, or in the copper mines of Bor, Serbia. The ghetto inhabitants were not organized for resistance, and did not have determined leaders able to set it in motion. Even if the conditions had been more auspicious, even if determined and self-sacrificing leadership had been available, the organization of the masses and the acquisition of weapons were made all but impossible by the barbarism with which the Jews were treated and the speed with which the ghettos were established and liquidated. By the time of the deportations the Jews had lost not only the power to resist, but often the will to live as well. Some of the young men and women who might have dared to engage in heroic actions were deterred by the Nazis' barbaric reprisals, usually directed against innocent hostages.

The majority of the Jews, psychologically unprepared and unenlightened about the Final Solution during the pre-occupation era, refused to believe the "horror stories" the young *Halutzim* revealed to them in at least some of the ghettos.[202] As described earlier, they were generally inclined to listen to the soothing advice and reassuring messages coming from the central Jewish leadership. However, a few provincial ghetto leaders took the warning of the *Halutzim* more seriously. But when, as in Munkács and Sátoraljaujhely, they tried to resist entrainment and the SS shot them, the other Jews entered the freight cars in an orderly fashion, surrendering to their fate.

In spite of the tremendous odds they faced, Hungarian Jews did manage some resistance—occasionally successful, at other times tragic. Although some sporadic acts of resistance were undertaken in a number of provincial towns, including Kolozsvár and Nagyvárad, the most daring ones took place in Budapest. Among these the mission of British-Palestinian parachutists of Hungarian-Jewish background, the illegal efforts to enlighten Hungarian public opinion, the attempts to arm the labor servicemen, and the rescue activities of the *Hehalutz* deserve special mention.

The Parachutists. The Jewish Agency offices in Jerusalem and Istanbul considered the possibility of sending a small mission to Hungary as early as January 1944. The mission, it was envisioned, would provide advice about and leadership for the organization of some kind of resistance and self-help in the event of a German occupation, which was presumably anticipated by the Jewish Agency leadership. The British reaction to this and several other related schemes advanced by the Jewish Agency was mixed at best. Many of the leading British officials, including Sir Harold MacMichael, the High Commissioner in Jerusalem, feared the possible postwar consequences for Palestine of the emergence of a corps of trained Jewish guerrillas. The British finally consented to the sending of a handful of Hungarian-speaking Palestinian Jews with the proviso that "they must be used as individuals under SOE [Special Operations Executive] Command, and not in groups under Palestinian Jewish direction."[203] The consent was also based on the expectation that the mission would be of service for the Allied cause as a whole. Specifically, the parachutists were expected to radio back to British headquarters military information that could be helpful in defeating the Nazis. The Budapest *Vaada* was informed about the plans early in 1944, when the Jewish Agency asked Dr. Moshe Schweiger, the local leader of the *Hagana,* the Jewish underground army, about a suitable place for the parachutists to make contact within Hungary. Schweiger identified a trusted Zionist colleague in Ujvidék, a town close to the partisan-held territory in Yugoslavia.

The three officers selected and trained by the British for organizational and intelligence operations in Hungary were volunteers who had emigrated to Palestine in the late 1930s. One of these was Hannah (Anikó) Szenes, formerly of Budapest, a woman of 23 whose passionate Zionism belied her bourgeois, assimilationist background. Her father, Béla, was a relatively well-known author and playwright. A romantic, sensitive soul with great interest in literature and poetry, she was a member of the S'dot Yam *Kibbutz,* near Caesarea.[204] The others were Peretz (Ferenc) Goldstein and Joel (Emil) Nussbecher of Kolozsvár.[205] All three had parents and other close relatives still living in Hungary.

After training in Egypt they were taken to Bari, Italy; from there they were dropped, along with some other agents, over partisan-held territory in Yugoslavia on March 13, 1944. They spent approximately three months among Tito's partisans, awaiting clearance from their British superiors for the crossing into Hungary. Szenes, who was in the company of Reuben Dafni,[206] crossed the border into Hungary on June 9. She was promptly arrested, reportedly after one of the professional smugglers who had helped her over the border betrayed her. A few days later, Nussbecher and Goldstein followed; they managed to get to Budapest, where their traces were picked up by the political police. By that time, Moshe Schweiger, their major contact in Budapest, had already been in the hands of the Gestapo for a long time, and the trusted Zionist of Ujvidék presumably was deported together with the other Jews of that community.

Szenes was imprisoned in Budapest, where the police tried to compel her to cooperate with them by arresting her widowed mother, Katherine (Kató) Szenes. For three months they were held in separate cells in the same prison. Katherine Szenes was freed toward the end of the Lakatos era, but all efforts for Hannah Szenes's release remained unsuccessful.[207] Following the Szálasi coup she was tried by a *Nyilas* court and executed on November 7.[208]

Equipped with false papers, Nussbecher and Goldstein arrived in Budapest around June 20. Under close surveillance by both the German and Hungarian counterintelligence services (they were presumably left unmolested at first in order to discover their contacts) they checked into a modest hotel. One of their first contacts was Kasztner, their former Zionist comrade in Kolozsvár. The following day, they went to the Síp Street headquarters of the Jewish Council, where they noticed that they were being shadowed. Nussbecher hid in a private apartment but was arrested on June 28. The same day, the 19-year-old

Goldstein, after having been hidden for two days, was taken to the Columbus camp for "prominent Jews" where his parents were waiting to board the train to freedom together with the other Jews selected from the Kolozsvár ghetto.

The mission that had been designed, among other things, to organize Hungarian Jewish youth for resistance turned into a nightmare for the parachutists and a source of grave anxiety for the *Vaada* leaders. The latter felt that all their rescue schemes—the Europa Plan, the Strasshof plan, as well as the plan relating to the "prominent Jews"—were being jeopardized by their involuntary implication in an espionage affair. Kasztner and Hansi Brand were once again arrested and pressured to reveal Goldstein's whereabouts. Allegedly once they were allowed to go free "to think the matter over" they reestablished contact with Goldstein; reportedly, after he heard about Nussbecher's arrest and its implication for the *Vaada*'s rescue mission, he decided to give himself up.

The parachutists were interrogated intensively by the Hungarians and the Germans in both Budapest and Pécs. The SS was kept fully informed, as was the German Foreign Office.[209] Apparently the Germans became convinced that Kasztner had not been directly involved in planning the mission, for they continued to deal with him and the *Vaada*.

After the parachutists had spent three months in prison, there seemed to be good prospects that they would be released concurrently with Horthy's extrication of Hungary from the war. But the Szálasi coup put an end to these hopes.[210] About two weeks after Szenes's execution, Goldstein and Nussbecher were entrained along with many other inmates and POWs, allegedly for transfer to Komárom. Nussbecher managed to escape and eventually returned to Budapest, where he survived the war along with other young *Halutzim*. Goldstein was deported and reportedly died in a German concentration camp.[211]

In terms of its original objectives, the mission was unsuccessful. In the sense that it contributed to the anxiety and burdens of the *Vaada* leaders it was perhaps even counterproductive. However, the personal courage of the parachutists and their readiness to sacrifice themselves for the rescuing of Jews undoubtedly had a positive influence on many of the Zionist pioneers and unaffiliated younger Jewish intellectuals who had become disillusioned with the leadership and policies of both the *Vaada* and the Jewish Council.

The Attempt to Enlighten Hungarian Public Opinion. The consequences of the Jewish leaders' failure to give wide publicity to the realities of the

Nazis' Final Solution program were revealed after the German occupation. The leaders' timid formalistic and legalistic posture, their reluctance to violate the censorship laws to the extent that they prohibited the dissemination of news about the destruction in the neighboring countries, their refusal to heed the warnings of the Polish and Slovak refugees, all contributed to the Jewish failure to take meaningful protective and defensive measures. Even after the occupation, when all signs pointed toward the imminent destruction of Hungarian Jewry, the Auschwitz Protocols, which according to some evidence were received weeks before the start of the deportations (see chapter 23), were treated as confidentially as the many other reports about the destruction of the Jews of Europe that had been arriving for several years.

It was only after the completion of the deportations from Carpatho-Ruthenia, northeastern Hungary, and Northern Transylvania, when the dejewification squads were beginning their operations in Hungary proper, that a minor revolt ensued against the Council. Following the suicide of Dr. Imre Varga, a young physician who unsuccessfully attempted to persuade the Council to change its course, a group of intellectuals consisting mostly of middle-echelon officials of the Council decided to prepare an appeal to the Hungarian Christians. The text was shown to Stern, who was willing to cooperate in the distribution if it was approved by the censorship authorities. The other members of the Council followed Stern's leadership. The intellectuals, including Rabbi Fábián Herskovits and Professors Fülöp Grünwald, Jenő Grünwald, and Dénes Láczer, defied the Council leaders and at great risk to themselves mimeographed 2,000 copies of the appeal (see chapter 20). It is not known how many of these copies were actually distributed; many that were supposed to have been taken along by people in the Kasztner group that left Budapest on June 30 were in fact destroyed by Hungarian officers who discovered them. A crude typewritten flyer was prepared early in July, calling upon the Jews of Budapest to resist being taken into the death camps. A similar flyer was addressed to Christian Hungarians, informing them about the deportation of the provincial Jews and imploring them to help prevent the destruction of the Budapest Jewish community.[212] It is not clear from the surviving evidence whether these flyers were actually mimeographed and distributed.

The courage and heroism of the participants notwithstanding, the attempts at enlightening Hungarian and Jewish public opinion proved of no great value. Most of those involved were soon arrested; the bulk of the literature was confiscated.

The Plan to Arm the Labor Servicemen. Toward the end of the Lakatos era, when the leaders of Hungary were planning the country's extrication from the Axis Alliance, some of the Jewish leaders, including some former officials of the Jewish Council, became involved in a more dramatic form of resistance—the arming of the labor servicemen in conjunction with a planned uprising by the anti-Nazi opposition.

The first step toward an involvement of the Jewish labor servicemen in a general armed uprising against the Germans and their Hungarian allies was taken on September 18. On that day, György Gergely, a leading official of the Council who was then associated with the International Red Cross, met Count György Pallavicini, Jr., a Legitimist leader who served on the executive committee of the Hungarian Front. They held an exploratory discussion concerning the possibility of placing the political and physical power represented by the Jewish youth and labor servicemen at the disposal of the Front. Later discussions also involved Otto Draksich (Pallavicini's secretary) and Count József Pálffy. Equipped with the latter's letter of recommendation, Gergely established contact on September 30 with General Károly Lázár, the commander of the Palace Guard, who was slated to become the commander-in-chief of the envisioned resistance forces. Gergely reminded the General that there were approximately 120,000 labor servicemen within the country alone, of whom 26,000 were in or around Budapest. He suggested that the others too be directed toward the capital and armed. Upon Lázár's request, a list of the various labor service companies were prepared.

On October 15, Pallavicini informed Gergely that the moment for action had arrived and that the following morning, on Lázár's instructions, he would identify for him the military barracks that would distribute arms to the labor servicemen. Gergely was also asked to prepare a proclamation to be read to the labor servicemen and to have 20 men available the following morning as couriers to instruct the companies and distribute copies of the proclamation. The proclamation was duly prepared and the couriers assembled in the apartment of Dr. János Beér, but the plans and all the hopes associated with them collapsed when the Regent, to the surprise of the leaders of the Hungarian Front, announced that very day—three days earlier than originally planned—Hungary's decision to sue for an armistice.[213]

Shortly after the coup on October 15–16, some labor servicemen in possession of arms barricaded themselves in two buildings—at 31 Népszinház Street and 4 Teleki Square—and engaged the *Nyilas* in combat. The tragic result was inevitable; with the support of the German forces, the *Nyilas* routed the labor servicemen. They later used this incident of Jewish resistance as an excuse to unleash their terror against the Jews of the capital.

Labor servicemen were involved in other forms of resistance as well. A unit of 25 men from Company No. 101/359, the so-called Clothes-Collecting Company (*Ruhagyüjtő Munkásszázad*), for example, provided special services to the persecuted Jews. Known as Section T of the International Red Cross, this unit, led by Dr. György Wilhelm, the son of Károly Wilhelm, engaged in many heroic rescue operations. The men of this unit, including István Békeffi, István Komlós, István Rádi, and Adorján Stella, rescued Jews from the death marches to Hegyeshalom and supplied the food made available by the International Red Cross to the children's homes and the ghetto. Ironically, they too had to be rescued on November 29, when they were scheduled for entrainment and deportation. This was achieved through the efforts of the rescue group headed by Sándor György Ujváry, a journalist of Jewish background, who was associated with the International Red Cross and the Papal Nuncio.[214] The rescue activities of Section T, like those of the Ujváry group, paralleled those undertaken by the *Halutzim*.

The Rescue Activities of the Hehalutz Youth: In contrast to the positions taken by the Jewish Council (see chapter 14) and the *Vaada,* the members of the young Zionist pioneers (and there were only a few hundred of them) took militant action for the rescuing of Jews. By doing so they were responsible for what were by far the shiniest hours in the tragic wartime history of Hungarian Jewry. They never engaged in open combat and they failed to sabotage any of the many rail lines leading to Auschwitz (they did not have this kind of power), but their heroic rescue operations can clearly be classified as acts of resistance.

The movement was under the leadership of young Zionists belonging primarily to the *Hashomer Hatzair* and *Dror* groups. The dominant role in the movement was played by young Polish and Slovak refugees who came to Hungary during the 1942–44 period. Among these were Zvi Goldfarb of Poland, and Rafi (Friedl) Ben-Shalom and Peretz Revesz of Slovakia.[215] These were soon joined by a number of equally brave young Hungarian *Halutzim*, who distinguished themselves during the underground struggle. Special mention must be made of the heroic activities of David (Gur) Grosz, Sándor (Alexander; Ben Eretz) Groszmann, Yitzhak (Mimish) Horváth, József Mayer, Moshe (Alpan) Pil, Moshe Rosenberg, and Efra (Agmon) Teichmann.[216]

With 500 members in Budapest, the leaders of the *Hehalutz* concentrated their attention on rescuing individuals, mostly their comrades and Zionist sympathizers; they had become convinced that there was no hope for the Jewish masses.[217] The nature and scope of their activities varied with the changing situation. Before the occupation, the *Hehalutz* was primarily engaged in the "legalization" of refugees whom they provided with the necessary (mostly Aryan) identification papers, and the rescue of Jews from Polish, Slovakian, and other camps. In this they worked closely with the *Vaada*, especially its *Tiyul* section.

Cooperation between the *Hehalutz* leaders and the Hungarian Jewish establishment and Zionist leaders was not always easy. The Slovak and Polish *Hehalutz* and refugee leaders were particularly scornful about the official leadership of Hungarian Jewry. In this they shared the views of Gisi Fleischmann, the leader of the Bratislava *Vaada*. Ben-Shalom identified Hungarian Jewry "as a particularly ugly lot" that did not want to know anything about events in the neighboring countries, although he and his fellow refugees were doing everything possible to enlighten them.[218]

The *Hehalutz* youth as a whole did not get along with the Hungarian Zionist establishment either. Ideological differences were compounded by generational conflicts. The older, traditional leaders of the weak Hungarian Zionist movement (the *Vatikim*) resented what they perceived as the intrusion, impatience, and militancy of the younger pioneers. The latter, in turn, became increasingly and ever more vocally scornful of the establishment leaders' complacency and bureaucratic tendencies. While they questioned some aspects of the *Vaada* leadership, their ire was directed especially against Krausz, the *Mizrachi* leader, for his allegedly improper and incompetent administration of the Palestine Office.[219] The dispute erupted into open conflict during the *Nyilas* era (see below).

Just before the occupation, the *Hashomer Hatzair* group decided to have all its members "aryanized" to assure their freedom of movement. While extremely risky, this enabled them to carry out their rescue operations more effectively. Under the leadership of Moshe Rosenberg they also established a *Hagana* Committee (composed of Pil, Menachem (Meno) Klein, Leon Blatt, and Dov Avramcsik) which, however, was short-lived. During the first phase of the occupation, the *Hehalutz* concentrated its attention on the production and distribution of false Aryan identification papers—including even Gestapo, SS, and *Nyilas* membership cards.[220] For reasons of security, the leaders in charge of this aspect of the underground operations, including Dan Zimmermann, Sraga Weil, Grosz, and Teichmann, had to shift their head-quarters at great risk to themselves. They naturally never wore the yellow star, which to their great consternation caused some establishment Jewish leaders to accuse them of trying to extricate themselves from the common lot. (Presumably unaware of the ominous implications of the badge, the latter were urging their fellow Jews to wear the yellow star in proud defiance.)[221]

Another important aspect of the *Hehalutz*'s work during this period was the organization of small groups of young men and women, mostly followers of one or another Zionist organization, for illegal transfer into Romania and Slovakia, where the anti-Jewish drive was at a standstill. A few groups were also directed toward Tito's Yugoslavia; however, after the capture of one of their comrades (Avri Lisszauer), this route was de-emphasized, especially since the *Vaada* leaders protested that its use was a threat to their negotiations with the Germans.[222] Interestingly, while the *Hehalutz* leaders questioned some of the activities of the *Vaada,* they tried to make sure that as many of their own followers as possible were included in the Kasztner group. And in fact on the night of June 30, when the transport left, hundreds of *Halutzim* climbed onto the train without leave.

Much of the illegal work of the *Hehalutz* was directed from the head-quarters of the Jewish Council, where the masses of people seeking help or inclusion in the Kasztner group gave them cover and allowed them to operate unobtrusively. (Some of their comrades, including Jenő Kolb and Yehuda Weisz, who were associated with the Council's Information Section, issued false Council certificates through which a number of Jews were brought to Budapest from the provincial ghettos.) In the relative calm that returned to the Council headquarters following the departure of the Kasztner group and the subsequent halting of the deportations, a conflict erupted between the official leaders and the *Hehalutz.* The latter's operations became more conspic-uous, causing considerable consternation among the establishment leaders. Particularly vitriolic was the reaction of the Jewish Combatant's League (*Zsidó Frontharcos Szövetség*), many of whose members enjoyed exemption from the anti-Jewish laws. The *Hehalutz* leaders, following a heated altercation that even led to violence, moved out of the Council headquarters and conducted their affairs from various public parks.[223]

After the Swiss-sponsored Glass House was established late in July, the *Hehalutz* gradually shifted their headquarters there. The *Hehalutz* leaders became Glass House staff members with considerable privileges, including virtual immunity. They exploited this haven to continue their "illegal" rescue operations—the organization of *Tiyul* groups as well as the production of falsified documents, especially Swiss protective passes. This led to a conflict with the official Zionist leaders of the House, above all Krausz and Arthúr Weisz, the owner and chief administrator of the building.[224] The latter were eager not only to safeguard the emigration scheme for which the Glass House operation was launched in the first place, but also to uphold scrupulously all the conditions under which the Swiss had agreed to cooperate. They were also concerned about their own welfare after *Magyar Szó* (Hungarian World) published an exposé on the Glass House. The dispute became so intense that on September 5, Krausz and Weisz allegedly threatened to call the police to forcibly evict Pil and Teichmann. A similar incident involved Rafi Ben-Shalom on October 15.[225]

Although the relationship between Krausz and the *Hehalutz* leaders remained tense, the latter continued to use the Glass House as the center of their operations. The relationship worsened after the *Nyilas* coup, when the Glass House became the refuge of close to 2,000 Jews.[226] To some extent, this was because the crowds that milled around daily included informers and occasionally even detectives, whose activities contributed to the misunderstanding and tension.

During the *Nyilas* era, the *Hehalutz* stepped up their daring efforts. Some of the young pioneers managed to acquire guns by taking advantage of the chaotic conditions on the day of the coup; others, especially those associated with the *Dror,* led by Goldfarb and other Polish refugees,[227] built bunkers in various parts of the capital. Seven or eight bunkers were built; there is no information as to the number of Jews actually saved in them. The one on Hungaria Boulevard was discovered by the *Nyilas* and in an exchange of fire there were casualties on both sides.

The production and distribution of false papers took on a new dimension. In addition to continuing the forging of Aryan papers, the *Hehalutz* intensified the mass production of protective passes (*Védőlevelek; Schutzpässe*) and related documents issued by the representatives of the Vatican and neutral states; especially valuable were copies of papers issued by the Swiss and Swedish authorities (figs. 29.4–29.11). They also reproduced all the stamps and seals used by these authorities as well as those used by the Hungarians and the Germans. (One of the stamps inadvertently led to the arrest of a number of people because it misspelled the word "Suisse" as "Susse.")

Perhaps the most heroic actions undertaken by the *Hehalutz* involved the rescue of Jews from the hands of the *Nyilas*. Dressed in the uniforms of the *Nyilas, Honvéd,* Levente, KISKA (*Kisegitő Katonai Alakulat;* Auxiliary Military Unit), and even the SS, and in possession of guns and automatic weapons as well as all the appropriate orders and documents, they rescued Jews from the locked Yellow-Star houses, internment camps, and the Óbuda brickyard, and snatched condemned Jews from prisons and even from columns being driven by the *Nyilas* gangs to execution along the banks of the Danube. It was in this manner that Goldfarb and Grosz were themselves rescued after their capture in December.

In cooperation with the International Red Cross (especially Komoly's Department A, with which some of the members were directly associated), the *Halutzim* also undertook to help supply food to the many children's homes, the so-called "protected houses," and the ghetto, and to protect the food stockpiles. One of the largest of these warehouses was in the Swiss building at 17 Wekerle Sándor Street, which was under the command of Sándor Groszmann. The *Halutzim* used the buildings assigned to Department A as additional centers of operation. Many of their activities were helped by the mutually rewarding contacts they established with several Hungarian officials eager to acquire alibis just before the end of the war. Among these were András Szentandrássy, the commander of the camp at the Óbuda brickyard, and Captain Leó L. Lullay, Ferenczy's deputy. Contact with the latter was often maintained through Vera Görög, the daughter of Frigyes Görög, who was then also associated with the International Red Cross.

During the Soviet siege of the capital, *Nyilas* gangs tried a number of times to invade the Glass House in search of food and in pursuit of their murderous aims. Sometimes they were talked into leaving peacefully; at other times, however, they shot into the crowds within the courtyard. In one of these forays they killed four Jews, including the mother of Sándor Scheiber, the postwar head of the National Theological Institute. Among the Vadász Street victims were also Arthúr Weisz, who was taken away on a ruse by First Lieutenant László Fábry and never returned, and Simcha Hunwald (alias János Kühne) who was shot on January 6, 1945.

In pursuit of their objectives, the *Hehalutz* members maintained contact with the small, loosely organized non-Jewish resistance organizations. The *Hehalutz* provided these organizations with whatever identification papers they requested; they in turn provided the *Hehalutz* members

A NEMZETKÖZI
VÖRÖSKERESZT BIZOTTSÁG
VÉDELME ALATT

UNTER DEM SCHUTZE
DES INTERNATIONALEN KOMITEES
VOM ROTEN-KREUZ

SOUS LA PROTECTION
DU COMITÉ INTERNATIONAL
DE LA CROIX-ROUGE

ПОД ПОКРОВИТЕЛЬСТВОМ
МЕЖДУНАРОДНОГО КОМИТЕТА
КРАСНОГО КРЕСТА

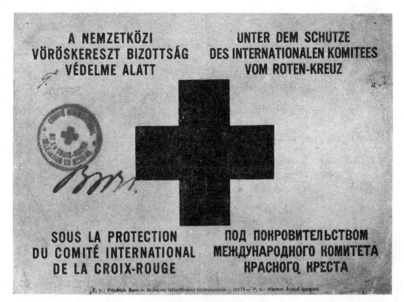

Figure 29.4.
Protective pass issued by the International Red Cross (used in the protection of buildings and institutions).

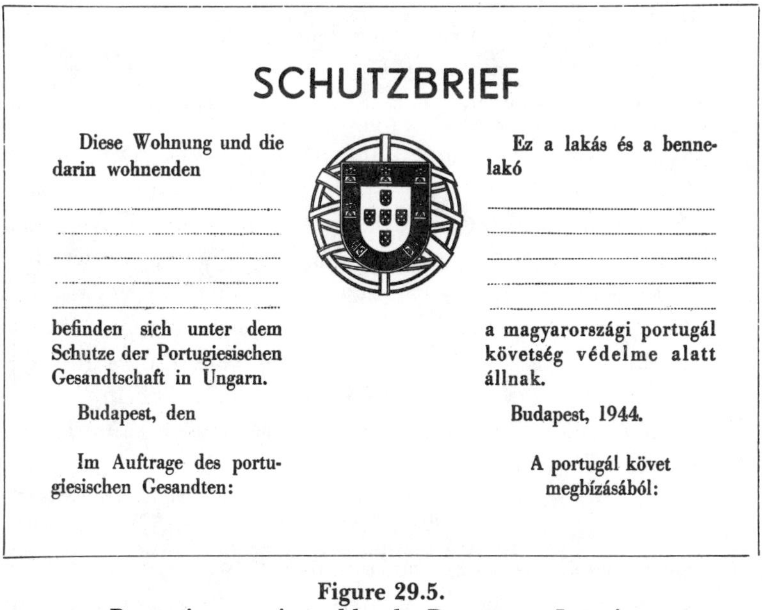

SCHUTZBRIEF

Diese Wohnung und die darin wohnenden

....
....
....
....
....

befinden sich unter dem Schutze der Portugiesischen Gesandtschaft in Ungarn.

Budapest, den

Im Auftrage des portugiesischen Gesandten:

Ez a lakás és a bennelakó

....
....
....
....
....

a magyarországi portugál követség védelme alatt állnak.

Budapest, 1944.

A portugál követ megbízásából:

Figure 29.5.
Protective pass issued by the Portuguese Legation.

LEGAÇÃO DE PORTUGAL NA HUNGRIA
A MAGYARORSZÁGI PORTUGÁL KÖVETSEG
DIE PORTUGIESISCHE GESANDSCHAFT

Ezennel igazolom, hogy

_____ úr
                                                 úrnő
_____ számú érvényes portugál útlevél tulajdonosa. Kérek tehát
minden polgári és katonai hatóságot, vegyék figyelembe, hogy **személye**
és lakása ennek a követségnek a védelme alatt áll.

Ich bestätige hiemit, dass

Herr _____
Frau
Inhaber(in) des gültigen portugiesischen Passes No. _____
Ich bitte alle Zivil- und Militärbehörden vor Augen zu halten, dass seine
                                                                      ihre
Person und Wohnung unter dem Schutze dieser Gesandschaft stehen.

Budapest, 1944 _____

Portugál Követ megbízásából:
Im Auftrage des Portugiesischen Gesandten:

Figure 29.6.
Form issued by the Portuguese Legation certifying that owner is in possession of a Portuguese passport.

PASSEPORT-PROVISOIRE

N°............

Nous, Consul de Portugal à Budapest

SIGNALEMENT:

Taille ....

Cheveux ....

Yeux .... ,. ....

Visage ....

Nez ....

Bouche ....

Barbe ....

Moustache ....

Signes particuliers:

Signature du porteur:

Faisons savoir à tous ceux qui verront le présent passeport

portugais que: ....

... . agé de: ....

de profession. ....

état civil:..

fils
fille de: ....

part de cette ville à destination de: ....

....

....

    Prions en conséquence toutes les autorités civiles et

militaires, auxquelles ce passeport sera présenté, de laisser

librement passer le porteur et de lui donner, en cas de

besoin, tout aide et protection pour son voyage.

    Le présent passeport est valable jusqu ....

....

pour ....

Consulat de Portugal à Budapest,

    le................. .... 19 ....

Le   Consul :

Figure 29.7.
Emergency passport form issued by the Portuguese Legation.

SCHUTZ-PASS

Nr. 0149

Name: **Frau Joseph M o s e r**
Név:

Wohnort: **Budapest**
Lakás:

Geburtsdatum: **24 Mai 1895**
Születési ideje:

Geburtsort: **Gols**
Születési helye:

Körperlänge: **162**
Magasság:

Haarfarbe: **grau**   Augenfarbe: **blau**
Hajszín: Szemszín:

Unterschrift: *Frau*
Aláírás: *Josef Moser*

SCHWEDEN ♛ SVÉDORSZÁG

Die Kgl. Schwedische Gesandtschaft in Budapest bestätigt, dass der Obengenannte im Rahmen der — von dem Kgl. Schwedischen Aussenministerium autorisierten — Repatriierung nach Schweden reisen wird. Der Betreffende ist auch in einen Kollektivpass eingetragen.

Bis Abreise steht der Obengenannte und seine Wohnung unter dem Schutz der Kgl. Schwedischen Gesandtschaft in Budapest.

Gültigkeit erlischt 14 Tage nach Einreise nach Schweden.

A budapesti Svéd Kir. Követség igazolja, hogy fentnevezett – a Svéd Kir. Külügyminisztérium által jóváhagyott — repatriálás keretében Svédországba utazik.

Nevezett a kollektív útlevélben is szerepel.

Elutazásáig fentnevezett és lakása a budapesti Svéd Kir. Követség oltalma alatt áll.

Érvényét veszti a Svédországba való megérkezéstől számított tizennegyedik napon.

Reiseberechtigung nur gemeinsam mit dem Kollektivpass. Einreisewisum wird nur in dem Kollektivpass eingetragen.

Budapest, den **17 August** 1944

KÖNIGLICH SCHWEDISCHE GESANDTSCHAFT

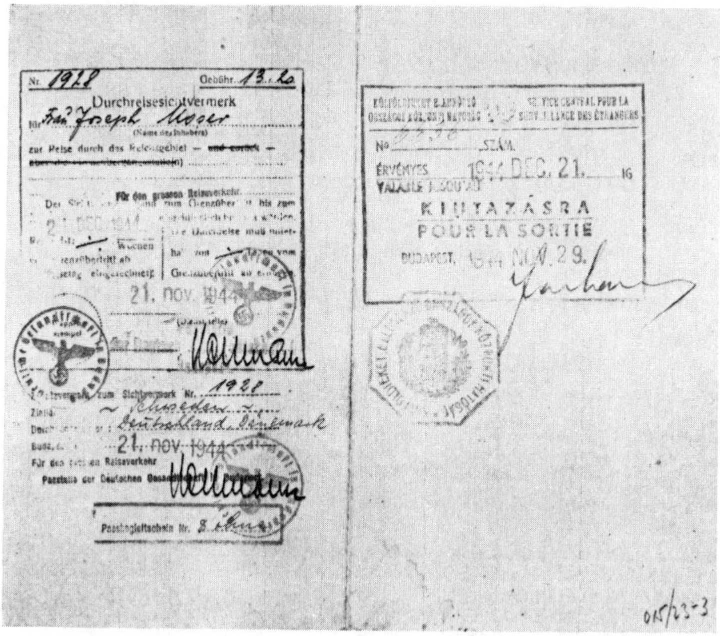
Nr. 1928 Gebühr 13.20
Durchreisesichtvermerk
für den grossen Reiseverkehr
21. nov. 1944
Für den kleinen Reiseverkehr
Passtelle der Deutschen Gesandtschaft
Passbegleitschein Nr.
No. SZÁM.
ÉRVÉNYES 1944 DEC. 21.
KIUTAZÁSRA
POUR LA SORTIE
BUDAPEST, 1944 NOV. 29.
015/23-3

Figure 29.8.
Protective pass issued by the Swedish Legation.

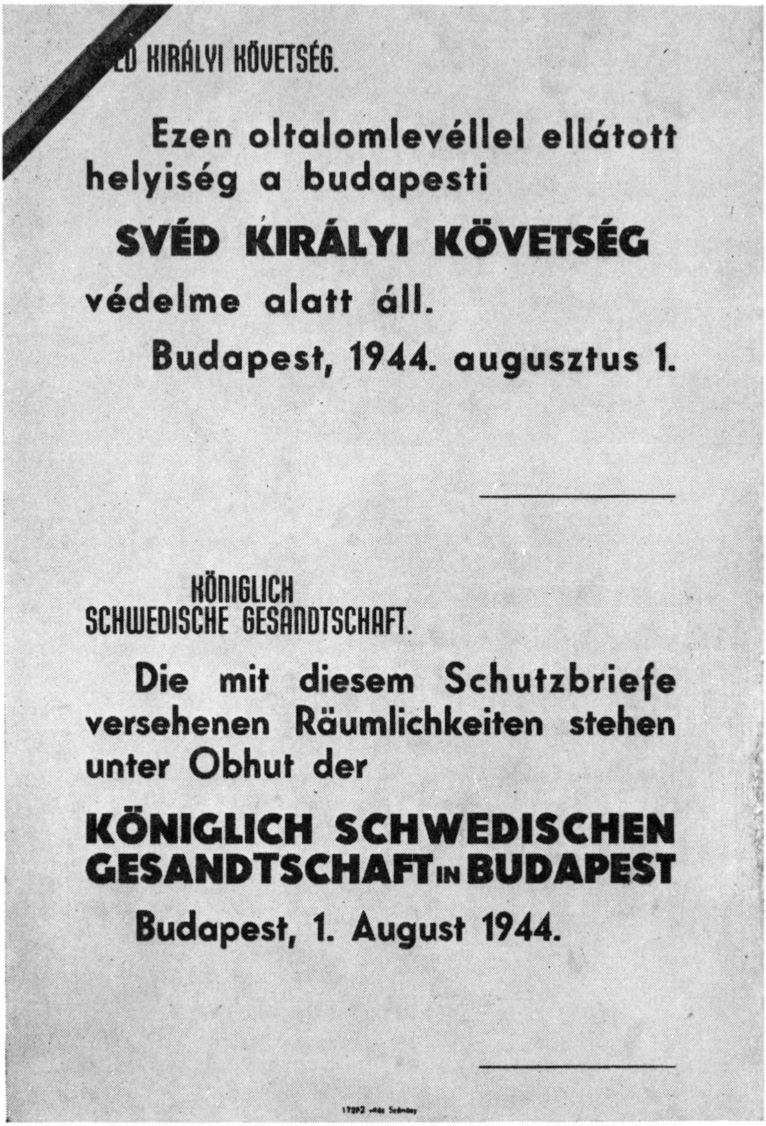

ED KIRÁLYI KÖVETSÉG.

Ezen oltalomlevéllel ellátott helyiség a budapesti

SVÉD KIRÁLYI KÖVETSÉG

védelme alatt áll.

Budapest, 1944. augusztus 1.

KÖNIGLICH
SCHWEDISCHE GESANDTSCHAFT.

Die mit diesem Schutzbriefe versehenen Räumlichkeiten stehen unter Obhut der

KÖNIGLICH SCHWEDISCHEN GESANDTSCHAFT in BUDAPEST

Budapest, 1. August 1944.

Figure 29.9.
Protective pass issued by the Swedish Legation.

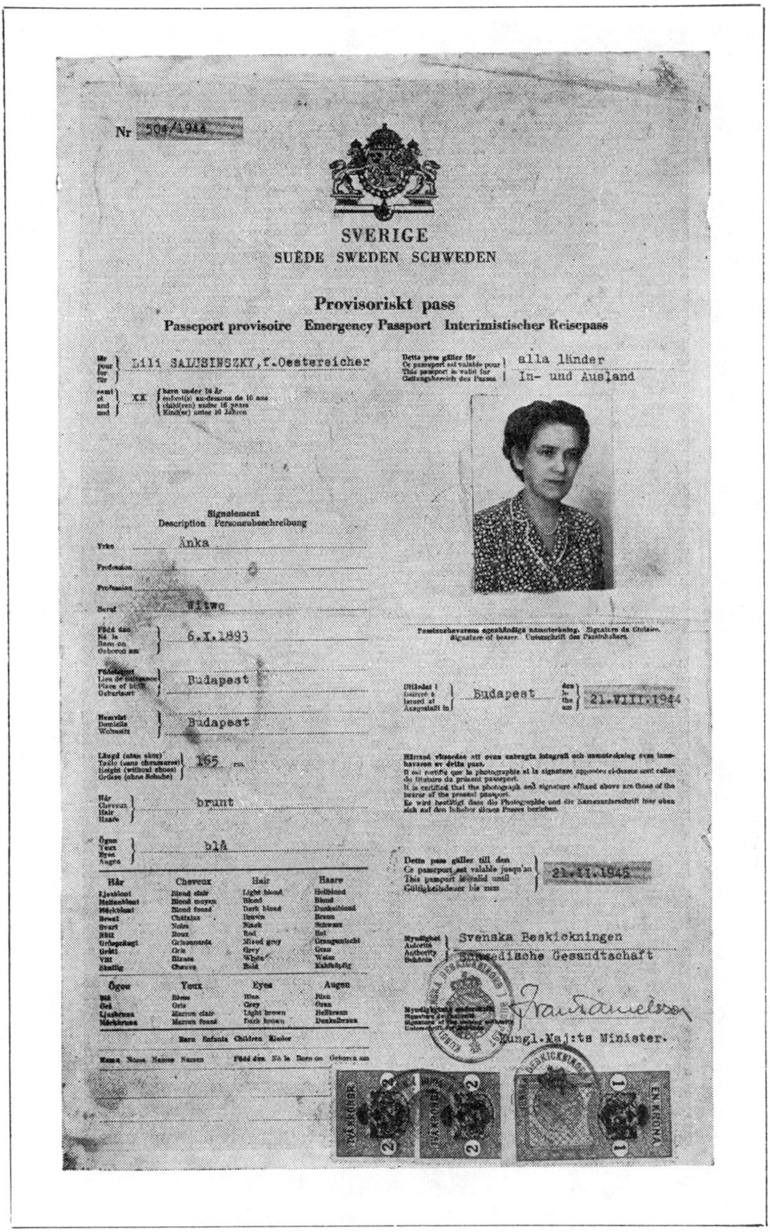

Nr 504/1944

SVERIGE
SUÈDE SWEDEN SCHWEDEN

Provisoriskt pass
Passeport provisoire Emergency Passport Interimistischer Reisepass

För / Pour / For / Für: Lili SALUSINSZKY, f. Oestersicher

Dette pass gäller för / Ce passeport est valable pour / This passport is valid for / Geltungsbereich des Passes: alla länder / In- und Ausland

samt / et / and / und: XX barn under 16 år / enfant(s) au-dessous de 16 ans / child(ren) under 16 years / Kind(er) unter 16 Jahren

Signalement
Description Personenbeschreibung

Yrke / Profession / Profession / Beruf: Änka / Witwe

Född den / Né le / Born on / Geboren am: 6.X.1893

Födelseort / Lieu de naissance / Place of birth / Geburtsort: Budapest

Hemvist / Domicile / Domicile / Wohnsitz: Budapest

Längd (utan skor) / Taille (sans chaussures) / Height (without shoes) / Grösse (ohne Schuhe): 165 cm.

Hår / Cheveux / Hair / Haare: brunt

Ögon / Yeux / Eyes / Augen: blå

Passinnehavarens egenhändiga namnteckning. Signature du titulaire. Signature of bearer. Unterschrift des Passinhabers.

Utfärdat i / Délivré à / Issued at / Ausgestellt in: Budapest den / le / the / am 21.VIII.1944

Härmed vitsordas att ovan anbragta fotografi och namnteckning avse innehavaren av detta pass.
Il est certifié que la photographie et la signature apposées ci-dessus sont celles du titulaire du présent passeport.
It is certified that the photograph and signature affixed above are those of the bearer of the present passport.
Es wird bestätigt dass die Photographie und die Namensunterschrift hier oben sich auf den Inhaber dieses Passes beziehen.

Detta pass gäller till den / Ce passeport est valable jusqu'au / This passport is valid until / Gültigkeitsdauer bis zum: 21.II.1945

Myndighet / Autorité / Authority / Behörde: Svenska Beskickningen / Schwedische Gesandtschaft

Kungl. Maj:ts Minister.

Figure 29.10.
Swedish emergency passport.

SVÁJCI KÖVETSÉG
IDEGEN ÉRDEKEK KÉPVISELETE

KIVÁNDORLÁSI OSZTÁLY
V., VADÁSZ-UTCA 29.

SCHWEIZERISCHE GESANDTSCHAFT
ABTEILUNG FÜR FREMDE INTERESSEN

ABTEILUNG AUSWANDERUNG
V., VADÁSZ-UTCA 29.

Die Schweizerische Gesandtschaft, Abteilung fremde Interessen, bescheinigt hiermit,
dass

im schweizerischen Kollektivpass zur Auswanderung eingetragen ist, daher ist der (die)
Betreffende als Besitzer eines
gültigen Reisepasses zu be-
trachten.

Budapest, 25. Oktober 1944.

A Svájci Követség, Idegen
Érdekek Képviselete, ezennel
igazolja, hogy

a svájci csoportos (collectiv)
utlevélben szerepel és ezért
nevezett érvényes utlevél bir-
tokában levő személynek tekin-
tendő.

Budapest, 1944. október 25.

Figure 29.11.
Collective passport certificate issued by the Swiss Legation.

with arms and occasional shelter. Among the units with which the *Hehalutz* cooperated was a POW group headed by a Dutch officer named Van der Walles (or Van-der-Vas) which consisted primarily of Dutch and British officers who had escaped from German camps. (It was through this group that the *Hehalutz* rescued Joel Nussbecher.) It also maintained contact with a Communist underground group headed by Pál Demény, and anti-German military and bourgeois groups represented by First Lieutenant Iván Kádár and Pál Fábry, respectively.[228] Unfortunately the non-Jewish resistance organizations were not very effective; this was a major factor limiting the scope and character of the *Hehalutz* operations. Another negative factor was the passivity of the general population, which in turn was influenced by the attitude of the Christian churches.[229]

Notes

1. Demands for the removal of the Jews from Hungary were made, for example, by Mátyás Matolcsy and Tamás Matolcsy, anti-Semitic brothers, in the House of Representatives of the Hungarian Parliament on November 26, 1940. *Képviselőházi Napló* (Records of the House of Representatives), Budapest, 8, session 160, p. 851; as cited in *FAA*, 1:xxxvii.

2. Some of these resignations were reported by Lieutenant-Colonel László Ferenczy, who was in charge of the deportations. See Jenő Lévai, *Szürke könyv magyar zsidók megmentéséről* (Gray Book on the Rescuing of Hungarian Jews) (Budapest: Officina, n.d.), pp. 101–6.

3. See, for example, *RAH*, pp. 465–590, 617–25. See also Frederick B. Chary, *The Bulgarian Jews and the Final Solution, 1940–1944* (Pittsburgh: University of Pittsburgh Press, 1972), 246 pp. On Romania, see chapter 28.

4. A small number of Jews were hidden in the countryside, especially in areas with Romanian or Serbian population, and a comparatively larger number of Jews were hidden in Budapest. Among those most actively involved in the rescue were the courageous nuns and priests of various convents, monasteries, and other religious institutions and charity organizations.

5. As of October 15, 1978, the Yad Vashem of Jerusalem has recognized 27 Hungarians as "Righteous Gentiles," awarding them various honors.

6. György Ránki, *1944. március 19* (March 19, 1944) 2nd ed. (Budapest: Kossuth, 1978), p. 244. A large number of the denunciations may be found in the *Országos Levéltár* (National Archives), Budapest, under no. P1434, László Endre Files 16–18. See also Lévai, "A magyar zsidóság tragédiája" (The Tragedy of Hungarian Jewry) in *Uj Élet* (New Life), Budapest, May 1, 1979.

7. Lévai, *Zsidósors Magyarországon*, p. 84.

8. *RLB*, Doc. 160.

9. Statement by Samu Stern in *HJS*, 3:12.

10. Philip Freudiger, *Five Months*. Manuscript dated November 21, 1972, p. 15.

11. *RLB*, Doc. 251.

12. *Magyarság* (Magyardom), Budapest, April 1, 1944.

13. *Uj Magyarság* (New Magyardom), Budapest, May 15, 1944.

14. Ránki, *1944, március 19,* 2nd ed., p. 244. For incidents of this kind, see also *Tribunalul Poporului, Cluj,* pp. 47–50, 58–65, 81–88, 115–16.

15. One of the statesmen who condemned the measures adopted against the Jews was Count Mihály Károlyi, who was then in exile in Britain. *NA,* Microcopy T-120, Roll 4664/2, Serial K1509/K350854–.

16. Eugene (Jenő) Lévai, *Black Book on the Martyrdom of Hungarian Jewry* (Zurich: The Central European Times, 1948), p. 139.

17. *Die Hauptverhandlung gegen das "Deportationstrio" Endre–Jaross–Baky vor dem ungarischen Volksgerichtshof* (The Main Trial of the Endre–Jaross–Baky "Deportation Trio" Before the Hungarian People's Court). YIVO Institute for Jewish Research, New York, Archives File no. 778, pp. 157–58. See also Elek Karsai, *Itél a nép* (The People Judge) (Budapest: Kossuth, 1977), pp. 209–10.

18. *Die Hauptverhandlung gegen das "Deportationstrio" Endre–Jaross–Baky,* pp. 141–42. See also Karsai, *Itél a nép,* p. 210., Lévai, *Zsidósors Magyarországon,* p. 101, and *Tribunalul Poporului, Cluj,* p. 19.

19. In his report of July 19, 1944, the Higher SS and Police Leader claimed that 15 Jews had been discovered in the ghetto of Nagyvárad and 11 Jews in the ghetto of Munkács. In Kassa, 30 to 40 Jews were apprehended almost two months after the first deportation train left the city. *RLB,* Doc. 289.

20. *NA,* Microcopy T-120, Roll 4665/4, Serial K1509/K350109–.

21. This was the case, for example, of the nine-member family of Rabbi Joseph Paneth of Nagyilonda, which escaped from the ghetto of Dés. Arnold David Finkelstein, *Fénysugár a borzalmak éjszakájában* (A Ray of Light in the Night of Horrors) (Tel Aviv: P. Solar and J. Nadiv, 1958), pp. 302–23. The Rabbi's family's escape is also described, together with other incidents of escape, rescue, and heroism in *"Volt egyszer egy Dés . . ."* (There Was Once Upon a Time a Dés . . .), ed. Zoltán Singer (Tel Aviv: A Dés és Vidékéről Elszármazottak Landsmannschaftja, n.d.), pp. 438–46.

22. Among these were the families of Albert Hirsch, Frigyes Ribáry, Henrik Hercz, Helmuth Bittner, and Ármin Erdős. Lévai, *Zsidósors Magyarországon,* p. 248.

23. We deal here only with the activities of the Jewish Council of Budapest. While the Jewish Councils of the various provincial communities did their best to alleviate the suffering of the Jews by negotiating with the local SS or Hungarian police officers, they were in existence for only a short while.

24. Freudiger, *Five Months,* p. 21.

25. Among the MIPI officials who distinguished themselves in this work were György Polgár, József Pásztor, István Földes, Imre Reiner, Lajos Klein, Nándor Eichel, Miklós Gál, and Sándor Bródy. Lévai, *Szürke könyv,* pp. 185–86.

26. *Ibid.,* pp. 206–9. See also chapter 26.

27. See chapter 14 and Lévai, *Zsidósors Magyarországon,* pp. 87–88.

28. Copies of these reports may be found in the archives of Yad Vashem, Jerusalem; Beth Lohamei Hagetaot; Moreshet; and the Central Zionist Archives, Jerusalem.

29. *Der Kastner-Bericht,* p. 53.

30. Note from Budapest *Vaada* to the Istanbul *Vaada,* dated January 20, 1944. The Central Zionist Archives, Jerusalem, S26/1190. By the end of the month, Weiss, Lichtenberg, Baumer, and Springmann had left Budapest for Istanbul en route to Palestine.

31. Technically, the Istanbul *Vaada* was a "delegation" of the Jewish Agency composed of various Zionist party representatives. For further details, see chapter 3.

32. The conflict within the Budapest *Vaada* was also recognized by Komoly. See his August 25, 1943, letter to Chaim Barlas in which he emphasized the differences of opinion between Brand and Baumer and their followers. The Central Zionist Archives, Jerusalem, S26/1190 a/b. The Istanbul *Vaada* was particularly caustic about the Budapest *Vaada*'s performance in the months before the occupation, especially in the field of res-

cue. See, for example, the exchange of correspondence in the archives of Beth Lohamei Hagetaot, Hungaria files, vols. 2 and 3.

33. *Der Kastner-Bericht,* p. 65.

34. Alex Weissberg, *Advocate for the Dead. The Story of Joel Brand* (London: Andre Deutsch, 1958), p. 27.

35. André Biss, *A Million Jews to Save* (London: Hutchinson, 1973), p. 35.

36. *RAH,* p. 7.

37. Freudiger, *Five Months,* pp. 2–5.

38. NG-4407 and NG-4553. See also *RAH,* p. 6.

39. Although Wisliceny asked to see Freudiger, Niszon Kahan, and Baroness Edith Weiss (the representatives of the Orthodox, Zionist, and Neolog factions of Hungarian Jewry), as recommended by Weissmandel, only Freudiger read the letter. The Baroness was already in hiding and Kahan, who accompanied Freudiger, was not invited in by Wisliceny. The letter was destroyed after Freudiger finished reading it. Freudiger, *Five months,* pp. 6–7.

40. See, for example, his letter addressed late in May 1944 to the *Hehalutz* center in Geneva in Livia Rothkirchen, *The Destruction of Slovak Jewry* (Jerusalem: Yad Vashem, 1961), pp. 237–42, and his July 16, 1944 letter in German translation in Yad Vashem, Jerusalem, Archives File M-20/47. See also his *Min Hametzar* (Out of the Depth). (New York: Amuna, 1960), 252 pp.

41. *Der Kastner-Bericht,* pp. 72–73. Brand, whose acccount is highly romanticized and full of gross inaccuracies, offers a completely different version of this first encounter with Wisliceny, asserting that Wisliceny guaranteed that there would be no deportations from Hungary, inasmuch as the Germans were the masters of Europe and the Hungarians could not initiate deportations without them. Weissberg, *Advocate for the Dead,* pp. 72 ff. This version of Brand is also at odds with the report Brand wrote for the *Vaada* leaders in Istanbul, detailing the background of his and Kasztner's dealings with the Germans until his departure. This report is available at Moreshet. Beit Edut al shem Mordchay Anielevicz, no D.1.721. The report bears no date or address and therefore it is difficult to determine whether Brand wrote it just before his departure or after his arrival in Istanbul.

42. The record is not clear about the participants at the various meetings with the SS and *Sonderkommando* leaders. In their memoirs, Kasztner, Brand, and the other Zionist figures all attempt to portray their own role as the most important one, while denigrating or ignoring those played by others.

43. At first Krausz had contacted Jean de Bavier, the representative of the International Red Cross, at whose urging the Sztójay government approved the emigration, and requested the Germans to grant the necessary exit permit. Lévai, *Zsidósors Magyarországon,* pp. 94–95.

44. Brand claims that the governing body of the Palestine Office was composed of himself, Komoly, Szilágyi, and Mihály Salamon. Weissberg, *Advocate for the Dead,* p. 46.

45. For Brand's account of the Kasztner-Krausz dispute, see *ibid.,* pp. 48–50. For an evaluation of Krausz's position see below.

46. For example, Kasztner claims that Eichmann saw Brand on May 8, and that the one million Jews were to have been Hungarian Jews. Cf. *Der Kastner-Bericht,* pp. 86–89, and Weissberg, *Advocate for the Dead,* pp. 83–89.

47. Details revealed by Grosz during his interrogation by N. J. Strachan, the British Intelligence officer, in the summer of 1944. Public Record Office, London. Fo.371/42810, S.I.M.E. Report no. 2, dated June 23, 1944. For an analysis of Grosz' role based on this document, see Béla Vágó, "The Intelligence Aspects of the Joel Brand Mission," in *YVS,* 10:111–28.

48. Minutes of Grosz's interrogation by Lieutenant N. J. Strachan, Cairo, June 24, 1944. S.I.M.E. Report no. 1. *PRO*, Fo.371/42810, pp. 79–81.

49. Grosz informed Brand about the substance of his own mission only after their arrival in Istanbul. Weissberg, *Advocate for the Dead*, pp. 126–27.

50. Biss claims that after several discussions with Klages, he became convinced that Himmler had attempted to "get guarantees covering him and his past deeds from Washington." See his *A Million Jews to Save*, p. 71.

51. Natan Eck, *Shoat haam ha'yehudi b'Europa* (The Holocaust of the Jewish People in Europe) (Jerusalem: Yad Vashem, 1977), pp. 313–14.

52. *RLB*, Doc. 291.

53. S.I.M.E. Report no. 2, p. 7.

54. Biss, *A Million Jews to Save*, p. 73.

55. *Ibid.*, p. 45.

56. Weissberg, *Advocate for the Dead*, p. 114.

57. Citing Klages, Biss claims that Kasztner's arrest was suggested by Brand, because Kasztner "had made no attempt to hide the serious objections to the despatch of Brand and Grosz on this mission." He further claims that "Brand and Grosz had gone so far as to reveal that Kasztner was in touch with the counterespionage services of the Hungarian army under General Ujszászy, and that since he knew Lieutenant-Colonel Garzoly well, Kasztner had no doubt informed him about the 'State Secret.'" Biss, *A Million Jews to Save*, pp. 46, 71, 122.

58. Kasztner claims that in proceeding against the *Abwehr* agents, the SS had requested the cooperation of the *Vaada* and that with the exception of Brand the *Vaada* leaders rejected the request. *Der Kastner-Bericht*, p. 87.

59. *Ibid.*, p. 93.

60. Moreshet, Archives Doc. D.1.718.

61. *Ibid.*

62. For text, see Weissberg, *Advocate for the Dead*, pp. 106–7. Grosz claimed that the letter was written on Krumey's orders. S.I.M.E. Report no. 1. *PRO*, Fo.371/42810, pp. 79–81.

63. For details on the background and affiliation of the various representatives attached to the Istanbul *Vaada*, see Dalia Ofer, "The Activities of the Jewish Agency Delegation in Istanbul in 1943," in *RAH*, pp. 435–50. See also chapter 3.

64. The map of Auschwitz and the demands to bomb the death camp and the railroads leading there were originally in the Auschwitz Protocols the Budapest *Vaada* leaders received late in April 1944.

65. Weissberg, *Advocate for the Dead*, pp. 119–20, 122.

66. The State Department was kept abreast of the Brand case by the British Foreign Office as well. Secretary of State Hull, in turn, forwarded these communications, along with the American position, to Steinhardt.

67. "Strictly Confidential" report prepared for Ambassador Steinhardt on June 4, 1944. Moreshet Archives D.1.721.

68. *PRO*, Fo.371/42813-819, p. 1399.

69. For text of the protocol, see Beth Lohamei Hagetaot, Archives, Hungaria-Slovakia, 2, Doc. U278. For a somewhat abbreviated English version of the text, see Weissberg, *Advocate for the Dead*, pp. 131–32.

70. See letter of the Istanbul *Vaada*, dated July 5, 1944, addressed to the Budapest *Vaada* at Moreshet, Archives Doc. D.1.748. It was received in Budapest on July 7, the day Horthy stopped the deportations. *Der Kastner-Bericht*, p. 148.

71. Beit Lohamei Hagetaot, Archives, Hungaria-Slovakia, 2, Doc. U275.

72. Shortly after he arrived in Istanbul, Grosz had begged the British authorities to admit him to the Middle East "since he feared the consequences of return to enemy terri-

tory." Because of his shady past, the British, after arresting him in Aleppo, decided to hold him in custody until the end of the war. *PRO*, Fo.371/42807-812, pp. 79, 81.

73. Preliminary report by Shertok dated June 27, 1944. Weizmann Archives, Rechovot, Israel.

74. *Ibid.*

75. Moreshet, Archives, Doc. D.1.713. These desperate pleas from Budapest were relayed to Jerusalem and from there by Shertok to Weizmann via the Foreign Office. He considered Brand's return as "imperative" and demanded that the Germans be urged to discontinue the slaughter of the Jews pending a meeting. See Randall's letter to Weizmann dated June 23. Weizmann Archives.

76. Moreshet, Archives, Doc. D.1.713.

77. For an evaluation of the attitude of the leaders and officials of the Grand Alliance toward Brand's mission, see chapter 31. For additional information on the Brand case, see Gustav Warburg, "Rescuing Hungarian Jews," in *The Jewish Monthly*, London, 1 (October 1947):26–37; "The Strange Case of Joel Brand," in *Jewish Observer and Middle East Review*, London, 3, (1954): April 9, pp. 3–4; June 11, pp. 5–6; June 18, pp. 11–13; June 25, pp. 11–13; July 2, p. 7; July 9, p. 5; August 20, p. 5; Leon Poliakov, "Juifs contre camions: l'histoire de Joel Brand" (Jews for Trucks: The Story of Joel Brand), in *Le Monde Juif* (The Jewish World), Paris, 11, no. 11 (October 1957):3–7.

78. While in Tel Aviv he wrote a 46-page report about the situation of the Jews of Hungary (*Memorandum über die jetztige Lage der Juden Ungarns . . .*) which apparently served as a basis for Weissberg's *Advocate for the Dead*. For copy of the memorandum, dated January 25, 1945, see The Central Zionist Archives, Jerusalem, S26/1190 a/b.

79. Weissberg, *Advocate for the Dead*, pp. 176–85.

80. In May 1964, while he was in Frankfurt, West Germany, testifying in the trial of Hermann Krumey and Otto Hunsche, Eichmann's former closest collaborators, Brand confessed that he made a "terrible mistake" in passing the Eichmann offer to the British. It became clear to him, he emphasized, that "Himmler sought to sow suspicion among the Allies as a preparation for his much-desired Nazi-Western coalition against Moscow." *The New York Times*, May 21, 1964.

81. Weissberg, *Advocate for the Dead*, p. 15.

82. *Ibid.*. pp. 178–79.

83. *The New York Times*, May 20, 1944.

84. Some of his telegrams to this effect may be found in the Weizmann Archives and in the *PRO*. See, for example, Fo.371/42807, p. 75.

85. Request transmitted to Rabbi Wise via Pinkerton on June 29, 1944.

86. See copies of his telegrams to these leaders, dated October 17, 1944, at the Central Zionist Archives, Jerusalem, S26/1190a/b.

87. See, for example, Aryeh Morgenstern, "Va'ad hatzala ha'meuchad shelid ha'Sochnut ha'yehudit upheulotov beshanim 1943–1945" (The United Rescue Committee of the Jewish Agency and Its Activities During 1943–1945). *Yalkut Moreshet*, Israel, no. 13, 1971, pp. 60–103. On Hungary, see especially pp. 84–92. See also Shabetai B. Beit-Zvi, *Ha'tsiyonut hapost Ugandit ba'mishvar ha'shoa* (Post-Ugandian Zionism in the Crucible of the Holocaust) (Tel Aviv: Bronfman, 1977), 495 pp.

88. Endre later disclaimed any knowledge of the Kasztner or Brand affairs. Baky stated that he had some knowledge about them and that he had ordered Hain to release Kasztner and his friends on the request of Hans Geschke, the head of the SD in Hungary. Sworn statements by Endre and Baky before Dr. Endre Pollák, the prosecutor in the Transylvanian war crimes trial cases, on December 17 and 18, 1945. Both original statements are in possession of this author.

89. *Der Kastner-Bericht*, p. 105.

90. In his confidential report from Geneva dated February 10, 1946, Zoltán Glatz

claims that the transport in Kolozsvár was put together with the cooperation of József Fischer (Kasztner's father-in-law), Hillel Danzig, Lajos Marton, Jenő Kertész, and Sándor Weiss. Citing examples of nepotism, Glatz claims that the transport included 32 members of the Fischer family, approximately 20 members of Zsigmond Léb's family, and approximately 14 members of Endre Balázs's family. Yad Vashem Archives M-20/95. For the names of those who eventually left for Budapest and from there to Bergen-Belsen, see the lists at Yad Vashem, Archives M-20/59 and M-20/68.

91. See Kaltenbrunner's letter of June 30, 1944, responding to the June 7 request by SS-*Brigadeführer* Blaschke, the Mayor of Vienna, concerning the "assignment of labor to essential war work in the city of Vienna." *RLB*, Doc. 184 (3803-PS). At Nuremberg, Kaltenbrunner tried to deny that he wrote this letter to Blaschke. *IMT*, 11:344–46.

92. Without identifying the source of his data, Lévai lists the various items handed over to the SS whose value was variously established as ranging from 3.2 to 11.0 million Swiss francs. See his *Zsidósors Magyarországon*, p. 356. See also *Der Kastner-Bericht*, pp. 150–51.

93. *Der Kastner-Bericht*, pp. 130–33.

94. Some passengers managed to send typewritten reports back to Budapest. See, for example, the letter by J. D. Bl., dated July 1944, in the archives of Yad Vashem, M-20/47.

95. According to Lajos Marton and other eyewitnesses, a few of the Jews who were aware of the realities of Auschwitz, including József Fischer, were reluctant or refused to take a bath.

96. *Der Kastner-Bericht*, p. 252. See also report by Siegfried Elek, one of the members of the group, addressed to A. Silberschein on November 12, 1944. Yad Vashem Archives, M-20/95.

97. According to Zoltán Glatz's report, cited above, the Jewish Council of that group consisted of Zsigmond Léb, Jenő László, József Fischer, József Moskowicz, Endre Balázs, Sándor Weiss, Jenő Kertész, and Endre Krémer. The report notes several economic abuses by some of these leaders.

98. See, for example, Weissmandel's passionate letter of July 16, 1944, cited above.

99. Kasztner periodically informed Schwalb and Saly Mayer about developments in Hungary, including his negotiations with the SS. For copies of his letters to Saly Mayer, see Israel State Archives, Jerusalem, File no. 31:124/53.

100. *Der Kastner-Bericht*, pp. 152–55.

101. See Komoly's letter to Schwalb dated July 24, 1944, in Moreshet Archives, Doc. D.1.976.

102. Biss, *A Million Jews to Save*, pp. 112–17.

103. The diplomatic correspondence on this plan does not make absolutely clear whether Freudiger's proposals as interpreted by the Sternbuch brothers involved the safeguarding of the Kasztner transport or the organization of a new convoy of "1200 prominent Orthodox Jews." See, for example, Harrison's telegram 4802 to the Secretary of State dated July 26, 1944. For further details on the Sternbuch brothers' difficulties with both Mayer and the *Vaada*, see below.

104. Freudiger was very bitter about the pressure from Komoly, Hansi Brand, and Offenbach. He claims that this incident induced him to join his family in the escape to Romania on August 9, 1944. See *Five Months*. Freudiger explained his position in a letter he wrote from Romania to Kasztner on August 20, 1944—shortly after his arrival in Romania. Kasztner mentions only the matter of the 200 trucks without revealing the background of the Freudiger "offer." *Der Kastner-Bericht*, pp. 155–56.

105. *RAH*, p. 15.

106. Pressure for the meeting was also exerted by the Istanbul *Vaada*, which in turn was constantly pressured by Budapest. See, for example, Istanbul's cable to Shertok in London, dated August 14, 1944. Weizmann Archives.

107. *RLB*, Docs. 294, 295.

108. Kasztner claims that the Germans were offered 15 million Swiss francs payable in three monthly installments and that *he* formulated the three conditions. *Der Kastner-Bericht*, p. 187. Yehuda Bauer of the Hebrew University in Jerusalem, who presents a very sympathetic evaluation of Mayer's wartime role, asserts that Mayer offered no specific sums and was himself responsible for the three preconditions. See his "The Negotiations Between Saly Mayer and the Representatives of the SS in 1944–1945," in *RAH*, pp. 5–45, especially p. 23. While Professor Bauer was given access to the Saly Mayer files which are in the archives of the AJDC in New York, this author was informed on May 31, 1978, that "the Saly Mayer files have not yet been opened to the public."

109. *RAH*, p. 31.

110. The marches were of course not halted on humanitarian grounds only. The Germans desperately needed able-bodied Jews to build trenches and other defense lines for the protection of Vienna.

111. *Der Kastner-Bericht*, p. 242.

112. In one of his many statements after the war, Becher claims that he persuaded Himmler sometime "between the middle of September and October 1944" to issue the following order for Kaltenbrunner and Pohl: "Effective immediately I forbid any liquidation of Jews and order that, on the contrary, hospital care is to be given to weak and sick persons. I hold you . . . personally responsible even if this order is not strictly adhered to by lower echelons." 3762-PS. For Kaltenbrunner's explanation of the background of this statement, see *IMT*, 11:334–36.

113. *Der Kastner-Bericht*, p. 246.

114. Cf. *Der Kastner-Bericht*, pp. 245–50; *RAH*, pp. 32–34.

115. Schwartz was born in Russia in 1899 and brought to America as a child. After receiving a doctorate from Yale, he served as an instructor at the American University in Cairo and on the faculty of Long Island University. He became director of European operations of AJDC in 1938. He died in New York on January 1, 1975.

116. *RAH*, p. 36.

117. Biss, *A Million Jews to Save*, pp. 209–10.

118. *Der Kastner-Bericht*, pp. 313–30. See also chapter 32.

119. Acting in the names of *Agudath Yisrael* and the Committee of Orthodox Rabbis in the United States (represented by the Sternbuch brothers), Musy persuaded Himmler to allow a transport of 1,200 Jews to leave Theresienstadt for Switzerland on February 3, 1945. Kersten had great influence on Himmler. He made it possible, for example, for Norbert Masur, a member of the Board of the Stockholm branch of the World Jewish Congress, to see Himmler on April 21, 1944. For Kersten's account see his *The Kersten Memoirs, 1940–1945* (New York: Macmillan, 1957), 314 pp; Masur's account is in his *En Jude talar med Himmler* (A Jew Speaks with Himmler) (Stockholm: Albert Bonniersforlag, 1945), 36 pp; Bernadotte's version is in his *The Curtain Falls. Last Days of the Third Reich* (New York: Knopf, 1945), 154 pp. For further details, see *RAH*, pp. 24–28, 37–41.

120. *RLB*, Doc. 326. See also Jenő Lévai, *Eichmann in Hungary* (Budapest: Pannonia, 1961), pp. 200–201, and chapter 25.

121. See note by Vischer, the Secretary of the Swiss Legation in Berlin, in *NA*, Microcopy T-120, Roll 4203, Frames K789/K209226–227, K789/K209228–247, 253–57.

122. For a facsimile of Kasztner's letter, see *YVS*, 8:16.

123. Ully Kertész and Julia Weisz were picked up the first day of the German occupation while they were trying to buy tickets, presumably to return to Kolozsvár. Lajos Marton, *A svájcba 1944 augusztusban és decemberben érkezett bergen-belseni csoport eseményeinek rövid kronográfiája* (A Short Chronology of the Bergen-Belsen Group That Arrived in Switzerland in August and December 1944) (Geneva, 1945), p. 2 (manuscript).

124. *Der Kastner-Bericht*, pp. 253–54. The girls were among the approximately 3,200

Hungarian Jewish women transferred from Auschwitz-Birkenau in the fall of 1944, following the Nazis' decision to destroy the camp before the arrival of the Soviet troops. Besides the *Bevorzugtenlager* for the Hungarians, there were similar camps in Bergen-Belsen for other "prominent" Jews with foreign passports, including 593 Polish and 660 Dutch Jews. Yad Vashem Archives, M-20/168. For some background information on the *Bevorzugtenlager* in Bergen-Belsen, see the diary of Rudolf Martin Cheim, a German-Dutch Jew who survived the war with his wife and daughter, in YIVO archives Record Group 804.

125. Some of the Jewish leaders in Switzerland made a special effort to free Fischer and his family from the camp. See, for example, Josef Mandl's letter to A. Silberschein, dated September 2, 1944. Yad Vashem Archives, M-20/46.

126. For the list of the Jews in these camps, see *ibid.*, M-20/59.

127. See his and Pozner's telegram exchanges of January–February 1945. *Ibid.* See also Marton, *A svájcba 1944 augusztusban.*

128. See, for example, the memoranda of April 18, April 19, and May 27, 1945, addressed to Dr. Hans Klee of *Relico—Komitee zur Hilfeleistung für die kriegsbetroffene jüdische Bevölkerung* (Committee for the Aid of War-Stricken Jewish Population), Geneva. *Ibid.*

129. On May 9, 1945, when the Third Reich offered its unconditional surrender, Kasztner sent a "mission accomplished" telegram to Neustadt in Tel Aviv, emphasizing his main achievements. Pazner Files, Yad Vashem.

130. *RLB*, Doc. 439 (2605-PS). It was used as USA exhibit 242 in the Nuremberg trials.

131. *Der Bericht des jüdischen Rettungskomitees aus Budapest, 1942–1945* (The Report of the Jewish Rescue Committee of Budapest, 1942–1945). (Basel: Va'ath Ezra ve'Hazalah beBudapest, 1946), xiii + 191 pp. Prepared for submission to the first postwar congress of the World Zionist Organization, it was published under the title *Der Kastner-Bericht.* A copy of Kasztner's report was given to Wisliceny while he was in a Bratislava jail awaiting execution. For his review of the report, see Doc. 901 of Bureau 06 of the Police of Israel used in preparation of Eichmann's trial.

132. Sternbuch's views were outlined in a lengthy rebuttal (July 5, 1948) addressed to Dr. Kubowitzki of the World Jewish Congress. The accusations directed against Kasztner and Mayer were amplified in a 16-page memorandum Sternbuch submitted on February 5, 1954, to Chaim Cohn, the legal counsel of the State of Israel, in connection with the impending Grünwald-Kasztner libel suit. The memorandum includes a harsh indictment of Kasztner.

133. Mayer's "exploits" were outlined by Dr. Joseph C. Hyman and Moses A. Leavitt, the Executive Vice-Chairman and Secretary of the AJDC.

These claims were vehemently denied by Kasztner, who rebutted them point by point in a lengthy letter addressed to Mayer on October 29, 1945. The press release and Kasztner's letter are in the possession of this author.

134. *RAH*, pp. 44–45. See also Bauer's " 'Onkel Saly.' Die Verhandlungen des Saly Mayer zur Rettung der Juden 1944/45" ('Uncle Saly.' The Negotiations of Saly Mayer on the Rescue of Jews in 1944–45). *Vierteljahrshefte für Zeitgeschichte* (Quarterly for Contemporary History), Munich, 25, no. 2 (April 1977):188–219, and his popularized account of the Nazis' attempt to "sell" Hungarian Jewry and Saly Mayer's positive role in *Maariv*, Tel Aviv, May 3, 1978. (Reproduced in Hungarian translation in *Uj Kelet*, Tel Aviv, May 5, 1978.) In their memoirs (which, like most, are tendentious and self-serving), Kasztner, Brand, and Biss are highly critical of Mayer's role, as are several leaders of the Bratislava *Vaada*, including Rabbi Weissmandel. The criticism of his "Germanic" attitude and secretive techniques was shared by many of the leaders of the major wartime Jewish organizations in Switzerland. The ultra-Orthodox Jewish groups are particularly vitriolic in their

accusations. See, for example, *The Holocaust Victims Accuse* by Reb Moshe Shonfeld. (Brooklyn, N.Y.: Neturei Karta of U.S.A., 1977), pp. 73–82. Kasztner's opinion is also reflected in his letter to Steger (March 9, 1947) in which he refers to Mayer as a "philanthropic gangster." *RAH,* p. 42.

135. Mayer died in 1950 at the age of 68. For biographical details, consult Bauer, "The Negotiations," pp. 42–45.

136. For unknown reasons, many of the statements collected by the police for the possible indictment of the *Vaada* and Jewish Council leaders are in the files involving the trial in Budapest (1945–47) of Dr. Béla Berend. NB. 2600/1946.

137. Testimony of Béla (Adalbert) Lewinger during Kasztner's trial in Israel in 1954. W. Z. Laqueur, "The Kastner Case. Aftermath of the Catastrophe." *Commentary,* 20, no. 6 (December 1955):507.

138. *Ibid.,* p. 503.

139. Ben Hecht, *Perfidy* (New York: Julian Messner, 1961), p. 78. Kasztner's statement was found in the files of the War Crimes Tribunal in Nuremberg by Uri Siegel, a Tel Aviv attorney. *The New York Times,* February 6, 1956. See also Laqueur, "The Kastner Case," p. 504.

140. The letter, which included a detailed accounting of the rescue monies received during the war, was used by the defense as Exhibit 22. Hecht, *Perfidy,* pp. 72–73, 259.

141. *Ibid.,* pp. 80–81, 259.

142. *Ibid.,* pp. 198–99, 269.

143. Becher outlined his role in the rescue of the Jews in a lengthy deposition signed on February 7, 1946, in which he devoted special attention to the questions relating to the Holocaust in Hungary, giving details on the background and activities of the principal German and Hungarian officials involved in it. *RLB,* Doc. 438 (NG-2972). For details on Becher's background and wartime activities, see *Criminals at Large,* eds. István Pintér and László Szabó. (Budapest: Pannonia, 1961), pp. 150–64, and Jenő Lévai, *A fekete SS "fehér báránya"* (The "White Lamb" of the Black SS) (Budapest: Kossuth, 1966), 191 pp.

144. Upon learning of the suit initiated by Kasztner, Sternbuch sent a 16-page memorandum to Chaim Cohn, the counsel for the State of Israel. Dated February 8, 1954, the memorandum, signed by a number of former associates of the HIJEF and of the European section of the Union of Orthodox Rabbis of the United States of America and Canada, catalogs the "reprehensible" activities of Kasztner. Citing Musy's statement of March 5, 1945, and Walter Schellenberg's sworn affidavit of June 18, 1948, the authors of the memorandum accuse both Kasztner and Mayer of having in fact undermined through their activities with Becher Musy's agreement with Himmler to have the approximately 750,000 Jews in the concentration camps freed. The memorandum also contains a critique of the report Kasztner had written after the war, especially with respect to its references to the HIJEF.

145. In a taped interview with this author (Tel Aviv, October 10, 1972), Hansi Brand was especially bitter about the performance of Kasztner's "friends" on the witness stand. She argued emphatically that it was "inconceivable that [these individuals] did not know what the German occupation meant in March–April 1944." She further insisted that the leaders of Kolozsvár had been informed exactly about what was happening to the Jews in Poland even before Kasztner's visit in May.

146. *Psak din shel beit-hamishpat hamehozi b'Yerushalayim betik pelili 124/53 hayoets hamishpati neged Malkiel Grünwald bifney nasi beit-hamishpat Dr. Benjamin Halevi* (Decision of the District Court of Jerusalem in Criminal Case 124/53, Attorney General v. Malkiel Grünwald Before the President of the Court, Dr. Benjamin Halevi) (Tel Aviv: Karni Publishing Company, 1957), p. 16. According to Ben Hecht, who had his own Revisionist-Zionist axe to grind, Danzig's answer to Tamir's question "Did Kasztner tell you they

were going to the gas chambers of Auschwitz?" was a laconic "No." See his *Perfidy*, p. 108.

147. Taped interview with this author, Tel Aviv, October 8, 1972.

148. Hecht, *Perfidy*, pp. 105–8. Kenyérmező was a fictitious place (although that had been the name of a military training camp in World War I, near Esztergom). Rumors about labor there and in Transdanubia were also spread by gendarmes just before the deportation. In Nagyvárad one rumor had it that the Jews would be sent to Mezőtúr, southeast of Budapest. See Andrei Paul, *Az északerdélyi zsidó lakosság deportálása 1944-ben* (The Deportation of the Jewish population of Northern Transylvania in 1944), manuscript. See also the account by István Marton in Béla Katona's *Várad a viharban* (Várad in the Storm) (Nagyvárad: Tealah Korháztámogató Egyesület, 1946), pp. 314–25.

149. For Rabbi Weinberger's account of his mission, see his *A kolozsvári zsidóság emlékkönyve* (The Memorial Book of Kolozsvár's Jewry) (New York: The Author, 1970), 313 pp. + Hebrew text.

150. Upon his arrival in Romania, Marton became associated with the International Red Cross and active in the promotion of assistance for the Jews of Hungary and Romania. See Béla Vágó, "Political and Diplomatic Activities for the Rescue of the Jews of Northern Transylvania," in *YVS*, 6:155–73.

151. Gideon Hausner, *Justice in Jerusalem* (New York: Harper & Row, 1966), pp. 340–41.

152. Laqueur, "The Kastner Case," p. 508.

153. The quotation is from Virgil, *Aeneid*, book II, line 49.

154. *Psak-din shel beit-hamishpat hamehozi b'Yerushalayim betik pelili 124/53*, pp. 22–24, 45. See also Hecht, *Perfidy*, pp. 178–83. For excerpts from the proceedings and copies of exhibits by both parties, consult Shalom Rosenfeld, *Tik pelili 124. Mishpat Grünwald-Kasztner* (Criminal Case 124. The Grünwald-Kasztner Case) (Tel Aviv: Karni Publishing Company, 1955), 470 pp. and Emanuel Porat, *Hamishpat hagadol. Parashat Kasztner* (The Great Trial. The Kasztner Case) (Tel Aviv: Or Publishers, 1955), 264 pp.

155. The three gunmen—Joseph Menkes, Zeev Ekstein, and Dan Shemer—were condemned to life imprisonment on January 7, 1958. *The New York Times*, January 8, 1958. According to Hecht, Ekstein, the actual triggerman, was until a few months before the shooting a paid undercover agent of the Israeli government's Intelligence Service. This gave rise to many speculations as to a possible conspiracy to silence Kasztner, who had obviously become a liability to certain Israeli political circles. See Hecht, *Perfidy*, p. 208.

156. *Arar pelili 232/55. Beirur shel hamearer: Hayoetz hamishpati lememshala neged hamegir: Malkiel Grünwald* (Appeal Civil Case No. 232/55. Appeal of Appellant, The Government Prosecutor, Against Accused, Malkiel Grünwald) (Jerusalem: Mifal Haschichpul shel Histadrut ha'Studentim shel ha'Universita Haivrit, 1957), 201 pp. It contains the opinions of Shimon Agranat (pp. 1–129), Moshe Silberg (pp. 130–63), Itzhak Olshan (pp. 164–74), Z. Chesin (pp. 174–97), and D. Goitein (pp. 197–201).

157. *Ibid.* See also Hecht, *Perfidy*, p. 272.

158. See, for example, Tamir's *Habakasha lekiyum diyun-chozer bemishpat Kasztner* (Petition for the Reopening of the Kasztner Case), which he submitted on July 22, 1962. (Mineographed, unpaged, available at Yad Vashem in Jerusalem.)

159. University of Haifa, Center of Historical Studies, File H3h27-A.M.E.2/15. A similar sentiment was expressed by Ernő Marton in a note to a justice in which he further speculated on the psychological reasons why some of the witnesses testified against Kasztner. *Ibid.*, File H3h26-A.M.E. 2/2.

160. Hannah Arendt, *Eichmann in Jerusalem* (New York: Viking, 1963), pp. 117–18. Communist historians, journalists, and propagandists have exploited the Kasztner affair ever since the launching of the drive against Zionism and cosmopolitanism late in 1948. Particularly vicious has been the campaign in the Soviet Union, where scores of books

continue to appear on the "evils of Zionism." See, for example, Yuri Ivanov's *Caution: Zionism!* (Moscow: Progress Publishers, 1970), 174 pp. For further details on the attitude of the Soviet Union toward the Jews during the war, see chapters 10 and 31.

161. On the basis of the results of the 1939 elections for the Zionist Congress, four seats were allotted to the *Mizrachi*, three to the General Zionists, three to *Hashomer Hatzair*, and one to *Ichud*.

162. See Brand's letter to Barlas, dated July 28, 1943, in Beit Lohamei Hagetaot, vol. 1, Hungary, Doc. U153.

163. For further details on the problems of the office and the difficulties with Krausz, see Komoly's letter to Barlas dated August 25, 1943, in The Central Zionist Archives, Jerusalem, S26/1190 a/b. See also the memorandum signed by Brand and the other representatives of the *Ichud* (November 10, 1943), protesting the arbitrary way in which Krausz was managing the affairs of the office, in Beit Lohamei Hagetaot, vol. 2, Hungary, Doc. U328. Criticisms of the way Krausz handled the affairs of the office were also expressed at the Transylvanian Zionist Conference (*Erdélyi Cionista Konferencia*), which was held on February 27, 1944. Marton, *A Svájcba 1944 augusztusban.*

164. According to his critics, Krausz worked alone in one of the two rooms of the office, usually coming in around 10:00 A.M. The other room was normally filled by hundreds of clients. As a result he could neither keep pace with the demands of the office (letters would be stacked on his desk unanswered) nor satisfy the many anxious clients. See, for example, Rafi (Friedl) Ben-Shalom, . . . *weil wir leben wollten* (Because We Wanted to Live), Moreshet, Archives D.2.88, pp. 25–26.

165. Lévai, *Zsidósors Magyarországon,* pp. 157–58. See also Lévai, *Szürke könyv,* pp. 168–70.

166. The evidence is overwhelming that it was Krausz's report of June 19, rather than the many similar reports sent by Kasztner and his colleagues, that became the focus of diplomatic activities in the summer of 1944. Copies or excerpts of the report were circulated between the U.S. State Department, the British Foreign Office, the Jewish Agency, and Weizmann's office. See, for example, the communications by A. W. G. Randall to Weizmann, dated July 1 and July 5, 1944, in the Weizmann Files, Rehovoth, Israel.

167. *RLB,* Docs. 324–26. See also chapter 25.

168. The details of the emigration scheme were discussed in the Ministry of Foreign Affairs on July 14. For a summary of the decisions relating to the issuance of a collective passport and to the technicalities of transportation, see Lévai, *Zsidósors Magyarországon,* p. 244. See also chapter 31.

169. For further details on this emigration scheme, see sections on "Switzerland" and "The Reaction of the Allies to the Horthy Offer" in chapter 31.

170. Lévai, *Zsidósors Magyarországon,* p. 245.

171. See, for example, Barlas's letter of August 12, 1944, addressed to the Budapest *Vaada* leaders in Beit Lohamei Hagetaot, vol. 2, Hungaria-Slovakia, Doc. U297. See also Komoly's letter to Nathan Schwalb, July 24, 1944, Moreshet Archives, Doc. D.1976.

172. For Bereczky's account see his *Hungarian Protestantism and the Persecution of Jews* (Budapest: Sylvester, 1945), 47 pp. For further details on the roleof the Christian churches, see chapter 30.

173. Komoly kept a diary of his activities during this period. The part covering August 21–September 16, 1944, is reproduced in English translation in *HJS,* 3:147–250. See also Béla Vágó, "Budapest Jewry in the Summer of 1944" in *YVS,* 8:81–105.

174. See Komoly's entries for August 29 and September 7, 1944, *HJS,* 3:186, 214.

175. Friedrich Born, *Bericht an das Internationale Komitee vom Roten Kreuz in Genf* (Report to the International Committee of the Red Cross in Geneva) (Geneva, June 1945), pp. 34–36.

176. For a listing of the children's and foundlings' homes and the number of children placed in them, see *ibid.*, p. 60; also *Der Kastner-Bericht*, pp. 303–4.

177. Among Komoly's closest associates in Department A were the members of the Budapest *Vaada* (Hansi Brand, Sholem Offenbach, Kasztner, and Biss) as well as Sándor Groszman, Dezső Billitzer, András Beregi, and András Fenyő. For a more nearly complete list of Department A's members, its organizational structure (together with the location of the various administrative units), and the hospitals it administered (as well as the physicians associated with them), see Born, *Bericht*, pp. 57–61.

178. For examples of such expressions of sympathy or aid given to Jews as reported by Ferenczy, see Lévai, *Szürke könyv*, pp. 101–6, 137–38.

179. *Ibid.*, pp. 114–17. See also chapter 10.

180. *Ibid.*, pp. 118–23. See also chapter 26.

181. *Ibid.*, pp. 124–30.

182. For details on the places of refuge, the people involved in the rescue effort, and the number of Jews rescued, see Dénes Sándor, "Szervezett segitség az üldözöttekért" (Organized Help for the Persecuted) in *A magyar katolikus egyház és az emberi jogok védelme* (The Hungarian Catholic Church and the Protection of Human Rights), ed. Antal Meszlényi (Budapest: A Szent István Társulat, 1947), pp. 169–78.

183. Bereczky, *Hungarian Protestantism and the Persecution of Jews*, pp. 41–43.

184. Among the typical works exaggerating the role of Hungarian resistance and especially of the minuscule Communist Party are Gyula Kállai, *A magyar függetlenségi mozgalom, 1936–1945* (The Hungarian Independence Movement, 1936–1945) (Budapest: Kossuth, 1965), 331 pp.; *Fegyverrel a fasizmus ellen* (With Guns Against Fascism), eds. József Gazsi and István Pintér (Budapest: Zrinyi Katonai Kiadó, 1968), 313 pp.; István Pintér, *Magyar antifasizmus és ellenállás* (Hungarian Anti-Fascism and Resistance) (Budapest: Kossuth, 1975), 488 pp.; István Pintér, *A Magyar Front és az ellenállás: 1944. március 19.–1945. április 4.* (The Hungarian Front and Resistance: March 19, 1944–April 4, 1945) (Budapest: Kossuth, 1970), 263 pp.; and József Gazsi, *Fények a Börzsönyben* (Lights in the Börzsöny) (Budapest: Kossuth, 1976), 236 pp.

185. Communication of Hillel Danzig, a leading figure of Hungarian Zionism. Danzig claims that the Party was at first favorably inclined to cooperate and even entrusted the nationalities committee, headed by Manó Buchinger, with the matter. However, no action was ever taken—to a large extent because some of the Jewish leaders, who belonged to the more radical left wing of the Party, opposed it. They presumably insisted on following a strictly class approach to the Jewish question. In a letter addressed to the Party leadership on June 30, 1946, Danzig expressed his bitterness over the wartime attitude of the Party, and above all over its postwar campaign against Zionism and the attempts to organize Jewish emigration to Palestine. See also chapter 23 concerning Kasztner's claim that he kept the Social Democratic Party leadership informed about the realities of Auschwitz.

186. The important role of the Kállay government (rather than the leftist forces) in opposing the German pressure is emphasized by Iván Boldizsár in his *A másik Magyarország. A magyar ellenállási mozgalom története* (The Other Hungary. The History of the Hungarian Resistance Movement) (Budapest: Az "Uj Magyarország" Röpiratai, 1946), 94 pp. Also available in a French edition: *L'"autre" Hongrie. Histoire du mouvement de resistance hongroise* (Budapest: Nouvelle Hongrie, 1946), 76 pp. See also chapter 7.

187. C. A. Macartney, 1:379–80.

188. See his *A Ludovikától Sopronkőhidáig* (From the Ludovika to Sopronkőhida) (Budapest: Magvető, 1978), p. 665.

189. The National Peasant Party (*Nemzeti Paraszt Párt*) was not formally organized until September 19, 1944, though Imre Kovács and his associates in the "Village Explorers" (*Falukutatók*) group (see chapter 2) had completed their plans to found it as early as July 1939. C. A. Macartney, 2:332. See also Imre Kovács, *Magyarország megszállása* (The Occupation of Hungary) (Toronto: Vörösváry Kiadó, 1979), 400 pp.

190. At the outbreak of World War II, the illegal party was known as the Communists' Party of Hungary (*Kommunisták Magyarországi Pártja*). Partly as a result of the 1936 Comintern decision on the dissolution of the party and partly because of embarrassment over the Hitler-Stalin Pact of August 1939, its (illegal) membership, according to an authority on Communist affairs, dwindled from 400 in 1936 to around 20 in 1942. In 1943, aiming to overcome its isolation, mislead the Horthy regime, and improve its image among the workers, it changed its name to Peace Party (*Békepárt*). It was still operating illegally, however. On September 12, 1944, it assumed the name of Communist Party under the initiative of such underground domestic leaders as László Rajk and Antal Apró.

By 1944, several rival Communist party groups also existed in Hungary. The "Moscovites" (Mátyás Rákosi, Ernő Gerő, József Révay, Mihály Farkas, and Zoltán Vas), who had headed the Foreign Committee (*Külföldi Bizottság*) in the Soviet capital before the liberation, established the Hungarian Communist Party (*Magyar Kommunista Párt*). The local Communists in the parts of Hungary liberated by the Red Army revived the Communists' Party of Hungary. In addition, there was the Communist group led by Pál Demény and Aladár Weisshaus, which was composed of workers employed in Csepel and some of the suburbs of Budapest. For further details on the conflicts within and among the various Hungarian Communist groups and parties, see the articles by Péter Gosztonyi in *Menora-Egyenlőség*, Toronto, June 8, 22, and July 20, 1974. See also Miklós Molnár, *A Short History of the Hungarian Communist Party* (Boulder, Col.: Westview Press, 1978), 168 pp., and C. A. Macartney, 2:332–33.

191. Gosztonyi, *Menora*, July 20, 1974.

192. C. A. Macartney, 2:313.

193. Joint memoranda of the parties composing the Hungarian Front were submitted to Horthy on September 8 and 24. For summaries, see *ibid.*, pp. 333–34, 364–65.

194. For some details, see *ibid.*, 2:365–66, 383–85; Lévai, *Fekete könyv*, p. 214. For further details on the possible use of labor servicemen in a general uprising, see below.

195. C. A. Macartney, 2:444.

196. *Ibid.*, p. 466.

197. Besides Bajcsy-Zsilinszky, Kiss, Tartsay, Nagy, and Révay, the *Nyilas* also indicted Miklós Makkay, Pál Almássy, Miklós Balassy, Róbert Schreiber, István Tóth, and József Kővágó. The court, headed by Vilmos Dominich, condemned Bajcsy-Zsilinszky, Kiss, Nagy and Tartsay to death. The latter three were executed on December 8 in Budapest; Bajcsy-Zsilinszky was executed in Sopronkőhida on December 24. For further details, see József Domokos, *Két per egy kötetben* (Two Trials in One Volume) (Budapest: Magvető, 1978), pp. 218–438. See also C. A. Macartney, 2:456–57, 462–63; Jenő Lévai, *A hősök hőse. Bajcsy-Zsilinszky Endre a demokrácia vértanuja* (The Hero of Heroes. Endre Bajcsy-Zsilinszky, the Martyr of Democracy) (Budapest: Müller Károly, 1945), 105 pp., and Ervin Hollós, *Rendőrség, csendőrség, VKF 2* (Police, Gendarmerie, VKF 2) (Budapest: Kossuth, 1971), pp. 407–15.

198. Dr. Géza Soós, a former minor official in the Ministry of Foreign Affairs, was flown in a stolen plane to San Severo, Italy, on December 9, 1944, to make an appeal to the Western Allies. According to OSS Field Memorandum 237, Dr. Soós brought along a microfilm copy of the Auschwitz Protocols, but it was not forwarded from Bari to the OSS London Headquarters until April 1945. Dr. Soós's mission was fruitless. C. A. Macartney, 2:457. A similar and equally fruitless mission had been undertaken earlier by Prince M. Odescalchi, a pilot in the Hungarian Air Force. In the summer of 1944, he landed in error in German-held Ancona instead of Foggia. He was executed by the *Nyilas* following his extradition from Italy late in the fall. *Ibid.*, 2:314, 462.

199. For details on the resistance groups involved in the production and distribution of false documents, including those led by Tibor Szalai and Mátyás Székely, see Lévai, *Szürke könyv*, pp. 131–36. Small, basically ineffective, partisan groups were organized by

the Soviets and dropped in the mountainous regions of northern Hungary beginning in August 1943. Among the Hungarians who participated in partisan activities as advisers or commanders were Ferenc Pataky, Sándor Nógradi, and Márton Szőnyi. Minor partisan operations were also conducted along the Yugoslav borders, especially in the Bácska, in conjunction with the Titoist forces. Veesenmayer made reports of these nuisance operations to the German Foreign Office. See, for example, *RLB*, Docs. 247–89.

200. Gosztonyi, *Menora*, June 8, 1974. For an explanation as to why the Peace (Communist) Party found it impossible to prepare and distribute a flyer about the deportations, see the reminiscences by one of the Party's former leaders: Lajos Fehér, *Igy történt* (This Is How It Happened) (Budapest: Magvető, 1978), 578 pp. See also *Menora*, June 30, 1979.

201. For additional background on Hungarian resistance, see Gosztonyi, "A magyar ellenállási mozgalom történetéből (1944)" (From the History of Hungarian Resistance [1944]), in *Új Látóhatár* (New Horizon), Munich, 8, no. 2 (March–April 1965):99–118, and *Magyarország története* (The History of Hungary), eds. György Ránki et al. (Budapest: Akadémiai Kiadó, 1976), pp. 1103–6, 1167–70, 1178–81, 1202–4. For additional references, consult Randolph L. Braham, *The Hungarian Jewish Catastrophe. A Selected and Annotated Bibliography* (New York: YIVO-Institute for Jewish Research, 1962), p. 42.

202. Many of these Zionist couriers acted in cooperation with Dr. Lajos Gottesmann, a Zionist from Kassa, who was one of the leaders in charge of maintaining illegal contact with the provincial ghettos.

203. Bernard Wasserstein, *Britain and the Jews of Europe, 1939–1945* (New York: Oxford University Press, 1979), pp. 290–95.

204. For additional biographical details consult Anthony Masters, *The Summer That Bled. The Biography of Hannah Szenesh* (London: Joseph, 1972), 349 pp.; *Hannah Szenesh: Her Life and Diary*. Introduction by Abba Eban (New York: Schocken Books, 1972), 257 pp.; *Szenes Chana élete, küldetése és halála* (The Life, Mission and Death of Hannah Szenes) (Tel Aviv: A Hakibuc Hameuchad Kiadása, 1954), 391 pp. See also Hecht, *Perfidy*, pp. 118–26.

205. After the war Nussbecher changed his name to Palgi. For his romanticized account, which contains many inaccuracies, see *És jött a fergeteg* (A Whirlwind Developed) (Tel Aviv: Alexander, n.d.), 376 pp. Born in Kolozsvár in 1918, Nussbecher went to Palestine in 1939 where he joined the Ofakim *Kibbutz*. After the war, he served in the Israeli air force and later was one of the leading officials of El Al Airlines. From 1963 to 1966, he served as Israel's Ambassador in Tanzania. He died in February 1978.

206. Dafni was of Yugoslav background. He remained with the partisans and carried out his military mission, which was to assist in the escape of Allied prisoners and airmen shot down over enemy territory.

207. Katherine Szenes was picked up after the *Nyilas* coup and taken to the brickyard of Óbuda. From there she was marched in November to Hegyeshalom, but managed to escape and return to Budapest. She survived the war with the aid of Christian friends. For her story see "On the Threshold of Liberation. Reminiscences" in *YVS*, 8:107–26.

208. Her remains were brought to Israel in 1950 and reinterred on Mount Herzl. For further details, see Katherine Szenes, "The Death of Hannah Szenes." *Midstream*, Autumn 1958, pp. 57–65. For additional references consult Braham, *The Hungarian Jewish Catastrophe*, p. 43.

209. See Veesenmayer's telegram of July 8, 1944. *RLB*, Doc. 287.

210. A tentative agreement to free the parachutists was reportedly reached on October 14 at a conference held in the Ministry of Defense with the participation of Kasztner, Friedrich Born of the International Red Cross, Lieutenant-Colonel József Garzoly of the Hungarian General Staff, Colonal Ottó Hatz, and István Oláh, the Secretary of the Ministry. Under the terms of the agreement, the parachutists were to go free and refrain

from engaging in any activities or leaving the city pending the final disposition of the case. *Der Kastner-Bericht*, p. 197.

211. For further details consult Dorothy and Pessach Bar-Adon, *Seven Who Fell* (Tel Aviv: The Zionist Organization Youth Department, 1947), pp. 81–124, 186–98; Marie Syrkin, *Blessed Is the Match* (Philadelphia: Jewish Publication Society of America, 1947), 361 pp.; and *Der Kastner-Bericht*, pp. 142–46.

212. *Vádirat*, 3:27–37. See also Munkácsi, *Hogyan történt*, pp. 118–24.

213. György Gergely, *Beszámoló a Magyarországi Zsidók Szövetsége Ideiglenes Intéző Bizottsága munkájáról* (Report on the Work of the Provisional Executive Committee of the Jewish Council of Hungary) (Budapest, 1945), pp. 36–37. (Manuscript).

214. Lévai, *Szürke könyv*, pp. 200, 203–6. For further details on Section T, see chapters 10 and 31; on Ujváry's activities, see section "The Vatican and the Budapest Nunciature" in chapter 31.

215. Goldfarb, "On 'Hehalutz' Resistance in Hungary," in *Extermination and Resistance* (Israel: Kibbutz Lohamei Hagetaot, 1958), 1:162–73; statement of April 1, 1962, in Moreshet, Archives File A.94. Goldfarb was a leader of the *Dror*. One of his closest associates in the movement was his wife, Neshka, a woman from Munkács. He died in Kibbutz Parod in January 1978. Ben-Shalom, *Weil wir leben wollten* (Because We Wanted to Live), 152 pp. Moreshet, Archives File D.2.88. Hebrew edition: *Neevaknu le'maan he'haim* (We Struggled for Our Lives) (Givet Haviva: Moreshet, 1977), 223 pp. A leader of the *Hehalutz*, Ben-Shalom came to Budapest in January 1944. A representative of the *Hashomer Hatzair* movement, he went to Israel in 1947. He later served as Israel's Ambassador in Mali, Cambodia, and Romania. Revesz, *Hashoa be'Hungaria* (The Holocaust in Hungary), statement available at the Center for Historical Studies at the University of Haifa, 14 pp.

216. An 18-year-old in 1944, Grosz was particularly active in the printing, storing, and distribution of false papers; He often went about disguised as a *Nyilas*, in uniform and armed. His account is reproduced in Ben-Shalom's *Neevaknu le'maan he'haim*, pp. 176–205. Mayer, whose underground name was Jóska Megyeri, also dressed in *Nyilas* uniform; he maintained close contact with several non-Jewish resistance groups. For his account see *ibid.*, pp. 149–60. For Pil's account see YIVO, Archives File 187/3619; for Teichmann's account see Ben-Shalom, *Neevaknu le'maan he'haim*, pp. 161–75.

217. Ben-Shalom, *Weil wir leben wollten*, pp. 32, 46.

218. See his *Weil wir leben wollten*, pp. 6, 8. See also chapter 23.

219. *Ibid.*, pp. 24–28.

220. The originals of these documents were usually purchased from Polish refugees who had access to Hungarian officials.

221. According to Ben-Shalom this was also the reaction of some Zionists, including Zvi Szilágyi of the *Vaada*. See his *Weil wir leben wollten*, p. 35.

222. *Ibid.*, p. 45.

223. *Ibid.*, pp. 69–70.

224. Formally, the building was administered by a Directorate that included Mihály Salamon, Albert Geyer, Jenő Frenkel, and Simcha Hunwald. In addition a number of officials, some of them associated with the Jewish Council, were actively involved in the processing of the emigration lists. Among these were Erzsébet Eppler and Rabbi Fábián Herskovits. For the accounts of Eppler, Herskovits, and Salamon, see YIVO, Files 768/3647, 768/3581, and 768/3648.

225. Ottó Komoly's diary, entry for September 6, 1944, in *HJS*, 3:210; Ben-Shalom, *Weil wir leben Wollten*, pp. 102–5.

226. The conflict between Krausz and the *Hehalutz* led to Krausz's ouster from the Palestine Office leadership soon after the liberation of Budapest. He was officially informed of his replacement on May 25, 1945, by Barlas. In the spring of 1946, he was also tried by a Zionist honor court. Among those who submitted detailed accusations against him were

Sándor Groszmann and Rafi Ben-Shalom. See Groszmann's *Adatok a Mosche Krausz, a Palamt volt titkára ügyében tartandó cionista becsületbirosági tárgyalásához* (Data Relating to the Planned Zionist Honor Court in the Case of Moshe Krausz, the Former Secretary of the Palestine Office) (Budapest, April 20, 1946), 2 pp. (typescript), and Ben-Shalom's (signed Rafi Friedl) *Klagesschrift gegen den früheren Leiter des Palestina-Amtes, Moshe Krausz* (Indictment Against Moshe Krausz, the Former Leader of the Palestine Office) (Prague, April 14, 1946), 4 pp. (typescript).

Krausz defended himself and his record in a memorandum submitted on March 4, 1946, to the Executive Committee of the Jewish Agency in Jerusalem. See his *Memorandum über die Tätigkeit des Palestina-Amtes in Budapest in den kritischen Kriegsjahren 1941–45* (Memorandum on the Activities of the Palestine Office in Budapest During the Critical War Years of 1941–45) (Budapest, March 4, 1946), 12 pp. (typescript).

Copies of all three documents are in the author's possession.

227. On the resistance activities of the Polish refugees, see *Bericht des Leiters des polnisch-jüdischen Flüchtlingscomités* (Report of the Leaders of the Polish-Jewish Refugee Committee), Yad Vashem Archives, M-20/99. See also Ben-Shalom, *Weil wir leben wollten,* pp. 37–38.

228. Statement by David (Gur) Grosz, pp. 189–91.

229. For references on Jewish and non-Jewish resistance in Hungary consult Braham, *The Hungarian Jewish Catastrophe,* pp. 42–43. See also Josef Shefer, "Hanhagat hamachteret hehalutzit beHungaria" (The Leadership of the *Halutz* Underground in Hungary) in *Hanhagat yehudei Hungaria bamivahan hashoa* (The Leadership of Hungarian Jewry in the Test of the Holocaust) (Jerusalem: Yad Vashem, 1975), pp. 135–49; *Tanúk vagyunk . . . !* (We Are Witnesses . . . !), ed. Ervin G. Galili (Tel Aviv: the editor, n.d.), 332 pp.; Lévai, *Szürke könyv,* pp. 210–14.

CHAPTER THIRTY

THE ATTITUDE AND REACTIONS OF THE CHRISTIAN CHURCHES

The Christian Churches and the Jews

THE CHRISTIAN CHURCHES must bear a great responsibility for the Hungarian Jewish catastrophe. Their attitude toward the Jews and their position on the Jewish question before and after World War I not only fostered the climate of anti-Semitism that determined the passivity if not open hostility of the masses, but also shaped the reaction to the Nazis' Final Solution program. Major pillars of the reactionary regimes, the Christian churches were in the forefront of the national-Christian campaigns that attempted to retain the antiquated semi-feudalistic social order and to protect the purity of the Christian spirit in the country. In practice, they interpreted this as a mandate to counter "radical" socialist ideas and movements and to protect the nation from the alleged damaging influence of the Jews—twin objectives they pursued with equal fervor.

While the potentially most damaging anti-Jewish policies of the Christian churches were adopted in the late 1930s, the foundation for the anti-Semitic climate that made the Final Solution possible had been laid in the so-called Golden Era of Hungarian Jewry. Although the anti-Semitic manifestations of this period were effectively controlled by the various Hungarian governments, the Christian churches provided added impetus to the anti-Jewish ideas and movements spearheaded by such political ideologists as Győző (Victor) Istóczy and Iván Simónyi (see chapter 1). The clergy, especially its lower echelon, played an important role in the anti-Semitic party founded by Istóczy shortly after the end of the notorious Tisza-Eszlár ritual murder case in 1882. It also embraced with great fervor the Vatican-sponsored movement for the establishment of Christian Socialist workers' associations, which were clearly designed to isolate and eventually destroy the genuine trade unions, generally labeled as Marxist. The movement was forcefully supported by the Catholic People's Party (*Katolikus Néppárt*), which was for a long time headed by Count Nándor Zichy. Backed by the pro-

Hapsburg aristocracy and the great landowners, this clerical, conservative party was particularly devoted to combatting the "destructive and anti-Christian" ideas associated with "Jewish liberalism and socialism." One of the central forces behind Christian Socialism was Bishop Ottokár Prohászka, whose spiritual leadership and sophisticated anti-Semitism exerted a profound influence on public opinion for several decades.

The churches did not welcome the liberal policies of the government and especially resented those providing for the equality of all accepted religions and the separation of church and state. The increasing militancy of the churches was expressed by their representatives in Parliament, from the pulpits, and through their major organs. For example, the *Alkotmány* (Constitution), the People's Party's daily founded in 1896, was the first respectable anti-Semitic national journal in the country. Edited by priests, it reflected a militant Catholicism which often found expression in rampant anti-Semitism. One of the leading experts on organizing and propagandizing for this form of Catholicism was Béla Bangha (1880–1940), the "Hungarian Savonarola." He crystallized the Catholic Church's ideological struggle against its two major opponents in his view—Judaism and socialism.[1]

The Christian churches' attitude toward the Jews took a turn for the worse after the disasters of World War I. The military debacle, the failure of the democratic-socialist coalition government of Count Mihály Károlyi to deal with the grave problems inherited from the past, and above all the radical revolutionary measures adopted during the short-lived proletarian dictatorship of Béla Kun induced the churches to wholeheartedly embrace the counterrevolution that brought Miklós Horthy to power. As in Germany, the Jews—along with Communists and Freemasons—were used as scapegoats and made responsible for the ills that befell Hungary. They had to suffer the fury of the counter-revolutionary "White Terror," whose ideological leitmotiv was "the Szeged Idea" (*A szegedi gondolat*). One of the most eloquent spokesmen of this ideology, whose central themes included anti-Bolshevism, anti-Semitism, revisionism, and chauvinistic nationalism, was Bishop István Zadravetz, the country's chief military chaplain and a leading figure of the Anti-Bolshevik Committee.[2] The idea was also propagated by newly founded ecclesiastical dailies, including the *Nemzeti Ujság* (National Journal) and *Uj Nemzedék* (New Generation), which frequently raised the subject of the "international Jewish conspiracy" responsible for Hungary's debacle. The theme was also picked up by priests who were elected to Parliament. In his speech of December 3, 1919, for example, Father Gyula Zakany claimed that it was "the fault of the Jews that Hungary's territorial integrity was destroyed." He evoked the same theme before gatherings of the Awakening Magyars (*Ébredő Magyarok*), one of the many ultra-chauvinistic anti-Jewish organizations that flourished during the period.[3]

Perhaps the most disastrous position taken by the leaders of the Christian churches came after the Nazis' acquisition of power in Germany and especially after the *Anschluss*. Though these leaders were fully aware of the dangers represented by Nazism to the Christian churches and organized religion, they fully supported, and occasionally even spearheaded, the policies aimed at the reacquisition of the lost territories with the aid of the Third Reich. They unwittingly provided a fertile ground for anti-Semitic propaganda by condoning the equation of Jews with Bolshevism and of National Socialism with Christianity. While many of these leaders lived to regret the position they had taken in the late 1930s, especially during the German occupation, they legitimized many of the extremist policies pursued by the representatives of the Right. Gyula Czapik, the Archbishop of Eger and the second-highest dignitary of the Catholic Church in Hungary, deplored "the fatal error" of the German Catholic Church not to identify itself with National Socialism. Bishop László Ravasz, the leading dignitary of the Reformed (Calvinist) Church, characterized the German drive for power as being motivated by ethical and religious principles. József Grösz, the Archbishop of Kalocsa, argued that the Arrow Cross was compatible with Christ's cross. Bishop Zoltán Turóczy, one of the leading figures of the Evangelical (Lutheran) Church, argued that "true Christianity is not pacifist but militarist, in the spirit of world-conquering totalitarian powers." István Hász, the bishop of the armed forces, concurred with National Socialist ideas, arguing that "against the Jews, the destroyers of the country, any offense is permissible."[4] Emboldened by the public position taken by their leaders, many clergymen had no scruples about spreading the anti-Jewish poison among the Hungarian masses, which had generally been tolerant until World War I.

The successful molding of public opinion by years of vicious anti-Semitic propaganda (which was reinforced by the social reform promises of the ultra-rightists at home and the successes of the Third Reich abroad) made the Christian churches' support of the major anti-Jewish laws both logical and praiseworthy. The leaders of the Christian churches supported the adoption of the first two anti-Jewish laws, albeit with decreasing enthusiasm. They mostly thought them to be in line with what they perceived to be Hungary's national interest, arguing at first that the laws would in fact "prevent the further exacerbation of the Jewish question and assure the disarming of anti-Semitism." While they had no compunction about supporting the First Anti-Jewish Law of 1938, which allegedly even some Hungarian Jewish leaders supported as a means of "taking the wind out of the *Nyilas* sails," some objected to a few provisions of the Second Anti-Jewish Law of 1939. Specifically, they objected to some openly racial aspects of the bill, which potentially affected even some Magyars, and insisted on amendments to protect the rights and interests of converts and to advance the cause of assimilationism and conversion among Jews. To counteract the reaction to these amendments, the leaders of the churches represented in the upper house, including Sándor Raffay of the Evangelical Church and Jusztinián Cardinal Serédi, the Catholic Prince Primate of Hungary, justified the adoption of the laws by emphasizing the "threat" that the cultural, political, and economic influence of the Jews represented for the national interests of Christian Hungary (see chapters 4 and 5).[5]

The church leaders showed the same insensitivity toward the adoption of Law No. II of 1939 and all its corollary decrees that led to the establishment and gradual expansion of the blatantly discriminatory labor service system. One of the few courageous voices of protest was that of Margit Schlachta, the mother superior of the Social Mission Society, who tried to arouse public opinion and induce the military authorities to put an end to the cruelties and harsh measures adopted against the labor servicemen.[6]

The leaders of the Christian churches did, however, oppose the Third Anti-Jewish Law, which was enacted shortly after Hungary's entry into the war against the Soviet Union in June 1941. Again, an important reason for their opposition was that the law, which incorporated the racist provisions of the Nuremberg Laws of 1935, directly affected many of their parishioners, both converts and Christian-born. As a result of their pressure and influence in the upper house, the law was amended to empower the Minister of Justice to waive the rules under exceptional conditions. Under the compromise solution, many potentially affected Hungarians, including several members of the aristocracy and of the governmental and political elite, were spared from being classified as Jews.[7]

The preoccupation with the special interests of converts and Christians of Jewish origin was characteristic of most church leaders' attitude throughout the war, including the occupation period. The record of their reaction to the Final Solution is at best mixed. Although they abhorred the methods employed by the Nazis and visibly sympathized with the suffering Jews, they undertook no effective measures to counteract the designs of the dejewification squads. Their measures may with generosity be classified as too little and too late. Dignitaries of the various Christian denominations usually acted singly and on their own when they contacted the leaders of the government in attempts to alleviate at least the means used in "solving" the Jewish question. Their primary concern even during the concentration and deportation of the Jews was the fate of the converts and non-Jews.

When the Jews were ordered to wear the yellow star, the church leaders only intervened to have the converts exempted. They never contemplated emulating the example of King Christian X of Denmark and of many Danes or of Reverend Géza Takaró, the pastor of the First Hungarian Reformed Church of New York, who together with his parishioners expressed their sympathy with the Jews by defiantly wearing the Star of David themselves.[8] Nor did they ever think of adopting the position taken by Metropolitan Stefan, the head of the Holy Synod of the Bulgarian Orthodox Church, and by other metropolitans, including Kiril of Plovdiv and Neofit of Vidin, who publicly preached against the anti-Semitic policies of their government.[9] Cardinal Serédi was aware of the more lenient treatment of Jews not only in Bulgaria, but also in Romania and Slovakia. He knew, for example, that the Romanians had halted the deportations at the very beginning and that the Romanian Jews did not have to wear badges.[10]

Although the national leaders of the Christian churches occasionally considered the desirability of taking a public stand, at no time did they actually arouse public opinion against the injustices being committed against the Jews. Some local clergy leaders, including Bishop Vilmos Apor of Győr, requested that Cardinal Serédi speak out in public against the violation of the most fundamental values of human rights; he failed to act (although he once threatened to take such action). His failure to take a public stand had a negative influence on the other leaders of the Catholic and Protestant churches of Hungary, and their common silence emboldened the enemies and discouraged the potential rescuers of Jewry.[11] The few bishops who dared to broach the Jewish persecutions in their sermons unfortunately could not stem the tide, for their messages reached only limited local audiences.

Lacking encouragement from the upper levels of the hierarchy, the junior members of the clergy failed, with a few exceptions, to become actively involved in protesting the concentration and deportation of the Jews. Individual clergymen, like the representatives of various church-related organizations, helped a few individual Jews and expressed shock over the way in which the ghettoization and deportation were carried out. Moved by the suffering of Jews in crammed freight cars, the National Association of Hungarian Catholic Women's Organizations (*A Magyar Katolikus Nőegyletek Országos Szövetsége*) and the National Hungarian Reformed Women's League (*A Magyar Református Országos Nőszövetség*), for example, appealed to Sztójay on June 20 through the Hungarian Red Cross (headed by Elemér Simon) to permit the setting up of refreshment stands in the major rail hubs to help alleviate the plight of the Jews. The Prime Minister, after pondering for three weeks, forwarded the request on July 14, through Lajos Huszovszky, to the Ministry of Foreign Affairs, which promptly approved it. By that time, July 18, the deportations had already been completed in the provinces and halted by Horthy.[12]

During the *Nyilas* era, when the situation of the Budapest Jews became critical, a number of clergymen and nuns became actively involved in various rescue operations (see below). These humanitarian activities, though affecting but one Jewish community, contrast painfully with the insensitivity and lack of urgency shown by the hierarchies of the churches.

The Attitude and Actions of the Catholic Church

After the passage of the new and harsher anti-Jewish measures after the German occupation, the leaders of Hungarian Jewry approached the dignitaries of the Christian churches for help. They took this step not only because of the vast influence of the churches, but also because many of the traditional supporters of Jewry, including the anti-Nazi conservative-aristocratic representatives of the former ruling elite, were themselves under arrest. The church leaders reacted swiftly; this may have been because the Germans and the newly installed Sztójay government were using the Third Anti-Jewish Law as a basis for defining who was and who was not a Jew. Cardinal Serédi first approached Sztójay toward the end of March 1944, taking along a memorandum prepared by the Holy Cross Society (*Szent Kereszt Egyesület*), the association of Jews who had converted to Catholicism. The Cardinal, echoing the views of the Society, expressed great consternation over the plans to make the wearing of the yellow star compulsory even for converts, some of whom were priests and nuns or active members of the church. He reminded the Prime Minister that the Star of David was a symbol of religion and not of the Jewish race and, consequently, its wearing by Christians would be a contradiction. Sztójay yielded on one point. On April 5, the day the Jews of Hungary began wearing the yellow star, Sztójay informed the Cardinal that priests, nuns, and lay church officials of Jewish background were to be exempted from the anti-Jewish measures.[13]

The Cardinal met again with Sztójay on April 13 to review the position of the Catholic Church. The only result was a suggestion that the Church ought better to concentrate its energies on the struggle against Communism. A week after the beginning of the ghettoization in Carpatho-Ruthenia and northeastern Hungary on April 16, Cardinal Serédi, having been informed of the cruelties perpetrated against the Jews, submitted a memorandum in the name of his fellow bishops to the Prime Minister, in which he protested the violations of human rights. Once again he entered a special plea in behalf of converts, arguing that they should be separated from the Jews since they had themselves already done so by virtue of their conversion. He summarized the Catholic Church's position by demanding:

- The exemption of Christians from the measures enacted against Jews.
- The removal of converts from the jurisdiction of the Jewish Council.
- The exemption of converts from wearing the Star of David.
- Permission for priests falling under the jurisdiction of anti-Jewish laws to have non-Jewish servants.
- Recognition by the government that the confiscation of Jewish property often affected children who were no longer Jewish.[14]

The Cardinal's failure to deplore the injustice and inhumanity of forcible removal of Jews from their homes, to condemn their concentration into ghettos and the spoliation of their property, or to warn about the possible consequences of the anti-Jewish measures undoubtedly encouraged Sztójay and the other members of the government to proceed with their other even more sinister designs involving the Jews. As if in gratitude for his not having raised these graver issues, the Prime Minister, in his reply of May 3, assured the Primate that the government had already exempted priests of Jewish origin and asserted that it would do everything possible to assure the economic interests of Christians whose parents were affected by the anti-Jewish laws. As to the yellow badge, Sztójay emphasized that it was not construed as a symbol of the Jewish religion, but "as a convenient means for the necessary identification from the administrative point of view of those of the Jewish race." He added that he would not object to the wearing by the converts of a cross as well.[15]

In the wake of the deportation from Kistarcsa (April 30) and the ghettoization in Northern Transylvania and other regions, which also affected many converts, the Cardinal approached Sztójay again, on May 10. This time too, his primary concern was not the plight of the Jews. He urged that within the ghettos, just as in the labor service companies, the converts be separated from the Jews and enabled to carry out their religious practices. In connection with the deportations, he urged Sztójay to see to it that the deportees did not lose their lives without due process. With respect to the ghettos, he was particularly concerned that many Christians were inconvenienced as a result of the forced relocations.

Two days after the beginning of the mass deportations on May 15, Cardinal Serédi issued a circular to the bishops summarizing the Church's activities and achievements in behalf of the converts. He rationalized his failure to publicize the measures adopted by the government and the interventions of the Church by claiming that such a move might have induced the government to rescind its concessions or given it an excuse to impose additional restrictions on Catholics or Catholic institutions.[16]

The public silence and apparent indifference of the Cardinal to the Jewish plight bewildered the Papal Nuncio and some bishops. On May 27, Bishop Apor deplored Cardinal Serédi's resolution not to publicize the persecutions and violations of human rights. He pleaded for the Cardinal, as head of the Hungarian Catholic Church, to issue a pastoral letter covering the religious and moral implications of the situation in a language understandable to the people, or at least to permit wide distribution of his memorandum of April 23 or give the bishops a free hand to inform and guide their parishioners. Angelo Rotta, the Nuncio, approached Cardinal Serédi on June 8, the day after the completion of the deportations from Carpatho-Ruthenia and Northern Transylvania, to inquire why he and the bishops of the Catholic Church were not taking a more resolute stand against the government. The Cardinal defended his position with arguments about the possible counterproductivity of public disclosures and the problems of censorship; he also informed the Nuncio that many sources were questioning the utility of the Apostolic Nunciature in Budapest, which "does nothing and nobody knows if it ever did anything; and it is deceitful for the Apostolic Holy See to maintain diplomatic relations with that German government which carries out the atrocities."[17]

Shortly thereafter, Sztójay sent some colleagues to "enlighten" the Cardinal about the government's anti-Jewish policies. On June 2, Cardinal Serédi was visited by István Antal, the Minister of Justice and of Cults and Public Education; on June 7, he was seen by Lajos Huszovszky, a ministerial secretary in the Council of Ministers; on June 8, Béla Imrédy called on him; finally, on June 17 István Bárczy invited him and the Catholic bishops to a government luncheon, ostensibly to clarify all the issues raised by the Church. In all of these discussions, the Cardinal deplored the harsh measures adopted against the Jews and argued that the Jews ought to have been "militarized" and employed in the country or perhaps sent to neutral countries instead of being deported. He rejected the luncheon invitation because acceptance might have been construed as an outright approval of the government's policies. Sztójay tried to disarm the Cardinal by informing him in a private letter on June 19 that the five demands expressed in his memorandum of April 23 were practically accepted and carried out by the government.[18]

In the meantime, the Cardinal was being subjected to additional pressure to take a public stand and to try to arouse public opinion. On June 15, László Ravasz, one of the leaders of the Reformed Church, approached him for the issuance of a joint public declaration. Two days later, Bishop Apor again urged the Cardinal to take a public stand. On June 27, the Nuncio conveyed the Pope's desire that the "Hungarian bishops take a public stand in defense of Christian principles and in support of those compatriots that were unjustly affected by the racial laws, and especially in behalf of the Christians." By that time the Cardinal was in fact working on a pastoral letter to be read in all churches during Sunday services. His draft was reworked by János Drahos, his deputy, and a number of bishops. The final text, which was adopted after consultation with Bishop Apor and Gyula Czapik, the Bishop of Eger, was dated June 29 and read as follows:

Our dear believers in Christ!

The successors of the Apostles, the everpresent visible Head of the Church and the other bishops are, in accordance with the will of God, the preachers and guardians of the unwritten or natural and written or revealed moral laws of God, mainly those of the Ten Commandments. Accordingly, in the nearly two-thousand-year-old history of our Church, they have often raised their voices as chief pastors when these laws have been violated by anyone; and they have stood up for those—regardless of origin, nationality, religion or social position—who suffered ills without determination by valid judicial decree of individual acts of crime in violation of the divine laws; because no one may be lawfully punished for the crimes of other human beings who belong to the same race, nationality or religion, if he personally had no part in the commission of such crime. For that reason they stood up for actual slaves, poor pariahs, etc., and strove to make them equal to free men, they supported the poor, and they strove to raise the oppressed working class.

According to the testament of our thousand-year-old history, the members of the Hungarian Council of Bishops also stood up for the poor and for those who suffered innocently, or were persecuted; and they helped them not only by practicing innovative Christian love, but also by endeavoring to have the case of the poor and also the social problem systematically resolved through the legislature, and trying to have justice prevail in every respect.

Above all, they supported the cause of the poor in every manner, because they knew that love is the highest commandment and that according to the words of Christ the poor will always be the ones toward whom love must be practiced. For that reason, even today, they maintain or support the old Catholic institutions of love even at great sacrifices, and establish new ones as well.

But our predecessor Hungarian bishops also saw to it that social and economic problems were solved systematically through the legislature, in a reasonable manner and free of politics. In the middle of the last century, they endeavored to promote the liberation of serfs, sacrificing a substantial part of their own income. They also brought mighty sacrifices for the later agrarian reforms. At the time the Parliament discussed these reforms, the Primate of the country, on behalf of the Council of Bishops, urged above all the allotting of land to poor families having many children, and proposed interest-free loans so they could secure the necessary working capital. According to the guidance of the socially minded Popes, Leo XIII and Pius XI, our predecessor Hungarian bishops urged the spiritual and material uplift of the working class, the elevation of its inherent human rights, the just determination of working hours and wages; they supported the bill on old-age and disability insurance, and at the same time they also urged similar insurance for agricultural workers.

And in the event anyone's inherent rights, such as the right to life, human dignity, individual freedom, religious practices, work, make a living, private property, etc., or rights obtained in a legal manner, are unjustly curbed or even taken away, whether by individuals or some communities or the representatives of the State itself, Hungarian bishops are obliged to raise their voices as chief pastors and point out that the aforementioned rights were given by God himself and not by individuals, by communities or even by the representatives of the State; therefore—except for legal and valid judicial decree—no one and no power on earth whatever can justifiably violate or deny it but God, or those upon whom God conferred legislative, governmental, judicial or executive power in this matter, because there is no power other than that coming from God. Nevertheless, the power received from God may only be practiced justly, i.e., in accordance with the moral laws of God, because God did not and could not empower anyone to practice injustice and violate His own laws.

Now therefore, our dear believers, we, the members of the Hungarian Council of Bishops, hereby fulfill our duty in these fateful times in defense of the innocent, by raising our protesting chief-pastoral voices in God's name against the type of warfare and bombardments condemned by Christian ethics. The destruction of the homes of peaceful citizens remote from any strategically significant site, the machine gunning of peaceful women and children from low-flying airplanes, the crippling of innocent children by the throwing of explosive toys: all these are acts which warfare claiming honesty cannot allow.

But we must also point out that when in this horrible world war God's help is so badly needed, when we ourselves should carefully avoid any word or act that would draw God's wrath upon us and our nation, we see with unspeakable sadness that in Christian Hungary a series of measures have been taken that are against the laws of God. To you, our dear believers, we need not list in detail the measures which are well known to you along with the manner of their execution, and which violate or even deny the inherent rights of some of our fellow citizens, even some who are together with us, members of our holy faith, only because of their origin. And all this without the determination of individual guilt and judicial decree. You could truly only understand all this, if the same deprivation of rights happened to you.

As the Chief Pastor of our believers as ordered by God, all partisan politics has been far from us, is still far from us, and will continue to be so, as well as any group interest or any individual interest. We also have no doubt that a part of Jewry has had a guilty subversive influence on the Hungarian economic, social and moral life. It is also a fact that the others did not stand up against their correligionists in this respect. We do not dispute the fact that the Jewish question must be resolved in a legal and just manner. Therefore we do not object, but actually hold it desirable, that in the economic system of the country the necessary measures be taken and the rightfully objectionable symptoms be remedied. However, we would neglect our moral and pastoral duty if we did not make very certain that the just shall not suffer, and our Hungarian fellow citizens and Catholic believers not be offended merely because of their origins; therefore we have endeavored for several months through oral and written negotiations to protect the just generally, and especially our fellow citizens and believers made victims of recently issued injurious measures: we have asked for the modification, and as it were, the repeal, of the injurious orders themselves.

Although we have occasionally been successful in reaching some mitigation which we accepted with gratitude, we are nevertheless deeply grieved that during our negotiations we simply could not obtain what we would have liked best, that the unjust violations and deprivation of rights, mainly the deportations, should finally be terminated. Since we were confident in Christianity, humanitarianism, and the humanity of the members of the government, we have not given up all hope despite the lack of success experienced until now; we have not issued statements to you but, other than taking the steps that were possible, we restrained ourselves and waited.

But now, when we see with great shock that our negotiations have been almost without success, especially in the most important respects, we solemnly disavow our responsibility. But in defense of the divine laws and by this means we also ask the competent authorities, recognizing their responsibility to God and history, to urgently remedy the injurious measures. These measures not only cause legal insecurity at this time of fighting for the existence of the nation, but they also disturb the unity of the nation, turn the common opinion of the Christian world against us, and more importantly they turn God against us.

Now as ever, we can have confidence in God above all, and therefore we ask you, dear believers, to pray together with us and work for the victory of justice and Christian love. Be careful that by approval or promotion of the objectionable acts you do not take the horrible responsibility upon yourselves before God and mankind. Do not forget that the true well-being of the homeland cannot be served through injustice. Pray and work for all our Hungarian co-citizens without exception, mainly for our Catholic brethren, for our Catholic Church and for our beloved Hungarian homeland.

Our chief-pastoral blessings on such intention, in the name of the Father, the Son and the Holy Ghost, Amen.[19]

The pastoral letter was brought to the attention of Antal, who promptly stopped its distribution, although some of the archdioceses, including those of Eger and Kalocsa, received the pastoral letter before Antal's order was issued. It was reportedly read in some of the churches in these dioceses. Following a resolution of the Council of Ministers, Antal visited Serédi on July 6 in Gerecse, the Cardinal's summer residence. Although he once again condemned the actions of the government, the Cardinal, especially after he was warned about the consequences of a possible *Nyilas* takeover of the government, expressed a readiness to withdraw the pastoral letter if the Prime Minister informed him officially that he had accepted the demands outlined in his earlier memoranda; the Christians were exempted from the anti-Jewish measures and the government did everything in its power to bring about the return of Christian deportees; the Church authorities could inform the parishioners that they were conducting negotiations with the government on the Jewish question and had already achieved certain concessions.

Upon Antal's immediate acceptance of the first two conditions, on July 7 Cardinal Serédi instructed all the parish heads by telegram to refrain from reading the pastoral letter. The following day, (the day after Horthy had stopped the deportations) some of the leading members of the government—among them Sztójay, Antal, Imrédy, and

Kunder—appeared in Gerecse in an effort to solve the outstanding issues still plaguing church-state relations. Sztójay brought along a letter he had written the day before to summarize the government's position and actions in response to the Church's demands. It read as follows:

In my reply dated June 19, 1944, to Your Eminence's letter dated May 10, 1944, I was as yet unable to inform you in full detail of the planned, and since then partially executed, measures concerning Jews of Christian faith. However in my present letter I can give you more detailed and in the case of some concrete questions more factual information.

According to the wish expressed repeatedly by Your Eminence, the Royal Hungarian Government has taken the following measures regarding the modification of the rules relating to Jews, beyond the already known ones:

1. On July 6, 1944, it established the Organization of Christian Jews, which takes care of and handles matters concerning Jews belonging to Christian denominations to protect their interests, independently from the Association of Jews of Hungary.

2. It has ordered a strict investigation to ascertain whether cruelties and ruthless procedures indeed happened in connection with the transportation and relocation of Jews. As a result of the investigation it has been ascertained that the rumors about cruelties and ruthless handling are generally untrue or at least strongly exaggerated. However, there is no doubt that in isolated cases irregular behavior by some authorities has actually happened, contrary to the intention of the Minister of Internal Affairs. In such cases, the Minister of Internal Affairs has applied the strictest sanctions, and he will prevent the reoccurence of similar cases with the same sanctions and other strict preventive measures in the future.

3. The deportation from the country of the Jews of Budapest has been suspended until further notice.

4. In the event it is necessary in the future that the Jews of Budapest be deported from the country, the Christian Jews will remain in the country. It is true that the Jews mentioned will still live in segregated apartments; however, organized care will be taken to ensure the free practice of their religion, and visits to churches and undisturbed spiritual care in general shall be secured by every means.

5. The relatives (parents, brothers and sisters, wives and children) of pastors of the Protestant churches will be excused from wearing the distinctive badge and all associated consequences.

In notifying Your Eminence of the above, may I express the hope that these measures, which under present circumstances may be regarded as far-reaching, will provide assurance concerning the protection of the lofty principles expressed by Your Eminence.[20]

Sztójay's assurances must have assuaged the Cardinal, for he agreed to a compromise formula under which on July 8 and 9 the state radio was to broadcast to all parishes the Cardinal's communication that the pastoral letter was designed only for the information of the priests and church officials, and was not to be read before the parishioners. Instead, the following note would be read:

Jusztinián Cardinal Serédi . . . informs the Catholic faithful in his name and in the name of the Council of Bishops that he has repeatedly approached the Royal Hungarian government in connection with the decrees relating to the Jews and especially the converts and is continuing his negotiations in this respect.[21]

Anticipating criticism for his apparent surrender to the government, on July 9 the Cardinal addressed a confidential letter to the bishops explaining the reasons for his actions. In it he reviewed his activities since May 17, the date of his first communication to them, emphasizing his efforts to bring about the suspension of the deportations, and he set forth his reasons for the preparation and eventual rescinding of the pastoral letter. He concluded with his belief that the faithful would realize, through the radio announcement and the brief text read from the pulpits, that the Church had done its duty and that the secret negotiations had yielded results that would have been impossible to achieve through an open conflict with the government.[22]

The short note was read in all the Catholic churches of Hungary on July 16, by which time the only Jews left in Hungary were in the labor service companies or Budapest. Although Bishop Apor approached the Cardinal once again, on July 15, to urge him to be on guard against violations by the government of its assurances and to propose additional measures, he no longer raised the question of arousing public opinion.[23]

Throughout, the Cardinal pursued a discreet and private approach in dealing with the government although he was fully informed about the problems that continued to plague the remnant of the Jewish community, including the "illegal" deportations from the Kistarcsa internment camp.[24] His failure to take a public stand was a cause of distress not only for the persecuted Jews, but also for many noted Hungarians living in exile. Petőfi Radio, for example, commenting on a speech the Cardinal made in mid-August, stated that the world, including Hungary's Christian society, had been without a pronouncement by him for five full months. The Cardinal's silence, the broadcast continued, led American-Hungarian Catholics to believe that he had been either imprisoned or murdered.[25]

The Attitude and Actions of the Protestant Churches

The reaction of the Protestant churches to the anti-Jewish measures was not fundamentally different from that of the Catholic Church.[26] In fact, in most cases the attitude and actions of the leaders of the two Protestant church associations—the Universal Convent of the Reformed Church of Hungary (*A Magyarországi Református Egyház Egyetemes Konventje*) and the Directorate of the Universal Evangelical Church of Hungary (*A Magyarországi Evangelikus Egyházegyetem Elnöksége*)—paralleled those of Cardinal Serédi.[27] Although they too agonized over the plight of the Jews, especially over the *manner* in which the Jewish question was being solved, their primary concern was the welfare of the converts. Like the Catholic hierarchy, they mostly expressed this concern discreetly, appealing individually or collectively to the local or central leaders of the government for the redress of injustices.

Bishop Ravasz approached Jaross and Gyula Ambrózy, the head of the Regent's Cabinet Office, on April 3, protesting the anti-Jewish measures and asking for exemptions from wearing the yellow star. On April 12 and 28, Ravasz visited Horthy with the same purpose. During the latter meeting, Horthy confirmed that he had indeed permitted the allocation of a few hundred thousand Jews "for labor in Germany."[28] In addition to such visits, appeals were submitted separately by the Convent and Directorate of the two Protestant churches.

The first joint action by the Reform (Calvinist) and Evangelical (Lutheran) church leaders was undertaken on April 4 on behalf of converts. In a memorandum addressed to Sztójay, Antal, and Jaross, they demanded that the converts be exempted from wearing the yellow badge, be allowed to employ non-Jewish servants, and not come under the jurisdiction of the Jewish Council. Sztójay's reply of May 10 was basically identical with the one given to Cardinal Serédi about the same requests.[29]

A day earlier Sztójay had also been visited by Bishop Ravasz in the company of Miklós Mester, the former Imrédyist secretary of state in the Ministry of Cults and Public Education who turned against the Germans and the *Nyilas* in the summer of 1944. They handed the Prime Minister a memorandum prepared by the Convent, deploring the atrocities committed during the concentration and ghettoization of the Jews.

On May 19, Károly Wilhelm, one of the leading members of the Jewish Council, informed Ravasz that mass deportations had been started a few days earlier. A young minister was sent to Kassa to check the veracity of the report. He returned almost immediately fully corroborating it. New memoranda (May 19 and 26) were submitted to Sztójay warning the government against the possible consequences of their unjust measures, but the response was always vague and noncommittal. While these memoranda included a condemnation of the deportations, their focus was on the fate of the converts. The church leaders demanded the right for the ministers of the various denominations to serve the spiritual needs of their congregants in the ghettos, and the identification as Christians of persons who had converted before their children reached seven years of age.[30]

With ample new evidence about the cruelties, the leaders of the Protestant churches approached Cardinal Serédi some time in May to undertake, along the example of the Dutch and Danish churches, a joint campaign to thwart the government's anti-Jewish measures. A meeting toward this end was actually held in the upper house of the Hungarian Parliament through the good offices of József Cavallier, the head of the Holy Cross Society, but it yielded no positive results.[31] Bishop Ravasz, who was absent from that meeting because of illness, approached Cardinal Serédi on June 15 via a letter that was taken to Esztergom, the Prince Primate's See, by Cavallier. Bishop Ravasz raised the right question, but offered an unfortunate loophole for temporizing over it. He asked: "When will the Christian churches deem the time ripe to voice their solemn declaration in protest, before the country and the world, against the inhuman methods currently being used in the handling of the Jewish question?" Although the mass deportations were in full swing, Bishop Ravasz suggested that before such a public stand were taken, a delegation of churches should hand the government leaders "a final earnest warning."[32] The Bishop was apparently still more concerned with the possible breach in church-state relations than with the plight of the Jews.

Cavallier took a copy of Bishop Ravasz's proposed protest memorandum to Serédi, but the Cardinal did not find it possible to cooperate.[33] The Protestant church leaders consequently decided to forward the memorandum without him. The text was not finalized until June 20, because it had to have the approval and signature of the nine bishops. The memorandum, addressed to Sztójay, conveyed the church leaders' dismay over the manner in which the Jewish question was being solved. While they implored the Prime Minister to put an end to the atrocities, they emphasized that for the time being at least, they would not bring this issue to public attention in order not to aggravate his political difficulties. The memorandum was handed to Sztójay on June 23 by a delegation composed of Bishops Ravasz and Kapi accompanied by Jenő Balogh and Baron Albert Radvánszky, the lay leaders of the Reformed and Evangelical churches.[34]

Sztójay told the church representatives that the accounts charging the Jews had been tortured were exaggerated. He referred to László Endre's assurances that the converts were being separated from the Jews, that they were adequately represented within the Jewish Council by the noted writer Sándor Török, and that the administrative and security organs of the state had been instructed to deal humanely with the Jews. Sztójay also repeated the standard lie that the Jews were merely being taken to Germany to work and the families were sent along to spare them from unnecessary worry about their loved ones. A copy of Endre's note of June 16 was forwarded by Huszovszky to Bishop Raffay on July 4.[35]

Probably frustrated by the failure of the delegation to get substantive concessions from Sztójay, on June 27 Raffay contacted Cardinal Serédi on his own, suggesting that the three long-established churches of Hungary submit a joint protest to either Horthy or Sztójay. The subject was once again "the shameful failure of the churches to protect their faithful" and the fact that the converts were concentrated together with Jews in camps and ghettos operating under the jurisdiction of Jewish Councils.[36] Once again, the Cardinal rejected the appeal, arguing that he was largely achieving his goals without such an approach and moreover that the churches could not expose themselves to the possibility of failure.[37]

Since the Protestant church leaders found the responses of the government unsatisfactory, they decided to issue a pastoral letter to inform the congregants about their efforts in behalf of the persecuted. The letter, which was to be read in all churches, was drawn up by Bishop Ravasz. It read in part:

> Brethren in Jesus Christ! The undersigned bishops of the Reformed Church in Hungary and the Evangelical Church in Hungary, turn to you to inform you, in the presence of God, of the steps they have taken, in the name of the Evangelical churches at the Royal government. We inform the holy congregations that, after several petitions made in writing and orally, on June 23 we presented a solemn memorandum of protest and plea to the Premier. In this memorandum we related the utterly regrettable events which accompanied the segregation and deportation of Jews of Hungary, whether Jews or Christians by faith. Having stated that this mode of solving the Jewish question violated

God's eternal laws, the memorandum went on as follows: God has ordained us, that we declare to this generation His eternal gospel, and to stand as witnesses by the unchangeable laws of His world order, whether or not it pleases men. Standing on the foundation of this divine commission, humble and sinful men as we are, yet testifying to God's word in the sacred communion of faith and obedience, we condemn all modes of action which violate human dignity, justice and mercy and bring upon the head of our people the frightful judgment of bloodshed.

At the same time, we earnestly besought the Royal government to put an end to the cruelties, condemned by members of the government themselves as well, and enforce the formal pronouncements on the one hand protesting against the assumption that the extermination of the Jews was a reality, and on the other hand containing instructions for the humane administration of the rules and regulations pertaining to the Jews.

We have to note that these pleas of ours led to no results. . . .[38]

Antal got wind of the Protestant church leaders' intentions and disarmed them by the same technique he had earlier used with the Cardinal. At a meeting held in Ravasz's home on July 11 attended also by Mester, Bishops Kapi and Révész, Reverend Albert Bereczky, and Szabolcs Lőrinczy, Antal gave the same assurances concerning the special treatment of the converts and the more humane treatment of the Jews. The church leaders yielded, rationalizing that an open break with the government might bring the *Nyilas* into power, which would be disastrous not only for the churches and the country but also for the Jews of Budapest. The formula of agreement was identical with the one reached with the Cardinal. On July 12, the ministers of the Protestant churches were instructed to read the following text to their congregants during the July 16 Sunday morning services:

The Bishops of the Reformed Church of Hungary and the Evangelical Church of Hungary wish to inform the congregations that in connection with the Jewish question, and particularly the baptized Jews, they have repeatedly taken steps with the appropriate government officials and will continue to do so.[39]

The efforts of the church leaders yielded some positive results. They gained exemption for church officials of Jewish background, as well as for persons living in mixed marriages. They also achieved a more lenient treatment of converts, for the defense of whose interest a special council—the Association of the Christian Jews of Hungary (*A Magyarországi Keresztény Zsidók Szövetsége*)—was established on July 14 (see chapter 14). Concurrently a campaign was launched to register those converted before August 1, 1941.[40] This move, coupled with the leaking of Sztójay's July 7 assurances to the Cardinal that converts would be exempted in case the deportations were resumed, caused many Jews to convert—to the dismay of both Orthodox Jews and the *Nyilas.*

The church leaders also undoubtedly contributed to the Regent's decision to halt the deportations. Nevertheless, their covert although well intentioned negotiations, and the failure to give clearcut guidance to the clergymen and the Christian masses, contributed to the climate that made the unhindered implementation of the Final Solution possible.

The Attitude and Actions of Individual Bishops

Most of the bishops of the various dioceses did everything in their power to induce the local authorities to alleviate the plight of the Jews. They also often contacted the central leaders of the Hungarian government. Again, with one or two exceptions the approach was private.

Among those who were indefatigable in their interventions in behalf of the Jews and especially the converts were Baron Vilmos Apor, the Bishop of Győr, and Gyula Czapik, the Bishop of Eger. The former was so relentless in his protests that Jaross threatened to imprison him. Bishops Lajos Shvoy and Endre Hamvas, the Bishops of Székesfehérvár and Csanád, expressed shock and consternation over the cruelties they had witnessed in their dioceses. This was also true of József Grösz, the Bishop of Kalocsa, Ferenc Virág, the Bishop of Pécs, and Sándor Kovács, the Bishop of Szombathely.[41] Most bishops also pressured the Cardinal to take more vigorous leadership in opposing the government's anti-Jewish policies.[42]

Three of the bishops publicly raised the issue of ghettoization and deportation on their own. During his Whitsunday sermon, Bishop Apor declared:

And he who denies the fundamental laws of Christianity about love and asserts that there are people and groups and races one is permitted to hate, and advocates that there are men whom one may torture, be they either Negroes or Jews, no matter how much he may boast of being Christian is in fact a pagan and clearly guilty. . . . And all those who approve such tortures and participate in their commission commit a serious crime and will not receive absolution until they make amends for their sin.[43]

Bishop Hamvas of Csanád, speaking at the ordination ceremony for new priests in the Szeged cathedral on June 25, when the Jews of the district were being deported, also expressed himself courageously and eloquently:

It is especially important now to proclaim the truth because men's reason has been very beclouded and their judgment impaired under the impact of one-sided propaganda. They consider as permissible, even praiseworthy, things that are forbidden by God as very grave sins and consider as Christian acts and feelings which are the most characteristic fruits of neo-paganism and cannot under any conditions be identified with Christianity. For what is happening nowadays? In the name of Christianity, hundreds and hundreds of thousands of people are deprived of their property and homes and are deported because of their race, which they are unable to do anything about, so that a flood of suffering descends upon them exposing their health and lives to uncertainty and denying their human dignity. Among these hundreds of thousands are innocent children, defenseless women, helpless old people and pitifully sick persons. . . . Some try to defend and explain the situation by simply labeling the entire race as guilty. But Christian morality states: The accused must be brought before a court and given an opportunity to defend himself, and may be condemned only after having been proven guilty; and the sentence must be proportionate to the crime. . . . God's laws protect the right of every man, even the Negro and the Jew, and defend their right to property, liberty, dignity, and health and life. We do not say this as friends of Jews but as friends of truth. God gave certain fundamental rights to all men, irrespective of their national, racial or class differences.[44]

Perhaps the most courageous public stand was taken by Bishop Áron Marton, whose diocese covered all of Transylvania and who frequently preached in Hungarian-held Northern Transylvania although his bishopric had its seat in the Romanian-held part of Transylvania, at Alba-Iulia. Speaking in St. Michael's Church of Kolozsvár on May 18, when the Jews of the surrounding area were still in the local ghetto, he movingly condemned the measures adopted against the Jews—in contrast to his Protestant counterparts in the area, who kept silent. His sermon, which was mimeographed and reportedly even distributed in other parts of the country, deserves extensive quotation:

Faithful to the command of its Godly founder, the Church, accepting and propagating man's love for his fellow man, has advocated the principle that the human race belongs to a single great family. In addition to the positive command to show love for one's fellow man, the basis of the Church's attitude and consistent position was the fundamental belief of Christianity that we are all God's children and are all brothers in Christ. The world is denying both these propositions, in both theory and practice. It has rejected the idea of everyone's being God's children and especially that of brotherhood in Christ, with the proclamation of high-sounding and misleading ideas in the name of science. It worked against the success of love for one's fellow man by pursuing one-sided and unjust interests under various slogans and often in the name of saintly pronouncements. We do not have the time (nor the proper forum) to challenge this: when we are confronted with passion and subjectivity, the rational mind cannot help much. Against spiritual blindness the only effective remedy is God's mercy, and theories, no matter how contemporary they are proclaimed to be, are buried by newer theories. For us, however, my dear brothers, the fundamental premise of our belief, the command to love one's fellow man, still holds, and its open acceptance and practice is even more of a duty today than in former times. The name of Christian, which has been used so many times as a symbol with so many meanings, compels us to do so, my brothers! He who sins against his fellow man endangers one of the great achievements of the 2000-year work of Christianity—the idea of the brotherhood of man. He proceeds not in a Christian but in a pagan spirit and willingly or unwillingly joins those drives that split the nations into races, separate social classes and selfish unions, and set the nations against each other in unpacifiable animosities. And finally, my brothers, our last, nonnegotiable treasure compels us to this stand: our people's honor. The people everywhere long for an order built on justice, on laws that are applied equally to all, and on love toward all, because they know through their innate feeling for justice and timeless experience that only this can give their life that sure framework within which they can work peacefully for themselves and the welfare of their families and the community. I have been informed that my parishioners, starting at the easternmost borders of the Church district, have been greatly shocked by news of the restriction of freedom and uncertain fate of certain persons, and have followed with great concern the measures that have lately been carried out against the Jews. I was most pleased to hear of this moral conception, opinion and judgment of my worshippers; I mention this with chief-pastoral pride because this is the conception, opinion and judgment of the broad masses and at the same time the happy sign that the true Catholic spirit is deeply rooted and still alive in our people's soul as a living force. In the defense of truth and the service of love, persecution and imprisonment are a mark not of shame but of honor.[45]

Bishop Marton's stand was not well received by the Hungarian authorities. Rebuked by Jaross, he returned to Alba-Iulia at the end of May and, having become a *persona non grata,* did not reenter Northern Transylvania until after the end of the war.[46]

One of the bishops whose attitude became the source of considerable controversy after the war was József Mindszenty, the Bishop of Veszprém, who later succeeded Cardinal Serédi as the Prince Primate of Hungary. Following the deportation of the Jews of Veszprém, Dr. Schimberna, the head of the local *Nyilas* party, reportedly approached the Franciscans to offer a solemn service and *Te Deum* in gratitude for the solution of the Jewish question in the city. The bishop protested against the plan, arguing that the deportees also included converts, but relented after the *Nyilas* threatened to distribute a flyer about his opposition. He finally permitted a special service on the condition that it not end with a *Te Deum* and that the *Nyilas* refrain from appearing in uniform. The services were held on July 25 in a church filled with worshippers with a monk in festive green vestments offering the mass. (The *Nyilas* did appear in uniform.)[47]

The incident at Veszprém was unique; there is no evidence that such special services were held in any other town. On the other hand, there is also no evidence that the brave stands taken by Bishops Apor, Hamvas, and Marton had any impact on the masses in their dioceses. The anti-Jewish measures were carried out in these areas with the same ease and with the population as passive as everywhere else in the country.

Source materials relating to the attitude and reactions of lower-ranking clergymen are scanty. The large number of personal narratives and memoirs, both published and unpublished, yield an incomplete picture. A number of priests and ministers took an active part in the weak Hungarian resistance movement and did their best to help the persecuted. Foremost among these were Reverend Albert Bereczky of the Reformed Church and Monsignor Béla Varga of the Roman Catholic Church.[48] Several became actively involved in supporting the Jews and converts, especially during the *Nyilas* era (see below). The overwhelming majority of the clergy, however—in the absence of guidance and encouragement from their superiors—reflected the passivity of the population at large. Some occasionally expressed dismay over the manner in which the Jews were being treated in their communities, usually showing special concern for the welfare of the converts. To alleviate the plight of the latter, they normally approached their immediate superiors or the central leaders of their faith. Their attitude is illustrated by that of Father Elek Oberndorf of the Evangelical Church in Mohács. In an appeal to Radvánszky in behalf of three local converted women, he articulated the views and feelings of many clergymen:

I know that Jewry was a foreign element in the nation's body, which had to be removed. It is not against this, but against the manner of its implementation that every Hungarian of good will has objections. I now restrict my complaints exclusively to my Protestant brethren of the Jewish race who were entrusted to me by God.

In concluding his plea, Father Oberndorf pointed out that he "never was a friend of the Jews, but was a friend and brother of those with whom he had become united in Christ."[49]

In contrast to the minority that tried to help and the many who were passive, a few clergymen actually sided with the *Nyilas,* giving them spiritual and occasionally even physical support in the implementation of anti-Jewish measures. For example, Dean Ignác László of Gyergyószentmiklós, a member of the upper house, advocated the physical annihilation of the Jewish people.[50] Another example is that of Father András Kun, a Minorite monk who was reportedly at odds with the church hierarchy. Wearing a gun and a *Nyilas* armband, he was involved in the torture-filled investigation of 300 protected Jews in the Budapest *Nyilas* headquarters at 14 Városház Street. Approximately 200 of these Jews were subsequently shot along the banks of the Danube. Father Kun was also involved in the January 11, 1945, massacre of the patients and staff of the Jewish Hospital on Maros Street, where he reportedly ordered the *Nyilas* to fire in the "holy name of Christ."[51]

The Christian Churches During the Nyilas Era

During the *Nyilas* era, the leaders of the Christian churches resumed their pleas on behalf of the Jews. Earlier in July, Antal had warned the church leaders that an open confrontation with the government might bring about a *Nyilas* takeover of power. Yet, when this very thing occurred, the church leaders continued to rely on the same tactics, even though the social order they so faithfully supported had been destroyed.

The Papal Nuncio again took the initiative in warning the new rulers of Hungary against resuming draconic measures against the Jews. Cardinal Serédi also contacted Szálasi on October 24 and 27 and submitted a memorandum on November 2; however, while he raised the Jewish question, his primary concern was with the government's planned actions in view of the worsening military situation. In light of the rapid advance of the Red Army, the Cardinal discussed the advisability of evacuation and urged that Budapest and Esztergom be declared open cities.

On November 8, following the start of the death marches to Hegyeshalom (chapter 26), the Cardinal protested the treatment of the Jews, demanding the safeguarding of their right to life and reminding Szálasi about the Sztójay government's assurances concerning the suspension of the deportations. Shortly afterwards Bishop Ravasz submitted a memorandum with five specific demands: declaration of Budapest as an open city; discarding the plans for the city's evacuation; adoption of humane methods in the treatment of Jews; termination of deportations; and security for the Jews' lives. Szálasi's response was delivered by Jenő Szöllősi, the Deputy Prime Minister, on November 24. The church leaders were told that Szálasi had obtained assurances from Hitler that the bridges and public works of Budapest would not be destroyed. They were also told that the Jews would be separated and the labor servicemen (including at this time all able-bodied Jewish men and women) would be transferred closer to the German border "in order to prevent their vengeance against Hungarians in case of a Russian occupation."

Dissatisfied with the government's reply, on November 26 Bishop Ravasz approached Cardinal Serédi via Valdemar Langlet, the representative of the Swedish Red Cross, suggesting that a delegation composed of the leaders of the three churches visit Szálasi. The Cardinal, who was already quite ill at the time, rejected the idea as useless. (Earlier, the Cardinal had given a similar reply to the leaders of the Jewish Council who in a telegram dated November 14 had appealed for his intervention because Jews were being rounded up and deported without regard to sex or state of health and in violation of existing decrees.) Seeing the reluctance of the Cardinal to cooperate, the bishops of the Reformed and Evangelical churches submitted a memorandum to Szálasi on their own. In this document, dated December 1, they proclaimed that the treatment accorded the Jews "mocks God's eternal laws which prescribe humane treatment even of one's enemies and brings God's anger on the head of the nation."[52]

While the church leaders tried to alleviate the situation of the Jews through direct appeals to the *Nyilas* leaders, some clergymen took an active role in trying to save Jewish lives. By far the most active among these were those associated with the ecclesiastical institutions of converts.

The Holy Cross Society

The major institution devoted to the protection and advancement of the interests of Jews converted to Catholicism was the Holy Cross Society. The establishment of a special committee to protect the interests of Jews converted to Catholicism was proposed in the fall of 1939 by Baron Móric Kornfeld, one of the country's leading industrialists. A convert himself, Baron Kornfeld was concerned with the possible impact of the anti-Jewish laws, which incorporated racial ideas with potentially ominous implications for Jews and converts alike. A committee of this kind was established under the leadership of Count Gyula Zichy, the Bishop of Kalocsa, following a meeting of the Catholic bishops on October 3, 1939.[53] Under the guidance of its secretary general, Dr. József Cavallier, the committee at first devoted its attention to the support of the refugees that began to enter the country after the outbreak of World War II. It also came to the aid of those affected by the anti-Jewish laws, cooperating in this regard with the major Jewish welfare organizations, including MIPI and OMZSA. Early in December 1940, the committee was amalgamated with the Holy Cross Society which, under the leadership of Professor József Jánossy, pursued similar objectives. Following the death of Bishop Zichy, Bishops Hamvas and Apor became its main patrons.

After the German occupation, the Holy Cross Society was heavily involved in protecting converts from the anti-Jewish measures. But it also was active in providing aid and comfort to the many refugees in the country, irrespective of their religious background. This part of its work was directed by Mrs. Béla Rónai, who for her generosity was deported by the Germans. Its medical services were organized and directed by Dr. Margit Kormos. The Society worked closely with the Catholic hierarchy as well as the Papal Nuncio, and was under the overall direction of Cavallier and Jánossy. It was a primary force in the establishment of the Association of the Christian Jews of Hungary and a champion of human rights. Its effectiveness was brought to an end late in November 1944, following a number of *Nyilas* raids on its offices. On November 17, Cavallier himself was shot and wounded and taken away by the *Nyilas* together with approximately 150 Jews who were applying for Papal protective passes. The Society's activities were to a large extent absorbed by the Good Shepherd Committee.[54]

The Good Shepherd Committee

The most visible cooperation between the Catholic and Protestant churches of Hungary in connection with the persecuted was between the Holy Cross Society and the Good Shepherd Committee (*A Jó Pásztor Bizottság*), the association of Jews converted to Protestantism.[55] This Committee was established on October 20, 1942, under the direction of Reverend Gyula Muraközy and the sponsorship of the Universal Convent of the Reformed Church of Hungary. The leadership of the Committee was entrusted to Reverend József Éliás, himself of Jewish background. Among his closest associates were Dr. Imre Kádár, the secretary of the Committee; Emil Hajos, deacon; and Reverend Károly Dobos, Dr. Ferenc Benkő, and Andor Borbás as well as a host of volunteers, who devoted their energies to social and charitable work as well as to serving the spiritual needs of the converts. The Evangelical

Church affiliated itself with the Committee in May 1944, when Bishop Raffay appointed Reverend Gábor Sztehló as its representative in charge of the children of labor servicemen and converts. Before the occupation, the Committee paid special attention to the physical and spiritual needs of converts affected by the various anti-Jewish laws, including those in labor service. It also helped Jewish and non-Jewish refugees, both by providing assistance for those interned in the camps of Csörgő, Garany, Ricse, and those on Magdolna, Páva, and Szabolcs streets in Budapest and by serving as a link to KEOKH, the police agency in charge of aliens.

After the occupation, the Committee acted in cooperation with the representatives of the various Protestant denominations to ease the plight of the Jews in general and of the converts in particular. Toward this end it worked closely with the Holy Cross Society and the Jewish Council.[56] During the Sztójay era, the Committee provided opportunities for conversions—either real or merely formal—and distributed protective passes issued by neutral state legations. Éliás was also active in bringing about the establishment of the Association of the Christian Jews of Hungary.[57]

The work of the Committee became especially important during the *Nyilas* era, when it included the sheltering of approximately 1,500 children in 32 homes.[58] The groundwork for these activities had been laid two years earlier, when the Committee set up a Protestant Orphans' Home in Noszvaj, near Eger, to shelter Jewish and non-Jewish refugee (mostly Slovak) children. Shortly before the coup, Reverends Éliás and Sztehló persuaded Géza Kiss, a legal adviser for the *Nyilas,* and Mihály Orosz, the propagandist appointed by László Baky to lead the "cultural struggle" against the churches, to permit the concentration of children into a special juvenile ghetto. The feeding, housing, and protection of the children were assured through the cooperation of the International Red Cross, which established a special department (Section B) for this purpose.[59] The Section, which was headed by Reverend Sztehló and included Dr. János Pétery and Professor Papp, acted in close cooperation with Komoly's Department A and with the Swedish Red Cross, headed by Valdemar Langlet. The program was largely financed by Heinrich and Ottó Haggenmacher and their families, who also provided large quantities of food as well as a number of homes.[60]

Since Reverend Éliás had to go into hiding almost immediately after the *Nyilas* coup (he had been blacklisted by the *Nyilas* for his philanthropic and political activities), responsibility for the protection of the children fell almost exclusively on Reverend Sztehló. He carried out his tasks with great courage and skill. Although some of the homes were subjected to *Nyilas* and police raids (one of these, around December 10 through 12, was led by László Endre himself) remarkably, no harm befell any of the children entrusted to his care. The children of the homes on Munkácsy Mihály, Király, and Perczel-Mór streets were taken into the ghetto only to be smuggled out with the connivance of Reverend Sztehló and the IRC.[61]

Following the establishment of the Budapest ghetto, the Committee served the spiritual needs of converts, providing solace and comfort for many Jews as well. The representatives of the Committee, including Reverends Gyula Nagy and Sándor Borsos, also managed on occasion to smuggle food and medicines into the ghetto. Reverend Nagy maintained close contact with Miksa Domonkos of the Jewish Council in his endeavors to help the persecuted.[62] The activities of these dedicated clergymen complemented the rescue and relief operations undertaken by the representatives of the International Red Cross and of the neutral states.

Notes

1. Robert Major, "The Churches and the Jews in Hungary." *Continuum*, Autumn 1966, p. 373.

2. For details on his political-ideological views see *Páter Zadravetz titkos naplója* (The Secret Diary of Pater Zadravetz), ed. György Borsányi (Budapest: Kossuth for Magyar Történelmi Társulat, 1967), 311 pp. See also chapter 1.

3. Major, "The Churches and the Jews in Hungary," pp. 374–75. See also his *25 év ellenforradalmi sajtó, 1919–1944* (25 Years of Counterrevolutionary Press, 1919–1944) (Budapest: Cserépfalvi, 1945), pp. 22–31.

4. Major, "The Churches and the Jews in Hungary," pp. 375–76.

5. For a sympathetic evaluation of the role of the Catholic Church with emphasis on its opposition to the Nazis and their supporters in Hungary, see Miklós Beresztóczy, "A magyar katolicizmus harca a nemzetiszocializmus ellen" (The Struggle of Hungarian Catholicism Against National Socialism) in *A magyar katolikus egyház és az emberi jogok védelme* (The Hungarian Catholic Church and the Protection of Human Rights) ed. Antal Meszlényi (Budapest: A Szent István Társulat, 1947), pp. 9–20. For a positive view of Cardinal Serédi's position, see Antal Meszlényi, "A hercegprímás a zsidótörvények enyhitéséért" (The Prince Primate for Easing the Impact of the Jewish Laws), *ibid.*, pp. 31–43. For a favorable view of the role of the Christian churches in general, see László, T. László, "Az egyházak szerepe a zsidó-mentésben Magyarországon. I. A zsidótörvények" (The Churches' Role in the Saving of Jews in Hungary. I. The Anti-Jewish Laws). *Katolikus Szemle* (Catholic Review), Rome, 31, no. 2 (1979):139–63.

6. Dr. Schlachta was also active in transmitting to the Vatican, and to Francis Cardinal Spellman of New York, documents relating to the destruction of the Jews of Poland and Slovakia which she had received from the MIPI representatives. Lévai, *Szürke könyv magyar zsidók megmentéséről* (Gray Book on the Rescuing of Hungarian Jews (Budapest:

Officina, n.d.), p. 168. Her heroism and humanitarianism were recognized by the Special Commission for the Designation of the Righteous of Yad Vashem, which honored her with its highest award: a medal, a certificate of honor, and the right to plant a tree on the Avenue of the Righteous at Yad Vashem.

7. For references to the various anti-Jewish laws and the reaction to them, consult Randolph L. Braham, *The Hungarian Jewish Catastrophe. A Selected and Annotated Bibliography* (New York: YIVO Institute for Jewish Research, 1962), pp. 8–14. See also chapters 4–6.

8. Popular resentment and the King's opposition prevented the introduction of the badge in Denmark. In the Netherlands, where opposition to the anti-Jewish measures was also strong, many people expressed their sympathies with the Jews by wearing the badge themselves. See Philip Friedman's "The Jewish Badge and the Yellow Star in the Nazi Era" in *Historia Judaica*, 17, no. 1 (April 1955):46–47, 66–68. *Vádirat*, 3:27, 86–87, 133–35.

9. Frederick B. Chary, *The Bulgarian Jews and the Final Solution, 1940–1944* (Pittsburgh: University of Pittsburgh Press, 1972), pp. 188–89.

10. A memorandum to this effect was sent to the Cardinal on August 14. *Vádirat*, 3:385–87.

11. For a highly sympathetic evaluation of Cardinal Serédi's role during the Sztójay and Szálasi eras, emphasizing his stand in support of the persecutees, see the three articles by Antal Meszlényi in *A magyar katolikus egyház és az emberi jogok védelme*, pp. 44–96. See also László T. László, "Az egyházak szerepe a zsidómentésben Magyarországon. II. A budapesti zsidóság megmenekülése" (The Churches' Role in the Saving of Jews in Hungary. II. The Rescue of Budapest's Jewry." *Katolikus Szemle* (Catholic Review), Rome, 31, no. 3 (1979):217–35.

12. *Vádirat*, 3:186–88.

13. Lévai, *L'église ne s'est pas tue. Dossier hongrois 1940–1945* (The Church Did Not Keep Silent. Hungarian Documents, 1940–1945) (Paris: Éditions du Seuil, 1966), pp. 83–84. See also chapter 15.

14. Lévai, *Zsidósors Magyarországon*, pp. 122–24.

15. *Ibid.*, pp. 124–25.

16. *Ibid.*, pp. 125–27. See also Lévai, *L'église ne s'est pas tue*, pp. 85–93. For the complete text of the circular, see *Vádirat*, 2:53–61.

17. Lévai, *Zsidósors Magyarországon*, p. 183–84.

18. *Ibid.*, pp. 184–87.

19. *Ibid.*, pp. 188–91.

20. *Ibid.*, p. 193. Cardinal Serédi included the text of the letter in his July 10 circular addressed to the bishops. See *Vádirat*, 3:126–29.

21. The text was brought to the attention of the bishops and priests together with the instruction that the pastoral letter not be read on July 10. *Ibid.*, pp. 128–29. The Council of Ministers was informed about the agreement by Antal on July 12. *Ibid.*, pp. 148–49.

22. *Ibid.*, 3:115–21.

23. The views of the Council of Ministers were summarized for the Cardinal by Miklós Beresztóczy, a ministerial counselor, on July 12. Lévai, *Zsidósors Magyarországon*, p. 195.

24. *Vádirat*, 3:312–17.

25. Petőfi Radio was a British-sponsored organ of the Independence Group (*Függetlenségi Csoport*) headed by Mihály Károlyi, the former Prime Minister; its broadcasts emanated from Alexandria, Cairo, and London. *Ibid.*, 3:412–13.

26. For a review of the Protestant churches' attitude during the Horthy era, see István Kónya, *A magyar református egyház felső vezetésének politikai ideologiája a Horthy korszakban* (The Political Ideology of the Higher Leadership of the Protestant Churches During the Horthy Era) (Budapest: Akadémiai Kiadó, 1967), 243 pp.

27. The nine leading figures of the Protestant churches were László Ravasz, Bishop of the Reformed Church District Along the Danube; János Vásárhelyi, Bishop of the Reformed Church District in Transylvania; Imre Révész, Bishop of the Reformed Church District in Tiszántul; Andor Enyedy, Bishop of the Reformed Church District in the Tiszáninneni ("Cis Tisza") area; Elemér Győry, Bishop of the Reformed Church District in Transdanubia; Béla Kapi, Bishop of the Evangelical Church District in Transdanubia; Sándor Raffay, Bishop of the Evangelical Church in the Bányai (Mining) District; Zoltán Turóczi, Bishop of the Evangelical Church in the Tisza District; and Dezső Kuthy, Bishop of the Evangelical Church District in the Cisdanubian Area.

28. Albert Bereczky, *Hungarian Protestantism and the Persecution of Jews* (Budapest: Sylvester, n.d.), pp. 14–18. See also chapter 11.

29. On the basis of Sztójay's communication, some bishops instructed the ministers in their diocese to carry out their responsibilities to the converts. Specifically, they were asked to go into the ghettos to serve the spiritual needs of their congregants and advise them that they could wear a white cross next to the Star of David. *Vádirat*, 3:130–33.

30. *Ibid.*, pp. 310–12.

31. Bereczky, *Hungarian Protestantism*, pp. 19–20.

32. *Ibid.*, pp. 19–20.

33. Lévai, *Zsidósors Magyarországon*, pp. 197–98.

34. *Ibid.*, pp. 198–200. See also *Vádirat*, 3:6–8, and Bereczky, *Hungarian Protestantism*, pp. 22–24.

35. *Vádirat*, 3:38–39.

36. *Ibid.*, pp. 9–10.

37. Cardinal Serédi responded on July 8, and included a copy of his planned pastoral letter of June 29. *Ibid.*, pp. 111–12.

38. Bereczky, *Hungarian Protestantism*, pp. 24–26.

39. *Ibid.*, p. 28. See also *Vádirat*, 3:153–55.

40. The registration of converts between July 12 and 17 was announced on posters issued by Ákos Doroghi Farkas, the Mayor of Budapest. The church leaders were eager to advance the conversion date to March 22, 1944, which caused some difficulties between the churches and the authorities. *Vádirat*, 3:49–52, 60–61, 155–58.

41. For a highly positive evaluation of the attitude of Catholic bishops during the occupation, see Antal Meszlényi, "A püspöki kar az emberi jogok védelmében" (The College of Bishops in Support of Human Rights) in *A magyar katolikus egyház és az emberi jogok védelme*, pp. 114–47. See also Lévai's *Zsidósors Magyarországon*, pp. 145–49, 185, and *Szürke könyv*, pp. 72–83.

42. Bishop Apor and Bishop Hamvas were most active in urging the Cardinal to intervene. See for example, Hamvas's note of July 15 in which he expressed shock over the way the searches for valuables were conducted in Makó and Szeged. *Vádirat*, 3:206–7.

43. Lévai, *Szürke konyv*, p. 79.

44. *Ibid.*, pp. 82–83.

45. Munkácsi, *Hogyan történt?*, pp. 144–45.

46. Béla Vágó, "The Destruction of the Jews of Transylvania" in *HJS*, 1:192–93. See also Márton Himler, *Igy néztek ki a magyar nemzet sírásói* (This Is What the Gravediggers of the Hungarian Nation Looked Like) (New York: St. Marks Printing Corp., 1958), pp. 60–62.

47. *RLB*, Doc. 289. For Cardinal Mindszenty's account, including his postwar ordeal, see his *Memoirs* (New York: Macmillan, 1974), 341 pp.

48. One of the leaders of the Smallholders' Party, Monsignor Varga served as the President of the Hungarian Parliament after the war. Following the Communist takeover in 1947, he settled in New York.

49. *Vádirat*, 3:19–22. Answering on behalf of Radvánszky, Sándor Vargha, the Secre-

tary General of the Directorate of the Evangelical Church, assured Father Oberndorf that the Directorate had done everything that was humanly possible to put an end to the inhumane treatment of the Jews. *Ibid.*, pp. 22–23.

50. László was tried after the war by a Romanian People's Tribunal in Kolozsvár and condemned to ten years imprisonment. Vágó, "The Destruction of the Jews of Transylvania," pp. 193, 219.

51. Lévai, *Fekete könyv*, pp. 254, 258. On Kun's conflict with his superiors, see *A magyar katolikus egyház és az emberi jogok védelme*, p. 18. Having been found guilty of war crimes, Father Kun was executed after the war.

52. Bereczky, *Hungarian Protestantism*, pp. 34–37; Lévai, *Zsidósors Magyarországon*, pp. 319–21. See also Gabriel Adriányi, *Fünfzig Jahre ungarischer Kirchengeschichte, 1895–1945* (Fifty Years of Hungarian Church History, 1895–1945) (Mainz: v. Hase & Kochler, 1974), pp. 106–16.

53. For details on the Society's historical background with emphasis on Bishop Zichy's role, see Antal Meszlényi, "Zichy Gyula kalocsai érsek lélek- és életmentő akciója" (The Campaign of Gyula Zichy, the Bishop of Kalocsa, for the Saving of Souls and Lives) in *A magyar katolikus egyház és az emberi jogok védelme*, pp. 97–113.

54. For details on the structure, membership, and wartime activities of the Society, see József Cavallier, "A püspöki kar és a magyar Szent Kereszt Egyesület embervédő munkája" (The College of Bishops and the Life Saving Work of the Hungarian Holy Cross Society) in *A magyar katolikus egyház és az emberi jogok védelme*, pp. 148–68. See also Lévai, *Szürke könyv*, pp. 84–85.

55. The Committee is often referred to as the Good Shepherd Mission (*Jó Pásztor Misszió*).

56. For example, at the request of Samu Stern, Mrs. A. Steckl, one of the members of the Committee, investigated the activities of the controversial Rabbi Béla Berend. See statement by Éliás in YIVO archives, File 768/3652/a. See also chapter 14.

57. Toward this end he worked closely with Sándor Török, who represented the converts in the Jewish Council. Munkácsi, *Hogyan történt?*, pp. 151–55. For Török's account see YIVO archives, File 768/3643.

58. Most of these were children of converts and Christian orphans. The protection of Jewish children was also the responsibility of Section A of the International Red Cross.

59. For the organizational structure of Section B, including a listing of the homes and the number of children placed in them, see Friedrich Born, *Bericht an das Internationale Komitee vom Roten Kreuz in Genf* (Report to the International Committee of the Red Cross in Geneva) (Geneva, June 1945), p. 56.

60. *Ibid.*, pp. 37–39. Heinrich (Henrik) Haggenmacher was the president of the National Association of Manufacturers (*A Gyáriparosok Országos Szövetsége*). For some additional details on him, see Gyula Kádár, *A Ludovikától Sopronkőhidáig* (From the Ludovika to Sopronkőhida) (Budapest: Magvető, 1978), pp. 511–12.

61. For Reverend Sztehló's statement see YIVO archives, File 768/3644. Some time after the war, Reverend Sztehló settled in Switzerland. His heroism and humanitarianism were recognized by the Special Commission for the Designation of the Righteous of Yad Vashem, which awarded him its highest honor: a medal, a certificate of honor, and the right to plant a tree on the Avenue of the Righteous at Yad Vashem.

62. Reverend Nagy was introduced to Domonkos by Lajos Gábor, the father of the well-known Gabor sisters. Personal communication. For additional information on the Good Shepherd Committee, see Bereczky, *Hungarian Protestantism*, pp. 19, 43–46; Lévai, *Szürke könyv*, pp. 86–87, and Munkácsi, *Hogyan történt?*, pp. 151–54.

CHAPTER THIRTY-ONE

INTERNATIONAL REACTION AND INTERVENTION

THE NAZIS' intensive and ruthless pursuit of the Final Solution program demonstrated the defenselessness of the Jewish communities under their control, the ineffectiveness and powerlessness of the Jewish leaders of the free world, and the basic indifference of the non-Nazi and anti-Nazi world to the plight of the Jews.

The leaders of the neutral and Allied countries and of the Vatican and the International Red Cross—although aware of the Nazis' genocidal plans since the summer of 1942—for the most part neither spoke up in defense of the Jews nor came to their rescue until late June 1944. They rationalized their silence and inaction in terms of their particular institutional and national interests. The Allies, while concerned, were reluctant to liberalize their immigration policies or to allow the Jewish tragedy to affect their war strategy. The neutral countries, some of which originally sympathized with the Axis, refused to engage in any operations that might jeopardize their neutrality or burden their societies with a larger number of Jews. The Vatican was careful to protect its special position and the worldwide interests of the Catholic Church. The International Red Cross feared that intervention in support of the Jews might jeopardize its traditional activities on behalf of prisoners of war.

The international reaction to the catastrophe of European Jewry took a more positive turn toward the end of June 1944. By that time, however, the deportations from the Hungarian countryside were coming to an end. This was also approximately three weeks after D-Day, when the defeat of the Third Reich was almost universally accepted as inevitable.

The International Red Cross

Until the middle of July 1944 the International Red Cross (IRC)[1] was not directly involved in the protection of the rights and interests of

Jews *per se*. In Hungary, as elsewhere, the IRC scrupulously adhered to the letter and spirit of the 1929 Geneva Convention, which restricted its activities primarily to matters relating to prisoners of war. It preferred not to get involved with matters affecting civil populations at large—the primary concern of the national Red Cross organizations—let alone with the defense and protection of minority groups against their own governments.

The IRC was not inclined to accept the suggestion of Jewish organizations, spearheaded by the World Jewish Congress, that it confer upon the Jews held in the ghettos and the labor and concentration camps the status of *civilian internees*—a procedure that would have enabled the IRC to carry out local inspection visits, send food parcels, provide medical aid, and in the process perhaps save hundreds of thousands of lives. Aryeh Tartakower and Aryeh L. Kubowitzki (later Kubovy) of the World Jewish Congress, in a sharply worded letter of December 10, 1943, suggested this to Dr. Marc Peter, the IRC's representative in the United States. This was followed by a personal discussion on January 5, 1944. Unfortunately, the IRC did not approach the German Foreign Office with the demand that it confer the status of civilian POWs on all foreigners detained in Germany and the occupied countries until October 2, 1944, when the collapse of the Third Reich was already evident to all.[2]

There were several reasons for the IRC's reluctance to get involved in the rescue of Jews. For one thing, the Germans had declared that the Jews were not *internees* but *detainees*—a penal rather than a civil category. Consequently the supervision the IRC was empowered to exercise over the treatment of prisoners and internees did not apply to them. The IRC also claimed that continued protests in support of the Jews would be resented by the authorities and prove detrimental to the Jews as well as to the other fields of IRC activities.[3] The IRC summarized its position as follows:

If help for the Jews had been the only cause which the International Committee was called upon to serve during the war, such a course, which could have put honour before the saving of life, might have been contemplated. But such was not the case. Relief for Jews, like relief for deportees, rested on no juridical basis. No convention provided for it, nor gave the International Committee even the shadow of a pretext for intervention. On the contrary, conditions were all against such an undertaking. Chances of success depended entirely on the consent of the Powers concerned. And there were all the other tasks, which the Conventions or time-honoured tradition permitted the International Committee to undertake, or which, with so great difficulty, it had succeeded in adding thereto. To engage in controversy about the Jewish question would have imperiled all this work, without saving a single Jew.[4]

Following this line of reasoning, the attitude of the IRC delegation in Hungary was at first identical with that manifested elsewhere in the world. The delegation restricted its activities to its traditional functions: responding to inquiries by foreigners and monitoring the treatment of prisoners of war, to whom it also forwarded parcels. These included thousands of Polish and Yugoslav prisoners and a smaller number of other Allied prisoners of war.[5]

During the first crucial months of the German occupation, the Budapest IRC, which was under the leadership of Jean de Bavier, continued its traditional policy in spite of the Final Solution measures, which its delegation was fully aware of. It maintained the same posture of neutrality even after de Bavier, who did not know German, was replaced in May by Friedrich Born, the director of the Swiss-Hungarian Chamber of Commerce of Budapest (*A Budapesti Svájci-Magyar Kereskedelmi Kamara*).[6] A change in the attitude of the IRC came about only after the Swiss press published some gruesome accounts of the Final Solution in Hungary based on the materials forwarded to Switzerland on June 19 by Miklós (Moshe) Krausz, the head of the Budapest Palestine Office (chapter 23). About two weeks after the interventions (in late June) of President Roosevelt, the King of Sweden, and the Pope, the IRC also decided to take a more active role in Hungary. The organization's visibility became higher in both Budapest and Geneva. Born began a more active campaign, visiting the Ministry of Foreign Affairs and other agencies in behalf of the deportees. He also contacted Theodor Horst Grell, the specialist on Jewish affairs in the German Legation, who assured him that the Hungarian Jews were being taken to Germany only to work and that since the Germans needed ablebodied and healthy Jews they themselves had berated the Hungarians for occasional mistreatments. Moreover, Grell assured Born, once the Jews arrived in Germany they were well taken care of and physically strengthened before assignment for labor. He rejected the suggestion that the IRC visit some of the camps; these were spread throughout Germany and Poland, he argued, and since they were engaged in the production of war materiel, their location had to be kept a secret.[7]

On July 7 (the day Horthy halted the deportations), Max Huber, the President of the IRC, approached the Hungarian Ministry of Foreign Affairs. He wanted all available information that would ease the worldwide restlessness over the alleged events in Hungary, as well as permission for an IRC delegate to visit some of the camps in which Jews were interned and distribute food and clothing.[8] A more specific request was submitted by Imre Tahy, the Hungarian chargé d'affaires in Berne, on July 19. Reporting on a meeting a day earlier with Carl J. Burckhardt of the IRC, Tahy urged that Hungary request the Germans to allow Dr. Robert Schirmer, the IRC delegate in Berlin, to visit Budapest. He emphasized that Schirmer was bringing a message for Horthy in connection with the Jewish question.[9]

Schirmer arrived in Budapest shortly thereafter, and on July 21 he met with Sztójay. Schirmer spelled out the requests earlier submitted by Huber, suggesting that he be allowed to visit some Yellow-Star houses; that the "shipment of Jews for labor abroad" cease and the Jews be concentrated in ghettos similar to the one in Theresienstadt (which an IRC delegation had visited·and approved on June 23);[10] and that the IRC be given an opportunity to investigate the fate of the British and American pilots shot down over Hungary.[11]

The response of Sztójay and Andor Jaross was transmitted to Schirmer on July 23 by Dénes Csopey, the head of the Political Department of the Hungarian Ministry of Foreign Affairs. The two leaders concurred with Schirmer's requests and suggested that the IRC delegation visit the Kistarcsa and Sárvár internment camps, which also contained non-Jewish political prisoners; visits to Yellow-Star houses were to be undertaken in consultation with József Szentmiklósy, the head of the social-political division in the mayor's office.[12] On July 27 and 28, a Schirmer-led IRC delegation visited the Kistarcsa and Sárvár camps, which were under the respective command of two decent men, István Vasdényei and Gribowszki. The situation in the camps was found quite acceptable. (Presumably the delegates were aware that the Germans had managed to deport approximately 1,300 Jews from Kistarcsa and around 1,500 Jews from Sárvár a short while before the visit in spite of Horthy's halting of the deportations and the assurances given to the IRC.)[13] The delegation also visited a few carefully selected Yellow-Star houses and Jewish institutions, finding the conditions generally satisfactory, although overcrowded.[14] The visits, of course, gave a false picture of the situation of Hungarian Jewry. The visit to Theresienstadt on June 23 had not revealed the realities of Auschwitz and Treblinka; the visit to Kistarcsa and Sárvár could not disclose the horror in the many brickyards and entrainment centers, let alone the ultimate fate of the deported Jews.

While in Budapest Schirmer approached Edmund Veesenmayer, the

Reich's Plenipotentiary in Hungary, requesting permission to send packages to the deportees, to visit a camp, and to accompany the inmates of a deportation train to Kassa. Veesenmayer, after consulting with Eichmann, sent a telegram to the German Foreign Office (August 2), in which he said he would be ready to approve the first two requests "if adequate preparations were made." However, he urged that the last one be rejected, asserting that "this would violate the secrecy related to the travel route and destination." Adolf Hezinger, the Foreign Office's expert on the treatment of Jews of foreign citizenship, was given responsibility for the reply. In a note to Horst Wagner, the head of *Inland II*, he suggested the same answer Hitler had given on July 10 to the Hungarians in connection with their earlier request to permit the emigration of some Jews. (This was in response to the appeals of Sweden, Switzerland, and the American War Refugee Board—see chapter 25.) Hezinger suggested that the distribution of packages was to be allowed "only after the resumption of the transfer of Jews into the Reich." He rejected the idea of anyone accompanying a deportation train, but left open the possibility of a camp visit "after thorough preparatory work in cooperation with Eichmann."[15]

The IRC confidentially informed the local and international Jewish organizations in Switzerland about its activities. On July 21, Burckhardt met with the leaders of a few Swiss Jewish organizations; this was followed by a larger meeting on August 10 attended by Huber and the representatives of the 17 largest domestic and international organizations and agencies in Switzerland, including the World Jewish Congress, the Jewish Agency for Palestine, the Palestine Office, and the AJDC. Burckhardt reviewed the situation of the Jews in Hungary, emphasizing the activities of the IRC. One of the objectives of the meeting was to impress upon the leaders of the local and international Jewish organizations the need to coordinate their activities.[16] Although the conferences, like the notes and memoranda handed to the Jewish organizations, were identified as confidential, the Germans became privy to their contents. (The Germans frequently intercepted the mail, including copies of such memoranda, that the Jewish leaders forwarded to their counterparts in Istanbul or Palestine.[17])

While the IRC never achieved the goals it outlined to Veesenmayer in July, in August it did become more involved in two other plans of great interest to the Jewish community: support of the Spanish, Swiss, and Swedish-initiated emigration schemes, and the protection of children. On July 12, the Jewish Council was informed that Spain was ready to accept 500 children. On the advice of Angel Sanz-Briz, the Spanish chargé d'affaires in Budapest, the Council persuaded the IRC to take the foreign-protected children under its aegis. The IRC, which consented to the suggestion early in August, thus acquired a legal framework by which to expand its activities to include the protection of "foreign" civilians.

The Spanish offer induced Burckhardt on August 9 to approach Baron Károly Bothmer, the head of the Hungarian Legation in Berne. He suggested that Hans Bachmann, the IRC's secretary general, meet Tahy, who had earlier assured the IRC that Hungarian Jews holding Palestine immigration certificates or visas from neutral states did have the right to leave the country. The Hungarian response, formulated by Csopey on August 26, asserted that the Hungarian government would recognize the competence of the IRC in all aid and emigration matters which it represented or initiated with the Hungarian government. The IRC took full advantage of this position, and intervened a number of times urging the Hungarian government to speed up the emigration of 2,000 Jews, which was being processed by the Swiss Legation in Budapest.[18] It also transmitted the notes of the Allied governments to the same effect. On August 16, for example, the British and American governments informed the Hungarians that they had accepted Hungary's earlier offer (see chapter 25) and would "make arrangements for the care of such Jews leaving Hungary who reach neutral or United Nations territory."[19] Though such efforts continued until the Soviet forces liberated Budapest, no groups were ever permitted to leave Hungary as a consequence.

By far the most important contributions of the IRC to the Jewish community in Budapest were the sheltering of children and the safeguarding and supplying of Jewish institutions, including the ghetto, during the *Nyilas* era. Plans for the protection of children were laid in August in light of the lingering threat of deportation, the continual dwindling of communal supplies, and the dangers associated with the rapidly approaching front.[20]

Under Born's leadership two sections dealing with children were established within the framework of the IRC: Section A, which was placed under the leadership of Ottó Komoly, the Zionist leader;[21] and Section B, which was entrusted to Reverend Gábor Sztehló of the Good Shepherd Committee.[22] In addition, Born was responsible for the establishment of Section T (*Transportgruppe;* Transportation Unit), which was composed of 25 to 35 recruits of Labor Service Company No. 101/359, the so-called Clothes-Collecting Labor Company (*Ruhagyüjtő*

Munkásszázad). Under the command of Dr. György Wilhelm, the son of Károly Wilhelm of the Jewish Council, and István Komlósi, Section T was engaged in relief, rescue, and resistance operations. It was particularly active in the rescuing of thousands of Jews from the death-marches to Hegyeshalom and in supplying the children's homes and the ghetto with food and fuel.[23]

During the *Nyilas* era, the IRC took under its protection a large number of Jewish and non-Jewish institutions—hospitals, public kitchens, homes for the handicapped and the aged, research and scientific institutes, and shops.[24] Each of these institutions was identified by a plate posted at the main entrance that read: "Under the Protection of the International Committee of the Red Cross" in Hungarian, German, French, and Russian. Born and his associates kept track of the anti-Jewish measures of the *Nyilas*, including those officially initiated by the government and those illegally perpetrated, and appeared frequently before the leaders, especially Baron Gábor Kemény, the Foreign Minister, to help alleviate the plight of the Jews. It was thanks to these interventions that on October 30 the government announced the recognition of protective passes issued by the Vatican and the foreign legations as well as the granting of exterritorial status to all institutions and buildings protected by the IRC.

Shortly after the Budapest ghetto was established, Hans Weyermann arrived from Geneva to assist Born. Though the relationship between the two IRC representatives was not the most harmonious one, they managed to divide their responsibilities during the critical weeks before the capital's liberation. Before the Soviet siege of Budapest began on Christmas day, Born withdrew to his home in Buda from where he directed the activities of the IRC in that part of the capital. Weyermann's responsibilities were concentrated in the Pest part, where the ghetto was located. The effectiveness of the IRC during this time was greatly enhanced by its cooperation with the Papal Nuncio and the representatives of the neutral states. In fact, some of the measures adopted in support of the beleaguered Jewish community, including the protection of the children's homes and the rescuing of Jews from the death marches, were conceived and carried out jointly (see below).[25]

The Vatican and the Budapest Nunciature

Though motivated by different considerations, the reactions of the Vatican to the catastrophe of European Jewry generally paralleled those of the IRC. According to the currently available evidence, Pope

Pius XII and the top officials of the Vatican were as aware of the Nazis' Final Solution program as the Jewish and non-Jewish leaders of the free world. This knowledge was also shared by some of the leading representatives of the Vatican abroad. Yet the Vatican, like the IRC, did not get actively involved in behalf of Jews as Jews until late in June 1944. Even then, the intervention was discreetly diplomatic, rather than public.

Evidence concerning awareness by the Catholic Church's leadership of the Final Solution was published by the Vatican itself in the 1970s. In its series of volumes on the papacy's role during World War II, the Vatican published a number of documents which though obviously selective reveal that Pope Pius XII had received repeated reports through diplomatic and private channels concerning the mass killing of Jews in Poland and the deportations to death camps from various parts of Nazi-dominated Europe. The Pope learned about the deportation of Jews early in 1941; from the beginning of 1942, he received a stream of detailed information about the anti-Jewish drive, including the fact that many of the deportees were destined for death. One of the first church dignitaries to alert the Pope about "the terrible fate" of the Jews was the Archbishop of Vienna, Theodor Cardinal Innitzer. Giuseppe Burzio, the papal envoy in Bratislava, kept the Vatican informed about the mass deportations from Slovakia from their beginning in March 1942. The Papal Nuncio in Berlin, Archbishop Cesare Orsenigo, reported to Monsignor Giovanni Battista Montini, then Acting Secretary of State to Pope Pius and the future Pope Paul VI, that "the most macabre suppositions about the fate of the non-aryans are admissible."[26]

In August 1942, SS-*Obersturmführer* Kurt Gerstein informed Dr. Winter, the legal adviser of Cardinal Count Preysing, the Bishop of Berlin, about the gassings he had witnessed at Belzec, near Lublin, and urged that this information be relayed to the Vatican.[27] A few months earlier, the representatives of the domestic and international Jewish organizations in Switzerland had an interview with Monsignor Filippo Bernardini, the Nuncio in Berne, informing him both orally and in writing about the plight of Jews in East Central Europe. A Jewish Agency memorandum, outlining the mass deportations from Western Europe and the executions of Jews in Poland, was forwarded to Monsignor Luigi Maglione, the Papal Secretary of State, in September 1942 via Harold H. Tittmann, Jr., the assistant of Myron C. Taylor, President Roosevelt's personal representative at the Vatican.[28]

One of the main sources of information about the Nazis' designs against the Jews was Archbishop Angelo Giuseppe Roncalli, the Apostolic Delegate in Istanbul (later to become Pope John XXIII). In his report of July 8, 1943, addressed to Monsignor Montini, Archbishop Roncalli stated that millions of Jews had been sent to Poland and annihilated there. He did not elaborate on the annihilation, presumably because the concentration camp system was by then sufficiently well known. Archbishop Roncalli also revealed his knowledge about the exterminations to Franz von Papen, the German Ambassador in Ankara, who replied by citing the Soviet massacre of Poles in the Katyn forest, near Smolensk.[29]

One of Archbishop Roncalli's sources of information was the Executive Committee of the Jewish Agency of Palestine, with which he had been in close contact since 1943. The leader of the Agency's delegation in Istanbul, Chaim Barlas, kept the Apostolic Delegate informed about the anti-Jewish measures in Europe. In fact, a few days after Hungary's occupation by the Germans, Barlas sent him a note thanking him for his readiness to get in touch with the Holy See and the Apostolic Delegate in Budapest in behalf of Hungarian Jewry.[30]

Although fully aware of the Nazis' drive to exterminate the Jews, the Pope consistently refused to take a public stand to condemn it. The Jewish leaders of the free world, including those associated with the World Jewish Congress, made numerous efforts to induce him to speak out against the exterminations and to threaten Hitler and those actively engaged in the drive with excommunication.[31] Similar appeals were also made by Western leaders. In July 1942, Tittmann reminded the Vatican that its silence was "endangering its moral prestige and is undermining faith both in the Church and in the Holy Father himself.[32]

The Pope refused to allow himself "to be drawn into any demonstrative statement against the deportation of the Jews" even when the Jews of Rome were being rounded up on October 16–17, 1943. Though the measure against the Roman Jews clearly demonstrated to the Vatican just what had happened elsewhere in Nazi-dominated Europe, the Pope refused to break his silence, for he did not want "to say anything that the German people might consider an act of hostility during a terrible war."[33]

The Jewish leaders of the free world tried to persuade prominent Catholic ecclesiastical and political figures to intercede with the Pope to end his silence. Most of their efforts were to no avail. Some of the Catholic dignitaries, including Edouard Theunis, the former Prime Minister of Belgium, refused to use their influence, arguing that "His

Holiness had serious reasons for not making his stand public."[34] Reportedly only one Catholic of world renown approached by the Jewish leaders had the courage to condemn the Pope's silence. He was Jacques Maritain, the noted French philosopher-theologian, then living in exile in the United States.[35]

The Vatican's standard response to the numerous appeals by Jewish groups was "The Holy See will do what it can."[36] The possible reasons for the Pope's silence are complex and not totally verifiable. According to some scholars, the Pontiff failed to speak out against the exterminations because of his "predilection for Germany" and because he "feared a Bolshevization of Europe more than anything else." The Pope's warmth for the German people, of which over 20 million were Catholic, and his undisguised appreciation of German culture can perhaps be traced to his twelve years of service in Germany as Papal Nuncio. The Vatican's abhorrence of Bolshevism was understandable; its leaders made no secret of their contempt for it. The Pope, according to Father Robert Leiber, one of his secretaries, "always looked upon Russian Bolshevism as more dangerous than German National Socialism." Following Italy's extrication from the war in the late summer of 1943, Monsignor Maglione declared that "the fate of Europe depends upon a German victory on the Eastern Front."[37]

Though he surely abhorred the crimes of the Nazis, the Pope presumably felt that he could not condemn the massacre of the Jews without deploring the mass killing of other groups, or single out the Germans without condemning the Soviets.[38] Perhaps the Pope did not want to risk the allegiance of the German Catholics, many of whom were in the forefront of the struggle against Bolshevism, or to jeopardize the neutrality of the Vatican. It is possible that the Pontiff adopted a low profile on the Jewish question because he, like many another Church leader in Europe, including Jusztinián Cardinal Serédi of Hungary, realized that all his previous diplomatic efforts had been basically futile. The most frequently offered explanation by the Vatican itself was that the Pontiff's policy of public silence on the plight of the Jews was calculated to avoid endangering its quiet diplomacy on their behalf.[39] The shortcoming of this position at the time the Jews were already being massacred was summarized by a student of the Catholic Church's wartime role as follows:

. . . A public denunciation of the mass murders by Pius XII, broadcast widely over the Vatican radio and read from the pulpits by the bishops, would have revealed to Jews and Christians alike what deportation to the East entailed. The

Pope would have been believed, whereas the broadcasts of the Allies were often shrugged off as war propaganda. Many of the deportees, who accepted the assurances of the Germans that they were merely being resettled, might thus have been warned and given an impetus to escape. Many more Christians might have helped and sheltered Jews, and many more lives might have been saved.[40]

While the threat of excommunication most probably would not have deterred the ultraradicals from pursuing their sinister designs, it might have had some influence on the many Catholics (and other Christians) all over Europe who were actively involved in the implementation of the Final Solution. The Pope's first direct involvement was the discreet diplomatic appeal directed to Horthy in behalf of the "unfortunate people" who had "peacefully endured" much suffering "on account of their national or racial origin" (see below). Even this appeal came when the deportations from the provinces were drawing to a close and in the wake of great pressure exerted by the Americans, following the exposés by the Swedish and the Swiss press based on the Auschwitz Protocols.

The Vatican reportedly was among the first to receive a copy of the Auschwitz Protocols, at the end of April 1944. They were forwarded through Giuseppe Burzio, the Nuncio in Bratislava.[41] Although the authenticity of the Protocols was fully corroborated, as were its ominous implications for Hungarian Jewry, the Vatican failed to react until late in June when one of its emissaries, Monsignor Mario, came to Slovakia to interview two of the escapees from Auschwitz (see chapter 23). It was only after Monsignor Mario's report and after the revelations of the Swiss press that the Pope decided to appeal to Horthy personally. While his telegram of June 25 was too late to do any good for the provincial Jews, it was influential in Horthy's decision to save the Budapest Jews.

The Vatican's position in Hungary was effectively put forth by Angelo Rotta, the Apostolic Delegate, who was also the dean of the diplomatic corps in Budapest.[42] An extremely able and compassionate man, the Nuncio took the leadership after the German occupation in warning the members of the newly established Sztójay government, individually and collectively, against any anti-Jewish excesses. Between March 23, when the Sztójay government was inaugurated, and May 15, when the mass deportations began, the Nuncio frequently contacted the Prime Minister and Mihály Arnóthy-Jungerth, the *de facto* Foreign Minister, pleading for moderation and the redressing of injustices.

These contacts were made either in person or through Gennaro Vero-lino, the secretary (*uditore*) of the Nunciature. The Nuncio was also in the forefront of the protest measures undertaken by the Christian churches of Hungary, urging their leaders to intervene ever more effectively in behalf of the persecuted. During the first phase of the Final Solution program, however, the Nuncio, like the Hungarian church leaders, was especially concerned with the fate of the converts and the Christians of Jewish origin.

By May 15, when the deportations began, the Nuncio realized the inadequacy of his approach and the failure of the government to heed his warnings. On that day, he submitted a note condemning the actions of the government, emphasizing that the whole world knew what the deportations meant. He appealed once again to the government not to overstep its bounds in the struggle against the Jews. Alluding to the deportations that were just beginning, the note stated:

The Office of the Apostolic Nuncio regards it as its duty to protest against such measures. Acting not out of a false sense of compassion but in the name of thousands of Christians, it requests the Hungarian government once again not to continue its war against the Jews beyond the limits prescribed by the laws of nature and God's commandments, and to avoid any action against which the Holy See and the conscience of the entire Christian world would feel obliged to protest.

The note contained three specific requests:

- That the government differentiate between Jews and converts, and that Christians be exempted, as in Slovakia, from the anti-Semitic measures.
- That fundamental human rights be observed in the implementation of measures deemed necessary by the government in defense of state interests.
- That the government take appropriate steps to prevent the repetition of abuses and assaults against church institutions and persons such as those the police had committed during the raid against the Holy Cross Society.

This note is of particular importance in the annals of the Vatican, because reportedly it was the first official protest against the deportation of Jews lodged by a representative of the Holy See.[43] Like all subsequent notes, it was diplomatic and personal in character. Although he revealed his awareness of the realities of the deportations, the Nuncio adhered to apparent Vatican policy. For, as one scholar of the Holocaust concluded, "no representative of the Vatican ever publicly told Catholics that they must not cooperate because Germany was killing Jews systematically and totally, and killing Jews was a sin."[44]

Along with the protest note, the Nuncio sent Sztójay a personal note, pleading that he support the three demands and pointing out that he was keeping the Holy See fully informed about developments in Hungary.[45]

The Council of Ministers took up the Nuncio's plea on May 17, after similar demands were advanced by the Hungarian church leaders. In accord with Sztójay's suggestions, the Council decided to:

- Request the Minister of the Interior to establish a special section within the Jewish Council to deal with the affairs of converts.
- Separate the converts from Jews in areas where the ghettoization was not yet completed.
- See to it that if there had to be transfer of labor abroad, from which converts could not be exempted, it would not be in the nature of deportation, and would be effectuated humanely, keeping the workers' families together.
- Set up a mechanism under which certain people might be exempted from the anti-Jewish laws for reasons of national interest.[46]

Reportedly, the Council of Ministers also received a message from Arnóthy-Jungerth, who was quite unsympathetic to the policies of the Jaross–Endre–Baky group in the Ministry of the Interior and particularly sensitive about the reaction abroad. He disclosed that the Nuncio had shown him Pope Pius XII's note warning that "Hungary is the land of the Blessed Virgin and of Saint Stephen, and the way it is behaving toward the Jews will be a permanent stain on its honor."[47]

The Nuncio was informed of the Council's decisions by the Ministry of Foreign Affairs on May 27. The note merely repeated the standard answer that the transfers were humane, and for labor abroad. As if to ease the anxiety of the Nuncio in connection with the converts, the note emphasized that the mass conversion of Jews in recent years had been motivated primarily by political and economic factors.[48]

The Nuncio was not persuaded by the government's obfuscating arguments. In his note of June 5, he deplored the deportations and the inclusion of the elderly, the ill, and the children. He expressed, somewhat sarcastically, his surprise that the government had extended to the Jewish laborers the favor of sending along their families when it provided no such opportunities for the thousands of Hungarian Christian workers who had been allowed to work in Germany for years.[49]

The campaign by the Nuncio, paralleling that undertaken by the Hungarian Christian churches, received a boost late in June, following the revelations in the Swiss press of the horrors of the deportations and of the concentration camp system. Among the world leaders who approached Horthy to put an end to these horrors was also Pope Pius XII.

In connection with the tragedy of Hungarian Jewry, Pope Pius XII had been under pressure to act ever since the occupation. The pleas of the Jewish Agency leaders, transmitted via Archbishop Roncalli, were joined by those emanating from other sources. On March 24, the U.S. War Refugee Board urged the Pope via the Apostolic Delegate in Washington to use his influence to protect the Jews of Hungary.[50] Another urgent appeal was advanced by the Board through Harold Tittmann, the U.S. State Department's Vatican representative, on May 26, following the start of the mass deportations:

We believe . . . that it is both timely and fitting that the Hungarian authorities and people should be reminded of the moral values involved and of the spiritual consequences that must flow from indulgence in the persecution and mass-murder of helpless men, women, and children. To that end we earnestly suggest that His Holiness may find it appropriate to express himself on this subject to the authorities and people of Hungary, personally by radio and through the Nuncio and clergy in Hungary as well as through a representative of the Holy See specially despatched to Hungary for that purpose. His Holiness, we deeply hope, may find it possible to remind the authorities and people of Hungary, among whom great numbers profess spiritual adherence to the Holy See, of the spiritual consequences of such acts and of the ecclesiastic sanctions which may be applied to the perpetrators thereof.[51]

The Pope was also approached by the Jewish leaders of the free world. On May 22, for example, Rabbis Isaac Herzog and Ben-Zion Meir Uziel, the Chief Rabbis of Palestine, approached him via the Apostolic Delegate in Cairo, with the request that he use his "great influence . . . to prevent the diabolical plan to exterminate the Jews of Hungary."[52] Toward the end of June, he was asked by Bernard Griffin, the Archbishop of Westminster (acting on behalf of the World Jewish Congress), to intervene in Hungary.[53] When the Pope yielded, his approach, like that of the Nuncio and the Hungarian church leaders, was both diplomatic and personal.

On June 25, the Pope sent the following telegram to the Regent:

Supplications have been addressed to Us from different sources that We should exert all Our influence to shorten and mitigate the sufferings that have, for so long, been peacefully endured on account of their national or racial origin by a great number of unfortunate people belonging to this noble and chivalrous nation. In accordance with our service of love, which embraces every human being, Our fatherly heart could not remain insensible to these urgent demands. For this reason we apply to Your Serene Highness, appealing to your noble feelings, in the full trust that Your Serene Highness will do everything in your power to save many unfortunate people from further pain and sorrow.[54]

Although the word "Jew" was not mentioned in the message, Horthy and his associates realized full well the intentions of the Pope. While the Sztójay government was clearing the last provincial areas of Jews, Horthy was already agonizing over the worldwide impact of the anti-Jewish measures. Cognizant of the rapidly deteriorating military situation, he became increasingly inclined to protect at least the Jews of Budapest. These conflicting positions were clearly reflected in the responses Sztójay and Horthy gave to the Nuncio and the Pope respectively.

In his response to the Nuncio's note of June 5, Sztójay identified on June 30 his government's position on the converts and on the nature of the deportations:

Though lacking the authority to alter the bases of the Hungarian legislative process through the regulation of the Jewish question, the Royal Government wishes to emphasize that it does not refuse the issuance of special considerations on behalf of converted Jews. It was in this spirit that the Royal Government has examined the recent note of the Apostolic Nunciature, and can summarize its opinion in connection therewith as follows:

1. As we have already stated, the interests of the converted Jews will be represented by a special section to be elected from within the Association of Jews in Hungary. Until the bylaws of the Association are approved, Mr. Sándor Török will represent the converted Jews in the Provisional Executive Committee. All necessary measures have been taken to promote the operations of this representative of the converted Jews.

b) We take this opportunity to mention that Hungarian Jews are not slated for deportation. A large number of Jewish manual laborers are being placed at the disposal of the German Government, and the fact that their families were sent together with them to Germany is the result of the decision to keep families undivided, since greater performance can be expected from Jews when they are relaxed by the presence of their families. In this connection, we saw to it that in the retention within the country of the manpower absolutely needed to maintain industrial and economic life, priority be given to the converted Jews and to their families.

c) The Royal Government has for the time being suspended approval of various emigration plans initiated by the Swedish Red Cross and the Swiss government, which envisioned the emigration of a certain number of persons into Sweden and the Near East. The Royal Government is examining these plans in good faith, and as soon as they are about to be realized, it will see to it that the converted Jews are given priority in the opportunities for emigration.

2. The Royal Government has put into effect the strictest measures so as to generally reassure the Jews with respect to the execution of the measures adopted against them; it has prescribed humane and equitable treatment and scrupulous care as guidelines for the executive organs, which are required to refrain from any violation of the principles of humanitarianism.[55]

In contrast to the devious explanations Sztójay gave to the Nuncio shortly after the important Crown Council meeting of June 26 (see chapter 25), Horthy, in his July 1 response to the Pope's plea, clearly intimated a resolution to act:

I have received the telegraphic message of Your Holiness with deepest understanding and gratitude. I beg Your Holiness to rest assured that I shall do everything in my power to enforce the claims of Christian and humane principles. May I beg Your Holiness not to withdraw Your blessing from the Hungarian people in its hours of deepest affliction.[56]

The Nuncio was incensed by the callousness with which the Prime Minister tried to cover up the realities of the anti-Jewish drive. He gave vent to his outrage during a discussion with Sztójay on July 6. Mincing no words, he identified the handling of the Jewish question as "abominable" and as "dishonorable" for Hungary. He complained especially about the cruelties perpetrated by the gendarmerie and about the fact that many Hungarians who were born as Christians or had lived as Christians for 30 to 40 years were being treated in the same outrageous manner as the Jews. In response, Sztójay repeated the arguments he had given in writing on June 30 and catalogued the government's concessions, which he had submitted in writing to Cardinal Serédi on July 7 (see chapter 30).[57] In fact, the Prime Minister urged the Nuncio during this meeting to use pressure on the Cardinal to make him desist from the planned distribution of the pastoral letter of June 29, which in his opinion was directed against the government. Sztójay invoked the threat of Bolshevism, which he claimed threatened both Hungary and the Christian churches. The Nuncio rejected the request, arguing that the Hungarian Catholic hierarchy was not engaged in any anti-government activity, but was merely trying to focus attention on the manner in which the Jewish question was being solved; he also warned against any limitations on the freedom of the church.[58] As it turned out, the Prime Minister achieved his objective despite the Nuncio's opposition.

In his attempt to at least partially recapture the good will of the Holy See, Sztójay supported a special request by the Nuncio to have 14 baptized Jews exempted from the anti-Jewish laws[59] and on July 22 assured him in writing of the governmental concessions he referred to on July 6. The Nuncio, while grateful for the concessions, identified them "as far from being satisfactory."[60]

The Nuncio also intervened on behalf of internees in response to Allied requests. On July 13, for example, he approached the Ministry of Foreign Affairs to support a request transmitted by the American government via the Holy See to have all those interned for political, religious, or racial reasons be treated in accord with the Geneva Convention, and be made eligible to receive food parcels from the IRC. Since there were only a few internment camps of this type in Hungary, including those of Kistarcsa and Sárvár, the Ministry, with the consent of the Prime Minister's office and of the Ministry of the Interior, responded affirmatively two days later.[61] On July 31, following the "illegal" deportations from Kistarcsa and Sárvár (see chapters 22 and 25), the Nuncio pleaded with István Antal, the Minister of Justice, on behalf of 3,000 political prisoners who were supposedly to be concentrated for deportation from Komárom.[62]

Although the deportations were officially suspended as of July 7, the threat of deportation lingered on (they continued in fact in the suburbs of Budapest on July 8 and 9), especially for nonconverted Jews. The several dates set for the deportation of the Budapest Jews, as well as the plans for their resettlement outside of the capital (generally viewed as a prelude to the deportations), induced the Nuncio to continue his efforts. Alarmed by the Jewish Council's communications concerning the planned "resettlement" of the Budapest Jews on August 25, Monsignor Rotta, in cooperation with the respresentatives of Portugal, Spain, Sweden, and Switzerland, on August 21 lodged a vigorous protest against the envisioned deportations.[63]

Even during this period of relative tranquillity, the Jewish leaders of the free world continued their efforts to see the Pope on behalf of the beleaguered Jews. Isaac Herzog, the Chief Rabbi of Palestine, desperately tried—by direct and indirect appeals—to obtain an audience with the Pope. But all his efforts were in vain. The best he could achieve was a meeting on September 5 with Monsignor Hughes, the Papal Delegate to Egypt and Palestine. Hughes claimed that the Pope had withheld an invitation for the Chief Rabbi to come to the Vatican out of fear that such a visit "in connection with measures to save the people of Israel might, perhaps, drive the Germans to wreak vengeance on the remnants of Jewry in Europe."

Similarly, when the Chief Rabbi suggested that "the Pope make a public appeal to the Hungarian people and call upon them to place obstacles in the way of the deportation; that he declare in public that any person obstructing the deportation will receive the blessing of the church, whereas any person aiding the Germans will be denounced," Monsignor Hughes rejected the suggestion. He claimed that "the Holy Father will fear that a public appeal to the Hungarian people may drive the Germans to liquidate the rest of the Hungarian Jews."

When Rabbi Herzog argued that it would be difficult for the Germans to continue the deportations "if Hungarian Bishops were to go into the camps and announce publicly that, if deportation of Jews went on they would go and die with them,"[64] Hughes remained adamant. Obviously the Chief Rabbi was as naïve about the position of the Vatican as he was about the historical role of the bishops in Hungary.

Following the *Nyilas* coup of October 15, the Nunciature expanded its operations on behalf of the persecuted Jews. In addition to pursuing its diplomatic approach, it also became actively involved in rescue operations, often acting in concert with the IRC and the legations of the neutral states. The Nuncio contacted Baron Gábor Kemény, the new Foreign Minister, on October 18, and Szálasi himself on October 21. He asked them to exercise great restraint and moderation in the handling of the Jewish question and to ensure that the concessions made during the Horthy era be honored. These interventions became ever more frequent as the *Nyilas* terror worsened. The mobilization of men and women for forced labor and the beginning of the death marches toward the Austrian border early in November led the Nuncio to conclude that Szálasi's earlier assurances that the Jews would be neither deported nor annihilated could not be trusted. On November 17, he and the Swedish Minister handed Szálasi a note—the second joint action of the Nunciature and the legations of the neutral states—requesting that the government:

- Revoke its decision to deport the Jews and halt the measures already in progress so that those separated from their families could return in the shortest time possible.
- Assure humane treatment (sufficient food, shelter, medical and religious care, respect for life) for those forced to live in concentration camps for labor service.
- Fully and loyally observe the assurances it had given earlier with regard to the Jews under the protection of the legations accredited to Budapest.[65]

That very day Szálasi issued his "final plan" for the solution of the Jewish question. He divided the Jews into six categories, one of which consisted of those to be lent to Germany; another, composed of approximately 15,000 persons holding foreign protective passes, was to be placed into an international ghetto.[66] Among the latter were the approximately 2,500 Jews and converts who had received protective passes from the Nunciature. On October 30, following the interventions of Friedrich Born of the IRC, the Szálasi government decided to recognize these passes. Taking advantage of this decision, the Nuncio ordered that all Roman Catholics affected by the anti-Jewish laws be issued passes stipulating that their holders were under the protection of the Vatican. Although the Nunciature was authorized to issue only 2,500 such certificates, it actually issued many more. In a short while, approximately 15,000 such safe-conduct certificates were in circulation. Many of these were issued by Rózsi Vájkay, the head of the safe-conduct office in the Nunciature, whose own special exemption had been arranged through the intervention of the Nuncio earlier in the year. Wanting to save as many of the persecuted as possible, she issued certificates of protection to all those who submitted baptismal papers without checking whether or not they were genuine.[67]

Many of the Jews holding safe-conduct certificates were housed in a few buildings in the international ghetto. They were identified by special name plates stating that they were under the protection of the Vatican. One of the persons primarily responsible for the safeguarding of these buildings was Tibor Báránszky, a secretary in the Nunciature.[68]

The Nuncio also authorized the issue of presigned blank safe-conduct certificates to be used for rescuing Jews from the Óbuda brickyards, where the victims were concentrated before deportation, and the death-march columns that were being driven toward Hegyeshalom.[69] In this he cooperated with the IRC, whose main representative was Sándor György Újváry. A writer-journalist and publisher of Jewish background, Újváry established contact with the Nuncio via János Tóth, the liaison between the Nunciature and the Ministry of Foreign Affairs.

Újváry became associated with the IRC in October and continued to head its Jewish rescue section until the capital's liberation in February 1945. In this capacity he was involved in the protection of the IRC-sponsored children's homes and the distribution of baptismal certificates which he obtained from Mrs. László Katona, a devout Catholic woman who managed a printing shop in Kassa. When the death marches began early in November, he decided to expand his rescue operations by involving the Nunciature as well. When he revealed his scheme for the "illegal" distribution of the presigned safe-conduct certificates, the Nuncio reportedly reassured him by stating: "What you are doing, my son, is pleasing to God and to Jesus, because you are saving innocent people. I give you absolution in advance. Continue your work to the honor of God."[70]

Újváry's effectiveness was enhanced by his role as liaison between the IRC and the gendarmerie, a position he had obtained through the cooperation of Lieutenant-Colonel László Ferenczy, the officer in charge of the deportations from the provinces. He exploited his triple role by establishing good relations with András Szentandrássy, a high-ranking police officer in the Óbuda brickyards, through whom he succeeded in saving many Jews just before their deportation. These Jews, supplied with baptismal certificates, were usually hidden in convents, monasteries, and other church institutions. These endeavors were supported by many notable Hungarians, among them Baroness Gizella Apor and Countess Mária Pejakevich. Újváry's rescue activities within the framework of the Nunciature were particularly helpful along the death route to Hegyeshalom. Equipped with a letter of authorization signed by the Nuncio and with presigned blank safe-conduct certificates, Újváry and his associates succeeded in saving thousands of Jews before they could be given to the Germans.[71] Among his closest collaborators were Dr. Géza Kiss, a textile merchant associated with the IRC, and Dr. István Biró, a Transylvanian member of the House of Representatives. Shortly after the establishment of the Budapest ghetto, Újváry also organized (December 7) a Department of Cooperation, whose task was to unify the rescue operations of the Nunciature with those of the neutral states under the umbrella of the IRC.[72]

Acting in cooperation with Sections A and B of the IRC, the Department of Cooperation devoted special efforts to the protection of children and children's institutions. Toward this end Újváry was in touch with Baron Kemény; his associates, including Milán Kosztich and József Eszterházy, maintained contact with Zoltán Bagossy, Kemény's deputy, who reportedly was also a leader of a *Nyilas* terror group. When the *Nyilas* authorities decided just before the beginning of the Soviet siege of Budapest to transfer the Jewish children into the ghetto, the Nuncio and the representatives of the neutral states forwarded their third and last collective protest memorandum to the Hungarian government. The memorandum, dated December 20, implored the government to "allow all children (together with their mothers when the children are not yet weaned) to remain outside the ghetto in the refuges organized by diplomatic missions or in the various Red Cross institutions."[73] The appeal was only partially heeded; thousands of children, especially Jewish ones in buildings administered by Section A of the IRC, were taken into the ghetto.

The Attitude and Reaction of the Neutral Countries

The participation of the representatives of the neutral states in the collective efforts undertaken by the IRC and the Nunciature during the *Nyilas* era was but a culmination of their activities in this sphere, which had begun shortly after the German occupation. Although the representatives of the neutral states were careful not to antagonize either the Third Reich or the Hungarian government, they did their best to alleviate the plight of the surviving Jews of Budapest.[74] By far the most active were the representatives of Switzerland and Sweden.

Switzerland. The involvement of Switzerland in Hungarian-Jewish affairs started shortly after Britain severed relations with Hungary on April 8, 1941, following its participation in the Axis campaign against Yugoslavia. The Swiss agreed to represent in Budapest the interests of Britain—and, after Pearl Harbor, of America and a number of other Allied states as well. In this capacity, they assumed responsibility for the handling of Palestinian immigration matters affecting Jews in Hungary. By coincidence, the Budapest branch of the Palestine Office of the Jewish Agency, which was headed by Miklós (Moshe) Krausz, received, via Chaim Barlas of the Jewish Agency's office in Istanbul 600 Palestine immigration certificates just three days before the German occupation. Although the newly installed Sztójay government yielded to the pleas of Jean de Bavier, the IRC representative, and issued its exit authorization early in April, the emigration could not be effectuated without German approval. This came late in the month in the wake of the Kasztner–Eichmann negotiations and served as a basis of various controversial rescue schemes (see chapter 29).

While Kasztner and the other members of the Budapest *Vaada* were dealing with the SS, Krausz, who originally concurred with this approach, eventually decided to concentrate on a different rescue attempt. At the Crown Council meeting of June 26, the Hungarian government decided to accept the offer of some neutral and Allied countries to sponsor the emigration of 7,800 Jews. Of these, from 300 to 400 were sponsored by the Swedes; the 7,000 who had Palestine immigration certificates or British offers of admission were sponsored by the Swiss. The Swiss Legation in Budapest applied for exit permits for these Jews on April 26.[75]

The decisions of the Crown Council were partially based on the reaction in Switzerland to the report (including an abbreviated version of the Auschwitz protocols) Krausz had sent to Geneva on June 19. The Swiss press published a series of exposés on the realities of the German concentration camps, paying special attention to the destruction of Hungarian Jewry.[76] The credence of the Krausz material was enhanced by its distribution with a covering letter dated July 4, signed by well-known Swiss academicians and theologians.[77] After this date the press campaign acquired such proportions that Imre Tahy, the Hungarian chargé d'affaires in Berne, felt compelled to alert his government about its possible implications. In his note of July 14, he identified the major newspapers and journals, emphasizing their sympathy for the Jews and their anti-Sztójay tone.[78]

The press campaign coincided with protest meetings organized by church groups and political organizations. On July 10, for example, the Swiss Social Democratic Party held a protest rally condemning the destruction of Hungarian Jewry. The speakers urged the government to end its silence and, as the representative of the home of the Red Cross, follow Sweden in condemning the "frightful events" in Hungary.[79] Similar demands were advanced by cantonal governmental organizations such as the Great Council of Basel, the Caritas Association, and an increasing number of ecclesiastical organs. Among those who condemned the horrors of the anti-Jewish drive in Hungary were the Church Council of Zurich Canton (July 7) and several leading clergymen, who spoke up during services in the Basel Cathedral on July 13.[80] Later in the month, the Cathedral was the scene of a demonstration by Swiss workers protesting the persecution of Hungarian Jewry.[81]

The press campaign, like the many anti-Nazi and anti-*Nyilas* demonstrations, was initiated primarily by the representatives of the many domestic and international Jewish organizations in the country. A special role was played by Georges (Mandl) Mantello, who then served as an official of El Salvador in Switzerland (see below).

Anti-Hungarian campaigns similar to the one in Switzerland were also launched in other neutral and Allied countries. Their cumulative effect was to make the Sztójay government more responsive to suggestions aimed at easing the lot of the surviving Jews. Sensing the changed atmosphere after Horthy's halting of the deportations, Charles Lutz, the Consul General in the Swiss Legation, took the initiative in arranging the emigration of the holders of the 7,000 Palestine immigration certificates or offers. Acting in close cooperation with Krausz,[82] Lutz soon emerged as one of the heroes of the Holocaust ·period in Hungary.

Lutz had been in the Swiss diplomatic service since his graduation from George Washington University in 1924. He served in Washington and Philadelphia until 1935, when he was assigned to Palestine; after the outbreak of World War II, he also represented German interests there. He was transferred to Budapest at the end of 1941 and on January 2, 1942, was appointed to head the Foreign Interests Division of the Swiss Legation. In this capacity, he represented the interests of Britain, the United States, and 14 other members of the Grand Alliance. As the spokesman of British interests, he also emerged after the German occupation as the representative of "foreign" Jews, including British and American nationals as well as Hungarian and other Jews in possession of Palestine immigration documents.[83]

Accompanied by Maximilian Jäger, the Swiss Minister,[84] Lutz visited Sztójay on July 21, requesting the Hungarian government's cooperation and assurances with respect to five specific points prior to starting the emigration of the Jews.

- Jews appearing on the emigration lists should neither be sent for labor abroad nor mobilized for labor service at home.
- The Hungarian government should verify whether the Germans were indeed resolved, as some rumors had it, to prevent the implementation of the Palestine emigration scheme.
- The Hungarian government should try to get the Germans to issue the necessary exit permits (*Durchlass-Schein*) in Budapest so that the Jews could be listed in collective passports.
- The Ministry of the Interior should cancel its directive to the Jewish Council to establish a camp for the prospective 9,000 emigrants, since the Germans might take advantage of such concentration and deport the Jews as they did in Kistarcsa a few days earlier.
- The Minister of the Interior should receive him personally if the technical details of the emigration required such a meeting.[85]

Sztójay's immediate response to Lutz's requests was reassuring. He promptly got in touch with Jaross and suggested that the Jews slated for emigration be left in their homes while awaiting the completion of the formalities. He also approached Veesenmayer and Otto Winkelmann, the Higher SS and Police Leader, who reportedly reconfirmed the Germans' position on the emigration plans advanced by Sweden and Switzerland. This was partially corroborated on July 23, at a meeting in the Hungarian Ministry of Foreign Affairs attended by Lutz, Dénes Csopey, the head of the Political Department; Oszkár Moór, a Ministerial Counselor; and Theodor Horst Grell, the expert on Jewish affairs in the German Legation. Csopey urged Lutz to continue the technical preparations for the emigration. Despite the positive tone of the meeting, two of the responses caused Lutz considerable anxiety. Csopey reported that Jaross had no objections to the Jews' being left in their homes, but suggested that they be concentrated in the Yellow-Star houses on certain specified streets. When he reviewed Veesenmayer's and Winkelmann's response to Lutz, Grell remarked that "the actual beginning of the departure, however, is dependent on the settlement of a political question between the German and Hungarian governments."[86]

The political question referred to by Grell involved the conditions under which Hitler had expressed readiness to cooperate with the scheme for the emigration of the 7,800 Jews. Heeding the advice of Veesenmayer and Ribbentrop, on July 10 Hitler had consented to the emigration of these Jews, "provided the Hungarians allowed the speedy resumption of the deportation of the remaining Jews."[87]

Though disturbed by Grell's remarks, Lutz proceeded with plans for the emigration in accordance with the assurances received from Sztójay. Working closely with Krausz, on July 24 he brought about the establishment of the Glass House at 29 Vadász Street (chapter 29).[88]

Those registered for emigration were classified as "foreign nationals," to be exempted from all anti-Jewish measures and relocated in specially assigned "Swiss-protected" buildings on Pozsonyi Road and its environs. They were eventually supplied with protective passes (*Schutzbriefe* or *Schutzpässe*), which stated that their owners were "included in a collective Palestine passport and until their departure under the protection of the Swiss Legation."[89] Two collective passports covering 2,195 names were in fact completed within a short time.[90]

After the Hungarian exit visa and the Romanian transit visa had been secured, the collective passports were submitted to the German Legation on August 3 for exit permits enabling the Jews to depart for Palestine via Romania.[91] In spite of their assurances to Sztójay and other members of the Hungarian government the Germans had apparently never really intended to let any of these Jews out unless, of course, Hitler's conditions were accepted.

But even these conditions were merely a ploy to induce the Hungarians to resume the deportations. This was partially revealed by Veesenmayer's July 25 communication to Ribbentrop. While reporting that the Swiss were holding Palestine immigration certificates for 40,000 Hungarian Jews, he hastened to reveal Eichmann's and Himmler's position on the subject. Eichmann had stated that Himmler would under no circumstances permit the emigration of the Jews to Palestine, for they were "without exception biologically valuable material." Eichmann was resolved to complete the Final Solution come what may. He was ready, if necessary, "to seek a new decision from the Führer, but he was confident that he would not have to resort to this ultimate step, for, as Veesenmayer reported, he intended "to carry out the expected expulsion of the Jews from Budapest once it is proceeded with, with the utmost suddenness and with such speed that they will be driven out before anyone has had a chance to obtain a travel document or visa to a foreign country."[92] In the meantime the "negotiations" were to continue but on a new basis. Instead of the route suggested by the Swiss (for which they already had the necessary Hungarian exit and Romanian transit visas), the Germans now insisted that the Jews were to be directed via Western Europe to Lisbon. The objective was to delay if not completely block the emigration: unlike the Romanian route, which required only permits that the Budapest German Legation could have issued, the Lisbon route required exit and transit permits from Berlin.

The Swiss request for exit permits so the Jews could leave via Romania was consequently rejected, on August 14. The rejection was based on Hezinger's suggestion of August 4, which coincided with Himmler's views. Hezinger and his colleagues argued that the Hungarians had failed to resume the deportation program under the conditions outlined in the Führer directive and that the emigration of Jews to Palestine would conflict with Germany's position toward the Grand Mufti of Jerusalem.[93]

The Swiss repeated their requests on August 25, August 31, and September 11. By that time Romania had switched sides and the Swiss suggested the possibility that 2,000 Germans interned in "enemy camps" might be released in exchange.[94] The Germans, still hoping eventually to find an opportunity to complete the Final Solution program, dragged out the negotiations. Following the Szálasi coup, the Swiss formally consented to a proposal under which 8,000 Hungarian Jews would be admitted to Switzerland[95] "for a short stay, provided that their quick emigration will be guaranteed and carried out by the American and British governments."[96] Under the plan, the Hungarian Jews were to be kept in Swiss transient camps until their departure for Palestine or Allied-controlled North Africa was arranged.[97] The British became apprehensive, expressing concern over the fact that the 8,000 Hungarian Jews might not be in possession of genuine Palestine immigration certificates. They were also worried about the possibility that the immigration quota might be exceeded if these Jews were allowed to enter Palestine.[98]

Among those the Swiss offered to accept on a provisional basis were 1,000 children whom they had originally offered to admit for a "vacation" in Switzerland on July 25.[99] Efforts to expedite the emigration were also made by the Jewish organizations in Switzerland, Istanbul, and Palestine. The Germans continued their delaying tactics, wanting clarification as to whether the 2,000 Jews in the collective passports were part of or in addition to the 7,000 whose emigration had been agreed to.[100] This was obviously a charade; the Germans by that time had neither the will nor the means to make possible the organized emigration of Jews. Following Romania's extrication from the Axis Alliance, the Swiss and Krausz, still unaware of the Germans' real intentions, devised a new plan for transporting the Jews listed in the collective passports to a Black Sea port via the Danube River. The Swiss asked the British government for safe conduct for the boats, but were rebuffed because the river was "thoroughly mined by Allied Air Forces."[101] The Germans subsequently invoked their friendship with the Arabs and intimated that "if these Jews were going to American or British territory their departure would be viewed more favorably."[102] Krausz apparently accepted these assurances at face value for he immediately informed the Jewish Agency delegation in Istanbul that the required exit permits would be secured and that the new route was through Switzerland and Portugal. He requested the WRB's aid in obtaining the necessary transit visas.[103] This engendered another round of correspondence between the Jewish organization leaders in Switzerland, Turkey, and Palestine, all eager to assure the emigration of the Jews and equally unaware of the Germans' lack of sincerity. The exchange of correspondence, involving also the WRB and the Swiss authorities in Budapest and Berne, continued until the Soviets liberated the capital.

In the meantime Lutz and his colleagues, including Dr. Peter

Zürcher and Ernst von Rufs, acting in close collaboration with Krausz and other Zionists, tried to save as many Jews as possible from the *Nyilas.* In its eagerness to be recognized by the neutral powers, the Szálasi regime permitted the issuance of a limited number of protective passes, including 7,000 for the Swiss-sponsored Jews.[104] At first, it was envisioned they would leave Hungary by November 15. When the emigration could not be implemented because of the opposition of the Germans, they were ordered into the so-called international ghetto. Despite the limitations imposed by the *Nyilas,* the number of protective passes increased phenomenally, primarily because of the illegal activities of the Zionists. Acting under the protective umbrella of the Swiss Legation, the *Hehalutz* youth distributed thousands of forged protective passed to Jews in the death march columns, saving them just prior to their transfer to the Germans. (Many Hungarian guards, either because they were bribed or out of pity, honored the passes without checking them closely.[105]) Occasionally, to the great chagrin of the SS and the *Nyilas,* an entire column would be rescued and brought back to Budapest. The RSHA got wind of these activities and Ribbentrop urged Veesenmayer to have Szálasi lodge a protest with the Swiss for "sabotaging the Hungarian-German war effort." Veesenmayer complied immediately, reminding the Swiss and Hungarian authorities in Budapest that protective passes could be issued only to Jews not yet mobilized for labor. He reassured the Foreign Office on November 16 that Jews in possession of protective passes would be screened and those with invalid ones would be "recaptured for labor."[106] Shortly thereafter raids were staged in the Swiss-protected buildings to winnow out persons in possession of forged passes. The raids were organized by the *Nyilas* in cooperation with *Obersturmbannführer* Theodor Dannecker, representing the Eichmann-*Sonderkommando.* Many of those caught were shot into the Danube or compelled to rejoin the death marches toward Hegyeshalom.

The raids did not stop the rescue campaign. Those associated with the Swiss rescue group continued their efforts. At the same time, others pursued their aid and rescue activities under the protective umbrella of other neutral states, especially Sweden.

Sweden. Sweden, the prestige and influence of which in Hungary can be traced to the great services it rendered the nation during both world wars, was in a unique position. During World War I, the Swedish Red Cross had provided care for the Hungarian wounded and protection for the Hungarian POWs; it had also played an important role after

World War I in the exchange of prisoners of war. The Sztójay govern-ment, like its predecessors, thus expected it to perform similar services once more. Moreover, Sweden was the power that represented Hungary in all the enemy countries. Some of these, including Britain and the United States, had a considerable number of citizens of Hun-garian origin, many of them quite well off, who might require protec-tion.

The Swedish leaders were acquainted with the Nazis' Final Solution program. They were kept abreast not only by their representatives abroad, who as neutrals were stationed in all the countries of Europe, but also by the spokesmen of the Swedish Jewish community, including Norbert Masur, an industrialist and the representative of the World Jewish Congress; Gunnar Josephson, the head of the Stockholm Jewish community; and Marcus (Mordechai) Ehrenpreis, the Chief Rabbi.[107] The latter were kept informed about the details of the anti-Jewish drive in Nazi-dominated Europe and urged to exert pressure on the Swedish government primarily by the representatives of the international and domestic Jewish organizations in Switzerland—who in turn received field reports from Bratislava, Budapest, and Istanbul. One of the direct links to Ehrenpreis was provided by Dr. Zwi Taubes, the Chief Rabbi of Zurich. Another major source of information was Vilmos Böhm, a former Hungarian political figure and journalist who lived in exile in Stockholm, where he was employed by the Press Reading Room of the British Legation. His reports, based on Hungarian newspapers and pe-riodicals as well as intelligence communications, were periodically sub-mitted to both the British and the Swedish authorities. Sweden also had a more direct experience with the Holocaust: in October 1943, it had helped rescue and offered haven to close to 8,000 Danish Jews.[108]

Sweden did not officially react to the anti-Jewish drive in Hungary until June 11, 1944, when the deportations from Carpatho-Ruthenia, northeastern Hungary, and Northern Transylvania had already been completed. On that day, Carl I. Danielsson, the Swedish Minister in Budapest, requested the Hungarian government to allow the Swedish Red Cross to join the Hungarian Red Cross in feeding and housing orphaned and abandoned children and in caring for victims of air-raids. He also asked the government to cooperate in allowing the emi-gration of 300 to 400 Jews. They were to receive Swedish citizenship from King Gustav V, because they had relatives in Sweden or had maintained long-term business connections with Sweden.[109]

The Crown Council meeting of June 26 acted favorably; Arnóthy-

Jungerth then accepted Danielsson's appointment of Dr. Valdemar Langlet as the Swedish Red Cross delegate.[110] Dr. Langlet, a member of the Swedish Legation and a Swedish-language lecturer at the University of Budapest, launched his humanitarian campaign without delay, working in close cooperation with Sarolta Lukács, the Deputy Chairman of the Hungarian Red Cross.[111]

Sweden became more deeply involved in aid and rescue work after June 30, when the King sent a telegram to Horthy urging him to save the remaining Jews. The King's appeal was part of the worldwide reaction to the horrors of the Final Solution program which were publicized in the Swiss and later also in the Swedish press. It was also partially a response to efforts by American as well as Jewish interests to influence Sweden.[112] Herschel Johnson, the United States Minister to Stockholm, and Ivor C. Olsen, the WRB representative, were most active among the Americans. They were advised on May 23 by Secretary of State Cordell Hull to urge the appropriate Swedish authorities to persuade the Hungarians "to desist from further barbarism."[113] The Jews exerted their influence through Rabbi Ehrenpreis, Masur, and Josephson. Occasionally they talked with Foreign Minister Christian Günther directly; at other times they used the good offices of Professor Hugo Valentin.[114] King Gustav's telegram was triggered by Dr. Taubes's appeal to Ehrenpreis, which had promptly been relayed to Günther. On the latter's recommendation, Prime Minister Per Albin Hansson obtained the Council of Ministers' approval for the King's intervention on June 28.[115]

The Swedish press intensified its campaign early in July, paying special attention to the background of the King's action and its perceived consequences, including Horthy's decision to halt the deportations.[116] The press accounts, including the exchange of telegrams between the two heads of state, were brought to the attention of the German Foreign Office by Hans Thomsen of the German Legation in Stockholm.[117] In the meantime, Veesenmayer was also disturbed by the activities of the Swedes in Budapest. On July 5, he complained that Swedish officials were enabling Jews who were not Swedish nationals to leave the country by issuing them regular passports.[118]

The Role of Raoul Wallenberg.   The humanitarian activities of Sweden were greatly enhanced after the arrival in Budapest of Raoul Wallenberg on July 9. Then 32 years'old, he had considerable political and business experience. Born into a well-known banking family in Stockholm on August 4, 1912, Wallenberg was brought up under the guidance of his grandfather, Gustav Oscar Wallenberg, the former Minister of Sweden to Japan and Turkey. (His father, Raoul Oscar, died shortly before he was born.) He inherited his penchant for diplomacy from many close relatives who served in the Swedish government. One of them, his great-uncle, Knut Wallenberg, was Foreign Minister during World War I; another great-uncle, Axel Wallenberg, served as Swedish Minister to Washington.[119] His background paralleled that of the Swiss humanitarian Lutz in at least two respects. He too had been educated in America and had spent some time in Palestine. Wallenberg graduated in 1935 from the University of Michigan, where he received a B.S. in architecture. In 1936, he spent six months in Haifa, where he worked in a Dutch-owned bank. While there, he met a number of German-Jewish refugees who made him conscious of the realities of National Socialism in the Third Reich, and acquainted him with the plight and the aspirations of the Jewish people. He first established contact with the Hungarian Jews in 1941, when he became associated with an export-import enterprise headed by Dr. Kálmán Lauer, a Swede of Hungarian-Jewish background. As the foreign trade representative of the firm, Wallenberg visited Budapest in February 1942 and again in the fall of 1943. On both occasions he had ample opportunities to observe at first hand the impact of the anti-Jewish laws as well as to learn about the excesses committed against Jews in Ujvidék and in the labor service companies.

Lauer and Henrik Wahl, a general director of the Weiss-Manfréd Works (both of whom were anxious to save their relatives) first hit upon the idea of sending Wallenberg to Budapest for rescue work. The possibility of expanding his role was raised in a discussion between Rabbi Ehrenpreis and Lauer at the end of May. Weeks elapsed before Wallenberg's mission was finally approved—primarily because Ehrenpreis at first had some misgivings about his youth and his request for large sums of money to bribe officials with. Ehrenpreis, however, was won over because of enthusiastic support by Johnson and Olsen.[120] The latter were advised by Secretary of State Hull on May 23 to impress upon the Swedes "the restraint which may result from the presence in Hungary of the greatest possible number of foreign observers . . . and to urge them in the interest of humanity, to take immediate steps to increase the numbers of Swedish diplomatic and consular personnel in Hungary."[121]

Wallenberg was therefore appointed third secretary to the Swedish Legation in Budapest and given the specific mission to organize mass-scale relief action and to follow and report "on the situation with re-spect to persecution of Jews and minorities."[122] He arrived one day after the last deportation train left Hungary.

In Budapest Wallenberg took over the leadership of Department C of the Legation, which was in charge of rescue. One of his first steps was to visit the headquarters of the Jewish Council and hand over to Samu Stern the letter of recommendation he had received from Rabbi Ehrenpreis.[123] He asked for and soon received a complete report on the situation of Hungarian Jewry, delivered to him by László Pető, the son of Ernő Pető, one of the Council leaders. Himself an official of the Council, László Pető knew Wallenberg personally: as students they had spent a summer in the same student hostel at Thenon-les-Baines, France—a chance encounter the Jewish Council exploited to its advan-tage.[124] Wallenberg quickly familiarized himself with the rescue activi-ties of the Swiss Legation as well as those already undertaken by Dan-ielsson and Langlet in his own Legation.

Wallenberg's first official report to Sweden was dated July 17. In it he gave an overview of the catastrophe that had befallen Hungarian Jewry under the German occupation.[125] This was soon followed by other reports as well as by private communications to his business part-ner, friends, and relatives—all including details about the persecutions.

To carry out the rescue campaign, Wallenberg set up an organization that included at the height of the operations 355 employees, 40 physi-cians, two hospitals and a soup kitchen. Most of the staff were Jews or converts who as a result of this work gained immunity for themselves and their families. Among those who played an important role in the rescue work, especially as intermediaries with the Hungarian authori-ties, were Hugo Wahl, Béla Forgács, and Vilmos Forgács, who had been given the status of Swedish subjects.

While at first Danielsson spoke in terms of granting Swedish citizen-ship to only the aforementioned 300 to 400 Jews with relatives or busi-ness connections in Sweden, the figure soon rose close to 650, thanks to a list Wallenberg carried with him to Budapest. These were given a provisional or emergency passport (*Provisoriskt Pass*). Within a few months after Wallenberg's arrival, this rescue effort was expanded; it eventually included 4,500 Jews, a figure approved by the *Nyilas* govern-ment on October 31 in the expectation of diplomatic recognition by Sweden. Originally expected to leave by November 15, these Jews were supplied with protective passes and transferred to "Swedish Houses" on Pozsonyi Road. As the *Nyilas* terror continued unabated, and especially during the Soviet siege, the number of those holding genuine or forged passes increased to well over 10,000. These were housed in 32 Swedish-protected buildings.[126]

The Germans were of course furious over the large-scale activities of the Swedes. Reportedly some of the Hungarian officials were also disturbed by them, as they were about the rescue measures undertaken by the Swiss. According to Grell, Csopey once expressed the indignation of Hungarian government circles over the "indiscriminate manner" in which the Swedes were issuing their protective passes. He allegedly declared that the Swedes and the Swiss were aiming at getting into the good graces of the Western Allies at the expense of Hungary.[127]

In August, Ferenczy ordered the relocation of the few hundred Swedish-protected Jews who lived in Yellow-Star houses in various parts of the city. He used the list handed to the Hungarian authorities by Wallenberg as an excuse to establish contact with the Jewish Council and the Regent (see chapter 25). The Council, which was entrusted with this task around August 22, was instructed to complete it by August 26. Some members of the Council, especially Lajos Stöckler, found the order very disquieting. In the first place Stöckler, reflecting the anxiety of the Jewish masses, saw the transfer of the privileged Jews as an additional indication that the deportation widely rumored for August 25–26 would actually be carried out. He was also concerned with the problem of the unprotected Jews who had to be evicted from the Pozsonyi Road buildings to make room for the Swedish-protected ones. Finally, he felt that the decision of some of the Jews to rescue themselves individually or collectively through Zionist emigration schemes or through the help of neutral powers, thus separating themselves from the Jewish masses, was reprehensible. In his anger over these rescue schemes, he suggested that the Council sever all relations with the protected Jews.[128]

Regardless of the feelings of some of its members, the Council of course had no alternative but to proceed with the implementation of the Ferenczy order. On August 23, it set up the machinery for the exchange of tenants.[129]

After the *Nyilas* coup, the rescue work of the Swedish Legation expanded. The officers of the Legation, including the Minister and his closest aides (Göte Carlsson, Lars Berg, and Per Anger), remained in Budapest, continuing to provide whatever assistance they could. The functions of Dr. Langlet acquired added importance as well. When the *Nyilas* decided to doublecheck the authenticity of the protective passes issued by the Swedish Red Cross, he and his wife Nina, and her secretary and interpreter Mária Kóla, did everything in their power to protect the Jews from being robbed or deported. Another unit of the Swedish Red Cross, headed by Asta Nilsson, was particularly active in protecting children. When the *Nyilas* raided some children's institutions and took the youngsters into the ghetto, they also took along Nilsson and Mrs. Bauer, a secretary in the Swedish Legation. (They were later freed through Wallenberg's intervention.)[130]

Wallenberg himself moved his offices from the Buda side of the capital to Pest, where most of the Jews were concentrated, to be in a better position to help them. The number of officially distributed emergency passports soon passed 7,000. Like the thousands of protective passes, both genuine and forged, these provided a modicum of security to their possessors. Under Wallenberg's guidance (and often with his personal assistance) Swedish rescue workers, including Mrs. István Csányi and Gedeon Dienes, saved hundreds of people from the death marches and the Óbuda brickyards by supplying them with protective passes. Wallenberg was also successful in saving the Swedish-protected labor servicemen just before they would have been put aboard trains at the Józsefvárosi station; those protected by the other neutral powers were less lucky.

For a while, the Szálasi government reluctantly tolerated the activities of the neutral powers in the hope of diplomatic recognition—Szálasi had hoped that these neutral powers would extend it immediately after he issued his "final plan" for the solution of the Jewish question on November 17. Early in December he became so exasperated that he informed Danielsson that he would apply the full vigor of the anti-Jewish laws to the Swedish-protected Jews as well. Shortly thereafter, when the Soviet siege was about to begin, Szálasi demanded that the Minister and his staff move to Western Hungary. When they refused, *Nyilas* units attacked the Legation (December 10).

Wallenberg's role took on heroic proportions during the siege. The government had relocated to the western parts of the country and the capital was in a state of anarchy, with armed *Nyilas* roaming the streets and venting their frustrations on the helpless Jews. Wallenberg's tasks were staggering: in addition to saving Jews from the hands of the *Nyilas*, he struggled to obtain food for the tens of thousands of Jews in the ghetto and the protected buildings (an extremely difficult task since the capital was cut off from its usual sources of supply). When the Jews became panic-stricken over the rumor that the Nazis and *Nyilas* planned to destroy the ghetto just before the arrival of the Soviet forces, Wallenberg warned both Ernö Vajna, the *Nyilas* leader entrusted with full powers for the defense of Budapest, and the German military commander against any massacres. In the midst of all these activities, he found time to submit his reports, giving specifics about the nature and magnitude of the catastrophe.[131]

The Disappearance of Wallenberg. Raoul Wallenberg provided a heartening and rare example of great personal courage and self-sacrificing humanitarianism. Sadly, like many another heroic figure in history, he ended up sharing the fate of the victims he had come to help. But in a cruel and ironic twist, his tragic end was brought about not by the Nazis, but by the Soviets who were eagerly awaited as the harbingers of a new era of freedom and equality. Indeed, the Soviet involvement in the disappearance of Wallenberg is doubly ironical, for it was Sweden which represented the interests of the USSR in Hungary during the war. On the day of the liberation of Pest (January 17, 1945), Wallenberg, who had been in touch with the Soviet officer in command of the fighting forces in Budapest since January 13, left for the Debrecen headquarters of Marshal Rodion Y. Malinovsky. Driven by Lajos Langfelder, an engineer who served as his Hungarian chauffeur, and accompanied by a Russian guard, Wallenberg had some forebodings about his coming encounter with the Soviet commander. As he was departing, he allegedly told his coworkers: "I don't know whether I am going as a prisoner or as a guest." Neither Wallenberg nor Langfelder returned from that trip.

S. Söderblom, Sweden's Minister in Moscow, reported Wallenberg's disappearance after receiving a telegram from the Swedish Legation in Bucharest. The Soviet response to frequent Swedish inquiries was dissembling. For example, in February 1945 Aleksandra M. Kollontay, the Soviet Ambassador in Stockholm, assured Wallenberg's mother as well as Foreign Minister Günther that Wallenberg was alive and well in the Soviet Union; on August 18, 1947, over a year after Söderblom took up the matter with Stalin (June 15, 1946), Soviet Foreign Minister Andrei J. Vishinsky declared: "As a result of a careful investigation it has been established that Wallenberg is not in the Soviet Union, and that he is unknown to us."[132]

The Soviet cover-up did not end with Stalin's death in March 1953. It was not until February 6, 1957, that the Khrushchev government acknowledged Soviet culpability in Wallenberg's disappearance. On that day, Andrei Gromyko, then Deputy Foreign Minister, informed Swedish Ambassador Sohlman that Wallenberg had died in Moscow's Lubianka prison on July 17, 1947. The Soviet leaders pinned the blame on Viktor S. Abakumov, former Minister for State Security, who was executed in December 1954 as an accomplice of Lavrenti P. Beria.[133] The Swedes reacted angrily, informing the Soviet leaders (February 19, 1957) that they could not disclaim responsibility for the abuses of the Stalinist regime by shifting blame to their secret police. They insisted that they would continue to hold the Soviet government responsible for Wallenberg's kidnapping and disappearance.[134]

Despite Soviet denials, the rumor that Wallenberg was still alive in some camp, prison, or mental institution in the Soviet Union continued unabated and was reinforced in the 1970s by several emigrants from the Soviet Union.[135] As a result of the new bits of information that filtered out of the USSR, there were new private and governmental attempts to induce the Soviet Union to free Wallenberg.[136] It is unlikely, however, that the Soviet leaders would be influenced by any humanitarian appeals. To admit that Wallenberg was still alive after they had officially declared him dead would place them in an embarrassing position both within and outside the USSR.[137]

Spain. Although openly sympathetic to the Axis powers, which had aided it during the civil war, the Franco regime offered asylum to a limited number of Jews who escaped from Nazi-dominated Europe. It was especially sympathetic to Sephardic Jews of Spanish origin. In 1943, for example, when the SS were engaged in the liquidation of Greek Jewry, the Spaniards showed a special interest in the approximately 600 Jews in Salonika, whom they identified as Spanish subjects. The Nazis offered to repatriate all of them, but the Spaniards were willing to admit only 50. The Spaniards managed to have the remainder transferred to the special camp for privileged people (*Bevorzugtenlager*) in Bergen-Belsen. Eventually, 365 of this group were allowed to enter Spain at the end of the war.[138]

As was the case with Switzerland and Sweden, Spain became involved only after the deportations from the provinces were ended. It entered the picture only after a meeting in Lisbon on July 5, 1944, among the Spanish Ambassador to Portugal, Eliahu Dobkin of the Executive Committee of the Jewish Agency for Palestine, and I. Weissmann of the World Jewish Congress. The Jewish leaders asked Spain's help for Sephardic Jews in the Nazi-dominated countries, to which request the

Ambassador explained that the Spanish government had already decided to grant protection to all Sephardic Jews who claimed "their Spanish origin or nationality at Spanish consulates."[139]

One week later, the Jewish Council of Budapest received a telegram from the Tangier Committee for Aid to Refugees (*Comité d'Assistance aux Refugiés Tanger*). Tangier, the Council was informed, would admit 500 children—200 of them specified on a list prepared by the Committee, and 300 to be selected by the Council. (Since the Tangier International Zone was under Spanish occupation during the war, this obviously reflected the position of the Spanish government.) A delegate of the Council immediately got in touch with Angel Sanz-Briz, the Spanish chargé d'affaires,[140] who suggested that the Council ask Madrid to instruct its Budapest Legation to issue the visas for the 500 children and also for 50 to 70 adults, who would accompany them. He also suggested that the Council try to implement the emigration through the IRC.[141] Negotiations were begun by Born and György Gergely, representing the Council, on July 29. They agreed, among other things, to immediately begin the registration of the children and place them in camps that would be protected by the IRC until their departure.[142] The matter was also the subject of discussions between Krausz and Zoltán Farkas, the Spanish Legation's legal counselor. While the talks were proceeding, the Spaniards followed the example of the Swiss and the Swedes and issued a limited number of protective passes.

The children's emigration never took place. Following the *Nyilas* coup the only question was immediate protection and survival. This task was no longer carried out by the Legation's ranking personnel; Sanz-Briz and his colleagues returned to Spain shortly after Szálasi was inaugurated. Leadership at the Spanish Legation was taken over by Giorgio (Jorge) Perlasca. An anti-Fascist Italian, he had already been a frequent visitor to the Legation (he had a personal friend there); his assumption of duties was therefore not viewed with suspicion by the lower-rank personnel or by the *Nyilas* Ministry of Foreign Affairs, which recognized him as the new chargé d'affaires. Perlasca and his colleagues issued approximately 3,000 protective passes. Like the other protected Jews, the Spanish-protected ones were relocated into the international ghetto after November 15. Early in January 1945, they were transferred into the large ghetto.[143]

The Germans, apparently unaware of Perlasca's personal role, were quite disturbed over the Spanish Legation's rescue activities. The accusatory reports on the Spanish government's involvement in the rescue of Hungarian Jews disturbed the Germans in Budapest, Berlin, and Madrid. On October 13, Thadden reported that on the initiative of the Americans, the Spanish government was ready to issue visas to 2,000 Jews. About ten days later Ballensiefen, the SS propaganda expert in Budapest, informed Rolf Günther, Eichmann's deputy in Berlin, that the Spanish Legation in Budapest had made an offer to the Jewish Council to protect Jewish orphans of 14 to 16 years. During the death marches, Veesenmayer reported (November 13) that the Spaniards requested exit visas for "additional Hungarian Jews having family relationships in Spain." [144]

Despite the frequent exchange of telegrams between the various representatives of the German Foreign Office and the many exchanges of notes between the Spaniards and the Hungarians, no Hungarian Jews were ever allowed to leave the country under the Spanish scheme; the Germans at no time issued the necessary exit and transit permits.

Portugal. The Germans made an exception to their policy of refusing to allow emigration for Carlos de Sampayo Garrido, the Portuguese Minister in Budapest. Three Jews were involved: Sampayo Garrido's secretary, Mrs. Bischowszky, and her parents, Mr. and Mrs. Gábor. The Hungarians, who were anxious to put an end to an embarrassing incident, heartily endorsed the scheme. In the early morning of April 30, the Hungarian police arrested the Minister and some of his Jewish friends in Galgagyörk, his summer residence just north of Budapest, on orders of Péter Hain, the head of the Hungarian Political Police. The police planned to free the Minister, who invoked his diplomatic immunity; however, he refused to leave unless the others were also let go. Following a high-level conference involving Sztójay, István Antal, László Baky, Hain, and Arnóthy-Jungerth, it was decided (on the latter's suggestion and to the great chagrin of Baky and Hain) to release all the captives. The order was communicated to the police chief as well as to Sampayo Garrido by Gyula Teleki, the chief of protocol in the Ministry of Foreign Affairs.

On May 3, Sampayo Garrido lodged a strongly worded protest and demanded a full investigation. He was recalled shortly thereafter, whereupon he asked that his secretary and her parents be allowed to leave with him. Arnóthy-Jungerth contacted Veesenmayer on May 23 and suggested that since the Minister would not leave without his secretary, nor she without her parents, all three be allowed to leave "to get rid of the Minister." [145] The German Foreign Office, after doublecheck-ing with Lisbon to see if President Antonio Salazar had any interest in his Minister's case, concurred with Arnóthy-Jungerth's recommendations and so instructed Veesenmayer.[146] The Germans issued the necessary papers to Mrs. Bischowszky immediately, but refused to issue them to her parents. The Minister left with his secretary on June 5; the Gábors were not allowed to leave until October 29.[147]

On July 15, the Portuguese chargé d'affaires Branquinho, and the Hungarian Ministry of Foreign Affairs applied to the German Legation for exit and transit permits for nine Hungarian Jews who had family or business relations in Portugal. The nine, including the Gábors, were given Portuguese passports valid till the end of the year. Veesenmayer was reluctant to act, although the departure of at least the Gábors was already authorized, because in the meantime the Führer had laid down his conditions for allowing the emigration of the Jews sponsored by the various neutral states. Consequently, the Portuguese request was treated for months in the same dilatory manner as the others.[148]

In the meantime, the chargé d'affaires authorized that passports be issued to all those Jews who could prove that they had relations in Portugal or Brazil. The petitions were handled by Gyula Gulden, who acted as Consul General, and Dr. Ferenc Bartha, who headed the special section in the Legation.

After the *Nyilas* coup, the Portuguese increased the number of their protective passes. Although they promised Foreign Minister Kemény that no more than 500 passes would be issued, in fact more than 700 were given out. The Germans at first refused to recognize them. However, Tovar, the Portuguese representative in Berlin, intervened; in addition, Szálasi was eager to obtain diplomatic recognition from the neutral states. The Germans therefore modified their position. Andor Hencke, the Chief of the Political Division of the German Foreign Office, offered a politically expedient concession on November 9, suggesting the recognition of protective passes "provided they are kept within reasonable limits." The Hungarians were advised (November 13) to recognize no additional protective passes.[149]

After November 15, the Portuguese-protected Jews too were ordered into special protected buildings. Most of them were relocated to 5 Ujpesti-rakpart, under the administration of Dr. Sándor Bródy. The dwellers were helped by Dr. Béla Richter, a state attorney who as air raid warden allowed them to use the shelters reserved for Christians. As the *Nyilas* rule became more barbaric, the status of the Portuguese-protected Jews became increasingly precarious. On November 26, the labor servicemen protected by the Portuguese were ordered to appear at the Albrecht barracks and from there, despite repeated assurances by the authorities, they were entrained and taken to the Sopron area to build the East Wall for the defense of Vienna. On January 4, 1945, at the height of the Soviet siege, the remaining Portuguese-protected Jews were transferred into the ghetto.[150]

Turkey. Turkey, although represented in Budapest, participated in only minimal activities. On May 24, 1944, Secretary of State Hull cabled Ambassador Laurence Steinhardt in Ankara to urge the Turks "in the interest of humanity, to take immediate steps to increase the numbers of Turkish diplomatic and consular personnel in Hungary" and to use all means available to persuade the Hungarians to desist from further barbarism. The Turks apparently were not persuaded. Late in June, Ambassador Steinhardt was asked by the U.S. Secretary of State to bring additional pressure on the Turkish government in light of the resolution then introduced by Congressman Sol Bloom, the Chairman of the House Committee on Foreign Relations. The resolution requested the Secretary of State "to urge that the Government of Turkey facilitate, in the interests of humanity, the entry of refugees who can escape from the Nazis into Turkey and establish a refugee camp in which such persons can be temporarily sheltered on its territory." Acting under pressure, the Turkish representative in Budapest issued a limited number of protective passes.[151]

The Attitude and Reaction of the Western Allies

As noted above, with the exception of the few who were permitted to go to Portugal to avoid a potentially embarrassing diplomatic issue, no Jews were ever allowed to leave Hungary under the various emigration schemes. The Germans firmly adhered to the Führer's directive under which, in order to protect the interests of the Arabs,[152] no Jews were to be allowed to go to Palestine; the 7,800 Jews sponsored by the neutral states were to be permitted, theoretically at least, to leave via Western Europe—a route requiring special transit permits from Berlin—and only if the deportation of the Jews of Budapest were resumed. The emigration schemes of the neutral powers were encouraged and supported by the Western Allies. The issue whether a more vigorous approach on the part of the Allies would have saved more Jews is one of the most controversial ones in Holocaust studies and continues, in light of the newly available evidence, to agitate scholars and laymen alike.

The Politics of Indifference. Beyond doubt, the Western Powers abhorred the cruel and immoral racial policies of the Third Reich. Their attitude and reaction to the Nazis' anti-Jewish measures, however, were determined almost exclusively by considerations of national interest. During the first years of the Nazi era, it was widely believed that the regime would be short-lived or that its racial policies would eventually be moderated. Although these expectations were of course overtaken by events, the Western Powers continued their policy of appeasement. In their myopic view of world history, they thought that they could secure peace by yielding to the continual "last demands" of Hitler. This also reflected their greater fear of the long-range danger represented by Bolshevism than of the immediate threat posed by National Socialism.

The *Anschluss* and the Nazis' ever-increasing barbarities presented the West with a dilemma: the Judeo-Christian ideals underlying the democratic credo came into conflict with national interest. Britain was dedicated to maintaining stability in the Middle East, which required the cultivation of good relations with the Arabs and consequently the restriction of Jewish immigration to Palestine; the depression-ridden United States was reluctant to change its restrictive quota-based immigration laws and policies. The two countries tried to find a way out of the dilemma by internationalizing the problem of refugees.

On President Roosevelt's initiative a conference was held in July 1938 at Evian-les-Bains, France. Representatives of 32 nations attended; Britain participated only on the condition that Palestine would not be discussed. The conference reviewed a number of plans for the absorption of refugees, none of which ever came to pass. Its only visible accomplishment was the establishment of an Intergovernmental Committee on Political Refugees (IGC) under the leadership of George Rublee, a Roosevelt protégé, which was envisioned to organize emigration and secure places of refuge on an orderly basis.

The IGC remained basically a paper organization, for no nation was truly willing to offer refuge to the Jews. Hitler goaded the conference participants for "oozing sympathy for the poor, tormented people, but remaining hard and obdurate when it comes to helping them." And indeed, as Ira Hirschmann accurately characterized the situation, Evian "was a facade behind which the civilized governments could hide their inability to act."[153] This assessment was corroborated 41 years later by U.S. Vice President Walter F. Mondale:

At Evian, they began with high hopes. But they failed the test of civilization. The civilized world hid in a cloak of legalisms. Two nations said they had reached the saturation point for Jewish refugees. Four nations said they could accept experienced agricultural workers only. One would only accept immigrants who had been baptized. Three declared intellectuals and merchants to be undesirable new citizens. One nation feared that the influx of Jews would arouse anti-Semitic feelings. And one delegate said this: As we have no real racial problem, we are not desirous of importing one.[154]

The indifference of the Western Allies to the plight of the Jews continued even after *Kristallnacht* and the subsequent dismemberment of Czechoslovakia, when the refugee problem became acute. Britain adopted a White Paper in May 1939, regulating its policy on immigration to Palestine for the 1939–1944 period. Under that policy 75,000 Jews were to be allowed to enter Palestine during the five years—50,000 "regular" immigrants and 25,000 refugees. The latter were to constitute Britain's "contribution toward the solution of the Jewish refugee problem."[155] The United States, for its part, steadfastly refused to liberalize its immigration policies, using the IGC as a cushion to absorb national and international pressure for changing them. The racial and political-ideological factors underlying the opposition to the liberalization of the immigration laws were reflected in the March 31, 1944, note from Henry L. Stimson, the Secretary of War, to John W. Pehle, the head of the WRB. Stimson argued that uncontrolled immigration from certain countries was bound to modify the proportion of the racial stocks already existing in the country, in violation of the intent of the immigration laws.[156]

Following the outbreak of World War II, Britain, and after Pearl Harbor the United States, subordinated all considerations of refuge and rescue to the exigencies of war. They consistently rejected specific pleas for rescue advanced by Jewish leaders in the free and Nazi-dominated world or by underground and resistance organizations, arguing that the concentration of resources for the quickest possible defeat of the Third Reich was the most effective way of helping the oppressed.

The leaders of the Western world were fully and accurately informed about the anti-Jewish policies of the Nazi occupation forces in Poland and Western Europe, as well as about the mass executions perpetrated by the *Einsatzgruppen* in the Soviet Union starting in June 1941. In the summer of 1942, they received authenticated reports about Hitler's resolve to bring about the destruction of European Jewry and about the techniques employed in various concentration camps. The sources of many of the reports were the neutral states, especially Switzerland, whose representatives had access to the national political leaders, as well as to Jewish and underground leaders in the Axis and occupied countries to which they were assigned. The major conduits through which the reports were transmitted to Washington and London were Leland Harrison and John Clifford Norton, the American and British ministers in Berne.[157] These reports were occasionally personally corroborated by emissaries of the underground who managed to reach London and Washington (see chapter 23).

Despite their awareness that the Nazis were bent on the total physical destruction of the Jews of Europe, the Western Allies clung to their resolve and consistently rejected any and all suggestions for an active involvement in rescue operations as incompatible with their need to marshal all their resources in the war against the Axis. However, in response to continuing pressure from both Jewish and non-Jewish public and ecclesiastical figures (in Britain the Archbishop of Canterbury was particularly active) and in light of the incontestable evidence about the Final Solution, they agreed to issue a joint declaration on December 17, 1942, condemning the Nazis' drive against the Jews. It took over six months of diplomatic wrangling to finally agree on the text of this document condemning the Nazi atrocities:

The German authorities . . . are now carrying into effect Hitler's oft-repeated intention to exterminate the Jewish people in Europe. . . . The above-mentioned governments and the French National Committee condemn in the strongest possible terms this bestial policy of cold-blooded extermination. . . . They reaffirm their solemn resolution to insure that those responsible for these crimes shall not escape retribution, and to press on with the necessary practical measures to this end.[158]

This declaration by the Allies was the first to define extermination of the Jews as a crime. Its effectiveness was somewhat undercut by its implication that nothing would be done before final victory and by its failure to provide for some immediate threat or possible retaliation against the Nazis and their allies; nevertheless, it was helpful in that it finally broke the conspiracy of silence. The mass slaughter of the Jews that had been going on since June 1941 was finally officially recognized as real and as criminal.

However, as was pointed out after the war by Gerhard Riegner, the representative of the World Jewish Congress in Switzerland who submitted the first reports on the Final Solution in 1942, until December

1942 "the Western Governments were afraid of being identified too much with the Jews and of being accused by their own populations of waging war for the Jews." When the facts of the extermination program became public knowledge, these governments, Riegner continued, "showed a lack of imagination in devising the extraordinary measures required outside the normal bureaucratic routine effectively to budge an enemy like Hitler, and lacked the determination and will to carry them out." [159]

While the Allies consistently refused to engage in any overt rescue operation in behalf of Jews, after December 1942 their broadcasts to other countries contained more specific information about the Nazi atrocities. These had, of course, not only an informative and psychological value for the Jews, but also and above all a propaganda value for the Allies.

The declaration of December 1942 by the Allies and the public disclosure of some details on the Nazis' extermination program resulted in requests from lay and religious leaders of all faiths, in both Britain and America, for concrete governmental efforts to rescue the victims of Nazism. In January 1943, the British Foreign Office suggested another conference to deal with the problems. After considerable wrangling over the location and agenda, the Western Allies met in April in Bermuda. The conference was doomed to failure from the beginning. As at Evian, Great Britain reiterated its opposition to any consideration of Palestine as a haven; the United States insisted on keeping its immigration laws intact. The British rejected the appeal of the Zionist leaders to make Palestine a place of refuge with a series of spurious arguments. [160] They expressed a fear that Germany might "change from a policy of extermination to one of extrusion . . . [and] aim as they did before the war at embarrassing other countries by flooding them with immigrants"; they were concerned about finding a place to settle large numbers of Jews; they were worried about the possibility that spies might be infiltrated with the refugees; and finally they raised the problem of the shortage of shipping. The debates were occasionally acrimonious: the British requested that the United States ease its immigration restrictions, while the Americans asked the British to facilitate the inflow of refugees to Palestine. The conference ended with a call for the revitalization of the IGC through a broadening of its scope and membership.

Like the earlier Evian meeting, the Bermuda conference had no visible results. The final report of the conference was not issued until

November 19, 1943. Commenting on its farcical character many years after the war, Richard K. Law (later Lord Coleraine), at the time the Parliamentary Undersecretary for Foreign Affairs, who led the British delegation, stated: "It was a conflict of self-justification, a façade for inaction."[161]

The Western Allies' recalcitrant position was revealed by their mishandling of certain specific rescue opportunities. For example, the Antonescu government of Romania was prepared to send 60,000 to 70,000 Jews to Palestine, on Romanian ships carrying Vatican insignia, in exchange for a ransom of £250 per capita.[162] The Allies also missed chances to rescue Jews in Bulgaria and approximately 6,000 Jewish children threatened by deportation in France. In each case, these opportunities were missed because of dilatory and antagonistic handling by Whitehall and Foggy Bottom. The British were once again concerned with "the difficulties of disposing of any considerable number of Jews should they be rescued from enemy territory."[163] The U.S. Department of State offered a variety of meretricious arguments—to the frustration of Treasury Secretary Henry Morgenthau, Jr., and his top assistants, who were also involved in the effort. By the end of 1943, the Treasury officials decided on a new approach: they suggested to the President that jurisdiction over rescue matters be transferred from the State Department to an independent agency.

The rationale for this approach was presented in a memorandum ("Report to the Secretary on the Acquiescence of This Government in the Murder of the Jews") prepared by Randolph Paul, the General Counsel of the Treasury Department. Paul documented the intransigence and foot-dragging of certain officials in the State Department, who had "willfully failed to act to rescue the Jews." Their procrastination, dating back to August 1942, Paul argued, had "facilitated mass murder in Nazi Europe."[164] During those "terrible eighteen months," Morgenthau reminisced after the war, "we knew in Washington . . . that the Nazis were planning to exterminate all the Jews of Europe. Yet . . . officials dodged their grim responsibility, procrastinated when concrete rescue schemes were placed before them, and even suppressed information about atrocities."[165] After the draft memorandum was revised to include the negative role of the British Foreign Office, Morgenthau first discussed it with Hull on January 11, 1944, and then submitted it personally to President Roosevelt on January 16. That same day, on Roosevelt's suggestion, he also met Under Secretary of

State Edward Stettinius. All three were reportedly shocked by the revelations.

On January 22, President Roosevelt issued Executive Order 9417, establishing the WRB under the Secretaries of State, Treasury, and War. The Order stated that "it is the policy of this government to take all measures within its power to rescue the victims of enemy oppression who are in imminent danger of death or otherwise to afford such victims all possible relief and assistance consistent with the successful prosecution of the war." The WRB was placed under the leadership of John W. Pehle, the head of Foreign Funds Control in the Treasury Department, and empowered to collaborate with private organizations, American and international agencies, and foreign governments in pursuing its objectives. The establishment of the WRB marked, officially at least, the end of the U.S. policy of indifference.[166]

The Western Allies and the Destruction of Hungarian Jewry. The views and policies of the WRB reflected the President's new resolve to insist on a more active American role in providing relief and rescue for Nazi victims.[167] Established after the bulk of European Jewry had already been destroyed, it faced its first major test in the case of Hungary.

The WRB began its operations with great zeal, expressing its concern for the treatment of the Jews of Hungary even before the German occupation. When it learned late in February that the Kállay government seemed to be yielding to German pressure "to deport foreign Jews and close its borders to refugees from Poland and elsewhere," the WRB expressed the American government's disapproval and warning on March 7 via the U. S. legations in Lisbon and Berne.[168] Its real test came after the occupation on March 19. Its good intentions notwithstanding, it proved no match for the Nazis and Hungarians bent on the quick implementation of the Final Solution program.

The first alarm about the possible fate of Hungarian Jewry, coupled with specific suggestions for action by the Allies, was sent to the Western Powers by Riegner on March 21. His telegram to the heads of the World Jewish Congress in Britain and the United States read:

Most anxious about destiny Hungarian Jewry, the only important section European Jewry still in existence, because of recent political developments. Am suggesting world wide appeal of Anglo-Saxon personalities [both] non-Jews and Jews including Chiefs of Protestant [and] Catholic Churches to the Hungarian people warning them not to allow application of policy of extermination of the Jews by the German butchers or Hungarian Quislings and to help Jews by all possible means in order to prevent their falling into the hands of the Germans. Warning should insist upon the fact that the attitude of the Hungarian people toward the Jews will be one of the most important tests of behaviour which allied nations will remember in the peace settlement after war. Similar broadcasts should be made every night in Hungarian language during the next weeks.[169]

The Western Powers complied. As part of the psychological warfare campaign devised by the WRB, President Roosevelt issued a statement on March 24, condemning the Nazis and their allies for the heinous crimes committed in the course of the war. In connection with Hungary, he declared:

In one of the blackest crimes of all history . . . the wholesale systematic murder of the Jews of Europe goes on unabated every hour. As a result of the events of the last few days hundreds of thousands of Jews, who while living under persecution, have at least found a haven from death in Hungary and the Balkans, are now threatened with annihilation as Hitler's forces descend more heavily upon these lands. That these innocent people, who have already survived a decade of Hitler's fury, should perish on the very eve of triumph over the barbarism which their persecution symbolizes, would be a major tragedy.

In an attempt to dissuade the Hungarians from collaborating, the President warned that "none who participate in these acts of savagery shall go unpunished."[170] That same day, Secretary of State Hull urged the Hungarians to resist the Germans, implying that only thus could Hungary "hope to regain the respect and friendship of free nations and demonstrate its right to independence."[171] The British government clung to its White Paper policies relating to Palestine immigration. Sir Harold MacMichael, the British High Commissioner in Jerusalem, reiterated on March 1, 1944, that the existing quota of 75,000 immigrants could not be exceeded, and that no further immigration quotas were planned after the expiration of the current one on March 31. Although he suggested that the 18,300 immigration permits not yet taken up be issued to refugees, he was reluctant to go along with the specific suggestions for their allocation by the Zionist leaders.[172] Nevertheless, eager not to appear totally callous, the British followed the U.S. lead. After Sidney Silverman, a member of the House of Commons and President of the British Section of the World Jewish Congress, raised the question of the anti-Jewish measures in Hungary, Foreign Secretary Anthony Eden (later Lord Avon) associated himself with the American President. In his statement of March 30, Eden emphasized that the "persecution of the Jews has in particular been of unexampled horror and intensity" and repeated the determination of the Allies to bring to justice all those guilty of such crimes. Like Roosevelt, Eden also called "upon the countries allied with or subject to Germany to join in preventing further persecution and cooperate in protecting and saving the innocent."[173]

The Allies' warnings and declarations had no effect on the dejewification-minded Nazis and their Hungarian hirelings. While they implemented their plans, the WRB engaged in a series of rescue-related activities that turned out to be useless—at least as far as the provincial Jews were concerned. The WRB continued to warn the Hungarians (April 12), explored the possibility of providing escape routes via partisan-held Yugoslav territories, contacted the Turks for the issuance of transit visas, and demanded that persons holding documents issued by any North or South American republic be accorded all rights and privileges of such nationals. On the theory that the presence of foreigners in official or unofficial capacities might have a deterrent effect, the WRB requested the IRC (March 25) to "send effective representation to Hungary in order to protect the well-being of groups facing persecution." On May 25–26, following receipt of reports on the beginning of the mass deportations, the WRB instructed the American missions in Ankara, Berne, Lisbon, Madrid, and Stockholm to prevail upon the governments of the neutral states "in the interest of most elementary humanity to take immediate steps to increase to the largest possible extent the number of . . . diplomatic and consular personnel in Hungary and to distribute them as widely as possible throughout the country."[174]

The WRB's expectations about the presence of foreign observers unfortunately proved unfounded. The determination of the Nazis, the reluctance of the IRC and the neutral powers, and the time consumed by diplomatic exchanges all conspired against the Jews. By the time Wallenberg arrived on July 9, the dejewification of the countryside had been completed and Horthy had halted the deportations.

The effectiveness of the WRB in the pursuit of relief and rescue operations was limited by the restrictions resulting from its general policy framework: it could undertake no measures that might be construed as inconsistent "with the successful prosecution of the war" or as violating British and American immigration policies relating to Palestine and the United States. The negative effect of these policies were clearly reflected in the attitude and reaction of the Allies to the Brand mission, the revelations of the Auschwitz Protocols, the demands for the bombing of Auschwitz, and the so-called Horthy offer relating to the emigration of Jews.

The Allies' Reaction to the Brand Mission. Brand's arrival in Istanbul on May 19, 1944, on his Eichmann-approved "blood for trucks" mission (see chapter 29) caught the Western Allies by surprise. Sir Harold Mac-Michael was briefed by Moshe Shertok (later Sharett) and David Ben-Gurion, the leaders of the Jewish Agency for Palestine, about the details of the supposed offer on May 25. That same day, Sir Harold informed his government, characterizing the offer as a "Nazi intrigue based on far other motives than the apparent ones."[175] The British War Cabinet took up the issue on May 31, and the immediate reaction of all those present was negative. A. W. G. Randall of the Foreign Office thought that "there were substantial reasons for having nothing to do with the proposals as they stood," but warned that the United States might have a different view. He asserted that "the scheme might secure sympathy beyond its merits in Washington, where the President's War Refugee Board, backed by Mr. Morgenthau, had, partly for electoral reasons [Roosevelt was campaigning for his fourth term], committed itself to the 'rescue' of Jews." Oliver Stanley, the Secretary of State for the Colonies, suggested that the scheme should not be considered because "the evacuation of a million refugees from occupied territories and their maintenance in neutral or allied countries could not be undertaken without a major alteration of the course of military operations." Therefore, the War Cabinet decided to inform the United States government of its decision not to engage in any dealings with the Gestapo. As one concession, they agreed to relay the information received from the Jewish Agency in Jerusalem to Chaim Weizmann and Nahum Goldman.[176]

Without revealing any details of the measures adopted by the War Cabinet meeting he had attended, G. H. Hall, the Parliamentary Under Secretary of State for Foreign Affairs, informed Weizmann about the details of the Brand mission—orally on June 2, in writing on June 5.[177]

Weizmann and the other Jewish leaders in London were eager to pursue the course of action that offered the best hope of saving Jewish lives, but were also extremely anxious that anything the Jewish Agency undertook toward this end "should be with the knowledge and approval of H. M. Government."[178] They had a series of discussions with the representatives of the British Foreign Office, including Anthony Eden, G. H. Hall, I. L. Henderson, A. W. G. Randall, and Alan Walker. On June 7, Weizmann met Eden and urged him to keep the Soviet government informed about the affair.[179] On June 22, 1944, Hall informed Weizmann about the findings of Shertok, emphasizing that Shertok was fully "convinced of Brand's reliability, and that Brand himself was convinced that the German proposition was a serious one." Hall added that in Ben-Gurion's view, however, "the whole business may quite likely be a trick."[180] The Jewish leaders in America were also somewhat skeptical, but emphatic on the need to keep the discussion open to save at least some Jewish lives. Nahum Goldman tended toward the theory that the offer was not part of psychological warfare, but a genuine offer "put up by Gestapo leaders (certainly Eichmann and possibly Himmler) with a view to obtaining foreign exchange for their own use when they would have to flee from a defeated and occupied Germany." Rabbi Stephen S. Wise was not sure of the motive behind the Gestapo offer, but thought it might be a move to discredit both the Allies and the Jews.[181]

Immediately after Shertok's arrival in London, a meeting of the Jewish leaders was held (June 28) to hear his report on the interview with Brand and on his and Joseph Linton's discussions with Randall, Walker, and Henderson of the Foreign Office that morning.[182] The Jewish leaders tried to persuade the British to allow Brand's speedy return to Hungary and to undertake some action toward the saving of Jewish lives. While the British were skeptical about the whole Brand issue "because the Germans were going on with their deportations and killing," they were also concerned about the possibility that the Germans might be serious and actually "offer to dump a million Jews on them." Randall remarked that difficulties arose even in connection with putting up a few thousand refugees. The British found a way out of their predicament by emphasizing that "they could not contemplate meeting the Germans without the Russians knowing about it."[183] Weizmann warned his colleagues that "they must not do anything which could be interpreted by the people with whom they are in contact or by public opinion as an attempt to force Britain to do something which might interfere with the war." He reminded them that "the shooting of 50 officers has done more to impress the public than the murder of four million Jews." He finally suggested that they tell Mr. Eden that the fiendish and diabolical German offer had put them on the horns of a dilemma. "On the one hand they might be able to save some Jews, but on the other hand there was danger that they might compromise themselves."[184]

Following their discussion with Shertok, the British officers informed

Washington that they had been reinforced in their conviction that the German offer was designed to:

- Extract material concessions of war materiel from Allied governments.
- Embroil the United Kingdom and United States Governments with the Soviet Government, by representing to the latter that the former were negotiating with the enemy.
- Elicit a rejection, which would then be represented as justification for extreme measures against Jews.

They labeled the German offer as not serious, especially as it came through such "insignificant or suspect channels" and added that Shertok himself appeared to agree with their analysis.[185] If their perception of Shertok's position was accurate, Shertok did not represent the view of the Jewish Agency in Jerusalem. On July 11, Ben-Gurion asked Nahum Goldman, via Pinkerton, to urge President Roosevelt "not to allow this unique and possibly last chance of saving remains of European Jewry to be lost." The President was asked, as the British were, to support the following Jewish Agency proposals:

First, [that] intimation to other side be made immediately through appropriate channels of readiness to nominate [a] representative to discuss rescue and transfer [the] largest possible number of Jews; second, intimation to other side that immediate discontinuance [of] deportations is [a] preliminary condition to any discussion.[186]

Since the British had decided to prevent or at least postpone Brand's return to Hungary, the idea was born to have Menachem Bader of the Istanbul *Vaada* fill in for him. The Germans were ready to cooperate and offered to grant Bader the necessary permits and guarantee of safe return. Weizmann and Shertok took up this proposal with Eden on July 6. Shertok was convinced that the Germans' offer to Bader clearly indicated that they were ready to discuss the release of Jews.[187] Eden expressed great reservations about a British national going into enemy territory.[188] Unaware of the British attitude, the Germans pressed on with the Bader idea. On July 8, Bader was contacted personally by Stiller, the German Consul General in Istanbul, informing him of a request he had received from the German Foreign Office to fly him to Berlin.[189] The matter was taken up by Shertok with the Foreign Office once again on July 12. Randall reiterated Eden's arguments.[190] Thereupon Shertok suggested that Kullmann of the IGC be sent instead. Kullmann, who was concerned with refugee matters, had already visited several parts of Nazi Europe during the war, and the objections raised in connection with Bader did not apply to him. The British rejected this idea as well, arguing that Kullmann was after all an official of the League of Nations.[191] Shertok then renewed the proposal advanced several times earlier that "all Jews in Nazi-occupied countries be declared to be British-protected or Anglo-American-protected persons." Randall rejected this proposal also by arguing that:

- Such a step would be treated with contempt by the other side.
- To make the offer appear serious it would have to be accompanied by an offer to exchange, for which no Germans were available.
- Giving asylum to hundreds of thousands of people was a practical impossibility.
- Such an offer might make the Germans feel that the Allies were so preoccupied with the Jewish problem as to make this a vulnerable point, with the result that they would tighten the screws even harder.[192]

The British were fearful that Brand's return might be construed as the first step in some form of negotiation which might lead them "into very dangerous issues."[193] The efforts of the Jewish leaders notwithstanding, Brand was therefore retained in British custody.[194] Escorted by a British officer, he was taken to Cairo, where he was treated as a "privileged prisoner." Bandi Grosz, who accompanied Brand on the mission, was mistrusted because of his dubious credentials (see chapter 29). He was less fortunate: shortly after he was picked up by the British in Syria, he was brought to Cairo where he was held in a military prison.

Both men were interrogated for days on end. At one point, Brand claims that he was even questioned by Lord Moyne, the Minister of State for the Middle East, who like Randall had expressed concern over acquiring responsibility for one million Jews in case the Germans kept their side of the bargain.[195]

Brand received a more sympathetic hearing from Ira A. Hirschmann, who arrived in Cairo late in June specifically to interview him and Grosz at the behest of the WRB.[196] Hirschmann had served as a special attaché of the American Embassy in Ankara, charged with the responsibility and duty of carrying out the WRB's program and policies in Turkey. When he undertook this special mission, he was already aware of the memorandum that Viscount Halifax had forwarded to Hull concerning the British government's opposition to any discussion with the "SS agents."[197] Overcoming the objection of the British authorities in Cairo, Hirschmann interviewed both agents, concluding that the British had erred in lumping the two in the same category. He informed Ambassador Steinhardt and the WRB that he could find no evidence to support the reservations of the British about Brand, underscoring his belief in Brand's integrity.[198]

The British were less inclined to differentiate between the two men and their missions, considering the German proposals "a sheer case of blackmail or political warfare . . . calculated to stave off Germany's defeat." They, like the Americans, were sensitive to the position of the Soviets, whose suspicion they did not want to arouse at that juncture. Averell Harriman, the American Ambassador to Moscow, informed the Kremlin about the affair on June 15, without mentioning the trucks. (Archibald Clark Kerr, the British Ambassador, had given Andrei J. Vishinsky, the Soviet Commissar for Foreign Affairs, a more complete report the day before.)[199] The Soviet reaction was communicated by Harriman in a June 19 cable to the State Department: Vishinsky had been instructed to state that the Soviet government did not consider it "expedient or permissible to carry on any conversations whatsoever with the German government on the question touched upon in the Embassy's note."[200]

The Americans were somewhat more flexible. Their position was reflected in a June 9 memorandum by Pehle. He emphasized President Roosevelt's view that the negotiations should be kept open and continued, in consultation with the British and the Soviet governments, in order to save the lives of as many intended victims as possible.[201] Again, Presidential politics conceivably influenced the American position. The British apparently thought so: In its note of July 12, prepared for the War Cabinet, the Foreign Office emphasized that "the only reason why, at the outset, H. M. Government did not dismiss the Gestapo proposals with contempt was that the U. S. Government, particularly in an election year, is desperately anxious to show that nothing, however fantastic, has been neglected which might lead to the rescue of Jews."[202] In the end, both the British and the Americans deferred to the Soviet opposition to negotiations with the Germans. On July 7, Harriman was asked to bring all the facts, including the matter of the trucks, to the attention of the Soviet government and to emphasize that neither the British nor the American government

has been deceived as to the character of this alleged offer of the German government and that the two governments are convinced that the offer is part and parcel of the psychological warfare effort of the German government. The alleged German willingness to guarantee that the trucks would not be used on the Western Front bears this out.[203]

Harriman was also asked to inform the Soviet government that while the British and the Americans were fully aware of the undesirability of direct contacts with the Germans, they were reluctant to shut the door completely to any possible "serious" offer by the Germans and were searching for a method of rescue which might be worked out through the intermediation of the Swiss.[204]

Though the Allies were possibly correct in assessing the Brand–Grosz mission as an attempt by the Germans to strike a wedge between the Soviet Union and the Western Powers and as an integral part of their psychological warfare strategy, they failed both to alleviate the anxiety of the Jewish leaders of the free world and to provide some more meaningful alternate means of rescue. Whatever hopes the Jewish leaders still had in connection with the mission dissipated in the evening of July 19, when the BBC brought it to public attention. The following day, the British press picked up the story, emphasizing that the "monstrous offer" of the Germans to barter Jews for munitions was a loathsome attempt to blackmail and sow suspicion among the Allies.

The BBC broadcast and the British press reports caught the attention of the Germans as well. Ribbentrop requested a full report from Veesenmayer about the background of the affair. When informed that the Brand mission was based on "a secret order of the *Reichsführer-SS*," Ribbentrop got in touch with Himmler, who presumably gave him a satisfactory response.[205] There is no evidence that the two rivals brought this issue before Hitler. The Hungarian Foreign Office denied the "allegations" of the British altogether and reiterated the resolve of the Hungarians to solve the Jewish question "in a humanitarian manner."[206]

The Allies' Reaction to the Auschwitz Protocols and the Krausz Report. The uproar over the Brand–Grosz affair became intertwined with the repercussions of the Krausz report of June 19, 1944, which included sections from the Auschwitz Protocols (see chapters 23 and 29). Distributed for publication in Switzerland by Mantello and relayed to Istanbul by Pozner on June 23, the report became the subject of numerous exchanges between the neutral capitals and London and Washington. These included frantic appeals for help by the Jewish leaders in Jerusalem (Gruenbaum), Geneva (Lichtheim), Lisbon (Dobkin), and Stockholm (Ehrenpreis). On June 24, Harrison informed Washington in a lengthy telegram about the realities of the deportations from Hungary and transmitted the request of Jewish leaders in Hungary and Slovakia that the Allies bomb the rail lines and bridges leading to Auschwitz.[207] Two days later, Norton forwarded Lichtheim's message to London. It included specific recommendations: a warning to the Hungarians, reprisals against Germans in Allied hands, and the bombing of Auschwitz and the rail lines leading to it as well as of all government buildings in Budapest.[208] The Western Allies were also subjected to considerable pressure by representatives of other governments,[209] rescue organizations, and numerous Jewish and non-Jewish lay and ecclesiastical leaders—all urging that the Allies act to save the remnant of Hungarian Jewry.

The United States reacted on June 26: through the Swiss Legation in Budapest, it sent a sharply worded warning to the Hungarian government, reiterating America's concern over the Jewish persecutions and calling attention to the President's statement of March 24 concerning the punishment of those found guilty of war crimes.[210] Two days later, the Office of War Information transmitted a message to the Hungarians from Archbishop Francis J. Spellman of New York. The Archbishop warned the Hungarians that the anti-Jewish measures, which "shocked all men and women who cherish a sense of justice and of human sympathy," were "in direct contradiction of the doctrines of the Catholic faith professed by the vast majority of the Hungarian people."[211] The Hungarian Ministry of Foreign Affairs did not respond to the note until July 18, and as always, they argued that the Jews had been placed at the disposal of the German government as workers.[212] In the meantime, the United States had reinforced its warning with a massive raid on Budapest (July 2).

The dismay of the British upon reconfirmation of the news they had already been acquainted with was expressed by Churchill in a succinct note to Eden (June 29) in reference to the Norton telegram: "What can be done? What can be said?"[213] Responding to questions raised by Silverman, Gallacher, and others in the House of Commons on July 5, Eden confirmed the "barbarous deportations." Noting that the repeated declarations and warnings by the Allies had failed to move the Germans and their Hungarian accomplices, Eden reiterated the oftstated position that "the principal hope of terminating this tragic state of affairs must remain the speedy victory of the Allied nations."[214]

This response was not found satisfactory by everyone: the public outcry by leading Jewish figures as well as by dignitaries of the Churches of England and Scotland continued unabated. William Temple, the Archbishop of Canterbury, who had approached Churchill on July 3,[215] appealed directly to the Hungarian people on July 8. He implored them to help the persecuted Jews "even if that involved great personal danger."[216] Similar messages were broadcast by the BBC. Frequently these also included information for the Hungarians about the true nature of the anti-Jewish measures and warnings to the members of the government and their accomplices about the consequences of their deeds.[217]

The restriction of British rescue policy to the issuance of warnings to the Hungarians was presumably sanctioned by Churchill. This was reflected by his July 11 note to Eden concerning the Norton telegram and the Brand mission. The Prime Minister dismissed the latter as not worthy of being taken seriously, especially since it was "put forward through a very doubtful channel." In connection with the former, he noted:

There is no doubt that this [persecution of Jews in Hungary and their expulsion from enemy territory] is probably the greatest and most horrible crime ever committed in the whole history of the world, and it has been done by scientific machinery by nominally civilized men in the name of a great State and one of the leading races of Europe. It is quite clear that all concerned in this crime who may fall into our hands, including the people who only obeyed orders by carrying out the butcheries, should be put to death after their association with the murders has been proved.[218]

The public reaction in the United States was more intense. The press published greater details about the catastrophe engulfing Hungarian Jewry,[219] eliciting expressions of indignation and horror from leading political figures as well as of hundreds of Jewish and non-Jewish private organizations.[220]

On June 3, the Senate Foreign Relations Committee called upon the Hungarian people to resist the orders of their government, help Jews to escape across the borders, and "watch and remember those who are accessories to murder and those who extend mercy, until the time when guilt and innocence will weigh heavily in the balance."[221] On June 21, the House Foreign Affairs Committee, in a highly unusual action, called on Hungary directly to halt the mistreatment of the Jews. In a statement issued by Committee Chairman Sol Bloom (Democrat of New York), Hungary was reminded that the tide of the war had changed in favor of the Allies and urged that country to "stem the tide of inhumanity toward the helpless people within her borders." The Committee also expressed its determination to bring to justice the criminals guilty of inhumane conduct.[222] A similar warning was issued by Secretary of State Hull in his statement of July 14, which publicly confirmed the mass killing of Hungarian Jews.[223]

The warnings and threats issued by the Allies had little, if any, effect on the Germans and Hungarians involved in the Final Solution program. The one approach that might have helped the Hungarian Jews was that suggested by the escapees from Auschwitz late in April and communicated by Rabbi Michael Dov Weissmandel and other leaders of the Bratislava *Vaada* early in May: the bombing of Auschwitz and of the rail lines and bridges leading to it, and of the major rail hubs along the route. The refusal of the Allies to act on these requests is well documented.[224] The stated reasons for the refusal was that the suggested air operations were "impracticable," counterproductive because they involved the diversion of aircraft needed for the success of military operations,[225] technically unfeasible, or difficult in the absence of accurate information on the location of the camps. These were basically spurious arguments, which aimed to camouflage the Allies' resolve not to be deterred by considerations of morality in the pursuit of their national interests.

Since the Germans were also using the rail lines and bridges to transport troops and war materiel, the bombing could easily have been justified even under the terms of Allied policy, which prohibited the use of armed forces for the rescuing of victims of enemy oppression "unless such rescues were the result of military operations conducted with the objective of defeating the armed forces of the enemy."[226] By the time of the German occupation of Hungary in March 1944, the Allies had achieved full control of the skies over Europe. In fact, starting in the summer of 1944, they carried out a number of massive air strikes on factory areas near Auschwitz.[227] The claim by the British Air Command (August 3, 1944) that it had no accurate information as to Birkenau's location[228] appears somewhat unfounded in light of the details included in the Auschwitz Protocols. Moreover, by late August the Allies had acquired an amazingly detailed aerial photograph of the camp with the aid of sophisticated photoanalysis techniques.[229]

While the Jewish leaders of the free world pleaded with the leaders of the Western Powers to act,[230] and while the political and military figures of these powers exchanged innumerable notes in their attempt to avoid doing so, the Hungarian Jews were being massacred at the rate of 12,000 a day. The exchange of memoranda continued well after Horthy had halted the deportations and the Auschwitz machinery of destruction had been demolished.

The Allies' Reaction to the Horthy Offer. The decision of the Hungarian Crown Council meeting of June 26 to permit the emigration of approximately 7,800 Jews (see above) came to be known to the Western Powers as the Horthy offer. This offer was communicated to Veesenmayer by Sztójay on June 27 and again by Horthy on July 8. The Swiss and the other interested legation representatives were informed a few days later. Unaware of Hitler's conditions for the approval of the limited emigration and of Eichmann's sinister plans in connection with the scheme, Krausz, with the support of the Swiss Legation (Lutz) and the IRC, proceeded with the organization of the emigration of "7,000 families" (approximately 40,000 Jews) to Palestine.[231] Taking considerable credit for the decision of the government, Krausz wrote two letters on July 13, one addressed to Barlas in Istanbul and the other to Pozner and Kahany in Geneva.[232] He reported without any basis in fact—unless he was misinformed by the low-ranking Hungarian officials he dealt with—that the German authorities in Berlin had already approved the emigration in principle and that they would not obstruct the departure of Hungarian Jews in possession of Palestine immigration certificates. Emphasizing that one of the conditions imposed by the authorities was that the emigration had to be effectuated swiftly, he urged Barlas to immediately provide Turkish ships to transport the Jews in weekly groups of 4,000 to 5,000 from either Constanţa, Romania, or Burgas, Bulgaria.

The Hungarian authorities spoke only in terms of 7,800 Jews; the Germans made no commitments concerning the issuance of the exit and transit permits beyond those stipulated by Hitler. The Swiss Legation, however, acting presumably on Krausz's assurances, nevertheless informed Geneva about the Hungarian offer in highly optimistic terms. The British Legation in Berne relayed the information to the Foreign Office on July 18; the following day, Harrison cabled to Washington:

A note from the Foreign Office, dated yesterday, states that according to a telegram from the Swiss Legation at Budapest, authorization has been given by the Government of Hungary for the departure of all Jews from Hungary who hold entry permits for another country, including Palestine.[233]

Later in the month, the offer was also transmitted via the IRC.[234] Relying on Krausz's reports to Barlas, Pozner, and Kahany as well as on the communication from the Swiss Legation in Budapest, the Jewish leaders of the free world began a concentrated drive to make possible the immigration to Palestine of 40,000 Jews. On July 20, Shertok and Linton urged Randall to take "immediate action to explore and take advantage of the offer."[235] The following day they met the leaders of the IGC, including Emerson, and urged them to act toward the same end.[236] On July 31, Eleanor F. Rathbone, a member of the House of Commons, addressed a note to Eden in behalf of the National Committee for Rescue from Nazi Terror, complaining that despite assurances received from Hall a few days earlier, the British Foreign Office had failed to inform the Hungarians about the British government's "determination to find transport and accommodation for all who could get out."[237]

The British, of course, had not yet decided to act on the offer. They were in fact concerned and worried about the possibility of large numbers of Jews suddenly arriving in Allied-held territories. Their anxiety was reflected in a memorandum addressed to Randall by Robert Maurice A. Hankey, an official of the Eastern Department of the Foreign Office, on July 20. Having learned of the Horthy offer from MacMichael, Hankey cautioned:

It is clear that the floodgates of Eastern Europe are now going to be opened and that we shall in a very short time have masses of Eastern European Jews on our hands. . . . The Eastern Department must remind you of the decision taken on a previous paper that a serious political situation would arise throughout the Arab world as soon as the Palestine quotas were filled. . . . It is vital that camps should be established . . . somewhere in the Mediterranean area, but not Palestine and preferably not too near Palestine.[238]

The War Cabinet took up the issue on August 3. Eden reviewed the offer and emphasized the objections of the Colonial Office over the ability of Palestine "to accept at the moment anything like so many immigrants."[239] As Eden saw it, the British could either refuse the "Horthy offer" (jointly with the United States Government or separately) and thus possibly arouse hostile public opinion, or accepting it, and risk civil war in Palestine thanks to an influx of Jews from Hungary into the Levant.[240]

The British were willing to admit into Palestine, within the framework of the White Paper, a limited number of Jews who held genuine immigration certificates. They urged the United States to accept more refugees and to induce the Latin American countries to do the same. They also proposed a joint approach to Lisbon to persuade the Portuguese to allow Jews to enter Angola.[241]

The United States adopted a more positive tone. Responding to some of the objections raised by the British in connection with difficulties over transportation and accommodation (objections clearly designed to delay a decision) the Americans argued that the Horthy offer "must be accepted as quickly as possible in order to save the largest number of lives possible." They also maintained that the Western Allies "must act immediately without waiting to consult or enlist the aid of other governments."[242] Its air of urgency notwithstanding, the United States showed no willingness to liberalize its own immigration policies. The only "concession" it made was to inform Germany and Hungary (via the Swiss) that

American consular officers in neutral countries have been authorized to issue an immigration visa to any person to whom an American immigration visa was issued or for whom a visa was authorized on or after July 1, 1941, and who has been in areas controlled by Germany or any of Germany's allies since December 8, 1941, provided that such person presents himself to an American consular officer in a neutral country and is found not to have become disqualified for the issuance of a visa.[243]

Notification to this effect was sent on July 26 to the American representatives in Portugal, Spain, Sweden, Switzerland, and Turkey. They were instructed to assure the affected governments of U.S. willingness to make arrangements for the maintenance and support of the refugees. While this position represented a slight departure in U.S. immigration policy, it had no impact on the plight of Hungarian Jewry. For even if the Germans and the Hungarians had agreed to let the affected Jews leave the country, their number, given the American quota for Hungary, would have been minimal.

The Western Allies wrangled for about three weeks over the response to be given to Hungary.[244] The compromise formula—a positive approach with no specific commitments—was incorporated in the statement issued on August 17:

The International Committee of the Red Cross has communicated to the Governments of the United Kingdom and the United States an offer of the Hungarian Government regarding the emigration and treatment of Jews. Because of the desperate plight of the Jews in Hungary and the overwhelmingly humanitarian considerations involved the two governments are informing the Government of Hungary through Intercross that, despite the heavy difficulties and responsibilities involved, they have accepted the offer of the Hungarian Government for the release of Jews and will make arrangements for the care of such Jews leaving Hungary who reach neutral or United Nations territory, and also that they will find temporary havens of refuge where such people may live in safety. Notification of these assurances is being given to the governments of neutral countries who are being requested to permit the entry of Jews who reach their frontiers from Hungary. The Governments of the United Kingdom and the United States emphasize that, in accepting the offer which has been made, they do not in any way condone the action of the Hungarian Government in forcing the emigration of Jews as an alternative to persecution and death.[245]

A few hours before the statement was issued, the Colonial Office sent a copy to High Commissioner MacMichael, noting that no departure from existing Palestine immigration policy was intended.[246] Subsequently, the IGC held a number of meetings attended by interested British agency representatives as well as Burckhardt and other members of the IRC to discuss the arrangements referred to in the declaration.[247] Contact was also established with the Allied and neutral countries who were likely to accept Jews. Neither the IGC nor the neutral and Allied countries showed any sense of urgency. The smaller Allies and the neutral countries were perplexed over the failure of the greater powers to absorb larger number of refugees, and fearful that once they admitted the immigrants they would be permanently stuck with them. The IGC itself became bogged down in questions of financing, accommodation, and transportation. Consequently even the few countries that showed some interest in the Allies' appeal were reluctant to accept more than a token number of Jews. This was anticipated by Pehle, who reminded the President in a memorandum dated May 8: "The necessity for unilateral action by this government lies in the fact that we cannot expect others to do what we ourselves will not do and if we are to act in time we must take the lead." The President was urged to make at least a symbolic gesture by establishing "temporary havens" for refugees, who would be classified as internees rather than immigrants. On June 9, President Roosevelt announced that such a temporary haven would be established for a maximum of 1,000 refugees at a former army post at Oswego, New York. On August 4, Secretary of the Interior Harold Ickes welcomed 987 carefully screened refugees to Oswego.[248] This meager contribution to the solution of the refugee problem by the leading power in the anti-Axis alliance certainly did not have a salutory effect upon the other nations that were called upon to act on the Horthy offer.

On September 6, Brazil expressed its readiness to admit 500 children, as long as it would have no "financial responsibilities in regard to transport or upkeep."[249] Two days later, the Republic of Ireland indicated its willingness to include Hungarian Jewish children among the 500 children it had earlier agreed to admit. It explained that it could take only children "for reasons of security," and that 500 was "the largest number which the Jewish population of Eire could reasonably be expected to support and that the Irish economy could be expected to absorb."[250] Australia, while sympathetic, was deterred by the "unpromising shipping position"; New Zealand . . . "decided that for the time being they were unable to help"; South Africa indicated that it already had its "hands full with war refugees and evacuees"; Southern Rhodesia reported that no additional refugees could be accommodated; Canada failed to reply.[251]

The greatest obstacle was the opposition of Britain to the liberalization of its Palestine immigration policies. The British continued to invoke their commitments under the White Paper, the need for security and stability in the Middle East, the problems of transportation, accommodation, and administration, and the potential diplomatic difficulties with Turkey and other countries on the transit routes.[252] They remained adamant in their position despite the great pressures exerted upon them, especially by the United States. The failure of Britain to admit the Hungarian Jews to Palestine was vehemently denounced in both houses of the Congress.[253] Jewish rescue and representative organizations in the United States submitted well-documented memoranda and sent deputations to the British Embassy in Washington.[254] All these moves were of no avail.

The dilatory manner in which the Western Allies treated the issue of rescue made the Horthy offer a moot question. Their anxiety, which in retrospect proved unfounded in view of the Germans' unwillingness to let a large number of Jews escape their net, was considerably relieved by the fast-moving military developments. The *volte face* of Romania on August 23 and the consequent swift Red Army offense made the Horthy-related emigration via Romania, Bulgaria, and the Black Sea all but impossible. After the *Nyilas* coup, the British and the Americans reverted back to the issuance of warnings of retribution as a means of protecting the Jewish community.[255] The WRB became involved in the rescue negotiations, which were carried out mostly by Saly Mayer of the AJDC and Kasztner and Becher. McClelland's personal involvement in the negotiations on November 4 may have had a decisive effect on their outcome, because Becher identified him to Himmler as "President Roosevelt's personal representative."[256]

The many pleas by the Jewish leaders for help were usually answered by the standard assurances that the Allies were doing everything possible to avert the danger of new persecutions in Hungary.[257] These assurances had no more effect on the Jews than the threats of retribution had on the *Nyilas*. The Jews remained as helpless as ever and the *Nyilas* continued their rampage until the arrival of the Soviet forces which liberated Pest on January 17 and Buda on February 13, 1945.

The USSR

While the Red Army played a determining role in saving the Jews of Budapest and thousands of Jews in the labor service companies, the USSR was not particularly involved in the political-diplomatic campaign for the rescue of Hungarian Jewry. The liberation of Jews was the consequence of the military operations of the Soviet forces against the Axis rather than the result of a conscious policy of rescue or considerations of humanitarianism. Like the other members of the Grand Alliance, the USSR too was motivated primarily by considerations of perceived national interests.[258]

Following the German occupation of Hungary, the Soviet Union condemned the measures adopted by the occupying forces and their Hungarian accomplices. Its messages were usually broadcast to Hungary by Radio Moscow and more frequently by Kossuth Radio, the station operated by Hungarian Communist exiles in the USSR. These usually called on the Hungarians to resist and on the Jews to remain confident of their ultimate liberation. Some of the messages, while well-intentioned, proved counterproductive. For example, Kossuth Radio advised the Jews on April 1 not to allow themselves to fall into a ghetto mood and to be ready to wear the Yellow Star proudly ("with their head up").[259] Since the Soviet press devoted little attention to the Final Solution and completely ignored the realities of Nazism during the period of the Hitler-Stalin Pact (August 23, 1939–June 22, 1941), it is possible that these Hungarian exiles and their Soviet colleagues were ignorant of the dangers associated with wearing the telltale badge.

The government of the Soviet Union, unlike those of Britain and the United States, did not comment officially on the likely consequences of the occupation for the Jews. The Soviet silence perplexed the Western Powers as well as the Jewish leaders of the free world. On May 16, the Emergency Committee to Save the Jewish People of Europe appealed to Stalin, urging him to intercede in behalf of the Hungarian Jews.[260] A day later, the American Embassy in Moscow was instructed to urge the Russians to broadcast warnings to those involved in the deportations that they would be held personally responsible for their actions. The Embassy was also instructed to induce the Soviet Ministry of Foreign

Affairs to use its influence upon the satellite governments and populations, encouraging them to resist the German demands for the deportation and persecution of minority groups.[261] On May 25, Harrison and McClelland suggested that the Soviet government "be prevailed upon in regard to the purpose of the occupation of Hungary by the Nazis, to associate itself with the declaration of March 24 by President Roosevelt." Such a declaration would carry great weight, they argued, "since the Soviet armies are standing on the frontiers of Hungary and the fear of the Russians in the hearts of a large number of 'collaborators' in Hungary is mortal." The suggestion was not cabled to the American ambassador in Moscow until June 10.[262] The British made a similar plea on July 13. Reminding the Soviet government of its participation in the December 17, 1942, declaration and of the Nazis' failure to desist "from their barbarous treatment of the Jews," Eden asked Molotov to arrange for a separate Soviet declaration, given the victorious advance of the Red Army. Such a declaration, Eden argued, "couched in terms of unambiguous frankness and proclaiming that the Soviet Armies and retribution for these crimes would enter Hungary together, might have the effect of at least reducing the scale of these horrible outrages against the Jewish population."[263] In a personal message to Eden (August 16), Molotov pointed out that the Soviet government had repeatedly made such declarations. He mentioned specifically the declaration issued on November 2, 1943, by Roosevelt, Churchill, and Stalin. (This declaration did not identify the Jews as a special target of the Nazis.) Molotov assured Eden that the Soviet government had issued directives "to the appropriate propaganda organizations to pay special attention to the unmasking of these crimes, and to issue warnings regarding the inevitable severe punishment to be meted out to all who are found guilty of such crimes."[264]

Long fearful of a possible rapprochement between the Western Allies and the Third Reich that might lead to an anti-Communist capitalist coalition, the Soviet leaders were highly suspicious of any attempt to deal with the Nazis on matters of rescue. Therefore, they ignored almost completely the plight of Nazi-oppressed groups and minorities. Jewish labor servicemen who escaped to the Soviet lines or who were captured as ordinary POWs were poorly treated; the government vehemently opposed any dealings with the Brand mission; the Horthy offer was condemned;[265] no official public declarations condemning the extermination of the Jews were ever issued. All this reflected the Soviet leaders' suspicions and political interests. Such attitudes were exacerbated after the war; in September 1948, the Soviet Union launched its campaign against Zionism and cosmopolitanism, a euphemism often identified with the Jewish people. In a large number of fictional and pseudo-historical works, Soviet and East European authors aimed to demonstrate the link that allegedly existed between Zionists and Nazis.[266]

El Salvador

The rescue activities of El Salvador were primarily the consequence of the efforts of a single person, Georges M. Mantello (formerly known as György Mandel or Mandl). A Hungarian Jew from the Transylvanian town of Beszterce, he arrived in Switzerland in December 1941, reportedly as a purchasing agent for the Romanians. Eventually he managed to have himself appointed First Secretary of the Consulate General of El Salvador in Geneva. In this capacity, he undertook several actions designed to help the victims of Nazism, especially Hungarian Jews. In connection with the latter, his achievements were twofold. First, with the cooperation of Colonel I. H. Castellanos, the Consul General, but originally without the knowledge of the government of El Salvador, Mantello sent a few hundred "nationality" certificates to Hungary. The possessors of these certificates were considered foreign nationals and exempted from the general anti-Jewish decrees.[267] Some complications arose over the fact that El Salvador had no nation to look after its interests in Hungary.[268] (The Swiss, and later the Swedish, representatives in Budapest had assumed that role somewhat informally.) Mantello's second major achievement, which was shared with Pozner, was to contact Krausz in Budapest via Florian Manoliu, a member of the Romanian Legation in Berne. It was through Manoliu that Krausz sent his June 19 report with the abbreviated version of the Auschwitz Protocols that evoked the worldwide reaction against the anti-Jewish drive in Hungary (see chapters 23 and 29).[269] Acting independently of the many domestic and international Jewish organizations in Switzerland, Mantello distributed the Krausz material to leading Swiss clergymen, political and academic figures and journalists. He was effectively supported in this campaign by Walter Garrett, the Zurich representative of the London-based Exchange Telegraph Company. On relief matters, he was aided by his brother Joseph (Iosip) Mandel.[270]

The Jewish Relief and Rescue Organizations

In addition to Mantello's operations, which were largely based on his personal social, political, and business contacts, Switzerland was the seat of a considerable number of domestic and international Jewish organizations devoted to relief and rescue activities. Among the domestic ones, by far the most important were the *Rabbinerverband der Schweiz* (Association of Rabbis of Switzerland) of St. Gallen; the *Schweizerischer Israelitischer Gemeindebund* (Association of Swiss Jewish Communities) of Zurich; the *Verband Schweizerischer Jüdischer Flüchtlingshilfen* (Association of Swiss Jewish Refugee Aid Societies) of Zurich; and the *Schweizerische Zentralstelle für Flüchtlingshilfe* (Swiss Refugee Aid Center) of Zurich. The community of international Jewish organizations included the *Agudath Yisrael World Organization* in Geneva; the *Union Internationale de Secours aux Enfants* (International Union for the Rescue of Children) in Geneva; and the *Union O.S.E.* of Geneva.

The international Jewish organizations that played a considerable role in connection with the tragedy of Hungarian Jewry were the AJDC, headed in St. Gallen by Saly Mayer;[271] the Jewish Agency for Palestine, headed in Geneva by Richard Lichtheim;[272] the Palestine Office of Switzerland (*Office Palestinien de Suisse*), headed in Geneva by Chaim Pozner and Samuel Schep; the Hehalutz World Center (*Weltzentrale des Hechaluz*), headed in Geneva by Nathan Schwalb; the World Jewish Congress, headed in Geneva by Gerhard Riegner;[273] RELICO (Committee for the Aid of War-Stricken Jewish Population), headed in Geneva by Abraham Silberschein;[274] and HIJEF (*Hilfsverein für jüdische Flüchtlinge im Auslande;* Society for the Aid of Refugees Abroad), headed by the Sternbuch brothers in Montreux (see chapter 29).

A committee devoted exclusively to the relief and rescue of Hungarian Jewry—the Swiss Committee of Assistance for the Jews in Hungary (*Comité d'entr'aide Suisse pour les Juifs en Hongrie; Schweizerisches Hilfskomitee für die Juden in Ungarn*)—was formed in Zurich on March 23, 1944.[275] Composed of Swiss citizens of Hungarian origin, the Committee was under the leadership of Dr. Mihály Bányai.[276] The Committee members maintained contact with the Swiss authorities, Hungarian and Anglo-American diplomats, the Papal Nuncio, and the representatives of the IRC and of the domestic and international Jewish organizations in Switzerland. They had a particularly close relationship with the WRB, whose delegate, László Hámori, was of Hungarian-Jewish background. The Committee collected and disseminated information about the Nazi drive against the Jews, and offered specific suggestions to the various contacts on possible relief and rescue.[277]

Despite the Nazis' claims about the power and influence of "international Jewry," the Jewish organizations were basically powerless. In addition to the transmission of information about the plight of the Jews, their activities consisted mostly of enlisting the support of governmental and international institutions, the disbursement of relatively small sums of money among some of the stricken communities, and the allocation of the limited number of Palestine immigration certificates made available by the British. Their staffs and operational budgets were pitifully small. (Their low budgets, which made large-scale relief and rescue operations all but impossible, resulted from the meager allocations by the increasingly impoverished free Jewish communities and by the foreign currency restrictions of the Allies.) As foreigners, the leaders of the international Jewish organizations abided strictly by the censorship and other regulations of the state, which while sympathetic to the plight of the Jews was reluctant to admit any sizable groups of refugees and aimed above all to preserve its neutrality. It was partially this fear of jeopardizing their status by upsetting their host country that prevented the "foreign" Jewish leaders from publicizing the news about the Final Solution, of which they had been aware at least since the summer of 1942. The same position was adopted by the Swiss Jewish leaders, though they were not so vulnerable as the foreign Jews. When, for example, Chaim Pozner first learned in 1942 about Hitler's secret order to exterminate the Jewish people, he relayed this information to V. C. Farrell, the head of the British Intelligence unit in Geneva, for transmission to the Allies and to Benjamin Segalowitz, the director of the press bureau of the Union of Jewish Communities in Switzerland, reportedly for possible dissemination. Segalowitz, a Swiss citizen, merely forwarded it to Gerhard Riegner, who, in turn, relayed it through the American Legation in Berne to Washington (see chapter 23). Although it was made public in the fall of 1942, it received but scant notice in the press. There was no meaningful attempt to motivate or inform the Jewish masses about the scope of the order. One can only speculate about the possible reaction of the world and of the impact on the Nazis' drive against the Jews had the order been publicized in 1942 as the Krausz report was late in June 1944. The same holds true for the Auschwitz Protocols, a copy of which was reportedly sent to Schwalb soon after their completion late in April 1944. A press campaign based on those Protocols, if launched early in May, might have had a sobering effect upon the political and governmental leaders of Hungary without whose cooperation the Germans could not have carried out their genocidal plans.

The limited effectiveness of the Jewish organizations was to a large extent the consequence of the lack of cooperation among them and the absence of central leadership. The leaders of world Jewry, including the heads of the World Jewish Congress, the Jewish Agency for Palestine, and the World Zionist Organization, lived during the war either in New York (Rabbi Stephen S. Wise and Dr. Nahum Goldman), or London (Dr. Chaim Weizmann) or Jerusalem (David Ben-Gurion and Moshe Shertok), serving as conduits to their particular governments. In the absence of the top leaders, the heads of the various organizations in Switzerland became embroiled in petty political, ideological, and personal animosities, each jealously guarding his own powers, prerogatives, and contacts. They exercised tight control over their separate limited budgets, usually keeping the source and amount of their allocations secret; they normally operated in isolation from each other, maintaining separate contact with their particular headquarters; and each tended to claim credit both during and after the war for whatever success was achieved in the field of rescue, accusing the others for the failure to accomplish more.[278] The lack of cooperation, the conflicting signals, caused duplicated efforts and occasionally delayed actions.

Starting in 1942, the Jewish Agency leadership in both Jerusalem and Istanbul tried to induce the leaders of the international Jewish organizations to coordinate their activities.[279] These efforts met with only limited success: the leaders affiliated with the *Histadrut* and the *Hehalutz* formed two separate aid commissions—both of which were short-lived and ineffective.[280] As Barlas pointed out after the war, differences of opinion among their members caused much conflict. Contact with Jerusalem and Istanbul "was maintained mainly through the officials of the different organizations, each on his own."[281]

Shortly before the German occupation of Hungary, Yitzhak Gruenbaum, the head of the Jewish Agency's Relief and Rescue Committee in Jerusalem, requested Lichtheim to establish a "relief and rescue committee" similar to those in Jerusalem and Istanbul. Lichtheim began such an attempt on March 6, 1944, but success eluded him.[282] He was reportedly unsuitable for the leadership position envisioned for him by Gruenbaum. He was at odds with many of the other organizational heads on both personal and political grounds, allegedly being convinced of the hopelessness of any rescue operations.[283] He was particularly bitter toward Barlas, whom he accused of regarding himself as the Jewish Agency Executive's Viceroy of Europe.[284] Gruenbaum made a last and equally unsuccessful effort on March 23, 1945, over a month after the Jews of Budapest were liberated. In a telegram to Lichtheim, he emphasized that his proposal aimed to prevent people from saying that "owing to the lack of coordination the rescue opportunities were not fully exploited at the last minute."[285]

Under a competent and respected central leadership, the effectiveness of the various organizations might have been enhanced; the bureaucratic way in which they treated the news of the Holocaust and the basically ineffective measures they adopted toward the alleviation of suffering might then have been replaced by more efficient modes of operation.[286] However, the ultimate fate of the Jewish people in the Nazi sphere of influence would most probably have been no different: the tragedy of the Jews lay not so much in the ineffectiveness of their organizational leaders, but in their total helplessness during the war. Some of the Jewish leaders occasionally subordinated the urgent tasks of rescue to their preoccupation with the future of the Jewish people and the establishment of a Jewish state;[287] but this was not the source of their impotence. They were handicapped by a lack of resources, by the absence of physical opportunities to reach the Diaspora Jews, by their lack of diplomatic status, by the limitations imposed by the British rule in Palestine, and above all by the lack of urgency with which the Allies viewed their plight. Although the Jews were singled out for total destruction by an enemy armed with all the resources of modern science, the leaders of the Grand Alliance rarely, if ever, heeded appeals by Jewish leaders to intervene on behalf of Jews. They insisted with considerable persuasiveness that the best way to save Jews was to defeat Nazi Germany as quickly as possible. But by the time victory finally came, close to 6 million Jews had perished. The staggering toll reflects not only the genocidal singlemindedness of the Nazis and their collaborators, but also and perhaps above all the indifference of the rest of the world.

Notes

1. The International Red Cross is frequently referred to as the International Committee of the Red Cross (ICRC).

2. Aryeh L. Kubovy, "The Silence of Pope Pius XII and the Beginnings of the 'Jewish Document'" in *YVS*, 6:7–11. See also *Unity in Dispersion* (New York: World Jewish Congress, 1948), pp. 167–69.

3. *Report of the International Committee of the Red Cross on Its Activities During the Second World War* (Geneva, 1948), 1:641. For a well documented account of the efforts of Gerhart M. Riegner and other leaders of the World Jewish Congress, often acting in cooperation with Jaromir Kopecky, the delegate of the Czechoslovak government-in-exile in Switzerland, to induce the IRC to act in behalf of the oppressed Jews, see Monty Noam Penkower, "The World Jewish Congress Confronts the International Red Cross During the Holocaust" in *Jewish Social Studies*, New York, 41, no. 3–4 (Summer–Fall 1979):229–56.

4. *Inter Arma Caritas* (Geneva: International Committee of the Red Cross, 1947), p. 76.

5. Since the outbreak of World War II, Hungary had interned approximately 3,000 military prisoners and 5,000 Polish civilians. Among these were a number of Polish Jewish officers and soldiers who were interned separately in Vámosmikola in a camp commanded by First Lieutenant Béla Turcsányi. They were treated quite well until November 19, 1944, when they were ordered to march toward the Austrian border along the Komárom-Hegyeshalom route. Questions relating to Polish internees were handled by Section P of IRC. For further details, see chapter 3. See also Friedrich Born, *Bericht an das Internationale Komitee vom Roten Kreuz in Genf* (Report to the International Committee of the Red Cross in Geneva) (Geneva, June 1945), pp. 2, 39–41. The number of Yugoslav internees and prisoners of war ranged from 6,000 to 8,000. These were handled by Section Y of IRC. There were also a relatively few British, Dutch, Belgian, French, and American officers and soldiers who had either escaped from German POW camps or been shot down (or were caught after parachuting) in Hungary. While Soviet POWs were normally handed over to the Germans, there was a camp in Veszkény with eight Soviet officers and 246 soldiers. There were also 109 pro-Badoglio Italian prisoners who were interned shortly after the German occupation. *Ibid.*, pp. 3–4, 41–45.

6. Born's closest associates in the Budapest Office included Cornel Wehner, Arthur Kárász, Edit Tölgyessy, Daisy Darányi, Elek and Klára Máthé, and Aliz Herceg. The IRC's economic bureau was headed by József Gál, the hospital bureau by Ernő Teleki, and the doctors' commission by Dr. Boldizsár Horváth. For details on the IRC's structure, see *ibid.*, pp. 54–55.

7. *Ibid.*, pp. 25–26.

8. *Vádirat*, 3:100–2.

9. *Ibid.*, pp. 226–27.

10. Prior to the Theresienstadt visit, the German authorities engaged in a nine-month beautification of the camp. For details on this deceitful project and on the composition and findings of the IRC delegation, see Meir Dworzecki, "The International Red Cross and Its Policy vis-à-vis the Jews in Ghettos and Concentration Camps in Nazi-Occupied Europe," in *RAH*, pp. 96–99.

11. *Vádirat*, 3:246–47.

12. *Ibid.*, pp. 249–50.

13. The leaders of the IRC complained about these deportations, arguing that they were a violation of Horthy's pledge. Baron Károly Bothmer, the Hungarian Minister in Berne, relayed the protest to Budapest, only to be assured by Lajos Reményi-Schneller, the then Acting Prime Minister, that the deportations were being carried out without the knowledge or consent of the Hungarian government. Lévai, *Szürke könyv magyar zsidók megmentéséről* (Gray Book on the Rescuing of Hungarian Jews) (Budapest: Officina, n.d.), pp. 187–90. See also *Vádirat*, 3:422–23.

14. Born, *Bericht*, pp. 27–28. See also *Notiz über die Situation der Juden in Ungarn* (Note on the Situation of the Jews in Hungary), November 14, 1944, Yad Vashem Archives M-20/47.

15. *RLB*, Docs. 336–38.

16. The IRC was obviously aware of the often conflicting operations and clearly dis-

cernible rivalries among some of the major Jewish organizations in Switzerland. For further details on this subject, see the last section in this chapter. For the minutes of the IRC conferences see Yad Vashem Archives M-20/47.

17. For example, the Foreign Correspondence Censorship Office in Vienna (*Auslandsbriefprüfstelle Wien*) intercepted an August 6 letter by Chaim Pozner addressed to S. Mandelblatt in Istanbul, which included copies of the reports by Born and Schirmer as well as details about the plans for the possible emigration of 7,800 families from Hungary. Copies of the intercepted materials were sent to the main censorship office in Berlin as well as to the *Wehrmacht* headquarters. *RLB*, Doc. 339.

18. These were the first of the 7,800 Jews whose emigration to Palestine the Swiss supported. The 2,000 Jews were provided with a collective passport through the efforts of the Palestine Office. For further details see the section on Switzerland below.

19. *Vádirat*, 3:362–66, 467–72, 481. This effort was supported by Alfred Zollinger, the representative of the IRC in the United States. For further details see Dworzecki, "The International Red Cross," pp. 102–4, and below.

20. According to one account, a plan for the protection of children was submitted to Born by Krausz shortly after his arrival in Budapest, but was not acted upon for a long time. Krausz reportedly complained about Born's alleged incompetence to Schirmer. For details on this and other accusations directed against Born, see Lévai, *Fehér könyv. Külföldi akciók zsidók megmentésére* (White Book. Foreign Activities for the Rescuing of Jews) (Budapest: Officina, n.d.), pp. 148–49, 152, 155–57.

21. Born, *Bericht*, pp. 27, 34–36. For details see "The Rescue Activities of Ottó Komoly" in chapter 29.

22. Born, *Bericht*, pp. 37–39. For details see "The Good Shepherd Committee" in chapter 30.

23. Born, *Bericht*, pp. 33, 36–37. See also Lévai, *Szürke könyv*, pp. 203–6, and the sections on the *Nyilas* Era and Jewish Resistance in chapters 10 and 29, respectively.

24. For a list of the institutions that enjoyed the protection of the IRC, see Born, *Bericht*, pp. 54–68. One of the institutions that was taken under the protection of the IRC was the Columbus Street Camp, which had previously housed the Jews in the so-called Kasztner group.

25. For further details on the activities of the IRC, consult David P. Forsythe, *Humanitarian Politics: The International Committee of the Red Cross* (Baltimore: The Johns Hopkins University Press, 1977), 298 pp.

26. Paul Hofmann, "Pius Knew in 1941 of Drive on Jews." *The New York Times*, April 27, 1974.

27. For Gerstein's statement of April 26, 1945, see PS-1553.

28. Nora Levin, *The Holocaust* (New York: Thomas Y. Crowell, 1968), pp. 686–87.

29. Paul Hofmann, "The Vatican Knew of Nazi Pogroms, Its Records Show." *The New York Times*, April 5, 1973.

30. Saul Friedländer, *Pius XII and the Third Reich. A Documentation* (New York: Alfred A. Knopf, 1966), p. 222. For further details, see chapter 23.

31. Kubovy, "The Silence of Pope Pius XII," p. 11. See also appeals by the British Section of the World Jewish Congress of June 26, and October 14, 1944, in behalf of Hungarian Jewry, in *PRO*, Fo.371/42807, p. 32, and Fo.371/42820, p. 22.

32. *Foreign Relations of the United States, Diplomatic Papers, 1942. Volume 3. Europe* (Washington: Government Printing Office, 1961), pp. 776–77. For additional documents on the subject, see section titled "Vatican. Efforts of the United States and Other Governments to Have the Pope Protest Publicly Against Nazi Atrocities in German Occupied Areas," *ibid.*, pp. 772–80. See also Levin, *The Holocaust*, p. 686.

33. Report of Ernst von Weizsäcker, former Secretary of State in the German Foreign

Office and then German Ambassador to the Holy See, dated October 28, 1943. Alvin Shuster, "Vatican Releases '43 Documents on Handling of Jewish Problems." *The New York Times*, January 24, 1976; Raul Hilberg, *The Destruction of the European Jews* (Chicago: Quadrangle, 1961), pp. 429–30.

34. Kubovy, "The Silence of Pope Pius XII," p. 11.

35. *Ibid.*

36. The standard response was usually given by Monsignor Montini on instructions from the Pope. It was revealed in a note attached by Monsignor Montini to a telegram received from an Orthodox Jewish group in December 1942, in which the Pope was requested to intervene in behalf of the Jews of Eastern Europe. Hofmann, "Pius Knew in 1941 of Drive on Jews," cited above.

37. Friedländer, *Pius XII and the Third Reich*, p. 236; Levin, *The Holocaust*, pp. 692–93; Guenter Lewy, *The Catholic Church and Nazi Germany* (New York: McGraw Hill, 1964), p. 305.

38. For example, in response to the October 14, 1944 appeal by Alex L. Easterman, the Political Secretary of the British Section of the World Jewish Congress, the Pope refused to make a public appeal, arguing that "if he made a public declaration about the treatment of Jews in Hungary he might have to yield to pressure to issue a similar statement in regard to Russian treatment of Poles and the Baltic populations." See telegram no. 701, dated November 20, 1944, from Sir D. Osborne, the British Minister to the Holy See, to the Foreign Office. *PRO*, Fo.371/42822, p. 86.

39. This theme was echoed in the 688-page volume of documents issued by the Vatican early in 1976. The volume also reflected the anti-Zionist bias of the Vatican, many of whose officers, including Cardinal Maglione, openly opposed the establishment of a Jewish state in Palestine. Alvin Shuster, "Vatican Releases '43 Documents on Handling of Jewish Problems." *The New York Times*, January 24, 1976. For a sympathetic evaluation of the Pope's role, see Carlo Falconi, *The Silence of Pius XII* (Boston: Little, Brown, 1970), 430 pp.; Robert A. Graham, *Pope Pius XII and the Jews of Hungary in 1944* (New York: The America Press for the United States Catholic Historical Society, 1964), 26 pp.; Jenő Lévai, *Hungarian Jewry and the Papacy* (London: Sands and Company, 1968), 132 pp; and Anthony Rhodes, *The Vatican in the Age of the Dictators, 1922–1945* (New York: Holt, Rinehart and Winston, 1973).

40. Lewy, *The Catholic Church and Nazi Germany*, p. 303. See also Friedländer, *Pius XII and the Third Reich*, pp. 103–47, 236–38.

41. Another copy of the Protocols—probably the one sent by Miklós (Moshe) Krausz on June 19—reached the Vatican via Monsignor Filippo Bernardini, the Apostolic Delegate in Berne, toward the end of June.

42. For the Nuncio's account see his "A budapesti nunciatura diplomáciai akciója a zsidók érdekében" (The Diplomatic Campaign of the Budapest Nunciature in Behalf of the Jews) in *A magyar katolikus egyház és az emberi jogok védelme* (The Hungarian Catholic Church and the Protection of Human Rights), ed. Antal Meszlényi (Budapest: A Szent István Társulat, 1947), pp. 21–30.

43. Friedländer, *Pius XII and the Third Reich*, p. 218.

44. Helen Fein, *Accounting for Genocide* (New York: The Free Press, 1979), p. 110.

45. *Vádirat*, 1:317–24.

46. *Ibid.*, pp. 324–25.

47. Lévai, *Hungarian Jewry and the Papacy*, p. 20.

48. *Vádirat*, 1:326–31.

49. Lévai, *Hungarian Jewry and the Papacy*, pp. 21–22.

50. *Summary Report of the Activities of the War Refugee Board with Respect to the Jews of Hungary* (Washington, October 9, 1944), p. 4. (Typescript). The report was prepared by

Lawrence S. Lesser, the assistant of John W. Pehle, the head of the WRB. A similar request was advanced a few days later by Mr. Osborne, the British Minister to the Vatican.

51. *Summary Report of the Activities of the War Refugee Board,* pp. 11–12. See also Fein, *Accounting for Genocide,* p. 109. The Jewish leaders of America and Europe, including Kubowitzki, were informed about the U.S. note to the Vatican by Lesser. Kubovy, "The Silence of Pope Pius XII," pp. 13–14.

52. Friedländer, *Pius XII and the Third Reich,* p. 223.

53. Graham, *Pope Pius XII,* p. 15.

54. *Ibid.,* p. 12.

55. Lévai, *Zsidósors Magyarországon,* pp. 182–83.

56. Graham, *Pope Pius XII,* pp. 12–13.

57. For the minutes of the Nuncio-Sztójay meeting, see *Vádirat,* 3:92–97. The pressure exerted by the Nuncio together with the Swiss and the Swedish representatives on Horthy and Sztójay was the subject of two telegrams sent by Veesenmayer to Ribbentrop early in July 1944. See *RLB,* Docs. 186–87.

58. *Vádirat,* 3:98–100.

59. See Sztójay's note to Jaross dated July 13. *Ibid.,* 170–71.

60. *Ibid.,* pp. 251–55.

61. *Ibid.,* pp. 167–70.

62. *Ibid.,* pp. 302–3.

63. The note was handed in person by the Nuncio and Carl I. Danielsson, the Swedish Minister, to Lajos Reményi-Schneller, the Acting Prime Minister at the time. For text of the note, see "New Deportation Threats" in chapter 25. This was the first collective action by the Apostolic Delegate and the representatives of the neutral states in Budapest.

64. Friedländer, *Pius XII and the Third Reich,* pp. 224–35.

65. Lévai, *Hungarian Jewry and the Papacy,* pp. 37–38. Unlike the first note, this one was signed by Rotta, Danielsson, Harald Feller, Jorge Perlasca, and Count Pongrácz. The latter three represented the Swiss, Spanish, and Portuguese legations respectively.

66. See "The International Ghetto" section in chapter 26.

67. Lévai, *Fehér könyv,* pp. 144–45.

68. In recognition of his wartime rescue activities, including the distribution of protective passes to Jews in the Óbuda brickyards and the death-march columns, Báránszky, who was only 21 years old at the time, was awarded the Medal of Righteous Gentile by Yad Vashem on January 10, 1979. Báránszky settled in the United States in 1961.

69. See section "The Death-Marches to Hegyeshalom" in chapter 26.

70. Lévai, *Hungarian Jewry and the Papacy,* p. 44.

71. The letter of authorization empowered Újváry to "search and bring home from camps and from en route those people of Jewish origin who were under the protection of the Apostolic Nunciature and who were taken or are en route to the West in violation of the agreement between the Apostolic Nunciature and the Hungarian Government." Sándor Újváry, "Szabálytalan önéletrajz" (Unorthodox Autobiography). *Menora,* Toronto, February 17, 1979, p. 8. See also Lévai, *Szürke könyv,* pp. 187–203.

72. In this endeavor, Ujváry had the cooperation of Biró, Géza Tolnay, Tibor Verebély, Milán Kosztich, József Eszterházy, László Helle, István Földiák, Imre Farkas, Major István Fehér, and Captain Zoltán Horváth. *Ibid.*

73. Lévai, *Hungarian Jewry and the Papacy,* pp. 50–51. See also his *Szürke könyv,* pp. 13–30, 68–69, and *Zsidósors Magyarországon,* pp. 179–83, 202–6, 319–20, 349–51.

74. The neutral states, like the IRC, did not really get involved in rescue and relief activities until after the completion of the deportations from the provinces.

75. See Sztójay's June 27 note to Veesenmayer in "The Crown Council Meeting of June 26" section of chapter 25.

76. The German Foreign Office was so concerned with the Swiss press reaction that it wanted to lodge a protest, but later rescinded this plan for fear that it would jeopardize the myth of Hungarian sovereignty. It therefore suggested that the Hungarians take such steps. *NA*, Microcopy T-120, Roll 4664, K1509/K350356-.

77. See "The Auschwitz Protocols" section in chapter 23.

78. *Vádirat*, 3:190–92.

79. The protest and appeal were monitored by the Press Department of the German Foreign Office. For text see *NA*, Microcopy T-120, Roll 4664, K1509/K350291-

80. *Ibid.*, K1509/K350354-. See also *RLB*, Doc. 369.

81. *Vádirat*, 3:296.

82. To increase the number of those to be rescued, Krausz and his Zionist colleagues interpreted the 7,000 to mean 7,000 family heads, which in effect meant from 30,000 to 40,000 Jews. For further details of this scheme, see 'The Krausz Line" section in chapter 29.

83. Lutz returned to Switzerland in April 1945. While en route in Istanbul he gave an interview in which he reviewed the tragedy and problems of Hungarian Jewry. For text see The Central Zionist Archives, Jerusalem, File S26/1190. Lutz died in Switzerland in February 1975 at 73 years of age. For further details on his background, see Alexander Grossmann, "Erinnerung an alt Generalkonsul Charles Lutz" (Remembering Consul General Emeritus Charles Lutz). *Neue Zürcher Zeitung* (New Zurich Newspaper), February 26, 1975.

84. Jäger left Budapest on November 10. His functions were assumed by Antoine J. Kilchmann and on December 9, following Kilchmann's departure, by Harald Feller, the Legation secretary. E. Szatmári, *Bericht über die Tätigkeit der neutralen Vertretungen in Budapest. . . .* (Report on the Activities of the Neutral Representatives in Budapest . . .) Manuscript, pp. 16, 23. Mr. Szatmári had served as an expert on the press in the Swiss Legation during the war.

85. *Vádirat*, 3:242–45.

86. *Ibid.*, pp. 247–49.

87. *RLB*, Docs. 324–26. See also chapters 25 and 29.

88. When the "International Ghetto" was established on November 15, 72 buildings were assigned to house persons under Swiss protection. These proved inadequate because of the large number of holders of forged protective passes. Lévai, *Szürke könyv*, p. 182. See also chapter 26.

89. Forged protective passes were produced in large numbers by the Zionist underground, which used them for the release of internees as well as for providing Jews, especially Zionists and their sympathizers, with a degree of security from further persecution. See chapter 29.

90. Many sources refer to either 2,000 or 2,200 Jews covered by the initial collective passports. Each collective passport was in fact a book containing more than 1,000 names with the vital statistics of and a photograph for each individual.

91. The Swiss request was also supported by the IRC. Both Huber and Burckhardt approached Baron Bothmer toward this end. Lévai, *Szürke könyv*, pp. 180–81.

92. *RLB*, Doc. 370. According to a communication from Reichel to Wagner dated August 15, Eichmann, presumably frustrated by his failure to proceed with his original plans, had a new idea: He was ready to grant a number of exit visas if the deportations resumed, but then he would stop the emigration of the visa holders. *Ibid.*, Doc. 330.

93. *Ibid.*, Docs. 329-30, 371–73.

94. *Ibid.*, Docs. 374-77, 383.

95. Marcel Pilet-Golaz, the Swiss Foreign Minister, informed Clifford J. Norton, the British Minister in Berne, on August 10, 1944, about the authority he had received from the Swiss Federal Council "to offer a temporary refuge in Switzerland to 8,000 Hungar-

ian Jews." See Norton's telegram no. 3747, dated August 10, 1944, addressed to the Foreign Office. *PRO*, Fo.371/42814, p. 12.

96. According to M. Kahany, an official of the Jewish Agency in Geneva, he approached the Swiss Political Department on October 20 upon learning of the renewed drive against the Jews. He also contacted Leland Harrison, the American Minister, and Douglas MacKillop, the British chargé d'affaires, who reportedly persuaded Pilet-Golaz, the Swiss Foreign Minister, about proceeding with the plan under the Anglo-American guarantees. Early in November, the Swedish representative in Switzerland persuaded the Anglo-Americans to extend their guarantee to the over 4,000 Hungarian Jews holding temporary Swedish passports, inasmuch as the route between Germany and Sweden was already severed. The Swiss reportedly agreed to admit the Swedish-protected Jews under the same conditions as the Swiss-protected Jews. Mr. Kahany's major source of information about developments in Budapest was Dr. Pozner. See Kahany's reports no. 103 and 104, dated October 30 and November 16, 1944, respectively in the "Pazner Files" at Yad Vashem.

97. The Swiss Legation in Budapest was informed about this decision of the Federal Council on October 31. Although the chances of the Jews leaving Hungary were minimal, the Swiss were seriously concerned with the practical difficulties involved in caring for the refugees. They approached the Allies to have the Jews transferred, shortly after their arrival, to Marseilles and to Phillipeville, Algeria. See cable dated November 13, 1944, by Acting Secretary of State Edward R. Stettinius, based on a communication received from McClelland. See also *PRO*, Fo.371/42824, pp. 31–32.

98. See note dated November 3, 1944, addressed by Christopher Eastwood of the Colonial Office, to Paul Mason of the Refugee Department in the Foreign Office. *Ibid.*, Fo.371/42821, p. 78.

99. On that date Jäger told Arnóthy-Jungerth he would accept children of 5 to 13 years irrespective of their national or racial background. Although at first (October 7) the Swiss rejected the German proposal that no Jewish or *Volksdeutsche* children be included, they later (October 24) relented after they were informally told that the Jewish children might be allowed to go to Palestine. *RLB*, Docs. 381, 385, 395–97. See also Lévai, *Fehér könyv*, pp. 112–13.

100. *RLB*, Docs. 400–4. See also *NA*, Microcopy T-120, Roll 4203, Frames K209276–285.

101. Cable no. 7394, September 8, 1944, addressed to the U.S. Secretary of State by John G. Winant, U.S. Ambassador in London.

102. Telegram no. 7998 of September 30, 1944, addressed by Secretary of State Hull to American Embassy in London, based on messages received from McClelland.

103. Telegram no. 2077, October 30, 1944, from Ambassador Steinhardt to U.S. Secretary of State.

104. This was agreed at the October 31 meeting held in Kemény's office in the Ministry of Foreign Affairs with the participation of Lieutenant-Colonel Ferenczy, Lutz, and Raoul Wallenberg, representing the Swedes. Szatmári, *Bericht*, p. 13.

105. *RLB.*, Docs. 389–90, 393.

106. *Ibid.*, Doc. 399. Kaltenbrunner was promptly informed of the contents of Veesenmayer's telegram. *NA*, Microcopy T-120, Roll 4355, Frame K213435. See also Lévai, *Fehér könyv*, pp. 120–26, and *Zsidósors Magyarországon*, pp. 311–16, 332–41, 359–60, 367–68.

107. Before becoming Chief Rabbi of Sweden in 1914, Ehrenpreis served in Bulgaria (1900–1914) and in Croatia (1896–1900). Born in Lvov (Lemberg) in 1869, he died in Stockholm in 1951.

108. For details on the rescuing of Danish Jews, see Hilberg, *The Destruction of the European Jews*, pp. 357–63, and Leni Yahil, "The Uniqueness of the Rescue of Danish Jewry"

in *RAH*, pp. 617–25. See also Yahil's *Hatzala ha'yehudim be'Dania* (The Rescue of the Jews of Denmark) (Jerusalem: The Hebrew University and Yad Vashem, 1967), 316 pp.

109. See Sztójay's note to Veesenmayer dated June 27 in chapter 25, under "The Crown Council Meeting of June 26." The note was based on Arnóthy-Jungerth's report to the Council of Ministers. For details, see Lévai, *Fehér könyv*, pp. 60–71.

110. The original plan called for the appointment of Count Oscar Bernadotte, the Deputy President of the Swedish Red Cross. Since Arnóthy-Jungerth feared that the Germans would not grant him a transit visa, he suggested Dr. Langlet, who was already in Budapest. Dr. Langlet's appointment was based on an oral note of July 4, which was followed up by a written one ten days later. It was acknowledged with a pledge of cooperation by Gyula Ambrózy, the head of Horthy's Cabinet Office, on July 25. *Ibid.*, pp. 167–70.

111. Professor Langlet became active in setting up children's homes as well as in the distribution of protective passes. For details on his activities, see his *Verk och dagar i Budapest* (Work and Days in Budapest) (Stockholm: Wahlstrom & Widstrand, 1946), 221 pp.

112. For the text of the King's telegram as well as Horthy's reply of July 10, see *Vádirat*, 3:58–60.

113. WRB cable no. 17 for Johnson and Olsen.

114. For Professor Valentin's account, see his "Rescue and Relief Activities in Behalf of Jewish Victims of Nazism in Scandinavia" in *YIVO Annual of Jewish Social Science*, New York, 8, 1953:224–52.

115. See exchange of telegrams between Rabbis Ehrenpreis and Taubes in Yad Vashem Archives M-20/47.

116. *Vádirat*, 3:56–58, 241–42.

117. *RLB*, Docs. 362, 364–65.

118. *Ibid.*, Doc. 361. On July 7, he alerted the Foreign Office about a Swedish request for the emigration of 186 Hungarian Jews to Sweden. *Ibid.*, Doc. 363.

119. For further biographical details, see Lévai, *Raoul Wallenberg regényes élete, hősi küzdelmei, rejtélyes eltűnésének titka* (Raoul Wallenberg's Adventurous Life, Heroic Struggles, and Secret of His Mysterious Disappearance) (Budapest: Magyar Téka, 1948), 311 pp., and G. B. Freed, "Humanitarianism vs. Totalitarianism: The Strange Case of Raoul Wallenberg," in *Papers of the Michigan Academy of Science, Arts, and Letters*, 46, 1961:503–28. For additional references, consult Braham, *The Hungarian Jewish Catastrophe. A Selected and Annotated Bibliography* (New York: YIVO-Yad Vashem, 1962), p. 45.

120. Lévai, *Raoul Wallenberg*, pp. 30–39.

121. WRB cable no. 17 cited above.

122. See Johnson's telegram of June 21 to the State Department in Freed, "Humanitarianism vs. Totalitarianism," pp. 507–8.

123. See text in Hungarian translation in Lévai, *Raoul Wallenberg*, p. 42. Shortly after the meeting, the leaders of the Council sent a letter of appreciation to King Gustav, including some specific suggestions for aiding the remaining Jews of Hungary. Munkácsi, *Hogyan történt?*, pp. 185–87.

124. Statement by Ernő Pető in *HJS*, 3:58–59.

125. The following day, Wallenberg wrote another report detailing some aspects of the tragedy, including information on some of the ghettos, the Kasztner transport, the Weisz-Manfréd deal, and the Yellow-Star houses in Budapest. He sent the two reports together with a copy of the Auschwitz Protocols. Lévai, *Raoul Wallenberg*, pp. 43–57.

126. Freed, "Humanitarianism vs. Totalitarianism," p. 509. According to Wallenberg, who presumably cited only official figures, the number of Jews protected by Sweden was only 7,000 and they were housed in 8 Swedish-protected buildings. See his report of December 8, 1944, in Lévai, *Fehér könyv*, pp. 134–36.

127. *RLB*, Doc. 367.

128. *Vádirat*, 3:427–28. After the completion of the relocations, Stöckler established a closer working relationship with Wallenberg. On October 5, for example, they discussed the possibility of sending clothing, food, and medicines for the deportees. *Ibid.*, p. 592.

129. At the Council headquarters, the operation was directed by Jenő Bleier. His two immediate assistants, Ernő Szalkai and Vilmos Vasadi, served as liaison to the Swedish Legation. At the site of the relocations on Pozsonyi Road, overall command was exercised by György Bognár, who also had the power to settle disputes arising from the apartment exchanges. Those dissatisfied with his decision had the right to appeal to a Council arbitration committee headed by Imre Váradi. To be eligible for relocation into the Swedish houses, a person had to be in possession of the Swedish *Schutzpass* as well as a transfer permit from the Council. *Ibid.*, pp. 428–31.

130. Lévai, *Fehér könyv*, pp. 172–74. In his *A pesti gettó* (p. 97), Lévai asserts that Nilsson (spelled Nielson) and Bauer were freed through the intervention of Born of the IRC.

131. Wallenberg's reports were forwarded from Stockholm in English translation to London and Washington. For a summary of Swedish help to Hungarian Jews, see *PRO*, Fo.371/42823, pp. 108–13. For further details on Wallenberg's activities during the *Nyilas* era, see Lévai, *Raoul Wallenberg*, pp. 82–215.

132. Freed, "Humanitarianism vs. Totalitarianism," pp. 513–14. For Lévai's version of Wallenberg's disappearance, see his *Raoul Wallenberg*, pp. 216–94.

133. For further details on Swedish–Soviet exchanges on the Wallenberg issue, consult Freed's study cited above, pp. 514–28. See also *The New York Times*, February 8, 1957.

134. *Ibid.*, February 21, 1957.

135. Among these were Alexander Solzhenitsyn, David Vendrovski, Menachem Melzer, Abraham Kalinski, and Jan Kaplan, former inmates of Soviet prisons. See Maurice Samuelson, "Soviet Said to Hide Fact Swedish Holocaust Hero Lives as Prisoner." *The Jewish Week*, New York, November 12, 1978; Elenore Lester, "Rescued Jews Insist Wallenberg Lives in Soviet Mental Prison," *ibid.*, June 24, 1979.

136. A number of Hungarian–Jewish Americans who were rescued in Budapest by Wallenberg, including Annette and Thomas P. Lantos of Alexandria, Virginia, and Robert Peter Held, formed a group called Concerned Citizens for Wallenberg toward this end. Nina Lagergren and Guy von Dardel, Wallenberg's half-sister and half-brother, managed to persuade Prime Minister Menachem Begin of Israel to take an interest in the case. (The Prime Minister suggested to President Carter that the latter take up the issue with the Soviet leaders.) They were also instrumental in bringing about the establishment in the United States of a Free Wallenberg Committee with Senators Daniel Patrick Moynihan (Democrat of New York), Frank Church (Democrat of Idaho), Claiborne Pell (Democrat of Rhode Island), and Rudy Boschwitz (Republican of Minnesota), as co-chairmen. In Great Britain a similar committee was formed under the co-chairmanship of Winston Churchill and Greville Janner, members of the House of Commons.

In July 1979, Annette Lantos and Lagergren were received by U.S. Secretary of State Cyrus R. Vance, who told them that the United States had recently raised the case with the Soviet government and were awaiting a reply. See "Raoul Wallenberg's Sister Sure Gulag Victim Is Alive, Gets Support of Senators," *ibid.*, July 29, 1979, and *The New York Times*, August 4, 1979. See also Elenore Lester and Frederick E. Werbell, "The Lost Hero of the Holocaust. The Search for Sweden's Raoul Wallenberg." *The New York Times Magazine*, March 30, 1980, pp. 20ff.

137. In 1960, Wallenberg was one of the first to be given the title of "Righteous Gentile" by Yad Vashem. On December 11, 1979, Yad Vashem again bestowed upon him its highest honor, which was accepted by his half brother, Professor Guy von Dardel of Geneva.

138. Hilberg, *The Destruction of the European Jews*, pp. 447–48.

139. See Weissmann's cable to Alex L. Easterman of the London branch of the World Jewish Congress in the Weizmann Archives files in Rehovoth, Israel.

140. Miguel Angel de Muguiro, the Spanish Minister in Budapest, had returned to Madrid soon after the German occupation.

141. This offer by Tangier provided the IRC with the legal framework for its involvement in rescue work in Hungary. See the "International Red Cross" section above and chapter 29.

142. The negotiations continued on August 2. See Gergely's notes on these meetings in Munkácsi's *Hogyan történt?*, pp. 208–12.

143. Lévai, *Fehér könyv*, pp. 143–44. L. Szamosi also played a crucial role.

144. *RLB*, Docs. 356–60. For further details on the wartime attitude of Spain, see Haim Avni, *Sefarad veha'yehudim bi'yeme ha'shoah veha'-emansipatsiah* (Spain and the Jews During the Holocaust and the Emancipation) (Jerusalem: The Hebrew University, 1975), 292 pp.

145. *RLB*, Doc. 344.

146. See Günther Altenburg's telegram of May 24, 1944, to the German Legation in Budapest. *NA*, Microcopy T-120, Roll 4355, Frame K213797 (NG-5583). See also Frames K213798–804.

147. Lévai, *Fehér könyv*, pp. 42–46.

148. *NA*, Microcopy T-120, Roll 4664, Serial K 1509/K348816–.

149. *Ibid.*, Roll 4203, Frames K209296–311, and *RLB*, Docs. 345–53.

150. Lévai, *Szürke könyv*, pp. 215–18.

151. WRB cables to Ambassador Steinhardt dated May 24 and June 28, 1944. See also Lévai, *Fehér könyv*, p. 174.

152. *NA*, Microcopy T-120, Roll 4203, Frames K209321–322.

153. Henry L. Feingold, *The Politics of Rescue. The Roosevelt Administration and the Holocaust, 1938–1945* (New Brunswick, N.J.: Rutgers University Press, 1970), p. 33.

154. Walter F. Mondale, "Evian and Geneva." *The New York Times*, July 28, 1979. For details on the Evian Conference and its antecedents, see Feingold, *The Politics of Rescue*, pp. 22–44, and Arthur D. Morse, *While Six Million Died. A Chronicle of American Apathy* (New York: Random House, 1967), pp. 199–220.

155. For details on Britain's "Palestine Statement of Policy, May 1939," as the White Paper was officially called, see Nathaniel Katzburg, "British Policy on Immigration to Palestine During World War II," in *RAH*, pp. 183–203. For a well-documented account of how Britain ignored the plight of the Jews during the war, see Bernard Wasserstein, *Britain and the Jews of Europe, 1939–1945* (New York: Oxford University Press, 1979), 389 pp.

156. See Michael Mashberg, "The West and the Holocaust." *Patterns of Prejudice*, London, 12, no. 3 (May–June 1978): 19–22, 29. For a detailed and well-documented account of the position taken by Breckinridge Long and Robert Borden Reams, George Warren, Robert Alexander and others of the Visa Division of the Department of State, and of many in other U.S. agencies and departments, in curtailing the inflow of refugees, see Feingold, *The Politics of Rescue*, pp. 45–166.

157. In 1944, the representatives of the Jewish organizations in Switzerland often dealt with Roswell McClelland, the WRB representative, and Douglas MacKillop, the British chargé d'affaires.

158. "German Policy of Extermination of the Jewish Race," *The Department of State Bulletin*, 7, no. 182 (December 19, 1942):1009. Noting the accounts based on the Riegner report and the demands for rescue as reported in the British and the American press, Josef Goebbels made the following entry in his diary for December 13, 1942: "The question of Jewish persecution in Europe is being given top priority by the English and the Americans. . . . At bottom, however, I believe both the English and the Americans are happy that we are exterminating the Jewish riff-raff." *The Goebbels Diaries, 1942–1943*, ed.

Louis P. Lochner (Garden City, N.Y.: Doubleday, 1948), p. 241. On December 17, 1942, Eden warned the German people in the House of Commons of their responsibility relating to the persecution of the Jews. *The New York Times*, December 18, 1942.

159. "British War Role on Jews Examined," *The New York Times*, November 19, 1967. Breckinridge Long's diary notes of April 20, 1943 emphasize Riegner's first point: "One danger in it all is that [the Jews'] activities may lend color to the charges of Hitler that we are fighting this war on account of and at the instigation and direction of our Jewish citizens." Feingold, *The Politics of Rescue*, p. 197.

160. For excerpts from Chaim Weizmann's memorandum suggesting that the conference consider Palestine as a place of refuge, see Herbert Druks, *The Failure to Rescue* (New York: Robert Speller, 1977), pp. 39–41.

161. Feingold, *The Politics of Rescue*, pp. 167–207. See also Morse, *While Six Million Died*, pp. 37–64.

162. Details of the ransom plan were revealed by Arthur Hays Sulzberger in the February 13, 1943, issue of *The New York Times*.

163. John Morton Blum, *Roosevelt and Morgenthau* (Boston: Houghton Mifflin, 1970), p. 527.

164. *Ibid.*, p. 531.

165. *Ibid.*, p. 518.

166. For further details on the attitude of the Western Allies, see Fein, *Accounting for Genocide*, pp. 166–85.

167. British and American critics of the Administration eager to impugn the President's motives rushed to point out that 1944 was a crucial election year.

168. *Summary Report of the Activities of the War Refugee Board*, p. 2.

169. Telegram no. 1249, March 23, 1944, from Norton to the British Foreign Office. *PRO*, Fo.371/39258, p. 61.

170. *The New York Times*, March 25, 1944. Leaflets with the text of the President's statement were dropped from the air over Hungary and other Axis-controlled countries. *Summary Report of the Activities of the War Refugee Board*, p. 3.

171. *The Department of State Bulletin*, 10, no. 248 (March 25, 1944): 278.

172. J. S. Conway, "Between Apprehension and Indifference: Allied Attitudes to the Destruction of Hungarian Jewry." *The Wiener Library Bulletin*, London, 27, no. 30/31 (1973–74): 39. See also the memorandum titled "Immigration" by the Zionist leadership, dated May 22, 1944, in the Weizmann Archives, Rehovoth, Israel.

173. Great Britain. *House of Commons. Parliamentary Debates (Hansard)*, Fifth Series, 398, March 30, 1944, pp. 1561–64.

174. *Summary Report of the Activities of the War Refugee Board*, pp. 3–10. The American representatives in the neutral capitals, especially Berne and Stockholm, were the conduits of many of the reports that emanated from Budapest and elsewhere concerning the fate of Hungarian Jewry.

175. *PRO*, Fo.371/42813–819, p. 1399.

176. For the minutes of the War Cabinet meeting chaired by Eden, see Yad Vashem Archives, M-27/4.

177. *PRO*, Fo.371/42813–819, p. 1390.

178. Letter from Weizmann to Eden dated June 6, 1944. Weizmann Archives.

179. Eden's memorandum to Churchill dated June 20, 1944. *PRO*, Fo.371/42813–819, p. 1391.

180. Letter from Hall to Weizmann (Confidential, W9647/109/Q), dated June 22, 1944. Weizmann Archives.

181. Letter from Randall to Weizmann dated June 24, 1944. *Ibid.*

182. The meeting of June 28 was attended by Chaim Weizmann, Shertok, Locker,

Agronsky, Bakatansky, Linton, Dugdale, and Namier. See minutes of that meeting, *ibid.*

183. *Ibid.* The British officials were guided by the position paper prepared in anticipation of Shertok's arrival in London. *PRO,* Fo.371/42807, pp. 59–62.

184. Minutes of June 28 meeting, Weizmann Archives. Shertok had kept Ben-Gurion informed about the negotiations in London. See, for example, his telegram of June 30, concerning his and Weizmann's meeting with Hall. *Ibid.*

185. *PRO,* Fo.371/42813–819, p. 1373.

186. Department of State, Confidential File 840.48 Refugees/7–1144.

187. See telegram no. 5891, dated July 19, 1944, addressed by Winant to the Secretary of State, transmitting message from Shertok for Nahum Goldman.

188. For a copy of the minutes of the meeting, which also involved Walker and Dickson of the Foreign Office, see Weizmann Archives.

189. Ben-Gurion's telegram to the British Foreign Office, dated July 13, 1944. *Ibid.* See also *PRO,* Fo.371/42809, pp. 69–70. The reference to Berlin is an error. The discussions actually were envisioned to be held in Budapest.

190. The Americans concurred with the British and opposed any meeting between Bader and the German agents or their contacts in Istanbul. They extended the same prohibition to Joseph J. Schwartz, the AJDC's representative in Europe. See Hull's telegram no. 2101, dated July 27, 1944, addressed to Norweb and McClelland, the WRB representatives in Lisbon and Berne. For further details, see chapter 29.

191. Shertok and Linton took up the question of Kullmann later in the month with Sir Herbert W. Emerson, the head of the IGC. He, like Randall, rejected the idea, arguing that "under our present mandate, negotiation with Governments at war with the Allies was not contemplated." A copy of Emerson's memorandum on the discussions was forwarded by John M. Allison, an officer of the American Embassy in London, to the Secretary of State on July 24, 1944.

192. Report by Shertok dated July 13, 1944. Weizmann Archives. The idea raised by Shertok was also advanced by Rabbi Baruch Korff in America and Joseph H. Hertz, the Chief Rabbi of England. In their response to the Korff and Hertz proposals, the British argued that special treatment of the Jews was not only contrary to H. M. Government, but would also create difficulties with many Allied governments "who might feel that their own nationals were without the benefits of such special protection." *PRO,* Fo.371/42808, pp. 92–96.

A similar proposal was advanced by Yitshak Ben Zvi of the *Vaad Leumi* to Rabbi Stephen Wise via Pinkerton and the War Refugee Board. See Pinkerton telegram to the State Department dated July 5, 1944.

193. Note by the Foreign Office, dated July 12, 1944. *PRO,* Fo.371/42810, p. 71.

194. He shared his captivity with, among others, Sámuel Springmann, a former Budapest *Vaada* leader who had been picked up by the British shortly after he was expelled by Turkey in March 1944.

195. Alex Weissberg, *Advocate for the Dead. The Story of Joel Brand* (London: Andre Deutsch, 1958), p. 167. Lord Moyne was assassinated in Cairo on November 6, 1944, by two Palestinian Jews.

196. For further details on Hirschmann's mission, see telegram no. 514, dated June 9, 1944, addressed by Stettinius to Steinhardt.

197. The British view, crystallized at the War Cabinet meeting of May 13, was forwarded to Washington on June 3, 1944. *PRO,* Fo.371/42813–819, p. 1398.

198. Ira A. Hirschmann, *Life Line to a Promised Land* (New York: Vanguard, 1946), pp. 107–32. Hirschmann identifies the date of his arrival as June 30 (p. 110); however, Shertok, in his report of June 27, claims that Hirschmann had already met Brand on June 22.

199. *PRO*, Fo.371/42807, pp. 46–48.
200. *Foreign Relations of the United States. Diplomatic Papers, 1944. Vol 1. General* (Washington: U.S. Government Printing Office, 1966), p. 1074.
201. This position was also made clear by the State Department. See Hull's telegram no. 683 addressed to Steinhardt on June 9, 1944. See also Viscount Halifax's telegram of June 22, 1944, addressed to the British Foreign Office. *PRO*, Fo.371/42807, p. 63.
202. *Ibid.*, pp. 71–72.
203. *Foreign Relations of the United States*, pp. 1089–91.
204. *Ibid.* See also Viscount Halifax's telegram dated July 9, 1944. *PRO*, Fo.371/42808, p. 84.
205. *RLB*, Docs. 290–92. See also *NA*, Microcopy T-120, Roll 4664/2, Serial K1509/K350354-, and German Foreign Office, Bonn, File no. 212 Inl. IIg. The latter contains reprints and German translation of the articles that appeared in the *Times, Daily Telegraph, Manchester Guardian,* and *Daily Herald* of July 20, 1944, as well as copies of articles that appeared in the Swedish press.
206. *RLB*, Doc. 293. For further details on the British attitude toward the Brand-Grosz affair, see Wasserstein, *Britain and the Jews of Europe*, pp. 249–62.
207. See Harrison's telegram no. 4041 addressed to the Secretary of State. See also *Summary Report of the Activities of the War Refugee Board*, p. 15.
208. Telegram no. 2949 dated June 26, 1944, addressed to the Foreign Office. *PRO*, Fo.371/42807, p. 107. The Germans intercepted Norton's telegram; Horst Wagner of the *Inland II* Section of the German Foreign Office brought it to the attention of Kaltenbrunner on July 5, 1944. *RLB*, Doc. 342.
209. On July 4, 1944, for example, Hubert Ripka, the Acting Czechoslovak Minister of Foreign Affairs, asked that the Allies issue an emphatic protest and warning to the Germans in connection with their crimes in Auschwitz and elsewhere. On July 10 and 15, J. Weytko of the Polish Embassy approached Henderson and Randall of the British Foreign Office in behalf of Jews in Nazi-occupied Europe in general and of Polish nationals in Hungary in particular. *PRO*, Fo.371/42809, pp. 34 and 157.
210. Lévai, *Fehér könyv*, pp. 56–57.
211. Graham, *Pope Pius XII*, pp. 5–6.
212. *PRO*, Fo.371/42815, pp. 116–18. The text was forwarded to Washington by Harrison on August 5 (Telegram no. 5040).
213. *PRO*, Fo.371/42807, p. 106.
214. Great Britain. *House of Commons. Parliamentary Debates (Hansard). 1944*, 401 (July 5, 1944): 1160–62. Eden's remarks were also reported by the German News Agency DNB that same day. *RLB*, Doc. 341.
215. In his letter of July 13, Churchill repeated for the Archbishop the arguments used by Eden in his House of Commons remarks of July 5. *PRO*, Fo.371/42809, p. 108.
216. *Vádirat*, 3:109–10. The Press Department of the German Foreign Office took note of the Archbishop's appeal to the Hungarians. *RLB*, Doc. 343.
217. For samples of such messages, see *Vádirat*, 3:238, 255–56. Toward the end of July, Allied planes dropped leaflets over Hungary, one side of which read "Is your conscience clear?" *Ibid.*, p. 357.
218. *PRO*, Fo.371/42809. p. 115.
219. Anne O'Hare McCormick wrote a particularly persuasive column in the July 15, 1944 issue of *The New York Times* ("Victims of the Last Fury of the Nazis"), urging the forces of humanity and Christianity to assert themselves to prevent the Germans from winning their "war against the spirit of man."
220. Among these were many American-Hungarian organizations. At a June 17 rally sponsored by the Emergency Committee to Save the Jewish People of Europe, the repre-

sentatives of these organizations denounced the extermination campaign directed against the Jews of Hungary. *The New York Times,* June 18, 1944.

221. *Ibid.,* June 4, 1944.

222. *Ibid.,* June 22, 1944. Although the move bypassed normal diplomatic channels, it was subsequently approved by Hull, *Ibid.,* June 27, 1944.

223. *The Department of State Bulletin,* Washington, 11, no. 264 (July 16, 1944):59.

224. David S. Wyman, "Why Auschwitz Was Never Bombed," *Commentary,* 65, no. 5 (May 1978):37–46; Erich Kulka, "Auschwitz Condoned," *The Wiener Library Bulletin,* London, 23, no. 1 (New Series No. 14, Winter 1968–69):2–5; "The Controversy About the Bombing of Auschwitz," *Ibid.,* 18, no. 2 (April 1964):20; Herbert Druks, "Why the Death Camps Were Not Bombed," *The American Zionist,* (December 1976):18–21; Roger M. Williams, "Why Wasn't Auschwitz Bombed?," *Commonweal,* November 24, 1978, pp. 746–51; Béla Vágó, "The British Government and the Fate of Hungarian Jewry in 1944" in *RAH,* pp. 215–19. See also *PRO,* Fo.371/PREM 4/51/10, pp. 1362–63, 1365–67, 371/42808, pp. 107–8, 371/42809, pp. 127–37, 142–49, and 371/42814, pp. 188–200.

225. See John J. McCloy's letter addressed to Pehle on July 4, 1944.

226. The policy statement was issued by the War Department to reassure the British after the establishment of the WRB. Wyman, "Why Auschwitz Was Never Bombed," p. 39.

227. While the Allies found it impossible to justify the effort required for the bombing of Auschwitz and the rail lines leading to it, they managed to divert 1,400 planes for the destruction of Dresden (Germany's "Florence on the Elbe") on February 13–14, 1945, though the city—a center of art and architecture—was free of all but a few light industries. For further details, see "Dresden Rebuilt," *Time,* February 23, 1970, p. 32.

228. Vágó, "The British Government and the Fate of Hungarian Jewry," p. 217.

229. For a view of the photograph, see *The New York Times,* February 24, 1979.

230. One of the Jewish leaders (Leon A. Kubowitzki) opposed the bombing of Auschwitz, fearing that the first victims would be the Jewish inmates. He suggested instead that "the Soviet government be approached with the request that it should dispatch groups of paratroopers to seize the buildings, to annihilate the squads of murderers, and to free the unfortunate inmates." See his letter addressed to Pehle on July 1, 1944, in Yad Vashem Archives M-2/H-18.

231. There is no evidence that either the Hungarians or the Germans ever went along with Krausz's interpretation that the 7,000 certificates were for entire families.

232. Both letters can be found in the Pazner Files at Yad Vashem.

233. *Summary Report of the Activities of the War Refugee Board,* p. 17.

234. Alfred E. Zollinger, the IRC representative in Washington, transmitted the offer on July 25. For text of the IRC note and of the U.S. reply of August 11, see *ibid.,* pp. 20–22. See also Conway, "Between Apprehension and Indifference," p. 44.

235. *PRO,* Fo.371/42810, pp. 174–75. Linton also had a discussion with Henderson on this issue on August 1. Weizmann approached Eden on September 6. For the minutes of the Linton-Henderson meeting and for a copy of Weizmann's letter, see Weizmann Archives.

236. *PRO,* Fo.371/42810, pp. 200–202. A copy of the minutes of the meeting with the IGC leaders was sent to Washington on July 24. See telegram no. 17024 from John W. Allison of the American Embassy in London to the State Department.

237. *Ibid.,* Fo.371/42812, p. 34.

238. *Ibid.,* 371/42810, p. 57.

239. *Ibid.,* 371/42814, pp. 27–28. See also minutes of the August 4 meeting of the War Cabinet Committee on the Reception and Accommodation of Refugees, *ibid.,* CAB.95/15.

240. *Ibid.,* 371/42814, pp. 69–70.

241. *Ibid.*, pp. 29–30. For a summary of the British position on the Horthy offer, prepared on August 8 for the War Cabinet, see *ibid.*, pp. 74–76.

Questions relating to the Horthy offer were raised a number of times in the House of Commons. On August 1, Edmund Harvey and others interpellated Dingle Foot, the Parliamentary Secretary to the Ministry of Economic Warfare; on August 2, Hewlett questioned Eden; and on November 8, Hammersley and Sir T. Moore questioned Eden. *Great Britain. House of Commons. Parliamentary Debates* (Hansard), 402, August 1, 1944:1140–41; August 2, 1944:1410; 404, November 8, 1944:1380.

242. *PRO*, Fo.371/42814, p. 31. For a summary of the American position, see Winant's August 15, 1944, note and memorandum addressed to Eden. *Ibid.*, 371/42815, pp. 55–58. See also *Summary Report of the Activities of the War Refugee Board*, pp. 17–22.

243. *Summary Report of the Activities of the War Refugee Board*, p. 19.

244. For some details, see Conway, "Between Apprehension and Indifference," pp. 44–46, and Vágó, "The British Government and the Fate of Hungarian Jewry," pp. 219–22.

245. *The Department of State Bulletin*, 11, no. 269 (August 20, 1944):175.

246. *PRO*, Fo.371/42815, pp. 78–79.

247. *Ibid.*, pp. 167–68, and Fo. 371/42816, pp. 148–50.

248. Feingold, *The Politics of Rescue*, pp. 259–65.

249. See note of Moniz de Aragao, Brazil's Ambassador in London, addressed to Sir Herbert Emerson, the head of the IGC, *PRO*, Fo.371/42817, pp. 95–96.

250. *Ibid.*, pp. 159–60.

251. Minutes of the October 23, 1944 meeting of the War Cabinet Committee on the Reception and Accommodation of Refugees, *ibid.*, Fo.371/42820, p. 94.

252. See, for example, the note of August 21 addressed by Christopher Eastwood of the Colonial Office to Henderson, and Lord Moyne's telegram no. 1960 addressed to the Colonial Office, *ibid.*, 42815, p. 140, and 42816, p. 40.

253. See, for example, *Congressional Record*, 90, Part 10, August 18, 1944, p. A3639 ("Hungarian Jews Must Be Saved," Extension of Remarks of Hon. Arthur G. Klein); August 22, 1944, p. A3698 ("Great Britain Must Act To Save Hungarian Jews," Extension of Remarks of Hon. Emanuel Celler); August 22, 1944, p. A3686 ("Britain's White Paper Bars Rescuing of Jews of Hungary," Extension of Remarks of Hon. Emanuel Celler); Part 11, September 8, 1944, p. A3949–50 ("Sanctuary for the Jews in Palestine," Extension of Remarks of Hon. William Langer); November 10, 1944, p. A4577 ("Rescuers or Accomplices?," Extension of Remarks of Hon. Thomas J. Lane).

254. On August 28, 1944, Rabbi Baruch Korff, representing the Union of Orthodox Rabbis of America, led a delegation composed of the representatives of the Emergency Committee to Save the Jewish People of Europe and a number of congressmen. In a memorandum submitted to the British Ambassador, the delegation requested that Britain open the doors of Palestine. (Rabbi Korff's approach to the setting up of the meeting was severely criticized by the British.) *PRO*, Fo.371/42818, pp. 108–12.

On September 25, Louis Lipsky, the Chairman of the Administrative Committee of the American Jewish Conference, submitted a detailed memorandum toward the same end. *Ibid.*, 371/42819, pp. 46–51. For further details on Britain's attitude toward the "Horthy offer," see Wasserstein, *Britain and the Jews of Europe*, pp. 262–70.

255. Copies of the American notes to the Szálasi government, transmitted via the Swiss, as well as the responses, usually found their way to the German Foreign Office. See, for example, *RLB*, Docs. 405–7.

256. For further details on the activities of the WRB, see Feingold, *The Politics of Rescue*, pp. 248–94. See also his "The Roosevelt Administration and the Effort to Save the Jews of Hungary" in *HJS*, 2:211–52. See also section "Kasztner's Negotiations With Becher" in chapter 29.

257. See, for example, the October 30 note from J. M. Martin, Churchill's secretary, to Weizmann. Weizmann Archives. For additional documentary references relating to the American reaction to the problem of refugees, see *Foreign Relations of the United States. Diplomatic Papers. 1944. Vol. 1. General*, pp. 981–1191.

258. For some details on the attitude of the USSR toward the Soviet and Polish Jews during World War II, see Dov Levin, "The Attitude of the Soviet Union to the Rescue of Jews" in RAH, pp. 225–36. See also Fein, *Accounting for Genocide*, pp. 185–89.

259. *Vádirat*, 1:90–91.

260. "Russia's Aid Sought for Jews in Hungary." *The New York Times*, May 17, 1944.

261. *Summary Report of the Activities of the War Refugee Board*, p. 7.

262. *Ibid.*, pp. 8–9.

263. *PRO*, Fo.371/42809, pp. 58, 137–39.

264. *Ibid.*, 371/42815, pp. 64 and 71.

265. The Soviets, ever suspicious of special plans to save Jews, considered Horthy's offer an attempt by the Hungarian governmental leaders to ingratiate themselves with the Western Powers in the drive to split the Grand Alliance. See Nikolai Fedorov's commentary on Moscow Radio (August 18, 1944) in *Vádirat*, 3:406–7.

266. See, for example, *The Promised Land*, a novel by Yuri Kolesnikov, which identifies Eichmann as having been a Zionist agent who arranged to send young and healthy Jews to Palestine while committing others to the gas chambers. See also Yuri Ivanov's *Caution: Zionism*, a pseudo-historical work, which identifies Zionism as a worldwide conspiracy allied with monopolistic circles. It viciously condemned the activities of the Budapest *Vaada*, paying special attention to Kasztner's dealings with Eichmann and the implications of the Brand mission (pp. 87–88). For additional references, consult Braham, *Jews in the Communist World. English Sources* (New York: Twayne, 1961), 64 pp.; and his *Jews in the Communist World. Non-English Sources* (with M. M. Hauer) (New York: Pro Arte, 1963), 144 pp.

267. Steiner, an official of the Swiss Legation, complained (July 11) to Jenő Miske-Gerstenberger of the Hungarian Ministry of Foreign Affairs that false El Salvador "nationality certificates" were being brought in from Switzerland and allegedly sold at high prices to Jews. *Vádirat*, 3:136.

268. See Harrison telegram no. 3867 (June 17) to the Department of State, transmitting McClelland message for WRB.

269. For a highly positive evaluation of Mantello's role, see Lévai, *Zsidósors Európában* (Jewish Fate in Europe) (Budapest: Magyar Téka, 1948), 335 pp.

270. Joseph Mandel (also known as Josef Mandl), a textile specialist for the I.N.C.O. firm of Bucharest, was sent to Switzerland in 1941 by the Ministry of National Defense of the Antonescu government to acquire aircraft cloth. Presumably he failed to carry out his assignment, for on October 21, 1942, the Ministry of the Interior asked N. Lahovary, the Romanian Minister in Berne, to bring about his extradition. (The Romanian authorities planned to deport him to Transnistria.) In Switzerland, Joseph Mandel maintained close contact with Abraham Silberschein, the head of RELICO, informing him periodically about developments in Hungary—news he usually obtained through his Romanian contacts. For pertinent documents, see Yad Vashem Archives M-20/46.

271. For details on the activities of the AJDC with emphasis on Mayer's role in the negotiations with the SS, see chapter 29. On the agency's role in Hungary after the liberation, see chapter 32.

272. Lichtheim's office was officially known as "The Executive of the Zionist Organization/The Jewish Agency for Palestine." One of his closest associates was Mieczeslav Kahany.

273. For details on the activities of the World Jewish Congress, see *Unity in Dispersion* (New York: World Jewish Congress, 1948), 381 pp., and Elizabeth E. Eppler, "The Res-

cue Work of the World Jewish Congress During the Nazi Period" in *RAH*, pp. 47–69.

274. Its French and German names were: *Comité pour l'assistance à la population juive frappée par la guerre; Komitee zur Hilfeleistung für die Kriegsbetroffene jüdische Bevölkerung.* Associated with the World Jewish Congress, Silberschein also headed SILBADO (*Comité international pour le placement des intellectuels réfugiés;* International Committee for the Placement of Refugee Intellectuals). One of his closest associates at RELICO was Hans Klee. For documentary sources on RELICO's activities, see "Rescue Efforts With the Assistance of International Organizations" in *YVS*, 8:64–80.

275. The Committee was formed through the cooperation of Rabbi Zwi Taubes of Zurich, Mrs. Lajos Buchwald, Rabbi Armin Kornfein, Mrs. Daniel Lowenstein, the Mandel brothers, and others. Lévai, *Zsidósors Európában*, pp. 37–38.

276. One of Bányai's closest associates was Géza Pallai, a member of the board of the Transimpex Import, Export & Transit Company of Zurich. Since he was a Hungarian citizen, Pallai was not formally a member of the committee.

277. For sources relating to the Committee's activities, see Yad Vashem Archives M-20/47.

278. The Sternbuch brothers, for example, were particularly bitter about the claims of success advanced by the World Jewish Congress and Rudolph Kasztner, and shared the negative views of the Budapest and Bratislava *Vaada* leaders about the activities of Saly Mayer. See, for example, Yitzhak Sternbuch's July 5, 1948 letter addressed to Kubowitzki and Kasztner's letter of October 29, 1945 addressed to Mayer, in Yad Vashem Archives M-20/46 and O15/19-5, respectively. The World Jewish Congress's claim of credit for the rescuing of 190,000 Hungarian Jews was also attacked by Andreas Biss of the Budapest *Vaada*. See his letter of July 10, 1948, addressed to Kubowitzki, in Yad Vashem Archives M-20/46.

279. See S. Mandelblatt's letter of December 24, 1942, addressed to Chaim Pozner. Pazner Files, Yad Vashem.

280. The Histadrut Aid Commission (*Hilfskommission der Histadruth*) was composed of Marc Jarblum, Pozner, Schwalb, and Silberschein; the Hehalutz Aid Commission (*Hilfskommission des Hechaluz*) was composed of Berkovitz, Bornstein, Muskat, Schloss, and Schwalb. See Lichtheim's letter of March 6, 1944, addressed to the heads of the major Jewish organizations in Switzerland in Pazner Files, Yad Vashem.

281. Chaim Barlas, *Hatzala bimi shoa* (Rescue in the Days of the Holocaust) (Israel: Beit Lohamei Hagetaot, 1975), p. 102.

282. See Gruenbaum's telegram to Lichtheim, dated February 10, 1944, and Lichtheim's letter of March 6 addressed to the prospective members of the Relief and Rescue Committee, in Pazner Files, Yad Vashem. For Pazner's response of April 3 and Schwalb's response of April 6, see *ibid* and Central Zionist Archives, File L 22/60.

283. *Der Kastner-Bericht*, p. 259.

284. See his especially bitter letter of July 3, 1944, addressed to Eliyahu Dobkin in Lisbon. He noted that institutions like the Red Cross were making jokes about the "disorder and disorganization" that characterized the behavior of the various Jewish organizations. Pazner Files, Yad Vashem.

285. *Ibid.* For a sympathetic review of Lichtheim's role during the war and of his fruitless efforts to arouse the Jewish leaders of the free world concerning the tragedy befalling European Jewry, see Walter Laqueur, "Jewish Denial and the Holocaust." *Commentary*, 68, no. 4 (December 1979):44–55.

286. For a basically negative view of these organizations, see Aryeh Morgenstern, "Va'ad hatzala ha'meuchad shelid ha'Sochnut he'yehudit upheulotov beshanim 1943–1945" (The United Rescue Committee of the Jewish Agency and Its Activities During 1943–1945). *Yalkut Moreshet*, Israel, no. 13 (1971):60–103. On Hungary, see especially

pp. 84–92. See also Shabetai B. Beit-Zvi, *Ha'tsiyonut hapost Ugandit ba'mishvar ha'shoa* (Post-Ugandian Zionism in the Crucible of the Holocaust) (Tel Aviv: Bronfman, 1977), 495 pp.

287. For a succinct self-critical appraisal of the failure of organized Jewry during the war, see *Unity in Dispersion,* pp. 193–96.

CHAPTER THIRTY-TWO

LIBERATION, RESTITUTION, RETRIBUTION

Liberation

THE REMNANT of Hungarian Jewry was liberated in stages, mostly by the victorious Soviet and Romanian troops (Romania had committed its forces to the war against the Nazis after it had changed sides). The first to be liberated, in September–October 1944, were the Jews in the labor service companies stationed in Northern Transylvania and the handful of exempted Jews and Jews holding false Aryan papers who lived in that province. As these were being liberated the bulk of the surviving Jews of Hungary (those of Budapest) were just beginning their long ordeal under the *Nyilas* terror. The surviving Jews of the capital were liberated early in 1945: those in the ghetto and those still somehow living in other sections of Pest were liberated on January 17–18; those in Buda, where the Nazi-*Nyilas* terror continued unabated, not until February 13.[1] Thousands of labor servicemen and many of the Jews who had been made to march from Budapest to build fortifications along the Austrian border were not liberated until April 4, when Hungary was finally cleared of German troops. The several thousand Jews who were taken along by the withdrawing Nazi forces were not liberated until May 9, when they were freed together with the surviving Jews in the concentration camps by the Allied armies.

As the Soviet-Romanian forces advanced across Hungary—a seven-month process that seemed agonizingly slow to the Jews and the other persecuted people of the country—the devastation suffered by the Jewish communities during the German occupation became painfully evident. The padlocked and looted homes, shops, farms, factories, and offices; the desecrated and demolished synagogues; the pilfered libraries and educational and cultural institutions; the overturned tombstones; the eerie absence of Jews—all served as vivid reminders of the fury with which the Nazis and their Hungarian accomplices had carried out the Final Solution program.

The Losses of Hungarian Jewry: A Statistical Overview

According to the census of 1941, Hungary at that time had a Jewish population of 725,005, representing 4.94 percent of the total population of 14,683,323. Of these, 400,981 lived in Trianon Hungary and 324,026 in the territories that were reacquired from Czechoslovakia, Romania, and Yugoslavia during 1938–1941.[2] Under the anti-Semitic legislation of 1941, approximately 100,000 converts and Christians of Jewish origin were also identified as racial Jews; 89,640 of them lived in Trianon Hungary (62,350 in Budapest alone). In the reacquired territories, which had a strong Orthodox tradition, there were only 10,360 converts (table 32.1).

Prior to the German occupation of March 19, 1944, the Jewish community suffered approximately 63,000 casualties during the war. Of these, around 42,000 were labor servicemen, most of whom were killed or died along the Ukrainian fronts; close to 20,000 were deported as "aliens" in July–August 1941 and slaughtered near Kamenets-Podolsk; and about 1,000 were killed in the Bácska area, including Ujvidék, in January–February 1942. Of the 63,000 pre-occupation casualties, 29,850 were from Trianon Hungary (15,350 from Budapest) and 33,150 from the reannexed territories.

At the time of the German occupation, Hungary had a (racially defined) total Jewish population of 762,007. Of these, 460,771 lived in Trianon Hungary (231,453 in Budapest) and 301,236 in the reacquired territories.

During the occupation, the deportations, the massacres perpetrated by the *Nyilas,* hunger, disease, and other causes, resulted in 501,507 casualties. The overwhelming majority of these were among the close to 440,000 Jews who were deported to Auschwitz between May 15 and July 8, 1944 (see table 19.1). Of the casualties during the occupation, 267,771 were Jews from Trianon Hungary—85,453 from Budapest and 182,318 from the provinces—and 233,736 from the ceded areas.

Thus, the overall losses of Hungarian Jewry during the Second World War, discounting those who fled abroad, come to 564,507—297,621 from Trianon Hungary (100,803 from Budapest) and 266,886 from the ceded areas.[3]

At the end of 1945, there were 255,500 Jews in the territories controlled by Hungary in 1944, of whom 190,000 lived in the Trianon part of the country—including 144,000 in Budapest, still by far the largest Jewish community in postwar Europe (excluding the USSR). Of the Budapest residents, 119,000 had been liberated in the city: 69,000 in

TABLE 32.1.
LOSSES OF HUNGARIAN JEWRY DURING WORLD WAR II

	Trianon Hungary			Ceded Areas	1944 Hungary, Total
	Budapest	Provinces	Total		
Number of Jews in 1941					
Jews	184,453	216,528	400,981	324,026	725,007
Converts and Christians of Jewish origin[a]	62,350	27,290	89,640	10,360	100,000
Total	246,803	243,818	490,621	334,386	825,007
Losses Prior to German Occupation on March 19, 1944					
Labor servicemen	12,350	12,500	24,850	17,150	42,000
Alien Jews deported in 1941[b]	3,000	2,000	5,000	15,000	20,000
Bácska massacres of 1942	–	–	–	1,000	1,000
Total	15,350	14,500	29,850	33,150	63,000
Number of Jews at the Time of the Occupation					
Total	231,453	229,318	460,771	301,236	762,007
Impact of the Occupation					
Fled abroad	2,000	1,000	3,000	2,000	5,000
Deported, killed, or died	105,453	222,318	327,771	290,236	618,007
Number of Jews on December 31, 1945					
Returned from deportation	20,000	40,000	60,000	56,500	116,500
Liberated labor servicemen	5,000	6,000	11,000	9,000	20,000
Liberated in Budapest	119,000	–	119,000	–	119,000
Total	144,000	46,000	190,000	65,500	255,500
Losses of Hungarian Jewry					
Losses prior to the occupation	15,350	14,500	29,850	33,150	63,000
Net losses during the occupation	85,453	182,318	267,771	233,736	501,507
Total	100,803	196,818	297,621	266,886	564,507
Loss to the community by escape abroad	2,000	1,000	3,000	2,000	5,000
Grand total	102,803	197,818	300,621	268,886	569,507

SOURCE: Based on data in *Hungarian Jewry Before and After the Persecution* (Budapest: Statistical Department of the Hungarian Section of the World Jewish Congress, n.d.), p. 2.

[a] Identified as racial Jews under the legislation in effect in 1941.

[b] Jews who could not prove their citizenship; deported and subsequently killed near Kamenets-Podolsk.

the ghetto, 25,000 in the protected houses of the international ghetto, and 25,000 who had been in hiding (most with false Aryan papers). The returnees to Budapest included 5,000 liberated from labor service and 20,000 from concentration camps.

Of the 46,000 Jews who lived in the provincial communities of Trianon Hungary at the end of 1945, there were 6,000 liberated from labor service companies and 40,000 returned from various concentration camps. Many of the latter had been deported in June 1944 to the family work camps in and around Strasshof, Austria. Of the 65,500 Jews who lived in the ceded territories at the end of 1945, 9,000 were former labor servicemen and 56,500 were returnees from concentration camps.

The staggering losses of Hungarian Jewry were compounded by the negative demographic structure of the surviving Jewish population, whose distribution by age and sex was highly unfavorable if a community were to be revived. The negative factors were particularly discernible in the countryside, where the dejewification process had been virtually completed; the returnees to the provinces consisted almost exclusively of persons 20 to 50 years old.[4] The demographic structure

TABLE 32.2.
DISTRIBUTION OF THE JEWS OF
TRIANON HUNGARY
IN 1941 AND
1946 BY AGE GROUPS

	Number of Jews		Losses	
	1941	1946	Total	Percent
Age Groups	*Countryside*			
0–20	60,132	7,566	52,566	87.42
20–40	62,925	22,559	40,366	64.15
40–60	58,514	13,745	44,769	76.52
60–	34,936	3,254	31,682	90.69
Total	216,507	47,124	169,383	78.24
	Budapest			
0–20	29,042	13,184	15,858	54.61
20–40	58,144	24,776	33,368	57.39
40–60	62,426	34,539	27,887	44.67
60–	34,861	24,001	10,860	31.16
Total	184,473	96,500	87,973	52.31

SOURCE: *Zsidó Világkongresszus*, no. 10, p. 7.

was considerably better in Budapest, where a large number of the elderly survived in the ghetto and thousands of children were rescued by the IRC and the various Christian denominations and orders.

The age distribution of the losses in Trianon Hungary's Jewish community, excluding converts and Christians of Jewish origin, is shown in table 32.2. Whereas in the countryside the number of Jews declined from 216,507 in 1941[5] to 47,124 in 1946 (a loss of 78.24 percent), the corresponding decline in Budapest was less pronounced: from 184,473 to 96,500 (52.31 percent). In the countryside, the losses were particularly high for those under 20 and above 60 years old.

When the survivors are compared by sex, however, Budapest does not fare as well as the rest of the country. Of the 96,500 Jews living in Budapest in 1946, 59,053 were women (a ratio of 1,576 females to 1,000 males—table 32.3). The greater survival rate of women in the capital was the consequence of Horthy's halting of the deportations on July 7, 1944 (when the rest of the country was already *Judenrein*) and

TABLE 32.3.
DISTRIBUTION OF THE JEWS OF HUNGARY BY
AGE GROUPS AND SEX IN 1946

	Males		Females		Total	
	Countryside	*Budapest*	*Countryside*	*Budapest*	*Countryside*	*Budapest*
Age Groups			*Number*			
0–1	49	92	68	127	117	219
1–6	427	1,011	464	1,072	891	2,083
6–14	1,134	2,654	1,119	2,495	2,253	5,149
14–20	1,831	2,556	2,474	3,177	4,305	5,733
20–40	11,238	8,986	11,321	15,790	22,559	24,776
40–60	8,381	12,400	5,364	22,139	13,745	34,539
over 60	1,544	9,748	1,710	14,253	3,254	24,001
Total	24,604	37,447	22,520	59,053	47,124	96,500
			Percent			
0–1	34.75	65.25	34.87	65.13	34.82	65.18
1–6	29.69	70.31	30.21	69.79	29.96	70.04
6–14	29.94	70.06	30.96	69.04	30.44	69.56
14–20	41.74	58.26	43.78	56.22	42.89	57.11
20–40	55.57	44.43	41.76	58.24	47.66	52.34
40–60	40.33	59.67	19.77	80.53	28.46	71.54
over 60	14.63	85.37	11.31	88.69	12.68	87.32
Total	39.65	60.35	27.02	72.98	32.82	67.18

SOURCE: *Zsidó Világkongresszus*, no. 10, p. 8.

the high losses among the males serving in the labor service system since 1942: wartime losses among the Budapest labor servicemen aged 20 to 40 were 68 percent, and among those 40 to 60, 57 percent.[6] The male–female ratio in the capital was particularly unfavorable in the age groups of most importance from the viewpoint of procreation and employment. With 37,929 females aged 20 to 60 as against 21,386 males, there resulted a ratio of 1,000 males to 1,756 and 1,784 females respectively, denoting a surplus of approximately 13,000 marriageable women unable to find Jewish spouses.[7] In the countryside, where the losses among the labor servicemen were somewhat lighter and the deportations affected the entire Jewish population, the male–female ratio of the survivors was considerably better. In 1946 there were 24,604 male survivors and 22,520 female survivors (915 females to 1,000 males). In the vital 20 to 60 age group, the number of males (19,619) exceeded that of females (16,685) by 2,934. The exact ratio, of course, varied from community to community.

Reconstruction

As the frontlines receded, the survivors began to resume their private activities, reestablish their organizations, and rebuild or rehabilitate their institutions. Outside of Budapest the initiative was usually taken by the returning labor servicemen, who were among the first to be liberated and return to their communities. Many of the communities very soon showed clear signs of possible regeneration. Religious services were resumed where a *minyan* was available; the synagogues (or at least a section of them) were once again made serviceable; the tombstones were re-erected; and the lay and religious schools in the few communities that still had children were reopened. One of the first communal tasks in many communities was to exhume the victims buried in the ghetto grounds and to transfer the corpses for burial in the Jewish cemeteries.

During the first phase of the post-liberation period, the returnees were preoccupied with the day-to-day problem of survival and with arrangements for the return of the liberated deportees. Many of them still suffered from severe camp-related mental and physical disabilities (particularly depression, malnutrition, and typhoid) and thousands would soon die. Because of the severe food shortages that plagued the country in the wake of its great wartime losses,[8] the survivors often lived under communal arrangements. They organized hostels and public kitchens, which were partially financed through funds and valuables reacquired by the returnees or "borrowed" from the assets of deported Jews. The principal source of funds was the AJDC and the "Ezra" (Relief) organization. These international organizations established contact with the liberated Jews of Hungary primarily through the efforts of Ernő Marton, the former publisher of *Uj Kelet* (New East), the Hungarian-language daily of Kolozsvár, who had escaped to Romania early in May 1944. While in Bucharest, Marton became active in organizing rescue and relief campaigns in support of the Jews of Hungary. Toward this end he cooperated with the new Romanian government in establishing the legal and political framework for the representation of the interests of the surviving Jews of Northern Transylvania, an area that was expected to revert to Romania,[9] and with the International Red Cross. His close relationship with the latter was developed early in 1945, when he was officially appointed to head the Southeast and Central European Section of the Campaign for Aiding the War-Aggrieved (*Oeuvre d'assistance pour les éprouvés de guerre, Section Europe Sud-Est et Centrale*), a newly established agency of the IRC.[10] The effectiveness of the *Oeuvre d'assistance* was enhanced by its close cooperation with the AJDC.

Almost immediately after the liberation of Northern Transylvania, a delegation of the AJDC entered the territory under the auspices of the IRC to survey the needs of the survivors. As the front receded, the *Oeuvre d'assistance* expanded its activities, with the permission of the Soviet occupation authorities, to include the liberated areas in Hungary, Czechoslovakia, and Poland. In the latter countries, the agency was particularly interested in locating concentration camp survivors and providing them with first aid. At the end of March 1945, the Romanian government placed a train at the disposal of the *Oeuvre d'assistance* to bring the surviving deportees back. The first trip to Poland was undertaken on April 12 under the command of Jacob Schmetterer and returned to Nagyvárad with 202 deportees. By the time the war ended on May 9, two additional trips were completed.[11]

In response to an appeal for food and drugs by the legations of the neutral countries in Budapest, a delegation of the *Oeuvre d'assistance* arrived in the Hungarian capital on March 6. The first supply-laden trucks arrived less than a week later. The relief operations in Budapest were organized under the leadership of Dr. Frigyes Görög, a distinguished lawyer and a highly respected community leader, who had been associated with Section A of the IRC.[12] Dr. Görög also became the head of the AJDC subcommittee which was established in March through the efforts of Marton acting in conjunction with the IRC. Hans Weyermann, the head of the IRC delegation in Hungary, took on the leadership of the Hungarian branch of the *Oeuvre d'assistance*. The AJDC subcommittee launched its relief activities with a grant of 2 million Swiss francs received through the *Oeuvre d'assistance*.

During the first three months of its operations, the AJDC subcommittee acted under the guidance of the Bucharest and Geneva offices of the AJDC. As the major source of relief, it was subjected to considerable pressure, especially by the representatives of the various Jewish communal organizations championing their particular relief or rehabilitation programs. Harmony was partially achieved on June 22, when the representatives of these organizations established a 12-member Joint Committee.[13] The appointment of Jenő Zeitinger as the representative of the Mayor of Budapest was also expected to enhance the effectiveness of the Committee.

At about the same time, the various welfare and relief organizations were united to form the National Jewish Aid Committee (*Országos Zsidó Segítő Bizottság*—OZSSB) also under the chairmanship of Görög. The OZSSB included representatives of the major Hungarian congregational and Zionist organizations, including the rabbinical council.[14] While concerned primarily with the return of the surviving deportees and the care of destitute Jews, the OZSSB was also in charge of approximately 5,000 orphans.

The National Committee for the Care of Deportees (*Deportáltakat Gondozó Országos Bizottság*—DEGOB), an agency of OZSSB, was given the task of touring the concentration camps in order to identify and return Hungarian Jewish survivors. By the end of 1945, DEGOB had undertaken 26 expeditions, returning thousands of survivors to Hungary. DEGOB also performed an important historical task by recording the testimonies of many survivors; among those interviewed were several members of the Budapest and provincial Jewish Councils, central and local communal leaders, labor servicemen, and hundreds of concentration camp survivors.[15] The activities of the OZSSB and DEGOB were financed almost exclusively by the AJDC.[16] By October 1945, the AJDC staff in Hungary had grown to 985 people, of whom 595 worked in the capital.[17]

Once the return of the remaining labor servicemen and deportees was largely accomplished, the survivors turned to the revitalization of their institutions and congregations, the pursuit of restitution and reparation for the losses suffered during the war, and the apprehension and punishment of war criminals.

The Revitalization of Communal Life

The surviving Jews of Hungary regained legal equality with all other citizens of the country under the Armistice Agreement of January 20, 1945 and the several legislative acts enacted in compliance with it. Under Article 5 of the Armistice agreement, Hungary undertook to immediately release all persons confined for racial and religious reasons and to repeal all discriminatory legislation and disabilities arising therefrom. Under the same article, it also undertook to assure that all displaced persons or refugees, including Jews and stateless persons, would be accorded the same protection and security as its own nationals.[18]

In accord with these provisions, on March 17 the Provisional National Government (*Ideiglenes Nemzeti Kormány*)[19] adopted Decree no. 200/1945. M.E. under which it repealed all the anti-Jewish laws and decrees that had been enacted during the Horthy and *Nyilas* eras.[20] The decree provided for the reestablishment of the equality of rights for all citizens and declared that the anti-Jewish measures had not been in accord with the constitutional sentiments of the Hungarian people. Similar provisions and views were expressed in several other legislative enactments, including Law XXV of 1946.[21]

The first Jewish communities to be formally reestablished were those in the capital and the larger cities. They consisted not only of the surviving indigenous Jews, but also of survivors from neighboring smaller towns and villages who had decided to leave their homes after the war because of their total isolation.

The Jewish community of Budapest had the strongest base for revitalization. The Neolog and the Orthodox communities resumed their operations almost immediately after the end of hostilities, under the leadership of Stöckler and Kahan-Frankl respectively. The latter was quickly also selected to head the Central Bureau of Orthodox Communities; after considerable maneuvering, Stöckler became the President of the National Bureau of Hungarian Jews.[22] During the first postarmistice phase, the National Bureau was led by a five-member provisional executive committee appointed by the government.[23]

In the countryside, the rebuilding of the congregations was pursued with great zeal. By the end of 1946, 258 congregations of the 704 that had been in existence in 1939 had been reestablished. Many of these, however, had barely enough members for a *minyan* and proved ephemeral.[24]

In Hungary as a whole, the number of Neolog congregations in 1946 was 102, as against 219 in 1930 (see chapter 3). The number of Orthodox congregations declined from 436 to 146 and of Status Quo ones from 54 to 15 during the same period. Of the provincial congregations, 55 had their own community offices in 1946, but only a few had the resources to reestablish such pre-occupation facilities as homes for the aged, hospitals, and ritual baths.[25] Although many of the synagogues were destroyed or suffered heavy damages, most of the reactivated communities had their own houses of worship.[26] Since with a few exceptions the rabbis of the provincial Jewish communities had been deported and perished with their parishioners, the postwar spiritual leadership consisted largely of newcomers, many from Romania. Because of the dearth of rabbis, many communities were compelled to share the services of itinerant spiritual leaders.[27] The same held true for ritual slaughterers.

Budapest was of course in a much more fortunate position. Its synagogues survived almost intact, as did many of its educational, cultural, and communal institutions.[28] It remained the center of Jewish communal life in Hungary, and some of its institutions have come to play an important role in the Jewish life of Eastern Europe. The Jewish Museum was enlarged to include a section on the Holocaust and the National Theological Institute (*Országos Rabbiképző Intézet*) emerged as the only institution in the Soviet sphere of influence for training rabbis.

The extent to which Jewish life was revitalized during the immediate postwar years varied from community to community, depending largely on the number of survivors and the resources available. The latter came from three sources: the personal funds of the survivors; contributions by foreign Jewish agencies, especially the AJDC; and assets acquired under a partial restitution and indemnification program.

Restitution, Indemnification, and Reparation

Hungary. The survivors pinned many of their hopes for the revitalization of their lives and communities on the understanding of the postwar government. At least during the first post-liberation phase, they were convinced that the central and local government authorities would find their demands both morally and legally correct. The survivors demanded the restitution of the movable and immovable property that had been Aryanized or confiscated; they requested indemnification for the injuries and damages they had suffered as a result of the anti-Jewish measures; and finally, they claimed reparations to enable them to reestablish their personal and communal lives.

Although the post-armistice Hungarian government sympathized with the plight of the survivors and hastened to express its moral outrage against the anti-Jewish regimes of the past by nullifying all discriminatory acts and reestablishing the coequality of all citizens, for political and economic reasons it could not meet the demands of the survivors. For one thing, the Soviet occupation authorities, acting in cooperation with the left radical forces not yet openly in power, were bent on guiding Hungary along a new political route. This required an appeasement of the population in the economic sphere and a manifestation of political generosity toward the former opponents. Many of those who had come into possession of Jewish property were working-class people whose allegiance to the Communist cause was eagerly sought. The complications hindering the restoration of confiscated Jewish property transcended these political considerations. In many cases, the Jewish property acquired by Christians had changed its characteristics, value, or ownership in the few years after its original transfer; many of the new owners had made additional investments or considerable improvements in the properties. In other cases, ownership had changed owing to inheritance or sales. Last but not least, many of the Christians in possession of Jewish property were themselves poor or war casualties. As a result, the survivors expected that much of the compensation for their losses would come from the government. However, both economic and political factors militated against these expectations.

Economically Hungary was in a desperate state. Ravaged by war, looted by two invading armies, and crippled by rampaging inflation, the country was in desperate need of economic aid. As an enemy state, it was subjected to maximum exploitation by the Soviet forces, which did not regard Jewish property as subject to special consideration. Moreover, the Soviets treated the Jewish property acquired by the Germans as a German asset, and it was therefore made subject to Soviet acquisition as part of German-Hungarian reparations.

After 26 years of rightist rule and a short but devastating Nazi-*Nyilas* reign of terror, the postwar government was cognizant of the anti-Semitic climate that still prevailed in the country. It feared that a massive restitution program at a time when the country was itself in ruin, the population impoverished, and the Soviet forces adamant on having their demands met, would only engender a new wave of anti-Semitism (see below). By the time the country's economic recovery was discernible, the Communist forces had acquired power (with the aid of the Soviet Union) and begun a collectivization and nationalization program that affected all property relations.

Shortly after the signing of the armistice agreement, the Jewish communal leaders submitted to the party leaders and to the government their demands in support of the deportees and for a swift and generous restitution and indemnification program. They argued that these were not designed to provide a privileged position for the Jews, but merely to compensate the survivors and enable them—the most persecuted segment of Hungarian society—to reestablish themselves. They insisted that their demands were not only morally and legally just, but also in the interests of Hungary itself. The reestablishment of Hungary's national honor and the more positive evaluation of the country's case in the forthcoming peace treaty negotiations, they argued, would depend on the extent to which the restitution and compensation program was fair and equitable.[29]

The government was sensitive to the implied accusations, at least in the legal sphere. In addition to reestablishing the civil rights and liberties of the Jews and the equality of the Jewish religion, it adopted an impressive number of laws and decrees relating to the survivors' economic grievances. These provided for the nullification of all contracts that had been made under duress in connection with Jewish commercial, business, and industrial enterprises and allowed Jews, under certain conditions, to reclaim their agricultural and forest lands. They also provided for the return of the shops, offices, personal property, and apartments that had been forcibly taken from the Jews. Special enactments regulated the status of the Jewish religion and Jewish employees and civil servants who had been dismissed before the liberation. Remedies were enacted concerning certain wartime marriages and declarations of death involving labor servicemen and deportees. Measures were also adopted with regard to professionals, war veterans, and students.[30]

Despite this array of legislative enactments and remedial statutes, many of which were implemented, the Jews enjoyed no tangible results with respect to restitution and indemnification. For one thing, the government never regulated the Hungarian state's responsibility for indemnifying the Jews for losses suffered during the Horthy and *Nyilas* eras. In view of the financial and economic difficulties that confronted the country, it was at one point proposed that the survivors be compensated from a "Jewish Indemnification Fund" (*Zsidó kártalanitási alap*) to be established primarily from abandoned or unclaimed Jewish properties. Nothing ever came of this proposal.[31] The suggestion was presumably made by Jewish leaders who were chagrined over a decision of the Provisional National Government in March 1945 to include these properties in the jurisdiction of the Government Commissioner for the Administration of Abandoned Properties (*Az Elhagyott Javak Kormánybiztosa*). Directly subordinate to the Prime Minister, the Government Commissioner also administered the properties of those Fascists who had fled with the Germans. Since the local boards consisted of political party representatives in the various cities and counties, the administration and uses of these properties largely reflected political interests. The lumping together of the two widely different categories of properties made the identification and restitution of the survivors' possessions considerably more difficult.[32]

The survivors encountered a series of other difficulties. The new owners were reluctant to yield their recently acquired properties; litigation was producing long delays; resistance by political leaders and parties with conflicting short and long-range interests were causing conflicts; the Communists acquired power and began to transform Hungary into a People's Democracy. All of this militated against the expectations of the Jews for restitution and compensation. Following the drive against the Smallholder and other anti-Communist parties in the spring of 1947 and the subsequent elections in August, the new Communist-dominated coalition government became ever more adamant in its position, despite its international obligations. The Paris Peace Treaty of February 10, 1947, for example, incorporated a number of provisions relating to the restoration of confiscated property. Paragraph 1 of Article 27 stipulated:

Hungary undertakes that in all cases where the property, legal rights or interests in Hungary of persons under Hungarian jurisdiction have, since September 1, 1939, been the subject of measures of sequestration, confiscation or control on account of the racial origin or religion of such persons, the said property, legal rights and interests shall be restored together with their accessories or, if restoration is impossible, that fair compensation shall be made therefor.[33]

These provisions, like the many other related ones in the armistice agreement and the peace treaty, proved merely declaratory. They embodied desiderata and principles rather than strict, legally binding orders; they were not self-executing (they needed appropriate municipal legislation and enforcement to prevail); and they did not provide for sanctions in case of non-compliance, other than the implied possible litigation before an international tribunal.

Reaction to Jewish Demands: Neo–Anti-Semitism

In the pursuit of anti-Fascist positions, the officials of the new order were with a few exceptions reluctant to treat Jewish suffering and losses differently from those of the other victims of war. The leftists (a group which included many Communists of Jewish origin) devoted most of their energies to the drive for the eventual liquidation of Fascism and the requirements of the class struggle; the rightist-oriented members of the postwar coalition were not interested in giving the Jews opportunities to pursue their demands for restitution and indemnification.

In the absence of a centrally guided and administered restitution and indemnification program, the survivors attempted, often successfully, to reacquire their properties, including their apartments and furnishings, with the aid of sympathetic local authorities. In many a community, Jews managed to acquire leadership positions in the party, trade union, police, and other local social and governmental organizations. Many of them were motivated by idealism, striving to participate in the building of a new socialist society; others were guided by opportunism or the desire to avenge the crimes of the past. In light of the total absence of Jews in these positions during the previous decades, their postwar visibility became a source of irritation and anti-Semitic manifestations.

Another irritant was an economic one. Under the extremely severe conditions of the immediate postwar period, when goods were scarce and inflation rampant, black-marketeering became highly visible as well as profitable, and the ranks of black-marketeers of course included a fair share of Jews. A whisper campaign against the Jews started, and was shortly followed by anti-Semitic outbursts in several communities. This may have been reinforced by the awareness that a considerable number of the top Communist party and state leaders were Marxists of Jewish background. In the minds of many people, who for years had been bombarded with warnings about the dangers of Judeo-Bolshevism, these leaders represented not only an alien ideology but also the interests of a foreign occupation power. This idea was fanned not only by inveterate anti-Semites, but also by many who had lost most of their wealth and privileges as a result of the debacle: the former land-owners, the industrial and business leaders, and the dismissed military officers and civil servants. Though many members of the aristocratic-conservative groups tolerated, if they did not openly sympathize with, the Jews before the Soviet liberation, in the wake of the socialization measures they too succumbed to the identification of Jewry with the evils of Communism.

Ironically and tragically, the anti-Jewish demonstrations were frequently sparked by leftist forces, which were guided by consider-ations of power and social change. In their drive for recruits, these for-ces, which included a proportionately large number of Jews, were pri-marily the ones which opposed the Jewish demands for restitution and compensation and championed the struggle against black-marketeers.

On March 25, 1945, for example, *Szabad Nép* (Free People), the organ of the Communist Party, called on the returning Jews to show understanding toward the Christians living in their confiscated apart-ments, even though many of these people had received their privileges because of their association with the ultra-rightists.[34] Soon after the lib-eration of the capital, the Budapest National Committee (*Budapesti Nemzeti Bizottság*) intimated that Jews could reacquire their apartments only by concluding agreements with the current occupants.[35] Early in the spring of 1945, József Darvas, the noted populist writer and leader of the National Peasant Party who was to become Minister of Construc-tion, published an article attacking the Jews for "always trying to take the easier road." He emphasized that "no one may claim any privileges on the basis of former suffering."[36] This was basically also the position of Péter Veres, Darvas's colleague, who was in charge of the agrarian reform that was carried out under the slogan "the land belongs to those who till it." Later in the year Veres is said to have declared that Hungary would rid itself of all foreigners, Jews as well as Germans.[37] The frictions caused by the conflicting interests of the feuding parties, at a time of great economic hardship, led to many anti-Semitic out-bursts. The anti-Jewish manifestations had a shattering effect both on the survivors, who were still suffering from the trauma of their experi-ences and losses, and on those many decent Hungarians who believed that the building of a harmonious democratic order based on justice and equality was possible.

By far the most shocking incidents took place in 1946, when the economic conditions were at their worst. The Communist leaders' campaign against black-marketeers, a term which often became a euphemism for Jews, led in February of that year to serious anti-Semitic outbursts in the working class centers of Ózd, Sajószentpéter, Szegvár, and Tótkomlós. Virtual pogroms broke out in Kunmadaras in May and in Diósgyőr in July, claiming several casualties. In Kunmadaras, anti-Semitic elements, resentful of the survivors' demands for restitution, incited the local population by spreading the rumor that the returning Jews were murdering Christian children. In Diósgyőr, near Miskolc, the anti-Jewish attacks followed a Communist-led demonstration of miners against black-marketeers—a demonstration that came ten days after a speech by Rákosi in Miskolc in which he demanded the scaffold for black-marketeers. In several other towns, the local population, incited by the beneficiaries of the wartime Jewish expropriations (*beati possidentes*) ordered the Jews to leave. In still others, local authorities not only rejected the lawful demands of the returned deportees, but actually passed resolutions to deny them employment. This was the case, for example, in a factory in Kispest, where the workers demanded (December 1945) the immediate dismissal of all Jewish employees.[38]

The anti-Semitic demonstrations that accompanied the struggle of the survivors for restitution and reparation reflected the political, social, and economic changes occurring in Hungary under Soviet tutelage. These became the subject of considerable discussion in both polemical and scholarly writings during the early postwar years. Some of the authors place much of the onus for the rise of neo–anti-Semitism on the Jews themselves. Their prevalent theme is that the Jews, having gone through a period of inhuman suffering, engaged in provocative action in an attempt to overcompensate for their ordeal. The Jews are further indicted for having acquired leadership positions in the political, administrative, and economic spheres and isolating themselves from the majority, thus enraging the masses. Last but not least, the Jews are accused of having invoked the dangerous weapon of collective responsibility by making the Hungarian people as a whole responsible for their suffering during the occupation.[39]

Several scholarly works offer a more balanced account, emphasizing that Hungarian Christians must share responsibility for the tragedy that befell their fellow citizens of the Jewish faith. But although they are sympathetic to the position of the Jews and astute in their socio-psychological analyses of the behavior patterns of the survivors and their opponents, some of these studies also impute to the Jews as a whole the negative behavior patterns of individuals in powerful positions.[40] The tendency to generalize and stereotype, of course, largely reflected the absence in the country of a tradition of democracy and toleration for the rights and interests of ethnic, national, and religious minorities. Underestimated (or ignored) by many of the postwar social critics was an essential consideration: that the bulk of the survivors not only were frustrated by their inability to reacquire what was rightfully theirs, but were also suffering the consequences of the postwar economic ills. In fact, many of the Jews lived through the hardships caused by famine, inflation, and black-marketeering only thanks to the modest aid doled out by the AJDC.

Postwar social critics, including some of the literary figures who showed considerable understanding toward the wartime plight of the Jews, tried to exculpate the Hungarian nation from moral and historical responsibility for what had happened to the Jews. Ignoring or distorting historical reality, they endeavored to place the blame almost exclusively upon the Germans. Oblivious to the record of other Axis-allied or German-occupied nations (e.g., Bulgaria, Denmark, Italy, Romania), these writers conveniently suppressed the fact that in no other country did the Germans receive such enthusiastic support for the implementation of the Final Solution as they did in Hungary. Some of the writers tried to mitigate Hungary's responsibility by arguing that the Hungarian Christians also had suffered during the war, and that the people at large could not be made responsible for the actions of the *Nyilas.* It is hard to understand this attempt to equate the plight of a people in the course of hostilities with the sufferings of a helpless minority that had for decades been subjected to systematic discrimination by a state that elevated anti-Semitism to official policy and at the end cooperated in the Final Solution.

The debate on the issue of responsibility was partially sparked by a resolution offered by Bishop László Ravasz shortly after the anti-Jewish demonstrations at Kunmadaras in May 1946. Adopted unanimously by the Hungarian Reformed (Calvinist) Church, the resolution stated:

The Council of the Convent of the Hungarian Reformed Church . . . confesses with deep humility the sin by which it has offended God's Majesty. It has offended God's Majesty by not fulfilling faithfully the prophetic mission received from Him. It failed to warn the people and their superiors when both entered on a path which went against God's laws, and it failed to step bravely forward to defend those who were innocently persecuted. We deem it necessary for the Hungarian nation to arrive at a salutary recognition of its sins under God's judgment and to confess them with repentance. . . . The Council orders penitential services to be held on one Sunday of every year in all congregations of the Hungarian Reformed Church.[41]

The conflicting perceptions on the issues of responsibility, restitution, and indemnification continued for several years. The Jews became increasingly convinced that their legitimate demands were being intentionally treated in a dilatory and bureaucratic fashion in order to frustrate the implementation of any meaningful restitution program. Their opponents argued that the Jews' demands were excessive, their behavior overzealous, and their participation in the drive for the liquidation of Fascism and the establishment of a new order tantamount to involvement in a witch hunt.

The conflict had a dual effect upon the Jews. Disillusioned with the new order, many decided to join the ranks of the Zionists, who had all along disclaimed the assimilationist solution of the Jewish question. Developing a new sense of Jewish national consciousness, many resolved to emigrate, especially after the establishment of the State of Israel. Many followed the route of emigration to the West, hoping to find new homes primarily in the United States and in the British Commonwealth nations. Their hopes for reparation and indemnification now rested primarily with the government of the Federal Republic of Germany.

The Federal Republic of Germany

Although Hungarian Jews were deported to and suffered in concentration camps located in all the postwar sovereign states that had formerly constituted the Third Reich, only the Federal Republic of Germany (West Germany) adopted a comparatively generous restitution and reparation program. Austria enacted a relatively modest act of restitution legislation, which however contained stringent Austrian citizenship requirements. The German Democratic Republic (East Germany), governed by a Soviet-supported regime, rejected any differentiation between classes of victims of Fascism based on race and religion. It also refused the adoption of restitution legislation as a matter of principle, insisting that it was not a "successor-in-interest" to the Third Reich. Like the other socialist states in East Central Europe, it took the position that by liquidating the heritage of Fascism and taking care of all the victims of the Third Reich residing in the country, it had fulfilled its historical and moral responsibilities.

Although West Germany rightly claimed it was not a "successor-in-interest" either, it nevertheless adopted a relatively generous and ambitious program to compensate the victims of Nazism. Although the willful extermination of 11 million civilians, among them 6 million Jews, and the unspeakable suffering by many other millions both during and after the war cannot really be expiated by monetary payments alone, the West German government showed a recognition of historical responsibility for the policies of the Third Reich, as well as a keen sensitivity toward the rightful claims of its victims. The West German government:

- Concluded a series of "international" agreements with Jewish organizations that had no governmental status.
- Offered compensation to Jewish victims of the Holocaust throughout the free world, irrespective of their citizenship.
- Entered into an indemnification agreement with Israel—a state that was not yet in existence at the time of the German persecution of the Jews.[42]

The generosity with which the West German government implemented these agreements may be gauged from the fact that by January 1, 1979, it had paid DM 85.3 billion, enabling hundreds of thousands of Jewish victims of Nazism to establish a new life and the State of Israel to bolster its economy and finances.[43] While the West German indemnification effort in relation to Hungarian Jews was less striking, it was nevertheless significant.[44] Some of the West German measures affected exclusively Jews still living in Hungary; others were of a more general nature, with some affecting Jews living in Hungary and others those residing in the free world.

The Federal Restitution Law of July 19, 1957, provided for the restitution of or compensation for identifiable assets the Nazis transferred or took along to the territories of the Federal Republic and Berlin. The value of the assets looted from Hungarian Jews could never be established with any degree of accuracy. While a sizable amount was taken along by individual Germans and Hungarians fleeing toward the West, a considerable proportion left the country in a "gold train," which ended up in the American and French zones of occupation in Austria.[45] Many valuables of Jewish origin were included in the assets handed over by Baron Gábor Kemény, the *Nyilas* Foreign Minister, to Jaques van Harten, the delegate of the IRC, on March 17, 1945, to be safeguarded as "part of the Hungarian state patrimony."[46]

Under the German restitution law, the Jews in Hungary encountered two initial difficulties. First, it was all but impossible for them to prove that their looted assets had actually reached the territories specified in the law. Second, there were no diplomatic relations between the Federal Republic of Germany and Hungary. These difficulties were overcome within a few years, though the compensation that was eventually authorized was but a fraction of the value of the looted assets. With the cooperation of the Hungarian authorities, over 66,000 applications were submitted to West Germany before the expiration of the April 1, 1959, deadline. Even before the establishment of diplomatic relations in December 1973, the West German government agreed on January 22, 1971, to pay DM 3 million (approximately $1.5 million) to Hungary in three yearly installments beginning in 1972. Under the agreement, the Hungarian government undertook to provide for the distribution of this amount among the applicants. Toward this end, it assigned immediate responsibility to the National Organization for the Protection of the Interests of Nazi Persecutees in Hungary (*A Nácizmus Magyarországi Üldözöttei Országos Érdekvédelmi Szervezete*).[47] In accordance with guidelines published on May 28, 1971, the eligible applicants were divided into four categories, entitled to payments ranging from approximately $80 to $400.[48] Although these payments were relatively modest, the recipients enjoyed an advantage over Hungarian Jews living abroad. Under the German-Hungarian agreement, the former did not need to prove the identity of looted assets in the areas under the jurisdiction of the West German government—a condition that remained binding for Hungarian Jews no longer residing in Hungary.

The Federal Indemnification Law of July 29, 1956,[49] provided for the compensation of the victims of Nazism for loss of life, liberty, and impairment of health, as well as for material losses, including the loss of real property and various types of assets, compulsory payments of fines, damage to careers, and losses in social security payments.[50] As originally designed, the legislation, for a variety of reasons, excluded residents of the Soviet bloc nations. Many framers of the draft bill feared that the inclusion of victims living in the Communist world would arouse opposition that might jeopardize the passage of the act. Others used fiscal arguments, emphasizing the large number of victims living in the Soviet Union and the Eastern European countries. Last but not least, there were those who raised the legal issue of recognition, arguing that payments to countries with which West Germany had no diplomatic relations were in conflict with some customs and principles of international law.

Although the law was designed primarily for the indemnification of

German Jews, it contained a section (part IV) which also covered persecutees from territories from which Germans had been expelled after the war. This section also covered stateless persons and political refugees. To be eligible for indemnification, an applicant who fulfilled all the other requirements had to prove that he had resided in the West as of October 1, 1953. Under the law, the West Germans undertook to compensate all those who had suffered as a result of persecution perpetrated either by the Germans, whether within or outside the Third Reich, or by foreign governments that had acted under German pressure or initiative.

In the case of Hungary, it was established, after considerable legal wrangling, that the persecution of Hungarian Jewry as of April 5, 1941, was the direct consequence of German pressure. The ruling made the labor servicemen eligible for indemnification, provided they met the law's residence requirements. The cutoff date of October 1, 1953, was a great disappointment for the many refugees who managed to escape Hungary after that date. (The problem became particularly acute after the exodus that followed the Hungarian Revolt of October–November 1956.) In March 1956, Hungarian Jewish leaders abroad began a concerted effort to have the benefits of the indemnification law extended to those reaching the West after October 1, 1953. These leaders were backed by former Prime Minister Kállay, of Hungary, who supported the thesis that the Hungarian Jews were persecuted because of German pressure.[51] Their efforts, also supported by several international Jewish organizations, contributed to the passage by the West Germans on September 14, 1965, of the so-called Final Act of the Federal Indemnification Law, which extended the eligibility date to December 31, 1965.[52] Although this law provided compensation for the thousands of Hungarian Jews who escaped to the West after November 1956, albeit at a somewhat lower scale than before, it leaves one last group of refugees without any benefits: the few thousand Hungarian-speaking Soviet Jews who were allowed to leave the province of Transcarpathian Ukraine of the Ukrainian SSR in the late 1970s. The province, formerly known as Carpatho-Ruthenia—an area that includes the once "Jewish towns" of Beregszász, Huszt, Munkács, Nagyszőllős, and Ungvár—belonged to Hungary during the war years (see chapter 5).

In addition to receiving compensation paid by the West German government under the Federal Indemnification Law, concentration camp inmates who had been used as slave laborers by such German firms as

I.G. Farben, Krupp, AEG, Telefunken, and Rheinmetall also became eligible for compensatory payments from these firms.[53] While this additional compensation did not generally equal the value of the labor rendered during the war, it represented an additional source of income for the former persecutees.

In Hungary, the applications of the former deportees who had worked as slave laborers were processed with the aid of the National Organization for the Protection of the Interests of Nazi Persecutees in Hungary, acting in conjunction with the General Bank for Trade of Valuables (*Általános Értékforgalmi Bank*). There are no data on the number of Hungarian Jews who benefited from any of the restitution-indemnification programs or the total amounts they received. It is safe to assume, however, that the compensation was commensurate neither with the percentage the Hungarian Jews represented among the Holocaust victims nor with their losses and suffering.

War Crimes Trials

Hungary. Under Article 14 of the Armistice Agreement of January 20, 1945, Hungary undertook to cooperate "in the apprehension and trial, as well as the surrender to the governments concerned, of persons accused of war crimes." In compliance with these provisions, the Provisional National Government adopted (January 25, 1945) Decree no. 81/1945.M.E., relating to the establishment of a system of tribunals designed to operate under "the people's jurisdiction" (*népbíráskodás*). These tribunals, it was envisioned, would continue until a permanent court system was established by a duly elected legislature.[54] The decree defined war crimes and crimes against the people and specified the types of penalties the tribunals could mete out. It also identified the procedures of the courts and specified the functions of the people's prosecutors. The decree provided for the establishment of two types of courts: people's tribunals (*népbíróságok*), lower trial courts to function in every court seat, and the National Council of People's Tribunals (*A Népbíróságok Országos Tanácsa*—NOT). Each people's tribunal (or panel) was composed of a professional judge and his deputy appointed by the Minister of Justice, and five lay judges who were to be representatives of the five political parties constituting the Hungarian National Independence Front (*Magyar Nemzeti Függetlenségi Front*).[55] The National Council of People's Tribunals was headed by a president appointed by the Minister of Justice. It had various appellate councils, which were composed of five professional judges (and their deputies) nominated by the five political parties.[56] The qualifications of the judges and of the prosecutors were determined by so-called certification committees, which paid special attention to the candidates' political background. In spite of their rigorous procedures, however, several prosecutors and judges managed to hide their *Nyilas* or ultra-rightist background. A few were caught taking bribes for failing to prosecute or for showing special leniency to the accused.[57]

The first trials were held even before the people's tribunals were formally established. These were conducted before ad hoc "revolutionary courts" and primarily involved labor service company guards accused of cruel behavior by their former victims.[58] In several localities liberated by the Red Army, many of the returning survivors (at the beginning almost exclusively labor servicemen) cooperated with the authorities in the identification and arrest of individuals suspected of having been involved in the ghettos and the deportations. These individuals were held for interrogation and subsequently transferred to the jurisdiction of the people's tribunals.

During the first phase of their operation, the people's tribunals—like the "revolutionary courts"—dealt primarily with cases involving labor service officers and guards. In Budapest, they also handled many cases involving *Nyilas* gang members who had terrorized the capital during the three months before the liberation. Among those tried for heinous crimes against the Jews were Dénes Bokor, who was charged with the torture and murder of 1,500 Jews; András Kun, a Menorite monk who was responsible for the execution of over 500 Jews; János Traum, József Mónos, Péter Pál Katona, and Endre Kovács, each accused of responsibility for the death of hundreds of Jews.[59] The priority devoted to these two types of cases was determined by the large number of arrests in the wake of the advancing Soviet forces and by the availability of witnesses willing and eager to testify.[60]

The first major trial was that of Zoltán Meskó, the former "National Socialist" member of the Hungarian Parliament, in May 1945. Meskó was sentenced to five years, but following an appeal by the prosecutor, NOT increased the sentence to life imprisonment.[61] While the prosecution was eager to proceed against those political and governmental leaders of the Horthy and *Nyilas* eras who were considered primarily responsible for the disasters that befell the country, the trial of those associated with the Szálasi regime, first scheduled for September 3, 1945,[62] had to be postponed because all of the accused were still in

American custody in the U.S. zones of occupation in Austria and Germany.

The Hungarian demands for the extradition of suspected war criminals, especially those of German nationality, caused considerable friction between the Hungarian and American authorities. The tensions were eased when most of the Hungarian suspects were returned and the Americans consented to the extradition of three top SS officials who had been active during the occupation (Kurt Becher, Edmund Veesenmayer, and Otto Winkelmann) to serve as witnesses in the major Hungarian war crimes trials.[63]

The series of trials involving the major war criminals began in the Academy of Music (*Zeneakadémia*)—one of the few relatively undamaged buildings available—on October 29, 1945. The first to be tried was former Prime Minister László Bárdossy, who was accused of involving Hungary in the war against the Soviet Union without the consent of Parliament. He was also held responsible for the massacre of Jews at Kamenets-Podolsk and the Ujvidék area, which had occurred during his tenure. Bárdossy was convicted on November 3. His appeal was rejected by NOT on December 28, and following the rejection of a clemency appeal he was executed by a firing squad on January 10, 1946.[64] Next to be tried (November 14–23) was former Prime Minister Béla Imrédy, who also played an important role in the Sztójay government. He was accused, among other things, of responsibility for the enactment of the anti-Jewish laws of 1938 and 1939 as well as of preparing the ground for the close cooperation with the Third Reich. He was convicted on November 23 and executed on February 28, 1946.[65]

The trial of Ferenc Rajniss followed on November 28. The ultrarightist journalist and founder of the anti-Semitic weekly *Magyar Futár* (Hungarian Courier) had served as Minister of Cults in the Szálasi government, and was indicted for war crimes and crimes against the people. Particularly, he was held responsible for conspiring against Horthy's attempts to extricate Hungary from the Axis alliance in September–October, 1944. Rajniss was convicted on December 7, and executed on March 12, 1946.[66]

Of greatest interest to the Jews was undoubtedly the trial of the three officials considered primarily responsible for the destruction of Hungarian Jewry—"the deportation trio" in the Sztójay government: László Baky, László Endre, and Andor Jaross. The trial opened under the chairmanship of Dr. Péter Jankó on December 18, 1945. By the time it ended on January 4, 1946, the country and the world at large had heard the gruesome details on the planning and implementation of the Final Solution program. In addition to responsibility for the destruction of the Jews, the three war criminals were accused of plotting and cooperating with the SS to the detriment of the national interests. They were sentenced to death on January 7, 1946. Baky and Endre were hanged on March 29 and Jaross was shot by a firing squad on April 11.[67]

The first of Szálasi's close associates to be tried were László Budinszky, the former Minister of Justice, and Count Fidél Pálffy, the former Minister of Agriculture. Budinszky's trial began on December 5, 1945. He was condemned to die on December 12 and hanged on March 9, 1946. Pálffy's trial began on December 12. Condemned to death on December 15, he was hanged on March 2, 1946.[68] Then came the turn of Szálasi and the remaining members of his government: Károly Beregfy, Sándor Csia, Dr. József Gera, Gábor Kemény, Jenő Szőllősi, and Gábor Vajna. The trial began on February 5, 1946, under the chairmanship of Dr. Péter Jankó. It attracted great attention, for the accused were considered chiefly responsible for having completely ruined the country when they prevented Horthy from extricating it from the Axis alliance. It gave the prosecution an opportunity to trace the background of the *Nyilas* movement, its relationship with the Nazi Party, and its role during the six months before the liberation of the country. The accounts of the accused were often contradicted by the testimonies of Veesenmayer and Winkelmann, who attempted to shift all blame on their former Hungarian henchmen. All of the accused were convicted and condemned to death on March 1. Beregfy, Gera, Szálasi, and Vajna were executed on March 12 and Csia, Kemény, and Szőllősi on March 19.[69]

The last major trial involved Döme Sztójay, the former Minister in Berlin who had been appointed Prime Minister after the German occupation and under whose tenure the bulk of Hungarian Jewry was liquidated. His chief codefendants were members of his government: Antal Kunder, Jenő Rátz, Lajos Reményi-Schneller, and Lajos Szász.[70] The trial began on March 14 before a panel headed by Dr. Béla Pálosi. The defendants were accused of sacrificing the interests of the nation by collaborating with the Third Reich. The proceedings called attention to Sztójay's role as Hungarian Minister in Berlin, the antecedents of the occupation, and the eagerness with which his government cooperated in fulfilling all German demands—including the Final Solution. Like most other major war criminals, the Sztójay group tried to pin all responsibility for the country's disaster on the Germans. The court nevertheless convicted all the defendants on March 22. Kunder was condemned to life imprisonment; the others were condemned to death and executed by firing squad shortly thereafter.[71]

Concurrently with these mass trials, the people's tribunals held individual trials of several persons who had played an important role in the destruction of Hungarian Jewry. Among these were Lieutenant-Colonel László Ferenczy, the gendarmerie officer in charge of the deportations, as well as Péter Hain and László Koltay, the leaders of the Hungarian State Security Police—"the Hungarian Gestapo." All three were executed in the spring of 1946. Several individuals who played a comparatively secondary role were also tried; these included István Antal, the former Minister of Justice and later Minister of Propaganda in the Sztójay government; Ferenc Basch, the leader of the *Volksbund;* Ferenc Fiala, the *Nyilas* press chief; Ferenc Kassai-Schallmayer, Szálasi's propaganda chief; Mihály Kolosváry-Borcsa, Sztójay's press chief; and Emil Kovarcz, a *Nyilas* organizer and member of the Hungarian dejewification unit. Also tried were Bálint Hóman, the former Minister of Cults and Public Education; General Iván Hindy, the military commander of Budapest during the *Nyilas* era; Kálmán Hubay, the anti-Semitic journalist and founder of the Hungarian National Socialist and Arrow Cross parties; and Ferenc Omelka, the journalist and former head of the *Nyilas* "Tribunal on Calling People to Account" (*Számonkérő Szék*). Antal was condemned to life imprisonment but was granted amnesty after 15 years. Fiala was condemned to life, but escaped and fled to the West during the Hungarian Revolt of 1956. Basch, Kassai, Kolosváry-Borcsa, and Kovarcz were executed. Hóman died in prison while serving life imprisonment; Hindy, Hubay, and Omelka were executed in the spring of 1946.[72]

Some major war criminals—including General Ferenc Feketehalmy-Czeydner, Major-General József Grassy, and Captain Márton Zöldi—were found guilty in connection with the massacres at Ujvidék. They were condemned to death on January 12, 1946, but were extradited to Yugoslavia, together with General Ferenc Szombathelyi, the former Chief of the General Staff, where they were tried once again and executed (see below).

The people's tribunals continued their activities for several years, handling cases of progressively less importance. By March 1, 1948, criminal proceedings had been initiated against 39,514 persons, and 31,472 cases had been disposed of. Of these, 5,954 were dismissed and

1168 LIBERATION, RESTITUTION, RETRIBUTION

9,245 ended with not guilty verdicts. Of the 16,273 convictions, 8,041 resulted in imprisonment of less than one year and 6,110 in terms between one and five years. Only 41 individuals were condemned to life terms at forced labor. In the country as a whole, 322 individuals were condemned to death; however, only 146 of these sentences were carried out, and the rest were commuted to life imprisonment.[73]

The record of the Hungarian people's tribunals is mixed. Dr. György Berend, the Deputy President of NOT, assessed it as follows:

If one takes into account how many leaders in responsible positions, how many warmongers and agitators against the people, and how many thousands of forced-labor-company murderer guards and *Nyilas* mass murderers were produced during the 25 years before the liberation, the above statistics elicit serious doubts even in the most ardent opponents of the people's tribunals.[74]

The people's tribunals, NOT, and the people's prosecution offices were supplanted on January 1, 1952, by new organs of justice established under Law no. III of 1951.[75] Nevertheless, war crimes trials continued to be held periodically. Two of these trials were especially important. The first was the June 1967 war crimes trial in Budapest of the so-called "Zugló *Nyilas*," the Hungarian Nazi goons who had preyed on the helpless Jews in the 14th (Zugló) District of Budapest. The accused were: Vilmos Kröszl, Lájos Németh, Alajos Sándor, György Bükkös, József Hollai, Antal Szőke, Kálmán Baráth, László Kálmán, Pál Füredi, Jenő Hernádi, János Erős, László Mészáros, Gyula Monostori, János Kovács, Ferenc Pataki, Gyula Kraut, József Kraut, István Kovács, and János Baráth. The first three were condemned to death, a new trial was ordered for Pataki, and the others were condemned to prison terms of 8 to 15 years.[76] In the second major trial of 1967, Mihály Schlei and Hermina Kraut (also known as Mrs. Sándor Bischoff), the so-called SS interpreters who had also been active in the *Volksbund* movement, were condemned to life imprisonment on December 10, 1967.[77]

The last war crimes trial in Hungary was reportedly that of Mihály Szemes, a *Nyilas* who had returned from a Soviet POW camp in 1950 and whose criminal past was not unmasked until the late 1960s. Accused of torturing, robbing, and killing many innocent people during the *Nyilas* era, he was condemned to death in the summer of 1970.[78]

Some Hungarian nationals were tried in Romania and Yugoslavia for crimes committed both before and during the German occupation. These trials dealt primarily with crimes committed in the territories acquired by Hungary from these countries in 1940 and 1941.

Romania. The Romanian people's tribunals were established by and operated under the provisions of Decree-Law no. 312 of the Ministry of Justice, dated April 21, 1945.[79] The crimes committed in Northern Transylvania, the area acquired by Hungary in August–September 1940, were the subject of two major trials before the People's Tribunals of Cluj (Kolozsvár). In the first of these, 63 individuals were accused of crimes against Romanians and some Jews during the occupation of Northern Transylvania by Hungarian troops in September 1940.[80]

The destruction of the Jews of Northern Transylvania was the subject of the second mass trial, involving 185 individuals. Among these were the government, military, police, and gendarmerie officers and officials of the counties and of the cities that had served as ghetto centers. The trial was held under the chairmanship of Dr. Nicolae Matei in the spring of 1946; the chief prosecutor was Andrei Paul (Endre Pollák).[81] The proceedings recorded the gruesome details of the Final Solution in the counties and communities of Northern Transylvania. The sentences handed down by the court were stiff—29 were condemned to death and many more to life imprisonment—but many of the accused were tried *in absentia.* Among the latter was Colonel Tibor Paksy-Kiss, the gendarmerie officer in charge of ghettoization in the province.[82]

Yugoslavia. In accordance with the provisions of Article 14 of the Armistice Agreement and Decree no. 4770/1945.M.E., the Hungarian authorities extradited to Yugoslavia several Hungarian officers charged with complicity in the massacre of thousands of Serbs and Jews in the Bácska area in January–February 1942 as well as with involvement in the murder of labor servicemen in the Ukraine and Bor, Serbia. Some of them, who were also charged with active participation in the Final Solution program, were first tried in Hungary and condemned to death. (The extradition agreement provided for their return to Hungary in case the Yugoslavs proved to be more lenient.)

The trial in Hungary of Grassy and Zöldi began on January 8, 1946. They were found guilty of the Ujvidék massacres and of participation in the ghettoization and deportation of the Jews in 1944, and were condemned to death by hanging on January 12. The Hungarian trial of Feketehalmy-Czeydner began on March 21 and that of Ferenc Szombathelyi, the Chief of the General Staff, on March 28. They too were found guilty by the court. All four were then handed over to the Yugoslavs, who retried them together with Lajos Gál, Ernő Bajsy (the former Deputy Prefect of the Bácska), Miklós Nagy (the former Mayor of Ujvidék), General Ferenc Bajor, and Pál Perepatits (the former representative of the counterintelligence service). The trial began on October 24, 1946, in Ujvidék and all 9 were condemned to death six days later: Feketehalmy-Czeydner, Grassy, and Zöldi by hanging and the others by firing squad. Feketehalmy-Czeydner was hanged on November 5 in Zsablya, where the Délvidék massacres began; the others were executed in Ujvidék one day earlier.[83]

Several major war crimes trials dealing with the destruction of Hungarian Jewry were held in the German Federal Republic, Austria, Czechoslovakia, Poland, and Israel. They involved members of the various agencies of the Third Reich, who were directly implicated in the planning and implementation of the Final Solution in Hungary.

The Federal Republic of Germany. In the area that eventually became West Germany, a number of trials dealt with the crimes committed against the Jews of Hungary. These included the trial of the 21 top leaders of the Third Reich before the International Military Tribunal at Nuremberg, the 12 cases involving 185 criminals tried before the U.S. Military Tribunals, the trials conducted in the British Zone of Occupation, and the trials conducted by German courts since the early 1950s.[84] At Nuremberg, the tragedy that befell Hungarian Jewry was dealt with in the cases involving Kaltenbrunner and Ribbentrop. The Americans brought up Hungary in connection with the cases involving Oswald Pohl, the Flick, I. G. Farben, and Krupp combines, and above all the Ministries; the British dealt with it primarily in the so-called Belsen trial involving Josef Kramer and 44 others associated with the Auschwitz, Natzweiler, and Bergen-Belsen camps.

By far the most important trial involving Hungarian Jewry was that of Edmund Veesenmayer, the former Plenipotentiary of the Third Reich in Hungary. As a leading defendant in the Ministries Case (1948), Veesenmayer was convicted on several counts of the indictment. In April 1949, he was sentenced to 20 years' imprisonment, but in January 1951, John J. McCloy, the U.S. High Commissioner for Germany, commuted his sentence to 10 years. He was freed the following year on the recommendation of a special U.S. clemency board.[85]

War crimes committed against Hungarian Jews were the subject of several trials conducted under the auspices of the French and Soviet military courts as well. The French courts were primarily concerned with crimes committed in concentration and forced labor camps.[86]

According to the report submitted by the West German Minister of Justice to the *Bundestag* early in 1965, the three Western occupying powers sentenced approximately 5,000 persons accused of National Socialist crimes.

The Soviet courts handled a much larger number of cases. Among these was that of Franz Jaeckeln, the Higher SS and Police Leader, *Ostland,* who was the commander of the forces that slaughtered the "alien" Jews from Hungary in and around Kamenets-Podolsk in August 1941. Jaeckeln was executed in 1946. Many of the cases prosecuted by the Soviet authorities were reportedly associated with the USSR's political objectives in East Germany. According to Soviet sources, 13,532 persons sentenced for various wartime activities were still imprisoned in Soviet camps in May 1950. Of the persons sentenced by Soviet military tribunals, 10,513 were handed over to the authorities of the Soviet Zone of Occupation in January 1950 "to serve their sentences."[87]

Although the German courts in the Western Zones of Occupation were reconvened toward the end of 1945, their competence in regard to a large part of National Socialist crimes was barred by Control Council Law no. 4 of October 30, 1945. They were particularly forbidden from prosecuting crimes committed against the Allies. Most of these restrictions, however, were abrogated by the Allied High Commission Law no. 13 of November 23, 1949, which went into effect on January 1, 1950. The courts of West Germany prosecuted a large number of groups of National Socialist crimes, ranging from the elimination of political opponents after the Nazi acquisition of power to crimes committed abroad.

Between 1945 and 1965, the West German courts sentenced 6,115 of the 61,761 individuals against whom the public prosecutor's offices had launched preliminary investigations. Of these, 4,419 were sentenced by the end of 1949, and 1,425 by the end of 1954. Early in 1965, proceedings against 13,892 were still pending. Proceedings against 542 were "temporarily suspended" because the whereabouts of the accused were unknown or foreign governments refused their extradition. Among these were SS-*Obergruppenführer* Martin Bormann, the Chief of the Party Chancellery, SS-*Gruppenführer* Heinrich Müller, Chief of Section IV of the Reich Security Main Office and Eichmann's immediate superior, and Drs. Horst Schumann and Josef Mengele, the Auschwitz physicians.[88]

With respect to the Hungarian Jewish catastrophe, by far the most important trials conducted in West German courts were those involving Hermann A. Krumey and Otto Hunsche, the two leading members of the Eichmann-*Sonderkommando* in Hungary. Krumey and Hunsche were first arrested in 1960. Freed by an appellate court, they were rearrested in the wake of an indictment prepared by Dr. Fritz Bauer, the Chief Prosecutor of the State of Hesse. Following a nine-month trial that began on April 27, 1964, before an assize court (*Schwurgericht*) in Frankfurt-am-Main, Hunsche was acquitted and Krumey was sentenced to five years at hard labor (February 3, 1965). Chief Judge Arnold Schmidt argued that "neither of the former Nazi officers has been proved to have initiated or taken a direct part in the slaughter of Jews." On the prosecution's appeal, the Appellate Court of Karlsruhe nullified the assize court's decision in 1968 and ordered a new trial. This time Krumey was condemned to life imprisonment while Hunsche was sentenced to 12 years (August 29, 1969).[89] The *Bundesgerichtshof* (Federal Court) of Karlsruhe upheld their conviction on January 17, 1973.[90]

Victor Capesius, one of the defendants in the so-called Auschwitz trial held from December 1963 to August 1965, was heavily involved in the Hungarian Jewish catastrophe. A Transylvanian pharmacist, he had assisted Mengele in the selection of which Jews would live. He was condemned to 9 years, but was freed shortly after the *Bundesgerichtshof* upheld the lower court decision on February 20, 1969. The Karlsruhe court ordered that the time Capesius spent in internment after the war be counted as part of his sentence.[91]

The West German authorities launched criminal proceedings against three other high-ranking officials of the Third Reich who had played an important role in the destruction of Hungarian Jewry: Horst Wagner and Eberhard von Thadden, the two leading officials of the *Inland II* section of the German Foreign Office, and Albert Theodor Ganzenmüller, the former State Secretary in charge of the railways in the Reich Ministry of Transport. The suit against Wagner and Thadden was initiated before the *Schwurgericht* in Essen in 1960, but the prosecution was not ready to try the case until May 1968. But Thadden was not present—he had died in an automobile accident on November 8, 1964—and Wagner, out on bail, managed to win one postponement after another by changing attorneys and claiming ill health. The trial finally began on May 29, 1972, but was almost immediately suspended because Wagner underwent an eye operation.[92] He died in Hamburg on March 13, 1977.

The trial of Ganzenmüller, accused of organizing the railroad cars necessary for the deportation of Jews, was set for June 2, 1971, before the *Schwurgericht* in Düsseldorf. His trial, which began on May 3, 1973, was indefinitely postponed because his lawyer was involved in another prolonged case.[93]

Austria. Two of the major war crimes trials held in Austria related directly to the catastrophe of Hungarian Jewry. The first one was that of Siegfried Seidl. At one time the commander of the Theresienstadt concentration camp, he subsequently served as a leading member of the Eichmann-*Sonderkommando* in Hungary. As an expert in the Final Solution program, he was particularly active in the roundup and deportation of the Jews in the Székesfehérvár area. Seidl was found guilty of war crimes and crimes against the people, and was executed in Vienna on October 4, 1946.

The second trial involved Franz Novak, the SS Captain who served as Eichmann's transportation officer and liaison with the Reich Ministry of Transport. In this capacity he was primarily responsible for the organization of the deportation trains. Novak, who had lived in Austria undisturbed for 15 years after the war, was finally arrested in 1961. He was first tried in November 1964, and was convicted on a subordinate count of brutality during the loading of railway cars: the prosecution established that Novak had known that the victims were being jammed into the cars without sufficient food or water. Since he was acquitted on the mass-murder charge, he was sentenced to only eight years' imprisonment. On appeal, the *Oberlandesgericht* (Appellate Court) of Vienna nullified the judgment and ordered a new trial. After the second trial, held in September 1966, the court ordered Novak's release (October 6, 1966) because the jury was deadlocked on whether Novak had been bound by orders he could not refuse. Novak was tried for a third time after the Vienna *Oberlandesgericht* nullified the acquittal in February 1968 on the grounds of "insufficient legal instruction" to the jury. As a result of this trial, which began on December 20, 1969, Novak was once again convicted on one count and sentenced to nine years' imprisonment. However, the *Oberlandesgericht* once again concurred with the appeal by the defense and ordered still another trial in August 1971. The fourth trial was held in March 1972, and the jury adopted the same position as its predecessor in the first trial. Therefore "the stationmaster of death" was convicted on one count of "jamming the freight cars." He was sentenced, on April 13, 1972, to seven years in prison.[94]

Also of interest in connection with the destruction of Hungarian Jewry was the trial in Vienna in 1972 of Walter Dejaco and Fritz Karl Ertl, the SS officers and architects who designed and built the Auschwitz gas chambers and cremation furnaces. Although Dejaco was denounced to the Austrian authorities in 1961, he remained at liberty for ten years. Following a trial that began on January 18, 1972, both defendants were acquitted of murder and released from custody on March 10. The jury was of the opinion that they were acting under military orders and were ignorant of the use to which the death ovens would be put.[95]

Other Countries. Trials of interest to Hungarian Jewry were held in Poland, Czechoslovakia, and Israel. In Poland, the liquidation of Hungarian Jewry was a subject in the trial of Rudolf Franz Ferdinand Höss, the former Commandant of Auschwitz. He was condemned to death by a Warsaw tribunal on March 29, 1947, and executed in Auschwitz a few days later. In Czechoslovakia the subject was highlighted in the trial of Dieter Wisliceny; in Israel of Adolf Eichmann—the two leading members of the *Sonderkommando.* Wisliceny was first interrogated in Nuremberg, where he served as a prosecution witness. He was subsequently extradited to Czechoslovakia. Tried in Bratislava, he was convicted on February 27, 1948, for his role in the liquidation of the Jews of Slovakia, Greece, and Hungary. He was hanged in Bratislava on May 4.[96]

Eichmann, who was captured by Israeli agents in Argentina in May 1960, was tried in Jerusalem. After a sensational trial that unfolded the record of the Final Solution in its complexity, Eichmann was hanged in Ramla on May 31, 1962.[97]

Those Who Escaped

While many leading members of the various Nazi agencies directly or indirectly involved in the destruction of Hungarian Jewry were tried and punished, many others managed to escape prosecution. Among these were Kurt Becher, who emerged as a rich grain merchant largely with the aid of Rudolph Kasztner, who signed a sworn affidavit in his behalf on August 4, 1947 (see chapter 29), and Otto Winkelmann, the former Higher SS and Police Leader in Hungary.[98] Many other leading officials of the German Foreign Office, Gestapo, intelligence, and security agencies in Hungary were equally fortunate.[99]

Those tried for war crimes and crimes against humanity, especially in West Germany and Austria, represent but a fraction of the Nazis and SS men who had to various degrees been active in "solving" the Jewish question. The blame must be shared by the Allies and the governments of Germany and Austria, which eventually acquired jurisdiction over the prosecution of war crimes cases. While during the war the Allies refused to engage in any rescue operations and instead offered a "solemn resolution to insure that those responsible for the [crimes against the Jews] shall not escape retribution," after the war their overriding concern became the advancement of their newly defined national interests. The Western Allies were eager to develop the areas under their control along democratic, anti-Communist lines; the Soviets were resolved to establish their version of "people's democratic," "anti-imperialist" regimes. Preoccupied with political and ideological objectives, they soon reneged on their wartime commitments.

The Allies, eager to appease German and Austrian public opinion and to hasten political evolution along their desired objectives, became increasingly reluctant to initiate proceedings against the thousands of individuals who had been actively involved in the Final Solution program; they also became progressively more lenient toward those already convicted. As a result of amnesties and arbitrary actions on the part of the occupation authorities and later of the respective governments, many convicted Nazis had their sentences reduced or were actually freed without going to prison. While the attitude of the Allies did not of course indicate that they had condoned or acquiesced in the act of Jewish exterminations, it clearly denoted the triumph of expediency over morality and justice.

Notes

1. For some details on the liberation of the Jews of Budapest, see Lévai, *Fekete könyv*, pp. 257–60, and Ilona Benoschofsky, "The Position of Hungarian Jewry After the Liberation" in *HJS*, 3:237–60.

2. The term "Trianon Hungary" is used to denote the area constituting all of Hungary in November 1938 and again after the armistice of January 1945. The areas acquired from the former Little Entente countries in 1938–1941, which were returned after the war, are identified in this section as "reacquired territories" or "ceded areas."

3. For additional and somewhat differing data, see Lévai, *Fekete könyv*, pp. 313–16.

4. The only exceptions were the communities whose Jewish populations had been transferred to Strasshof. See chapter 21.

5. The sources do not explain the slight difference in the absolute number of Jews given for 1941 in tables 32.1 and 32.2.

6. *Zsidó Világkongresszus*, no. 10, p. 7.

7. *Ibid.*, p. 8.

8. According to one account, Hungary lost 40.1 percent of its national wealth during the war. This loss amounted to 21.9 billion *Pengős* (1930 rate)—five times the national income of 1938. Sándor Ausch, *1945–46 évi infláció és stabilizáció* (The Inflation and Stabilization of 1945–46) (Budapest: Kossuth, 1958), p. 63. In 1941–42, the official value

of the *Pengő* was approximately 20 cents. The black market price of the dollar, however, ranged from 11 to 13 *Pengős*. *Ibid.*, pp. 30–31.

9. He worked most closely with Romulus Pop, the new Minister of Minorities, and with Ionel Pop, the newly appointed High Commissioner for the Administration of Liberated Transylvania (*Înalt Comisar pentru administrarea Transilvaniei eliberate*). For further details, see chapter 28.

10. Marton worked especially closely with Wl. von Steiger and Charles Kolb, the IRC delegates in Bucharest. For his certificate of appointment, see Haifa University, Center of Historical Studies, File R4b21-A.M.E.1/29. See also Ernő Marton Files, Yad Vashem Archives JM/2625/1.

11. Marton's report of May 22, 1945. *Ibid.* See also chapter 28.

12. Until the adoption of the First Anti-Jewish Law in 1938, Frigyes Görög was also a bank director. After his immigration to the United States in 1948, he founded and for a long time headed the World Federation of Hungarian Jews. He died in New York in 1978 at 87 years of age. For his account, see interviews with him by Yehuda Bauer of March 14 and April 19, 1968, at Hebrew University of Jersualem, Institute of Contemporary Jewry, Oral History Division, no. (47)/15. See also chapter 29.

13. The meeting of June 22 was chaired by Marton and attended by Lajos Stöckler as the representative of the Jewish Community of Pest and the Central Bureau of Hungarian Jewry; Samu Kahan-Frankl, the head of the Orthodox community; Albert Geyer, the head of the Hungarian Zionist Association; Károly Wilhelm, as the representative of the Bucharest and Geneva offices of the AJDC; Sándor Offenbach, a Zionist leader; and Görög. The new Joint Committee consisted of André Biss, István Földes, Rafi Friedl, Geyer, Görög, Kahan-Frankl, Offenbach, Imre Reiner, Mihály Salamon, Stöckler, Siegfried Roth, and Wilhelm. Ernő Marton Files, Yad Vashem, JM/2625/1. See also Haifa University, Center for Historical Studies, File H4b17-A.M.E. 2/27.

14. The Jewish Community of Pest was represented by István Földes, the Orthodox by Imre Reiner, and the Zionists by Mihály Salamon, Siegfried Roth, Moshe Pil, and Gyula Zink. In addition there were the representatives of the provincial communities (Márton Stern, Alfred Züszmann, and Miklós Vida), of the rabbinical council (Ferenc Hevesi and Imre Benoschofsky), and of the labor servicemen (Dezső Simor). Lévai, *Fekete könyv*, pp. 263–64.

15. Most of these testimonies and personal narratives were translated into English under the auspices of the Documentation Department of the Jewish Agency for Palestine and are available in the Yad Vashem Archives under files no. 0–2, 0–3, 0–7, 0–11, 0–15, 0–33, 0–37, and 0–39, and in the YIVO archives under files 768–81.

16. By the end of 1945, the AJDC had distributed 9 million Swiss francs in Budapest alone. It maintained 32 children's hostels in Budapest and 6 in the provincial towns. It distributed food, medicines, and money in 210 communities. Lévai, *Fekete könyv*, p. 264.

17. February 6, 1946 memorandum from Karbach to Kubowitzki at Haifa University, Center for Historical Studies, File H4c13-A.M.E. 1/13.

18. Hungary was the last of the Axis satellites to sign an armistice agreement with the three major Allies. It was enacted on September 14, 1945 as Law no. V. For the text of the English and Russian originals and of the Hungarian translation, see *1945. évi országos törvénytár* (National Code of Laws for 1945) (Budapest, September 16, 1945), pp. 1–22.

19. The Provisional National Government was elected by the Provisional National Assembly (*Ideiglenes Nemzetgyülés*) on December 22, 1944, in Debrecen. The Provisional National Assembly, chaired by Dr. Béla Zsedényi, had 230 deputies representing the various anti-Nazi parties. The Provisional National Government was headed by General Béla Miklós and included two representatives each from the Communist, Smallholders, and Social Democratic parties. It also included General Gábor Faraghó and Count Géza

Teleki, the two emissaries that were sent by Horthy to Moscow to negotiate the armistice agreement in September 1944. The provisional government and assembly moved to Budapest in April 1945. Although a permanent government was established after the general elections of November 4, 1945, in which the Smallholders Party won 59.9 percent of the votes (245 of the 409 parliamentary seats), real power continued for some time to lie largely with the Soviet-dominated Allied Control Commission. Among the Smallholder deputies elected to Parliament were three Jews: Ödön Antl, Mihály Borsa, and Alfred Offner. Jews and politicians of Jewish background played an important role in the Social Democratic and Communist parties as well. Manó Buchinger, Pál Justus, Miklós Kertész, István Ries, Ferenc Szeder, and László Faragó were prominent among the Social Democrats while Mátyás Rákosi, Zoltán Vas, Ernő Gerő, and József Révay played a leading role among the Communists.

20. For the text see *Magyar Közlöny* (Hungarian Official Gazette), Budapest, no. 9, March 17, 1945. For a somewhat abridged version together with several related acts, see *Két év hatályos jogszabályai, 1945–1946* (The Valid Legal Provisions of Two Years, 1945–1946), ed. Ferenc Bacsó, et al. (Budapest, 1947), pp. 262–63.

21. For text see *Hatályos jogszabályok gyüjteménye, 1945–1958* (Collection of Legal Provisions in Effect, 1945–1958) (Budapest, 1960), pp. 34–35. For an evaluation of the postwar legislative enactments relating to the Jews, see Endre Déry, Endre Elbert, Endre Friedmann, and József Vági, *A fasizmus üldözötteit védő jogszabályok, 1945–1946* (Rules of Law Relating to the Victims of Fascism, 1945–1946) (Budapest : Az American Joint Distribution Committee Magyarországi Bizottsága, 1946), 179 pp.

22. After the liberation Samu Stern, the old-time leader of the Jewish Community of Pest and of Hungarian Jewry, had been compelled to resign his position, primarily by the Zionists who were highly critical of his role during the occupation. Several accounts allege that Stöckler, who originally acquired his postwar leadership position with the aid of the Zionists, became an instrumentality of the increasingly dominant Communist faction. See, for example, Eugene Duschinsky, "Hungary," in *The Jews in the Soviet Satellites* (Syracuse, N.Y.: Syracuse University Press, 1953), pp. 405, 414–15, 442–50.

23. The members of this committee were Stöckler (President), representing the Jewish Community of Pest; Samu Csobádi, the head of the Jewish Community of Buda; Albert Geyer, the president of the Hungarian Zionist Association; Robert Papp, the honorary president of the Jewish community of Szeged; and Samu Szemere, the former head of the Jewish Teacher-Training Institute. Lévai, *Fekete könyv*, pp. 265–66.

24. For a list of Jewish congregations active in 1947, see *Zsidó Világkongresszus*, no. 8–9 (April 1, 1948):17–19.

25. Of the 55 offices, however, only 18 were operational at the end of 1946. At that time, the following communal institutions were in operation in the provinces: 10 shelters, 24 cultural homes, 11 homes for the aged, 7 ritual baths, 4 hospitals, and 3 daycare centers. These were mostly concentrated in the larger Jewish communities such as Debrecen, Miskolc, Pécs, and Szeged. *Ibid.*, p. 15.

26. The 258 provincial Jewish communities had 249 synagogues in 1946. Of these, 125 were unusable because of the damages suffered during the German occupation. The furnishings, equipment, and ritual objects were totally destroyed in 184 synagogues and 50 percent destroyed in 65. *Ibid.*

27. At the beginning of 1947, the Neolog and Status Quo communities had 80 rabbis and deputy rabbis. Of these, 44 served in Budapest. The Orthodox congregations were served by 27 rabbis and 37 assistant rabbis, of whom 17 were in Budapest. *Ibid.*

28. Of the many synagogues of the congregations of Budapest, 15 were damaged. With the exception of two which had been ruined, they were rebuilt by the end of 1946. Early in 1947, 29 of the 35 Orthodox houses of worship were once again in operation.

For data on the educational institutions in operation in Budapest during the 1946–47 and 1947–48 school years, see *ibid.*, pp. 16–17. See also Duschinsky, "Hungary," pp. 398–99, 412–15.

29. The first appeal was submitted on March 5, 1945. This was followed by several others in the course of the year. For extracts, see Lévai, *Fekete könyv*, pp. 266–70.

30. For details on and references to these statutes and legislative enactments, see Déry, et al., *A fasizmus üldözötteit védő jogszabályok.*

31. Law XXV of 1946 cited above referred to a fund to be administered by a three-man committee, but it was reportedly never enacted.

32. Déry, *et al., A fasizmus üldözötteit védő jogszabályok*, pp. 13–14. See also Duschinsky, "Hungary," pp. 404–5.

33. The Peace Treaty was enacted on July 25, 1947, as Law XVIII. For the English, Russian, and Hungarian texts, see "A Párisban 1947. évi február hó 10. napján kelt békeszerződés becikkejezése tárgyában" (Concerning the Enactment of the Paris Peace Treaty of February 10, 1947) in *Országos törvénytár, 1944–1947* (National Code of Laws, 1944–1947) (Budapest: Athenaeum Nyomda, 1948), pp. 167–237.

34. Duschinsky, "Hungary," p. 404.

35. Lévai, *Fekete könyv*, p. 265.

36. *Szabad Nép* (Free People), Budapest, March 25, 1945, as quoted by Duschinsky, "Hungary," pp. 404 and 410. See also extracts from his interview for the *Uj Élet* (New Life) of November 22, 1945, in *ibid.*, pp. 410–11. Darvas's statement attracted the attention of Western correspondents. See, for example, John MacCormac, "Anti-Semitism Rife in Central Europe." *The New York Times*, September 9, 1945.

In an election speech on August 26, 1945, Darvas reiterated the same thesis. Speaking in the Budapest Municipal Theater, he declared that "a certain group should not demand preferential treatment on the ground of racial prerogatives." János Kovács, "Neo-Antisemitism in Hungary." *Jewish Social Studies*, 8, no. 3 (July 1946):159.

37. For details on Veres's allegedly anti-Semitic position, see Duschinsky, "Hungary," pp. 403, 414, 429, 451. For further details, see Asher Cohen, "Giz'anut v'antishemiut basmol hapopulisti beHungaria. Hasofer vehamedinai Péter Veres" (Racism and Anti-Semitism in the Populist Left in Hungary. The Writer and Politician Péter Veres) in *Dapim lecheker tekufat hashoa* (Studies on the Holocaust Period) (Tel Aviv: Kakibbutz Hameuchad, 1978), 1:176–88. See also Kovács, "Neo-Antisemitism in Hungary," p. 159.

38. Kovács, "Neo-Antisemitism in Hungary," pp. 158, 160. For further details on anti-Semitic incidents during the immediate postwar period and on the domestic and foreign reactions to them, see Duschinsky, "Hungary," pp. 418–31. See also *European Jewry Ten Years After the War* (New York: Institute of Jewish Affairs of the World Jewish Congress, 1956), pp. 60–81.

39. See, for example, E. R. Kutas, "Judaism, Zionism and Anti-Semitism in Hungary." *Journal of Central European Affairs*, 8, no. 4 (January 1949):377–89.

40. By far the most seminal among these authors was István Bibó, who was to emerge as one of the heroes of the Hungarian Revolution in 1956. See his "Zsidókérdés Magyarországon 1944 után" (Jewish Question in Hungary After 1944) in *Válasz* (Response), 8 (October–November 1948):778–877. The long essay, which discusses the responsibility of the Hungarians for the Holocaust, the historical and philosophical-psychological bases of anti-Semitism, the issues of assimilation and Jewish national consciousness, and the postwar causes of anti-Semitism, is reproduced in *Harmadik út* (The Third Road), Zoltán Szabó, ed. (London: Magyar Könyves Céh, 1960), pp. 227–354. The essay elicited considerable interest and controversy. See for example, Ferenc Kőrösy, "Válasz Bibó István: A zsidókérdés Magyarországon 1944 után c. tanulmányára" (Response to István Bibó's Study on the Jewish Question in Hungary After 1944) in *Huszadik Század* (Twentieth Century), Budapest, 36, no. 6 (December 1948):454–56, and Sebestyén

Molnár, "Észrevételek Bibó István tanulmányához" (Observations Regarding István Bibó's Study," *ibid.*, 37, no. 1 (February–March 1949):40–47. While Kőrösy agrees that the Jews were used as scapegoats after the war, Molnár aims to absolve the Hungarian people of their collective responsibility for the crimes committed against the Jews.

41. Duschinsky, "Hungary," p. 414, as quoted in English translation from *Uj Élet* (New Life), Budapest, June 5, 1946.

42. Direct German-Israeli talks on reparation followed shortly after Chancellor Konrad Adenauer addressed the *Bundestag* on September 27, 1951. The Chancellor emphasized that the Bonn government was not only aware of the crimes perpetrated against the Jews, but also would do everything in its power to make amends. The Luxemburg Treaty, covering various agreements between the Federal Republic of Germany and Israel, was signed on September 10, 1952. For details on the background and implementation of the treaty, see Nicholas Balabkins, *West German Reparations to Israel* (New Brunswick, N.J.: Rutgers University Press, 1971), 384 pp.

43. Of the DM 85.3 billion, DM 51.910 billion were paid from the Federal Treasury. The disbursements were as follows: DM 70 billion were distributed under the Federal Indemnification Law *(Bundesentschädigungsgesetz*—BEG); DM 4.250 billion under the Federal Restitution Law *(Bundesrückerstattungsgesetz*—BRÜG); DM 3.450 billion under the agreement with Israel; DM 1.0 billion under agreement with 12 different states; and DM 6.6 billion for other services. Rolf Vogel, "Das Gesetzwerk der Widergutmachung" (The Legal Framework for Reparations). *Aufbau* (Reconstruction), New York, May 18, 1979, p. 14. See also issue of December 14, 1979, p. 23.

The value of the DM ranged from $1 = DM 4.20 in the 1950s, when the Germans started reparation payments, to $1 = DM 1.80 in 1979. For further details on West German restitution, see Raul Hilberg, *The Destruction of the European Jews* (Chicago: Quadrangle, 1961), pp. 738–59. For other references consult *Guide to Jewish History Under Nazi Impact,* eds. Jacob Robinson and Philip Friedman. (New York: YIVO-Institute for Jewish Research, 1960), pp. 283–94.

44. There are no statistical data on the value of restitution and indemnification received by Hungarian Jews either from the West Germans or the Hungarians.

45. For some details on the spoliation of Jewish property during the German occupation and the transfer of a trainload of valuables to the West during the *Nyilas* era under the command of Árpád Toldy, the former Prefect of Székesfehérvár, and László Avar, the former Mayor of Zenta, see chapter 16. In the French zone in Austria, 36 crates laden with gold or gold objects and 12 kilograms of diamonds were found soon after the end of hostilities. Hervé Alphand, then the head of the Economics Section of the French Ministry of Foreign Affairs, and Miklós Nyárády, the Hungarian Minister of Finance, agreed on the return of the assets (consisting primarily of jewelry, precious metals, and works of art made of precious metals) on the condition that they be returned to their original Hungarian Jewish owners "if ascertainable." Reportedly, the Hungarian government held that none of the former owners could be identified and transferred the value of the assets to the Jewish Indemnification Fund, which was never activated.

In the American zone of occupation, jurisdiction over captured loot was exercised by Major Felix T. Simpson, the head of the Reparation and Restitution Branch. One of the complications regarding the return of the valuables confiscated from Hungarian Jews was that the Russians claimed that they belonged to them, inasmuch as the valuables had been taken along by German military units, and thus became part of their war booty. The American Military Government returned a considerable part of the identified assets, including machinery, equipment, radium, and works of art, to Hungary. However, very little, if any, of these were ever used for the benefit of individual victims of Nazism. Personal communication by Andrew Freeman. For further details on the assets taken to the American and French zones of occupation, see "Jelentés a francia zónában zárlat alatt levő zsidó vagyon történetéről" (Report on the History of the Jewish Wealth Sequestered in the French Zone) and "Jelentés az amerikai zonában zárlat alatt levő zsidó vagyon ügyében folytatott tárgyalásokról" (Report on the Negotiations Relating to the Jewish Wealth Sequestered in the American Zone) at Haifa University, Center for Historical Studies, File H3h25-A.M.E.1/31.

46. On April 30, 1945, van Harten informed Dr. Chaim Pozner, the co-director of the Palestine Office in Geneva, that much of the jewelry had originally belonged to Hungarian Jews. For documents relating to the empowerment of van Harten by Kemény and of van Harten's correspondence with Pozner, see Pazner Files, Yad Vashem Archives.

47. "21/1971. (V.25) Korm. számu rendelet egyes kártalanitási igényeknek a Nácizmus Magyarországi Üldözöttei Országos Érdekvédelmi Szervezete utján történő rendezéséről" (Government Decree No. 21/1971 [V.25] Concerning the Regulation of Certain Indemnification Claims by the National Organization for the Protection of the Interests of Nazi Persecutees in Hungary). *Hatályos jogszabályok gyüjteménye 1945–1972* (Collection of Statutory Provisions in Effect, 1945–1972) (Budapest: Közgazdasági és Jogi Könyvkiadó, 1974), p. 639.

48. Eligible were claimants (or heirs) who resided in Hungary on January 1, 1971.

49. For text see *Bundesgesetzblatt* (Federal Gazette), Bonn, 1, 1956:562 ff.

50. The law included a number of restrictions. For example, only injuries to health that resulted in the inability (or decreased ability) of the claimants to make a living were to be compensated for. This restriction, as well as some others, was remedied by subsequent legislation.

51. Kállay signed a six-page sworn affidavit before Franz Josef Hoffmann, the German Consul General in New York on March 6, 1956. In response to a request by the United Restitution Organization, the World Federation of Hungarian Jews, a New York-based organization, prepared a position paper that was submitted to the West German authorities, titled *Gutachten des Weltverbandes der Ungarischen Juden in der Frage ob und inwieweit die Verfolgungsmassnahmen gegen die Juden in Ungarn in den Jahren 1938–1944 von deutscher Seite veranlasst wurden* (Expert Opinion of the World Federation of Hungarian Jews on the Question Whether and to What Extent the Persecution Measures Against the Jews in Hungary in 1938–1944 Were Brought About by the Germans) (New York, 1957), 63 pp., mimeographed. See also *Judenverfolgung in Ungarn* (Persecution of Jews in Hungary) (Frankfurt am Main: United Restitution Organization, 1959), 235 pp.; *Gutachten des Institutes für Staats- und Rechtswissenschaften der Ungarischen Akademie der Wissenschaften über die Völkerrechtliche Lage Ungarns nach dem 19. März 1944* (Expert Opinions of the Institute of Political Science and Law of the Hungarian Academy of Sciences Concerning the International Legal Status of Hungary After March 19, 1944), comp. Géza Herczegh (Budapest: Komitee der Verfolgten des Nazismus in Ungarn, 1965), 52 pp., mimeographed; and Géza Herczegh, "Einige Fragen des Völkerrechts hinsichtlich der Entschädigung der Verfolgten des Nazismus in Ungarn" (A Few International Legal Questions Concerning the Indemnification of Nazi Persecutees in Hungary). *Acta Juridica Academiae Scientiarum Hungaricae*, Budapest, 9, no. 3–4 (1967):307–30.

52. *Bundesgesetzblatt*, 1(1965):1315.

53. Compensation payments for slave labor were determined as a result of a test case initiated in the late 1950s by Norbert Wollheim, a New York accountant, who had worked as a slave laborer for I.G. Farben while interned at Buna (Auschwitz) during the war. For details see Benjamin B. Ferencz, *Less Than Slaves: Jewish Forced Labor and the Quest for Compensation* (Cambridge: Harvard University Press, 1979), 249 pp.

54. The decree went into effect on February 5, 1945. It was amended by Decree no. 1.440/1945.M.E. of April 27, 1945, Decree no. 5.900/1945.M.E. of August 1, 1945, and Decree no. 6.750/1945.M.E. of August 16, 1945. These government decrees were formally enacted into law by the Provisional National Assembly on September 14, 1945, as

Law no. VII of 1945. For text see "1945. évi VII. törvénycikk a népbiráskodás tárgyában kibocsátott kormányrendeletek törvényerőre emeléséről" (Law no. VII of 1945 Concerning the Enactment Into Law of the Government Decrees Relating to the People's Jurisdiction). *1945. évi országos törvénytár* (National Code of Laws for 1945) (Budapest: Athenaeum, 1945), pp. 33–52.

55. These were the Democratic Bourgeois Party (*Demokratikus Polgári Párt*), the Independent Smallholders' Party (*Független Kisgazdapárt*), the Hungarian Communist Party (*Magyar Kommunistapárt*), the National Peasant Party (*Nemzeti Parasztpárt*), and the Social Democratic Party (*Szocialdemokrata Párt*). The representatives of the National Trade Union Council (*Országos Szakszervezeti Tanács*) were subsequently added (Decree no. 1.440/1945.M.E. of April 27, 1945). In 1947, the Democratic Bourgeois Party withdrew its representatives from the tribunals.

56. After 1948, the president of the National Council of People's Tribunals was Dr. Béla Bojta. The appellate councils were headed by one of the party-nominated judges appointed by the Minister of Justice. Once appointed, the appellate judges were no longer subject to recall by the parties.

57. For instances of corruption and examples of rightist judges, see Jenő Lévai, "The War Crimes Trials Relating to Hungary" in *HJS*, 2:258–60.

58. In Budapest, the first such trial began on January 28, 1945, under the chairmanship of Dr. Ákos Major. The two labor service guards, Péter Rotyis and Sándor Szivós, were hanged on February 4—nine days before the Buda part of the capital was liberated. *Ibid.*, pp. 254–55.

59. The listed persons were all convicted and executed. For a succinct review of their activities and for additional information on other related trials, see Lévai, *Fekete könyv*, pp. 304–6.

60. References to trials involving labor service officers and guards, including that concerning Lieutenant-Colonel Lipót (Metzl) Muray, "the hangman of Nagykáta," are given in chapter 10.

61. *HJS*, 2:267–68.

62. The trial date was set by the People's Tribunal of Budapest on August 3 (NB 1948/1945/2); the accused were Károly Beregfy, László Budinszky, Sándor Csia, Vilmos Hellebronth, Béla Jurcsek, Ferenc Kassai-Schallmayer, Gábor Kemény, Emil Kovarcz, Ferenc Rajniss, Lajos Reményi-Schneller, Ferenc Szálasi, Jenő Szőllősi, and Gábor Vajna. Elek Karsai, *Itél a nép* (The People Judge) (Budapest: Kossuth, 1977), p. 14.

63. The Hungarians demanded the arrest and extradition of 483 Hungarian and 38 German war criminals. The Hungarian war criminals were rounded up and first interrogated by a team headed by Martin Himler, a Hungarian-American who headed the Hungarian Section of the Office of Strategic Services in Salzburg, Austria. Eventually 390 Hungarian war criminals were returned to Hungary in October 1945 under the command of Lieutenant George Granville, an American Air Force officer of Hungarian background. Among these were practically all the leading figures of the Sztójay and Szálasi governments. These were handed over to Major-General Gábor Péter, the head of the Political Police (*Politikai Rendészeti Osztály*). The Americans rejected the extradition of the Germans, arguing that the "charges against . . . the alleged war criminals were found insufficient and not of a war crimes nature." *HJS*, 2:263–64, 291–93. For Himler's account and excerpts from the interrogations, see his *Igy néztek ki a magyar nemzet sírásói* (This Is What the Gravediggers of the Hungarian Nation Looked Like) (New York: St. Marks Printing, 1958), 196 pp. For a psychological portrayal of the major Hungarian war criminals based on interviews conducted in prison, see István Kelemen, *Intervjúk a rács mögött. Beszélgetés a háborús főbűnösökkel* (Interviews Behind Bars. Discussion with the Major War Criminals) (Budapest: Müller Károly, 1946), 188 pp., and Rezső Szirmai, *Fasiszta lelkek. Pszichoanalitikus beszélgetések a háborús főbűnösökkel a börtönben* (Fascist Souls.

Psychoanalytical Interviews in the Prison with the Major War Criminals) (Budapest: Faust, 1946), 299 pp. For information on Hungarians accused of war crimes living in the West, see *Criminals at Large*, eds. István Pintér and László Szabó. (Budapest: Pannonia, 1961), pp. 298–314.

64. The trial was held under the chairmanship of Ákos Major. For further details, see *A Bárdossy per. A vád, a vallomások és az itélet* (The Bárdossy Trial. The Indictment, the Testimonies and the Verdict) eds. Ferenc Ábrahám and Endre Kussinszky. (Budapest: Hiradó Könyvtár, 1945), 64 pp., and Karsai, *Itél a nép*, pp. 17–71.

65. The trial was held under the chairmanship of Dr. Károly Nagy. For details, including excerpts from the testimonies, see *Az Imrédy per. A vád, a vallomások és az itélet* (The Imrédy Trial. The Indictment, the Testimonies, and the Verdict) eds. Ferenc Ábrahám and Endre Kussinszky. (Budapest: Hiradó Könyvtár, 1945), 127 pp., Karsai, *Itél a nép*, pp. 72–119, and YIVO Archives, File 779.

66. See Karsai, *Itél a nép*, pp. 120–39, and YIVO Archives, File 779.

67. For excerpts from the transcript see *Die Hauptverhandlung gegen das "Deportations-trio" Endre-Jaross-Baky vor dem ungarischen Volksgerichtshof* (The Trial Proceeding Against the Endre-Jaross-Baky "Deportation Trio" Before the Hungarian People's Tribunal), 249 pp., manuscript. YIVO Archives File 778. See also Karsai, *Itél a nép*, pp. 185–215.

68. For excerpts from the trial proceedings, see *Ladislas Budinszky, the "Lord Privy Seal" of Szálasi, Faces the People's Judges*, 43 and 61 pp., typescript, YIVO Archives, Files 777, 779, and *Count Fidél Pálffy, Szálasi's Minister of Agriculture, Before the Hungarian People's Court*, 82 pp. typescript, *ibid.*, File 778.

69. *A Szálasi per. Szálasi, Szőllősi, Csia, Gera, Vajna, Beregfy, Kemény bűnügyének főtárgya-lása és az itélet* (The Szálasi Trial. The Main Trial and the Verdict in the Criminal Case Against Szálasi, Szőllősi, Csia, Gera, Vajna, Beregfy, and Kemény), eds. Ferenc Ábrahám and Endre Kussinszky. (Budapest: Hiradó Könyvtar, 1946), 192 pp. See also Karsai, *Itél a nép*, pp. 216–74.

70. Béla Jurcsek, Sztójay's Minister of Agriculture and one of Veesenmayer's closest confidants, died while in American custody in the U.S. Zone of Germany in the summer of 1945. Emil Szakváry, a leading official in the Ministry of Industry, who was indicted with Sztójay's group, was tried separately at a later date because of illness. *HJS*, 2:273, and Karsai, *Itél a nép*, p. 171.

71. For excerpts from the testimonies, see Karsai, *Itél a nép*, pp. 140–84.

72. Lévai, "The War Crimes Trials," *HJS*, 2:275–76.

73. *Ibid.*, p. 277.

74. *Ibid.*, p. 278.

75. NOT was disbanded under Decree no. 73/1950.M.T. of March 11, 1950. The people's prosecution office was discontinued under Decree no. 21.400/1950 of the Ministry of Justice. *Ibid.*, pp. 278, 294.

76. For details on the trial see József Sólyom *and* László Szabó, *A zuglói nyilasper* (The Trial of the Zugló Nyilas) (Budapest: Kossuth, 1967), 384 pp. See also chapter 26 and Lévai, "The War Crimes Trials," in *HJS*, 3:251–57.

77. For details, see *ibid.*, pp. 257–62.

78. *Ibid.*, pp. 262–63. See also Oszkár Zsadányi, "Százötvenszeres nyilasgyilkos a Fővá-rosi Biróság elött" (*Nyilas* Murderer One Hundred Fifty Times Over Before the Capital's Tribunal). *Uj Élet* (New Life), Budapest, 25, July 15, 1970, p. 1.

79. *Monitorul Oficial* (Official Gazette), Bucharest, Part I, April 24, 1945, pp. 3362–64.

80. The accused were members of the Hungarian armed forces as well as Transylvanian Hungarians. Many of them were tried *in absentia*. See Tribunalul Poporului, Cluj. *Completul de judecată Dosar Nr. 1/1946. Hotărârea Nr. 1. Şedinţa publică din 13 Martie 1946.* (Judgment Panel. File no. 1/1946. Decision no. 1. Public Session of March 13, 1946), 57 pp. typescript. (Copy of the official judgment is in possession of this author.)

81. The court included Dr. Nerva Hăgăduş, an assessor, and seven people's judges: Pavel Bojan, Augustin Mesesan, and Mihaiu Covaciu representing the Ploughmen's Front (*Frontul Plugarilor*); Ştefan Belovai, representing the Communist Party (*Partidul Comunist Român*); Gheorghe Dan, representing the General Confederation of Labor (*Confederaţia Generală a Muncii*); Alexandru Gligorin, representing the Social Democratic Party (*Partidul Social Democrat*); and Victor Taflan, representing the National Liberal Party (*Partidul Naţional Liberal*).

82. *Tribunalul Poporului, Cluj.* (A copy of the 177-page judgment of May 22, 1946, is in the possession of this author.) See also Lévai, "The War Crimes Trials," *HJS*, 2:283–85.

83. Artur Geyer, "Az 1942 évi ujvidéki 'razzia' " (The Ujvidék 'Raid' of 1942) in *Uj Élet naptár 1959* (New Life Calendar, 1959) (Budapest: A Magyar Izraeliták Országos Képviselete, 1959), pp. 50–51. For further information on these criminals, their crimes and trials, consult: Demokratska Federativna Yugoslaviya, *Saopštenya Br. 7–33 o zlocinima okupatora i njihovih pomagača* (Reports No. 7–33. The Atrocities Committed by the Occupants and Their Collaborators) (Belgrade: Drzavna Shtampariya, 1945), pp. 242–301; Pokrajinska Komisija za utvrdjivanje zločina okupatora i njihovih pomagača u Vojvodini, *Saopštenja o. zlocinima okupatora i njihovih pomagača u Vojvodini od 1941–1944* (Reports on the Crimes of the Enemy Occupation Forces and Their Collaborators in Vojvodina, 1941–1944) (Novi Sad, 1946), 2 vols. (vol. 1: Bačka i Baranja, 355 pp.; vol. 2: Srem, 338 pp.); Zdenko Lowenthal, *Zločini fašističkih okupatora i njihovih pomagača protiv Jevreja u Jugoslaviji* (The Crimes of the Fascist Occupants and Their Collaborators Against the Jews in Yugoslavia) (Belgrade: Izdanje Saveza Jevrejskih Opština Jugoslavije, 1952), 245 pp. See also Lévai, "The War Crimes Trials," *HJS*, 2:288–89.

84. For a succinct evaluation of these trials, see Hilberg, *The Destruction of the European Jews*, pp. 684–715. For references to all aspects of all war crimes trials and related document collections, including those published under the IMT, NMT, and NCA series, consult *Guide to Jewish History Under Nazi Impact*, pp. 175–210.

85. The recommendation was due at least partially to a desire to improve the psychological climate in West Germany, to assist Chancellor Konrad Adenauer in his plans for the eventual adherence of his country to the NATO pact. For the composition of the clemency board, see Hilberg, *The Destruction of the European Jews*, p. 696.

Veesenmayer died in Darmstadt on December 24, 1977. For further details on his trial and postwar life in West Germany, see *NMT*, 14:625–31, 646–60, 812–17, 858–59, and *Criminals at Large*, pp. 22–70. See also his affidavit signed in Nuremberg, NG-1628. For the transcript of Veesenmayer's trial, including his testimony and the testimonies of Miklós Horthy, Rudolph Kasztner, Ernst Kienast, and Otto Winkelmann, see *Ministries Case* (Court 4, Case 11), transcript pp. 2702–50, 3617–59, 7143–58, 13062–460, and 26156–189.

86. For references to these and other trials in which France was involved consult *Guide to Jewish History Under Nazi Impact*, pp. 190–210.

87. *News From the German Embassy*, Washington, 9, no. 4 (March 11, 1965):2. See also *Guide to Jewish History Under Nazi Impact*, pp. 209–10.

88. *News From the German Embassy*, p. 3. Bormann is believed to have been killed by a Russian shell on leaving Hitler's bunker on April 30, 1945. Müller, who reportedly disappeared from the bunker the day before, is widely believed to have been recruited by Soviet security forces. Dr. Schumann was living in the mid 1960s in Ghana, which refused to extradite him. Dr. Mengele eventually found refuge in Paraguay. For further details on Dr. Mengele see chapter 22.

89. *Schwurgericht*, Frankfurt-am-Main, File 4 Ks 1/63. See also "Lebenslanges Zuchthaus für Krumey" (Life Imprisonment for Krumey) in *Frankfurter Allgemeine Zeitung* (General Newspaper of Frankfurt), August 30, 1969, p. 7.

90. Lévai, "The War Crimes Trials," *HJS*, 3:278–80. See also Krumey's affidavit of

September 30, 1947, and text of his interrogation by Rudolph L. Pins on August 15, 1947. Both documents and the *Bundesgerichtshof* decision are in possession of this author.

91. Bernd Naumann, *Auschwitz. A Report on the Proceedings Against Robert Karl Ludwig Mulka and Others Before the Court at Frankfurt* (New York: Praeger, 1966), 433 pp. See also Lévai, cited above, pp. 274–78.

92. *Schwurgericht*, Essen, Criminal Case Files 29 Ks 1/60 and 29a Ks 4/67. See also *Time*, November 6, 1972, and Lévai, "War Crimes Trials," pp. 280–81.

93. *Schwurgericht*, Düsseldorf, Criminal Case File 8 Ks 1/71. See also *Time* and Lévai, "War Crimes Trials," pp. 283–85. The information concerning the indefinite postponement of Ganzenmüller's trial was communicated to this author in August 1979 by the *Zentrale Stelle der Landesjustizverwaltungen* (Center for the State Administration of Justice) of Ludwigsburg.

94. Lévai, "War Crimes Trials," pp. 264–66.

95. *Ibid.*, pp. 266–67. See also *The New York Times*, March 11, 1972.

96. For Wisliceny's affidavit relating to the Final Solution program, see *NCA*, 8:606–21. For extracts from this affidavit emphasizing the Eichmann-*Sonderkommando*'s role in Hungary, see *RLB*, Doc. 440. See also Wisliceny's affidavit concerning Veesenmayer's activities (NG-1823). For his Nuremberg testimony relating to Hungary, see *IMT*, 4:355–73.

97. For references to all aspects of Eichmann's activities and to his pursuit, capture, and trial, see Randolph L. Braham, *The Eichmann Case: A Source Book* (New York: World Federation of Hungarian Jews, 1969), 186 pp.

98. *Criminals at Large*, pp. 71–116, 150–64. Winkelmann died at Bordesholm, West Germany, on September 24, 1977. For his Nuremberg affidavit see NO-4139. For Becher's affidavit in connection with the Jewish question in Hungary see NG-2972, which is reproduced in *RLB* as Doc. 438.

99. For information on many of these officials, including Wilhelm Höttl, Kurt Krumholz, Erhard Olbrich, Karl Werkmeister, Gerhart Feine, Horst Grell, Kurt Brunhoff, and Otto Skorzeny, see *Criminals at Large*. For information on Alfred Trenker, the former head of the security police in Budapest, see *Menóra*, Toronto, June 28, 1969. See also *The Murderers Among Us. The Wiesenthal Memoirs*, ed. Joseph Wechsberg (New York: McGraw-Hill, 1967), 340 pp.

APPENDIX ONE

Administration of the Labor Service System in the Ministry of Defense: 1944

All Labor Service system matters were handled by the following sections or divisions.

Section 41. *Competence:* The administration of the military (public, auxiliary, and special) labor service units as well as of all labor services under military command; the assurance of close contact with related ministries. *Head:* Col. Sándor Vályi.

Division XI. *Head:* Maj.-Gen. Ernő Horny, who also doubled as the head of KMOF.

Section 42. *Competence:* The organization, training, and specialization of the military (public, auxiliary, and special) labor service units. *Head:* Col. Gusztáv Hibbey.

Section 43. *Competence:* The deployment of the military (public, auxiliary, and special) labor service units; personal matters and complaints. *Head:* Col. Egon Gátföldy.

Section 44. *Competence:* The standardization, registration, acquisition, handling, and issuance of tools; the determination of needs and the keeping of records on national stockpiles; the preparation of the budget relating to labor service. *Head:* Col. János Heinrich.

Division XII. *Head:* Col. Lajos Fábián, who also doubled as the National Superintendent of Labor Service for National Defense (*Honvédelmi Munkaszolgálat Országos Felügyelője*).

Section 45. *Competence:* The allocation of mass labor over and above the labor force provided by virtue of national mobilization; the organization and allocation of mass labor for the clearing or rehabilitation of the damage or destruction caused by penetrating enemy aircraft; the supervision of the economic utilization, housing, treatment, and discipline of the labor force employed under military command; the maintenance of labor discipline. *Head:* Col. Ernő Ács.

Section 46. *Competence:* Matters relating to labor service for national defense by women; the supervision of the economic use, placement, treatment, and labor discipline of the female labor force employed; the maintenance of labor discipline. *Head:* Col. Dénes Marton, who also doubled as the National Superintendent of the Labor Service for Women (*A Női Munkaszolgálat Országos Felügyelője*); the general and physical education of youth for national defense. *National commander:* Gen. Alajos Béldy.

SOURCE: *FAA*, 2:838–39.

APPENDIX TWO

Labor Service Companies Authorized for Transfer to the Germans

By Virtue of Decree No. 975/M. 42-1944 of the Hungarian Minister of Defense Dated October 26, 1944.

Labor Service Company	Deployment in October 1944	Date of Transfer
101/605	Manfréd Weiss Works, Csepel	Oct. 27–Nov. 2
104/7	Polgári Brewery of Kőbánya, Budapest	Oct. 27–Nov. 2
108/5	Dréher Brewery, Budapest	Oct. 27–Nov. 2
109/35	Repair Works of Nagybátony Újlak, Budapest	Oct. 27–Nov. 2
701/306	Industrial Plants of Pestszentlőrinc	Oct. 27–Nov. 2
109/20	Air Defense Works, Budapest	Oct. 26–Nov. 3
109/21	Army Construction, Budapest	Oct. 28–Nov. 3
110/63	Törökbálint	Oct. 28–Nov. 3
701/17	"Igy. ép. vez.," Budapest	Oct. 28–Nov. 3
701/302	United Incandescent Works, Újpest	Oct. 28–Nov. 3
1/2 101/67	Rákos Railyards, Budapest	Oct. 29–Nov. 4
1/2 101/210	Manfréd Weiss Works, Csepel	Oct. 29–Nov. 4
1/2 101/342	Machine-Building Company, Kapuvár	Oct. 29–Nov. 4
1/2 101/351	Dréher Brewery, Budapest	Oct. 29–Nov. 4
1/2 101/353	Domestic Worsted Mills, Budapest	Oct. 29–Nov. 4
1/2 101/209	Manfréd Weiss Works, Csepel	Oct. 29–Nov. 4
1/2 102/204	Manfréd Weiss Works, Csepel	Oct. 29–Nov. 4
102/14	Motor Vehicle Works, Mátyásföld	Oct. 29–Nov. 4
107/300	4/b Reiter Ferenc Street	Oct. 29–Nov. 4
107/304	"Ferenc József gy. lkt."	Oct. 29–Nov. 4
102/205	Polgári Brewery, Budapest	Oct. 29–Nov. 4
101/208	Manfréd Weiss Works, Csepel	Oct. 29–Nov. 2
1/2 108/304	Sziklaközpont	Oct. 29–Nov. 4
1/2 108/304	Hungarian Cotton Works, Budapest	Oct. 29–Nov. 4
1/2 107/23	Parquet and Furniture Plant, Budapest	Oct. 29–Nov. 4
1/2 105/303	Manfréd Weiss Works, Csepel	Oct. 29–Nov. 4
1/2 101/354	Dréher Brewery, Budapest	Oct. 30–Nov. 5
102/212	Gas Works, Budapest	Oct. 30–Nov. 5
102/18	Free Port of Csepel	Oct. 30–Nov. 5
105/501	Szentkirályszabadja (Bor Company)	Oct. 30–Nov. 6
105/508	" "	Oct. 30–Nov. 6
105/503	" "	Oct. 30–Nov. 6
105/504	" "	Oct. 30–Nov. 6
105/505	" "	Oct. 30–Nov. 6
105/506	" "	Oct. 30–Nov. 6

Labor Service

Company	Deployment in October 1944	Date of Transfer
1/2 110/65	Budakalász (Bor Company)	Oct. 31–Nov. 6
110/69	" "	Oct. 31–Nov. 6
101/35	" "	Oct. 31–Nov. 6
VI./5	" "	Oct. 31–Nov. 6
1/2 701/305	Szilárd J. "Bérfürészelő," Budapest	Oct. 31–Nov. 6
1/2 108/62	Csillebérc, Budapest	Oct. 31–Nov. 6
102/303	Gánt Aluminum Mines	Nov. 1–Nov. 6
1/2 101/342	Igmándi Erőd, Komárom	Nov. 4–Nov. 6
1/2 101/358	M.Á.V.A.G., Győr	Nov. 4–Nov. 6
1/2 101/365	M.A.O.R.T., Szőny	Nov. 4–Nov. 6
1/2 101/356	M.A.O.R.T., Szőny	Nov. 4–Nov. 6
1/2 104/303	Hungarian Car and Machine Works, Győr	Nov. 5–Nov. 6
1/2 101/357	Nyergesújfalui Wiscosa, Inc.	Nov. 2–Nov. 6
103/301	Szombathely	Nov. 1–Nov. 6
102/301	Győr	Nov. 5–Nov. 6
104/302	Péti Nitrogen Works	Nov. 1–Nov. 7
1/2 101/353	" " "	Nov. 1–Nov. 7
1/2 105/304	" " "	Nov. 1–Nov. 7
1/2 701/305	" " "	Nov. 1–Nov. 7
103/302	Pusztaszabolcs	Nov. 1–Nov. 7
1/2 101/356	Újdörögd	Nov. 1–Nov. 7
1/2 101/357	"	Nov. 1–Nov. 7
104/2	Artillery Camp, Hajmáskér	Nov. 1–Nov. 7
701/15	Lőrinci Ganz and Company	Nov. 1–Nov. 11
109/36	M.A.V.A.G., Hatvan	Nov. 1–Nov. 11
107/321	Seventh District, Hatvan	Nov. 1–Nov. 11
107/322	" "	Nov. 1–Nov. 11
108/1	" "	Nov. 3–Nov. 17
105/35	" "	Nov. 3–Nov. 17
101/310	Dunaszekcső	Nov. 3–Nov. 17
110/27	"	Nov. 3–Nov. 17
Company of Jászberény	"	Nov. 1–Nov. 7
105/507	Szentkirályszabadja	Nov. 3–Nov. 11
105/508	"	Nov. 3–Nov. 11
105/509	"	Nov. 3–Nov. 11

SOURCE: *FAA,* 2:655–57.

APPENDIX THREE

Major Anti-Jewish Decrees Issued Between March 29 and December 6, 1944

1. Decree no. 1.140/1944. M.E. of the Hungarian Royal Ministry Concerning the Obligation of Jewish Telephone Subscribers to Submit Data. *Budapesti Közlöny. Hivatalos Lap* (The Gazette of Budapest. Official Journal), no. 71, March 29, 1944, pp. 1–2. (The journal is referred to hereafter as *BK*.)

2. Decree no. 1.200/1944. M.E. of the Hungarian Royal Ministry Concerning the Prohibition of the Employment of Non-Jews in Jewish Households. *BK*, no. 73, March 31, 1944, p. 1.

3. Decree no. 1.210/1944. M.E. of the Hungarian Royal Ministry Concerning the Termination of the Employment of Jews in Public Service and Public Commissions and of the Activities of Jewish Lawyers. *BK*, no. 73, March 31, 1944, p. 2.

4. Decree no. 1.220/1944. M.E. of the Hungarian Royal Ministry Concerning the Termination of the Membership of Jews in the Chambers of the Press, Theatrical Arts, and Film Arts. *BK*, no. 73, March 31, 1944, p. 2.

5. Decree no. 1.230/1944. M.E. of the Hungarian Royal Ministry Concerning the Declaration of Jewish-Owned Motor Vehicles. *BK*, no. 73, March 31, 1944, pp. 2–3.

6. Decree no. 1.240/1944. M.E. of the Hungarian Royal Ministry Concerning the Marking of the Jews for Purposes of Their Differentiation. *BK*, no. 73, March 31, 1944, p. 3.

7. Decree no. 1.310/1944. M.E. of the Hungarian Royal Ministry Concerning the Prohibition of Listening to Foreign Radio Stations. *BK*, no. 75, April 2, 1944, p. 6.

8. Decree no. 358/1944. B.M. of the Royal Hungarian Minister of the Interior Concerning the Listening to Foreign Radio Stations. *BK*, no. 75, April 2, 1944, p. 6.

9. Decree no. 26.666/Elnökség 1944. H.M. of the Royal Hungarian Minister of Defense Concerning the Revocation of the Right of Individuals Identified as Jews to Wear Military Uniforms. *BK,* no. 77, April 5, 1944, p. 4.

10. Decree no. 1.450/1944. M.E. of the Hungarian Royal Ministry Concerning the Amendment of Paragraph 3 of Decree no. 1.240/1944. M.E. on the Marking of the Jews for Purposes of Their Differentiation. *BK,* no. 77, April 5, 1944, p. 4.

11. Decree no. 1.270/1944. M.E. of the Hungarian Royal Ministry Concerning the Restriction on Travel by Jews. *BK,* no. 79, April 7, 1944, p. 4.

12. Decree no. 1.300/1944. M.E. of the Hungarian Royal Ministry Concerning the Obligation of Jewish Radio Subscribers to Submit Data. *BK,* no. 79, April 7, 1944, p. 4.

13. Decree no. 1.370/1944. M.E. of the Hungarian Royal Ministry Concerning the Regulation of the Pharmacy Licenses of Jews. *BK,* no. 83, April 14, 1944, pp. 1–2.

14. Decree no. 1.600/1944. M.E. of the Hungarian Royal Ministry Concerning the Declaration and Sequestration of the Wealth of the Jews. *BK,* no. 85, April 16, 1944, pp. 1–3.

15. Decree no. 396/1944. B.M. of the Royal Hungarian Minister of the Interior Concerning the Declaration of the Termination of the Employment of Non-Jewish Household Workers in Jewish Households in Budapest. *BK,* no. 87, April 19, 1944, p. 2.

16. Decree no. 1.490/1944. M.E. of the Hungarian Royal Ministry Concerning the Declaration of Radio Receivers Obtained Under Whatever Title From Jews or Persons Considered as Jews After March 22, 1944. *BK,* no. 89, April 21, 1944, p. 2.

17. Decree no. 33.000/Eln. 18.-1944. of the Royal Hungarian Minister of Defense Concerning the Requisitioning of Radio Receivers Owned by Jewish Radio Subscribers. *BK,* no. 89, April 21, 1944, p. 2.

18. Decree no. 217.300/1944. K.K.M. of the Royal Hungarian Minister of Trade and Transportation Concerning the Submission of the Requisitioned Jewish-Owned Radio Receivers. *BK,* no. 89, April 21, 1944, p. 2.

19. Decree no. 50.500/1944. K.K.M. of the Royal Hungarian Minister of Trade and Transportation Concerning the Requisitioning of the Stocks and Equipment in the Stores Owned by Jewish Traders. *BK,* no. 89, April 21, 1944, pp. 2–3.

20. Decree no. 1.520/1944. M.E. of the Hungarian Royal Ministry Concerning the Representation and Self-Government of the Jews. *BK,* no. 90, April 22, 1944, pp. 1–2.

21. Decree no. 27.800/Eln.-1944. H.M. of the Royal Hungarian Minister of Defense Amending Decree no. 55.000/Eln.-1942. H.M. *BK,* no. 90, April 22, 1944, p. 2.

22. Decree no. 108.500/1944. K.M. of the Royal Hungarian Minister of Supplies Concerning the Regulation of the Food Supplies for Jews. *BK,* no. 91, April 23, 1944, p. 3.

23. Decree no. 1.540/1944. M.E. of the Hungarian Royal Ministry Concerning the Termination of the Hiring and Employment of Jews in White-Collar Positions. *BK,* no. 92, April 25, 1944, pp. 1–2.

24. Decree no. 1.540/1944. M.E. of the Hungarian Royal Ministry Concerning the Termination of the Hiring and Employment of Jews in White-Collar Positions. *BK,* no. 93, April 26, 1944, pp. 1–2.

25. Decree no. 108.510/1944. K.M. of the Royal Hungarian Minister of Supplies Concerning the Submission of Data by Persons Considered as Jews from the Point of View of Food Supplies. *BK,* no. 94, April 27, 1944, pp. 10–11.

26. Decree no. 1.610/1944. M.E. of the Hungarian Royal Ministry Concerning the Regulation of Certain Questions Relating to the Determination of the Jews' Apartments and Living Places. *BK,* no. 95, April 28, 1944, pp. 2–3.

27. Decree no. 1.630/1944. M.E. of the Hungarian Royal Ministry Concerning the Restriction on the Purchase and Ownership by Jews of Fire Arms, Ammunition, and Explosive Materials. *BK,* no. 95, April 28, 1944, p. 3.

28. Decree no. 20.500/1944. Ip.M. of the Royal Hungarian Minister of Industry Concerning the Obligation by Certain Jewish Industrialists to Supply Data. *BK,* no. 96, April 29, 1944, pp. 1–3.

29. Decree no. 1.077/1944. P.M. VI, fő. of the Royal Hungarian Minister of Finance Concerning the Implementation of Some of the Provisions of Decree no. 1.600/1944. M.E. on the Declaration and Sequestration of the Wealth of the Jews. *BK,* no. 96, April 29, 1944, p. 3.

30. Decree no. 123.000/1944. P.M. of the Royal Hungarian Minister of Finance Concerning Fees Relating to Travel by Jews. *BK,* no. 96, April 29, 1944, p. 4.

31. Decree no. 10.800/1944. M.E. of the Hungarian Royal Ministry Concerning the Protection of Hungarian Intellectual Life from the Literary Works of Jewish Authors. *BK,* no. 97, April 30, 1944, pp. 5–6.

32. Decree no. 1.530/1944. M.E. of the Hungarian Royal Ministry Concerning the Review of Exemption Documents Relating to Jews. *BK,* no. 97, April 30, 1944, p. 2.

33. Decree no. 444/1944. B.M. of the Royal Hungarian Minister of the Interior Concerning the Prohibition on the Attendance of Public Baths by Jews. *BK,* no. 98, May 2, 1944, pp. 1–2.

34. Decree no. 1.580/1944. M.E. of the Hungarian Royal Ministry Concerning the Revocation of Profit-Bringing Governmental Licenses Held by Jews. *BK,* no. 102, May 6, 1944, pp. 1–2.

35. Decree no. 8.700/1944. V.K.M. of the Royal Hungarian Minister of Cults and Public Education Concerning the Prohibition on Wearing of School Uniforms by Jewish Students. *BK,* no. 102, May 6, 1944, p. 4.

36. Decree no. 231.300/1944. B.M. of the Royal Hungarian Minister of the Interior Concerning the Appointment of Trustees for Absentee Jews. *BK,* no. 104, May 9, 1944, pp. 1–2.

37. Decree no. 1.141/1944. P.M. of the Royal Hungarian Minister of Finance Concerning the Consideration of the Property Tax Base and of the Net Income of Real Estate Per Cadaster for Purposes of Calculating the Remuneration of Real Estate Acquired Under Law no. XV/1942 Relating to the Agricultural and Forestry Estates of Jews. *BK,* no. 104, May 7, 1944, p. 9.

38. Decree no. 8.960/1944. V.K.M. of the Royal Hungarian Minister of Cults and Public Education Concerning the Revocation of the Permits Granted to Jews for the Maintenance of Schools,

Courses, and Students' Hostels. *BK,* no. 107, May 12, 1944, p. 9.

39. Decree no. 160.765/1944. É.M.K. of the Royal Hungarian Commissioner on Matters of Intellectual Unemployment Concerning the Registration of Jewish Employees with a Level of Schooling of Four Secondary School Grades or Higher Employed in Non-White-Collar Positions. *BK,* no. 107, May 12, 1944, p. 9.

40. Decree no. 1.730/1944. M.E. of the Hungarian Royal Ministry Concerning the Unitary Regulation of Persons Exempted from the Provisions Established for the Jews. *BK,* no. 108, May 13, 1944, pp. 1–2.

41. Decree no. 176.774/1944. VII.b. B.M. of the Royal Hungarian Minister of the Interior Concerning the Appointment of the Provisional Executive Committee of the Association of the Jews of Hungary. *BK,* no. 108, May 13, 1944, p. 3.

42. Decree no. 23.200/1944. Ip.M. of the Royal Hungarian Minister of Industry Concerning the Appointment of Enterprise Managers to Some of the Industrial, Mining, and Smelting Works of Jews. *BK,* no. 109, May 14, 1944.

43. Decree no. 1.204/1944. P.M. of the Royal Hungarian Minister of Finance Concerning the Implementation of Decree no. 1.580/1944. M.E. of the Hungarian Royal Ministry on the Revocation of Profit-Bringing Governmental Licenses Held by Jews. *BK,* no. 111, May 17, 1944, pp. 2–4.

44. Decree no. 24.200/1944. Ip.M. of the Royal Hungarian Minister of Industry Concerning the Revocation of the Licenses of Jewish Patent Agents. *BK,* no. 112, May 18, 1944, pp. 2–3.

45. Decree no. 11.000/1944. M.E. of the Hungarian Royal Ministry Concerning the Revocation of Certain Industrial Licenses Issued to Jews. *BK,* no. 113, May 20, 1944, pp. 3–4.

46. Decree no. 500/1944. B.M. of the Royal Hungarian Minister of the Interior Concerning the Restriction on the Visiting of Restaurants and Restaurant-Related Enterprises by Jews. *BK,* no. 113, May 20, 1944, p. 4.

47. Decree no. 510/1944. B.M. of the Royal Hungarian Minister of the Interior Concerning the Prohibition on the Attendance of

Public Entertainment Places by Jews. *BK,* no. 113, May 20, 1944, p. 4.

48. Decree no. 56.455/1944. É.M.K. of the Royal Hungarian Commissioner on Matters of Intellectual Unemployment Concerning the Declarations Relating to the Replacement of the Labor Shortages Arising from the Termination of the Hiring and Employment of Jews in White-Collar Positions and the Application for the Labor Forces Needed as Replacement. *BK,* no. 113, May 20, 1944, p. 9.

49. Decree no. 1.252/1944. VI. P.M. of the Royal Hungarian Minister of Finance Concerning the Implementation of Decree no. 1.600/1944. M.E. Relating to the Declaration and Sequestration of the Wealth of the Jews. *BK,* no. 113, May 20, 1944, p. 9.

50. Decree no. 60.000/1944. K.K.M. of the Royal Hungarian Minister of Trade and Transportation Concerning the Declaration of the Termination of the Relation of Employment of Non-Jewish Employees Employed by Jewish Traders. *BK,* no. 114, May 21, 1944, p. 3.

51. Decree no. 58.000/1944. K.K.M. of the Royal Hungarian Minister of Trade and Transportation Concerning the Further Restriction on the Industrial (Trade) Activities of Jews. *BK,* no. 114, May 21, 1944, p. 2.

52. Decree no. 1.870/1944. M.E. of the Hungarian Royal Ministry Concerning the Expulsion of the Jewish Members and Council Members of the Stock Markets and the Dismissal of Their Jewish Employees. *BK,* no. 116, May 24, 1944, pp. 1–2.

53. Decree no. 66.500/1944. K.K.M. of the Royal Hungarian Minister of Trade and Transportation Concerning the Implementation of Decree no. 1.580/1944. M.E. Relating to the Revocation of Profit-Bringing Governmental Licenses Held by Jews. *BK,* no. 116, May 24, 1944, pp. 5–6.

54. Decree no. 1.830/1944. M.E. of the Hungarian Royal Ministry Concerning the Inventory and Safeguarding of the Objects of Art Sequestered from Jews. *BK,* no. 117, May 25, 1944, pp. 1–2.

55. Decree no. 66.658/1944. K.K.M. of the Royal Hungarian Minister of Trade and Transportation Concerning the Amending of

Decree no. 50.500/1944. K.K.M. on the Requisitioning of the Stocks and Equipment in the Stores Owned by Jewish Traders and Decree no. 58.000/1944. K.K.M. on the Further Restriction of the Industrial (Trade) Activities of Jews. *BK,* no. 117, May 25, 1944, p. 5.

56. Decree no. 7.700/1944. XIII.a. P.M. of the Royal Hungarian Minister of Finance Concerning the Implementation of the Provisions Relating to the Tobacco-Producing Licenses in Decree no. 1.580/1944 M.E. on the Revocation of Profit-Bringing Governmental Licenses Held by Jews. *BK,* no. 118, May 26, 1944, pp. 2–3.

57. Decree no. 100.100/1944. B.M. of the Royal Hungarian Minister of the Interior Concerning the Implementation of the Provisions Relating to the Permits Granted by the Police Authorities under Decree no. 1.580/1944. M.E. on the Revocation of Profit-Bringing Governmental Licenses Held by Jews. *BK,* no. 119, May 27, 1944, pp. 2–3.

58. Decree no. 550/1944. B.M. of the Royal Hungarian Minister of the Interior Concerning the Payment of the Expenses Involved in the Determination of the Value of the Pharmaceutical Stock, Furnishings and Equipment and in the Estimation of the Value of the Furnishings and Equipment in the Case of the Reissuance of Pharmaceutical Licenses for Jews. *BK,* no. 124, June 3, 1944, p. 4.

59. Decree no. 1.990/1944. M.E. of the Hungarian Royal Ministry Concerning the Restriction on the Shopping by Jews to a Specific Period of the Day. *BK,* no. 125, June 4, 1944, p. 2.

60. Decree no. 74.187/1944. F.M. of the Royal Hungarian Minister of Agriculture Concerning the Implementation of Decree no. 1.580/1944. M.E. on the Revocation of Profit-Bringing Governmental Licenses Held by Jews. *BK,* no. 130, June 11, 1944, pp. 5–6.

61. Decree no. 2.120/1944. M.E. of the Hungarian Royal Ministry Concerning the Utilization of the Jewish Business Establishments. *BK,* no. 132, June 14, 1944, pp. 1–2.

62. Decree no. 147.501/1944.-IX. of the Mayor of the Capital City of Budapest Concerning the Determination of the Buildings in

Which Jews Could Live in the Capital's Administrative District no. I. *BK,* no. 135, June 17, 1944, pp. 3–4.

63. Decree no. 147.502/1944.-IX. of the Mayor of the Capital City of Budapest Concerning the Determination of the Buildings in Which Jews Could Live in the Capital's Administrative District no. II. *BK,* no. 135, June 17, 1944, p. 4.

64. Decree no. 147.503/1944.-IX. of the Mayor of the Capital City of Budapest Concerning the Determination of the Buildings in Which Jews Could Live in the Capital's Administrative District no. III. *BK,* no. 135, June 17, 1944, pp. 4–5.

65. Decree no. 147.504/1944.-IX. of the Mayor of the Capital City of Budapest Concerning the Determination of the Buildings in Which Jews Could Live in the Capital's Administrative District no. IV. *BK,* no. 135, June 17, 1944, p. 5.

66. Decree no. 147.505/1944.-IX. of the Mayor of the Capital City of Budapest Concerning the Determination of the Buildings in Which Jews Could Live in the Capital's Administrative District no. V. *BK,* no. 135, June 17, 1944, p. 5.

67. Decree no. 147.506/1944.-IX. of the Mayor of the Capital City of Budapest Concerning the Determination of the Buildings in Which Jews Could Live in the Capital's Administrative District no. VI. *BK,* no. 135, June 17, 1944, p. 5.

68. Decree no. 147.507/1944.-IX. of the Mayor of the Capital City of Budapest Concerning the Determination of the Buildings in Which Jews Could Live in the Capital's Administrative District no. VII. *BK,* no. 135, June 17, 1944, p. 6.

69. Decree no. 147.508/1944.-IX. of the Mayor of the Capital City of Budapest Concerning the Determination of the Buildings in Whcih Jews Could Live in the Capital's Administrative District no. VIII. *BK,* no. 135, June 17, 1944, p. 6.

70. Decree no. 147.509/1944.-IX. of the Mayor of the Capital City of Budapest Concerning the Determination of the Buildings in Which Jews Could Live in the Capital's Administrative District no. IX. *BK,* no. 135, June 17, 1944, p. 6.

71. Decree no. 147.510/1944.-IX. of the Mayor of the Capital City of Budapest Concerning the Determination of the Buildings in

Which Jews Could Live in the Capital's Administrative District no. X. *BK*, no. 135, June 17, 1944, pp. 6–7.

72. Decree no. 147.511/1944.-IX. of the Mayor of the Capital City of Budapest Concerning the Determination of the Buildings in Which Jews Could Live in the Capital's Administrative District no. XI. *BK*, no. 135, June 17, 1944, p. 7.

73. Decree no. 147.512/1944.-IX. of the Mayor of the Capital City of Budapest Concerning the Determination of the Buildings in Which Jews Could Live in the Capital's Administrative District no. XII. *BK*, no. 135, June 17, 1944, p. 7.

74. Decree no. 147.513/1944.-IX. of the Mayor of the Capital City of Budapest Concerning the Determination of the Buildings in Which Jews Could Live in the Capital's Administrative District no. XIII. *BK*, no. 135, June 17, 1944, p. 7.

75. Decree no. 147.514/1944.-IX. of the Mayor of the Capital City of Budapest Concerning the Determination of the Buildings in Which Jews Could Live in the Capital's Administrative District no. XIV. *BK*, no. 135, June 17, 1944, pp. 7–8.

76. Decree no. 111.200/1944. K.M. of the Royal Hungarian Minister of Supplies Concerning the Implementation of Decree no. 1.580/1944. M.E. on the Revocation of the Profit-Bringing Governmental Licenses Held by Jews. *BK*, no. 138, June 21, 1944, pp. 3–4.

77. Decree no. 2.250/1944. M.E. of the Hungarian Royal Ministry Concerning the Medical Practice of Jews and Their Membership in the Medical Chamber. *BK*, no. 140, June 23, 1944, p. 2.

78. Decree no. 2.230/1944. M.E. of the Hungarian Royal Ministry Concerning the Supervision Over the Administration of the Agricultural and Forestry Estates of Certain Jewish Foreign Nationals. *BK*, no. 140, June 23, 1944, p. 1.

79. Decree no. 8.200/1944. V.K.M. of the Royal Hungarian Minister of Cults and Public Education Concerning the Submission of the Jewish Religious-Communal and School Registers. *BK*, no. 141, June 24, 1944, p. 5.

80. Decree no. 148.451/1944.-IX. of the Mayor of the Capital City of Budapest Concerning the Definitive Determination of the

Buildings in Which Jews Could Live in the Buda Part of the Capital. *BK,* no. 141, June 24, 1944, pp. 6–7.

81. Decree no. 148.452/1944.-IX. of the Mayor of the Capital City of Budapest Concerning the Definitive Determination of the Buildings in Which Jews Could Live in the Pest Part of the Capital. *BK,* no. 141, June 24, 1944, pp. 7–9.

82. Decree no. 11.300/1944. M.E. of the Hungarian Royal Ministry Concerning the Protection of Hungarian Intellectual Life and the Removal of the Works of Jewish Authors from Public Circulation. *BK,* no. 142, June 25, 1944, pp. 14–15.

83. Decree no. 31.100/1944. Ip.M. of the Royal Hungarian Minister of Industry Concerning the Implementation of Decree no. 1.580/1944. M.E. on the Revocation of the Profit-Bringing Governmental Licenses Held by Jews. *BK,* no. 142, June 25, 1944, pp. 8–10.

84. Decree no. 286.275/1944. B.M. of the Royal Hungarian Minister of the Interior Concerning the Implementation of the Provisions Relating to the Permits for the Production of Immunological and Diagnostical Bacteriological Products Used in Human Medicine and to the Production of Smallpox Vaccine in Decree no. 1.580/1944. M.E. on the Revocation of the Profit-Bringing Governmental Licenses Held by Jews. *BK,* no. 146, July 1, 1944, pp. 1–2.

85. Announcement no. 418/1944. Eln. 107. of the President of the Royal Hungarian Patent Court Concerning the Revocation of the Licenses of Jewish Patent Agents and the Appointment of Trustees for Their Offices. *BK,* no. 147, July 2, 1944, p. 12.

86. Decree no. 2.540/1944. M.E. of the Hungarian Royal Ministry Amending Decree no. 1.520/1944. M.E. Concerning the Representation and Self-Government of the Jews. *BK,* no. 157, July 14, 1944, p. 4.

87. Decree no. 2.650/1944. M.E. of the Hungarian Royal Ministry Concerning the Regulation of Certain Questions Relating to the Property of Jews. *BK,* no. 165, July 23, 1944, p. 2.

88. Decree no. 191.449/1944. VII.b. B.M. of the Royal Hungarian Minister of the Interior Concerning the Filling of Vacancies on

the Provisional Executive Committee of the Association of the Jews of Hungary. *BK*, no. 169, July 28, 1944, p. 12.

89. Decree no. 91.647/1944. K.K.M. of the Royal Hungarian Minister of Trade and Transportation Concerning the Assignment of Enterprise Managers to the Industrial (Trade) Enterprises of Jews. *BK*, no. 169, July 28, 1944, pp. 12–13.

90. Decree no. 2.750/1944. M.E. of the Hungarian Royal Ministry Amending Law no. XVII:1923 Relating to the Statutes of Engineers. *BK*, no. 169, July 28, 1944, pp. 9–12.

91. Decree no. 188.358/1944. É.M.K. of the Royal Hungarian Commissioner on Matters of Intellectual Unemployment Concerning the Petitioning for Permits for Temporary Exemption from Auxiliary Military Service and for Travel to Their Work Place by Jews Who Were Retained in Their Positions Under Paragraph 2 of Decree no. 1.540/1944. M.E. *BK*, no. 174, August 3, 1944, p. 15.

92. Decree no. 2.880/1944. M.E. of the Hungarian Royal Ministry Amending Decree no. 2.120/1944. M.E. Concerning the Utilization of Jewish Business Establishments. *BK*, no. 177, August 6, 1944, p. 3.

93. Decree no. 95.600/1944. K.K.M. of the Royal Hungarian Minister of Trade and Transportation Concerning the Transfer of Certain Responsibilities to the Royal Hungarian Foreign Trade Office in Connection with the Utilization of the Business Establishments of Jews. *BK*, no. 177, August 6, 1944, p. 7.

94. Decree no. 189.821/1944. É.M.K. of the Royal Hungarian Commissioner on Matters of Intellectual Unemployment Concerning the Declaration and Employment of Labor Requested for the Replacement of Dismissed Jewish Employees. *BK*, no. 183, August 13, 1944, pp. 8–9.

95. Decree no. 2.040/1944. M.E. of the Hungarian Royal Ministry Concerning the Exemption of Certain Persons from the Legal Provisions Relating to Jews. *BK*, no. 189, August 22, 1944, p. 1.

96. Decree no. 3.050/1944. M.E. of the Hungarian Royal Ministry Amending Decree no. 1.600/1944. M.E. Concerning the Declaration and Sequestration of the Wealth of the Jews. *BK*, no. 191, August 24, 1944, p. 2.

97. Decree no. 3.100/1944. M.E. of the Hungarian Royal Ministry Concerning the Termination of the Management by Jews of Agricultural and Forestry Estates Owned by Non-Jews. *BK,* no. 194, August 26, 1944, pp. 2–3.

98. Decision no. 4.980/1944. of the Royal Hungarian Commissioner of Leather Materials Concerning the Bringing into Circulation of the Leather Materials Found in the Sequestered Jewish Stores. *BK,* No. 201, September 3, 1944, p. 4.

99. Decree no. 3.400/1944. M.E. of the Hungarian Royal Ministry Concerning the Certification of Non-Jewish Origin. *BK,* no. 205, September 8, 1944, p. 3.

100. Decree no. 3.230/1944. M.E. of the Hungarian Royal Ministry Concerning the Advancement of the Utilization of the Agricultural Estates Acquired Under Law no. XV:1942 Relating to the Agricultural and Forestry Estates of Jews. *BK,* no. 206, September 10, 1944, pp. 2–3.

101. Decree no. 16.000/1944. I.M. of the Royal Hungarian Minister of Justice Amending Decree no. 70.000/1941. I.M. Relating to the Implementation of the Provisions Concerning the Prohibition of Marriages Between Jews and Non-Jews. *BK,* no. 214, September 20, 1944, p. 2.

102. Decree no. 3.520/1944. M.E. of the Hungarian Royal Ministry Concerning the Utilization of the Merchandise Stocks, Materials, and Other Property Assets Found in Jewish Stores (Works). *BK,* no. 222, September 29, 1944, pp. 2–3.

103. Decree no. 120,971. K.K.M. of the Royal Hungarian Minister of Trade and Transportation Concerning Certain Actions Relating to the Utilization of Jewish Business Establishments in Cases of Negative Decisions by the Industrial Authority of First Instance. *BK,* no. 235, October 15, 1944, p. 10.

104. Decree no. 3.780/1944. M.E. of the Hungarian Royal Ministry Concerning the Revision of the Exemption Documents Issued Under Decree no. 3.040/1944. M.E. *BK,* no. 247, October 29, 1944, p. 1.

105. Decree no. 3.840/1944. M.E. of the Hungarian Royal Ministry Concerning the Property of the Jews. *BK,* no. 250, November 3, 1944, pp. 2–4.

106. Decree no. 49.500/1944. Ip.M. of the Royal Hungarian Minister of Industry Concerning the Abrogation of Decree no. 23.200/1944. Ip.M. Relating to the Appointment of Enterprise Managers to Some of the Industrial, Mining, and Smelting Works of Jews. *BK,* no. 258, November 12, 1944, p. 2.

107. Decree no. 960/1944. B.M. of the Royal Hungarian Minister of the Interior Concerning the Changing of the Names of Streets, Roads, and Squares. *BK,* no. 279, December 6, 1944, p. 5.

APPENDIX FOUR

Hungarian and Foreign Jewish Authors Whose Works Were Banned

Hungarian-Jewish Authors *

Imre Abádi (Dunajecz), Andor Adorján (Lachenbacher), Adolf Ágai (Rosenzweig), Ernő Andai (Axelrad), Sándor Antal (Adler), Béla Balázs (Bauer), Ernő Ballagi (Bloch), Endre Barát (Breuer), Lajos Barta, Sándor Barta, Jób Bede (Rosenberg), László Békefi (Békeffy; Kann), Sándor Benamy (Berger), Béla Bernstein, Lajos Bíró (Blau), László Boros (Beimer), Mihály Boross (Weimer), Vilmos Böhm, Sándor Bródy, Manó Buchinger, Miklós Buk, László Bús-Fekete (Trauerschwartz), Gyula Dénes (Freireich), Zsófia Dénes (Deutsch), Jenő Dévény (Deutsch), Gábor Drégely (Dressauer), René Erdős (Ehrenthal), Béla Fábián (Feuermann), László Falus (Frank), Jenő Faragó (Frankfurter), Imre Fazekas, László Feleky (Füchsel), Jenő Fényes (Feurerwerker), Samu Fényes (Fein), Miksa Fenyő (Fleischmann), László Fodor, Pál Forró (Friedmann), Imre Földes (Fleischmann), Jolán Földes (Grünfeld), Mihály Földi (Frank), Milán Füst (Fürst), Andor Gábor (Greiner), Imre Gál (Grünfeld), Mariska Gárdos (Grünfeld), Mór Gelléri (Glück), Oszkár Gellért (Goldmann), Győző Gergely (Ungár), Sándor Gergely, Andor Gervai, János Giszkalay (Widder), Ferenc Göndör (Krausz), Bódog Halmi, József Halmi, Baron Lajos Hatvany (Deutsch), Baroness Lili Hatvany (Deutsch), Pál Ignotus (Veigelsberg), Ottó Indig, Oszkár Jászi (Jakubovits), Samu Jászai, Dániel Jób (Ziffer), Ede Kabos (Rosenberg), Illés Kaczér (Katz), Mózes Kahána, Ede Kenéz-Kurländer, József Kiss, Izidor Knerr, Tamás Kóbor (Bermann), Noémi Kóbor, Nándor Korcsmáros (Reich), Zsigmond Kunfi (Kohn), László Lakatos (Kellner), Miklós Lázár (Léderer), Menyhért Lengyel (Lebovits), Henrik Lenkei (Guttmann), György Lukács (Löwinger), Rodion Markovits, József Márkus (pen name: Satanelló), Ernő Mezei (Grünfeld), Mór Mezei (Grünfeld), Vilmos Mezőfi (Grünfeld), Ákos Molnár, Ferenc Molnár (Neumann), Jenő Molnár (Müller), Illés Mónus (Brandstein), Sándor Nádas (Neumann), Imre Nagy (Fischer), Károly

Nóti, Ernő Osváth (Roth), Árpád Pásztor (Pikler), Andor Peterdi (Pollák), József Pogány (Schwartz), Sándor Propper, József Radnóti (Glat-
ter), Ferenc Ráskai (Kraus), Pál Relle (Reichmann), Béla Révész (Roth),
Mihály Révész (Reisner), Imre Roboz, Géza Róheim, Irén Sass (Kell-
ner), Zoltán Somlyó (Schwartz), Béla Somogyi (Steiner), Endre Sós
(Schlesinger), Ervin Szabó, Lajos Szabolcsi (Weinstein), Mór Szatmári
(Gottlieb), Ernő Szép (Schön), Géza Szilágyi (Silbermann), István Szo-
maházy (Steiner), Dezső Szomory (Weisz), Szőke Szakáll (Gerő-
Grünwald), Nándor Ujhelyi, László Vadnai (Wolf), Zseni Várnai
(Weisz), Vilmos Vázsonyi (Weiszfeld), Jakab Weltner, and Béla Zsolt
(Steiner).

Foreign Jewish Authors

Shalom Asch, Vicki Baum, Tristan Bernhard, Eduard Bernstein,
Henrik Bernstein, Hugo Bettauer, Jean Bloch, Max Brod, Martin
Buber, Maurice Dekobra, Osip Dymov, Ilya Ehrenburg, Lion
Feuchtwanger, Sigmund Freud, Bernhard Kellermann, Alfred Kerr,
Egon Ervin Kisch, Lili Körber, Ferdinand Lassalle, Emil Ludwig,
André Maurois, Karl Marx, Rabbach Miasa, Max Nordau, Josef Opa-
toshu, Felix Salten, Arthur Schnitzler, Mendele Mocher Szfurim, Jakob
Wassermann, Franz Werfel, Otto Zarek, Otto Zweig, Stefan Zweig, and
Israel Zangwill.

Hungarian-Jewish Authors: Supplemental List

Lajos Aczél (Adler; pen name: László Aczél), Klára Ács (Adler),
Miklós Adler (pen name: Miklós Ákos), Sándor Adorján (Weisz), Béla
Ágai (Schäffer), Ernő Ágoston (Adler), Nevis Alba (Ilona Ungár),
György Andersen, Károly Aszlányi (Ausländer), Pál Avar (Auer), Emil
Balassa (Berger), Dezső Bálint (Beck), Imre Bálint (Österreicher), László
Bánoczi (Weisz), Imre Bárd (Beck), Arthúr Bárdos (Burstein), Lajos
Báttaszéki (Hoffmann), Ferenc Baumgarten, Róza Bédi-Schwimmer,
István Békefi (Kann), Izor Béldi (Goldstein), Tibor Bencze (Bruch; pen
name: Tibor Benczés), László Berend (Braun), Imre Berkes (Bergl),
Mór Bogdányi (Bienenstock), Malvin Bokor (Bruck), László Bródy,
Miksa Bródy; Hugó Csergő (Hónig), Gyula Csermely, Tibor Déri
(Deutsch), László Dormándi, Viktor Egri, Tamás Emőd (Ernő Fleis-
cher), Pál Farkas (Wolfner), Mátyás Feld (Rosenfeld), László Fenyő,
János Fóthy (Fleiner), Ákos Gara (Gottlieb), Andor Garami (Goldstein),

Andor Gellért, Attila Gerő (Guttmann), Lajos Gró (Grosz), Soma Guthi (Guttmann), István Haáz (Háász), Sándor Hajó (Hoffmann), László Hars (Herczog), Jenő Heltai (Herczl), Frigyes Hervay (Herczfeld), Károly Heumann, József Hevesi (Kronstein), Ede Horn (Einhorn), Henrik Incze (Izrael), Sándor Incze (Stein), Mrs. Oszkár Jászi (Amália Moskovitz; pen name: Anna Lesznai), Imre Kádár, Marcel Kadosa (Krieszhaber), Jenő Kálmán (Kreisler), Izor Kálnoki (Kaufmann), Benő Karácsony, Vilmos Karczag (Krammer), László Kardos (Katz), Frigyes Karinthy, Dezső Keér, Simon Kemény (Kohn), Pál Kéri (Krammer), Sámuel Kohn, Aladár Komját (Korah), Aladár Komlós (Katz), András Komor (Kohn), Gyula Komor (Kohn), Imre Kőműves, Sándor Kuthi (Schönborn; pen name: Sándor Térey), Andor Latzkó, Lehel Lendvay (Léderer), Géza Lengyel, Sándor Lestyán (Lichstein), Ernő Ligeti (Lichstein), László Loránth, Gyula Lukács (Lichstein), Lajos Magyar, Emil Makai (Fischer), Imre Mezei (Rosenfeld), Jutka Miklós (Militzer), Henrik Miskolczi (Weiszmann), Tamás Moly, Endre Nagy (Grosz), Samu Nagy (Neuhaus), Zoltán Nagy, Jób Paál, Lajos Palagyi (Silberstein), Menyhért Palagyi (Silberstein), Ede Pályi (Klein), Károly Papp, József Patai (Klein), Miklós Radnóti (Glatter), Piroska Reichard, Andor Roboz (Rosenzweig), Mihály András Rónai, Miklós Rózsa (Rosenthal), László Sas, Sándor Sásdi, Imre Szabó (Steiner), György Szántó, Nándor Székely, Béla Szenes (Schlesinger), Rezső Szirmai (Schwartzkopf), Emil Szomori, Kornél Tábori (Tauber), Sári Tamás, Jenő Ujvári (Groszmann), László Ujvári (Groszmann), Péter Ujvári (Groszmann), Ernő Vajda (Weisz), Iván Vándor (Weisz), Rusztem Vámbéry (Wamberger), Dániel Várnai (Weisz), Andor Vér (Weisz), György Verő (Weisz), József Vészi (Weisz), Marcel Vidor (Weinberger), Andor Villányi (Schwabach), Jenő Wallesz, Zoltán Zelk, Gyula Zempléni (Pollak), and Béla Zerkovits.

Foreign Jewish Authors: Supplemental List

Chaim Nachman Bialik, Afred Döblin, Avigdor Hameiri, Heinrich Heine, Theodor Herzl, Catulle Mandes, Marcel Proust, Moritz Gottlieb Saphir, Nachum Sokolov, Ernst Toller, and Gudio de Verona.

SOURCE: The original list was included as an appendix to Decree no. 10.800/1944. M.E. in *Budapesti Közlöny* (Official Gazette of Budapest), no. 97, April 30, 1944, pp. 5–6; the supplemental list was part of Decree no. 11.300/1944. M.E., *Ibid.*, no. 142, June 25, 1944, pp. 14–15.

APPENDIX FIVE

Chronology

1867–1937

December 22, 1867: Hungarian Jewry acquires equality of rights under Emancipation Law no. XVII:1867.

December 1868–February 1869: Congress of Hungarian Jewry, which failed to reconcile the differences between the Neolog (assimilationist) and Orthodox factions.

May 4, 1884: Beginning of the infamous Tisza-Eszlár blood libel suit, which fanned the flames of anti-Semitism.

October 1, 1895: The Jewish religion is recognized as one of the "received" religions under Law no. XLII:1895.

October 31, 1918: Following the end of World War I, a new Hungarian government is formed under Count Mihály Károlyi.

March 21–August 1, 1919: Communist rule under Béla Kun, who proclaimed Hungary a Soviet Republic on June 25.

November 1919: Establishment of a counterrevolutionary regime under Admiral Miklós Horthy in the midst of a "White Terror."

September 1920: Adoption of Law no. XXV:1920, the so-called *Numerus Clausus* Act (the first anti-Jewish law in post-World War I Europe) limiting the admission of Jews to institutions of higher learning.

April 14, 1921: Appointment of Count István Bethlen as Prime Minister and the beginning of the "Consolidation Era" (1921–1932).

1928: Revision of the *Numerus Clausus* Act under the provisions of Law no. XIV:1928.

October 1, 1932: Gyula Gömbös, a leader of the Right and of the defunct "Race Defense Party," becomes Prime Minister.

1938

March 5: Prime Minister Kálmán Darányi outlines his government program at Győr and announces Hungary's readiness to come to grips with the Jewish question.

May 28: The first major anti-Jewish law (no. X:1938) is adopted.

July: Conference at Evian-les-Baines, France, on the problem of refugees, establishes the Intergovernmental Committee on Political Refugees.

November 2: Signing of the First Vienna Award under which Hungary acquired the Upper Province (*Felvidék*) from Czechoslovakia.

1939

February 15: Béla Imrédy is replaced by Count Pál Teleki as Prime Minister.

March 11: Law no. II:1939, which provided the legal basis for the introduction of the labor service system (Article 230), is promulgated.

March 14–18: Hungary conquers Carpatho-Ruthenia from Czechoslovakia.

May: British issue "White Paper" limiting Jewish immigration to Palestine to 75,000 in five years.

May 4: the second major anti-Jewish law (no. IV:1939) goes into effect.

May 28–29: General elections are held in Hungary in which the ultra-Rightist (*Nyilas*) parties which had won only 2 seats in 1935, now win 49.

1940

August 30: Signing of the Second Vienna Award under which Hungary acquired Northern Transylvania from Romania.

1941

April 11: Hungary joins the Third Reich in the war against Yugoslavia and acquires the Délvidék area.

June 27: Under the leadership of Prime Minister László Bárdossy, Hungary joins the Third Reich in declaring war against the Soviet Union.

August 2: The Nuremberg-type racial law (no. XV:1941) goes into effect.

August 27–28: The majority of the 16,000 to 18,000 "alien" Jews deported from Hungary are slaughtered near Kamenets-Podolsk.

1942

January: Hungarian military units massacre over 3,300 people in and around Ujvidék, including close to 1,000 Jews.

January 5–7: Major-General József Heszlényi informs Karl Clodius and a number of top *Wehrmacht* officers that Hungary was interested in the transfer of 12,000 "alien" Jews to Russia.

January 20: Wannsee Conference is held under the chairmanship of SS-*Obergruppenführer* Reinhard Heydrich on the Final Solution of the Jewish question in Europe.

March 9: Miklós Kállay is sworn in as the new Prime Minister of Hungary, replacing László Bárdossy.

April 11: Beginning of the deployment of approximately 50,000 Jewish labor servicemen in the Ukraine.

July 12: Lieutenant-General Sándor Homlok, the Hungarian Military Attaché in Berlin, reminds the *Wehrmacht* of Major-General Heszlényi's offer of January 5–7, 1942.

September 25: Adolf Eichmann, reacting to Major-General Heszlényi's offer, rejects the idea of mobilizing the entire deportation apparatus for only a "few thousand" Jews. Suggests the inclusion of these Jews in a general Final Solution program.

October 6: The Third Reich formally requests the Hungarian government to solve the Jewish question along the lines pursued in Nazi-occupied Europe.

December 2: The Kállay government rejects the German demand for the Final Solution.

December 17: Allies issue joint declaration, condemning the Nazis' drive against the Jews.

1943

January 12: The Second Hungarian Army is destroyed in battle near Voronezh.

April 17–18: Horthy and Hitler meet at Schloss Klessheim.

April 19: Beginning of the Bermuda Conference on Refugees, resulting in a call for the revitalization of the Intergovernmental Committee on Political Refugees.

April 28: Ribbentrop meets Döme Sztójay, the Hungarian Minister in Berlin, and summarizes the Third Reich's views on the Jewish question.

April 30: Edmund Veesenmayer, serving as special emissary of the German Foreign Office, submits his first comprehensive report on conditions in Hungary. Jewish labor servicemen are massacred at Doroshich (Dorosics), the Ukraine.

July 2: A German-Hungarian agreement is signed, permitting the transfer of Jewish labor service companies for deployment in the copper mines of Bor, Serbia.

July 31: Representatives of the opposition parties, including Endre Bajcsy-Zsilinszky, submit a memorandum to the Kállay government, urging that it change its course.

September 30: German General Staff completes its plans for the possible occupation of Hungary.

December 10: Edmund Veesenmayer submits his second comprehensive report on conditions in Hungary.

1944

January 22: President Roosevelt issues Executive Order 9417, establishing the War Refugee Board.

January 24: General Ferenc Szombathelyi, the Chief of the General Staff, meets Hitler and Field Marshal Wilhelm Keitel concerning the possible withdrawal of the Hungarian forces from the Soviet front.

February 12: Horthy writes to Hitler asking permission to withdraw the Hungarian forces from the Eastern front "to use them for the unaided defense of the Carpathians."

February 14: Göring asks Himmler for concentration camp labor to build underground aircraft factories.

March 9: Himmler assures Göring of 100,000 concentration camp inmates for use in the construction of underground aircraft factories.

March 12: Hitler issues his order for the implementation of "Operation Margarethe" concerning the occupation of Hungary.

March 14: Josef Winninger, a member of the Budapest branch of the *Abwehr*, informs Rudolph Kasztner, the executive officer of the *Vaada*, about the impending German occupation of Hungary.

March 17–18: Horthy and members of his delegation, Foreign Minister Jenő Ghyczy, Defense Minister Lajos Csatay, and Szombathelyi, meet Hitler at Schloss Klessheim.

March 19: German forces occupy Hungary. Horthy reports on his meeting with Hitler at an emergency Crown Council meeting. Hermann A. Krumey and Dieter Wisliceny, two of the leading members of the Eichmann-*Sonderkommando*, appear at the headquarters of the Jewish community and order László Bánoczi to convene the Hungarian Jewish leaders for a meeting the following morning.

March 20: Krumey and Wisliceny issue instructions to the national leaders of Hungarian Jewry, ordering them to form a Jewish Council that would exercise jurisdiction over all the Jews in the country.

March 21: A coalition eight-member Jewish Council is established under the leadership of Samu Stern, the President of the Jewish Community of Pest.

March 22: A new government under the leadership of Döme Sztójay is sworn in.

March 23: The Jewish Council issues its first appeal to the Jews of Hungary.

March 24: President Roosevelt warns the Hungarian authorities against taking any harsh measures against the Jews.

March 28: Krumey meets the leaders of the Budapest and of the other major Jewish communities of Hungary. László Baky is appointed Secretary of State in the Ministry of the Interior, replacing András Gergelyffy.

March 29: The Sztójay-led Council of Ministers issues a series of anti-Jewish decrees, including the one requiring the wearing of the Star of David. Ottó Komoly, the President of the Hungarian Zionist Association, meets Miklós Mester in an attempt to contact Béla Imrédy.

March 31: The leaders of the Central Jewish Council meet Eichmann, who issues a series of instructions.

April 1: Carpatho-Ruthenia and Northern Transylvania are declared *ex post* as military operational zones.

April 3: American aircraft bomb Budapest. Eichmann and Péter Hain, the head of the Hungarian Security Police, demand that the Jewish Council provide 500 apartments to compensate the Christian air raid victims.

April 4: Baky chairs meeting at the Ministry of the Interior on the ghettoization of the Jews. Ministry of the Interior issues decree requiring the registration of Jews. Authorities order the confiscation of 1,500 Jewish apartments to compensate the Christian victims of the April 3 raid.

April 5: Jews all over the country begin to wear the yellow star. Baky issues decree appointing Dr. Lajos Meggyesi, the head of the Prosecution Section of the Center for State Defense (*Államvédelmi Központ*), to supervise the implementation of the anti-Jewish measures. Jewish leaders hand over 500 apartments for the compensation of Christian victims of air raids. Kasztner and Joel Brand meet Wisliceny for the first time.

April 6: Central Jewish Council appeals to Hungarian Jewry for obedience and calm.

April 7: Baky issues top secret decree concerning the ghettoization of Hungarian Jewry. Baky confers with Endre, Colonel Győző Tölgyesy, the Commander of Gendarmerie District VIII (Kassa), and representatives of the Eichmann-*Sonderkommando,* on the implementation of ghettoization in Carpatho-Ruthenia.

April 9: Hitler informs Field Marshal Milch of the assignment of 100,000 Hungarian Jews for the construction of underground aircraft factories.

April 11: Endre is formally appointed Secretary of State in the Ministry of the Interior and entrusted with the handling of the Jewish question.

April 12: A conference is held in Munkács under the chairmanship of Endre concerning the ghettoization of Jews in Carpatho-Ruthenia and in northeastern Hungary. Bishop László Ravasz visits Horthy concerning the measures taken against the Jews of Hungary.

April 16: The Jews of Carpatho-Ruthenia and northeastern Hungary are driven "illegally" into ghettos.

April 19: The Sztójay government issues decree establishing a new Jewish Council.

April 21: Kasztner hands over to the SS 2.5 million *Pengős,* the second installment relating to an agreement on the "rescue" of Hungarian Jewry. (The first installment of 3 million *Pengős* was delivered to Krumey and Hunsche a few days earlier.)

April 24: Central Jewish Council issues summonses to Jewish professionals identified on lists received from the Hungarian police authorities. Eichmann, Endre, and their colleagues tour the ghettos of Carpatho-Ruthenia and northeastern Hungary.

April 25: Eichmann summons Brand and makes his "blood for trucks" offer. Rudolf Vrba (Walter Rosenberg) and Josef Lanik (Alfred Wetzler), two escapees from Auschwitz, tell their story to the leaders of Slovak Jewry and warn about the impending disaster of Hungarian Jewry.

April 26: The Sztójay government issues a number of anti-Jewish decrees, including the one relating to the concentration (ghettoization) of the Jews. The Sztójay government places 50,000 Jewish labor servicemen at the immediate disposal of the Germans. Dejewification leaders hold meeting at Szatmárnémeti under the chairmanship of Endre concerning the ghettoization of the Jews of Northern Transylvania.

April 27: Central Jewish Council forwards letter to Andor Jaross, the Minister of the Interior, concerning the plight of the Jews of Carpatho-Ruthenia and northeastern Hungary.

April 28: Bishop László Ravasz visits Horthy concerning the measures taken against the Jews only to be reassured about the "lending of workers" to an ally. The first trainload of deportees is taken to Auschwitz from the Kistarcsa internment camp.

May 3: The Jews of Northern Transylvania are taken into ghettos. Kasztner arrives in Kolozsvár in the company of Dr. Rudi Sedlaczek.

May 4–6: A Conference is held in Vienna with the participation of Leó L. Lullay and Franz Novak, representing the Hungarian Gendarmerie and the Eichmann-*Sonderkommando,* respectively, concerning the schedule and route of the deportations from Hungary.

May 8: Wisliceny confidentially informs Kasztner about the decision on the "total deportation" of the Jews of Hungary. Endre formally appoints members of the new Central Jewish Council.

May 9: Plans for the deportation of Hungarian Jewry are completed at a conference held in Munkács.

May 12: Inauguration of the Hungarian Institute for the Researching of the Jewish Question, headed by Zoltán Bosnyák.

May 15: The systematic mass deportation of the Jews of Hungary begins. Angelo Rotta, the Papal Nuncio, condemns the actions of the Sztójay government directed against the Jews.

May 17: Brand, accompanied by Bandi (György) Grosz, leaves on his controversial "blood for trucks" mission. The SS acquire control over the Weisz-Manfréd Works under an agreement worked out by Kurt Becher.

May 18: Bishop Áron Marton condemns the anti-Jewish measures in a sermon in St. Michael's Church in Kolozsvár.

May 22: Lajos Szász, the Minister of Industry, issues a misleading statement on the government's plans for the Jews. Eichmann informs Kasztner about his agreement to allow the emigration of 600 holders of Palestine immigration certificates.

May 25: Conference is held in the Ministry of the Interior concerning the dejewification of northern Hungary, the areas encompassing Gendarmerie Districts II and VII.

May 25–26: Eberhard von Thadden, a leader of the *Inland II* Section of the German Foreign Office, arrives in Budapest to assess the activities of the German agencies involved in the Final Solution program.

June 6: Sztójay meets Hitler in his military headquarters.

June 7: The deportations from Carpatho-Ruthenia, northeastern Hungary, and Northern Transylvania are completed. Brand is arrested by the British in Aleppo, Syria.

June 10: In an agreement with Eichmann, 388 Jews are transferred from the Kolozsvár ghetto to Budapest to be included in the Kasztner group.

June 11: Carl I. Danielsson, the Swedish Minister in Budapest, offers the possible immigration to Sweden of 300 to 400 Hungarian Jews.

June 16: The deportation of the Jews of Northern Hungary, the areas encompassing Gendarmerie Districts II and VII, is completed.

June 17: The Jews of Budapest begin their relocation into specially designated Yellow-Star houses.

June 19: Miklós Krausz sends an abbreviated version of the Auschwitz Protocols together with a report on the fate of Hungarian Jewry to Switzerland.

June 21: The Council of Ministers hears a report from Mihály Arnóthy-Jungerth, the Deputy Foreign Minister, on the impact of the measures taken against the Jews of Hungary. Baky and Endre report to the Council of Ministers on the deportations.

June 22: The Central Jewish Council sends a petition to Sztójay on the plight of Hungarian Jewry.

June 23: Arnóthy-Jungerth continues his report on the impact of the anti-Jewish measures. Endre reads a long report concerning the character of the measures taken against the Jews.

June 25: Pope Pius XII appeals to Horthy on behalf of the persecuted.

June 26: Following a decision of the Crown Council, the Hungarian government approves the emigration of 7,800 Jews sponsored by neutral states. The Swiss Legation transmits President Roosevelt's warning to the Hungarians concerning the measures enacted against the Jews.

June 27: Arnóthy-Jungerth reports to the Council of Ministers on the international reaction to the handling of the Jewish question in Hungary. Secretary of State Cordell Hull issues a warning to the Hungarians concerning the treatment of the Jews.

June 28: The deportation of the Jews from southeastern Hungary, the area encompassing Gendarmerie Districts V and VI, is completed. Sztójay informs Veesenmayer about the decisions taken by the government on the Jewish question, including the plan to allow the emigration of 7,800 Jews.

June 29: Jusztinián Cardinal Serédi completes a pastoral letter to be read in all Catholic churches, but its distribution is halted following an understanding with István Antal, the Minister of Cults and Public Education.

June 30: King Gustav V of Sweden appeals to Horthy on behalf of the Jews. The Kasztner group leaves Budapest.

July 2: Allied aircraft stage a massive daylight raid on Budapest. A coup attempt engineered by Baky is foiled.

July 6: The deportation of the Jews of western and southwestern Hungary, the areas encompassing Gendarmerie Districts III and IV, is completed.

July 7: Horthy decides to suspend the deportations from Hungary. Sztójay informs Cardinal Serédi about Horthy's decision to halt the deportations. Max Huber, the President of the International Committee of the Red Cross, contacts Horthy with respect to the handling of the Jewish question in Hungary.

July 8: The deportation of the Jews from the communities surrounding Budapest is completed. Jaross relieves Baky and Endre at Horthy's request. The Kasztner group arrives in Bergen-Belsen and is placed in a special camp for the prominent (*Bevorzugtenlager*).

July 9: Raoul Wallenberg, the Swedish diplomat, arrives in Budapest on a humanitarian mission.

July 10: Hitler agrees with the Hungarians' plans to permit the emigration of 7,800 Jews, provided that the remaining Jews are deported from Hungary.

July 12: Sztójay informs the Council of Ministers about Hitler's reaction to the Hungarian plan to permit the emigration of 7,800 Jews. Spain offers the admission of 500 children to Tangier.

July 14: The Association of the Christian Jews of Hungary is formed as a concession to the Christian churches. Horthy orders the return of the Kistarcsa Jews deported on Eichmann's orders.

July 17: Veesenmayer warns Horthy that Hitler is resolved that Hungary follow a "correct" course. Veesenmayer suggests a public relations campaign to "explain" the character of the deportations.

July 18: Hungarian Foreign Ministry informs Hungarian legations abroad about the nature of the anti-Jewish measures taken the months before. Hungarian gendarmerie units associated with Lieutenant-Colonel László Ferenczy arrest Kasztner and keep him incommunicado for nine days.

July 19: In his second attempt within a week, Eichmann manages to deport 1,450 inmates from the Kistarcsa internment camp against Horthy's will.

July 22: Lajos Stöckler and Ernő Boda replace Sándor Török and Samu Kahan-Frankl on the Jewish Council.

July 24: 'Close to 1,500 inmates of the Sárvár internment camp are deported "illegally." Imre Tahy of the Hungarian Legation in Berne reports on the reaction of the Swiss press to the anti-Jewish measures in Hungary. The "Glass House" at 29 Vadász Street is opened as an annex of the Swiss Legation for the registration of prospective emigrants.

July 28: Himmler expresses concurrence with Horthy's decision to halt the deportations.

August 7: Antal Kunder, Béla Imrédy, and Andor Jaross are relieved by Horthy. Miklós Bonczos becomes Minister of the Interior.

August 9–10: Fülöp Freudiger and his family and friends escape to Romania.

August 17: Western Allies accept the so-called Horthy offer concerning the emigration of several thousand Hungarian Jews.

August 21: First meeting between Saly Mayer, Kasztner and Kurt Becher on a bridge linking Switzerland and Austria. 318 Hungarian Jews from the Kasztner group arrive from Bergen-Belsen to Switzerland. Horthy issues decree exempting certain categories of Jews from the provisions of the anti-Jewish laws.

August 22: Horthy repeats his opposition to the deportations. Representatives of the neutral states and the Papal Nuncio meet to jointly protest the pending anti-Jewish measures, especially the rumored deportation of the Budapest Jews on August 25.

August 23: Romania extricates itself from the Nazi Alliance and soon joins the war against the Third Reich and Hungary.

August 24: Eichmann and some of his associates leave Hungary.

August 25: Lajos Reményi-Schneller, the acting Prime Minister, officially informs Veesenmayer about the government's opposition to further deportations. The Jews of Budapest, according to a rumor, were to be deported.

August 28: László Ferenczy announces that he is solely authorized to deal with the Jewish question.

August 29: Horthy appoints General Géza Lakatos Prime Minister and entrusts him with the formation of a new government.

September 3–5: Second series of meetings is held between Saly Mayer, Kasztner, and Becher's representatives on the bridge linking Switzerland and Austria.

September 5: Baky is relieved as Secretary of State in the Ministry of the Interior.

September 7: Endre is relieved as Secretary of State in the Ministry of the Interior.

September 28: Kasztner leaves for his third meeting with Saly Mayer in Switzerland.

October 7–8: Labor servicemen evacuated from Bor, Serbia, are massacred at Cservenka.

October 15: Horthy announces decision to extricate Hungary from the Axis Alliance. Szálasi, assisted by the Germans, stages coup and takes power.

October 17: Eichmann and his associates return to Budapest.

October 20: Able-bodied Jews of Budapest, ranging in age from 16 to 60, are mobilized for digging of trenches and fortifications.

November 4–5: Saly Mayer, Kasztner, Becher, and Roswell McClelland meet in St. Gallen and Zurich.

November 7: Hannah Szenes is executed in a Budapest prison by the *Nyilas.*

November 8: The death marches to Hegyeshalom and the Austrian border begin.

November 9: The Jews of Budapest are forbidden from leaving their homes for three days to enable the authorities to doublecheck compliance with the labor obligations.

November 12: Jews in possession of protective passes or temporary passports from neutral countries are ordered to relocate into specially designated "protected houses."

November 17: Szálasi reveals a "final plan" for the solution of the Jewish question, placing the Jews into six categories. SS-*Obergruppenführer* Hans Jüttner reportedly orders the halting of the death marches to Hegyeshalom.

November 21: Eichmann orders the resumption of the death marches.

November 26: Becher returns to Budapest from a meeting with Himmler.

November 28: Kasztner departs for Switzerland in the company of Krell.

November 29: Agreement is reportedly reached between Hans Geschke and the *Nyilas* for the delivery of 17,000 labor servicemen. Minister of the Interior Gábor Vajna issues decree on the establishment of the ghetto of Budapest.

December 2: The transfer of the Jews of Budapest into the ghetto is completed.

December 3: The *Nyilas* attack the Columbus Street camp, which was under the protection of the International Red Cross.

December 5: Saly Mayer, Kasztner, and Krell meet on the Swiss border.

December 7: The second group in the Kasztner transport, consisting of 1,368 Jews, arrives in Switzerland.

December 10: The ghetto of Budapest is surrounded by a fence. The headquarters of the Jewish Council are heavily damaged in an air raid.

December 22: Meeting in Debrecen, the Provisional National Assembly elects a Provisional National Government.

December 24: Soviet troops begin the siege of Budapest. Eichmann and his colleagues together with many *Nyilas* escape from Budapest.

1945

January 1: Ottó Komoly is murdered by the *Nyilas*.

January 9: Kasztner meets Wisliceny in Vienna.

January 11: *Nyilas* gangs massacre the patients, nurses, and physicians in the Maros Street Jewish Hospital in Buda.

January 14: *Nyilas* gangs massacre approximately 150 patients and medical personnel at the Orthodox Jewish Hospital at Városmajor.

January 16: Soviet troops liberate the area of Pest containing the "International Ghetto."

January 17–18: Soviet troops complete the liberation of Pest, including the ghetto.

January 20: Hungary signs Armistice Agreement with the Allies.

January 25: The Provisional National Government adopts decree establishing a system of people's tribunals for the trial of war criminals.

February 11: Saly Mayer, Kasztner, Becher, and Krell meet at Swiss border.

February 13: Buda is liberated by Soviet troops.

March 17: The Provisional National Government adopts decree repealing all anti-Jewish laws and decrees.

April 4: Hungary is freed of all Nazi-*Nyilas* troops.

June 22: The Budapest Committee of the AJDC is established.

October 3: The Americans return to Budapest the first group of major Hungarian war criminals, including László Bárdossy, Béla Imrédy, Ferenc Szálasi, Andor Jaross, and László Endre.

October 29: Trials of the major war criminals begin.

November 4: Elections are held in Hungary with the Smallholders' Party winning 59.9 percent of the votes.

1946–1965

February–July, 1946: Anti-Semitic demonstrations and pogroms are staged in several Hungarian towns, including Ózd, Sajószentpéter, Szegvár, Kunmadaras, and Diósgyőr.

February 10, 1947: Peace Treaty with Hungary is signed.

August 4, 1947: Kasztner signs an affidavit in support of Kurt Becher.

January 1, 1954: The Grünwald-Kasztner libel suit begins in Jerusalem.

June 22, 1955: Judge Benjamin Halevi finds that Kasztner had "sold his soul to the Devil."

July 29, 1956: The Federal Republic of Germany adopts the Federal Indemnification Law.

March 4, 1957: Kasztner is assassinated in Tel Aviv and dies eleven days later.

July 19, 1957: The Federal Republic of Germany adopts a Federal Restitution Law.

January 15–17, 1958: The Supreme Court of Israel posthumously exonerates Kasztner.

September 14, 1965: The Federal Republic of Germany adopts the so-called Final Act of the Federal Indemnification Law.

Glossary

Abwehr: The German counter-espionage organization headed by Admiral Wilhelm Canaris. Its chief representative in Hungary was Dr. Schmidt, head of *Abwehrstelle* III "F"—Vienna.

AJDC: American Joint Distribution Committee; also known as the American Jewish Joint Distribution Committee or simply as Joint. An American philanthropic organization dedicated to helping distressed Jews the world over.

Aktion: Action or operation, a Nazi term denoting police action against Jews for subsequent "special treatment." See also *Sonderaktion*.

Aliya: Hebrew for ascent; a term commonly used to denote the emigration of Jews to Palestine (Israel).

Aliya Beth: A term denoting the illegal emigration movement to Palestine.

AR (*Állambiztonsági Rendészet*): State Security Police: The Hungarian Gestapo, headed by Péter Hain.

Arrow Cross Party: See *Nyilaskeresztes Párt*.

Chevra Kadisha: Jewish ritual burial society.

Churban: Hebrew word denoting the Holocaust.

DEGOB (*Deportáltakat Gondozó Országos Bizottság*): National Committee for the Care of Deportees, 1945–48.

Dejewification: A term denoting a policy or activity relating to the physical elimination of Jews from a particular area. See also MZsK.

DM (*Deutsche Miliz*): German Militia.

Dror: Hebrew for freedom; the Zionist youth organization of the Labor movement.

Einsatzgruppen: Mobile formations of the German Security Police and Security Service used after the invasion of the Soviet Union on June 22, 1941, for the liquidation of Jews and other "dangerous" persons, including Communist party functionaries.

EKSz (*Etelközi Szövetség*): Etelköz Association. A secret Hungarian patriotic ultra-rightist organization.

ÉME (*Ébredő Magyarok Egyesülete*): Association of Awakening Magyars. An ultra-rightist Hungarian organization.

Final Solution or Final Solution of the Jewish Question (*Endlösung der Judenfrage*): A Nazi euphemism used in correspondence and other forms of communication, denoting the program relating to the extermination of the Jews.

Gestapo (*Geheime Staatspolizei*): Secret State Police in the Third Reich.

Hagana: The Jewish underground army from which the Israeli Army was evolved after the establishment of the State of Israel.

Hashomer Hatzair: Hebrew for Young Guard; a Socialist-Zionist youth movement to train members for life in a Kibbutz in Israel.

Hazkara, or Yom Zikaron (Memorial day): Day devoted to the commemoration of the murdered Jews and the Jewish communities destroyed by the Nazis.

HB (*Hadviseltek Bizottsága*): Jewish Veterans' Committee.

Hehalutz: Hebrew for pioneer; organization of pioneering youth which trained young Jewish men and women for agricultural work in Israel (Palestine).

Herut ("Freedom Movement"): A rightist Israeli political party guided by the Zionist Revisionist views of Vladimir Y. Jabotinsky. The parliamentary heir to the clandestine *Irgun Zvai Leumi* (National Military Organization), the guerrilla organization that fought the British troops and Arab militants during the Mandate era.

HHU (*Hadviseltek Hitközségi Ügyosztálya*): Communal Section of Veterans. A Jewish veterans' organization affiliated with the Jewish Community of Pest.

HIJEF (*Hilfsverein für jüdische Flüchtlinge im Auslande*): Society for the Aid of Refugees Abroad, a rescue and relief organization headed by the Sternbuch brothers in Montreux, Switzerland.

Histadrut: Hebrew acronym for the General Federation of Labor of Israel.

Höherer SS- und Polizeiführer: Higher SS- and Police Leader, a position held in Hungary by Otto Winkelmann.

Honszeretet ("Love of the Fatherland"): A Hungarian Nazi organization.

Honvéd: Popular name of a member of the Hungarian armed forces.

Honvédség: Term used to denote the Hungarian armed forces.

Ichud: The name by which the Mapai, the centrist labor party of Israel, was known in the Diaspora.

IGC: The Intergovernmental Committee on Political Refugees, formed in the wake of the Evian Conference of 1938.

IMIT (*Izraelita Magyar Irodalmi Társulat*): Hungarian Jewish Literary Society. Dissolved in the post-World War II period.

IRC: International Red Cross. Used also to denote the International Committee of the Red Cross.

Irgun Zvai Leumi: See Herut.

Joint: See AJDC.

Judenrat: Council of Jewish Elders or Jewish Council; a body appointed by the Nazis to administer Jewish affairs under their supervision. See also *Zsidó Tanács*.

Kapo(s): A Nazi term derived from the Italian *Capo* (head) denoting a concentration camp inmate in charge of other inmates, especially during work.

Kenyérmező: A basically fictitious geographic name used during the deportations as the alleged ultimate destination of the Jews.

KEOKH (*Külföldieket Ellenőrző Országos Központi Hatóság*): National Central Alien Control Office. With headquarters in Budapest, it was in charge, among other things, of the Jews with foreign citizenship living in Hungary.

Kibbutz: Hebrew for gathering, collective agricultural settlement in Israel.

KMOF (*A Közérdekű Munkaszolgálat Országos Felügyelője*): National Superintendent of the Public Labor Service System.

KMSZ (*Keresztény Munkaszolgálatos Század*): Christian Labor Service Company. A Hungarian labor service company composed of Christians of Jewish descent considered as Jews under the Hungarian racial law of 1941.

Knesset: Hebrew for assembly; the Parliament of the State of Israel.

Kripo (*Kriminalpolizei*): Nazi Criminal Police.

Kristallnacht: German for Crystal Night; the night of November 9–10, 1938, during which synagogues were burned and Jewish homes and businesses were looted and demolished throughout the Third Reich.

KZ (*Konzentrationslager*): Concentration camp.

Labor Service Company (*Munkaszolgálatos Század*): Established by virtue of Paragraph 230 of Law no. II of 1939. Jews served in these companies in lieu of compulsory military service.

Landsmanschaften: Societies of Jewish immigrants that were originally set up in order to help newly arrived countrymen.

MAOIH (*A Magyarországi Autonom Orthodox Izraelita Hitfelekezet*): Autonomous Orthodox Jewish Community of Hungary.

Mapai: The centrist labor party of Israel that dominated the government during the first decades of the state's existence.

MAZOT (*Magyar Zsidók Országos Tanácsa*): National Council of Hungarian Jews. Dissolved in the late 1940s.

MCSz (*Magyar Cionista Szövetség*): Hungarian Zionist Association.

MÉP (*Magyar Élet Pártja*): Hungarian Life Party. The Hungarian ruling party during the Horthy era.

MIKÉFE (*Magyar Izraelita Kézműves és Földmüvelő Egyseület*): Hungarian Jewish Artisan and Agricultural Association.

MINOSZ (*Magyar Izraelita Nők Országos Szövetsége*): National Association of Hungarian Jewish Women.

MIOI (*Magyar Izraeliták Országos Irodája*): National Bureau of Hungarian Jews.

MIOK (*Magyar Izraeliták Országos Képviselete*): National Representation of Hungarian Jews. Since the 1950s the central body of the Jews of Hungary.

MIPI (*Magyar Izraeliták Pártfogó Irodája*): Benevolent Society of Hungarian Jews. Dissolved in the postwar period.

Mizrachi: A centrist Zionist political party and movement of Orthodox Jews.

MKZsSz (*Magyarországi Keresztény Zsidók Szövetsége*): Association of the Christian Jews of Hungary.

MONE (*Magyar Orvosok Nemzeti Egyesülete*): National Association of Hungarian Physicians. A former Hungarian professional association discriminating against Jews and other "non-Hungarian elements."

MOVE (*Magyar Országos Véderő Egyesület*): Hungarian Association for National Defense, an ultra-rightist organization.

MÜNE (*Magyar Ügyvédek Nemzeti Egyesülete*): National Association of Hungarian Lawyers. Like the MONE, a nationalistic association.

Mussulman: Name given to an emaciated concentration camp inmate.

MUSZ (*Munkaszolgálatosok Szövetsége*): Association of Labor Servicemen. Also the popular name for a former draftee.

MZsK (*Magyar Zsidótlanitó Különitmény*): Hungarian Dejewification Unit, composed of László Endre, László Baky, Lajos Meggyesi, Márton Zöldi, and Péter Hain.

MZsSz (*Magyarországi Zsidók Szövetsége*): Association of the Jews of Hungary. The official name of the central Jewish Council.

NG: Nuremberg Government. Documents dealing principally with the activities of various Reich ministries.

NO: Nuremberg, Organizations. Documents pertaining to the activities of organizations of the Nazi Party.

NOKW: Nuremberg, *Oberkommando der Wehrmacht*. Documents pertaining to the High Command of the German Armed Forces.

NOT (*Népbiróságok Országos Tanácsa*): National Council of People's Tribunals.

NSDAP (*Nationalsozialistische Deutsche Arbeiterpartei*): National Socialist German Workers' (Nazi) Party.

Nyilas: A member or follower of the Arrow Cross Party.

Nyilaskeresztes Párt: Arrow Cross Party. The Hungarian Nazi party headed by Ferenc Szálasi, who was executed for war crimes in 1946.

OKW (*Oberkommando der Wehrmacht*): Armed Forces High Command.

OMIKE (*Országos Magyar Izraelita Közművelődési Egyesület*): National Hungarian Jewish Cultural Society. Dissolved during the postwar period.

OMZSA (*Országos Magyar Zsidó Segitő Akció*): National Hungarian Jewish Aid Campaign. Dissolved during the postwar period.

Operation Margarethe: German military code name for the occupation of Hungary in March 1944.

Operation Marita: German military code name for the plan to invade Greece in execution of which both Yugoslavia and Greece were attacked on April 6, 1941.

Operation "Mickey Mouse": German code name for the arrest and kidnapping of Miklós Horthy Jr. in October 1944, forcing the Regent to "recognize" the Arrow Cross leader, Ferenc Szálasi, as the new head of government.

Operation Panzerfaust: German military code name for helping Szálasi's coup d'état of October 15, 1944.

ORPO (*Ordnungspolizei*): Order Police.

ORT: Organization for Rehabilitation and Training.

OT (*Organisation Todt*): Todt Organization. The labor corps organized and headed by Fritz Todt.

OZSSB (*Országos Zsidó Segitő Bizottság*): National Jewish Aid Committee. A relief organization formed after the liberation.

PIH (*A Pesti Izraelita Hitközség*): The Jewish Community of Pest.

Prefect: Term used to denote the official head of a county (*Főispán*). Responsibility for administration was exercised by the Deputy Prefect (*Alispán*).

PRO: Public Record Office, London.

Protective Pass: See *Schutzpass*.

PS: "Paris-Storey." Code for the principal series of documents collected by the United States Prosecution in preparation of the Nuremberg Trials. The collection was started in Paris under the direction of Colonel Storey, first Chief of the Document Division, and later greatly extended in Nuremberg.

Reichsführer-SS: Reich Leader of the SS, the position held in the Third Reich by Heinrich Himmler.

RSHA (*Reichssicherheitshauptamt*): Reich Security Main Office. Operating under the auspices of the *Reichsführer*-SS it was headed until 1942 by Reinhard Heydrich and then by Ernst Kaltenbrunner.

SA (*Sturmabteilung*): Storm Troops of NSDAP—Brown Shirts.

Schutzpass: Protective pass issued to many Jews in Budapest by legations or embassies of neutral states and by the Nunciature.

SD (*Sicherheitsdienst*) Security Service. Intelligence and counter-intelligence agency of the SS.

Secretary of State (*Államtitkár*): A Hungarian governmental title roughly equivalent to an American departmental Under Secretary.

Sheerit ha-Pleta: Biblical phrase which denotes displaced persons; it is taken from I Chron. 4:43: "And they smote the remnant of the Amalekites that were escaped, and dwelt there unto this day."

SIPO *(Sicherheitspolizei)*: Security Police. The name given to the Gestapo and Kripo jointly.

Sonderaktion: Special action: A Nazi term denoting the rounding up of Jews for deportation and extermination.

Sonderkommando: Special Commando in charge of implementing the Final Solution. In Hungary, it was headed by Adolf Eichmann.

SS *(Schutzstaffel)*: Elite Corps of the NSDAP—Black Shirts.

TESz *(Társadalmi Egyesületek Szövetsége)*: Federation of Social Associations, an ultra-rightist umbrella organization.

Tiyul: Hebrew word for "trip"; the code name of the section of the Budapest Rescue and Relief Committee *(Vaada)* which dealt with the smuggling of refugees from Poland and Slovakia.

UNRRA: United Nations Relief and Rehabilitation Agency.

Vaada *(Vaadat ha'Ezra ve'ha'Hatzalah)*: Relief and Rescue Committee, established in Budapest in January 1943.

VDU *(Volksbund der Deutschen in Ungarn)*: Association of the Germans in Hungary. A pro-Nazi organization dissolved with defeat of the Axis.

Veranlassung: Term used in the *Bundesentschädigungsgesetz* (Federal Law of Compensation) to indicate the limits of German responsibility for damages caused to Jews outside Germany; such responsibility exists if the anti-Jewish measures were taken on German *Veranlassung*.

Volksdeutsche: Ethnic (racial) Germans who lived outside the Reich in various European countries and who were citizens of these countries.

Waldsee: A fictitious geographic name used by the Nazis to pacify the Hungarian Jews awaiting deportation. Deported Jews, many of them just prior to being gassed, were asked to write home messages of well-being from this "locality."

Wannsee Conference: The conference held in Berlin (in the office of the International Criminal Police Commission, Am Grossen Wannsee, No. 56/8) on January 20, 1942, on the "Final Solution of the Jewish Question in Europe."

WRB: War Refugee Board, established by order of President Roosevelt in January 1944.

WVHA *(Wirtschaft- und Verwaltungs Hauptamt)*: Economic and Administration Main Office of the SS in Charge of Concentration Camps.

Yellow-Star House: One of a series of buildings in Budapest identified by a yellow star in which thousands of Jews were concentrated in 1944.

Yeshivah: Hebrew for sitting; school devoted to the study of the Talmud and rabbinical literature.

Yishuv: Hebrew for settlement; usually denoting the Jewish community of Israel (Palestine).

YIVO: YIVO-Institute for Jewish Research, New York.

Yizkor Books: Memorial books to commemorate the Jewish communities destroyed by the Nazis.

Zsidó Tanács: Hungarian name of the Council of Jewish Elders; see also *Judenrat*.

Zsidókérdést Kutató Magyar Intézet: A Hungarian Institute for the Researching of the Jewish Question. Established after the German occupation, it was headed by Zoltán Bosnyák.

Name Index*

Abeles, Sándor, 958
Abetz, Otto, 263
Ábrahám, Dezső, 17
Ábrahám, József, 587
Abromeit, Franz, 396, 568, 579
Abrudbányai, Zoltán, 200
Acél, Dezső, 851, 882
Ács, Ernő, 1185
Adamovic-Waagstaetten, Franz von, 388, 890
Adenauer, Konrad, 1179, 1183
Adler, Hermann, 704-5
Ághy (Hungarian officer), 202
Agranat, Shimon, 975
Agy, Zoltán, 544
Ajtay, Gábor, 203, 408
Alapi, Béla, 86
Albrecht, Archduke, 214, 235, 236
Álgya-Pap, Zoltán, 539
Alphand, Hervé, 1179
Ambró, Ferenc, 413, 811
Ambrózy, Gyula, 755, 783, 806, 824, 1041
Andrássy (Gendarmerie officer), 673
Andrássy, Count Gyula, 16, 20
Andréka, Ödön, 876
Anger, Per, 899, 1088
Angya, János, 577
Antal, István, 46, 135, 148, 370, 374, 402, 491, 1035, 1038, 1044, 1073, 1093, 1167
Antal, Sándor, 466
Antalffy, Pál, 574
Antl, Ödön, 475, 1177
Antonescu, Ion, 367, 902, 904, 909
Antonescu, Mihai, 908, 910, 911; letter of June 17, 1944, addressed to A. L. Zissu, 908-9
Apor, Baroness Gizella, 1076
Apor, Bishop Vilmos, 621, 773, 1045, 1048, 1051; appeals to Jusztinián Cardinal

Serédi, 1034, 1035, 1040; opposition to the deportations from Győr, 1045
Apor, Count Gábor, 811
Apponyi, Count Albert, 16, 19, 24
Apponyi, György, 480
Arendt, Hannah, 784, 976
Argalás, Lajos, 406, 450
Argermayer (SS official), 648, 650, 651
Arndt (Gestapo officer), 670
Arnóthy-Jungerth, Mihály, 611, 657, 744, 746, 747, 751, 752, 755, 756, 762, 766, 769, 792-93, 889, 1067, 1069, 1093
Aschner, Lipót, 480
Auer, György, 466, 739
Auguszt, József, 854
Auringer (Gestapo officer), 668
Avar, László, 514, 1179
Avramcsik, Dov, 999
Avriel, Echud, 948, 971
Axmann, János, 200-201

Babos, József, 212
Bach, Gabriel, 711
Bacher-Bodrog, Pál, 441
Bachman, Hans, 1062
Bach-Zelewski, Erich von dem, 823, 828, 877
Bacsó, Béla, 19
Bader, Menachem, 116, 494, 700, 942, 971, 1106, 1107
Baeck, Rabbi Leo, 721-22
Bagossy, Zoltán, 1076
Bágyoni, Ferenc, 110, 942
Bajcsy-Zsilinszky, Endre, 36, 45, 53, 206, 208, 212, 213, 215, 253, 327, 365, 394, 407, 480, 481, 986, 989, 990
Bajor, Ferenc, 642, 1170
Bajóti, Antal, 201

* Names of local community and Jewish Council leaders are not listed in this index. For references to them check under the name of the community in the Geographic Index.

Geographic Index*

*The geographic names of localities in the territories acquired by Hungary from Czechoslovakia, Romania, and Yugoslavia in 1938-41 are rendered in their Hungarian version. Their Romanian, Serbo-Croatian, and Slovak equivalents are given in the Geographic List of Names (vol. 1, p. xxxi).

Turda, 904, 905, 906
Turjaporoskő, 541
Tűrje, 670
Túrkeve, 649
Turkey, 887, 889, 1095. *See also* Neutral
    states *in Subject Index*
Tüskevár, 687

Udvard, 621
Udvarhely County, 168, 169, 534, 566, 583,
    585
Ugocsa County, 133, 534
Ugod, 687
Ujfehértó, 547
Ujkécske, 647
Ujpest, 671, 672, 673, 836
Ujverbász, 181
Ujvidék, 181, 642-43; massacres at, 208-11
Ukraine, 228, 240, 307-21
Üllő, 807
Ung County, 133, 146, 534, 541, 552
Ungdorocz, 541
Ungvár, 132, 133, 533, 540, 551, 552, 554,
    588; ghetto of, 541-42
United States, 1100-101; attitude toward
    the Brand mission, 1108-9; reaction of the
    U.S. Congress, 1111-12, 1117; reaction to
    the "Horthy offer," 1114-18; relief and
    rescue efforts of, 758; restrictive immi-
    gration policies of, 1097; warning to Hun-
    gary, 756, 1110. *See also* War Refugee
    Board; Western Allies *in Subject Index*
Uraiujfalu, 688
Urmező, 146
USSR, 1118-20, 1175; attitude toward
    Jewish labor servicemen, 318, 347-49,
    1119; campaign against Zionism, 720,
    1120; declaration of war against, 185;
    involvement in Raoul Wallenberg's dis-
    appearance, 1090-91; liberation of Hun-
    gary, 1142; reaction to the Brand mission,
    1108

Vajta, 666
Vámfalu, 578
Vámosmikola, 104, 1125
Vámospércs, 641

Váncsfalva, 544
Varjac, 542
Városszalónak, 688
Vas County, 180, 688
Vásárosnamény, 542
Vasmegyer, 547
Vasvár, 670, 688
Végsellye, 621
Vencsellő, 547
Vereb, 623
Verebély, 133, 623
Veresegyháza, 573
Veszprém, 19, 531, 666
Veszprém County, 531
Vésztő, 649
Vetéle, 543
Vilmány, 626
Visk, 146, 543
Visóoroszi, 168
Voronezh, 198, 318
Vulchovec, 543

"Waldsee," 653, 663
Weitra, 652
Westerbork, 262, 266, 900
Wiener-Neustadt, 652

Yugoslavia: acquisition of territories from,
    180; attack on, 180; Hungarian policy
    toward, 178-79; war crimes trials in,
    1169-70. *See also* Croatia

Zagyvapálfalva, 626
Zagyvarékás, 626
Zalabár, 670
Zala County, 180, 549, 550, 608
Zalaegerszeg, 667, 670-71
Zalalővő, 670
Zalaszentgrót, 670
Zemplén County, 133, 543
Zenta, 181, 642
Zilah, 168
Zirc, 668, 687
Zomba, 664
Zombor, 181, 334, 643
Zsablya, 207, 208
Zseliz, 623

Subject Index*

*For the identification of acronyms, consult the Glossary.

patho Ruthenia, Jewish population of;
Northern Transylvania, Jew of *in*
Georgraphic Index
Orthodox Public Table, 860
Orthodox Relief and Rescue Committee,
108-9
OT *see* Todt Organization
OZSSB, 1149

Palestine Office, Budapest, 92, 885, 941,
977. *See also* Miklós Krausz *in Name Index*
Palestine Office, Geneva, 945, 949, 1121. *See
also* Chaim Pozner *in Name Index*
Palestine press, 715-16
Papal Nuncio *see* Monsignor Angelo Rotta
Parachutists, 993-95. *See also* Resistance,
Jewish
Parliament, Jewish members of, 72, 91, 105,
239, 252, 1177
Party of Hungarian Renewal, 120, 161,
174-75, 297, 400
Patriotic associations, 17, 20-23. *See also*
Rightist parties and movements
Peace Party *see* Communist Party
Peace Treaty of February 10, *1947*, 1154-55
People's tribunals: establishment of,
1163-64; record of, 1167-68; replacement
of, 1168. *See also* War crimes trials
People's Unity Party of the Ruthenians of
Carpatho-Ruthenia, 498
Petőfi Radio, 1040, 1054
PIH, 86, 99, 150, 344-45, 778
Police, Hungarian, 405-7. *See also* Ministry
of the Interior
Polish Government-in-Exile, 694, 695, 716
Polish-Jewish Refugee Committee, 107-8
Polish Jewry, reports on its extermination,
694-96
Political opposition, 245-46
POWs in Hungary, 115, 1011, 1060, 1073,
1125
Press: ecclesiastical, 1028; opposition, 499;
rightist, 160-63, 175
Proclamation of October 15, *1944*, 826-27
Proletarian dictatorship of *1919*, 14-16,
1028
Protected buildings, 789; relocation of Jews
into, 795, 796
Protected Jews, 853; number of, 847, 848;
treatment of, 843-44, 847-48. *See also*
International ghetto; Protective passes

Protected labor service companies, 843-44
Protective passes, 840, 843, 896, 1075, 1080,
1083, 1087, 1088, 1092, 1094; check of,
848-49, 1083; privileges associated with,
845; production of, 1001, 1083; samples
of, 1003-10
Protestant churches, 1041-45; church leaders' appeal to Cardinal Serédi, 1042;
draft pastoral letter of, 1043-44. *See also*
Christian churches
Provisional Executive Committee of the National Association of the Jews of Hungary
see Jewish Council
Provisional National Government, 883

Rabbinate, attitude of, 467-68, 776, 785
Race-Protecting Party, 22, 45-46
Rationalizations of Jews, 100-101, 126-27,
537-38, 570, 775
Reconstruction, 1147-51
Refugees, 88, 103-10, 151, 200, 885; legali-
zation of, 999; revelations on the Final
Solution by, 700-705
RELICO, 1121
Religious activities, 800, 817, 866-67. *See also*
Rabbinate
Reparation *see* Restitution
Reprisals, 487
Requisitions, 484-90. *See also* Expropria-
tions
Rescue, 928-30; activities of Miklós Krausz,
977-82; activities of Ottó Komoly, 982-85;
involvement of the *Hehalutz*, 1001-11;
involvement of non-Jews, 985-87; in-
volvement of the *Vaada*, 932-68;
Kasztner's role in, 932-41, 951-68;
Romania's role in, 906-13
Resistance, 987-1011; Jewish, 840,
991-1011; by *Hehalutz* youth, 998-1011;
by labor servicemen, 830, 997-98; non-
Jewish, 988-91; the parachutists, 993-95;
Veesenmayer's view of, 990; Yugoslav,
207
Restitution, 1151-63; Hungary, 1151-55;
the Federal Republic of Germany,
1159-63
Righteous Gentile, Yad Vashem award, 355,
502, 1011, 1053-54, 1056, 1128, 1132
Rightist parties and movements, 56-69
Ritual murder case, 9, 1027
Rökk Szilárd Street internment camp *see*
National Theological Institute

DATE DUE

DEC 2 1 2005
JAN 1 7 2006
OCT 0 1 2012